THE CRICKETERS' WHO'S WHO

5/7

THE CRICKETERS' WHO'S WHO

1985

compiled and edited by

IAIN SPROAT

associate editor

RALPH DELLOR

Queen Anne Press

A *Queen Anne Press* book

© Iain Sproat, 1985

First published in Great Britain in 1985 by
Queen Anne Press, Macdonald & Co (Publishers) Ltd
Maxwell House, 74 Worship Street, London EC2A 2EN
in association with The Cricketers' Who's Who

A BPCC plc company

British Library Cataloguing in Publication Data
The Cricketers' who's who.
  1. Cricket players—Biography
  I. Sproat, Iain
  796.35′8′0922   GV915.A1

  ISBN 0-356-12002 3

  ISBN 0-356-10856 2 PBK.

Cover design: Clare Forte
Cover photographs, left to right: Brian Hardie *Jan Traylen for Patrick Eagar*
                                  Graham Stevenson *Patrick Eagar*
                                    Chris Gladwin *Jan Traylen for Patrick Eagar*
Portraits: Bill Smith

Typeset by Margaret Spooner Typesetting,
Dorchester, Dorset.

Printed in Great Britain at
The Pitman Press, Bath.

PREFACE

EACH YEAR I try to add something new to *The Cricketers' Who's Who* to make the book more full, informative and amusing. These ideas, for the most part, come from the county cricketers themselves and from other readers: I am most grateful to them for this help.

This year I have made several new additions to players' entries: I have changed the order in which the cricketers' biographies are listed from alphabetical by individual name to alphabetical by county. And to the individual entries I have added details of a cricketer's best performance, the number of 100s and 50s a player has scored in one-day cricket, the number of times a player has taken 5 wickets in a first-class innings and 10 wickets in a match, and the number of catches a player has taken in the previous season and in his whole career.

As in last year's edition, I am making use of some of the spaces that inevitably occur occasionally on certain pages to include cricket quiz questions — some easy, some not — to help while away those rain-spoilt hours of an English summer. Answers are at the back of the book.

If you have any ideas for information to be added to next year's edition, please write and tell me.

The cricketers listed in this volume include all those who played for their county at least once last season, either in the county championship, John Player Special League, Benson & Hedges or NatWest matches. The statistics are accurate up to the end of the last English season — with one exception: it has proved impossible to guarantee the accuracy of the statistics of certain matches, classified as first-class, in India and Pakistan. However, Test match figures in those countries have been included. Figures about 50 wickets and 1000 runs etc. in a season refer to matches in England only.

The following abbreviations apply: * means not out; J.P.L. means John Player Special League and B & H means Benson & Hedges. Where there are two lines of bowling figures, the top line refers to eight ball overs, the bottom line to six. Normally there is only one line, referring to six ball overs. The figures for batting and bowling averages refer to 1984, followed in brackets by the 1983 figures. Inclusion in the first-class batting averages depends on a minimum of eight innings, and an average of at least 10 runs; a bowler has had to have taken at least 10 wickets in at least 10 innings.

Readers will notice certain occasional differences in the way the same kind of information about cricketers is presented. This is because I have usually tried to follow the way in which the cricketers themselves have provided the relevant information.

I should like to acknowledge with particular gratitude the very wide-ranging help I have had from Mr Ralph Dellor, the cricket broadcaster, journalist and N.C.A. staff coach. I should also like to thank Mr G.J.T.V. Vyvyan for his advice. Once again I am indebted to Mr Robert Brooke for this splendidly professional work on the collection of the statistics, and to Mr Bill Smith, F.R.P.S. who personally took most of the photographs. Above all I am grateful to the county cricketers themselves without whose generous support this book could not have been compiled.

Iain Sproat

Derbyshire

ANDERSON, I.S.

Full Name: Iain Stuart Anderson.
Role: Right-hand bat (opener), off-break bowler.
Born: 24 April 1960, Derby.
Height: 6′ 0″ **Weight:** 11st 2lbs.
Nickname: Tommy, Tom.
County debut: 1978.
County cap: No.
Test debut: —
No. of Tests: 0.
No. of One-Day Internationals: 0.
1000 runs in a season: 1.
50 wickets in a season: 0.
1st-Class 50s scored: 15.
1st-Class 100s scored: 2.
1st-Class 200s scored: 0.
1st-Class 5 w. in innings: 0.
1st-Class 10 w. in match: 0.
One-day 50s: 1.
One-day 100s: 0.

Place in batting averages: 198 average: 29.64; (1983: 65 average: 37.36).
Place in bowling averages: — average: —; (1983: — average: —).
1st-Class catches 1984: 14 (career: 78).
Parents: May and Norman Anderson.
Marital status: Single.
Education: Dovecliff Grammar School; Wulfric School, Burton.
Qualifications: 8 'O' levels, 3 'A' levels, Preliminary Coaching Certificate.
Family links with cricket: Father and brother played club cricket.
Overseas tours: England Young Cricketers Tour Australia 1979.
Overseas teams played for: Berguliet, (Cape Town) 1979–80 and 1980–81; Kew, (Melbourne) 1982; Ellerslie, (Auckland) 1982; Boland (S. Africa) 1983–84.
Equipment used: Duncan Fearnley.
Other sports: Soccer, squash.

Relaxations: Reading, listening to music.
Best batting performance: 112 Derbyshire v Kent, Chesterfield 1983.
Best bowling performance: 4-35 Derbyshire v Australia, Derby 1981.

LAST SEASON: BATTING

	I.	N.O.	R.	H.S.	AV.
TEST					
OTHER FIRST CLASS	23	1	454	79	20.64
INT					
J.P.L.	3	0	33	23	11.00
NAT.W.					
B & H					

CAREER: BATTING

	I.	N.O.	R.	H.S.	AV.
TEST					
OTHER FIRST CLASS	146	21	2994	112	23.95
INT					
J.P.L.	24	1	419	54	18.22
NAT.W.	3	0	81	47	27.00
B & H	1	0	32	32	–

LAST SEASON: BOWLING

	O.	M.	R.	W.	AV.
TEST					
OTHER FIRST CLASS	55	10	176	3	58.67
INT					
J.P.L.					
NAT.W.					
B & H					

CAREER: BOWLING

	O.	M.	R.	W.	AV.
TEST					
OTHER FIRST CLASS	352.5	66	1271	20	63.55
INT					
J.P.L.	7.1	2	28	2	14.00
NAT.W.					
B & H					

BARNETT, K.J.

Full Name: Kim John Barnett.
Role: Right-hand bat, leg-break bowler, or seamers.
Born: 17 July 1960, Stoke-on-Trent.
Height: 6' 1" **Weight:** 11st. 12lbs.
Nickname: Wristy.
County debut: 1979.
County cap: 1982.
Test debut: —
Number of Tests: 0.
No. of One-Day Internationals: 0.
1000 runs in a season: 2.
50 wickets in a season: 0.
1st-Class 50s scored: 32.
1st-Class 100s scored: 13.
1st-Class 200s scored: 0.
1st-Class 5 w. in innings: 0.
1st-Class 10 w. in match: 0.
One-day 50s: 5.
One-day 100s: 1.

Place in batting averages: 30 average: 45.63; (1983: 60 average: 38.46).
Place in bowling averages: — average: —; (1983: — average: —).

1st-Class catches 1984: 21 (career: 80).

Parents: Derek and Doreen Barnett.

Wife and date of marriage: Nancy, 31 September 1984.

Education: Leek High School, Staffs.

Qualifications: 7 0-levels.

Equipment used: Gray-Nicolls.

Jobs outside cricket: Bank clerk, National Westminster Bank 1978.

Overseas tours: With England Schools to India 1977; Young England to Australia 1978–79; Derrick Robins XI to New Zealand and Australia 1979–80.

Other sports: Football. Has played soccer semi-professionally for Cheshire League side, Leek Town F.C. Follows horse-racing.

Extras: Played for Northants. 2nd XI when aged 15. Played one Minor County match for Staffordshire; also for Warwickshire 2nd XI. Became youngest captain of a first-class county when appointed in 1983.

Opinions on cricket: "Would like to see the introduction of four day cricket to the County Championship to make the difference between Test match cricket and the County·Championship smaller and hopefully promote more attacking cricket."

Best batting performance: 144 Derbyshire v Middlesex, Derby 1984.

Best bowling performance: 4-76 Derbyshire v Warwickshire, Edgbaston 1980.

LAST SEASON: BATTING

	I.	N.O.	R.	H.S.	AV.
TEST					
OTHER FIRST CLASS	41	3	1734	144	45.63
INT					
J.P.L.	14	1	460	131*	35.38
NAT.W.	2	0	53	37	26.50
B & H	4	0	88	34	22.00

CAREER: BATTING

	I.	N.O.	R.	H.S.	AV.
TEST					
OTHER FIRST CLASS	199	22	5888	144	33.27
INT					
J.P.L.	77	15	1780	131*	28.70
NAT.W.	12	2	349	88	34.90
B & H	19	1	298	34	16.56

LAST SEASON: BOWLING

	O.	M.	R.	W.	AV.
TEST					
OTHER FIRST CLASS	43	6	162	0	–
INT					
J.P.L.	17	0	131	2	65.50
NAT.W.	9.2	0	24	6	4.00
B & H	9	2	33	2	16.50

CAREER: BOWLING

	O.	M.	R.	W.	AV.
TEST					
OTHER FIRST CLASS	409.2	66	1567	18	84.83
INT					
J.P.L.	38.3	2	256	7	36.57
NAT.W.	18.3	2	73	8	9.12
B & H	9	2	33	2	16.50

BROOME, I.

Full Name: Ian Broome.
Role: Right-hand bat, right arm
medium fast bowler, fields
anywhere except slips.
Born: 6 May 1960, Bradenstoke,
Wiltshire.
Height: 5' 11¾" **Weight:** 12½st.
Nickname: Broomie, Aus (short
for Aussie).
County debut: 1984.
County cap: No.
Test debut: —
No. of Tests: 0.
No. of One-Day Internationals: 0.
1000 runs in a season: 0.
50 wickets in a season: 0.
1st-Class 50s scored: 0.
1st-Class 100s scored: 0.
1st-Class 200s scored: 0.
1st-Class 5 w. in innings: 0.
1st-Class 10 w. in match: 0.
One-day 50s: 0.
One-day 100s: 0.

Place in batting averages: — average: —; (1983: — average: —).
Place in bowling averages: — average: —; (1983: — average: —).
1st-Class catches 1984: 1 (career: 1).
Parents: George Derrick and Vicky Broome.
Marital status: Single.
Education: Warrandyte Primary School, Mitcham Technical School, Box Hill
Technical College (started P.E. course but left to pursue a career in cricket).
Qualifications: Leaving Certificate.
Jobs outside cricket: Selling sunglasses 1980, working on a farm and working
for Action World Sports in Melbourne.
Off-season 1984–85: Playing grade cricket for Collingwood C.C. in Australia
and maybe Sheffield Shield with Victoria.
Equipment used: Duncan Fearnley.
Overseas tours: 1980 tour to Barbados and Trinidad, Middlesex County
League, and with Gloucestershire to Barbados again in 1980.
Overseas teams played for: Melbourne grade cricket Fitzroy C.C. 1977–78,
Collingwood C.C. 1977–78, started playing with Warrandyte C.C. U14, U16
and Seniors from 1974-77 and South Brisbane C.C. 1983 (only ½ season).
Cricketers particularly learnt from: Frank Tyson (still learning).
Other sports: Basketball, golf, tennis, backgammon and fruit machines. Follow
golf, horse jumping, athletics.

Significant injuries in 1984: Pinched nerve during May and a little bit of June.
Relaxations: Sleeping, listening to music—Supertramp, George Benson, Joan Armatrading, Eurythmics, Dire Straits, Roy Buchannon etc. "depends what mood I'm in". Fishing.
Best batting performance: 26* Derbyshire v Kent, Derby 1984.

LAST SEASON: BATTING

	I.	N.O.	R.	H.S.	AV.
TEST					
OTHER FIRST CLASS	4	3	35	26	–
INT					
J.P.L.	5	2	18	9*	6.00
NAT.W.	1	1	2	2*	–
B & H					

CAREER: BATTING

	I.	N.O.	R.	H.S.	AV.
TEST					
OTHER FIRST CLASS	4	3	35	26	17.50
INT					
J.P.L.	6	3	18	9*	6.00
NAT.W.	1	1	2	2*	–
B & H					

LAST SEASON: BOWLING

	O.	M.	R.	W.	AV.
TEST					
OTHER FIRST CLASS	19.1	6	62	2	41.00
INT					
J.P.L.	38	1	193	8	24.13
NAT.W.	12	0	74	2	37.00
B & H					

CAREER: BOWLING

	O.	M.	R.	W.	AV.
TEST					
OTHER FIRST CLASS	19.1	6	82	2	41.00
INT					
J.P.L.	45	1	231	8	28.88
NAT.W.	12	0	74	2	37.00
B & H					

FINNEY, R.J.

Full name: Roger John Finney.
Role: Right-hand bat, left arm medium bowler.
Born: 2 August 1960, Darley Dale, Derbyshire.
Height: 6′ 1″ **Weight:** 12st. 10lbs.
Nickname: Albert.
County debut: 1982.
County cap: No.
Test debut: —
No. of Tests: 0.
No. of One-Day Internationals: 0.
1000 runs in a season: 0.
50 wickets in a season: 1.
1st-Class 50s scored: 7.
1st-Class 100s scored: 0.
1st-Class 200s scored: 0.
1st-Class 5 w. in innings: 3.
1st-Class 10 w. in match: 0.
One-day 50s: 1.

One-day 100s: 0.
Place in batting averages: 192 average: 21.22; (1983: 197 average: 17.52).
Place in bowling averages: 53 average: 28.55; (1983: 81 average: 36.33).
1st-Class catches 1984: 5 (career: 10)
Parents: Roy and Janet Finney.
Marital status: Single.
Family links with cricket: Father played and captained local side for many years.
Education: Lady Manners School, Bakewell.
Qualifications: O-Levels.
Jobs outside cricket: Production clerk and sports salesman.
Off-season 1984–85: Playing and coaching in Pietermaritzburg, South Africa.
Cricket superstitions: "Always put left pad on first."
Equipment used and endorsed: Gunn & Moore.
Overseas teams played for: Alexandrians, Pietermaritzburg, South Africa, 1980–81 and 1981–82.
Cricketers particularly learnt from: "Phil Russell, Derbyshire coach, Don Wilson, Head coach at Lord's."
Other sports: Rugby, football, golf.
Relaxations: "Music, movies, good beer, eating at a good restaurant."
Extras: Before joining Derbyshire, spent two years with the M.C.C. Young Professionals.
Best batting performance: 78 Derbyshire v Lancashire, Buxton 1984.
Best bowling performance: 5-55 Derbyshire v Lancashire, Buxton 1984.

LAST SEASON: BATTING

	I.	N.O.	R.	H.S.	AV.
TEST					
OTHER FIRST CLASS	37	5	679	78	21.22
INT					
J.P.L.	9	2	140	50*	20.00
NAT.W.	1	1	2	2*	–
B & H	4	0	89	46	22.25

CAREER: BATTING

	I.	N.O.	R.	H.S.	AV.
TEST					
OTHER FIRST CLASS	73	7	1296	78	19.64
INT					
J.P.L.	22	6	363	50*	22.69
NAT.W.	2	1	19	14*	–
B & H	5	0	110	46	22.00

LAST SEASON: BOWLING

	O.	M.	R.	W.	AV.
TEST					
OTHER FIRST CLASS	584	130	1770	62	28.55
INT					
J.P.L.	89	5	475	14	33.93
NAT.W.	8	3	8	2	4.00
B & H	35	5	143	2	71.50

CAREER: BOWLING

	O.	M.	R.	W.	AV.
TEST					
OTHER FIRST CLASS	879.5	173	2780	93	29.89
INT					
J.P.L.	158.5	11	815	25	32.60
NAT.W.	32	7	86	3	28.67
B & H	46	5	187	4	46.75

FOWLER, W.P.

Full Name: William Peter Fowler.
Role: Right-hand bat, left arm spin bowler. Bat/pad fielder.
Born: 13 March 1959, St. Helens, Lancs.
Height: 5' 10" **Weight:** 13st.
Nickname: Twister, Chook.
County debut: 1982.
County cap: No.
Test debut: —
No. of Tests: 0.
No. of One-Day Internationals: 0.
1000 runs in a season: 0.
50 wickets in a season: 0.
1st-Class 50s scored: 12.
1st-Class 100s scored: 2.
1st-Class 200s scored: 0.
1st-Class 5 w. in innings: 0.
1st-Class 10 w. in match: 0.
One-day 50s: 2.
One-day 100s: 0.
Place in batting averages: 113 average: 30.58; (1983: 140 average: 24.62).
Place in bowling averages: — average: —; (1983: — average: —).
1st-Class catches 1984: 17 (career: 34).
Parents: Robert Alan and Mary Catherine Fowler.
Marital status: Single.
Education: Tawa College; Kamo High School; Otago University and Auckland University.
Jobs outside cricket: Builder's labourer, and works in sports shop in New Zealand.
Off-season 1984–85: Playing and coaching in Northland, New Zealand.
Family links with cricket: "Father once captained his House 2nd XI!"
Cricketing superstitions: "Never have lunch on a Sunday."
Overseas tours: Toured Australia with New Zealand Secondary Schools, 1975–76.
Overseas teams played for: Northern Districts, 1979–80, 80–81; Auckland 1981–82, 82–83.
Cricketers particularly learnt from: "I admire Richard Hadlee, and have learnt from most of the senior players at the club, especially John Wright."
Equipment used: Newbery bats.
Other sports: Squash. Watching anything sporting at all.
Relaxations: Reading, listening to music, and lazing about the house.
Opinions on cricket: "1) 117 is a good number of overs per day. Players should be able to maintain 18 overs per hour. 2) Qualifying period for England is too

short—the players should have had to live in England as long as they have lived overseas. 3) 3-day county cricket is more positive than 4-day games — although at times results do have to be manufactured. If 4-day cricket is introduced the pitches must be brought up to standard so the matches last 4 days!"

Best batting performance: 116 Derbyshire v Glamorgan, Derby 1984.

LAST SEASON: BATTING

	I.	N.O.	R.	H.S.	AV.
TEST					
OTHER FIRST CLASS	38	8	948	116	30.58
INT					
J.P.L.	14	2	276	51	23.00
NAT.W.	1	0	1	1	–
B & H	4	0	76	53	19.00

CAREER: BATTING

	I.	N.O.	R.	H.S.	AV.
TEST					
OTHER FIRST CLASS	82	13	1823	116	26.42
INT					
J.P.L.	26	2	448	51	18.67
NAT.W.	3	1	17	9*	8.50
B & H	5	0	80	53	16.00

LAST SEASON: BOWLING

	O.	M.	R.	W.	AV.
TEST					
OTHER FIRST CLASS	117.3	23	398	5	79.60
INT					
J.P.L.	23	1	132	5	26.40
NAT.W.	2	0	6	0	–
B & H	14	1	77	3	25.67

CAREER: BOWLING

	O.	M.	R.	W.	AV.
TEST					
OTHER FIRST CLASS	315.2	67	1058	14	75.57
INT					
J.P.L.	37	2	182	8	22.75
NAT.W.	2	0	6	0	–
B & H	14	1	77	3	25.67

HAMPSHIRE, J.H.

Full Name: John Harry Hampshire.
Role: Right-hand bat, leg-break and googly bowler.
Born: 10 February 1941, Thurnscoe, near Rotherham, Yorkshire.
Height: 6' 0" **Weight:** 13st.
Nickname: Hamps.
County debut: 1982 (Derbys.).
County cap: 1982 (Derbys.).
Test debut: 1969.
No. of Tests: 8.
No. of One-Day Internationals: 3.
Benefit: £28,425 in 1976.
1000 runs in a season: 15.
50 wickets in a season: 0.
1st-Class 50s scored: 142.
1st-Class 100s scored: 43.
1st-Class 200s scored: 0.
1st-Class 5 w. in innings: 1.
1st-Class 10 w. in match: 0.

One-day 50s: 39.
One-day 100s: 7.
Place in batting averages: 131 average: 28.29; (1983: 93 average: 31.63).
Place in bowling averages: — average: —; (1983: — average: —).
1st-Class catches 1984: 20 (career: 444).
Wife and date of marriage: Judith, 5 September 1964.
Children: Ian, 6 January 1969; Paul, 12 February 1972.
Education: Oakwood Technical High School, Rotherham.
Family links with cricket: Father played pre-war for Yorkshire C.C.C. (six games); also brother.
Other sports: Golf.
Relaxations: Gardening, golf, reading.
Extras: Scored 107 in his first Test Match, v West Indies at Lord's. Top of Yorkshire batting averages in his last year with Yorkshire. Made debut for Yorkshire in 1961, winning his cap in 1963. Captain of Yorkshire in 1979–80. Moved to Derbyshire for 1982 season. Retired after 1984 season.
Best batting performance: 183* Yorkshire v Sussex, Hove 1971.
Best bowling performance: 7-52 Yorkshire v Glamorgan, Cardiff 1963.

LAST SEASON: BATTING

	I.	N.O.	R.	H.S.	AV.
TEST					
OTHER FIRST CLASS	32	4	792	101*	28.29
INT					
J.P.L.	5	1	54	22	13.50
NAT.W.					
B & H	3	1	27	21*	13.50

CAREER: BATTING

	I.	N.O.	R.	H.S.	AV.
TEST	16	1	403	107	26.87
OTHER FIRST CLASS	908	111	27063	183*	33.96
INT	3	1	48	25*	24.00
J.P.L.	172	20	4994	119	32.85
NAT.W.	33	5	930	110	33.21
B & H	45	6	1091	85*	27.97

LAST SEASON: BOWLING

	O.	M.	R.	W.	AV.
TEST					
OTHER FIRST CLASS	1	1	0	0	–
INT					
J.P.L.					
NAT.W.					
B & H					

CAREER: BOWLING

	O.	M.	R.	W.	AV.
TEST					
OTHER FIRST CLASS	16.6 402.5	1 85	1637	30	54.57
INT.					
J.P.L.	4	1	22	1	–
NAT.W.	2	0	4	0	–
B & H					

Q. 1. Which county has a bear on its crest?
Q. 2. What animal has Leicestershire on its county crest?
Q. 3. Which county has fruit on its county crest, and what fruit?

HILL, A.

Full Name: Alan Hill.
Role: Right-hand bat, off-break
bowler.
Born: 29 June 1950, Buxworth,
Derbyshire.
Nickname: Bud.
County debut: 1972.
County cap: 1976.
Test debut: —
No. of Tests: 0.
No. of One-Day Internationals: 0.
1000 runs in a season: 4.
50 wickets in a season: 0.
1st-Class 50s scored: 61.
1st-Class 100s scored: 14.
1st-Class 200s scored: 0.
1st-Class 5 w. in innings: 0.
1st-Class 10 w. in match: 0.
One-day 50s: 12.
One-day 100s: 2.

Place in batting averages: 96 average: 32.98; (1983: 63 average: 37.46).
Place in bowling averages: — average: —; (1983 — averagge: —).
1st-Class catches 1984: 13 (career: 85).
Parents: Hilda and Jack.
Wife and date of marriage: Linda, 18 March 1978.
Children: Elizabeth Anne, Eleanor Jane, Laura Louise.
Education: Buxworth Primary School; New Mills Grammar School; Chester
College of Education.
Qualifications: B.Ed. Physical Education teacher. Advanced Cricket Coaching
Award.
Jobs outside cricket: Teaching posts, clerical work, promotional assistant.
Family links with cricket: Father and brother both played local league cricket.
Brother, Bernard, played for Derbyshire 2nd XI.
Cricketers particularly admired: Sir Garfield Sobers.
Overseas teams played for: Orange Free State in 1976–77 Currie Cup
Competition.
Equipment used: Gunn & Moore.
Relaxations: Other sports, particularly football; music, reading.
Extras: England Schoolboy cricketer 1968; also represented National
Association of Young Cricketers.
Opinions on cricket: "In favour of (a) reduction in amount of cricket played
with one 3- or 4-day game per week and 1-day games on Saturday and Sunday,
leaving one day off; (b) more specialised coaching required at all levels,
including county. Video equipment a necessity at professional level; (c) would

like to see the abolition of the current benefit system in favour of a fairer system whereby all professional cricketers would receive a sum at the end of their careers, that sum being dependent upon their length of service."

Best batting performance: 160* Derbyshire v Warwickshire, Coventry 1976.
Best bowling performance: 3-5 Free State v N. Transvaal, Pretoria 1976–77.

LAST SEASON: BATTING

	I.	N.O.	R.	H.S.	AV.
TEST					
OTHER FIRST CLASS	44	3	1352	125	32.98
INT					
J.P.L.	11	0	206	43	18.73
NAT.W.	2	1	38	25	–
B & H	3	0	186	87	62.00

CAREER: BATTING

	I.	N.O.	R.	H.S.	AV.
TEST					
OTHER FIRST CLASS	393	38	10585	160*	29.82
INT					
J.P.L.	76	4	1577	120	21.90
NAT.W.	15	1	306	72	21.86
B & H	23	1	748	102*	34.00

LAST SEASON: BOWLING

	O.	M.	R.	W.	AV.
TEST					
OTHER FIRST CLASS	50	10	191	3	63.67
INT					
J.P.L.	8	0	32	3	10.67
NAT.W.					
B & H					

CAREER: BOWLING

	O.	M.	R.	W.	AV.
TEST					
OTHER FIRST CLASS	83.2	16	343	8	42.88
INT					
J.P.L.	8	0	32	3	10.67
NAT.W.					
B & H					

MAHER, B.J.M.

Full Name: Bernard Joseph Michael Maher.
Role: Wicket-keeper, batsman.
Born: 11 February 1958, Hillingdon.
Height: 5' 10" **Weight:** 11st. 6lbs.
Nickname: "Tends to vary. 'Sewer Rat' or 'Rodders' most popular at present."
County debut: 1981.
County cap: No.
Test debut: —
No. of Tests: 0.
No. of One-Day Internationals: 0.
1000 runs in a season: 0.
50 wickets in a season: 0.
1st-Class 50s scored: 2.
1st-Class 100s scored: 0.
1st-Class 200s scored: 0.
1st-Class 5 w. in innings: 0.
1st-Class 10 w. in match: 0.
One-day 50s: 0.

One-day 100s: 0.
Place in batting averages: 230 average: 16.22; (1983: 212 average: 15.00).
Place in bowling averages: — average: —; (1983: — average: —)
Parents: Francis J. and Mary Ann Maher.
Marital status: Single.
Family links with cricket: Brother kept wicket for school; father follows Derbyshire C.C.C. quite closely.
Education: Abbotsfield Comprehensive, Bishopsmalt Grammar, Harrow College, Loughborough University.
Qualifications: B.Sc. Hons in Economics and Accountancy; 3 A-levels, 10 O-levels. Nearly qualified accountant. N.C.A. coaching award 1982.
Jobs outside cricket: "While playing and coaching abroad 1982–83 and 1983–84 my contract entailed working as an accountant 5 mornings a week."
Equipment used: Slazenger and Puma.
Off-season 1984–85: Playing in Auckland, New Zealand.
Overseas tours: With the Middlesex Cricket League touring team to Trinidad and Tobago, 1978. Amsterdam with Loughborough University 1981.
Cricketers particularly learned from: "Bob Taylor, John Hampshire, Phil Russell, the Derbyshire coach, Alan Knott, George Barton (Hillingdon C.C.) who taught me how to keep, Grayson Heath (Natal manager)."
Other sports: Tennis, squash, badminton, windsurfing, skiing, riding, rugby union.
Relaxations: Reading cricketers' autobiographies, golf, "not too well", hiking (especially around the Lake District and Snowdonia). Listening to music.
Extras: Caught 5 catches in innings on debut v. Gloucs. 2nd XI. Cap in August 1982.
Opinions on cricket: "1a) The qualification laws enabling overseas players to play for England are being and should be drastically reviewed, as the vast majority of professional players think they are too slack. 1b) The emphasis with overseas qualification appears to be where a person is born. I think it should be with where a person is bred. A person who was born overseas, but has lived most of his life in England should be allowed to play for England. A person who was born in England but lived most of his life abroad shouldn't! 2) I do not blame the demise of English cricket on the 3-day game on too much county cricket, the blame in my opinion can be put to a large extent on the wickets. We should produce fast, bouncy pitches with consistant bounce. 3) I think any restrictions on short pitched bowling should be removed; English players should have to learn to cope with intimidatory bowling. 4) More one day cricket should be played even at the expense of 3-day cricket, as it is this type of cricket that the sponsors and public want! 5) More points should be given to teams that win a county championship game. 6) I think that the Combined Universities side playing in the Benson and Hedges competition should be extended to include players from the other universities in England. There are enough good players outside Oxbridge to justify this. 7) The problems regarding South Africa's exclusion from international cricket should be resolved. Their presence would be a great boost for the game."
Best batting performance: 66 Derbyshire v Essex, Chesterfield 1984.

LAST SEASON: BATTING

	I.	N.O.	R.	H.S.	AV.
TEST					
OTHER FIRST CLASS	11	2	146	66	16.22
INT					
J.P.L.	4	1	14	8*	4.67
NAT.W.					
B & H					

CAREER: BATTING

	I.	N.O.	R.	H.S.	AV.
TEST					
OTHER FIRST CLASS	37	10	351	66	13.00
INT					
J.P.L.	10	2	33	13	4.13
NAT.W.					
B & H					

LAST SEASON: WICKET KEEPING

	C.	ST.			
TEST					
OTHER FIRST CLASS	18	–			
INT					
J.P.L.	1	1			
NAT.W.					
B & H					

CAREER: WICKET KEEPING

	C.	ST.			
TEST					
OTHER FIRST CLASS	50	5			
INT					
J.P.L.	11	6			
NAT.W.					
B & H					

MALCOLM, D.E.

Full Name: Devon Eugene Malcolm.
Role: Right-hand bat, right arm bowler.
Born: 22 February 1963, Kingston, Jamaica.
Height: 6′ 2″ **Weight:** 14st.
County debut: 1984.
County Cap: No.
Test debut: —
No. of Tests: 0.
No of One-Day Internationals: 0.
1000 runs in a season: 0.
50 wickets in a season: 0.
1st-Class 50s scored: 0.
1st-Class 100s scored: 0.
1st-Class 200s scored: 0.
1st-Class 5 w. in innings: 0.
1st-Class 10 w. in match: 0.
One-day 50s 0.
One-day 100s: 0.
Place in batting averages: — average: —; (1983: — average: —).
Place in bowling averages: 122 average: 42.13; (1983: — average: —).
1st-Class catches 1984: 4 (career: 4).
Parents: Albert Malcolm and Brendale Malcolm (deceased).
Marital status: Single.
Education: St. Elizabeth Technical High School and Richmond College.
Qualifications: College certificates.

Off-season 1984–85: Training for summer 1985.
Equipment used: Gunn & Moore bats.
Cricketers particularly admired: Michael Holding, Richard Hadlee.
Other sports: Football, table tennis.
Significant injuries in 1984: Back injuries.
Relaxations: Watching Karate films, music.
Best batting performance: 23 Derbyshire v Nottinghamshire, Trent Bridge
1984.
Best bowling performance: 3-78 Derbyshire v Kent, Maidstone 1984.

LAST SEASON: BATTING

	I.	N.O.	R.	H.S.	AV.
TEST					
OTHER FIRST CLASS	8	1	40	23	5.72
INT					
J.P.L.					
NAT.W.					
B & H					

CAREER: BATTING

	I.	N.O.	R.	H.S.	AV.
TEST					
OTHER FIRST CLASS	8	1	40	23	5.72
INT					
J.P.L.					
NAT.W.					
B & H					

LAST SEASON: BOWLING

	O.	M.	R.	W.	AV.
TEST					
OTHER FIRST CLASS	156.2	24	674	16	42.13
INT					
J.P.L.					
NAT.W.					
B & H					

CAREER: BOWLING

	O.	M.	R.	W.	AV.
TEST					
OTHER FIRST CLASS	156.2	24	674	16	42.13
INT					
J.P.L.					
NAT.W.					
B & H					

MILLER, G.

Full Name: Geoffrey Miller.
Role: Right-hand bat, off-break
bowler.
Born: 8 September 1952,
Chesterfield.
Height: 6′ 2″ **Weight:** 11st. 6lbs.
Nickname: Dusty.
County debut: 1973.
County cap: 1976.
Benefit: 1985.
Test debut: 1976.
No. of Tests: 34.
No. of One-Day Internationals: 25.
1000 runs in a season: 0.
50 wickets in a season: 4.
1st-Class 50s scored: 60.
1st-Class 100s scored: 1.

DERBYSHIRE

1st-Class 200s scored: 0.
1st-Class 5 w. in innings: 0.
1st-Class 10 w. in match: 0.
One-day 50s: 16.
One-day 100s: 0.
Place in batting averages: 107 average: 32.17; (1983: 97 average: 30.39).
Place in bowling averages: 32 average: 25.70; (1983: 92 average: 34.54).
1st-Class catches 1984: 27 (career: 202).
Parents: Gwen and Keith Miller.
Wife: Carol.
Children: Helen Jane; Anna Louise; James Daniel.
Education: Chesterfield Grammar School.
Family links with cricket: Father played local cricket in Chesterfield. Brother plays for Chesterfield C.C.
Overseas tours: With England Young Cricketers to India 1970–71 and West Indies 1972. Toured with England to India, Sri Lanka, Australia 1976–77; Pakistan, New Zealand 1977–78; Australia 1978–79 and 1979–80 but had to return December 1979 through injury. W. Indies 1981; Australia and New Zealand 1982–83.
Cricketers particularly learnt from: E.J. Barlow, R. Illingworth, F. Titmus.
Equipment used: Gray-Nicolls.
Other sports: Golf, table-tennis, football.
Relaxations: Crosswords, reading, television, family life. Watching Chesterfield F.C. particularly, and all sports in general.
Extras: Became Captain of Derbyshire half-way through 1979 season, but relinquished it half-way though 1981 season in favour of Barry Wood. Declined to sign for Derbyshire for 1982 season, and was released. Negotiated with several other counties, but signed again. Dropped out of Lord's Test v. Pakistan, August 1982, because of chicken-pox.

LAST SEASON: BATTING

	I.	N.O.	R.	H.S.	AV.
TEST	4	0	42	22	10.50
OTHER FIRST CLASS	30	5	891	130	35.64
INT	3	1	20	10	10.00
J.P.L.	10	5	284	78*	56.80
NAT.W.	1	0	1	1	–
B & H	4	1	123	65*	41.00

CAREER: BATTING

	I.	N.O.	R.	H.S.	AV.
TEST	51	4	1212	98*	25.78
OTHER FIRST CLASS	359	63	8226	130	27.79
INT	18	2	136	46	8.50
J.P.L.	120	25	1956	84	20.58
NAT.W.	14	3	273	59*	24.82
B & H	41	7	858	88*	25.24

LAST SEASON: BOWLING

	O.	M.	R.	W.	AV.
TEST	28	1	142	1	–
OTHER FIRST CLASS	869.2	256	2094	86	24.35
INT	30	4	111	6	18.50
J.P.L.	60.3	4	303	11	27.55
NAT.W.	24	7	39	0	–
B & H	44	6	128	5	25.60

CAREER: BOWLING

	O.	M.	R.	W.	AV.
TEST	280.1 484.4	79 140	1859	60	30.98
OTHER FIRST CLASS	256.2 6298.1	48 1744	16335	650	25.13
INT	13 194	1 19	813	25	32.52
J.P.L.	699.1	52	2955	108	27.36
NAT.W.	173	41	462	16	28.88
B & H	399	79	1134	43	26.37

Best batting performance: 130 Derbyshire v Lancashire, Old Trafford 1984.
Best bowling performance: 8-70 Derbyshire v Leicestershire, Coalville 1982.

MOIR, D.G.

Full Name: Dallas Gordon Moir.
Role: Right-hand bat, left arm
slow bowler.
Born: 13 April 1957, Imtarfa, Malta
("am Scottish however").
Height: 6' 8" **Weight:** 16st.
Nickname: "Usual nicknames for a
Scotsman in England."
County debut: 1981.
County cap: No.
Test debut: —
No. of Tests: 0.
No. of One-Day Internationals: 0.
1000 runs in a season: 0.
50 wickets in a season: 2.
1st-Class 50s scored: 3.
1st-Class 100s scored: 1.
1st-Class 200s scored: 0.
1st-Class 5 w. in innings: 0.
1st-Class 10 w. in match: 0.
One-day 50s: 1.
One-day 100s: 0.

Place in batting averages: 168 average: 24.27; (1983: 232 average: 12.44).

LAST SEASON: BATTING

	I.	N.O.	R.	H.S.	AV.
TEST					
OTHER FIRST CLASS	28	6	534	107	24.27
INT					
J.P.L.	9	0	141	79	15.67
NAT.W.	1	0	23	23	–
B & H	1	1	1	1*	–

CAREER: BATTING

	I.	N.O.	R.	H.S.	AV.
TEST					
OTHER FIRST CLASS	57	11	990	107	21.52
INT					
J.P.L.	12	0	156	79	13.00
NAT.W.	1	0	23	23	–
B & H	6	1	81	44	16.20

LAST SEASON: BOWLING

	O.	M.	R.	W.	AV.
TEST					
OTHER FIRST CLASS	822.5	206	2419	65	37.22
INT					
J.P.L.	80	4	372	9	41.33
NAT.W.	24	6	58	3	19.33
B & H	11	1	43	0	–

CAREER: BOWLING

	O.	M.	R.	W.	AV.
TEST					
OTHER FIRST CLASS	2193.5	578	6159	187	32.94
INT					
J.P.L.	119	8	541	12	45.08
NAT.W.	24	6	58	3	19.33
B & H	43	4	174	0	–

Place in bowling averages: 106 average: 37.22; (1983: 93 average: 3~..
1st-Class catches 1984: 18 (career: 57).
Parents: Douglas Lennox and Anthea Gillian Moir.
Marital status: Single.
Family links with cricket: Father and brother play league cricket in Aberdeen.
Education: Hazlehead Primary School, Aberdeen; Aberdeen Grammar School; Aberdeen College of Commerce.
Jobs outside cricket: Computer operator.
Cricketing superstitions: Puts right pad on first.
Equipment used: Gunn & Moore.
Other sports: Rugby, basketball, golf.
Relaxations: Girl friend, music, crosswords.
Extras: Played for Scottish Under-21 XI for five years (1974–78). Played for Scotland in their first year in Benson & Hedges Cup (1980). Played for Scotland in 1980 against Holland, Ireland, Worcestershire and West Indies. Top wicket taker for Derbyshire in 1982 with 76 wickets. Declined offer of new contract for "personal" (non-cricketing) reasons at end of 1982 season, but then changed mind and was a regular member of the side.
Best batting performance: 107 Derbyshire v Warwickshire, Chesterfield 1984.
Best bowling performance: 6-60 Derbyshire v Nottinghamshire, Trent Bridge 1984.

MORRIS, J.E.

Full Name: John Edward Morris.
Role: Right-hand bat;
right arm medium bowler.
Born: 1 April 1964, Crewe, Cheshire.
Height: 5′ 10″ **Weight:** 11st. 8lbs.
Nickname: Animal.
County debut: 1982.
County cap: No.
Test debut: —
No. of Tests: 0.
No. of One-Day Internationals: 0.
1000 runs in a season: 0.
50 wickets in a season: 0.
1st-Class 50s scored: 4.
1st-Class 100s scored: 3.
1st-Class 200s scored: 0.
1st-Class 5 w. in innings: 0.
1st-Class 10 w. in match: 0.
One-day 50s: 3.
One-day 100s: 1.

Place in batting averages: 78 average: 35.11; (1983: 186 average: 19.00).
Place in bowling averages: — average: —; (1983: — average: —).
1st-Class catches 1984: 4 (career: 8).
Parents: George (Eddie) and Jean Morris.
Marital status: Single.
Education: Shavington Comprehensive School, and Dane Bank College of Further Education.
Qualifications: O-levels.
Jobs outside cricket: Worked as a carpet fitter.
Off-season 1984–85: Abroad.
Overseas tours: Umbilo C.C. Durban, S. Africa 1982–83, 1983–84.
Family links with cricket: "Father played for Crewe C.C. for many years as an opening bowler."
Cricketers particularly learnt from: "Tony Borrington, Phil Russell and my father."
Equipment used: Duncan Fearnley.
Other sports: Football, basketball and snooker. Watching athletics and motor-racing.
Significant injuries in 1984: Hit on knee at short leg; missed one month.
Relaxations: Movies, music, good food.
Opinions on cricket: "There are too many overseas players qualifying to play for England. The rules should be tightened up."
Best batting performance: 135 Derbyshire v Leicestershire, Leicester 1984.

LAST SEASON: BATTING

	I.	N.O.	R.	H.S.	AV.
TEST					
OTHER FIRST CLASS	28	1	948	135	35.11
INT					
J.P.L.	12	1	380	104	34.54
NAT.W.	1	0	8	8	–
B & H	3	0	80	51	26.67

CAREER: BATTING

	I.	N.O.	R.	H.S.	AV.
TEST					
OTHER FIRST CLASS	50	2	1327	135	27.65
INT					
J.P.L.	20	1	548	104	29.84
NAT.W.	2	0	15	8	7.50
B & H	3	0	80	51	26.67

LAST SEASON: BOWLING

	O.	M.	R.	W.	AV.
TEST					
OTHER FIRST CLASS	11	0	73	1	–
INT					
J.P.L.					
NAT.W.					
B & H					

CAREER: BOWLING

	O.	M.	R.	W.	AV.
TEST					
OTHER FIRST CLASS	13	2	73	1	–
INT					
J.P.L.					
NAT.W.					
B & H					

MORTENSEN, O.H.

Full Name: Ole Henrik Mortensen.
Role: Right-hand bat, right arm fast bowler.
Born: 29 January 1958, Vejle, Denmark.
Height: 6′ 4″ **Weight:** 14st. 2lbs.
Nickname: Stan (coined by Bob Taylor after England footballer Stan Mortenson).
County debut: 1983.
County cap: No.
Test debut: —
No. of Tests: 0.
No. of One-Day Internationals: 0.
1000 runs in a season: 0.
50 wickets in a season: 1.
1st-Class 50s scored: 0.
1st-Class 100s scored: 0.
1st-Class 200s scored: 0.
1st-Class 5 w. in innings: 3.
1st-Class 10 w. in match: 1.
One-day 50s: 0.
One-day 100s: 0.
Place in batting averages: 233 average: 15.75; (1983: — average: —).
Place in bowling averages: 78 average: 31.67; (1983: 33 average: 24.32).
1st-Class catches 1984: 4 (career: 9).
Parents: Willy Ernst and Inge Wicka Mortensen.

LAST SEASON: BATTING

	I.	N.O.	R.	H.S.	AV.
TEST					
OTHER FIRST CLASS	8	4	63	40*	15.75
INT					
J.P.L.	2	0	7	5	3.50
NAT.W.					
B & H	–	–	–	–	–

CAREER: BATTING

	I.	N.O.	R.	H.S.	AV.
TEST					
OTHER FIRST CLASS	31	19	139	40*	11.58
INT					
J.P.L.	6	4	12	5	6.00
NAT.W.	1	1	2	2*	–
B & H	–	–	–	–	–

LAST SEASON: BOWLING

	O.	M.	R.	W.	AV.
TEST					
OTHER FIRST CLASS	212.3	55	570	18	31.67
INT					
J.P.L.	53	5	202	10	20.20
NAT.W.					
B & H	11	2	30	3	10.00

CAREER: BOWLING

	O.	M.	R.	W.	AV.
TEST					
OTHER FIRST CLASS	731	163	2175	84	25.89
INT					
J.P.L.	130.5	9	542	24	22.58
NAT.W.	24	7	66	4	16.50
B & H	11	2	30	3	10.00

Wife and date of marriage: Jette Jepmond.
Children: Julie Jepmond Mortensen, 30 August 1982.
Family links with cricket: "My small brother Michael Mortensen used to play cricket. He is now a professional tennis player, and has played in Davis Cup for Denmark."
Education: Brondbyoster School; Avedore School.
Jobs outside cricket: Worked as a tax assistant in Denmark.
Equipment used: Gunn & Moore.
Overseas tours: Touring East Africa in 1976 with the Danish national side.
Overseas teams played for: Ellerslie in Auckland, New Zealand, 1983–84 and Svanholm C.C. Denmark.
Cricketers particularly learnt from: Torben Jensen, Jorgen Janson, Peter Hargreaves and many others.
Cricketers particularly admired: Dennis Lillee, Bob Taylor.
Other sports: Tennis, golf, handball, ice-hockey, football.
Relaxations: Music, books, movies.
Extras: *Derbyshire's Dane* by Peter Hargreaves, published 1984. Has played for Denmark.
Best batting performance: 40* Derbyshire v Glamorgan, Derby 1984.
Best bowling performance: 6-27 Derbyshire v Yorkshire, Sheffield 1983.

NEWMAN, P.G.

Full Name: Paul Geoffrey Newman.
Role: Right-hand bat; right arm fast medium bowler, outfielder.
Born: 10 January 1959, Leicestershire.
Height: 6' 3" **Weight:** 13st. 3lbs.
Nickname: Judge ("from the film *Judge Roy Bean*, starring my namesake").
County debut: 1980.
County cap: No.
Test debut: —
No. of Tests: 0.
No. of One-Day Internationals: 0.
1000 runs in a season: 0.
50 wickets in a season: 1.
1st-Class 50s scored: 0.
1st-Class 100s scored: 0.
1st-Class 200s scored: 0.
1st-Class 5 w. in innings: 0.
1st-Class 10 w. in match: 0.
One-day 50s: 0.

One-day 100s: 0.
Place in batting averages: 251 average: 14.16; (1983: — average: —).
Place in bowling averages: 96 average: 34.34; (1983: — average: —)
1st-Class catches 1984: 3 (career: 16).
Marital status: Single.
Education: Alderman Newton's Grammar School, Leicester.
Qualifications: Six O-levels.
Jobs outside cricket: Has worked as a cashier in a dairy, and to strengthen his back, lifting packing cases in a toy factory warehouse.
Off-season 1984–85: At home relaxing.
Equipment used and endorsed: Gunn & Moore.
Overseas teams played for: Queensland Cricket Assn. Colts XI 1981–82, Old Collegians S.A. 1983–84.
Cricketers particularly learnt from: "Learnt from many, especially my colleagues at Derby."
Other sports: Golf, football, 10 pin bowling, snooker.
Relaxations: Crosswords, music, T.V., watching Leicester F.C. and Leicester basketball.
Significant injuries in 1984: Sore shins and muscle tear in back.
Extras: Played for Leicestershire 2nd XI in 1978 and 1979, but was released. As a schoolboy was a wicket-keeper. Took 50 wickets in his first season with Derbyshire. Won Commercial Union Under-23 Bowling Award for 1981. Won Whitbread Scholarship to Brisbane, Australia 1981–82.
Best batting performance: 40 Derbyshire v Lancashire, Old Trafford 1984.
Best bowling performance: 7-104 Derbyshire v Surrey, The Oval 1984.

LAST SEASON: BATTING

	I.	N.O.	R.	H.S.	AV.
TEST					
OTHER FIRST CLASS	21	2	269	40	14.16
INT					
J.P.L.	5	1	41	24	10.25
NAT.W.	1	0	35	35	–
B & H	3	2	41	21	–

CAREER: BATTING

	I.	N.O.	R.	H.S.	AV.
TEST					
OTHER FIRST CLASS	67	13	640	40	11.52
INT					
J.P.L.	17	4	116	24	8.92
NAT.W.	3	1	50	35	25.00
B & H	7	5	62	21	31.00

LAST SEASON: BOWLING

	O.	M.	R.	W.	AV.
TEST					
OTHER FIRST CLASS	505.2	89	1717	50	34.34
INT					
J.P.L.	58	3	290	13	22.31
NAT.W.	24	3	98	1	–
B & H	44	4	180	6	30.00

CAREER: BOWLING

	O.	M.	R.	W.	AV.
TEST					
OTHER FIRST CLASS	1452.5	254	5046	151	33.42
INT					
J.P.L.	293.2	17	1259	51	24.69
NAT.W.	63.4	6	220	8	27.50
B & H	129.5	17	510	19	26.84

ROBERTS, B.

Full Name: Bruce Roberts.
Role: Right-hand bat, right arm
medium pace bowler.
Born: 30 May 1962, Lusaka,
Zambia.
Height: 6′ 1″ **Weight:** 14st.
County debut: 1983.
County cap: No.
Test debut: —
No. of Tests: 0.
No. of One-Day Internationals: 0.
1000 runs in a season: 0.
50 wickets in a season: 0.
1st-Class 50s scored: 7.
1st-Class 100s scored: 0.
1st-Class 200s scored: 0.
1st-Class 5 w. in innings: 0.
1st-Class 10 w. in match: 0.
One-day 50s: 0.
One-day 100s: 0.
Place in batting averages: 151 average: 26.38; (1983: — average —).
Place in bowling averages: 130 average: 47.45; (1983: — average: —).
1st-Class catches 1984: 12 (career: 19).
Parents: Arthur William and Sarah Anne Roberts.
Marital status: Single.
Education: Puzawi, Peterhouse, Prince Edward, Rhodesia.
Qualifications: O-levels.
Off-season 1984–85: In Johannesburg.

LAST SEASON: BATTING

	I.	N.O.	R.	H.S.	AV.
TEST					
OTHER FIRST CLASS	26	5	554	80	26.38
INT					
J.P.L.	9	2	169	47	24.14
NAT.W.	1	0	3	3	–
B & H	3	1	13	11	6.50

CAREER: BATTING

	I.	N.O.	R.	H.S.	AV.
TEST					
OTHER FIRST CLASS	48	7	1167	89	28.46
INT					
J.P.L.	9	2	169	47	24.14
NAT.W.	1	0	3	3	–
B & H	3	1	13	11	6.50

LAST SEASON: BOWLING

	O.	M.	R.	W.	AV.
TEST					
OTHER FIRST CLASS	277	43	1044	22	47.45
INT					
J.P.L.	67.4	1	435	20	21.75
NAT.W.	16	1	84	2	42.00
B & H	30	2	151	4	37.75

CAREER: BOWLING

	O.	M.	R.	W.	AV.
TEST					
OTHER FIRST CLASS	469	82	1613	48	33.60
INT					
J.P.L.	67.4	1	435	20	21.75
NAT.W.	16	1	84	2	42.00
B & H	30	2	151	4	37.75

Equipment used and endorsed: Slazenger.
Overseas teams played for: Transvaal B 1982–83 and 1983–84.
Cricketers particularly admired: Mike Proctor, Ian Chappell.
Other sports followed: Rugby.
Relaxations: Family.
Best batting performance: 89 Transvaal B v Free State, Johannesburg 1983–84.
Best bowling performance: 4-32 Transvaal B v Free State, Johannesburg 1982–83.

TAYLOR, J.P.

Full Name: Jonathan Paul Taylor.
Role: Left-hand bat, left arm fast medium bowler.
Born: 8 August 1964, Ashby-de-la-Zouch, Leicestershire.
Height: 6' 2" **Weight:** 12st. 10lbs.
Nickname: Arthur, Nasty.
County debut: 1984.
County cap: No.
Test debut: —
No. of Tests: 0.
No. of One-Day Internationals: 0.
1000 runs in a season: 0.
50 wickets in a season: 0.
1st-Class 50s scored: 0.
1st-Class 100s scored: 0.
1st-Class 200s scored: 0.
1st-Class 5 w. in innings: 0.
1st-Class 10 w. in match: 0.
One-day 50s: 0.
One-day 100s: 0.
Place in batting averages: — average: —; (1983: — average: —).
Place in bowling averages: — average: —; (1983: — average: —).
1st-Class catches 1984: 2 (career: 2).
Parents: Roland Derek and Janet Elizabeth Taylor.
Marital status: Single.
Family links with cricket: Father and brother played local league cricket.
Education: Pingle School, Swadlincote.
Qualifications: 6 O-levels.
Jobs outside cricket: Mining craft apprentice for National Coal Board.
Off-season 1984–85: Playing and coaching in Auckland, New Zealand.
Equipment used: Gunn & Moore.
Cricketers particularly learnt from: John Lever, Bob Taylor.

Other sports: Basketball, squash, badminton, football, swimming.
Best batting performance: 11 Derbyshire v Middlesex, Derby 1984.
Best bowling performance: 2-92 Derbyshire v Somerset, Taunton 1984.

LAST SEASON: BATTING

	I.	N.O.	R.	H.S.	AV.
TEST					
OTHER FIRST CLASS	2	0	11	11	5.50
INT					
J.P.L.	3	0	5	4	1.67
NAT.W.					
B & H					

CAREER: BATTING

	I.	N.O.	R.	H.S.	AV.
TEST					
OTHER FIRST CLASS	2	0	11	11	5.50
INT					
J.P.L.	3	0	5	4	1.67
NAT.W.					
B & H					

LAST SEASON: BOWLING

	O.	M.	R.	W.	AV.
TEST					
OTHER FIRST CLASS	49.2	6	188	2	94.00
INT					
J.P.L.	31	1	172	5	34.40
NAT.W.					
B & H					

CAREER: BOWLING

	O.	M.	R.	W.	AV.
TEST					
OTHER FIRST CLASS	49.2	6	188	2	94.00
INT					
J.P.L.	31	1	172	5	34.40
NAT.W.					
B & H					

TAYLOR, R.W.

Full Name: Robert William Taylor.
Role: Right-hand bat; wicket-keeper.
Born: 17 July 1941, Stoke-on-Trent.
Height: 5' 8" **Weight:** 10st 10lbs.
Nickname: Chat.
County debut: 1961.
County cap: 1962.
Test debut: 1970.
No. of Tests: 57.
No. of One-Day Internationals: 27.
Testimonial: £6,672 in 1973, and
£54,000 in 1981.
1000 runs in a season: 0.
50 wickets in a season: 0.
1st-Class 50s scored: 22.
1st-Class 100s scored: 1.
1st-Class 200s scored: 0.
1st-Class 5 w. in innings: 0.
1st-Class 10 w. in match: 0.
One-day 50s: 0.
One-day 100s: 0.

Place in batting averages: 201 average: 20.10; (1983: 204 average: 15.91).

Place in bowling averages: — average: —; (1983: — average: —).
Wife and date of marriage: Catherine, 1962.
Children: Mark (21), Claire (11).
Family links with cricket: Son keeps wicket at club level.
Overseas tours: Australia, New Zealand 1970–71 and 1974–75; Australia with Rest of the World team 1971–72; West Indies 1973–74 with England; Pakistan, New Zealand 1977–78, 1983–84; Australia 1978–79 and 1979–80. India, 1981–82, 1982–83.
Cricketers particularly learnt from: Godfrey Evans, Keith Andrew.
Equipment endorsed: Mitre.
Jobs outside cricket: Promotional work with Mitre Sports, Huddersfield.
Other sports: Golf and squash. Follows equestrianism, point-to-point, racing.
Significant injuries in 1984: Tennis elbow.
Relaxations: Pipe-smoker, reading, gardening, music.
Extras: First wicket-keeper to 100 dismissals and to 100 catches, in John Player League. Dismissed 10 batsmen in a match, all caught, v Hampshire at Chesterfield in 1963, and seven in one innings, all caught, v Glamorgan at Derby in 1966. Played for Staffordshire 1958–60. Debut for Minor Counties v South Africans at Stoke-on-Trent in 1960. Has written "Anyone for Cricket" jointly with David Gower about the 1978–79 Australian Tour. Also "Wicket-Keeping." In 15 years, he used only 2 pairs of his blue-backed wicket-keeping gloves, and one of those was stolen. Even when Alan Knott was keeping Bob

LAST SEASON: BATTING

	I.	N.O.	R.	H.S.	AV.
TEST					
OTHER FIRST CLASS	22	7	303	46	20.20
INT					
J.P.L.	5	4	46	29*	–
NAT.W.	1	0	1	1	–
B & H	2	1	12	6*	–

CAREER: BATTING

	I.	N.O.	R.	H.S.	AV.
TEST	83	12	1156	97	16.28
OTHER FIRST CLASS	795	155	10884	100	17.06
INT	17	7	130	26*	13.00
J.P.L.	147	53	1341	43*	14.26
NAT.W.	30	11	349	53*	18.37
B & H	40	16	323	31*	13.46

LAST SEASON: BOWLING

	O.	M.	R.	W.	AV.
TEST					
OTHER FIRST CLASS	6.2	1	23	1	–
INT					
J.P.L.					
NAT.W.					
B & H					

CAREER: BOWLING

	O.	M.	R.	W.	AV.
TEST	2	0	6	0	–
OTHER FIRST CLASS	17.4	3	69	1	–
INT					
J.P.L.					
NAT.W.					
B & H					

LAST SEASON: WICKET KEEPING

	C.	ST.			
TEST					
OTHER FIRST CLASS	27	5			
INT					
J.P.L.	7	1			
NAT.W.	2	1			
B & H	10	–			

CAREER: WICKET KEEPING

	C.	ST.			
TEST	167	7			
OTHER FIRST CLASS	1304	168			
INT	26	6			
J.P.L.	187	49			
NAT.W.	58	8			
B & H	65	12			

Taylor out of the England team, Knott acknowledged Taylor was the better wicket-keeper. His house is named "Hambledon" after the famous early cricketing village. Celebrated his 40th birthday by playing for England v Australia. Awarded M.B.E., 1981. Waited 20 years to hit first century: v Yorkshire at Sheffield 19 June 1981. It took him 2 hrs. 48 mins. 1st first-class wicket 1984 (A. Stovold of Gloucestershire). Retired at end of 1984 season to take up post with 2nd XI.

Best batting performance: 100 Derbyshire v Yorkshire, Sheffield 1981.

TUNNICLIFFE, C.J.

Full Name: Colin John Tunnicliffe.
Role: Right-hand bat; left arm fast medium bowler.
Born: 11 August 1951, Derby.
Nickname: Tunners.
County debut: 1973.
County cap: 1977.
Test debut: —
No. of Tests: 0.
No. of One-Day Internationals: 0.
1000 runs in a season: 0.
50 wickets in a season: 1.
1st-Class 50s scored: 6.
1st-Class 100s scored: 0.
1st-Class 200s scored: 0.
1st-Class 5 w. in innings: 0.
1st-Class 10 w. in match: 0.

LAST SEASON: BATTING

	I.	N.O.	R.	H.S.	AV.
TEST					
OTHER FIRST CLASS					
INT					
J.P.L.	2	1	7	4	–
NAT.W.					
B & H	–	–	–	–	–

LAST SEASON: BOWLING

	O.	M.	R.	W.	AV.
TEST					
OTHER FIRST CLASS					
INT					
J.P.L.	8.4	0	92	0	–
NAT.W.					
B & H	22	8	57	3	19.00

CAREER: BATTING

	I.	N.O.	R.	H.S.	AV.
TEST					
OTHER FIRST CLASS	176	30	2092	91	14.33
INT					
J.P.L.	75	28	646	51*	13.74
NAT.W.	9	1	47	15*	5.88
B & H	21	5	181	28	11.31

CAREER: BOWLING

	O.	M.	R.	W.	AV.
TEST					
OTHER FIRST CLASS	3511.3	820	10265	319	32.18
INT					
J.P.L.	758.2	57	3209	122	26.30
NAT.W.					
B & H	126.2	17	458	19	24.10

One-day 50s: 1.
One-day 100s: 0.
Place in batting averages: — average: —; (1983: 191 average: 18.44).
Place in bowling averages: — average: —; (1983: 95 average: 35.18).
1st-Class catches 1984: 0 (career: 65).
Qualifications: N.C.A. Advanced Coach.
Equipment used: Stuart Surridge.
Jobs outside cricket: Commercial activities with Derbyshire.
Extras: Left staff after 1974 season but re-appeared in 1976. Renowned as a dressing-room raconteur. Released again in 1983, but made occasional appearances during 1984.
Best batting performance: 91 Derbyshire v Hampshire, Portsmouth 1983.
Best bowling performance: 7-36 Derbyshire v Essex, Chelmsford 1980.

WARNER, A.E.

Full name: Allan Esmond Warner.
Role: Right-hand bat, right arm
fast bowler, outfielder.
Born: 12 May 1959, Birmingham,
England.
Height: 5′ 8″ **Weight:** 10st.
Nickname: Esis.
County debut: 1982.
County cap: No.
Test debut: —
No. of Tests: 0.
No. of One-Day Internationals: 0.
1000 runs in a season: 0.
50 wickets in a season: 0.
1st-Class 50s scored: 0.
1st-Class 100s scored: 0.
1st-Class 200s scored: 0.
1st-Class 5 w. in innings: 1.
1st-Class 10 w. in match: 0.
One-day 50s: 0.
One-day 100s: 0.

Place in batting averages: — average: —; (1983: 225 average: 13.10).
Place in bowling averages: 123 average: 42.13; (1983: 23 average: 22.52).
1st-Class catches 1984: 5 (career: 10).
Parents: Edgar and Sarah Warner.
Children: Alvin, 6 September 1980.
Education: Tabernacle School, St. Kitts, West Indies.
Qualifications: C.S.E. Maths, Bricklaying.
Cricketers particularly learnt from: John Browny, Henry Benjamin.

Cricketers particularly admired: M. Marshall and M. Holding.

Equipment endorsed: Duncan Fearnley.

Off season 1984–85: Playing cricket in St. Kitts and Leeward Islands.

Other sports: Football, table-tennis. Follow football, boxing and athletics.

Relaxations: Watching movies; music (soul, reggae and calypso).

Extras: Released by Worcestershire at end of 1984 and joined Derbyshire.

Opinions on cricket: "Too many overs bowled in a day. And, in the John Player Special League, bowlers must come off a longer run."

Best batting performance: 67 Worcestershire v Warwickshire, Edgbaston 1982.

Best bowling performance: 5-27 Worcestershire v Glamorgan, Worcester 1984.

LAST SEASON: BATTING

	I.	N.O.	R.	H.S.	AV.
TEST					
OTHER FIRST CLASS	7	2	62	27	12.40
INT					
J.P.L.	1	0	2	2	–
NAT.W.					
B & H	1	0	2	2	–

CAREER: BATTING

	I.	N.O.	R.	H.S.	AV.
TEST					
OTHER FIRST CLASS	39	9	480	67	16.00
INT					
J.P.L.	15	4	45	14	4.09
NAT.W.	1	0	2	2	–
B & H	5	2	39	24*	13.00

LAST SEASON: BOWLING

	O.	M.	R.	W.	AV.
TEST					
OTHER FIRST CLASS	185	33	632	15	42.13
INT					
J.P.L.	15	0	73	1	–
NAT.W.					
B & H	22	1	93	1	–

CAREER: BOWLING

	O.	M.	R.	W.	AV.
TEST					
OTHER FIRST CLASS	597.4	106	1947	61	31.92
INT					
J.P.L.	130.3	5	604	19	31.79
NAT.W.	19.3	2	83	2	41.50
B & H	66.5	6	248	8	31.00

Q. 4. Which is the latest country to become an associate member of the I.C.C., but without voting power?

Q. 5. How many times has Geoffrey Boycott captained England?

Q. 6. Which counties finished, respectively, top and bottom in the 1984 county championship?

Q. 7. Which three players scored centuries on the last day of the 1984 county championship?

WRIGHT, J.G.

Full Name: John Geoffrey Wright.
Role: Left-hand bat, right arm
medium bowler.
Born: 5 July 1954, Darfield,
New Zealand.
Height: 6′ 1″ **Weight:** 12st. 6lbs.
Nickname: Wrighty, Shake.
County debut: 1977.
County cap: 1977.
Test debut: 1977–78.
No. of Tests: 31.
No. of One-Day Internationals: 52.
1000 runs in a season: 6.
50 wickets in a season: 0.
1st-Class 50s scored: 71.
1st-Class 100s scored: 34.
1st-Class 200s scored: 0.
1st-Class 5 w. in innings: 0.
1st-Class 10 w. in match: 0.
One-day 50s: 34.
One-day 100s: 4.

Place in batting averages: 10 average: 60.05; (1983: 21 average: 46.54).
Place in bowling averages: — average: —; (1983: — average: —).
1st-Class catches 1984: 10 (career: 138).
Parents: Geoff and Helen Wright.
Marital status: Single.
Education: Christ's College, Christchurch, New Zealand; University of Otago, Dunedin, N.Z.
Qualifications: B.Sc. Biochemistry.
Family links with cricket: "Father played first-class cricket."
Overseas tours: Toured England with New Zealand 1978. Australia 1980–81, Sri Lanka and Pakistan 1984–85.
Overseas teams played for: Northern Districts, Kent 2nd XI.
Cricketers particularly learnt from: "Greg Chappell, Eddie 'Bunter' Barlow, David 'Razor' Steele– he taught me the true value of a run."
Off-season 1984–85: Playing in New Zealand.
Cricket superstitions: "Ironed shirts are bad luck."
Equipment used and endorsed: Gray-Nicolls.
Other sports: Golf, horse-racing, skiing.
Relaxations: "Music, watching movies, filling out questionnaires."
Extras: Holds record of 7 centuries for Derbyshire in a season– beating record of 6 held by Peter Kirsten in previous season, after record of 5 had stood for 49 years. Vice-captain of New Zealand 1984.
Opinions on cricket: County cricket is a business and should be administered

at all levels by persons who are qualified to do so. The County Championship should be restricted to 16 four-day games.

Best batting performance: 190 Derbyshire v Yorkshire, Derby 1982.

LAST SEASON: BATTING

	I.	N.O.	R.	H.S.	AV.
TEST					
OTHER FIRST CLASS	21	1	1201	177	60.05
INT					
J.P.L.	15	0	294	46	19.60
NAT.W.	2	1	119	73*	–
B & H	4	0	95	39	23.75

CAREER: BATTING

	I.	N.O.	R.	H.S.	AV.
TEST	54	2	1586	141	30.50
OTHER FIRST CLASS	332	25	12996	190	42.33
INT	52	1	1465	84	28.72
J.P.L.	91	6	2710	108	31.88
NAT.W.	12	2	555	87*	55.50
B & H	30	2	1005	102	35.89

LAST SEASON: BOWLING

	O.	M.	R.	W.	AV.
TEST					
OTHER FIRST CLASS	22	2	114	1	–
INT					
J.P.L.					
NAT.W.					
B & H					

CAREER: BOWLING

	O.	M.	R.	W.	AV.
TEST	1	0	2	0	–
OTHER FIRST CLASS	36.4	4	179	2	89.50
INT	3	1	2	0	–
J.P.L.					
NAT.W.					
B & H					

COUNTY QUIZ

Q. 1. When was the club founded?

Q. 2. Who made the most first-class runs for the county last season, and how many?

Q. 3. What's the highest ever county total, and against whom?

Q. 4. Who took most wickets for the county last season, and how many?

Q. 5. What's the highest individual score for the county, who hit it, and when?

Q. 6. What's the highest scoring partnership for the county for any wicket?

Q. 7. How many times has the club won the County Championship?

Q. 8. What's the lowest ever total made by the county in one innings, when, and against whom?

Q. 9. Which bowler took the most first-class wickets in one season, when, and how many?

Q. 10. Which batsman hit the most runs in one season, when and how many?

Essex

ACFIELD, D.L.

Full Name: David Laurence Acfield.
Role: Right-hand bat, off-break bowler.
Born: 24 July 1947, Chelmsford, Essex.
Height: 5′ 9½″ **Weight:** 11st 2lbs.
Nickname: Ackers.
County debut: 1966.
County cap: 1970.
Test debut: —
No. of Tests: 0.
No. of One-Day Internationals: 0.
1000 runs in season: 0.
50 wickets in a season: 7.
1st-Class 50s scored: 0.
1st-Class 100s scored: 0.
1st-Class 200s scored: 0.
1st-Class 5 w. in innings: 0.
1st-Class 10 w. in match: 0.
One-day 50s: 0.
One-day 100s: 0.

Place in batting averages: — average: —; (1983: — average: —).
Place in bowling averages: 63 average: 29.74; (1983: 57 average: 28.42).
1st-Class catches 1984: 10 (career: 126).
Benefit: 1981: £42,788
Parents: Robert and Ena Acfield.
Wife and date of marriage: Helen, 27 October 1973.
Children: Clare Louise, 10 December 1977, Rosemary Helen, 16 March 1982.
Education: Brentwood School; Christ's College, Cambridge.
Qualifications: M.A. Cantab, History.
Jobs outside cricket: Schoolmaster.
Family links with cricket: Late elder brother, Ian 1944–68, member of M.C.C., Incogniti, Cambridge University Crusaders, etc.
Equipment used: Stuart Surridge.

Overseas tours: With M.C.C. to East Africa 1973–74.
Other sports: Fencing (sabre), British Olympic team 1968 and 1972. Commonwealth Games Gold Medal (team event) 1970, British champion 1969–70–71–72, now retired. Cambridge blue for fencing.
Relaxations: Bird-watching; films, especially Westerns.
Extras: Cambridge cricket blue 1967, 1968.
Best batting performance: 42 Cambridge University v Leicestershire, Leicester 1967.
Best bowling performance: 8-55 Essex v Kent, Canterbury 1981.

LAST SEASON: BATTING

	I.	N.O.	R.	H.S.	AV.
TEST					
OTHER FIRST CLASS	22	9	41	7*	3.15
INT					
J.P.L.	4	2	5	4	2.50
NAT.W.	1	0	1	1	–
B & H	1	1	5	5*	–

CAREER: BATTING

	I.	N.O.	R.	H.S.	AV.
TEST					
OTHER FIRST CLASS	377	191	1545	42	8.31
INT					
J.P.L.	45	30	78	9*	5.20
NAT.W.	7	6	3	2*	–
B & H	4	3	15	8*	–

LAST SEASON: BOWLING

	O.	M.	R.	W.	AV.
TEST					
OTHER FIRST CLASS	577.4	174	1368	46	29.74
INT					
J.P.L.	68	3	290	5	58.00
NAT.W.	24	12	25	4	6.25
B & H	23	5	65	2	32.50

CAREER: BOWLING

	O.	M.	R.	W.	AV.
TEST					
OTHER FIRST CLASS	10293.1	2975	24214	876	27.64
INT					
J.P.L.	715.2	68	2794	113	24.72
NAT.W.	93.3	21	281	8	35.13
B & H	273.5	27	879	28	31.39

Q. 8. Who was top of the first-class bowling averages in 1984, with how many wickets at what average?

Q. 9. Who was top of the first batting averages in 1984, with how many runs at what average?

Q. 10. What English player scored over 2000 runs in the 1984 season and took 38 wickets and 27 catches?

Q. 11. What was the best first-class bowling performance of the English 1984 season and by whom?

Q. 12. Who took the most first-class catches in the English 1984 season?

EAST, D.E.

Full Name: David Edward East.
Role: Right-hand bat, wicket-keeper.
Born: 27 July 1959, Clapton.
Height: 5' 10" **Weight:** 12st. 7lbs.
Nickname: "Various insults, but
Ethel seems popular."
County debut: 1981.
County cap: 1982.
Test debut: —
No. of Tests: 0.
No. of One-Day Internationals: 0.
1000 runs in a season: 0.
50 wickets in a season: 0 ("unless
you count benefit matches").
1st-Class 50s scored: 8.
1st-Class 100s scored: 0.
1st-Class 200s scored: 0.
1st-Class 5 w. in innings: 0.
1st-Class 10 w. in match: 0.
One-day 50s: 0.
One-day 100s: 0.
Place in batting averages: 245 average: 14.57; (1983: 159 average: 22.68).
Place in bowling averages: — average: —; (1983: — average: —).
Parents: Edward William and Joan Lillian East.
Wife and date of marriage: Jeanette Anne, 14 September 1984.
Family links with cricket: Father played club cricket for Hadley C.C., an
Essex touring side.
Education: Millfields Primary; Hackney Downs School; University of East
Anglia.
Qualifications: B.Sc. Hons in Biological Sciences. Advanced cricket coach.
Jobs outside cricket: Shipping clerk, Byron Shipping, 1979; Field sales
manager, M.C. Kirby Ltd., Norwich; insurance clerk, Flett Sinclair Ltd., Ilford,
Essex.
Off-season 1984–85: Playing and coaching in Cape Town, South Africa.
Cricketing superstitions: The number 111.
Equipment used: Duncan Fearnley.
Cricketers particularly learnt from: Bill Morris, Ilford Cricket School, Alan
Knott.
Other sports: Hockey, squash, interested in most but loathes horse racing.
Relaxations: Playing the piano, listening to various types of music, video.
Extras: In spite of frequent jokes about the same name, he is no relation to his
Essex colleague, Ray East. Says David: "He doesn't mind being thought of as
my brother, but he has been a bit aggrieved that anyone has mistaken him for my
father!" Spent 1980 season with Northants. 2nd XI. Played for Essex 2nd XI at

16. Gordon's Gin Wicket-keeper of the Year 1983.

Opinions on cricket: "I believe that good fielding is penalised unfairly in that when an accurate throw hits the stumps runs can be scored from overthrows. I believe the ball should be 'dead' if the batsman is not out. Also felt that 117 overs a day was set too high. Games finished very late and the sponsors of the day's cricket often left dissatisfied because they were unable to meet the players after the game. Sponsorship is vital to our game and we should ensure that these people are kept happy."

Best batting performance: 91 Essex v Sussex, Hove 1983.

LAST SEASON: BATTING

	I.	N.O.	R.	H.S.	AV.
TEST					
OTHER FIRST CLASS	37	2	510	81	14.57
INT					
J.P.L.	9	5	89	25*	22.25
NAT.W.	2	1	25	25*	–
B & H	2	0	55	33	27.50

CAREER: BATTING

	I.	N.O.	R.	H.S.	AV.
TEST					
OTHER FIRST CLASS	118	17	1814	91	17.96
INT					
J.P.L.	25	10	206	43	13.73
NAT.W.	9	4	72	25*	14.40
B & H	9	0	129	33	14.33

LAST SEASON: BOWLING

	O.	M.	R.	W.	AV.
TEST					
OTHER FIRST CLASS	3	0	11	0	–
INT					
J.P.L.					
NAT.W.					
B & H					

CAREER: BOWLING

	O.	M.	R.	W.	AV.
TEST					
OTHER FIRST CLASS	3	0	11	0	–
INT					
J.P.L.					
NAT.W.					
B & H					

LAST SEASON: WICKET KEEPING

	C.	ST.			
TEST					
OTHER FIRST CLASS	76	1			
INT					
J.P.L.	12	1			
NAT.W.	–	1			
B & H	8	–			

CAREER: WICKET KEEPING

	C.	ST.			
TEST					
OTHER FIRST CLASS	235	20			
INT					
J.P.L.	46	10			
NAT.W.	11	2			
B & H	24	–			

Q. 13. What's the highest innings total in a NatWest/Gillette match?

Q. 14. What's the lowest innings total in a NatWest match?

EAST, R.E.

Full Name: Raymond Eric East.
Role: Right-hand bat, slow left arm orthodox bowler.
Born: 20 June 1947, Manningtree, Essex.
Height: 6' 1" **Weight:** 12st.
Nickname: Easty. Spindle.
County debut: 1965.
County cap: 1967.
Test debut: —
No. of Tests: 0.
No. of One-Day Internationals: 0.
Benefit: 1978.
1000 runs in a season: 0.
50 wickets in a season: 9.
1st-Class 50s scored: 22.
1st-Class 100s scored: 1.
1st-Class 200s scored: 0.
1st-Class 5 w. in innings: 0.
1st-Class 10 w. in match: 0.
One-day 50s: 1.
One-day 100s: 0.

Place in batting averages: — average: —; (1983: 185 average: 19.09).
Place in bowling averages: — average: —; (1983: 98 average: 35.56).
1st-Class catches 1984: 2 (career: 256).
Parents: Eric Edward and Paula East.
Wife and date of marriage: Barbara Wilms, July 1974.
Children: James Peter, 26 November 1976, John Raymond, 24 January 1979.
Education: East Bergholt Comprehensive.
Qualifications: Advanced coaching course.
Jobs outside cricket: Has been fuel representative. Gave up apprenticeship as electrician to take up one-year contract with Essex. Now runs a pub, The Red Lion at East Bergholt.
Other sports: Golf, soccer.
Relaxations: Keen Ipswich F.C. fan.
Extras: One of the best known "characters" in the game. Does excellent comic act on and off the field. Did a hole-in-one playing golf in the 156-yard 16th at Royston in the Cricketers v. Golfers annual match in 1981. Has taken 5 wickets in a John Player League innings four times—a record he shares with D.P. Hughes and D.A. Marriott. Gave up regular cricket to become 2nd XI captain and coach in 1984, but still makes occasional appearances in first team. Published autobiography *A Funny Turn* in 1983.
Best batting performance: 113 Essex v Hampshire, Chelmsford 1976.
Best bowling performance: 8-30 Essex v Nottinghamshire, Ilford 1977.

LAST SEASON: BATTING

	I.	N.O.	R.	H.S.	AV.
TEST					
OTHER FIRST CLASS	2	0	30	22	15.00
INT					
J.P.L.	1	1	2	2*	–
NAT.W.					
B & H					

CAREER: BATTING

	I.	N.O.	R.	H.S.	AV.
TEST					
OTHER FIRST CLASS	517	112	7178	113	14.21
INT					
J.P.L.	105	38	654	25*	9.76
NAT.W.	23	5	199	38*	11.06
B & H	32	15	259	54	15.24

LAST SEASON: BOWLING

	O.	M.	R.	W.	AV.
TEST					
OTHER FIRST CLASS	152.4	48	324	11	29.45
INT					
J.P.L.	19	0	79	2	39.50
NAT.W.					
B & H					

CAREER: BOWLING

	O.	M.	R.	W.	AV.
TEST					
OTHER FIRST CLASS	10998.1	3226	26210	1119	23.42
INT					
J.P.L.	1107.5	103	4504	187	24.08
NAT.W.	259.3	50	657	26	25.27
B & H	417	64	1262	49	25.76

FLETCHER, K.W.R.

Full Name: Keith William Robert Fletcher.
Role: Right-hand bat, leg-break bowler.
Born: 20 May 1944, Worcester.
Height: 5' 11" **Weight:** 10st. 7lbs.
Nickname: Gnome, Fletch.
County debut: 1962.
County cap: 1963.
Test debut: 1968.
No. of Tests: 59.
No. of One-Day Internationals: 24.
1000 runs in a season: 20.
50 wickets in a season: 0.
1st-Class 50s scored: 187.
1st-Class 100s scored: 62.
1st-Class 200s scored: 2.
1st-Class 5 w. in innings: 1.
1st-Class 10 w. in match: 0.
One-day 50s: 54.
One-day 100s: 2.
Place in batting averages: 95 average: 33.00; (1983: 89 average: 32.64).
Place in bowling averages: — average: —; (1983: — average: —).
1st-Class catches 1984: 22 (career: 586).
Parents: Joseph and Doris Fletcher.
Wife and date of marriage: Susan Elizabeth, 22 March 1969.
Children: Tamara Jane, 2 August 1970; Sara Jane, 19 December 1972.

Jobs outside cricket: Has worked as oil representative.
Overseas tours: Pakistan 1966–67. Ceylon and Pakistan 1968–69. Australia and N.Z. 1970–71 and 1974–75. India, Sri Lanka and Pakistan 1972–73. W. Indies 1973–74. India, Sri Lanka and Australia 1976–77. India and Sri Lanka 1981–82, as captain.
Equipment used: Duncan Fearnley.
Other sports: Golf, fishing, "Shooting partridge – my second favourite sport after cricket."
Relaxations: Gardening.
Significant injuries in 1984: Damaged ankle in M.C.C. v Champion County match when trod on the ball.
Extras: Played for Essex at age of 17. Led Essex to first county championship in 1979, second in 1983 and third in 1984. Also Benson & Hedges Cup in 1979 and John Player Special League in 1981 and 1984. Scored two centuries in a match, 111 and 102 not out, v Notts., at Nottingham in 1976. Captain since 1974. Awarded O.B.E. in 1985 New Year's honours list.
Best batting performance: 228* Essex v Sussex, Hastings 1968.
Best bowling performance: 5-41 Essex v Middlesex, Colchester 1979.

LAST SEASON: BATTING

	I.	N.O.	R.	H.S.	AV.
TEST					
OTHER FIRST CLASS	37	5	1056	131	33.00
INT					
J.P.L.	14	4	357	84*	35.70
NAT.W.	2	0	15	8	7.50
B & H	4	0	125	76	31.25

CAREER: BATTING

	I.	N.O.	R.	H.S.	AV.
TEST	96	14	3272	216	39.90
OTHER FIRST CLASS	966	137	31741	228*	38.29
INT	22	3	757	131	39.84
J.P.L.	198	28	5202	99*	30.60
NAT.W.	38	3	884	97	25.26
B & H	60	10	1750	101*	35.00

LAST SEASON: BOWLING

	O.	M.	R.	W.	AV.
TEST					
OTHER FIRST CLASS	9	2	28	0	–
INT					
J.P.L.					
NAT.W.	4.3	0	27	1	–
B & H					

CAREER: BOWLING

	O.	M.	R.	W.	AV.
TEST	20 20.5	1 5	193	2	96.50
OTHER FIRST CLASS	64.3 361.3	6 52	2002	48	41.71
INT.					
J.P.L.	70.2	3	319	9	35.44
NAT.W.	10.3	1	43	2	21.50
B & H					

Q. 15. What's the highest individual score in a NatWest match?
Q. 16. When was the first Gillette Cup?
Q. 17. Who won the first Gillette Cup?

FOSTER, N.A.

Full Name: Neil Alan Foster.
Role: Right-hand bat, right arm fast
medium bowler, outfielder.
Born: 6 May 1962, Colchester.
Height: 6' 4" **Weight:** 12st. 7lbs.
Nickname: Fozzy.
County debut: 1980.
County cap: 1983.
Test debut: 1983.
No. of Tests: 6.
No. of One-Day Internationals: 8.
1000 runs in a season: 0.
50 wickets in a season: 2.
1st-Class 50s scored: 1.
1st-Class 100s scored: 0.
1st-Class 200s scored: 0.
1st-Class 5 w. in innings: 0.
1st-Class 10 w. in match: 0.
One-day 50s: 0.
One-day 100s: 0.
Place in batting averages: 206 average: 18.73; (1983: 183 average: 19.33).
Place in bowling averages: 25 average: 24.11; (1983: 29 average: 23.39).
1st-Class catches 1984: 9 (career: 18).
Parents: Jean and Alan Foster.
Marital status: Engaged to Miss Romany King.
Family links with cricket: Father and brother both play local cricket.
Education: Broomgrove Infant & Junior Schools; Philip Morant Secondary
Comprehensive, Colchester.
Qualifications: 1 A-level, 9 O-levels.
Overseas tours: N.C.A. tour of Canada 1978; Young England XI tour of West
Indies 1980. Whitbread Scholarship 1981–82 in Tasmania (Glencory and
District). England tour of New Zealand and Pakistan 1983–84.
Off-season 1984–85: England tour to India and Australia.
Jobs outside cricket: Played semi-pro. football some years.
Cricketing superstitions: None.
Equipment used: Gray-Nicolls.
Cricketers particularly learnt from: Essex players and Graham Saville.
Cricketers particularly admired: Dennis Lillee and Imran Khan.
Other sports: Plays nearly any sport and has had football trials with Colchester
and Ipswich. Golf.
Extras: Was summoned from school at short notice to play for Essex v Kent at
Ilford to open bowling. First ball went for 4 wides, but he went on to dismiss
Woolmer, Tavaré and Ealham for 51 runs in 15 overs. Played for Young
England v Young India 1981.

Opinions on cricket: "117 overs in a day was too many. As the public left at 6.30 p.m. for dinner there seems little point in trying to entertain empty stands. The principle is fine but the number of overs too many."
Best batting performance: 54* Essex v Sussex, Eastbourne 1984.
Best bowling performance: 6-46 Essex v Sussex, Ilford 1983.

LAST SEASON: BATTING

	I.	N.O.	R.	H.S.	AV.
TEST	2	1	15	9*	–
OTHER FIRST CLASS	25	7	341	54*	18.94
INT	2	1	28	24	–
J.P.L.	3	0	17	10	5.67
NAT.W.	1	0	3	3	–
B & H	2	0	9	9	4.50

CAREER: BATTING

	I.	N.O.	R.	H.S.	AV.
TEST	8	2	62	18*	10.33
OTHER FIRST CLASS	47	14	663	54*	20.09
INT	5	2	35	24	11.67
J.P.L.	5	0	35	10	7.00
NAT.W.	1	0	3	3	–
B & H	3	0	9	9	3.00

LAST SEASON: BOWLING

	O.	M.	R.	W.	AV.
TEST	18	0	82	0	–
OTHER FIRST CLASS	669.1	146	2016	87	23.18
INT	32	1	147	1	–
J.P.L.	19	1	79	1	–
NAT.W.	19	5	43	2	21.50
B & H	33	4	214	6	35.67

CAREER: BOWLING

	O.	M.	R.	W.	AV.
TEST	223	53	647	13	49.78
OTHER FIRST CLASS	1284.1	270	3907	163	23.97
INT	74	8	302	5	60.40
J.P.L.	70.2	3	319	9	35.44
NAT.W.	43	9	106	8	13.25
B & H	91	8	331	12	27.58

GLADWIN, C.

Full Name: Christopher Gladwin
Role: Left-hand bat, right arm medium bowler.
Born: 10 May 1962, East Ham.
Nickname: Gladders.
County debut: 1981.
County cap: 1984.
Test debut: —
No. of Tests: 0.
No. of One-Day Internationals: 0.
1000 runs in a season: 1.
50 wickets in a season: 0.
1st-Class 50s scored: 12.
1st-Class 100s scored: 1.
1st-Class 200s scored: 0.
1st-Class 5 w. in innings: 0.
1st-Class 10 w. in match: 0.
One-day 50s: 3.
One-day 100s: 0.
Place in batting averages: 94 average: 33.24; (1983: 83 average: 33.57).

Place in bowling averages: — average: —; (1983: — average: —).
1st-Class catches 1984: 13 (career: 17).
Education: Langdon Comprehensive, Newham.
Overseas tours: Toured West Indies with Young England team, 1980.
Best batting performance: 162 Essex v Cambridge University, Cambridge 1984.

LAST SEASON: BATTING

	I.	N.O.	R.	H.S.	AV.
TEST					
OTHER FIRST CLASS	45	3	1396	162	33.24
INT					
J.P.L.	16	0	382	75	23.87
NAT.W.	2	0	1	1	0.50
B & H	5	0	135	41	27.00

CAREER: BATTING

	I.	N.O.	R.	H.S.	AV.
TEST					
OTHER FIRST CLASS	60	3	1919	162	33.67
INT					
J.P.L.	23	0	453	75	19.69
NAT.W.	2	0	1	1	0.50
B & H	5	0	135	41	27.00

LAST SEASON: BOWLING

	O.	M.	R.	W.	AV.
TEST					
OTHER FIRST CLASS	15	1	48	0	–
INT					
J.P.L.					
NAT.W.					
B & H					

CAREER: BOWLING

	O.	M.	R.	W.	AV.
TEST					
OTHER FIRST CLASS	18	1	59	0	–
INT					
J.P.L.					
NAT.W.					
B & H					

GOOCH, G.A.

Full Name: Graham Alan Gooch.
Role: Right-hand bat, right arm medium bowler.
Born: 23 July 1953, Leytonstone.
Height: 6' 0" **Weight:** 13st.
Nickname: Zap, Goochie.
County debut: 1973.
County cap: 1975.
Benefit: 1985.
Test debut: 1975.
No. of Tests: 42.
No. of One-Day Internationals: 37.
1000 runs in a season: 8.
50 wickets in a season: 0.
1st-Class 50s scored: 95.
1st-Class 100s scored: 47.
1st-Class 200s scored: 3.
1st-Class 5 w. in innings: 2.
1st-Class 10 w. in match: 0.

One-day 50s: 48.
One-day 100s: 14.
Place in batting averages: 6 average: 67.34; (1983: 52 average: 40.03).
Place in bowling averages: 15 average: 22.37; (1983: 128 average: 52.00).
1st-Class catches 1984: 27 (career: 272).
Parents: Alfred and Rose Gooch.
Wife and date of marriage: Brenda, 23 October 1976.
Children: Hannah.
Education: Norlington Junior High School, Leytonstone.
Qualifications: Four-year apprenticeship in toolmaking.
Jobs outside cricket: Toolmaker.
Family links with cricket: Father played local cricket for East Ham Corinthians. Second cousin, Graham Saville, played for Essex C.C.C. and is now N.C.A. coach for Eastern England.
Overseas tours: West Indies with England Young Cricketers 1972. Australia 1978–79 and 1979–80; West Indies 1981; India 1981–82.
Overseas teams played for: Perth C.C., W. Australia, W. Province, S. Africa.
Cricketers particularly admired: Bob Taylor, a model sportsman; Mike Procter for his enthusiasm; Barry Richards for his ability.
Equipment endorsed: Duncan Fearnley.
Other sports: Squash, soccer, golf.
Relaxations: "Relaxing at home."

LAST SEASON: BATTING

	I.	N.O.	R.	H.S.	AV.
TEST					
OTHER FIRST CLASS	45	7	2559	227	67.34
INT					
J.P.L.	16	2	613	125*	43.78
NAT.W.	2	0	197	133	98.50
B & H	5	0	143	57	28.60

CAREER: BATTING

	I.	N.O.	R.	H.S.	AV.
TEST	75	4	2540	153	35.78
OTHER FIRST CLASS	418	39	16423	227	43.33
INT	36	1	1046	108	29.89
J.P.L.	146	12	3862	176	28.82
NAT.W.	23	0	736	133	32.00
B & H	53	3	2313	198*	46.26

LAST SEASON: BOWLING

	O.	M.	R.	W.	AV.
TEST					
OTHER FIRST CLASS	321.1	75	850	38	22.37
INT					
J.P.L.	79	3	413	13	31.77
NAT.W.					
B & H	19	2	58	3	19.33

CAREER: BOWLING

	O.	M.	R.	W.	AV.
TEST	6 148.1	1 42	348	8	43.50
OTHER FIRST CLASS	20 1533	1 387	31201	132	23.64
INT.	1 131.5	0 7	612	16	38.25
J.P.L.	498.3	31	2218	80	27.72
NAT.W.	96.1	11	325	10	32.50
B & H	273.5	27	879	28	31.39

Extras: Good mimic—"particularly of Geoffrey Boycott." Impersonates bowlers on the field and voices off it. Published book (Pelham Books) entitled "Batting" in 1980. Wrote a diary of 1981 cricket year, published in April 1982 by Stanley Paul. Trains with West Ham. Hit a century before lunch v Leicester, 28 June 1981. Kept wicket for England v. India in 2nd innings at Madras, 1982. Captained English rebel team in S. Africa, 1982 and was banned from Test cricket for 3 years. Holds record 1-day innings of 198 n.o. v. Sussex, May 1982. Hit a hole in one at Tollygunge Golf Club during England's tour in India, 1981–82. First bowler to bowl both right and left handed in a Test match (v. India at Calcutta, imitating Dilip Doshi). Shared in second wicket record partnership for county, 321 with K.S. McEwan v Northants. at Ilford in 1978. Holds record (jointly) for Essex for catches in match (6) and innings (5) v. Gloucestershire, 1982.

Best batting performance: 227 Essex v Derbyshire, Chesterfield 1984.
Best bowling performance: 7-14 Essex v Worcestershire, Ilford 1982.

HARDIE, B.R.

Full Name: Brian Ross Hardie.
Role: Right-hand bat, right arm medium bowler, bat/pad fielder.
Born: 14 January 1950, Stenhouse-muir.
Height: 5' 10" **Weight:** 12st.
Nickname: Lager.
County debut: 1973.
County cap: 1974.
Benefit: 1983 (£48,486).
Test debut: —
No. of Tests: 0.
No. of One-Day Internationals: 0.
1000 runs in a season: 9.
50 wickets in a season: 0.
1st-Class 50s scored: 65.
1st-Class 100s scored: 14.
1st-Class 200s scored: 0.
1st-Class 5 w. in innings: 0.
1st-Class 10 w. in match: 0.

One-day 50s: 22.
One-day 100s: 1.
Place in batting averages: 80 average: 34.74: (1983:104 average: 29.77).
Place in bowling averages: — average: —; (1983: — average: —).
1st-Class catches 1984: 27 (career: 241).
Parents: James Millar and Elspeth Hardie.
Wife and date of marriage: Fiona, 28 October 1977.

Education: Stenhousemuir Primary School, Larbert High School.
Qualifications: Three Higher Levels, seven O-levels, N.C.A. Advanced cricket coach.
Jobs outside cricket: Computer operator, bank clerk, shipping clerk.
Off-season 1984–85: Working with Essex C.C.C. on promotions and sponsorships.
Family links with cricket: Father and brother, Keith, played for Scotland.
Overseas teams played for: Two seasons in New Zealand club cricket 1980–81 and 1981–82.
Cricketers particularly learnt from: "Everyone has something to offer."
Equipment used: Stuart Surridge.
Other sports: Football, golf.
Relaxations: Sport.
Extras: Played for Stenhousemuir in East of Scotland League. Debut for Scotland 1970. Scored two centuries for Scotland v M.C.C. at Aberdeen in 1971, but not then regarded as first-class match.
Best batting performance: 162 Essex v Warwickshire, Edgbaston 1975.

LAST SEASON: BATTING

	I.	N.O.	R.	H.S.	AV.
TEST					
OTHER FIRST CLASS	38	7	1077	99	34.74
INT					
J.P.L.	10	3	171	52	24.42
NAT.W.	2	0	22	22	11.00
B & H	4	3	93	62*	–

CAREER: BATTING

	I.	N.O.	R.	H.S.	AV.
TEST					
OTHER FIRST CLASS	421	51	12579	162	34.00
INT					
J.P.L.	141	13	3078	108*	24.04
NAT.W.	22	0	689	83	31.32
B & H	48	11	942	62*	25.46

LAST SEASON: BOWLING

	O.	M.	R.	W.	AV.
TEST					
OTHER FIRST CLASS					
INT					
J.P.L.	2	0	11	0	–
NAT.W.	8	1	16	1	–
B & H					

CAREER: BOWLING

	O.	M.	R.	W.	AV.
TEST					
OTHER FIRST CLASS	15	1	80	2	40.00
INT					
J.P.L.	4.5	0	24	1	–
NAT.W.	8	1	16	1	–
B & H					

Q. 18. Who won the last Gillette Cup?
Q. 19. When was the first NatWest Trophy?
Q. 20. Who won the first NatWest Trophy?
Q. 21. Which team has won the Gillette Cup three times running and when?

LEVER, J.K.

Full Name: John Kenneth Lever.
Role: Right-hand bat, left arm fast medium bowler.
Born: 24 February 1949, Stepney.
Height: 6' 0" **Weight:** 13st.
Nickname: Jake, J.K. Stanley.
County debut: 1967.
County cap: 1970.
Test debut: 1976.
No. of Tests: 20.
No. of One-Day Internationals: 22.
Benefit: 1980, £66,250.
1000 runs in a season: 0.
50 wickets in a season: 14.
1st-Class 50s scored: 2.
1st-Class 100s scored: 0.
1st-Class 200s scored: 0.
1st-Class 5 w. in innings: 73.
1st-Class 10 w. in match: 11.
One-day 50s: 0.
One-day 100s: 0.
Place in batting averages: 258 average: 12.13; (1983: 210 average: 15.07).
Place in bowling averages: 12 average: 21.98; (1983: 2 average: 16.28).
1st-Class catches 1984: 10 (career: 169).
Parents: Ken and Doris Lever.
Wife and date of marriage: Chris, 30 July 1983.
Education: Highlands Junior, Dane County Secondary School.
Qualifications: Three G.C.E.s, three R.S.A.s.
Jobs outside cricket: Clerk with Access Social Club; Byron Shipping; Dominion Insurance.
Off-season 1984–85: Coaching in South Africa.
Cricketing superstitions: "Too many to mention."
Family links with cricket: None.
Overseas tours: India, Sri Lanka and Australia, 1976–77; Pakistan and New Zealand, 1977–78; Australia, 1978–79 and 1979–80.
Cricketers particularly learnt from: "A little from a lot."
Equipment used: Stuart Surridge.
Equipment endorsed: Sponsors – Access and Tolly Cobbold.
Other sports: "All sports." Football, squash, badminton, tennis, golf.
Relaxations: Music, cooking.
Significant injuries during 1984: Knee operation to remove a small chip of bone.
Extras: Took 10 wickets in his Test debut in 1976 v India at Delhi. Took 106 wickets at an average of 15.80 in 1978, and 106 wickets at an average of 17.30

in 1979, and 106 wickets at an average of 16.28 in 1983. Last season was first to 100 wickets with 116 at 21.98. Also, season's best return of 8-37 v Gloucestershire. President of Blythswood C.C. Member of Ilford C.C. since the age of 14. Another of the renowned Essex comedians. Has reputation of "not breaking down". On the executive of the Cricketers Association. Banned from Test Cricket for 3 years for joining rebel tour of S. Africa in 1982.

Opinions on cricket: "I look forward to the 1985 season with the hope that we shall be allowed to finish at 6.30 p.m."

Best batting performance: 91 Essex v Glamorgan, Cardiff 1970.

Best bowling performance: 8-37 Essex v Gloucestershire, Bristol 1984.

LAST SEASON: BATTING

	I.	N.O.	R.	H.S.	AV.
TEST					
OTHER FIRST CLASS	22	7	182	37	12.13
INT					
J.P.L.	3	2	19	14*	–
NAT.W.	1	1	15	15*	–
B & H	2	1	14	13	–

CAREER: BATTING

	I.	N.O.	R.	H.S.	AV.
TEST	29	4	306	53	12.24
OTHER FIRST CLASS	424	167	2761	91	10.74
INT	11	4	56	27*	8.00
J.P.L.	94	58	361	23	10.02
NAT.W.	21	14	81	15*	11.57
B & H	23	15	92	13	11.50

LAST SEASON: BOWLING

	O.	M.	R.	W.	AV.
TEST					
OTHER FIRST CLASS	874.5	195	2550	116	21.98
INT					
J.P.L.	89.4	7	385	23	16.73
NAT.W.	16.1	2	50	2	25.00
B & H	53.5	11	153	6	25.50

CAREER: BOWLING

	O.	M.	R.	W.	AV.
TEST	166.7 463.2	27 104	1785	67	26.64
OTHER FIRST CLASS	210.4 11618	40 2453	32615	1391	23.45
INT.	33 148	5 15	713	24	29.71
J.P.L.	1566.3	188	5548	310	17.89
NAT.W.	386.3	72	855	57	15.00
B & H	655.5	135	1940	113	17.17

Q. 22. Which team won the NatWest Trophy twice?

Q. 23. What's the highest total in a Benson & Hedges match?

Q. 24. What's the lowest total in a Benson & Hedges match?

Q. 25. What's the highest individual innings in a Benson & Hedges match, and by whom?

LILLEY, A.W.

Full Name: Alan William Lilley.
Role: Right-hand bat, wicket-keeper.
Born: 8 May 1959, Ilford, Essex.
Height: 5′ 11″ **Weight:** 13st. 4lbs.
Nickname: Shacky.
County debut: 1978.
County cap: No.
Test debut: —
No. of Tests: 0.
No. of One-Day Internationals: 0.
1000 runs in a season: 0.
50 wickets in a season: 0.
1st-Class 50s scored: 7.
1st-Class 100s scored: 1.
1st-Class 200s scored: 0.
1st-Class 5 w. in innings: 0.
1st-Class 10 w. in match: 0.
One-day 50s: 3.
One-day 100s: 0.

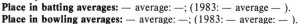

Place in batting averages: — average: —; (1983: — average —).
Place in bowling averages: — average: —; (1983: — average: —).
1st-Class catches 1984: 0 (career: 16).
Parents: Min and Ron Lilley.
Marital status: Single.
Education: Caterham High School, Ilford.
Family links with cricket: Father played for Osborne C.C. as a bowler for 18 years.

LAST SEASON: BATTING

	I.	N.O.	R.	H.S.	AV.
TEST					
OTHER FIRST CLASS	–	–	–	–	–
INT					
J.P.L.	6	0	54	21	9.00
NAT.W.	1	1	59	59*	–
B & H					

CAREER: BATTING

	I.	N.O.	R.	H.S.	AV.
TEST					
OTHER FIRST CLASS	48	2	1175	100*	25.54
INT					
J.P.L.	60	3	811	60	14.22
NAT.W.	5	1	143	59*	35.75
B & H	15	1	367	119	26.21

LAST SEASON: BOWLING

	O.	M.	R.	W.	AV.
TEST					
OTHER FIRST CLASS	5.2	2	11	2	5.50
INT					
J.P.L.	0.3	0	0	2	–
NAT.W.	7	3	19	2	9.50
B & H					

CAREER: BOWLING

	O.	M.	R.	W.	AV.
TEST					
OTHER FIRST CLASS	8.2	2	21	2	10.50
INT					
J.P.L.	2.3	0	19	3	6.33
NAT.W.	8	3	33	2	16.50
B & H					

Overseas teams played for: Perth C.C. Western Australia, 1979–80.
Cricketers particularly learnt from: Stuart Turner (his coach in early days).
Equipment used: Duncan Fearnley.
Other sports: Badminton, swimming.
Extras: Was on M.C.C. Young Pro staff at Lord's one season after leaving
school. Scored century in second innings of debut v Notts. Plays for Ilford.
Best batting performance: 100* Essex v Nottinghamshire, Trent Bridge 1978.
Best bowling performance: 2-11 Essex v Surrey, Chelmsford 1984.

McEWAN, K.S.

Full Name: Kenneth Scott McEwan.
Role: Right-hand bat, off-break
bowler and occasional wicket-
keeper.
Born: 16 July 1952, Bedford, Cape
Province, South Africa.
Height: 5′ 9″ **Weight:** 11st. 11lbs.
Nickname: Kenny.
County debut: 1974.
County cap: 1974.
Benefit: 1984.
Test debut: —
No. of Tests: 4 in 1983 v 'Rebel'
West Indians.
No. of One-Day Internationals: 11
for S. Africa v. 'Rebel' West Indians,
1983.

1000 runs in a season: 11.
50 wickets in a season: 0.
1st-Class 50s scored: 97.
1st-Class 100s scored: 56.
1st-Class 200s scored: 2.
1st-Class 5 w. in innings: 0.
1st-Class 10 w. in match: 0.
One-day 50s: 41.
One-day 100s: 11.
Place in batting averages: 29 average: 46.18; (1983: 5 average: 64.00).
Place in bowling averages: — average: —; (1983: — average: —).
1st-Class catches 1984: 20 (career: 320).
Education: Queen's College, Queenstown, South Africa.
Overseas teams played for: Eastern Province and Western Province, South
Africa; Western Australia.
Equipment endorsed: Duncan Fearnley.
Other sports: Tennis, rugby, golf and watches most sports.

Extras: Debut for Eastern Province in 1972–73 Currie Cup Competition. Played for T.N. Pearce's XI v West Indies at Scarborough in 1973. Was originally recommended to Sussex C.C.C. by Tony Greig, who coached him at school. "Quietest member of Essex XI." (i) Has played in team winning domestic competitions in three different countries— County Championships with Essex 1979, 1983 and 1984; Sheffield Shield with W. Australia 1980–81; Currie Cup with Western Province 1981–82; (ii) scored four consecutive centuries in 1977; (iii) has made century against every county; (iv) only wicket keeper to score 100 in same John Player League game (v. Worcester in 1980). Voted Players' Player of the Year 1983.

Best batting performance: 218 Essex v Sussex, Chelmsford 1977.

LAST SEASON: BATTING

	I.	N.O.	R.	H.S.	AV.
TEST					
OTHER FIRST CLASS	44	6	1755	142*	46.18
INT					
J.P.L.	16	1	535	89	35.67
NAT.W.	2	0	76	75	38.00
B & H	5	1	178	72	44.50

CAREER: BATTING

	I.	N.O.	R.	H.S.	AV.
TEST					
OTHER FIRST CLASS	589		52	21842	218	40.67
INT					
J.P.L.	163	15	4948	162*	33.43
NAT.W.	22	2	694	119	34.70
B & H	53	4	1749	133	35.69

LAST SEASON: BOWLING

	O.	M.	R.	W.	AV.
TEST					
OTHER FIRST CLASS					
INT					
J.P.L.					
NAT.W.					
B & H					

CAREER: BOWLING

	O.	M.	R.	W.	AV.
TEST					
OTHER FIRST CLASS	39.4	3	281	3	93.67
INT					
J.P.L.	2	0	7	0	–
NAT.W.	1	0	5	0	–
B & H					

Q. 26. When was the first Benson & Hedges match?

Q. 27. Who won the first Benson & Hedges Cup?

Q. 28. Which is the only team to have won the Benson & Hedges two years running?

PHILLIP, N.

Full Name: Norbert Phillip.
Role: Right-hand bat, right arm fast medium bowler.
Born: 12 June 1948, Bioche, Dominica, West Indies.
Height: 6′ 0″ **Weight:** 12st 4lbs.
Nickname: Nobbie in England and Zidi in Dominica.
County debut: 1978.
County cap: 1978.
Test debut: 1977.
No. of Tests: 9.
No. of One-Day Internationals: 1.
1000 runs in a season: 1.
50 wickets in a season: 5.
1st-Class 50s scored: 18.
1st-Class 100s scored: 1.
1st-Class 200s scored: 0.
1st-Class 5 w. in innings: 0.
1st-Class 10 w. in match: 0.
One-day 50s: 6.
One-day 100s: 0.

Place in batting averages: 204 average: 19.53; (1983: 205 average: 15.88).
Place in bowling averages: 40 average: 26.79; (1983: 13 average: 20.42).
1st-Class catches 1984: 3 (career: 69).
Parents: Philbert and Irene Phillip.
Wife and date of marriage: Elizabeth, 31 October 1975.
Children: Twin boys, Frank and Franklyn, 28 February 1972.
Education: Dominica Grammar School.
Qualifications: O Level History. National Cricket Association coaching certificate.
Jobs outside cricket: Sports officer with Government of Dominica.
Overseas tours: India and Sri Lanka with W. Indies, 1978–79.
Overseas teams played for: Windward Islands; Combined Islands.
Equipment used: Stuart Surridge.
Other sports: Football, athletics.
Relaxations: Reading and listening to music, "specially reggae, soul and calypso".
Extras: "I acted as Assistant-Secretary of the Dominica Cricket Association, and Chairman of the Association's Youth Sub-Committee. I am involved in cricket coaching as a Sports Officer to the Government of Dominica." Captain of Windward Islands.
Best batting performance: 134 Essex v Gloucestershire, Gloucester 1978.
Best bowling performance: 7-33 Windwards v Leewards, Roseau 1980–81.

LAST SEASON: BATTING

	I.	N.O.	R.	H.S.	AV.
TEST					
OTHER FIRST CLASS	17	2	293	71	19.53
INT	.				
J.P.L.	13	3	154	44*	15.40
NAT.W.	2	0	7	7	3.50
B & H	1	0	0	0	–

CAREER: BATTING

	I.	N.O.	R.	H.S.	AV.
TEST	15	5	297	47	29.70
OTHER FIRST CLASS	306	32	6397	134	23.35
INT	1	0	0	0	–
J.P.L.	91	18	1426	95	19.53
NAT.W.	15	2	201	45	15.46
B & H	19	7	229	33*	19.08

LAST SEASON: BOWLING

	O.	M.	R.	W.	AV.
TEST					
OTHER FIRST CLASS	275.2	48	911	34	26.79
INT					
J.P.L.	89.3	5	371	19	19.52
NAT.W.	10	3	24	2	12.00
B & H	11	2	30	1	–

CAREER: BOWLING

	O.	M.	R.	W.	AV.
TEST	303.2	46	1041	28	37.18
OTHER FIRST CLASS	5068.2	999	14955	640	23.37
INT	7	0	22	1	–
J.P.L.	662.3	44	2628	127	20.69
NAT.W.	129	16	473	21	22.52
B & H	282.1	36	1011	38	26.61

PONT, K.R.

Full Name: Keith Rupert Pont.
Role: Right-hand bat, right arm
medium bowler.
Born: 16 January 1953, Wanstead.
Height: 6′ 2″ **Weight:** 13st.
Nickname: Monty, Plod, Ponty,
Rodney Port, Vintage.
County debut: 1970.
County cap: 1976.
Test debut: —
No. of Tests: 0.
No. of One-Day Internationals: 0.
1000 runs in a season: 0.
50 wickets in a season: 0.
1st-Class 50s scored: 33.
1st-Class 100s scored: 7.
1st-Class 200s scored: 0.
1st-Class 5 w. in innings: 2.
1st-Class 10 w. in match: 0.
One-day 50s: 5.
One-day 100s: 0.

Place in batting averages: — average: —; (1983: 77 average: 34.87).
Place in bowling averages: — average: —; (1983: — average: —).
1st-Class catches 1984: 1 (career: 87).
Wife: Veronica.
Education: Secondary school.

Jobs outside cricket: Has been furniture representative, insurance clerk and in road haulage management.

Off-season 1984–85: Working for air freight company.

Family links with cricket: Younger brother Ian, played for England Under 19, and Notts. Elder brother, Kelvin, was on M.C.C. staff.

Equipment used: Stuart Surridge.

Cricketing superstitions: "None really, touch wood."

Other sports: Scuba diving, golf. Watch skiing.

Extras: Strong comic sense, e.g. has been known to field outside ground when Ray East comes on to bowl. The first person to pedal on a bicycle from third man to third man whilst a first-class match is in progress, while playing for Essex.

Best batting performance: 125* Essex v Glamorgan, Southend 1983.

Best bowling performance: 5-17 Essex v Glamorgan, Cardiff 1982.

LAST SEASON: BATTING

	I.	N.O.	R.	H.S.	AV.
TEST					
OTHER FIRST CLASS	3	0	61	32	20.33
INT					
J.P.L.					
NAT.W.					
B & H					

CAREER: BATTING

	I.	N.O.	R.	H.S.	AV.
TEST					
OTHER FIRST CLASS	277	40	6122	125*	25.83
INT					
J.P.L.	134	28	1838	55*	17.33
NAT.W.	20	2	245	39	13.61
B & H	40	10	624	60*	20.80

LAST SEASON: BOWLING

	O.	M.	R.	W.	AV.
TEST					
OTHER FIRST CLASS					
INT					
J.P.L.					
NAT.W.					
B & H					

CAREER: BOWLING

	O.	M.	R.	W.	AV.
TEST					
OTHER FIRST CLASS	936.5	183	2689	83	32.40
INT					
J.P.L.	497.4	36	2277	88	25.87
NAT.W.	76.5	9	283	12	23.58
B & H	226.2	19	878	33	26.60

Q. 29. What's the highest total in a John Player Special League match?

Q. 30. What's the lowest completed total in a John Player Special League match?

PRICHARD, P.J.

Full Name: Paul John Prichard.
Role: Right-hand bat, cover
fielder.
Born: 7 January 1965, Brentwood.
Height: 5' 0" **Weight:** 11st.
Nickname: Digger, Pablo.
County debut: 1984.
County cap: No.
No. of Tests: 0.
No. of One-Day Internationals: 0.
1000 runs in a season: 0.
50 wickets in a season: 0.
1st-Class 50s scored: 6.
1st-Class 100s scored: 1.
1st-Class 200s scored: 0.
1st-Class 5 w. in innings: 0.
1st-Class 10 w. in match: 0.
One-day 50s: 0.
One-day 100s: 0.
Place in batting averages: 98 average: 32.89; (1983: — average: —).
Place in bowling averages: — average: —; (1983: — average: —).
1st-Class catches 1984: 10 (career: 10).
Parents: Margaret and John.
Marital status: Single.
Family links with cricket: Father played club cricket in Essex.
Education: Brentwood County High School.
Qualifications: N.C.A. Coaching Award.
Jobs outside cricket: Working on the County Ground at Chelmsford.

LAST SEASON: BATTING

	I.	N.O.	R.	H.S.	AV.
TEST					
OTHER FIRST CLASS	29	2	888	100	32.89
INT					
J.P.L.					
NAT.W.					
B & H					

CAREER: BATTING

	I.	N.O.	R.	H.S.	AV.
TEST					
OTHER FIRST CLASS	29	2	888	100	32.89
INT					
J.P.L.					
NAT.W.					
B & H					

LAST SEASON: BOWLING

	O.	M.	R.	W.	AV.
TEST					
OTHER FIRST CLASS	1	0	5	0	–
INT					
J.P.L.					
NAT.W.					
B & H					

CAREER: BOWLING

	O.	M.	R.	W.	AV.
TEST					
OTHER FIRST CLASS	1	0	5	0	–
INT					
J.P.L.					
NAT.W.					
B & H					

Off-season 1984–85: Working on the County Ground.
Cricketing superstitions: "None touch wood!"
Equipment used and endorsed: Gray-Nicolls.
Overseas tours: Kingfishers tour South Africa January 1981.
Overseas teams played for: V.O.B. Cavaliers (Cape Town) October 1981–March 1982.
Cricketers particularly learnt from: All at Essex.
Cricketers particularly admired: "Too many to mention."
Other sports: Football, golf. Follow rugby, football, skiing.
Relaxations: Playing golf, listening to music.
Opinions on cricket: "117 overs a day is too many."
Best batting performance: 100 Essex v Lancashire, Old Trafford 1984.

PRINGLE, D.R.

Full Name: Derek Raymond Pringle.
Role: Right-hand bat, right arm medium bowler, 1st slip fielder.
Born: 18 September 1958, Nairobi, Kenya.
Height: 6' 4½" **Weight:** 14st 7lbs.
Nickname: Suggs.
County debut: 1978.
County cap: 1982.
Test debut: 1982.
No. of Tests: 10.
No. of One-Day Internationals: 7.
1000 runs in a season: 0.
50 wickets in a season: 1.
1st-Class 50s scored: 21.
1st-Class 100s scored: 6.
1st-Class 200s scored: 0.
1st-Class 5 w. in innings: 7.
1st-Class 10 w. in match: 1.
One-day 50s: 10.
One-day 100s: 0.

Place in batting averages: 174 average: 23.50; (1983: 79 average: 34.47).
Place in bowling averages: 48 average: 27.87; (1983: 24 average: 22.63).
1st-Class catches 1984: 15 (career: 81).
Parents: Donald James, deceased, and Doris May Pringle.
Marital status: Single.
Education: St Mary's School, Nairobi; Felsted School, Essex; Cambridge.
Qualifications: Two S-levels, three A-levels, eight O-levels. B.A. (Hons.) Cantab.

Family links with cricket: Father represented Kenya and East Africa (played in World Cup 1975).

Off-season 1984–85: On the dole.

Overseas tours: With England Schools to India 1978–79; Oxbridge tour of Australia 1979–80, England to Australia and New Zealand 1982–83.

Cricketers particularly learnt from: "Main influence was my father, and also Gordon Barker (ex-Essex) the coach at Felsted."

Cricketers particularly admired: "None from close quarters, many from afar."

Cricket superstitions: "Ignore the popular press."

Equipment endorsed: Gray-Nicolls and Jockey sportswear.

Other sports: Squash, golf. Watch Man. Utd. and rugby union.

Relaxations: Reading novels, especially by V.S. Naipaul and Günter Grass; photography.

Extras: "Took all ten wickets for Nairobi Schools Under-13½ v Up Country Schools Under-13½. Captain of Cambridge 1982 season. Narrowly missed an Oscar for best ad-libbing extra in "Chariots of Fire'."

Opinions on cricket: "An imposed maximum of 117 overs per day not possible. It does not seem to prevent even the most ardent supporter from missing a prompt 7.00 p.m. supper. Therefore it appears to be superfluous and must be amended."

Best batting performance: 127* Cambridge University v Worcestershire, Cambridge 1981.

Best bowling performance: 7-32 Essex v Middlesex, Chelmsford 1983.

LAST SEASON: BATTING

	I.	N.O.	R.	H.S.	AV.
TEST	6	1	81	46*	16.20
OTHER FIRST CLASS	29	6	577	96	25.87
INT	3	1	16	8	8.00
J.P.L.	12	2	387	81	38.70
NAT.W.	1	0	0	0	–
B & H	5	2	120	51*	40.00

CAREER: BATTING

	I.	N.O.	R.	H.S.	AV.
TEST	17	3	247	47*	17.64
OTHER FIRST CLASS	151	32	3718	127*	31.24
INT	5	2	61	34*	20.33
J.P.L.	29	8	642	81	30.57
NAT.W.	2	0	19	19	9.50
B & H	24	5	679	68	35.74

LAST SEASON: BOWLING

	O.	M.	R.	W.	AV.
TEST	71.3	10	257	5	51.40
OTHER FIRST CLASS	508.4	117	1527	59	25.89
INT	29	3	123	4	30.75
J.P.L.	81	3	363	7	51.86
NAT.W.	10	2	32	1	–
B & H	53	13	177	16	11.06

CAREER: BOWLING

	O.	M.	R.	W.	AV.
TEST	253.2	53	752	16	47.00
OTHER FIRST CLASS	2330	556	6560	244	26.89
INT	65	4	320	8	40.00
J.P.L.	292.5	14	1360	42	32.38
NAT.W.	33	6	105	3	35.00
B & H	250.4	34	857	42	20.40

TURNER, S.

Full Name: Stuart Turner.
Role: Right-hand bat; right arm fast medium bowler.
Born: 18 July 1943, Chester.
Height: 6' 0½" **Weight:** 12st 7lbs.
Nickname: Stu.
County debut: 1965.
County cap: 1970.
Test debut: —
No. of Tests: 0.
No. of One-Day Internationals: 0.
Benefit: 1979.
1000 runs in a season: 0.
50 wickets in a season: 6.
1st-Class 50s scored: 41.
1st-Class 100s scored: 4.
1st-Class 200s scored: 0.
1st-Class 5 w. in innings: 27.
1st-Class 10 w. in match: 1.
One-day 50s: 9.
One-day 100s: 0.

Place in batting averages: 160 average: 24.63; (1983: 245 average: 10.41).
Place in bowling averages: 58 average: 29.38; (1983: 28 average: 23.11).
1st-Class catches 1984: 4 (career: 217).
Parents: Arthur Leonard and Alice Turner.
Wife and date of marriage: Jacqueline Linda, 9 April 1966.
Children: Jeremy Paul, 12 February 1968; Emma Louise, 21 January 1970.
Education: Epping Junior School; Epping Secondary Modern.
Qualifications: Advanced M.C.C. cricket coach.
Jobs outside cricket: Insurance claims broker. Coaching cricket both in South Africa and England.
Overseas tours: Toured West Indies 1974 with Derrick Robbins XI; South Africa 1975 with Derrick Robins XI.
Overseas teams played for: Played for Natal in Currie Cup and Gillette Cup, Competitions 1976–77–78. Won both in 1976–77.
Cricketers particularly learnt from: "Learnt from so many—one never stops learning."
Cricketers particularly admired: "G. Sobers – a great privilege to play against him."
Cricket records: First player to take 200 wickets and score 2,000 runs in the John Player League.
Equipment used: Stuart Surridge.
Other sports: Golf, squash, occasional football, enjoy as many sports as possible, watching and playing.

Relaxations: "Reading, playing records, watching television, driving, doing anything that takes my fancy and just enjoying life."

Extras: A century before lunch against Kent (108 mins.) 3 May 1979, Chelmsford. Hat-trick against Surrey at the Oval 4 May 1971. Spent 1966 and 1967 out of the game, returning in 1968.

Best batting performance: 121 Essex v Somerset, Taunton 1970.

Best bowling performance: 6-26 Essex v Northamptonshire, Northampton 1977.

LAST SEASON: BATTING

	I.	N.O.	R.	H.S.	AV.
TEST					
OTHER FIRST CLASS	13	5	197	59	24.63
INT					
J.P.L.	10	3	96	36*	13.72
NAT.W.					
B & H	3	1	4	4	2.00

CAREER: BATTING

	I.	N.O.	R.	H.S.	AV.
TEST					
OTHER FIRST CLASS	502	100	9261	121	23.04
INT					
J.P.L.	199	40	3099	87	19.49
NAT.W.	27	3	439	50*	18.29
B & H	50	16	597	55*	17.56

LAST SEASON: BOWLING

	O.	M.	R.	W.	AV.
TEST					
OTHER FIRST CLASS	285	95	617	21	29.38
INT					
J.P.L.	98.5	9	482	17	28.35
NAT.W.					
B & H	55	10	120	5	24.00

CAREER: BOWLING

	O.	M.	R.	W.	AV.
TEST					
OTHER FIRST CLASS	8737.1	2240	20892	808	25.86
INT					
J.P.L.	1645.5	162	6605	290	22.77
NAT.W.	308.5	67	873	42	20.81
B & H	659.2	113	1845	93	19.84

COUNTY QUIZ

Q. 1. When was the club founded?

Q. 2. Who made the most first-class runs for the county last season, and how many?

Q. 3. What's the highest ever county total, and against whom?

Q. 4. Who took most wickets for the county last season, and how many?

Q. 5. What's the highest individual score for the county, who hit it, and when?

Q. 6. What's the highest scoring partnership for the county for any wicket?

Q. 7. How many times has the club won the County Championship?

Q. 8. What's the lowest ever total made by the county in one innings, when, and against whom?

Q. 9. Which bowler took the most first-class wickets in one season, when, and how many?

Q. 10. Which batsman hit the most runs in one season, when and how many?

Glamorgan

BARWICK, S.R.

Full Name: Stephen Royston Barwick.
Role: Right-hand bat, right-arm
medium pace bowler.
Born: 6 September 1960, Neath.
Height: 6′ 2″ **Weight:** 13st. 7lbs.
Nickname: Baz.
County debut: 1981.
County cap: No.
Test debut: —
No. of Tests: 0.
No. of One-Day Internationals: 0.
1000 runs in a season: 0.
50 wickets in a season: 1.
1st-Class 50s scored: 0.
1st-Class 100s scored: 0.
1st-Class 200s scored: 0.
1st-Class 5 w. in innings: 4.
1st-Class 10 w. in match: 0.
One-day 50s: 0.
One-day 100s: 0.

Place in batting averages: 267 average: 10.50; (1983: — average: —).
Place in bowling averages: 37 average: 26.28; (1983: 125 average: 34.84).
1st-Class catches 1984: 6 (career: 14).
Parents: Margaret and Roy Barwick.
Marital status: Single.
Family links with cricket: "My uncle David played for Glamorgan 2nd XI."
Education: Cwrt Sart Comprehensive School; Dwr-y-Felin Comprehensive
School.
Qualifications: "Commerce, human biology, mathematics, English."
Jobs outside cricket: Ex-steel worker.
Significant injuries in 1984: Stress fracture of lower region of the vertebrae.
Other sports: Badminton, squash, table-tennis, football (watching Swansea City).
Extras: Made debut on 25 April 1981 v Oxford University, and took 4 wickets
in 1st innings.
Best batting performance: 25 Glamorgan v Derbyshire, Derby 1984.

Best bowling performance: 8-42 Glamorgan v Worcestershire, Worcester 1983.

LAST SEASON: BATTING

	I.	N.O.	R.	H.S.	AV.
TEST					
OTHER FIRST CLASS	19	9	105	25	10.50
INT					
J.P.L.	–	–	–	–	–
NAT.W.	1	1	2	2*	–
B & H	3	2	26	18	–

CAREER: BATTING

	I.	N.O.	R.	H.S.	AV.
TEST					
OTHER FIRST CLASS	48	23	282	25	11.28
INT					
J.P.L.	4	3	20	12*	–
NAT.W.	3	2	9	6	–
B & H	7	5	30	18	15.00

LAST SEASON: BOWLING

	O.	M.	R.	W.	AV.
TEST					
OTHER FIRST CLASS	477.4	123	1314	50	26.28
INT					
J.P.L.	46	3	213	1	–
NAT.W.	4.2	0	15	0	–
B & H	16	2	64	0	–

CAREER: BOWLING

	O.	M.	R.	W.	AV.
TEST					
OTHER FIRST CLASS	1002.3	257	2960	100	29.60
INT					
J.P.L.	167.4	10	831	17	48.88
NAT.W.	23.2	7	62	5	12.40
B & H	75	10	266	13	20.46

DAVIES, T.

Full Name: Terry Davies.
Role: Wicket-keeper,
right-hand bat.
Born: 25 October 1960, St Albans,
Hertfordshire.
Height: 5' 6" **Weight:** 10st. 4lbs.
Nickname: Sid.
County debut: 1979.
County cap: 1984.
Test debut: —
No. of Tests: 0.
No. of One-Day Internationals: 0.
1000 runs in a season: 0.
50 wickets in a season: 0.
1st-Class 50s scored: 4.
1st-Class 100s scored: 0.
1st-Class 200s scored: 0.
1st-Class 5 w. in innings: 0.
1st-Class 10 w. in match: 0.
One-day 50s: 0.
One-day 100s: 0.

Place in batting averages: 250 average: 14.21; (1983: 146 average: 23.64).
Place in bowling averages: — average: —; (1983: — average: —).

Parents: Harry and Peggy Davies.
Wife: Noele.
Education: Townsend Secondary School, St. Albans.
Jobs outside cricket: Carpet-fitter; also worked in a sports shop.
Off-season 1984–85: Playing and coaching.
Family links with cricket: Brother playing club cricket in Sydney, Australia. "Father a fantastic back-garden bowler!"
Overseas teams played for: Played grade cricket in Sydney, Australia, for Central Cumberland in 1978–79. Bankstown Canterbury in 1980–81. Mosman, Sydney 1982–83.
Cricketers particularly learnt from: Bob Taylor, Javed Miandad, David Evans.
Cricket superstitions: "I bat in a short sleeved shirt, and strap right pad on first."
Equipment endorsed: Stuart Surridge, Slazenger.
Other sports: Playing football, squash, tennis.
Relaxations: Music, darts, fishing.
Extras: Played soccer for Hertfordshire Under-16 and for Watford and West Ham in the South-East Counties League. Had trials with West Ham F.C., Tottenham Hotspur and Luton. Trained with Watford for a season. On Lord's ground staff 1977–78.
Best batting performance: 69* Glamorgan v Kent, Cardiff 1983.

LAST SEASON: BATTING

	I.	N.O.	R.	H.S.	AV.
TEST					
OTHER FIRST CLASS	35	7	398	43	14.21
INT					
J.P.L.	10	8	102	38*	51.00
NAT.W.	1	0	1	1	–
B & H	3	0	44	23	14.67

CAREER: BATTING

	I.	N.O.	R.	H.S.	AV.
TEST					
OTHER FIRST CLASS	68	15	956	69*	18.04
INT					
J.P.L.	16	11	185	46*	37.00
NAT.W.	1	0	1	1	–
B & H	4	0	54	23	13.50

LAST SEASON: WICKET KEEPING

	C.	ST.			
TEST					
OTHER FIRST CLASS	43	11			
INT					
J.P.L.	10	7			
NAT.W.	–	–			
B & H	5	1			

CAREER: WICKET KEEPING

	C.	ST.			
TEST					
OTHER FIRST CLASS	89	15			
INT					
J.P.L.	21	11			
NAT.W.	–	–			
B & H	9	3			

Q. 31. What's the highest individual John Player Special League score and by whom?

Q. 32. When was the first John Player Special match?

DAVIS, W.W.

Full Name: Winston Walter Davis.
Role: Right-hand bat, right arm fast
medium bowler.
Born: 18 September 1958,
St. Vincent, Windward Islands.
County debut: 1982.
County cap: No.
Test debut: 1982–83 (W. Indies).
No. of Tests. 9.
No. of One-Day Internationals: 12.
1000 runs in a season: 0.
50 wickets in a season: 2.
1st-Class 50s scored: 2.
1st-Class 100s scored: 0.
1st-Class 200s scored: 0.
1st-Class 5 w. in innings: 0.
1st-Class 10 w. in match: 0.
One-day 50s: 0.
One-day 100s: 0.

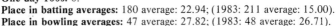

Place in batting averages: 180 average: 22.94; (1983: 211 average: 15.00).
Place in bowling averages: 47 average: 27.82; (1983: 48 average: 26.71).
1st-Class catches 1984: 8 (career: 27).
Overseas tours: Young West Indies to Zimbabwe 1981–82, West Indies to
India 1983–84.
Overseas teams played for: Windward Islands, Combined Islands.
Off-season 1983–84: Playing for West Indies.
Extras: Member of West Indies World Cup squad 1983. Bowled over 250 no

LAST SEASON: BATTING

	I.	N.O.	R.	H.S.	AV.
TEST	1	0	77	77	–
OTHER FIRST CLASS	23	7	313	50	19.56
INT					
J.P.L.	2	0	8	5	4.00
NAT.W.	1	0	5	5	–
B & H	3	0	14	8	4.67

CAREER: BATTING

	I.	N.O.	R.	H.S.	AV.
TEST	10	4	141	77	23.50
OTHER FIRST CLASS	97	34	742	60	11.78
INT	2	2	7	7*	–
J.P.L.	4	2	10	5	5.00
NAT.W.	3	1	6	5	3.00
B & H	3	0	14	8	4.67

LAST SEASON: BOWLING

	O.	M.	R.	W.	AV.
TEST	23	3	77	2	38.50
OTHER FIRST CLASS	524.5	115	1648	60	27.47
INT					
J.P.L.	68.1	4	295	8	36.88
NAT.W.	8	1	29	0	–
B & H	38.2	5	149	9	16.56

CAREER: BOWLING

	O.	M.	R.	W.	AV.
TEST	286.3	32	894	22	40.64
OTHER FIRST CLASS	2200.2	443	5429	244	22.25
INT	121.3	13	489	12	40.75
J.P.L.	156.4	14	649	30	21.63
NAT.W.	30.5	4	108	4	27.00
B & H	38.2	5	149	9	16.56

balls for Glamorgan in 1983. Holds record of 33 wickets in a Shell Shield season.
Best batting performance: 77 West Indies v England, Old Trafford 1984.
Best bowling performance: 7-101 Glamorgan v Nottinghamshire, Swansea 1982.

DERRICK, J.

Full name: John Derrick.
Role: Right-hand bat, right arm medium fast bowler.
Born: 15 January 1963, Aberdare, South Wales.
Height: 6' 1" **Weight:** 13st. 8lbs.
Nickname: J.D., Bo.
County debut: 1983.
County cap: No.
Test debut: —
No. of Tests: 0.
No. of One-Day Internationals: 0.
1000 runs in a season: 0.
50 wickets in a season: 0.
1st-Class 50s scored: 3.
1st-Class 100s scored: 0.
1st-Class 200s scored: 0.
1st-Class 5 w. in innings: 0.
1st-Class 10 w. in match: 0.
One-day 50s: 0.
One-day 100s: 0.
Place in batting averages: 34 average: 43.88; (1983: — average: —).
Place in bowling averages: — average: —; (1983: — average: —).
1st-Class catches 1984: 8 (career: 11).
Parents: John Raymond and Megan Irene Derrick.
Marital Status: Single.
Family links with cricket: Father and brother, Anthony play Club Cricket for Aberdare.
Education: Glynhafod and Blaengwawr Primary Schools and Blaengwawr Comprehensive School.
Qualifications: School Certificate.
Jobs outside cricket: Coaching cricket in St. Joseph's College, Brisbane.
Off-season 1984–85: Coaching cricket in Australia (Brisbane).
Overseas teams played for: Toombul C.C. Brisbane.
Equipment used: Duncan Fearnley.
Cricketers particularly learnt from: Tom Cartwright, Don Wilson, Andy Wagner.

Cricketers particularly admired: Geoff Boycott, John Snow, Dennis Lillee.
Other sports: Soccer, squash, tennis and golf; follow rugby and racing.
Relaxations: Listening to Lionel Richie.
Extras: Spent 3 years on M.C.C. groundstaff 1980–82. Coached at Lord's in
winter of 1981.
Best batting performance: 69* Glamorgan v Surrey, Swansea 1984.
Best bowling performance: 3-42 Glamorgan v Derbyshire, Swansea 1984.

LAST SEASON: BATTING

	I.	N.O.	R.	H.S.	AV.
TEST					
OTHER FIRST CLASS	15	7	351	69*	43.88
INT					
J.P.L.	6	3	37	17*	12.33
NAT.W.					
B & H					

CAREER: BATTING

	I.	N.O.	R.	H.S.	AV.
TEST					
OTHER FIRST CLASS	20	10	403	69*	40.30
INT					
J.P.L.	6	1	73	18*	14.60
NAT.W.					
B & H					

LAST SEASON: BOWLING

	O.	M.	R.	W.	AV.
TEST					
OTHER FIRST CLASS	133.5	31	441	8	55.13
INT					
J.P.L.	38	0	211	8	26.38
NAT.W.					
B & H					

CAREER: BOWLING

	O.	M.	R.	W.	AV.
TEST					
OTHER FIRST CLASS	141.5	7	472	8	59.00
INT					
J.P.L.	79.3	1	421	13	32.38
NAT.W.					
B & H					

FRANCIS, D.A.

Full Name: David Arthur Francis.
Role: Right-hand bat, off-break
bowler.
Born: 29 November 1953, Clydach,
Glamorgan.
Nickname: Arthur.
County debut: 1973.
County cap: 1982.
Test debut: —
No. of Tests: 0.
No. of One-Day Internationals: 0.
1000 runs in a season: 1.
50 wickets in a season: 0.
1st-Class 50s scored: 23.
1st-Class 100s scored: 3.
1st-Class 200s scored: 0.
1st-Class 5 w. in innings: 0.
1st-Class 10 w. in match: 0.

One-day 50s: 2.
One-day 100s: 1.
Place in batting averages: — average: —; (1983: 128 average: 26.56).
Place in bowling averages: — average: —; (1983: — average: —).
1st-Class catches 1984: 2 (career: 62).
Education: Cwmtawe Comprehensive School, Pontardawe.
Extras: Played for Glamorgan 2nd XI in 1971 and 1972. Played for Gowerton in 1979 in South Wales League. Released at end of 1984 season.
Best batting performance: 142* v Kent, Canterbury 1982.

LAST SEASON: BATTING

	I.	N.O.	R.	H.S.	AV.
TEST					
OTHER FIRST CLASS	3	0	27	20	9.00
INT					
J.P.L.	1	0	2	2	–
NAT.W.					
B & H	1	0	23	23	–

CAREER: BATTING

	I.	N.O.	R.	H.S.	AV.
TEST					
OTHER FIRST CLASS	237	36	4938	142*	24.57
INT					
J.P.L.	65	11	885	101*	16.38
NAT.W.	6	1	158	62*	31.60
B & H	18	0	220	59	12.22

LAST SEASON: BOWLING

	O.	M.	R.	W.	AV.
TEST					
OTHER FIRST CLASS					
INT					
J.P.L.					
NAT.W.					
B & H					

CAREER: BOWLING

	O.	M.	R.	W.	AV.
TEST					
OTHER FIRST CLASS	5	0	31	0	–
INT					
J.P.L.					
NAT.W.					
B & H					

Q. 33. Who was the first team to win the John Player Special League?

Q. 34. Who was the first player to take 50 catches in the John Player Special League?

Q. 35. When was the first County Championship?

GREEN, R.C.

Full Name: Russell Christopher
Green.
Role: Right-hand bat, right arm
medium fast bowler.
Born: 30 July 1959, St. Albans.
County debut: 1984.
County cap: No.
Test debut: —
No. of Tests: 0.
No. of One-Day Internationals: 0.
1000 runs in a season: 0.
50 wickets in a season: 0.
1st-Class 50s scored: 0.
1st-Class 100s scored: 0.
1st-Class 200s scored: 0.
1st-Class 5 w. in innings: 0.
1st-Class 10 w. in match: 0.
One-day 50s: 0.
One-day 100s: 0.
Place in batting averages: — average: —; (1983: — average: —).
Place in bowling averages: — average: —; (1983: -- average: —).
1st-Class catches 1984: 1 (career: 1).

LAST SEASON: BATTING

	I.	N.O.	R.	H.S.	AV.
TEST					
OTHER FIRST CLASS	1	1	3	3*	–
INT					
J.P.L.	–	–	–	–	–
NAT.W.					
B & H	–	–	–	–	–

CAREER: BATTING

	I.	N.O.	R.	H.S.	AV.
TEST					
OTHER FIRST CLASS	1	1	3	3*	–
INT					
J.P.L.	–	–	–	–	–
NAT.W.	1	1	8	8*	–
B & H	–	–	–	–	–

LAST SEASON: BOWLING

	O.	M.	R.	W.	AV.
TEST					
OTHER FIRST CLASS	31.5	11	92	2	46.00
INT					
J.P.L.	3	0	13	0	–
NAT.W.					
B & H	11	2	36	1	–

CAREER: BOWLING

	O.	M.	R.	W.	AV.
TEST					
OTHER FIRST CLASS	31.5	11	92	2	46.00
INT					
J.P.L.	3	0	13	0	–
NAT.W.	12	4	14	1	–
B & H	11	2	36	1	–

HENDERSON, S.P.

Full Name: Stephen Peter Henderson.
Role: Left-hand bat, right arm
medium pace bowler, slip fielder.
Born: 24 September 1958, Oxford.
Height: 6' 2" **Weight:** 14st.
Nickname: Hendo.
County debut: 1983 (Glamorgan).
County cap: No.
Test debut: —
No. of Tests: 0.
No. of One-Day Internationals: 0.
1000 runs in a season: 0.
50 wickets in a season: 0.
1st-Class 50s scored: 11.
1st-Class 100s scored: 2.
1st-Class 200s scored: 1.
1st-Class 5 w. in innings: 0.
1st-Class 10 w. in match: 0.
One-day 50s: 3.
One-day 100s: 0.
Place in batting averages: 118 average: 30.44; (1983: 122 average: 29.33).
Place in bowling averages: — average: —; (1983: — average: —).
1st-Class catches 1984: 4 (career: 43).
Parents: Derek and Ann.
Marital status: Single.
Family links with cricket: Father Oxford Blue 1950.
Education: Downside School; Durham University; Magdalene College, Cambridge.

LAST SEASON: BATTING

	I.	N.O.	R.	H.S.	AV.
TEST					
OTHER FIRST CLASS	17	1	487	108	30.44
INT					
J.P.L.	7	2	186	65*	37.20
NAT.W.					
B & H	4	1	11	7*	3.67

CAREER: BATTING

	I.	N.O.	R.	H.S.	AV.
TEST					
OTHER FIRST CLASS	104	13	2305	209*	25.33
INT					
J.P.L.	13	3	298	65*	29.80
NAT.W.	2	0	50	33	25.00
B & H	11	1	127	82	12.70

LAST SEASON: BOWLING

	O.	M.	R.	W.	AV.
TEST					
OTHER FIRST CLASS					
INT					
J.P.L.					
NAT.W.					
B & H					

CAREER: BOWLING

	O.	M.	R.	W.	AV.
TEST					
OTHER FIRST CLASS	29.4	6	185	3	61.67
INT					
J.P.L.	1.4	0	17	0	—
NAT.W.					
B & H	8	0	48	3	16.00

Qualifications: BA (Durham); BA (Cantab).
Jobs outside cricket: Chartered Surveyor; spot welder; barman.
Off-season 1984–85: Coaching.
Cricketing superstitions: "Getting out in the 60s."
Equipment used: Slazenger.
Overseas tours: Barbados 1980 with Worcester C.C.C.; U.S.A. 1981 with M.C.C.; Africa 1983 with McAlpines.
Cricketers particularly learnt from: Gordon Wilcock, Basil D'Oliveira.
Other sports: Rugby, squash, hockey, tennis, golf.
Relaxations: Photography, television, reading, conservation of hedgehogs.
Extras: Captained Cambridge University 1983. Blues 1982 & 83. Made debut for Worcestershire in 1977, but left staff in 1981.
Opinions of cricket: "Clubs should have a one-day game every weekend. Abolish 117 overs in a day, have 112 with allowance for wickets and injuries."
Best batting performance: 209* Cambridge University v Middlesex, Cambridge 1982.

HOLMES, G.C.

Full Name: Geoffrey Clark Holmes.
Role: Right-hand bat, right arm medium bowler, cover fielder.
Born: 16 September 1958, Newcastle-on-Tyne.
Height: 5′ 10″ **Weight:** 10st 10lbs.
County debut: 1978.
County cap: No.
Test debut: —
No. of Tests: 0.
No. of One-Day Internationals: 0.
1000 runs in a season: 1.
50 wickets in a season: 0.
1st-Class 50s scored: 9.
1st-Class 100s scored: 1.
1st-Class 200s scored: 0.
1st-Class 5 w. in innings: 0.
1st-Class 10 w. in match: 0.
One-day 50s: 3.
One-day 100s: 0.

Place in batting averages: 123 average: 29.68; (1983: — average: —).
Place in bowling averages: — average: —; (1983: — average: —).
1st-Class catches 1984: 10 (career: 29).
Parents: George and Rita Holmes.
Wife: Christine.
Education: West Denton High School.

Qualifications: A-levels in Maths and Chemistry, six O-levels. Advanced cricket coach.
Jobs outside cricket: Trainee estimator, has worked as milkman.
Overseas teams played for: Villa C.C. 1980–81; Bathurst C.C. 1983–84.
Cricketers particularly learnt from: Javed Miandad.
Off-season 1984–85: Playing and coaching in Cape Town (Fish Hock C.C.).
Family links with cricket: Father played in the Northumberland League.
Other sports: Soccer.
Relaxations: Reading, especially cricket books.
Best batting performance: 100 * Glamorgan v Gloucestershire, Bristol 1979.
Best bowling performance: 5-86 Glamorgan v Surrey, The Oval 1980.

LAST SEASON: BATTING

	I.	N.O.	R.	H.S.	AV.
TEST					
OTHER FIRST CLASS	37	2	1039	90	29.68
INT					
J.P.L.	12	1	350	73	31.82
NAT.W.	1	0	13	13	–
B & H	–	–	–	–	–

CAREER: BATTING

	I.	N.O.	R.	H.S.	AV.
TEST					
OTHER FIRST CLASS	122	24	2435	100*	24.85
INT					
J.P.L.	43	9	678	73	19.94
NAT.W.	2	0	24	13	12.00
B & H	6	1	62	30	12.40

LAST SEASON: BOWLING

	O.	M.	R.	W.	AV.
TEST					
OTHER FIRST CLASS	70	8	253	3	84.33
INT					
J.P.L.	45.2	3	226	13	17.38
NAT.W.					
B & H					

CAREER: BOWLING

	O.	M.	R.	W.	AV.
TEST					
OTHER FIRST CLASS	339.1	59	1270	29	43.79
INT					
J.P.L.	160.3	9	806	30	26.87
NAT.W.	8	1	33	0	–
B & H	39	5	144	6	24.00

Q. 36. Who won the first County Championship?
Q. 37. Which side has won the championship the most times running, and how many?
Q. 38. What was the title of the autobiography, published last year, of Bob Woolmer, Kent & England?

HOPKINS, J.A.

Full Name: John Anthony Hopkins.
Role: Right-hand bat, occasional
wicket-keeper.
Born: 16 June 1953, Maesteg.
Nickname: Ponty.
County debut: 1970.
County cap: 1977.
Test debut: —
No. of Tests: 0.
No. of One-Day Internationals: 0.
1000 runs in a season: 7.
50 wickets in a season: 0.
1st-Class 50s scored: 49.
1st-Class 100s scored: 15.
1st-Class 200s scored: 1.
1st-Class 5 w. in innings: 0.
1st-Class 10 w. in match: 0.
One-day 50s: 21.
One-day 100s: 2.
Place in batting averages: 93 average: 33.33; (1983: 121 average: 27.39).
Place in bowling averages: — average: —; (1983: — average: —).
1st-Class catches 1984: 18 (career: 173).
Education: Trinity College of Education, Carmarthen.
Qualifications: Trained as a teacher.
Jobs outside cricket: Teacher.
Family links with cricket: Younger brother of J.D. Hopkins who appeared for
Middlesex C.C.C. and formerly on Glamorgan staff.

LAST SEASON: BATTING

	I.	N.O.	R.	H.S.	AV.
TEST					
OTHER FIRST CLASS	50	5	1500	128*	33.33
INT					
J.P.L.	13	0	315	73	24.23
NAT.W.	1	0	29	29	–
B & H	4	1	124	62*	41.33

CAREER: BATTING

	I.	N.O.	R.	H.S.	AV.
TEST					
OTHER FIRST CLASS	426	27	11305	230	28.66
INT					
J.P.L.	132	11	2590	130*	21.40
NAT.W.	14	0	282	63	20.14
B & H	32	2	926	103*	30.87

LAST SEASON: BOWLING

	O.	M.	R.	W.	AV.
TEST					
OTHER FIRST CLASS	2.2	0	18	0	–
INT					
J.P.L.					
NAT.W.					
B & H					

CAREER: BOWLING

	O.	M.	R.	W.	AV.
TEST					
OTHER FIRST CLASS	13.2	1	68	0	–
INT					
J.P.L.					
NAT.W.					
B & H					

Extras: In 1979 dropped down order from opener, then regained form, and returned to opening bat. Known as fine baritone singer and raconteur in the Glamorgan 'cabaret' act.
Best batting performance: 230 Glamorgan v Worcestershire, Worcester 1977.

JAVED MIANDAD

Full Name: Miandad Khan Javed.
Role: Right-hand bat, leg-break and googly bowler.
Born: 12 June 1957, Karachi.
Height: 5' 9" **Weight:** 11st 7lbs.
Nickname: J.J., Mum 'n Dad.
County debut: 1980 (Glam.).
County cap: 1980.
Test debut: 1976–77.
No. of Tests: 60.
No. of One-Day Internationals: 58.

1000 runs in a season: 4.
50 wickets in a season: 0.
1st-Class 50s scored: 95.
1st-Class 100s scored: 51.
1st-Class 200s scored: 1.
1st-Class 5 w. in innings: 0.
1st-Class 10 w. in match: 0.
One-day 50s: 39.
One-day 100s: 3.
Place in batting averages: 7 average: 64.00; (1983 — average: —).
Place in bowling averages: — average: —; (1983: — average: —).
1st-Class catches 1984: 4 (career: 263).
Marital status: Single.
Education: C.M.S. Secondary School, Karachi.
Jobs outside cricket: Assistant Vice-President in Habib Bank of Pakistan.
Family links with cricket: Father played in India. Two brothers play for a bank in Pakistan.
Overseas tours: Toured with Pakistan to Australia and West Indies 1976–77; England 1978 and 1982; India 1978–79, Australia 1983–84.
Overseas teams played for: Karachi Whites; Karachi; Sind; Habib Banks.
Equipment used: Gray-Nicolls.
Other sports: Hockey, soccer, swimming.
Relaxations: Reading sports books, spending time with family, watching television.
Significant injuries in 1984: Hit on head by Lillee bouncer in Calcutta benefit match and missed much of season.

Extras: Was Vice-Captain of Pakistan Under-19 team in England in 1974 and was Captain of Under-19 side in Sri Lanka 1974–75. Made debut for Sussex in 1976, gaining his cap in 1977. Left Sussex for Glamorgan at end of 1980 season. Scored a century on debut for Glamorgan, and was immediately awarded his cap. Topped Glamorgan first-class batting averages, 1981 and 1982. Captain of Glamorgan for that part of 1982 when he was not playing for Pakistan. Youngest-ever double century maker in Test cricket at age of 19 years 4 months. (Scored 163 for Pakistan v New Zealand on Test debut, Lahore, 1966–67, and 206 v New Zealand at Karachi in third Test.) Pakistan captain 1980–81. Second Pakistani to top 4,000 runs in Test cricket.

Best batting performance: 311 Karachi Whites v Nat. Bank Karachi 1974–75.

Best bowling performance: 7-39 Habib Bank v I.D.B.P. Lahore 1980–81.

LAST SEASON: BATTING

	I.	N.O.	R.	H.S.	AV.
TEST					
OTHER FIRST CLASS	15	2	832	212*	64.00
INT					
J.P.L.	6	0	244	69	40.67
NAT.W.					
B & H					

CAREER: BATTING

	I.	N.O.	R.	H.S.	AV.
TEST	95	14	4519	280*	55.79
OTHER FIRST CLASS	365	60	15888	317	52.00
INT	56	11	1641	119*	36.48
J.P.L.	82	14	2564	107*	37.70
NAT.W.	9	1	328	75	41.00
B & H	18	2	700	95	43.75

LAST SEASON: BOWLING

	O.	M.	R.	W.	AV.
TEST					
OTHER FIRST CLASS	51.2	9	187	6	31.17
INT					
J.P.L.					
NAT.W.					
B & H					

CAREER: BOWLING

	O.	M.	R.	W.	AV.
TEST	130.6 62.4	20 9	661	17	38.88
OTHER FIRST CLASS			5531	170	32.53
INT	50	3	209	5	41.80
J.P.L.	13.5	0	68	2	34.00
NAT.W.	2	0	12	0	–
B & H	2	0	14	0	–

Q. 39. What county cricketer's autobiography, recently re-issued, is entitled *A Funny Turn*?

Q. 40. What current county cricketer wrote a collection of essays entitled *Slices of Cricket*?

JONES, A.L.

Full Name: Alan Lewis Jones.
Role: Left-hand bat.
Born: 1 June 1957, Alltwen, near Swansea.
Height: 5′ 8½″ **Weight:** 10st 4lbs.
Nickname: Jonah, occasionally Posh.
County debut: 1973, at age of 16 years 99 days. Youngest player for Glamorgan.
County cap: 1983.
Test debut: —
No. of Tests: 0.
No. of One-day Internationals: 0.
1000 runs in a season: 2.
50 wickets in a season: 0.
1st-Class 50s scored: 31.
1st-Class 100s scored: 5.
1st-Class 200s scoreed: 0.
1st-Class 5 w. in innings: 0.
1st-Class 10 w. in match: 0.
One-day 50s: 7.
One-day 100s: 0.
Place in batting averages: 66 average: 36.96; (1983: 94 average: 31.39).
Place in bowling averages: — average: —; (1983: — average: —).
1st-Class catches 1984: 30 (career: 86).
Parents: Ieuan and Marion Jones.
Wife and date of marriage: Diane, 27 September 1980.

LAST SEASON: BATTING

	I.	N.O.	R.	H.S.	AV.
TEST					
OTHER FIRST CLASS	51	2	1811	132	36.96
INT					
J.P.L.	14	0	319	71	22.79
NAT.W.	1	0	7	7	–
B & H	3	0	42	20	14.00

CAREER: BATTING

	I.	N.O.	R.	H.S.	AV.
TEST					
OTHER FIRST CLASS	230	18	5483	132	25.86
INT					
J.P.L.	71	3	1525	82	22.42
NAT.W.	5	0	80	36	16.00
B & H	14	0	191	36	13.64

LAST SEASON: BOWLING

	O.	M.	R.	W.	AV.
TEST					
OTHER FIRST CLASS	10	0	86	1	
INT					
J.P.L.					
NAT.W.					
B & H					

CAREER: BOWLING

	O.	M.	R.	W.	AV.
TEST					
OTHER FIRST CLASS	14.5	0	128	1	
INT					
J.P.L.	0.4	0	5	0	–
NAT.W.					
B & H					

Education: Ystalyfera Grammar School; Cwmtawe Comprehensive School; Cardiff College of Education.
Qualifications: Eight O-levels. Teacher training certificate. Qualified advanced coach.
Jobs outside cricket: Working in chartered accountant's office training to be certified accountant. Has worked as life assurance salesman.
Off-season 1984–85: Playing in Auckland, New Zealand.
Equipment used and endorsed: Slazenger.
Overseas tours: West Indies with England Young Cricketers 1976. Australasia with Derrick Robins XI in 1980.
Overseas teams played for: Played with Hamilton-Wickham in Newcastle, Australia, in 1978–79.
Cricketers particularly learnt from: Alan Jones.
Cricketers particularly admired: Alan Jones, Gordon Greenridge, Andy Roberts.
Other sports: Squash, golf. Watch soccer and rugby.
Relaxations: Keeps up-to-date with previous biology studies; keep-fit enthusiast.
Extras: Made debut for Glamorgan 2nd XI in 1972, aged 15. Played for Briton Ferry Town in 1979 in South Wales League.
Best batting performance: 132 Glamorgan v Hampshire, Cardiff 1984.

LLOYD, B.J.

Full Name: Barry John Lloyd.
Role: Right-hand bat, off-break bowler.
Born: 6 September 1953, Neath.
Height: 6′ 0″ **Weight:** 12st.
Nickname: Lloydy.
County debut: 1972.
County cap: 1982.
Test debut: —
No. of Tests: 0.
No. of One-Day Internationals: 0.
1000 runs in a season: 0.
50 wickets in a season: 2.
1st-Class 50s scored: 0.
1st-Class 100s scored: 0.
1st-Class 200s scored: 0.
1st-Class 5 w. in innings: 3.
1st-Class 10 w. in match: 0.
One-day 50s: 0.
One-day 100s: 0.

Place in batting averages: — average: —; (1983: 223 average: 13.50).

Place in bowling averages: — average: —; (1983: 120 average: 41.72).
1st-Class catches 1984: 0 (career: 87).
Parents: Leslie John and Patricia Mary Lloyd.
Wife and date of marriage: Janice Prydderch, 11 September 1976.
Children: Hannah Jayne, 25 August 1979, Elinor Hâf, 5 September 1983 (Hâf is Welsh for summer).
Education: Llangatwg Comprehensive School, Cadoxton, Neath, West Glamorgan; Bangor Normal College, North Wales.
Qualifications: Advanced coaching award. Teaching certificate.
Jobs outside cricket: Teacher.
Family links with cricket: Father and grandfather played cricket with Pontneddfechan C.C., a small village in the Neath Valley.
Equipment used: Gunn & Moore.
Cricketers particularly learnt from: "Javed Miandad – I think he is the best batsman in the world." Alan Jones.
Other sports: Plays rugby for Bryncoch R.F.C., Neath.
Relaxations: Any sport, including fishing; gardening, family life.
Extras: Formerly on M.C.C. ground staff. Captain while Malcolm Nash was injured. Took over Glamorgan captaincy when Javed was playing for Pakistan. Released at end of 1984 season.
Best batting performance: 48 Glamorgan v Sussex, Cardiff 1982.
Best bowling performance: 8-70 Glamorgan v Lancashire, Cardiff 1981.

LAST SEASON: BATTING

	I.	N.O.	R.	H.S.	AV.
TEST					
OTHER FIRST CLASS					
INT					
J.P.L.	1	0	27	27	—
NAT.W.					
B & H					

CAREER: BATTING

	I.	N.O.	R.	H.S.	AV.
TEST					
OTHER FIRST CLASS	184	47	1631	48	11.91
INT					
J.P.L.	40	16	325	32	13.54
NAT.W.	5	0	16	12	3.20
B & H	7	2	50	38*	10.00

LAST SEASON: BOWLING

	O.	M.	R.	W.	AV.
TEST					
OTHER FIRST CLASS					
INT					
J.P.L.	7	0	47	0	—
NAT.W.					
B & H					

CAREER: BOWLING

	O.	M.	R.	W.	AV.
TEST					
OTHER FIRST CLASS	3418.3	778	10133	247	41.04
INT					
J.P.L.	427.4	31	1827	48	38.06
NAT.W.	71	20	166	5	33.20
B & H	83.4	12	271	10	27.10

MORRIS, H.

Full Name: Hugh Morris.
Role: Left-hand bat.
Born: 5 October 1963, Cardiff.
Height: 5′ 8″ **Weight:** 12st.
Nickname:"H", Huge, Gnasher.
County debut: 1981.
County cap: No.
Test debut: —
No. of Tests: 0.
No. of One-Day Internationals: 0.
1000 runs in a season: 0.
50 wickets in a season: 0.
1st-Class 50s scored: 6.
1st-Class 100s scored: 0.
1st-Class 200s scored: 0.
1st-Class 5 w. in innings: 0.
1st-Class 10 w. in match: 0.
One-day 50s: 1.
One-day 100s: 0.

Place in batting averages: 88 average: 33.87; (1983: 173 average: 20.72).
Place in bowling averages: — average: —; (1983: — average: —).
1st-Class catches 1984: 2 (career: 10).
Parents: Roger and Anne Morris.
Marital status: Single.
Education: Blundell's School, S. Glamorgan Institute.
Qualifications: 9 O-levels and 3 A-levels, 1 AO level. N.C.A. Coaching Award.
Jobs outside cricket: Student.
Family links with cricket: Brother played for Wales Under-16, and Glamorgan Under-19. Father played club cricket.
Off-season 1984–85: Studying at College.
Cricketing superstitions: "Getting off '0' and '111'. Put right pad on first."
Equipment used: Gray-Nicolls.
Overseas tours: December-January 1980–81, with English Public Schoolboy tour to West Indies (Trinidad, Tobago, Barbados), 1982–83 to Sri Lanka, 1984 to USA (Los Angeles).
Cricketers particularly learnt from or admired: Javed Miandad, Alan Jones, Viv Richards, Tom Cartwright.
Other sports: Rugby, squash, tennis "amongst others".
Relaxations: Watching rugby, listening to music, travelling and having a few drinks.
Extras: Highest schoolboy cricket average in 1979 of 89.71 and highest in 1981 of 184.6 and highest in 1982 of 149.2. Captain of England Under-19 Schoolboys in 1981 and 1982. Played for Young England v. Young West Indies

1982, and captained Young England v. Australians. Won Gray-Nicholls "Most Promising Schoolboy" Award 1981, and Young Cricketer of 1982.
Opinions on cricket: "The 117 overs rule has to be changed as several games were being played after 8 o'clock and most spectators do not plan to watch cricket at that time."
Best batting performance: 114* Glamorgan v Yorkshire, Cardiff 1984.

LAST SEASON: BATTING

	I.	N.O.	R.	H.S.	AV.
TEST					
OTHER FIRST CLASS	20	4	542	114*	33.87
INT					
J.P.L.	5	1	101	55*	25.25
NAT.W.					
B & H	1	0	10	10	–

CAREER: BATTING

	I.	N.O.	R.	H.S.	AV.
TEST					
OTHER FIRST CLASS	42	10	1004	114*	31.38
INT					
J.P.L.	7	1	143	55*	23.83
NAT.W.					
B & H	1	0	10	10	–

LAST SEASON: BOWLING

	O.	M.	R.	W.	AV.
TEST					
OTHER FIRST CLASS	9	1	45	1	–
INT					
J.P.L.					
NAT.W.					
B & H					

CAREER: BOWLING

	O.	M.	R.	W.	AV.
TEST					
OTHER FIRST CLASS	12.5	1	68	1	–
INT					
J.P.L.					
NAT.W.					
B & H					

ONTONG, R.C.

Full Name: Rodney Craig Ontong.
Role: Right-hand bat, right arm fast medium bowler.
Born: 9 September 1955, Johannesburg, South Africa.
County debut: 1975.
County cap: 1979.
Test debut: —
No. of Tests: 0.
No. of One-Day Internationals: 0.
1000 runs in a season: 4.
50 wickets in a season: 3.
1st-Class 50s scored: 51.
1st-Class 100s scored: 15.
1st-Class 200s scored: 1.
1st-Class 5 w. in innings: 20.
1st-Class 10 w. in match: 2.
One-day 50s: 9.
One-day 100s: 1.

Place in batting averages: 72 average: 35.67; (1983: 59 average: 38.52).

Place in bowling averages: 57 average: 29.12; (1983: 102 average: 36.66).
1st-Class catches 1984: 15 (career: 117).
Education: Selbourne College, East London, South Africa.
Overseas teams played for: Made debut in 1972–73 for Border in Currie Cup Competition. Transferred to Transvaal for 1976–77 season, before returning to Border.
Extras: Took over Glamorgan captaincy during 1984.
Best batting performance: 204* Glamorgan v Middlesex, Swansea 1984.
Best bowling performance: 7-60 Border v N. Transvaal, Pretoria 1975–76.

LAST SEASON: BATTING

	I.	N.O.	R.	H.S.	AV.
TEST					
OTHER FIRST CLASS	45	8	1320	204*	35.67
INT					
J.P.L.	14	2	304	48*	25.33
NAT.W.	1	0	2	2	–
B & H	3	0	124	81	41.33

CAREER: BATTING

	I.	N.O.	R.	H.S.	AV.
TEST					
OTHER FIRST CLASS	414	46	10477	204*	28.47
INT					
J.P.L.	96	11	2029	100	23.87
NAT.W.	11	1	309	64	30.90
B & H	24	3	382	81	18.19

LAST SEASON: BOWLING

	O.	M.	R.	W.	AV.
TEST					
OTHER FIRST CLASS	837.4	231	2155	74	29.12
INT					
J.P.L.	83	6	422	13	32.46
NAT.W.	12	3	34	1	–
B & H	33	8	73	3	24.33

CAREER: BOWLING

	O.	M.	R.	W.	AV.
TEST					
OTHER FIRST CLASS	5422.2	1169	16530	555	29.78
INT					
J.P.L.	583.4	28	2809	90	31.21
NAT.W.	98	18	380	9	42.22
B & H	218.4	43	659	34	19.38

Q. 41. Whose cricket autobiography is entitled *The Sun Has Got His Hat On*?

Q. 42. Who published his autobiography last season entitled *Hooked on Opening*?

Q. 43. Which counties did umpire Harold Bird play first-class cricket for?

Q. 44. How many cricketers called Smith have played for England?

PRICE, M.R.

Full Name: Mark Richard Price.
Role: Right-hand bat, left arm
spin, slip fielder.
Born: 20 April 1960, Liverpool.
Height: 6' 2" **Weight:** 13st.
Nickname: Grimbo, Dale.
County debut: 1984.
County cap: No.
Test debut: —
No. of Tests: 0.
No. of One-Day Internationals: 0.
1000 runs in a season: 0.
50 wickets in a season: 0.
1st-Class 50s scored: 0.
1st-Class 100s scored: 0.
1st-Class 200s scored: 0.
1st-Class 5 w. in innings: 0.
1st-Class 10 w. in match: 0.
One-day 50s: 0.
One-day 100s: 0.
Place in batting averages: — average: —; (1983: — average: —).
Place in bowling averages: — average: —; (1983: — average: —).
Parents: Alan and Nellie.
Wife and date of marriage: Caroline, March 1984.
Family links with cricket: Father played Lancashire League for Ramsbottom.
Education: Harper Green High, Farnworth, Bolton.
Qualifications: 7 C.S.E.s. Engineer.

LAST SEASON: BATTING

	I.	N.O.	R.	H.S.	AV.
TEST					
OTHER FIRST CLASS	2	0	8	7	4.00
INT					
J.P.L.					
NAT.W.					
B & H					

CAREER: BATTING

	I.	N.O.	R.	H.S.	AV.
TEST					
OTHER FIRST CLASS	2	0	8	7	4.00
INT					
J.P.L.					
NAT.W.					
B & H					

LAST SEASON: BOWLING

	O.	M.	R.	W.	AV.
TEST					
OTHER FIRST CLASS	31	4	109	2	54.50
INT					
J.P.L.					
NAT.W.					
B & H					

CAREER: BOWLING

	O.	M.	R.	W.	AV.
TEST					
OTHER FIRST CLASS	31	4	109	2	54.50
INT					
J.P.L.					
NAT.W.					
B & H					

Jobs outside cricket: Engineering; building sites.
Off-season 1984–85: Playing in New Zealand.
Equipment used: Slazenger.
Cricketers particularly admired: Ian Botham, Bishen Bedi.
Other sports: Football, snooker, table tennis, boxing.

ROWE, C.J.C.

Full Name: Charles James Castell Rowe.
Role: Right-hand bat, off-break bowler.
Born: 27 November 1951, Hong Kong.
Height: 5′ 9½″ **Weight:** 11st 10lbs.
Nickname: Charlie, Chas.
County debut: 1982 (Glamorgan).
County cap: 1983.
Test debut: —
No. of Tests: 0.
No. of One-Day Internationals: 0.
1000 runs in a season: 2.
50 wickets in a season: 0.
1st-Class 50s scored: 30.
1st-Class 100s scored: 6.
1st-Class 200s scored: 0.
1st-Class 5 w. in innings: 3.
1st-Class 10 w. in match: 1.
One-day 50s: 7.
One-day 100s: 0.

Place in batting averages: 225 average: 17.22; (1983: 153 average: 23.26).
Place in bowling averages: — average: —; (1983: 119 average: 41.36).
1st-Class catches 1984: 2 (career: 63).
Parents: George and Betty Rowe.
Wife and date of marriage: Susan, 12 March 1977.
Children: Lucy, 25 September 1977; James, 4 July 1979.
Education: Hawkhurst Court Prep. School; King's School, Canterbury.
Qualifications: 4 A-levels, 6 O-levels. M.C.C. coach (intermediate).
Overseas tours: England Under-19 XI to India 1970–71; with Hong Kong to Sri Lanka, Singapore, Sabah 1971.
Cricketers particularly learnt from: Colin Cowdrey, Bob Woolmer.
Cricket superstitions: Always buckle left pad on first.
Equipment used: Slazenger.
Other sports: Played rugby, hockey, tennis, squash and soccer at school, also table-tennis. Plays squash for Beckenham in the winter to keep fit. Also swims.

Relaxations: Reading, particularly historical novels and science fiction, cars, cinema, travel, photography and music, mainly non-classical. "I enjoy going for a drive in the country on days off."

Extras: Known in the dressing-room for being absent-minded. Took one wicket with right arm and one wicket with left arm in same innings in championship match v Sussex, Hove 1980. Hat-trick for Kent 2nd XI v Surrey 2nd XI 1980. Used to be on the committee of the Stragglers of Asia C.C. Wife, Susie, played tennis for Kent, reaching finals of Junior Wimbledon and in Junior Wightman Cup squad. Father-in-law, George Morgan represented Kent at rugby and brother-in-law, Guy Morgan, has captained Kent at squash for several years. Was one of the few opening batsmen not to wear a helmet. Released by Kent in 1981, having made his debut in 1974, and won county cap in 1977. Released by Glamorgan at end of 1984.

Best batting performance: 147* Kent v Susex, Canterbury 1979.
Best bowling performance: 6-46 Kent v Derbyshire, Dover 1976.

LAST SEASON: BATTING

	I.	N.O.	R.	H.S.	AV.
TEST					
OTHER FIRST CLASS	11	2	155	60*	17.22
INT					
J.P.L.	1	0	25	25	–
NAT.W.	1	0	30	30	–
B & H	1	0	5	5	–

CAREER: BATTING

	I.	N.O.	R.	H.S.	AV.
TEST					
OTHER FIRST CLASS	277	43	6408	147*	27.39
INT					
J.P.L.	65	16	1184	61	24.16
NAT.W.	9	2	99	30	14.14
B & H	22	0	280	54	12.73

LAST SEASON: BOWLING

	O.	M.	R.	W.	AV.
TEST					
OTHER FIRST CLASS	135	41	356	12	29.67
INT					
J.P.L.	1	0	10	0	–
NAT.W.	10	3	37	2	18.50
B & H					

CAREER: BOWLING

	O.	M.	R.	W.	AV.
TEST					
OTHER FIRST CLASS	1676	399	5127	128	40.06
INT					
J.P.L.	51.1	2	307	12	25.58
NAT.W.	37	5	146	5	29.20
B & H	12	1	75	1	–

Q. 45. What legendary England Test cricketer had the nickname of "Smith" in his Cambridge days?

Q. 46. What current Hampshire cricketer has played in every place in the county's batting order?

Q. 47. Who hit the fastest first-class century in the England 1984 season?

Q. 48. Who came bottom of the John Player Special League in 1984?

SELVEY, M.W.W.

Full Name: Michael Walter William Selvey.
Role: Right-hand bat, right arm fast medium bowler. Captain 1983–
Born: 25 April 1948, Chiswick.
Height: 6' 2" **Weight:** 14st.
Nickname: Walter or Walt.
County debut: 1983 (Glamorgan).
County cap: 1983.
Benefit: 1982 (with Middlesex).
Test debut: 1976.
No. of Tests: 3.
No. of One-Day Internationals: 0.
1000 runs in a season: 0.
50 wickets in a season: 7.
1st-Class 50s scored: 4.
1st-Class 100s scored: 0.
1st-Class 200s scored: 0.
1st-Class 5 w. in innings: 38.
1st-Class 10 w. in match: 4.
One-day 50s: 0.
One-day 100s: 0.
Place in batting averages: 264 average: 11.10; (1983: 236 average: 11.90).
Place in bowling averages: 114 average: 39.88; (1983: 80 average: 32.31).
1st-Class catches 1984: 9 (career: 79).
Parents: Walter and Edith Selvey.
Wife and date of marriage: Mary, 29 August 1970.
Children: Nichola, 12 May 1975.
Education: Battersea Grammar School; Manchester University; Cambridge University.
Qualifications: B.Sc. Certificate of Education.
Jobs outside cricket: Various teaching posts, overseas coaching and playing.
Equipment used: Duncan Fearnley, Gola Boots.
Equipment endorsed: Vehicle supplied by U.B.M. Cardiff Chartered Trust.
Cricketing superstitions: "Used to be 'Nelson' (i.e. 111, 222, etc.). Now superstitious about ignoring Nelson."
Overseas tours: With M.C.C. to India, Sri Lanka, and Australia 1976–77; International Team to Pakistan 1981.
Cricketers particularly learnt from: "Learned something from all cricketers, but especially Fred Titmus."
Overseas teams played for: Orange Free State in 1973–74 Currie Cup Competition. 1978–79–80 off-seasons spent playing and coaching in Auckland, New Zealand.
Other sports: Played soccer for Cambridge but now only plays golf.

Relaxations: Reading, rock music "especially Bruce Springsteen", Times, Guardian and Telegraph crosswords, real ale.

Extras: Debut for Surrey 1968. Cambridge Blue 1971. Took four West Indies wickets in Test debut at Manchester 1976. Known for very informal dress. Wife was a model. Famous round the county circuit for always wearing a long blue scarf. Took 3 wickets in first 20 balls in Test cricket. Released by Middlesex at end of 1982 season and joined Glamorgan as captain. Injury forced retirement during 1984.

Best batting performance: 67 Middlesex v Zimbabwe, Bulawayo 1980–81.

Best bowling performance: 7-20 Middlesex v Gloucestershire, Gloucester 1976.

LAST SEASON: BATTING

	I.	N.O.	R.	H.S.	AV.
TEST					
OTHER FIRST CLASS	18	8	111	20	11.10
INT					
J.P.L.	4	3	25	9	–
NAT.W.	1	1	6	6*	–
B & H	3	2	17	13	–

CAREER: BATTING

	I.	N.O.	R.	H.S.	AV.
TEST	5	3	15	5*	7.50
OTHER FIRST CLASS	273	85	2390	67	12.71
INT					
J.P.L.	86	40	560	38*	12.17
NAT.W.	17	7	90	14	9.00
B & H	29	8	144	27*	6.86

LAST SEASON: BOWLING

	O.	M.	R.	W.	AV.
TEST					
OTHER FIRST CLASS	311.3	69	997	25	39.88
INT					
J.P.L.	60.1	1	310	7	44.29
NAT.W.					
B & H	28	3	78	5	15.60

CAREER: BOWLING

	O.	M.	R.	W.	AV.
TEST	82	9	343	6	57.17
OTHER FIRST CLASS	7466.2	1884	20239	766	26.42
INT	28.2	2			
J.P.L.	1208.2	122	4747	208	22.82
NAT.W.	316.2	70	829	40	20.73
B & H	511.1	98	1512	74	20.43

Q. 49. How many sixes were hit in all 1984 John Player Special League matches?

Q. 50. What was the one change in the West Indies tour squad for Australia in 1984–85 from their squad for England in 1984?

STEELE, J.F.

Full Name: John Frederick Steele.
Role: Right-hand bat, slow left arm orthodox bowler.
Born: 23 July 1946, Stafford.
Height: 5' 10½" **Weight:** 11st 7lbs.
Nickname: Steeley.
County debut: 1970 (Leicestershire), 1984 (Glamorgan).
County cap: 1971 (Leicestershire).
Benefit: With Leicestershire in 1983 (£33,470).
Test debut: —
No. of Tests: 0.
No. of One-Day Internationals: 0.
1000 runs in a season: 6.
50 wickets in a season: 2.
1st-Class 50s scored: 69.
1st-Class 100s scored: 20.
1st-Class 200s scored: 0.
1st-Class 5 w. in innings: 16.
1st-Class 10 w. in match: 0.
One-day 50s: 14.
One-day 100s: 1.
Place in batting averages: 132 average: 28.28; (1983: 184 average: 19.24).
Place in bowling averages: 44 average: 27.46; (1983: 77 average: 31.60).
1st-Class catches 1984: 34 (career: 394).
Parents: Alfred and Grace Steele.
Wife and date of marriage: Susan, 16 April 1977.

LAST SEASON: BATTING

	I.	N.O.	R.	H.S.	AV.
TEST					
OTHER FIRST CLASS	41	12	820	60*	28.28
INT					
J.P.L.	9	4	102	38*	20.40
NAT.W.	1	0	31	31	–
B & H	3	0	53	28	17.67

CAREER: BATTING

	I.	N.O.	R.	H.S.	AV.
TEST					
OTHER FIRST CLASS	576	77	14489	195	29.04
INT					
J.P.L.	131	34	1838	92	18.94
NAT.W.	21	4	452	108*	26.59
B & H	49	6	1122	91	26.09

LAST SEASON: BOWLING

	O.	M.	R.	W.	AV.
TEST					
OTHER FIRST CLASS	673	175	1867	68	27.46
INT					
J.P.L.	120	9	411	23	17.86
NAT.W.	8	3	20	1	–
B & H	44	6	124	7	17.71

CAREER: BOWLING

	O.	M.	R.	W.	AV.
TEST					
OTHER FIRST CLASS	6175.5	1957	14603	564	25.89
INT					
J.P.L.	1117.2	95	4409	184	23.96
NAT.W.	217	44	647	22	29.41
B & H	543	89	1624	61	26.64

Education: Endon Secondary Modern, Staffordshire.
Jobs outside cricket: Work Study Officer. Junior Fireman, Staffs. Fire Brigade.
Family links with cricket: Younger brother of David Steele of Derbyshire and England, and cousin of former Northants player B.S. Crump. Uncle, Stan Crump, played as professional in Lancashire League.
Overseas teams played for: Natal in 1973–74 and 1977–78 Currie Cup Competitions. Pinetown Cricket Club, Natal, S. Africa.
Other sports: Golf.
Relaxations: Music. Reading.
Extras: Was 12th man for England v Rest of the World at Lord's in 1970, only a month after making debut. Played for Leicestershire 1970–1983.
Best batting performance: 195 Leicestershire v Derbyshire, Leicester 1971.
Best bowling performance: 7-29 Natal B v Griqualand West, Umzinto 1973–74; 7-29 Leicestershire v Gloucestershire, Leicester 1980.

THOMAS, J.G.

Full Name: John Gregory Thomas.
Role: Right-hand bat, right arm medium fast bowler.
Born: 12 August 1960, Trebanos, Swansea.
Height: 6′ 3″ **Weight:** 14st.
County debut: 1979.
County cap: No.
Test debut: —
No. of Tests: 0.
No. of One-Day Internationals: 0.
1000 runs in a season: 0.
50 wickets in a season: 0.
1st-Class 50s scored: 2.
1st-Class 100s scored: 0.
1st-Class 200s scored: 0.
1st-Class 5 w. in innings: 5.
1st-Class 10 w. in match: 1.
One-day 50s: 0.
One-day 100s: 0.

Place in batting averages: 241 average: 14.95; (1983: 235 average: 12.00).
Place in bowling averages: 89 average: 33.51; (1983: 53 average: 27.84).
1st-Class catches 1984: 9 (career: 24).
Parents: Illtyd and Margaret Thomas.
Marital status: Single.
Family links with cricket: Father played village cricket.

Education: Cwmtawe Comprehensive School; South Glamorgan Institute of Higher Education.
Qualifications: Qualified teacher, advanced cricket coach.
Off-season 1984–85: East London, South Africa.
Cricketing superstitions: The number 111.
Equipment endorsed: Gray-Nicolls.
Overseas tours: To West Indies with British Colleges March–April 1982.
Overseas teams played for: Border Cricket Union, South Africa.
Other sports: Watches rugby.
Relaxations: Any sport, music.
Extras: Top of Glamorgan first-class bowling averages in 1982. Bowling award for 4 wickets or more most times in 1983, John Player Special League (3 occasions).
Best batting performance: 84 Glamorgan v Surrey, Guildford 1982.
Best bowling performance: 5-56 Glamorgan v Somerset, Cardiff 1984.

LAST SEASON: BATTING

	I.	N.O.	R.	H.S.	AV.
TEST					
OTHER FIRST CLASS	26	5	314	36*	14.95
INT					
J.P.L.	13	2	176	33	16.00
NAT.W.					
B & H	3	0	23	17	7.67

CAREER: BATTING

	I.	N.O.	R.	H.S.	AV.
TEST					
OTHER FIRST CLASS	68	9	865	84	14.66
INT					
J.P.L.	26	7	316	37	16.63
NAT.W.	2	0	39	24	19.50
B & H	3	0	23	17	7.67

LAST SEASON: BOWLING

	O.	M.	R.	W.	AV.
TEST					
OTHER FIRST CLASS	435.2	95	1575	47	33.51
INT					
J.P.L.	91.3	9	436	19	22.94
NAT.W.					
B & H	33.3	3	137	2	68.50

CAREER: BOWLING

	O.	M.	R.	W.	AV.
TEST					
OTHER FIRST CLASS	1037.1	217	3778	128	29.52
INT					
J.P.L.	179.1	11	910	41	22.19
NAT.W.	11	0	72	0	–
B & H	33.3	3	137	2	68.50

Q. 51. What is/was the weight of bat used by a) Ian Botham; b) Denis Compton; c) Don Bradman?

Q. 52. How many first-class centuries had Dennis Amiss scored by the end of the 1984 season?

YOUNIS AHMED

Full Name: Mohammed Younis Ahmed.
Role: Left-hand bat, left arm medium bowler.
Born: 20 October 1947, Lahore, Pakistan.
Height: 5' 10" **Weight:** 11st. 7lbs.
Nickname: Yoon.
Benefit: "Not been so lucky."
County debut: 1979 (Worcs.). 1984 (Glamorgan).
County cap: 1979 (Worcs.).
Test debut: 1969–70.
No. of Tests: 2.

No. of One-Day Internationals: 0.
1000 runs in a season: 12.
50 wickets in a season: 0.
1st-Class 50s scored: 113.
1st-Class 100s: 37.
1st-Class 200s scored: 1.
1st-Class 5 w. in innings: 0.
1st-Class 10 w. in match: 0.
One-day 50s: 45.
One-day 100s: 5.
Place in batting averages: 33 average: 44.16; (1983: — average: —).
Place in bowling averages: — average: —; (1983: — average: —).
1st-Class catches 1984: 13 (career: 232).
Parents: Father, Inaitullah Ahmed; mother, Shamin Akthir.
Wife and date of marriage: Gloria Ahmed, 15 September 1972.
Children: Samir Ahmed, 2 January 1975; Yasmine Ahmed, 16 January 1979.
Education: Moslem High School, Lahore.
Qualifications: Matriculation. B.A. degree, Government College, Lahore.
Jobs outside cricket: Has coached in Rhodesia and South Africa which led to ban on playing for Pakistan. Owns and runs own travel agency.
Family links with cricket: Younger brother of Saeed Ahmed who played for Pakistan.
Equipment used and endorsed: Duncan Fearnley.
Overseas tours: West Indies 1970; Commonwealth tour Pakistan–Kuwait, 1971; South Australia 1972–73; South Africa 1973–74; International XI to Rhodesia 1974–75.
Overseas teams played for: Pakistan Inter Board Schools. South Australia in 1972–73 Sheffield Shield. Universal Club, Rhodesia, 1974–75–76–77.
Cricketers particularly learnt from or admired: John Edrich, Fred Titmus, Alf Gover. Saeed Ahmed (brother), Sir Gary Sobers.

Other sports: Squash, tennis, golf.

Relaxations: "Evenings spent with my children. Reading cricket books."

Extras: Debut in 1962 at age of 14yrs 4mths for Pakistan School v South Zone (counts as first-class). Debut for Surrey in 1965, cap 1969. Is now eligible to play for England. Suffers from hay fever. Sacked by Worcestershire in 1983 season.

Opinions on cricket: "I would like to see 4-day cricket matches played in England rather than 3-day matches. This will provoke the full opportunity to middle over batsmen, not possible in 3-day matches."

Best batting performance: 221* Worcestershire v Nottinghamshire, Trent Bridge 1979.

Best bowling performance: 4-10 Surrey v Cambridge University, Cambridge 1975.

LAST SEASON: BATTING

	I.	N.O.	R.	H.S.	AV.
TEST					
OTHER FIRST CLASS	35	4	1369	158*	44.16
INT					
J.P.L.	13	2	321	103*	29.18
NAT.W.	1	0	18	18	–
B & H	3	0	76	48	25.33

CAREER: BATTING

	I.	N.O.	R.	H.S.	AV.
TEST	4	0	89	62	22.25
OTHER FIRST CLASS	689	104	23033	221*	39.26
INT					
J.P.L.	204	22	5621	113	30.88
NAT.W.	25	2	731	87	31.78
B & H	54	7	1373	115	29.21

LAST SEASON: BOWLING

	O.	M.	R.	W.	AV.
TEST					
OTHER FIRST CLASS	12	3	34	0	–
INT					
J.P.L.					
NAT.W.					
B & H					

CAREER: BOWLING

	O.	M.	R.	W.	AV.
TEST					
OTHER FIRST CLASS	108.5 457.5	11 116	1639	39	42.03
INT					
J.P.L.	124	0	608	14	43.42
NAT.W.	34	2	125	4	31.25
B & H	51	2	208	9	23.11

COUNTY QUIZ

Q. 1.   When was the club founded?

Q. 2.   Who made the most first-class runs for the county last season, and how many?

Q. 3.   What's the highest ever county total, and against whom?

Q. 4.   Who took most wickets for the county last season, and how many?

Q. 5.   What's the highest individual score for the county, who hit it, and when?

Q. 6.   What's the highest scoring partnership for the county for any wicket?

Q. 7.   How many times has the club won the County Championship?

Q. 8.   What's the lowest ever total made by the county in one innings, when, and against whom?

Q. 9.   Which bowler took the most first-class wickets in one season, when, and how many?

Q. 10.   Which batsman hit the most runs in one season, when and how many?

Gloucestershire

ATHEY, C.W.J.

Full Name: Charles William Jeffrey Athey.
Role: Right-hand bat, occasional seamer.
Born: 27 September 1957, Middlesborough, Yorkshire.
Height: 5′ 10″ **Weight:** 12st.
Nickname: Bumper, Wingnut.
County debut: 1976 (Yorkshire), 1984 Gloucestershire.
County cap: 1980 (Yorkshire).
Test debut: 1980.
No. of Tests: 3.
No. of One-Day Internationals: 2.
1000 runs in a season: 3.
50 wickets in a season: 0.
1st-Class 50s scored: 42.
1st-Class 100s scored: 15.
1st-Class 200s scored: 0.
1st-Class 5 w. in innings: 0.
1st-Class 10 w. in match: 0.
One-day 50s: 31.

One-day 100s: 1.
Place in batting averages: 63 average: 37.75; (1983: 143 average: 24.45).
Place in bowling averages: — average: —; (1983: — average: —).
1st-Class catches 1984: 26 (career: 176).
Parents: Peter and Maree Athey.
Wife and date of marriage: Janet Linda, 9 October 1982.
Education: Linthorpe Junior School; Stainsby Secondary School; Acklam Hall High School.
Qualifications: Four 0-levels, some CSEs. National Cricket Coaching Certificate, New South Wales, Australia.
Family links with cricket: "Father played league cricket in North Yorkshire and South Durham League for 29 years, 25 of them with Middlesbrough. President of Middlesbrough C.C. since 1975. Brother-in-law Colin Cook

played for Middlesex, other brother-in-law (Martin) plays in Thames Valley League. Father-in-law deeply involved in Middlesex Youth cricket."

Jobs outside cricket: Barman, building labourer, sports shop assistant.

Overseas tours: D.H. Robbins XI to Canada in 1976, South America 1979, Australasia 1980. England Under-19 to West Indies in 1976 and with England to West Indies in 1981. Barbican XI to Gulf States.

Overseas teams played for: Manly Warringah, Sydney, Australia 1977–78, 1978–79, 1979–80; Balmain, Sydney, Australia 1980–81; Schoeman Park, Bloemfontein, South Africa 1981–82; Papatoetoe, Auckland, N.Z. 1983–84.

Cricketers particularly learnt from: D. Padgett

Cricketers particularly admired: G. Greenidge, M. Marshall.

Off-season 1984–85: Staying home.

Equipment used: Slazenger.

Other sports: Squash, tennis, soccer. Follow most sports.

Relaxations: Music, good films, good food!

Extras: Played for Teeside County Schools Under-16s at age 12, also 1971–72–73, and approached by Northamptonshire County Cricket Club. Made debut in 1972 North Yorkshire and South Durham League. Played for Yorkshire Colts 1974; played for North of England Young Cricketers XI v West Indies Young Cricketers at Old Trafford in 1974. Played football for Middlesbrough Schools Under-16 XI 1972–73, 1973–74. Played for Middlesbrough Juniors 1974–75. Offered but declined apprenticeship terms with Middlesbrough F.C. Captained North Riding Under-19 XI 1975–76.

Opinions on cricket: "Must play on better wickets."

Best batting performance: 134 Yorkshire v Derbyshire, Derby 1982.

Best bowling performance: 3-38 Yorkshire v Surrey, The Oval 1978.

LAST SEASON: BATTING

	I.	N.O.	R.	H.S.	AV.
TEST					
OTHER FIRST CLASS	52	4	1812	114*	37.75
INT					
J.P.L.	14	0	435	79	31.87
NAT.W.	2	1	77	70*	–
B & H	4	1	51	35*	17.00

CAREER: BATTING

	I.	N.O.	R.	H.S.	AV.
TEST	6	0	17	9	2.83
OTHER FIRST CLASS	314	25	8598	134	29.75
INT	2	0	83	51	41.50
J.P.L.	100	8	2995	118	32.55
NAT.W.	17	3	562	115	40.14
B & H	30	5	659	94*	26.36

LAST SEASON: BOWLING

	O.	M.	R.	W.	AV.
TEST					
OTHER FIRST CLASS	13	1	54	0	–
INT					
J.P.L.	23.1	0	174	4	43.50
NAT.W.	8	0	51	0	–
B & H	34	2	143	8	17.88

CAREER: BOWLING

	O.	M.	R.	W.	AV.
TEST					
OTHER FIRST CLASS	353.1	70	1114	21	52.90
INT					
J.P.L.	84.4	1	489	18	27.17
NAT.W.	18	1	92	1	–
B & H	52.4	4	218	12	18.17

BAINBRIDGE, P.

Full Name: Philip Bainbridge.
Role: Right-hand bat, right arm
medium fast bowler. Cover fielder.
Born: 16 April 1958, Stoke-on-Trent.
Height: 5' 10" **Weight:** 11st. 13lbs.
Nickname: Bains, Robbo.
County debut: 1977.
County cap: 1981.
Test debut: —
No. of Tests: 0.
No. of One-Day Internationals: 0.
1000 runs in a season: 4.
50 wickets in a season: 0.
1st-Class 50s scored: 32.
1st-Class 100s scored: 3.
1st-Class 200s scored: 0.
1st-Class 5 w. in innings: 2.
1st-Class 10 w. in match: 0.
One-day 50s: 7.
One-day 100s: 0.

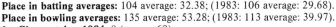

Place in batting averages: 104 average: 32.38; (1983: 106 average: 29.68).
Place in bowling averages: 135 average: 53.28; (1983: 113 average: 39.97).
1st-Class catches 1984: 9 (career: 60).
Parents: Leonard George and Lilian Rose Bainbridge.
Wife and date of marriage: Barbara, 22 September 1979.
Children: Neil, 11 January 1984.
Education: Hanley High School; Stoke-on-Trent Sixth Form College;
Borough Road College of Education.
Qualifications: B.Ed; M.C.C. Coaching Certificate; two A-levels, nine 0-levels.
Jobs outside cricket: P.E. Lecturer.
Family links with cricket: Cousin, Stephen Wilkinson, played for Somerset
1969–72.
Overseas tours: Holland with N.C.A. North of England Youth team 1976;
Barbados, Trinidad and Tobago with British Colleges 1978; Barbados 1980
with Gloucestershire C.C.C.; Pakistan 1983 for 2 Zaheer benefit matches.
Overseas teams: Alberton C.C. 1979–80, 1981–82.
Cricketers particularly learnt from: All senior players at Gloucestershire—
and county coach.
Cricketers particularly admired: Mike Procter.
Off-season 1984–85: Lecturing at Brunel Technical College.
Equipment endorsed: Gray-Nicolls.
Other sports: All sports – football, rugby, squash, horse-riding.
Relaxations: Photography, wine-making, beer-making, listening to music,

"walking in the country with my Golden Retriever dog and my wife. Entertaining my son."

Significant injuries in 1984: Twice broke right thumb.

Extras: Enjoys coaching. While at College coaches at Lord's indoor school. Played for four 2nd XIs in 1976: Gloucestershire, Derbyshire, Northamptonshire and Warwickshire. Played for Young England v Australia 1977. Won Commercial Union Under-23 Batsman of the Year 1981. Scored first century for Stoke-on-Trent aged 14. Played scrum-half for Clifton Rugby Football Club 4th XV. Run a part-time mail order business with Chris Broad marketing gold and silver cricket bat pendants (Rosga Sporting Jewellery). Run Gloucestershire Cricketers' Charity football team, helping to raise about £1500 for various charities last winter.

Opinions on cricket: "Introduction of minimum number of overs a day, although a good thing in principle, leads to too many late finishes when there is a 117 over requirement."

Best batting performance: 146 Gloucestershire v N. Zealanders, Bristol 1983.

Best bowling performance: 6-59 Gloucestershire v Glamorgan, Swansea 1982.

LAST SEASON: BATTING

	I.	N.O.	R.	H.S.	AV.
TEST					
OTHER FIRST CLASS	42	7	1133	134*	32.37
INT					
J.P.L.	13	2	240	50*	21.82
NAT.W.	2	1	56	51	–
B & H	1	0	48	48	–

CAREER: BATTING

	I.	N.O.	R.	H.S.	AV.
TEST					
OTHER FIRST CLASS	213	34	5453	146	30.46
INT					
J.P.L.	67	11	955	55	17.05
NAT.W.	8	2	292	75	48.67
B & H	16	4	306	80	25.50

LAST SEASON: BOWLING

	O.	M.	R.	W.	AV.
TEST					
OTHER FIRST CLASS	303.2	73	959	18	53.28
INT					
J.P.L.	95	0	505	14	36.07
NAT.W.	24	4	59	1	–
B & H	11	1	38	1	–

CAREER: BOWLING

	O.	M.	R.	W.	AV.
TEST					
OTHER FIRST CLASS	1617.5	390	4885	122	40.04
INT					
J.P.L.	464.1	12	2310	74	31.21
NAT.W.	96	13	299	10	29.90
B & H	148.2	19	511	19	26.89

Q. 53. Is it true or false that, as England's last pair needing 15 runs to win against Australia, George Hirst said to Wilfred Rhodes: "We'll get 'em in singles"?

BRASSINGTON, A.J.

Full Name: Andrew James
Brassington.
Role: Wicket-keeper.
Born: 9 August 1954, Bagnall,
Stoke-on-Trent.
Height: 6' **Weight:** 11st 9lbs.
Nickname: Imma.
County debut: 1974.
County cap: 1978.
Test debut: —
No. of Tests: 0.
No. of One-Day Internationals: 0.
1000 runs in a season: 0.
50 wickets in a season: 0.
1st-Class 50s scored: 0.
1st-Class 100s scored: 0.
1st-Class 200s scored: 0.
1st-Class 5 w. in innings: 0.
1st-Class 10 w. in match: 0.
One-day 50s: 0.
One-day 100s: 0.
Place in batting averages: — average: —; (1983: — average: —).
Place in bowling averages: — average: —; (1983: — average: —).
Parents: Joan Ursula and John Reginald.
Wife and date of marriage: Rosalyn, 26 February 1977.
Children: Emma Louisa.
Education: Endon Secondary Modern.
Qualifications: 6 C.S.E.

LAST SEASON: BATTING

	I.	N.O.	R.	H.S.	AV.
TEST					
OTHER FIRST CLASS	3	1	22	22	11.00
INT					
J.P.L.	1	1	1	1*	—
NAT.W.					
B & H					

CAREER: BATTING

	I.	N.O.	R.	H.S.	AV.
TEST					
OTHER FIRST CLASS	153	44	878	35	8.06
INT					
J.P.L.	21	12	93	14*	10.33
NAT.W.	1	0	20	20	—
B & H	7	2	21	9	4.20

LAST SEASON: WICKET KEEPING

	C.	ST.			
TEST					
OTHER FIRST CLASS	2	1			
INT					
J.P.L.	1	—			
NAT.W.					
B & H					

CAREER: WICKET KEEPING

	C.	ST.			
TEST					
OTHER FIRST CLASS	209	48			
INT					
J.P.L.	33	8			
NAT.W.	3	—			
B & H	8	2			

Jobs outside cricket: Salesman and promotional work.
Off-season 1984–85: Working.
Equipment used: Slazenger.
Overseas tours: Malawi – Gloucestershire 1978.
Cricketers particularly learnt from: Bob Taylor.
Cricketers particularly admired: Alan Knott, Bob Taylor, Greg Chappell, Rod Marsh, Viv Richards, Mike Procter.
Other sports: Football (goalkeeper) and follows football and rugby.
Significant injuries in 1984: Broken right hand (v Warwickshire at Edgbaston in June).
Relaxations: Watching TV, playing Scrabble and music.
Opinions on cricket: "The new rule for 117 overs should be abolished. Games went on until after 8 o'clock in 1984."
Best batting performance: 35 Gloucestershire v Sussex, Hastings 1982.

BURROWS, D.A.

Full Name: Dean Andrew Burrows.
Role: Right-hand bat, right-arm quick bowler.
Born: 20 June 1966, Easington, Co. Durham.
Height: 6' 3" **Weight:** 13st 5lbs.
Nickname: Deano.
County debut: 1984.
County cap: No.
Test debut: —
No. of Tests: 0.
No. of One-Day Internationals: 0.
1000 runs in a season: 0.
50 wickets in a season: 0.
1st-Class 50s scored: 0.
1st-Class 100s scored: 0.
1st-Class 200s scored: 0.
1st-Class 5 w. in innings: 0.
1st-Class 10 w. in match: 0.
One-day 50s: 0.
One-day 100s: 0.
Place in batting averages: — average: —; (1983: — average: —).
Place in bowling averages: — average: —; (1983: — average: —).
Parents: Michael Alec John and Barbara Michelle Burrows.
Marital status: Single.
Education: Shotton Hall School, Peterlee, Co. Durham.
Qualifications: 5 O-levels.
Jobs outside cricket: None at the moment.

Off-season 1984–85: Keeping fit and preparing for next season.
Cricketers particularly learnt from: Dennis Lillee had everything.
Cricketers particularly admired: Dennis Lillee, Bob Willis, Michael Holding.
Other sports: Soccer, swimming, some tennis.
Significant injuries in 1984: Missed two weeks due to shin soreness.
Relaxations: "Enjoy watching films, videos etc. I also love music."
Extras: Won Sunday Sun Cricketer of the Month August 1983 for taking 10 wickets for 15 runs (all clean bowled) including 4 in 4 balls. Represented Durham County in the Minor counties when I was 17.
Opinions on cricket matters: "The County circuit seems very hectic. Players are very open to injury through strain and stress, because of the constant cricket each day. Maybe something can be done to give players a chance to recover. It must be very hard for Test players coming out 5 days and going straight into another championship game."

LAST SEASON: BATTING

	I.	N.O.	R.	H.S.	AV.
TEST					
OTHER FIRST CLASS	1	0	0	0	–
INT					
J.P.L.	1	1	0	0*	–
NAT.W.					
B & H					

CAREER: BATTING

	I.	N.O.	R.	H.S.	AV.
TEST					
OTHER FIRST CLASS	1	0	0	0	–
INT					
J.P.L.	1	1	0	0*	–
NAT.W.					
B & H					

LAST SEASON: BOWLING

	O.	M.	R.	W.	AV.
TEST					
OTHER FIRST CLASS	15	0	76	0	–
INT					
J.P.L.	5	0	32	1	–
NAT.W.					
B & H					

CAREER: BOWLING

	O.	M.	R.	W.	AV.
TEST					
OTHER FIRST CLASS	15	0	76	0	–
INT					
J.P.L.	5	0	32	1	–
NAT.W.					
B & H					

Q. 54. What was the date and destination of the first M.C.C./England touring side to travel overseas by air?

Q. 55. Who was the first Englishman to score 1000 runs in the 1984 season?

CHILDS, J.H.

Full Name: John Henry Childs.
Role: Left-hand bat, slow left arm orthodox bowler.
Born: 15 August 1951, Plymouth.
Height: 6' 0" **Weight:** 12st 2lbs.
Nickname: Charlie.
County debut: 1975.
County cap: 1977.
Test debut: —
No. of Tests: 0.
No. of One-Day Internationals: 0.
1000 runs in a season: 0.
50 wickets in a season: 2.
1st-Class 50s scored: 0.
1st-Class 100s scored: 0.
1st-Class 200s scored: 0.
1st-Class 5 w. in innings: 21.
1st-Class 10 w. in match: 2.
One-day 50s: 0.
One-day 100s: 0.

Place in batting averages: — average: —; (1983: — average: —).
Place in bowling averages: 132 average: 49.07; (1983: 103 average: 36.69).
1st-Class catches 1984: 2 (career: 63).
Parents: Sydney and Barbara Childs.
Wife and date of marriage: Jane Anne, 11 November 1978.
Children: Lee Robert, 28 November 1980.
Education: Audley Park Secondary Modern, Torquay.
Qualifications: Advanced Cricket Coach.
Jobs outside cricket: Signwriter.
Overseas tours: Zambia, 1977, Barbados, 1983.
Overseas teams played for: Spent winter 1979–80 coaching in Gisborne, New Zealand and 1982–83 in Auckland for Howice-Pakuranga.
Equipment endorsed: 3D.
Cricketers particularly admired: G. Sobers and M. Procter.
Other sports: Golf, most ball games.
Relaxations: Watching rugby, decorating at home, "walking on moors and beaches. My family."
Extras: Played for Devon 1973–74. Released by Gloucestershire at end of 1984.
Best batting performance: 34* Gloucestershire v Nottinghamshire, Cheltenham 1982.
Best bowling performance: 9-56 Gloucestershire v Somerset, Bristol 1981.

LAST SEASON: BATTING

	I.	N.O.	R.	H.S.	AV.
TEST					
OTHER FIRST CLASS	6	2	12	4*	3.00
INT					
J.P.L.	1	1	10	10*	–
NAT.W.					
B & H	1	1	6	6*	–

CAREER: BATTING

	I.	N.O.	R.	H.S.	AV.
TEST					
OTHER FIRST CLASS	151	72	535	34*	6.77
INT					
J.P.L.	17	9	74	16*	9.25
NAT.W.	4	3	22	14*	–
B & H	7	5	25	10	12.50

LAST SEASON: BOWLING

	O.	M.	R.	W.	AV.
TEST					
OTHER FIRST CLASS	296	83	736	15	49.07
INT					
J.P.L.	11	0	66	1	–
NAT.W.					
B & H	11	1	53	0	–

CAREER: BOWLING

	O.	M.	R.	W.	AV.
TEST					
OTHER FIRST CLASS	4974.4	1441	13464	421	31.98
INT					
J.P.L.	318.1	17	1444	39	37.02
NAT.W.	48	12	132	7	18.86
B & H	156	35	466	14	33.29

CUNNINGHAM, E.J.

Full Name: Edward James Cunningham.
Role: Left-hand bat; right arm off-break bowler.
Born: 16 May 1962, Oxford.
Height: 6' 2" **Weight:** 12st 10lbs.
Nickname: Auntie, Cobra.
County debut: 1982.
County cap: No.
Test debut: —
No. of Tests: 0.
No. of One-Day Internationals: 0.
1000 runs in a season: 0.
50 wickets in a season: 0.
1st-Class 50s scored: 1.
1st-Class 100s scored: 0.
1st-Class 200s scored: 0.
1st-Class 5 w. in innings: 0.
1st-Class 10 w. in match: 0.
One-day 50s: 2.
One-day 100s: 0.
Place in batting averages: 200 average: 20.25; (1983: — average: —).
Place in bowling averages: — average: —; (1983: — average: —).
1st-Class catches 1984: 0 (career: 4).
Parents: Charles John and Ann Maria Cunningham.
Marital Status: Single.
Education: Marlborough College.

Qualifications: 2 A-Levels.

Family links with cricket: Uncle and great-uncle were F.T. Mann and F.G. Mann.

Cricket superstitions: "Any successful match induces a series of new superstitions."

Overseas tours: Schoolboy tour to Australia, 1979–80. Schoolboy tour to West Indies, 1980–81.

Cricketers particularly admired: David Gower, Clive Lloyd.

Equipment used: Gray-Nicolls.

Other sports: Squash, tennis; watch tennis, athletics, wrestling.

Relaxations: Music, travelling, cars, gambling.

Significant injuries in 1984: Broken finger (missed one match).

Extras: Made record score of 203 in the Western league (Bristol 45 overs competition) in 1981. Was captain of Marlborough 1st XI.

Opinions on cricket: "117 overs a day is far too many for players and spectators. Concerted effort should be made to produce faster and more even wickets as there are so many dead wickets around which, in the long run, is detrimental to the standard of the game."

Best batting performance: 61* Gloucestershire v Sri Lanka, Cheltenham 1984.

LAST SEASON: BATTING

	I.	N.O.	R.	H.S.	AV.
TEST					
OTHER FIRST CLASS	11	3	162	61*	20.25
INT					
J.P.L.	8	1	286	56	40.86
NAT.W.	1	0	18	18	–
B & H					

CAREER: BATTING

	I.	N.O.	R.	H.S.	AV.
TEST					
OTHER FIRST CLASS	23	5	271	61*	15.06
INT					
J.P.L.	13	1	331	56	27.58
NAT.W.	1	0	18	18	–
B & H					

LAST SEASON: BOWLING

	O.	M.	R.	W.	AV.
TEST					
OTHER FIRST CLASS	21	3	70	0	–
INT					
J.P.L.					
NAT.W.					
B & H					

CAREER: BOWLING

	O.	M.	R.	W.	AV.
TEST					
OTHER FIRST CLASS	74	13	264	4	66.00
INT					
J.P.L.	8	0	35	0	–
NAT.W.					
B & H					

Q. 56. Which Surrey & England cricketer said to which other Surrey & England cricketer "You are wearing Surrey colours. You are a Surrey cricketer. You should be proud of that. Behave like one. Never let me hear you swear in the dressing-room again"?

DALE, D.A.

Full Name: Dean Andrew Dale.
Role: Right-hand bat, right arm medium fast bowler.
Born: 20 June 1966, Peterlee, Co. Durham.
County debut: 1984.
County cap: 1984.
Test debut: —
No. of Tests: 0.
No. of One-Day Internationals: 0.
1000 runs in a season: 0.
50 wickets in a season: 0.
1st-Class 50s scored: 0.
1st-Class 100s scored: 0.
1st-Class 200s scored: 0.
1st-Class 5 w. in innings: 0.
1st-Class 10 w. in match: 0.
One-day 50s: 0.
One-day 100s: 0.
Place in batting averages: 226 average: 16.67; (1983: — average: —).
Place in bowling averages: — average: —; (1983: — average: —).
1st-Class catches 1984: 1 (career: 1).
Extras: Finished top of Gloucestershire 2nd XI bowling averages in 1983.
Best batting performance: 49 Gloucestershire v Yorkshire, Bradford 1984.
Best bowling performance: 3-10 Gloucestershire v Oxford University, Oxford 1984.

LAST SEASON: BATTING

	I.	N.O.	R.	H.S.	AV.
TEST					
OTHER FIRST CLASS	8	2	100	49	16.67
INT					
J.P.L.	1	0	0	0	–
NAT.W.					
B & H					

CAREER: BATTING

	I.	N.O.	R.	H.S.	AV.
TEST					
OTHER FIRST CLASS	8	2	100	49	16.67
INT					
J.P.L.	1	0	0	0	–
NAT.W.					
B & H					

LAST SEASON: BOWLING

	O.	M.	R.	W.	AV.
TEST					
OTHER FIRST CLASS	125.1	22	467	7	66.72
INT					
J.P.L.	23	0	139	2	69.50
NAT.W.					
B & H					

CAREER: BOWLING

	O.	M.	R.	W.	AV.
TEST					
OTHER FIRST CLASS	125.1	22	467	7	66.72
INT					
J.P.L.	23	0	139	2	69.50
NAT.W.					
B & H					

DOUGHTY, R.J.

Full Name: Richard John Doughty.
Role: Right-hand bat, right arm fast
medium bowler.
Born: 17 November 1960,
Bridlington, Yorkshire.
Height: 6' ½" **Weight:** 13st.
Nickname: Dicky Doubts,
Dangerous Dick.
County debut: 1981.
County cap: No.
Test debut: —
No. of Tests: 0.
No. of One-Day Internationals: 0.
1000 runs in a season: 0.
50 wickets in a season: 0.
1st-Class 50s scored: 0.
1st-Class 100s scored: 0.
1st-Class 200s scored: 0.
1st-Class 5 w. in innings: 1.
1st-Class 10 w. in match: 0.
One-day 50s: 1.
One-day 100s: 0.
Place in batting averages: — average: —; (1983: 125 average: 27.00).
Place in bowling averages: — average: —; (1983: — average: —).
1st-Class catches 1984: 0 (career: 2).
Parents: Mary and Trevor Doughty.
Wife and date of marriage: Elizabeth, 2 April 1982.
Education: Scarborough College, N. Yorkshire.

LAST SEASON: BATTING

	I.	N.O.	R.	H.S.	AV.
TEST					
OTHER FIRST CLASS	1	0	4	4	–
INT					
J.P.L.	5	2	34	21*	11.33
NAT.W.					
B & H	3	0	69	31	23.00

CAREER: BATTING

	I.	N.O.	R.	H.S.	AV.
TEST					
OTHER FIRST CLASS	19	7	214	32*	17.83
INT					
J.P.L.	14	6	146	50*	18.25
NAT.W.	1	1	5	5*	–
B & H	4	0	69	31	17.25

LAST SEASON: BOWLING

	O.	M.	R.	W.	AV.
TEST					
OTHER FIRST CLASS					
INT					
J.P.L.	15.5	0	108	2	54.00
NAT.W.					
B & H	30	4	111	2	55.50

CAREER: BOWLING

	O.	M.	R.	W.	AV.
TEST					
OTHER FIRST CLASS	266	40	939	23	40.83
INT					
J.P.L.	102.3	0	647	13	49.77
NAT.W.	15	2	60	2	30.00
B & H	44	4	193	3	64.33

Qualifications: 3 0-levels, 3 C.S.E.
Jobs outside cricket: "Anything I can get!"
Cricketers particularly learnt from: Don Wilson, Imran Khan, D.K. Lillee, Richard Edwards.
Other sports: Golf, rugby, skiing, surfing, squash. Watching motor-racing, high diving.
Relaxations: Music, eating, watching T.V., drawing, photography.
Best batting performance: 32* Gloucestershire v Worcestershire, Bristol 1983.
Best bowling performance: 6-43 Gloucestershire v Glamorgan, Bristol 1982.

GRAVENEY, D.A.

Full Name: David Anthony Graveney.
Role: Right-hand bat, slow left arm orthodox bowler.
Born: 2 January 1953, Bristol.
Height: 6' 4" **Weight:** 14st.
Nickname: Gravity, Grav.
County debut: 1972.
County cap: 1976.
Test debut: —
No. of Tests: 0.
No. of One-Day Internationals: 0.
1000 runs in a season: 0.
50 wickets in a season: 4.
1st-Class 50s scored: 14.
1st-Class 100s scored: 2.
1st-Class 200s scored: 0.
1st-Class 5 w. in innings: 28.
1st-Class 10 w. in match: 4.
One-day 50s: 0.
One-day 100s: 0.
Place in batting averages: 231 average: 15.93; (1983: 169 average: 21.35).
Place in bowling averages: 59 average: 29.41; (1983: 82 average: 32.38).
1st-Class catches 1984: 18 (career: 134).
Parents: Ken Graveney and Jeanne (deceased).
Wife and date of marriage: Julie, 23 September 1978.
Education: Millfield School, Somerset.
Jobs outside cricket: Company director. Accountant.
Family links with cricket: Son of J.K. Graveney, Captain of Gloucestershire, who took 10 wickets for 66 runs v Derbyshire at Chesterfield in 1949, and nephew of Tom Graveney of Gloucestershire, Worcestershire and England. Brother, John, selected for English Public Schools v English Schools at Lord's.

Equipment endorsed: Slazengers.
Other sports: Golf, soccer, squash.
Relaxations: "Playing sport, TV and cinema, and taking the wife out for a good meal and visit to the local pub."
Extras: Treasurer of the County Cricketers' Association.
Best batting performance: 119 Gloucestershire v Oxford University, Oxford 1980.
Best bowling performance: 8-85 Gloucestershire v Nottinghamshire, Cheltenham 1974.

LAST SEASON: BATTING

	I.	N.O.	R.	H.S.	AV.
TEST					
OTHER FIRST CLASS	40	13	430	33	15.93
INT					
J.P.L.	6	1	53	22	10.60
NAT.W.	1	1	20	20*	–
B & H	3	0	62	31	20.67

CAREER: BATTING

	I.	N.O.	R.	H.S.	AV.
TEST					
OTHER FIRST CLASS	365	95	5087	119	18.84
INT					
J.P.L.	105	34	1033	49	14.54
NAT.W.	19	6	238	44	18.31
B & H	31	7	316	49*	13.17

LAST SEASON: BOWLING

	O.	M.	R.	W.	AV.
TEST					
OTHER FIRST CLASS	665.4	202	1588	54	29.41
INT					
J.P.L.	62	2	252	5	50.40
NAT.W.	18	5	52	2	26.00
B & H	26	2	92	2	46.00

CAREER: BOWLING

	O.	M.	R.	W.	AV.
TEST					
OTHER FIRST CLASS	6548.5	1945	17150	594	28.87
INT					
J.P.L.	739.4	46	3393	108	31.41
NAT.W.	209.5	32	705	26	27.12
B & H	289.5	30	1087	39	27.87

Q. 57. Who said, when and why: "It's not easy to bat with tears in your eyes"?

Q. 58. How many fathers and sons have played for England, and who were they?

Q. 59. Which immortal Australian Test cricketer was so superstitious that he kept the same pair of batting trousers throughout his career until they were threadbare?

LAWRENCE, D.V.

Full Name: David Valentine Lawrence.
Role: Right-hand bat, right arm fast bowler, outfielder.
Born: 28 January 1964, Gloucester.
Height: 6' 3" **Weight:** 15st.
Nickname: Syd, Bruno.
County debut: 1981.
County cap: No.
Test debut: —
No. of Tests: 0.
No. of One-Day Internationals: 0.
1000 runs in a season: 0.
50 wickets in a season: 0.
1st-Class 50s scored: 0.
1st-Class 100s scored: 0.
1st-Class 200s scored: 0.
1st-Class 5 w. in innings: 3.
1st-Class 10 w. in match: 0.
One-day 50s: 0.
One-day 100s: 0.
Place in batting averages: — average: —; (1983: — average: —).
Place in bowling averages: 107 average: 37.34; (1983: average: —)
1st-Class catches 1984: 2 (career: 3).
Parents: Joseph and Joyce Lawrence.
Education: Linden School, Gloucester.
Equipment used: Gray-Nicolls.

LAST SEASON: BATTING

	I.	N.O.	R.	H.S.	AV.
TEST					
OTHER FIRST CLASS	25	4	135	17	6.43
INT					
J.P.L.	3	2	28	17	–
NAT.W.	1	0	0	0	–
B & H	1	1	1	1*	–

CAREER: BATTING

	I.	N.O.	R.	H.S.	AV.
TEST					
OTHER FIRST CLASS	34	8	157	17	6.04
INT					
J.P.L.	3	2	28	17	–
NAT.W.	1	0	0	0	–
B & H	1	1	1	1*	–

LAST SEASON: BOWLING

	O.	M.	R.	W.	AV.
TEST					
OTHER FIRST CLASS	455.1	80	1531	41	37.34
INT					
J.P.L.	85.4	1	466	21	22.19
NAT.W.	22	3	116	2	58.00
B & H	22	2	100	6	16.67

CAREER: BOWLING

	O.	M.	R.	W.	AV.
TEST					
OTHER FIRST CLASS	654.1	108	2294	50	45.88
INT					
J.P.L.	115.4	1	628	31	20.25
NAT.W.	50.5	7	219	5	43.80
B & H	22	2	100	6	16.67

Off-season 1984–85: Playing in Perth, Western Australia.
Cricketers particularly learnt from: Michael Holding, Richard Hadlee.
Cricketers particularly admired: Viv Richards.
Other sports: Rugby football.
Relaxations: "Like listening to jazz, funk and dancing."
Opinions on cricket: "I would like to see the JPSL rules changed to allow the two opening bowlers to come off their full runs."
Best batting performance: 17 Gloucestershire v Nottinghamshire, Trent Bridge 1984.
Best bowling performance: 5-58 Gloucestershire v Somerset, Bristol 1984.

LLOYDS, J.W.

Full Name: Jeremy William Lloyds.
Role: Left-hand bat, off-spin bowler, close fielder.
Born: 17 November 1954, Penang, Malaya.
Height: 5' 11½" **Weight:** 11st. 7lbs.
Nickname: Jo'burg, J.J. or Jerry.
County debut: 1979.
County cap: 1982.
Test debut: —
No. of Tests: 0.
No. of One-Day Internationals: 0.
1000 runs in a season: 0.
50 wickets in a season: 0.
1st-Class 50s scored: 21.
1st-Class 100s scored: 5.
1st-Class 200s scored: 0.
1st-Class 5 w. in innings: 6.
1st-Class 10 w. in match: 1.
One-day 50s: 1.
One-day 100s: 0.
Place in batting averages: 48 average: 40.60; (1983: 123 average: 27.30).
Place in bowling averages: 133 average: 49.79; (1983: 70 average: 30.83).
1st-Class catches 1984: 22 (career: 84).
Parents: Edwin William and Grace Cicely Lloyds.
Marital status: Single.
Education: St Dunstan's Prep. School; Blundell's School.
Qualifications: N.C.A. advanced coach. 10 O-levels.
Jobs outside cricket: Lloyds Bank, Taunton, for 1½ years. M.C.C. Young Professionals at Lord's 1975 for four years.
Family links with cricket: Father played Blundell's 1st XI 1932–35, selected for Public Schools Rest v Lord's Schools at Lord's 1935, Inter-State cricket in

Malaya and Singapore 1950–55. Brother, Christopher Edwin Lloyds, played for Blundell's 1st XI 1964–66 and Somerset 2nd XI in 1966.

Overseas tours: With Somerset in Antigua, 1981.

Overseas teams played for: St Stithian's Old Boys, Johannesburg, 1978–79, 79–80, Toombul D.C.C., Brisbane, 1980–81, 1981–82, North Sydney District 1982–83, Orange Free State 1983–84.

Cricketers particularly learnt from: Don Wilson and Derek Taylor.

Cricketers particularly admired: John Hampshire and Graeme Pollock.

Off-season 1984–85: Playing and coaching in Johannesburg.

Equipment used: Duncan Fearnley.

Other sports: Rugby, soccer, golf, tennis, swimming, squash. Watches motor-racing.

Significant injuries in 1984: Thigh injury.

Relaxations: Music, cinema, driving, reading.

Extras: Scored 132 n.o. and 102 n.o. for Somerset in same Championship match, June 1982. Took 30 catches in 1982 season for Somerset. Moved to Gloucestershire for 1985 season to get more opportunities.

Opinions on cricket: "To emphasise the distinction between Test and County cricket and on the other hand, the one-day game, why not use coloured clothing and white balls for all one-day cricket?"

Best batting performance: 132* Somerset v Northamptonshire, Northampton 1982.

Best bowling performance: 7-88 Somerset v Essex, Chelmsford 1982.

LAST SEASON: BATTING

	I.	N.O.	R.	H.S.	AV.
TEST					
OTHER FIRST CLASS	30	10	812	113*	40.60
INT					
J.P.L.	6	2	42	28*	10.50
NAT.W.	1	0	7	7	–
B & H	2	0	9	8	4.50

CAREER: BATTING

	I.	N.O.	R.	H.S.	AV.
TEST					
OTHER FIRST CLASS	163	21	4050	132*	28.52
INT					
J.P.L.	35	9	354	33	13.62
NAT.W.	6	2	85	28*	21.25
B & H	11	0	153	51	13.91

LAST SEASON: BOWLING

	O.	M.	R.	W.	AV.
TEST					
OTHER FIRST CLASS	240.2	69	697	14	49.39
INT					
J.P.L.	18	3	84	0	–
NAT.W.	9	1	18	0	–
B & H					

CAREER: BOWLING

	O.	M.	R.	W.	AV.
TEST					
OTHER FIRST CLASS	1498.1	357	4667	135	34.57
INT					
J.P.L.	28.5	3	134	3	44.67
NAT.W.	9	1	18	0	–
B & H	2	0	6	0	–

ROEBUCK, P.G.P.

Full Name: Paul Gerard Peter Roebuck.
Role: All rounder.
Born: 13 October 1963, Bath, Somerset.
Height: 6′ 0″ **Weight:** 13st 7 lbs.
Nickname: Roebi, Roebers.
County debut: 1984.
county cap: No.
Test debut: —
No. of Tests: 0.
No. of One-Day Internationals: 0.
1000 runs in a season: 0.
50 wickets in a season: 0.
1st-Class 50s scored: 2.
1st-Class 100s scored: 0.
1st-Class 200s scored: 0.
1st-Class 5 w. in innings: 0.
1st-Class 10 w. in match: 0.
One-day 50s: 0.
One-day 100s: 0.

Place in batting averages: 130 average: 28.60; (1983: — average: —).
Place in bowling averages: — average: —; (1983: — average: —).
1st-Class catches 1984: 2 (career: 3).
Parents: James and Elizabeth Roebuck.
Marital status: Single.
Family links with cricket: Sister played for Oxford University, brother plays for Somerset.
Education: Millfield School; Emmanuel College, Cambridge.
Qualifications: Part I Law.
Off-season 1984–85: "Studying for my Law finals.
Cricketing superstitions: "If I had a good day, I do everything I did yesterday."
Equipment used: Stuart Surridge.
Cricketers particularly learnt from: Barry Duddleston.
Cricketers particularly admired: Mike Procter, Ian Botham.
Other sports: Tennis, squash and golf. Follow football (Spurs).
Significant injuries in 1984: "Both my 1983 and 1984 seasons have been severely disrupted by a stress-fracture in my back.
Relaxations: Reading well written literature and listening to a wide range of music.
Extras: "September to January I am going to be in a plaster cast. In January I am undergoing an operation similar to that done to Neil Foster of Essex. With luck I shall be fit for the start of the season — the first time for four years!"

Opinions on cricket: There are many who would like to have played professional cricket. Those who are fortunate enough to be able to do so should perhaps try to set an example while on the field of play, since it is their actions that will be watched and copied.

Best batting performance: 62 Cambridge University v Nottinghamshire, Trent Bridge 1984.

LAST SEASON: BATTING

	I.	N.O.	R.	H.S.	AV.
TEST					
OTHER FIRST CLASS	12	2	286	62	28.60
INT					
J.P.L.					
NAT.W.					
B & H	1	0	13	13	–

CAREER: BATTING

	I.	N.O.	R.	H.S.	AV.
TEST					
OTHER FIRST CLASS	19	5	368	62	26.29
INT					
J.P.L.					
NAT.W.					
B & H	4	0	53	23	13.25

LAST SEASON: BOWLING

	O.	M.	R.	W.	AV.
TEST					
OTHER FIRST CLASS					
INT					
J.P.L.					
NAT.W.					
B & H	2	0	9	0	–

CAREER: BOWLING

	O.	M.	R.	W.	AV.
TEST					
OTHER FIRST CLASS	75.5	17	269	6	44.83
INT					
J.P.L.					
NAT.W.					
B & H	25	1	86	1	–

ROLL, L.M.

Full Name: Lawson Macgregor Roll.
Role: Right-hand bat, off-spinner.
Born: 8 March 1965, Thornbury.
Height: 5′ 10½″ **Weight:** 10st.
Nickname: Loo.
County debut: 1984.
County cap: No.
Test debut: —
No. of Tests: 0.
No. of One-Day Internationals: 0.
1000 runs in a season: 0.
50 wickets in a season: 0.
1st-Class 50s: 0.
1st-Class 100s: 0.
1st-Class 200s: 0.
1st-Class 5 w. in innings: 0.
1st-Class 10 w. in match: 0.
One-day 50s: 0.
One-day 100s: 0.
Place in batting averages: — average: —; (1983: — average: —).

Place in bowling averages: — average: —; (1983: — average: —).
Parents: Michael and Yvonne Roll.
Marital status: Single.
Family links with cricket: Grandfather played for Warwickshire C.C.C.
Education: Colston's School, Bristol.
Jobs outside cricket: Student.
Off-season 1984–85: University.
Equipment used: Gray-Nicolls.
Cricketers particularly admired: Barry Richards.
Other sports: Squash, hockey. Follows football and rugby.
Significant injuries in 1984: Struck on leg by ball, damaging nerves.
Relaxations: Music.
Extras: Played for Glos. Y.C. XI which won national competition for Young Cricketers.

LAST SEASON: BATTING

	I.	N.O.	R.	H.S.	AV.
TEST					
OTHER FIRST CLASS					
INT					
J.P.L.					
NAT.W.					
B & H					

CAREER: BATTING

	I.	N.O.	R.	H.S.	AV.
TEST					
OTHER FIRST CLASS					
INT					
J.P.L.					
NAT.W.					
B & H					

LAST SEASON: BOWLING

	O.	M.	R.	W.	AV.
TEST					
OTHER FIRST CLASS	15	1	49	0	–
INT					
J.P.L.					
NAT.W.					
B & H					

CAREER: BOWLING

	O.	M.	R.	W.	AV.
TEST					
OTHER FIRST CLASS	15	1	49	0	–
INT					
J.P.L.					
NAT.W.					
B & H					

Q. 60. Who is the only bowler ever to take 10 wickets in two county championship matches, first for county A v county B and then for county B v county A, and what were the counties?

ROMAINES, P.W.

Full Name: Paul William Romaines.
Role: Right-hand opening bats-
man.
Born: 25 December 1955, Bishop
Auckland, Co. Durham.
Height: 6″ 0′ **Weight:** 12st. 8lbs.
Nickname: Canny, Human.
County debut: 1982 (Glos.).
County cap: 1983.
Test debut: —.
No. of Tests: 0.
No. of One-Day Internationals: 0.
1000 runs in a season: 2.
50 wickets in a season: 0.
1st-Class 50s scored: 16.
1st-Class 100s scored: 8.
1st-Class 200s scored: 0.
1st-Class 5 w. in innings: 0.
1st-Class 10 w. in match: 0.
One-day 50s: 10.
One-day 100s: 0.
Place in batting averages: 77 average: 35.46; (1983: 78 average: 34.76).
Place in bowling averages: — average: —; (1983: — average: —)
1st-Class catches 1984: 12 (career: 27).
Parents: George and Freda Romaines.
Wife and date of marriage: Jule Anne, 1979.
Education: Leeholme School, Bishop Auckland.
Qualifications: 8 0-levels. N.C.A. Qualified Coach.
Jobs outside cricket: Sales representative for L'Oreal.
Off-season 1984–85: Playing for Kimberley in South Africa.
Family links with cricket: Father played local cricket and is still an avid
watcher. Grandfather, W.R. Romaines, represented Durham in Minor
Counties cricket, and played v Australia in 1926.
Cricket superstitions: "Put left pad on first and when opening always walk out
on the right-hand side."
Cricketers particularly learnt from or admired: P. Willey, Zaheer Abbas,
David Graveney, Barry Duddleston.
Equipment used: Duncan Fearnley.
Other sports: Squash, golf, soccer, follow motor-racing.
Relaxations: "Listening to music, (Dire Straits, Elton John, George Benson).
Having a good pint (with a head on it) with friends, collecting antique furniture."
Extras: Joined Northants in 1973, played until 1976 when was not retained.
Debut for Northants 1975. Minor county cricket with Durham County C.C.
between 1977–1981.

Opinions on cricket: "Don't agree that cricket should change to the four-day game. However, the pressures of travelling in between matches increases the strain on cricketers. Certainly the rest that the four-day game allows would be appreciated."

Best batting performance: 186 Gloucestershire v Warwickshire, Nuneaton 1982.

LAST SEASON: BATTING

	I.	N.O.	R.	H.S.	AV.
TEST					
OTHER FIRST CLASS	52	0	1844	141	35.46
INT					
J.P.L.	14	0	283	82	20.21
NAT.W.	2	0	108	56	54.00
B & H	4	1	170	98*	56.67

CAREER: BATTING

	I.	N.O.	R.	H.S.	AV.
TEST					
OTHER FIRST CLASS	126	7	3795	185	31.89
INT					
J.P.L.	36	3	894	82	27.09
NAT.W.	10	1	293	82	32.55
B & H	5	1	179	98*	44.75

LAST SEASON: BOWLING

	O.	M.	R.	W.	AV.
TEST					
OTHER FIRST CLASS	0.3	0	8	0	–
INT					
J.P.L.					
NAT.W.					
B & H					

CAREER: BOWLING

	O.	M.	R.	W.	AV.
TEST					
OTHER FIRST CLASS	5.3	2	17	0	–
INT					
J.P.L.					
NAT.W.					
B & H					

RUSSELL, R.C.

Full Name: Robert Charles Russell.
Role: Left-hand bat, wicket-keeper.
Born: 15 August 1963, Stroud.
Height: 5′ 8½″ **Weight:** 9st 7lbs.
Nickname: Jack.
County debut: 1981.
County cap: 1984.
Test debut: —
No. of Tests: 0.
No. of One-Day Internationals: 0.
1000 runs in a season: 0.
50 wickets in a season: 0.
1st-Class 50s scored: 4.
1st-Class 100s scored: 0.
1st-Class 200s scored: 0.
1st-Class 5 w. in innings: 0.
1st-Class 10 w. in match: 0.
One-day 50s: 0.
One-day 100s: 0.

Place in batting averages: 166 average: 24.43; (1983: 164 average: 22.04).
Place in bowling averages: — average: —; (1983: — average: —).
Parents: Derek John and Jenifer Mary Anne Russell.
Marital status: Single.
Family links with cricket: Younger brother plays for Stroud C.C. and Gloucestershire Young Cricketers. Father plays for Chalford C.C.
Education: Uplands Primary; Archway Comprehensive School.
Qualifications: 2 A-levels, 7 O-levels.
Off-season 1984–85: Playing and coaching in New Zealand (Takapuna C.C.).
Cricketing superstitions: "The numbers 37 and 87. Prefer not to change equipment if possible."
Equipment endorsed: Slazenger.
Overseas tours: Denmark with N.C.A. Young Cricketers 1981.
Overseas teams played for: Takapuna C.C. New Zealand 1983–84.
Cricketers particularly learnt from or admired: Andy Brassington, Geoff Boycott, Alan Knott, Bob Taylor.
Others sports: Football.
Relaxations: Watching cricket videos; going to the Prince Albert pub, technical illustrating.
Extras: Record for most dismissals in a match for first-class debut: eight (7 caught, one stumped) for Gloucestershire v Sri Lanka 1981. Youngest wicket-keeper for Gloucestershire (17 years 307 days). Represented Young England against Young West Indies in the Agatha Christie "Test Match" series, 1982. Gordon's Gin Wicket-keeper of the Month, July 1984.
Opinions on cricket: "Too many overs have to be bowled in a day. 110 would be plenty. The season is long and hard enough as it is without having to play until gone 8 every evening. Nobody finds it harder than a first-class umpire!"
Best batting performance: 64* Gloucestershire v Worcestershire, Bristol 1983.

LAST SEASON: BATTING

	I.	N.O.	R.	H.S.	AV.
TEST					
OTHER FIRST CLASS	27	6	513	63	24.43
INT					
J.P.L.	9	4	101	43	20.20
NAT.W.	1	0	16	16	–
B & H	3	0	22	10	7.33

CAREER: BATTING

	I.	N.O.	R.	H.S.	AV.
TEST					
OTHER FIRST CLASS	66	17	1102	64*	22.49
INT					
J.P.L.	15	8	123	43	17.57
NAT.W.	5	1	45	16	11.25
B & H	5	2	68	36*	22.67

LAST SEASON: WICKET KEEPING

	C.	ST.			
TEST					
OTHER FIRST CLASS	26	9			
INT					
J.P.L.	8	1			
NAT.W.	2	1			
B & H	5	1			

CAREER: WICKET KEEPING

	C.	ST.			
TEST					
OTHER FIRST CLASS	83	29			
INT					
J.P.L.	17	4			
NAT.W.	2	1			
B & H	6	4			

SAINSBURY, G.E.

Full Name: Gary Edward Sainsbury.
Role: Left arm medium fast bowler.
Born: 17 January 1958, Wanstead,
London.
Height: 6' 3" **Weight:** 12st.
Nickname: Sains, Noddy.
County debut: 1983 (Glos.).
County cap: No.
Test debut: —
No. of Tests: 0.
No. of One-Day Internationals: 0.
1000 runs in a season: 0.
50 wickets in a season: 1.
1st-Class 50s scored: 0.
1st-Class 100s scored: 0.
1st-Class 200s scored: 0.
1st-Class 5 w. in innings: 5.
1st-Class 10 w. in match: 0.
One-day 50s: 0.
One-day 100s: 0.
Place in batting average: — average: —; (1983: — average: —).
Place in bowling averages: 88 average: 33.25; (1983: 88 average: 33.39).
1st-Class catches 1984: 8 (career: 9).
Parents: Gordon and Muriel Sainsbury.
Marital status: Single.
Education: Redbridge Primary School, Beal Grammar School, Bath
University.

LAST SEASON: BATTING

	I.	N.O.	R.	H.S.	AV.
TEST					
OTHER FIRST CLASS	20	15	40	10*	8.00
INT					
J.P.L.	4	2	15	6*	7.50
NAT.W.	1	0	3	3	–
B & H	3	2	2	1*	–

CAREER: BATTING

	I.	N.O.	R.	H.S.	AV.
TEST					
OTHER FIRST CLASS	45	25	112	13	5.60
INT					
J.P.L.	8	4	20	6*	5.00
NAT.W.	2	1	5	3	–
B & H	3	2	2	1*	–

LAST SEASON: BOWLING

	O.	M.	R.	W.	AV.
TEST					
OTHER FIRST CLASS	566.2	141	1596	48	33.25
INT					
J.P.L.	87.3	10	424	13	32.62
NAT.W.	24	5	80	4	20.00
B & H	42	4	143	4	33.75

CAREER: BOWLING

	O.	M.	R.	W.	AV.
TEST					
OTHER FIRST CLASS	1062	303	3801	114	33.34
INT					
J.P.L.	193.2	16	907	22	41.22
NAT.W.	54	14	180	6	30.00
B & H	71.4	11	223	10	20.27

Qualifications: 11 O-levels, 3 A-levels, BSc (Hons) Statistics. First stage of the N.C.A. Coaching Award.

Jobs outside cricket: Computer programmer– C.E. Heath & Co. Ltd., Assistant in Finance Section of Tower Hamlets Council's Social Services Department, Assistant in Research Department for Bristol and West Building Society.

Off-season 1984–85: Resume with Bristol and West Building Society.

Equipment used: Symonds.

Overseas teams played for: Hamilton-Wickham C.C. In Newcastle, N.S.W. 1981–82.

Cricketers particularly learnt from: Bill Morris, (Ilford Cricket School), John Gray (Wanstead C.C.), Mike Denness, John Lever.

Significant injuries in 1984: Strained muscles under ribs.

Other sports: Squash, badminton, football, golf.

Relaxations: T.V., reading, listening to music.

Extras: "Played for Essex C.C.C. 1977–1982. First class appearances limited to three matches. In my last season with them I was named Young Player of the Year."

Best batting performance: 13 Gloucestershire v Glamorgan, Cheltenham 1983.

Best bowling performance: 6-66 Gloucestershire v Worcestershire Worcester 1983

SHEPHERD, J.N.

Full Name: John Neil Shepherd.

Role: Right-hand bat, right arm medium bowler.

Born: 9 November 1943, St Andrew, Barbados.

Height: 5' 10½" **Weight:** 12st 11lbs.

Nickname: Shep, Walter.

County debut: 1982 (Glos.).

County cap: 1983.

Test debut: 1969.

No. of Tests: 5.

No. of One-Day Internationals: 0.

Benefit: 1979. £58,537.

1000 runs in a season: 2.

50 wickets in a season: 11.

1st-Class 50s scored: 66.

1st-Class 100s scored: 10.

1st-Class 200s scored: 0.

1st-Class 5 w. in innings: 54.

1st-Class 10 w. in match: 2.

One-day 50s: 13.
One-day 100s: 1.
Place in batting averages: 140 average: 27.66; (1983: 68 average: 36.61).
Place in bowling averages: 71 average: 30.90; (1983: 67 average: 30.55).
1st-Class catches 1984: 13 (career: 290).
Parents: Ollie and Kathleen Shepherd.
Wife and date of marriage: Terri, 14 December 1968.
Children: Caroline, 31 May 1976; Jacqueline, 21 September 1978.
Education: St Andrew's Boys (primary); Alleyn's School, Barbados.
Family links with cricket: Grandfather and two younger brothers all played.
Overseas tours: South Africa in 1973 with Derrick Robins XI, being first black cricketer to tour there.
Overseas teams played for: Debut 1964–65 in one match for Barbados. Played for Rhodesia in 1975–76 Currie Cup Competition. Five tests for the West Indies 1969 and 1970–71 but never played again for them after playing in Rhodesia.
Equipment used: Gray-Nicolls.
Relaxations: Music, golf, squash.
Extras: Introduced to Kent by Colin Cowdrey. Released by Kent at end of 1981 season, having made debut for Kent in 1966, and won cap in 1967.
Opinions on cricket: "I would like to see youngsters appear to enjoy the game a bit more and bring back some fun into it."
Best batting performance: 170 Kent v Northamptonshire, Folkestone 1968.
Best bowling performance: 8-40 West Indians v Gloucestershire, Bristol 1969.

LAST SEASON: BATTING

	I.	N.O.	R.	H.S.	AV.
TEST					
OTHER FIRST CLASS	39	7	885	87	27.66
INT					
J.P.L.	12	3	178	52*	19.77
NAT.W.	1	0	2	2	–
B & H	3	0	19	10	6.33

CAREER: BATTING

	I.	N.O.	R.	H.S.	AV.
TEST	8	0	77	32	9.62
OTHER FIRST CLASS	603	106	13277	170	26.71
INT					
J.P.L.	169	46	2934	94	23.85
NAT.W.	32	3	517	101	17.83
B & H	50	7	751	96	17.47

LAST SEASON: BOWLING

	O.	M.	R.	W.	AV.
TEST					
OTHER FIRST CLASS	800.3	208	2225	72	30.90
INT					
J.P.L.	94.1	3	415	11	37.73
NAT.W.	24	4	88	5	17.60
B & H	43.3	7	156	9	17.33

CAREER: BOWLING

	O.	M.	R.	W.	AV.
TEST	240.5	70	479	19	25.21
OTHER FIRST CLASS	12261.5	3657	31456	1136	27.69
INT					
J.P.L.	1394.1	109	5436	261	20.82
NAT.W.	443.4	80	1388	60	23.13
B & H	605.1	82	1961	96	20.43

STOVOLD, A.W.

Full Name: Andrew Willis Stovold.
Role: Right-hand bat, wicket-keeper.
Born: 19 March 1953, Bristol.
Height: 5' 7" **Weight:** 12st 4lbs.
Nickname: Stumper, Squeak, Stov, Stovers.
County debut: 1973.
County cap: 1976.
Test debut: —
No. of Tests: 0.
No. of One-Day Internationals: 0.
1000 runs in a season: 6.
50 wickets in a season: 0.
1st-Class 50s scored: 76.
1st-Class 100s scored: 14.
1st-Class 200s scored: 1.
1st-Class 5 w. in innings: 0.
1st-Class 10 w. in match: 0.
One-day 50s: 27.
One-day 100s: 2.
Place in batting averages: 110 average: 31.75; (1983: 36 average: 42.85).
Place in bowling averages: — average: —; (1983: — average: —).
1st-Class catches 1984: 14 (career: 238).
Parents: Lancelot Walter and Dorothy Patricia Willis-Stovold.
Wife and date of marriage: Kay Elizabeth, 30 September 1978.
Children: Nicholas, 18 June 1981; Neil, 24 February 1983.
Education: Olveston Primary; Filton High School; Loughborough College of Education.
Qualifications: Certificate of Education.
Jobs outside cricket: Teacher at Tockington Manor Prep. School.
Cricketing superstitions: "Keeping the same routine until I have a bad run, then trying something else. Always prepare for batting in the same order."
Family links with cricket: Father played local club cricket for Old Down C.C. and is Chairman. Brother, Martin, also played county cricket for Gloucestershire.
Overseas tours: With England Schools to India, 1970–71. With England Young Cricketers to West Indies 1972.
Overseas teams played for: Orange Free State, 1974–75, and 1975–76.
Off-season 1984–85: Teaching at Tockington Manor Prep. School.
Equipment used: Gray-Nicolls.
Other sports: Football, golf, hunting, horse-racing.
Relaxations: Gardening, walking.
Best batting performance: 212* Gloucestershire v Northamptonshire, Northampton 1982.

LAST SEASON: BATTING

	I.	N.O.	R.	H.S.	AV.
TEST					
OTHER FIRST CLASS	50	2	1524	139*	31.75
INT					
J.P.L.	14	3	315	62	28.63
NAT.W.	2	0	64	53	32.00
B & H	4	0	169	78	42.25

CAREER: BATTING

	I.	N.O.	R.	H.S.	AV.
TEST					
OTHER FIRST CLASS	450	24	13292	212*	31.20
INT					
J.P.L.	146	18	3095	98*	24.17
NAT.W.	21	2	547	82	28.79
B & H	41	5	1459	123	40.53

LAST SEASON: BOWLING

	O.	M.	R.	W.	AV.
TEST					
OTHER FIRST CLASS					
INT					
J.P.L.					
NAT.W.					
B & H					

CAREER: BOWLING

	O.	M.	R.	W.	AV.
TEST					
OTHER FIRST CLASS	25.3	6	99	2	49.50
INT					
J.P.L.					
NAT.W.					
B & H					

LAST SEASON: WICKET KEEPING

	C.	ST.		
TEST				
OTHER FIRST CLASS	4	2		
INT				
J.P.L.	1	–		
NAT.W.				
B & H				

CAREER: WICKET KEEPING

	C.	ST.		
TEST				
OTHER FIRST CLASS				
INT				
J.P.L.	57	13		
NAT.W.				
B & H				

TREMBATH, C.R.

Full Name: Christopher Richard Trembath.
Role: Right-hand bat, right arm fast medium bowler.
Born: 27 September 1961, London.
Height: 6′ 2″**Weight:** 12st. 10lbs.
Nickname: Trembers.
County debut: 1982.
County cap: No.
Test debut: —
No. of Tests: 0.
No. of One-Day Internationals: 0.
1000 runs in a season: 0.
50 wickets in a season: 0.
1st-Class 50s scored: 0.
1st-Class 100s scored: 0.
1st-Class 200s scored: 0.
1st-Class 5 w. in innings: 1.
1st-Class 10 w. in match: 0.
One-day 50s: 0.

One-day 100s: 0.
Place in batting averages: — average: —; (1983: — average: —).
Place in bowling averages: — average: —; (1983: — average: —).
1st-Class catches 1984: 0 (career: 1).
Parents: Richard and Robina Trembath.
Marital status: Single.
Family links with cricket: Father played for army.
Education: Dulwich College, London; Clifton College, Bristol.
Qualifications: O- and A-levels and degree in Mining Engineering.
Jobs outside cricket: Trainee accountant.
Off-season 1984–85: Training as an accountant.
Equipment used: Symonds.
Overseas tours: School tour to Bermuda; the Dragons tours to West Indies.
Cricketers particularly learnt from: Jim Andrew, coach at school.
Cricketers particularly admired: Mike Brearley.
Other sports: Rugby, hockey, squash, golf. Follow most sports.
Relaxations: Sports, music, reading and beer.
Extras: Giving up professional cricket in order to pursue a career in accountancy.
Opinions on cricket: A greater effort must be made to prepare wickets that will produce more attacking cricket. Low, slow wickets are boring for the crowd and the players.
Address: 11 Manilla Road, Clifton, Bristol.
Best batting performance: 17* Gloucestershire v Middlesex, Lord's 1984.
Best bowling performance: 3-106 Gloucestershire v Middlesex, Lord's 1984.

LAST SEASON: BATTING

	I.	N.O.	R.	H.S.	AV.
TEST					
OTHER FIRST CLASS	3	2	25	17*	—
INT					
J.P.L.	2	0	6	5	3.00
NAT.W.					
B & H					

CAREER: BATTING

	I.	N.O.	R.	H.S.	AV.
TEST					
OTHER FIRST CLASS	4	3	33	17*	—
INT					
J.P.L.	5	1	21	7	5.25
NAT.W.					
B & H					

LAST SEASON: BOWLING

	O.	M.	R.	W.	AV.
TEST					
OTHER FIRST CLASS	46.5	5	225	5	45.00
INT					
J.P.L.	12.1	0	80	0	—
NAT.W.					
B & H					

CAREER: BOWLING

	O.	M.	R.	W.	AV.
TEST					
OTHER FIRST CLASS	96.2	12	444	11	40.36
INT					
J.P.L.	40.1	1	247	6	41.17
NAT.W.					
B & H					

WALSH C.A.

Full Name: Courtney Andrew Walsh.
Role: Right-hand bat, right arm
fast bowler.
Born: 30 October 1962, Kingston,
Jamaica.
Height: 6' 5½" **Weight:** 13st 7lbs.
Nickname: Mask, Walshy.
County debut: 1984.
County cap: No.
Test debut: —
No. of Tests: 0.
No. of One-Day Internationals: 0.
1000 runs in a season: 0.
50 wickets in a season: 0.
1st-Class 50s scored: 0.
1st-Class 100s scored: 0.
1st-Class 200s scored: 0.
1st-Class 5 w. in innings: 0.
1st-Class 10 w. in match: 0.
One-day 50s: 0.
One-day 100s: 0.
Place in batting averages: — average: —; (1983: — average: —).
Place in bowling averages: 104 average: 36.84; (1983: — average: —).
1st-Class catches 1984: 1 (career: 9).
Parents: Joan Wollaston and Erick Walsh.
Marital status: Single.
Education: Excelsior High School.
Qualifications: G.C.E. and C.X.L.

LAST SEASON: BATTING

	I.	N.O.	R.	H.S.	AV.
TEST					
OTHER FIRST CLASS	15	3	98	30	8.17
INT					
J.P.L.					
NAT.W.	2	0	23	14	11.50
B & H					

CAREER: BATTING

	I.	N.O.	R.	H.S.	AV.
TEST					
OTHER FIRST CLASS	41	8	258	30	7.82
INT					
J.P.L.					
NAT.W.	2	0	23	14	11.50
B & H					

LAST SEASON: BOWLING

	O.	M.	R.	W.	AV.
TEST					
OTHER FIRST CLASS	341.1	80	1179	32	36.84
INT					
J.P.L.	21.4	5	72	2	36.00
NAT.W.					
B & H					

CAREER: BOWLING

	O.	M.	R.	W.	AV.
TEST					
OTHER FIRST CLASS	840.4	173	2816	100	28.16
INT					
J.P.L.	21.4	5	72	2	36.00
NAT.W.					
B & H					

Equipment used: Gray-Nicolls.
Overseas tours: To England 1984, Australia 1984–85, with West Indies.
Overseas teams played for: West Indies, Jamaica.
Other sports: Football; follow basketball and track and field events.
Relaxations: Music and watching T.V.
Extras: Took record 10-43 in Jamaican school cricket in 1979.
Best batting performace: 30 Gloucestershire v Lancashire, Bristol 1984.
Best bowling performance: 6-35 Jamaica v Guyana, Kingston 1983–84.

WOOTTON, S.H.

Full Name: Simon Howard Wootton.
Role: Left-hand bat, left arm medium bowler, cover fielder.
Born: 24 February 1959.
Height: 5′ 9″ **Weight:** 10st 9lbs.
County debut: 1981 (Warwickshire), 1984 (Gloucestershire).
County cap: No.
Test debut: —
No. of Tests: 0.
No. of One-Day Internationals: 0.
1000 runs in a season: 0.
50 wickets in a season: 0.
1st-Class 50s scored: 2.
1st-Class 100s scored: 1.
1st-Class 200s scored: 0.
1st-Class 5 w. in innings: 0.
1st-Class 10 w. in match: 0.
One-day 50s: 0.
One-day 100s: 0.
Place in batting averages: 139 average: 27.72; (1983: — average: —).
Place in bowling averages: — average: —; (1983: — average: —).
1st-Class catches 1984: 4 (career: 8).
Parents: Bernard Arthur and Irene Maria Wootton.
Wife and date of marriage: Drenagh Helen, 3 December 1983.
Family links with cricket: Father played for Middlesex Club Cricket Conference side and R.A.F.
Education: Ley Hill Junior School; Arthur Terry School.
Qualifications: O-levels and N.C.A. cricket coaching award.
Jobs outside cricket: Assistant Promotions Manager Sondico International 1979–80.
Off-season 1984–85: Working in the "Slug and Lettuce" wine bar, Stratford-upon-Avon.
Cricketing supersitions: The number 13. Put right pad on first.

Equipment used: Duncan Fearnley. Sondico Sports for pads and gloves.
Overseas teams played for: Springs High School Old Boys, South Africa
1980–81. Berea Park, Pretoria, South Africa, 1982–82.
Cricketers particularly learnt from: Don Wilson, M.C.C. coach.
Cricketers particularly admired: Dennis Amiss.
Other sports: Plays badminton for Warwickshire County 1st team. Watch
football and golf.
Relaxations: Walking the dog.
Extras: Spent two years on M.C.C. Young Professional Staff at Lord's, 1979–
80. Badminton English Nationals Under-21 Mixed Doubles Champion 1980;
ranked No. 6 in England at Badminton when under 18. Member of England
Youth Squad (Badminton) Under-18. On debut, became Gloucestershire's
500th player (scored 97).
Best batting performance: 104 Warwickshire v Cambridge University,
Cambridge 1983.

LAST SEASON: BATTING

	I.	N.O.	R.	H.S.	AV.
TEST					
OTHER FIRST CLASS	8	1	194	97	27.72
INT					
J.P.L.					
NAT.W.					
B & H					

CAREER: BATTING

	I.	N.O.	R.	H.S.	AV.
TEST					
OTHER FIRST CLASS	24	3	561	104	26.71
INT					
J.P.L.	10	4	135	28*	22.50
NAT.W.	1	0	2	2	–
B & H	1	0	33	33	–

LAST SEASON: BOWLING

	O.	M.	R.	W.	AV.
TEST					
OTHER FIRST CLASS					
INT					
J.P.L.					
NAT.W.					
B & H					

CAREER: BOWLING

	O.	M.	R.	W.	AV.
TEST					
OTHER FIRST CLASS	1	0	7	0	. –
INT					
J.P.L.					
NAT.W.					
B & H					

Q. 61. Which Sussex & England player achieved greater fame
as a Hollywood actor?

Q. 62. Which current county player wrote a diary of the 1983
English season entitled *It Never Rains . . .*?

WRIGHT, A.J.

Full Name: Anthony John Wright.
Role: Right-hand bat; right arm
medium bowler.
Born: 27 July 1962, Stevenage.
Height: 6′ 0″ **Weight:** 13st.
Nickname: Paul Getty, Billy.
County debut: 1982.
County cap: No.
Test debut: —
No. of Tests: 0.
No. of One-Day Internationals: 0.
1000 runs in a season: 0.
50 wickets in a season: 0.
1st-Class 50s scored: 10.
1st-Class 100s scored: 1.
1st-Class 200s scored: 0.
1st-Class 5 w. in innings: 0.
1st-Class 10 w. in match: 0.
One-day 50s: 1.
One-day 100s: 0.
Place in batting averages: 145 average: 26.97; (1983: 135 average: 25.33).
Place in bowling averages: — average: —; (1983: — average: —).
1st-Class catches 1984: 11 (career: 19).
Parents: Patricia and Michael.
Marital status: Single.
Education: Alleyn's Grammar School, Stevenage.
Qualifications: 6 O-levels.
Jobs outside cricket: Plasterers labourer.

LAST SEASON: BATTING

	I.	N.O.	R.	H.S.	AV.
TEST					
OTHER FIRST CLASS	39	3	971	139	26.97
INT					
J.P.L.	5	1	26	14	6.50
NAT.W.					
B & H	3	0	14	7	4.67

CAREER: BATTING

	I.	N.O.	R.	H.S.	AV.
TEST					
OTHER FIRST CLASS	75	7	1750	139	25.74
INT					
J.P.L.	19	3	187	52	11.69
NAT.W.	1	0	14	14	–
B & H	3	0	14	7	4.67

LAST SEASON: BOWLING

	O.	M.	R.	W.	AV.
TEST					
OTHER FIRST CLASS					
INT					
J.P.L.					
NAT.W.					
B & H					

CAREER: BOWLING

	O.	M.	R.	W.	AV.
TEST					
OTHER FIRST CLASS	1	0	3	0	–
INT					
J.P.L.	4	0	18	0	–
NAT.W.					
B & H					

Equipment used: Slazenger.
Overseas tours: Barbados 1980 with Gloucestershire.
Overseas teams played for: Port Melbourne 1981–82, 1982–83.
Cricketers particularly learnt from: John Childs, Barry Duddleston.
Cricketers particularly admired: Zaheer Abbas, Vivian Richards.
Other sports: Rugby, golf, squash, snooker.
Extras: Played for 2nd XI since 1979. Played twice in John Player League in 1980. Did not play in 1981. Hit 65 in his first-class debut v. Warwickshire.
Best batting performance: 139 Gloucestershire v Surrey, Cheltenham 1984.

ZAHEER ABBAS

Full Name: Syed Zaheer Abbas.
Role: Right-hand bat; off-break bowler.
Born: 24 July 1947, Sialkot, Pakistan.
Height: 5' 11½" **Weight:** 11st. 3lbs.
Nickname: Zed.
County debut: 1972 (Gloucs.).
County cap: 1975.
Benefit: 1983.
Test debut: 1969–70.
No. of Tests: 69.
No. of One-Day Internationals: 49.
1000 runs in a season: 11.
50 wickets in a season: 0.
1st-Class 50s scored: 144.
1st-Class 100s scored: 97.

1st-Class 200s: 9.
1st-Class 5 w. in innings: 0.
1st-Class 10 w. in match: 0.
One-day 50s: 56.
One-day 100s: 18.
Place in batting averages: 115 average: 30.75; (1983: 24 average: 45.63).
Place in bowling averages: — average: —; (1983: — average: —).
1st-Class catches 1984: 2 (career: 260).
Parents: Syed Gaulam Shabbir and Kaneez Fatima.
Education: High School Jehangir Road, Islamia College, Karachi.
Wife and date of marriage: Najma October 1972.
Children: Two daughters, Rudaba and Roshana.
Overseas tours: England 1971 and 1974; Australia and New Zealand 1972–73; Australia and West Indies, 1976–77. Australia and New Zealand, 1978–79, 1983–84.
Equipment used: Gunn & Moore.

Cricketers particularly admired: Hanif Mohammed, but "Rohan Kanhai was my greatest hero of all."

Overseas teams played for: Karachi Whites; Pakistan International Airways; Dawood Club.

Relaxations: Cinema, music.

Extras: Debut for Karachi Whites 1965–66. Was dismissed for hitting the ball twice for Pakistan International Airways v Karachi Blues at Karachi in 1969–70. Played for Rest of the World v Australia 1971–72. Scored two centuries in a match three times: twice in 1976 (216 not out and 156 not out, v Surrey at the Oval; 230 not out and 104 not out, v Kent at Canterbury) and once in 1977 (205 not out and 108 not out, v Sussex at Cheltenham). Shared in second wicket record partnership for Pakistan, 291 with Mushtaq Mohammed v England at Birmingham in 1971. Wears spectacles. In 1981, was the first man to score 1000 runs in a calendar month–June– for 22 years. Played World Series Cricket. Vice-captain of Pakistan 1981–. Scored century before lunch for Pakistan v. Derby, 1982. Top of Gloucestershire 1st class batting averages in 1982 and 1983. Captained Pakistan for first time in 1983. Published "Zed"— autobiography. 70% of fan mail comes from India. Returned to Pakistan in July 1984.

Opinions on cricket: "Batting is my religion, after being a Muslim. . . . I'm of the same mind as Geoff Boycott. It's his religion to get runs. . . . Wherever a cricketer comes from in the world, I don't believe he can do better than play county cricket in England. It teaches you so much . . . The standard of umpiring in England is I believe the best in the world."

Best batting performance: 274 Pakistan v England, Edgbaston 1971.

Best bowling performance: 5-15 Dawood v Railways, Lahore 1975–76.

LAST SEASON: BATTING

	I.	N.O.	R.	H.S.	AV.
TEST					
OTHER FIRST CLASS	28	4	738	157*	30.75
INT					
J.P.L.	7	0	264	102	37.72
NAT.W.	1	0	21	21	–
B & H	4	0	115	67	28.75

CAREER: BATTING

	I.	N.O.	R.	H.S.	AV.
TEST	112	10	4747	274	46.53
OTHER FIRST CLASS	621	78	29097	230*	53.59
INT	49	6	2177	123	50.62
J.P.L.	132	17	4663	129*	40.54
NAT.W.	22	1	980	158	46.67
B & H	47	6	1455	98	35.49

LAST SEASON: BOWLING

	O.	M.	R.	W.	AV.
TEST					
OTHER FIRST CLASS	5.4	4	1	0	–
INT					
J.P.L.					
NAT.W.					
B & H					

CAREER: BOWLING

	O.	M.	R.	W.	AV.
TEST	146	17	93	1	–
OTHER FIRST CLASS			927	25	37.08
INT	29.1	2	129	6	21.50
J.P.L.	16	0	73	2	36.50
NAT.W.	11.3	0	41	2	20.50

COUNTY QUIZ

Q. 1.   When was the club founded?

Q. 2.   Who made the most first-class runs for the county last season, and how many?

Q. 3.   What's the highest ever county total, and against whom?

Q. 4.   Who took most wickets for the county last season, and how many?

Q. 5.   What's the highest individual score for the county, who hit it, and when?

Q. 6.   What's the highest scoring partnership for the county for any wicket?

Q. 7.   How many times has the club won the County Championship?

Q. 8.   What's the lowest ever total made by the county in one innings, when, and against whom?

Q. 9.   Which bowler took the most first-class wickets in one season, when, and how many?

Q. 10.   Which batsman hit the most runs in one season, when and how many?

Hampshire

ANDREW, S.J.W.

Full Name: Stephen Jon Walter Andrew.
Role: Right-hand bat, right arm medium-fast bowler.
Born: 1 January 1966, London.
Height: 6′ 3″ **Weight:** 13st.
Nickname: Rip.
County debut: 1984.
County cap: No.
Test debut: —
No. of Tests: 0.
No. of One-Day Internationals: 0.
1000 runs in a season: 0.
50 wickets in a season: 0.
1st-Class 50s scored: 0.
1st-Class 100s scored: 0.
1st-Class 200s scored: 0.
1st-Class 5 w. in innings: 0.
1st-Class 10 w. in match: 0.
One-day 50s: 0.
One-day 100s: 0.

Place in batting averages: — average: —; (1983: — average: —).
Place in bowling averages: 131 average: 48.18; (1983: — average: —).
1st-Class catches 1984: 1 (career: 1).
Parents: Jon Trevor and Victoria Julia Maud Andrew.
Marital status: Single.
Education: Hordle House Prep School; Milton Abbey Public School.
Qualifications: 3 O-levels.
Off-season 1984–85: Coaching in Durban, South Africa and Young England tour of West Indies.
Overseas teams played for: Pirates C.C. Durban, South Africa 1983–84.
Cricketers particularly learnt from: Peter Sainsbury, Tim Tremlett, David Turner.
Cricketers particularly admired: Richard Hadlee, Michael Holding, D.K. Lillee.

Other sports played: Squash, golf. Interested in most sports.
Relaxations: Listening to music.
Extras: Youngest bowler to have opened bowling for Hampshire.
Opinions on cricket: "Politics should not interfere with any sport. I feel very strongly about the isolation of South Africa as a sporting nation."
Best batting performance: 6* Hampshire v Middlesex, Bournemouth 1984.
Best bowling performance: 4-30 Hampshire v Sussex, Hove 1984.

LAST SEASON: BATTING

	I.	N.O.	R.	H.S.	AV.
TEST					
OTHER FIRST CLASS	6	4	12	6*	6.00
INT					
J.P.L.					
NAT.W.					
B & H	1	1	1	1*	–

CAREER: BATTING

	I.	N.O.	R.	H.S.	AV.
TEST					
OTHER FIRST CLASS	6	4	12	6*	6.00
INT					
J.P.L.					
NAT.W.					
B & H	1	1	1	1*	–

LAST SEASON: BOWLING

	O.	M.	R.	W.	AV.
TEST					
OTHER FIRST CLASS	162.2	43	530	11	48.18
INT					
J.P.L.	62.3	0	304	6	50.67
NAT.W.					
B & H	18	1	60	6	10.00

CAREER: BOWLING

	O.	M.	R.	W.	AV.
TEST					
OTHER FIRST CLASS	162.2	43	530	11	48.18
NAT.W.					
J.P.L.	62.3	0	304	6	50.67
NAT.W.					
B & H	18	1	60	6	10.00

CONNOR, C.A.

Full Name: Cardigan Connor.
Role: Right-hand bat, right arm fast-medium bowler.
Born: 24 March 1961, West End, Anguilla.
Height: 5′ 10″ **Weight:** 11st. 6lbs.
Nickname: "Christy, Cardy and many more."
County debut: 1984.
County cap: No.
Test debut: —
No. of Tests: 0.
No. of One-Day Internationals: 0.
1000 runs in a season: 0.
50 wickets in a season: 1.
1st-Class 50s scored: 0.
1st-Class 100s scored: 0.
1st-Class 200s scored: 0.

1st-Class 5 w. in innings: 2.
1st-Class 10 w. in match: 0.
One-day 50s: 0.
One-day 100s: 0.
Place in batting averages: — average: —; (1983: — average: —).
Place in bowling averages: 76 average: 31.43; (1983: — average: —).
1st-Class catches 1984: 7 (career: 7).
Parents: Ethleen Snagg.
Marital status: Single.
Education: Valley Secondary School, Anguilla, B.WI.; Langley College.
Qualifications: Engineer.
Jobs outside cricket: Timko Engineering, Slough Trading Estate.
Off season 1984–85: Playing club cricket in Newcastle, N.S.W., Australia.
Cricketing superstitions: Never change before the end of the day's play.
Equipment used: Duncan Fearnley.
Overseas tours: C.C.C. tour of Hong Kong, Singapore, New Zealand and Australia in 1983.
Overseas teams played for: Merriweather C.C. Newcastle, Australia 1983–84. West End C.C. Anguilla 1973–76.
Cricketers particularly learnt from: Tim Tremlett. "He helped me a great deal in my first season."
Cricketers particularly admired: Viv Richards, Andy Roberts, Richard Hadlee.
Other sports: Most other sports; follow football, boxing, tennis etc.
Significant injuries in 1984: Shoulder injury.
Relaxations: Music, wine bars, meeting people.
Extras: Played for Buckinghamshire in Minor Counties before joining Hampshire. First Anguillan-born player to appear in the County Championship.
Opinions on cricket: "Play 16 4-day championship matches instead of 24 3-day."

LAST SEASON: BATTING

	I.	N.O.	R.	H.S.	AV.
TEST					
OTHER FIRST CLASS	23	9	65	13*	4.64
INT					
J.P.L.	2	2	0	0*	–
NAT.W.	1	1	3	3*	–
B & H					

CAREER: BATTING

	I.	N.O.	R.	H.S.	AV.
TEST					
OTHER FIRST CLASS	23	9	65	13*	4.64
INT					
J.P.L.	2	2	0	0*	–
NAT.W.	1	1	3	3*	–
B & H					

LAST SEASON: BOWLING

	O.	M.	R.	W.	AV.
TEST					
OTHER FIRST CLASS	642.5	155	1949	62	31.43
INT					
J.P.L.	97.2	6	439	20	21.95
NAT.W.					
B & H					

CAREER: BOWLING

	O.	M.	R.	W.	AV.
TEST					
OTHER FIRST CLASS	642.5	155	1949	62	30.45
INT					
J.P.L.	97.2	6	439	20	21.95
NAT.W.	18	4	63	1	–
B & H					

Best batting performance: 13* Hampshire v Kent, Bournemouth 1984.
Best bowling performance: 7-37 Hampshire v Kent, Bournemouth 1984.

COWLEY, N.G.

Full Name: Nigel Geoffrey Cowley
Role: Right-hand bat, off-break bowler.
Born: 1 March 1953, Shaftesbury, Dorset.
Height: 5' 7" **Weight:** 11st 7lbs.
Nickname: Dougall.
County debut: 1974.
County cap: 1978.
Test debut: —
No. of Tests: 0.
No. of One-Day Internationals: 0.
1000 runs in a season: 1.
50 wickets in a season: 5.
1st-Class 50s scored: 25.
1st-Class 100s scored: 2.
1st-Class 200s scored: 0.
1st-Class 5 w. in innings: 4.
1st-Class 10 w. in match: 0.
One-day 50s: 5.
One-day 100s: 0.
Place in batting averages: 116 average: 30.65; (1983: 181 average: 19.50).
Place in bowling averages: 79 average: 31.77; (1983: 40 average: 25.68).
1st-Class catches 1984: 9 (career: 81).

CAREER: BATTING

	I.	N.O.	R.	H.S.	AV.
TEST					
OTHER FIRST CLASS	302	42	5767	109*	22.18
INT					
J.P.L.	109	21	1723	74	19.57
NAT.W.	15	2	259	63*	19.92
B & H	29	2	389	59	14.41

LAST SEASON: BATTING

	I.	N.O.	R.	H.S.	AV.
TEST					
OTHER FIRST CLASS	38	4	1042	80	30.65
INT					
J.P.L.	13	3	124	33	12.40
NAT.W.	2	0	30	30	15.00
B & H	3	1	35	23*	17.50

CAREER: BOWLING

	O.	M.	R.	W.	AV.
TEST					
OTHER FIRST CLASS	4057.4	1095	11095	327	33.93
INT					
J.P.L.	631.1	35	2958	99	29.88
NAT.W.	159.1	27	433	17	26.06
B & H	222.3	42	67	17	39.41

LAST SEASON: BOWLING

	O.	M.	R.	W.	AV.
TEST					
OTHER FIRST CLASS	588.1	133	1779	56	31.77
INT					
J.P.L.	115	11	571	17	33.59
NAT.W.	23.2	2	67	5	13.40
B & H	40	12	103	1	—

Parents: Geoffrey and Betty Cowley.
Wife: Susan.
Children: Mark and Darren.
Family links with cricket: Father played good club cricket.
Education: Mere Dutchy Manor, Mere, Wilts.
Off-season 1984–85: Coaching in Durban.
Cricketing superstitions: "None".
Equipment used: Duncan Fearnley.
Overseas tours: To Sri Lanka 1977 and West Indies 1980.
Cricketers particularly learnt from: Peter Sainsbury.
Other sports: Football, badminton, golf — 10 handicap.
Extras: In charge of pre-season and match day training.
Best batting performance: 109* Hampshire v Somerset, Taunton 1977.
Best bowling performance: 6-48 Hampshire v Leicestershire, Southampton 1982.

GOLDIE, C.F.E.

Full name: Christopher Frederick
Evelyn Goldie.
Role: Wicket-keeper, right-hand bat.
Born: 2 November 1960,
Johannesburg.
Height: 5′ 6″ **Weight:** 9st 7lbs.
Nicknames: Stumpy, Pygmy,
Manders and many others which are
unprintable.
County debut: 1983.
County cap: No.
Test debut: —
No. of Tests: 0.
No. of One-Day Internationals: 0.
1000 runs in a season: 0.
50 wickets in a season: 0.
1st-Class 50s scored: 1.
1st-Class 100s scored: 0.
1st-Class 200s scored: 0.
1st-Class 5 w. in innings: 0.
1st-Class 10 w. in match: 0.
One-day 50s: 0.
One-day 100s: 0.

Place in batting averages: — average —; (1983: — average: —).
Place in bowling averages: — average: —; (1983: — average: —)
Parents: Thomas Hugh Evelyn and Eva Johanna (Janet) Goldie.
Marital status: Single.

Family links with cricket: Father played for Somerset II before war, for Oxfordshire and premier league in Jo'burg for Old Johannians. Uncle played for Devon and still plays aged 73; and brother is a keen club cricketer. Both father and brother play for Richmond C.C.

Education: St. Pauls School, Barnes, Pembroke College, Cambridge.

Qualifications: 8 'O' levels, 3 'A' levels. BA Hons (Cantab), studied Arabic for two years (very badly) and history for one year (a little bit better).

Jobs outside cricket: Spent winter 1982–83 working as an insurance broker for Willis Faber & Dumas, who also employ Mike Griffiths (ex-Sussex) and the present chairman of selectors.

Equipment used: Duncan Fearnley.

Overseas tours: M.C.C. tour to U.S.A. September 1982. Vic Lewis Allstars tours to Finland August 1981 and Holland August 1982. Gordon Greenidge Benefit tour to Paris September 1983.

Overseas teams played for: Grosvenor-Fynnland C.C. Durban 1983–84.

Cricketers particularly learnt from: Ted Whitfield (ex-Northants and Surrey) and Gwyn Hughes (ex-Cambridge and Glamorgan) whilst at school. Brian 'Tonker' Taylor at Cambridge and latterly Peter Sainsbury. "Above all, all credit or blame must go to my father."

Cricketers particularly admired: Bob Taylor.

Other sports: Golf, squash— both badly. Knee injury forced early retirement from soccer. Watch rugby— supporter of Cambridge Univ. and Rosslyn Park F.C. soccer and American football.

Relaxations: Reading, films, good T.V., good company, Everton F.C. and fruit machines that pay out lots of money.

Extras: Spent two years on Middlesex staff but never came anywhere near to a first team game. Cambridge blue 1981 and 1982, scoring 77 as nightwatchman in 1981, set a latter day record for dismissals by a Cambridge keeper in 1982–83.

Opinions on cricket: "Whilst appreciating the need for improved over rates, I

LAST SEASON: BATTING

	I.	N.O.	R.	H.S.	AV.
TEST					
OTHER FIRST CLASS					
INT					
J.P.L.					
NAT.W.					
B & H					

CAREER: BATTING

	I.	N.O.	R.	H.S.	AV.
TEST					
OTHER FIRST CLASS	24	3	302	77	14.38
INT					
J.P.L.					
NAT.W.					
B & H	4	1	6	3*	2.00

LAST SEASON: WICKET KEEPING

	C.	ST.			
TEST					
OTHER FIRST CLASS	2	1			
INT					
J.P.L.					
NAT.W.					
B & H					

CAREER: WICKET KEEPING

	C.	ST.			
TEST					
OTHER FIRST CLASS	34	8			
INT					
J.P.L.					
NAT.W.					
B & H					

have got the impression that the 117 minimum over rule is enjoyed by neither players nor spectators, whose days are proving longer and whose routines are becoming more and more disrupted."

Best batting performance: 77 Cambridge University v Oxford University, Lords 1981.

GREENIDGE, C.G.

Full Name: Cuthbert Gordon Greenidge.

Role: Right-hand bat, right arm medium bowler.

Born: 1 May 1951, St Peter, Barbados.

County debut: 1970.

County cap: 1972.

Benefit: 1983 (£28,648).

Test debut: 1974–75.

No. of Tests: 57.

No. of One-Day Internationals: 60.

1000 runs in a season: 13.

50 wickets in a season: 0.

1st-Class 50s scored: 123.

1st-Class 100s scored: 56.

1st-Class 200s scored: 7.

1st-Class 5 w. in innings: 1.

1st-Class 10 w. in match: 0.

One-day 50s: 58.

One-day 100s: 19.

Place in batting averages: 1 average: 82.83; (1983: 2 average: 65.36).

Place in bowling averages: — average: —; (1983: average: —).

1st-Class catches 1984: 5 (career: 386).

Wife and date of marriage: Anita, September 1977.

Children: Carl, born 1978.

Education: Black Bess School; St Peter's Boys' School; Sutton Secondary School, Reading, Berkshire.

Qualifications: Studied accountancy and book-keeping.

Jobs outside cricket: Working for Sutton's Seeds, Reading; Dimplex, Southampton.

Family links with cricket: Wife is cousin of West Indian and Leicestershire fast bowler Andy Roberts.

Overseas tours: Toured with West Indies to India, Sri Lanka and Pakistan 1974–75; Australia 1975–76; England 1976; Australia 1979–80. Pakistan, 1980. Australia, 1981–82, India 1983, England 1984, Australia 1984–85.

Overseas teams played for: Barbados.

Equipment used: Gray-Nicolls.

Other sports: "Played some soccer but particularly I enjoyed rugby." Golf.

Extras: Could have played for either England or West Indies. Persuaded to join Hampshire by John Arlott after playing for Berkshire U-19s. Suffered badly from knee injury but continued to play in 1979. Scored two centuries in one match (134 and 101) for West Indies v England at Manchester 1976, and v Kent at Bournemouth (136 and 120) in 1978. When he left school, he thought of joining the church: "Certainly, as a 17 year-old, it seemed a much more feasible career than playing cricket." Shared in partnership of 285 for second wicket with D.R. Turner v Minor Counties South at Amersham in 1973, being the record partnership for all one-day competitions.

Best batting performance: 273* Robins' XI v Pakistan, Eastbourne 1974.

LAST SEASON: BATTING

	I.	N.O.	R.	H.S.	AV.
TEST	8	1	572	223	81.72
OTHER FIRST CLASS	8	2	497	138	82.83
INT	3	0	61	32	20.33
J.P.L.					
NAT.W.					
B & H					

CAREER: BATTING

	I.	N.O.	R.	H.S.	AV.
TEST	96	11	4338	223	51.03
OTHER FIRST CLASS	545	44	22104	273*	44.12
INT	60	6	2545	115	47.13
J.P.L.	153	8	5066	163*	34.93
NAT.W.	26	1	1068	177	42.72
B & H	45	2	1522	173*	35.39

LAST SEASON: BOWLING

	O.	M.	R.	W.	AV.
TEST					
OTHER FIRST CLASS	9	6	11	1	–
INT					
J.P.L.					
NAT.W.					
B & H					

CAREER: BOWLING

	O.	M.	R.	W.	AV.
TEST	1.3	1.2	4	0	–
OTHER FIRST CLASS	148.5	36	445	17	26.18
INT.	10	0	45	1	–
J.P.L.	18	0	89	1	–
NAT.W.	0.5	0	4	0	–
B & H	12.1	1	57	0	–

Q. 63. Who was X.C. Balaskas?

Q. 64. What was the highest not-out score ever made in first-class cricket? Who made it for whom and when?

HARDY, J.J.E.

Full Name: Jonathan James Ean
Hardy.
Role: Left-hand bat.
Born: 2 October 1960, Nakuru,
Kenya.
Height: 6′ 3″ **Weight:** 14st.
Nickname: Greigy, J.J.
County debut: 1984.
County cap: No.
Test debut: —
No. of Tests: 0.
No. of One-Day Internationals: 0.
1000 runs in a season: 0.
50 wickets in a season: 0.
1st-Class 50s scored: 4.
1st-Class 100s scored: 0.
1st-Class 200s scored: 0.
1st-Class 5 w. in innings: 0.
1st-Class 10 w. in match: 0.
One-day 50s: 1.
One-day 100s: 0.
Place in batting averages: 68 average: 36.64; (1983: — average: —).
Place in bowling averages: — average: —; 81983: — average: —).
1st-Class catches 1984: 9 (career: 9).
Parents: Ray and Petasue Hardy.
Marital status: Single.
Family links with cricket: Father played for Yorkshire Schools; related to
Nottinghamshire Gunn's.

LAST SEASON: BATTING

	I.	N.O.	R.	H.S.	AV.
TEST					
OTHER FIRST CLASS	20	6	513	94*	36.64
INT					
J.P.L.	9	2	140	58	20.00
NAT.W.					
B & H					

CAREER: BATTING

	I.	N.O.	R.	H.S.	AV.
TEST					
OTHER FIRST CLASS	20	6	513	94*	36.64
INT					
J.P.L.	9	2	140	58	20.00
NAT.W.					
B & H					

LAST SEASON: BOWLING

	O.	M.	R.	W.	AV.
TEST					
OTHER FIRST CLASS	1	0	3	0	–
INT					
J.P.L.					
NAT.W.					
B & H					

CAREER: BOWLING

	O.	M.	R.	W.	AV.
TEST					
OTHER FIRST CLASS	1	0	3	0	–
INT					
J.P.L.					
NAT.W.					
B & H					

Education: Pembroke House, Gilgil, Kenya; Canford School, Dorset.
Qualifications: 10 O-levels, 3 A-levels (English, Economics, Geography).
Off-season 1984–85: Captaining Multi-Racial 'pirates' in Durban Inter-city league and coaching.
Equipment used: Slazenger.
Overseas teams played for: Pirates, Durban 1981–84.
Cricketers particularly admired: Graeme Pollock, Greg Chappell.
Other sports: Hockey (capt. Dorset U-19), rugby, squash.
Relaxations: Photography, walking.
Extras: Suffered from Bilharzia, a tropical parasitic disease from January 1981 to July 1983. Scored 94* on debut championship innings while Hampshire followed on.
Best batting performance: 94* Hampshire v Somerset, Taunton 1984.

JESTY, T.E.

Full Name: Trevor Edward Jesty.
Role: Right-hand bat, right arm medium bowler.
Born: 2 June 1948, Gosport, Hampshire.
Height: 5′ 9″ **Weight:** 11st 10lbs.
Nickname: Jets.
County debut: 1966.
County cap: 1971.
Benefit: 1982.
Test debut: —
No. of Tests: 0.
No. of One-Day Internationals: 10.
1000 runs in a season: 7.
50 wickets in a season: 2.
1st-Class 50s scored: 78.
1st-Class 100s scored: 26.
1st-Class 200s scored: 1.
1st-Class 5 w. in innings: 18.
1st-Class 10 w. in match: 0.
One-day 50s: 33.
One-day 100s: 6.
Place in batting averages: 47 average: 40.62; (1983: 35 average: 42.88).
Place in bowling averages: 99 average: 35.16; (1983: 109 average: 38.29).
1st-Class catches 1984: 16 (career: 213).
Parents: Aubrey Edward and Sophia Jesty.
Wife and date of marriage: Jacqueline, 12 September 1970.
Children: Graeme Barry, 27 September 1972; Lorna Samantha, 7 November 1976.

Education: Privet County Secondary Modern, Gosport.

Jobs outside cricket: Cricket coach in South Africa and New Zealand. Representative for wine company.

Family links with cricket: Brother, Aubrey Jesty, wicket-keeper and left-hand bat. Could have joined Hampshire staff, but decided to continue with his apprenticeship.

Overseas teams played for: Border in 1973–74, and Griqualand West in 1974–75 and 1975–76, South Africa, in the Currie Cup Competition.

Cricketers particularly learnt from: Barry Richards.

Equipment used: Slazenger.

Other sports: Soccer, golf.

Relaxations: Watching soccer, and gardening.

Extras: Took him 10 years to score maiden first-class century. Missed most of 1980 season through injury. Made Vice-Captain in 1981. Top of Hampshire first-class batting averages in 1982. Considered to be most unlucky not to be chosen for England tour of Australia 1982–83 after brilliant 1982 season, then was called in as a replacement. Left Hampshire at end of 1984 season when not appointed captain.

Best batting performance: 248 Hampshire v Cambridge University, Cambridge 1984.

Best bowling performance: 7-75 Hampshire v Worcestershire, Southampton 1976.

LAST SEASON: BATTING

	I.	N.O.	R.	H.S.	AV.
TEST					
OTHER FIRST CLASS	44	4	1625	248	40.62
INT					
J.P.L.	16	0	300	62	18.75
NAT.W.	2	0	37	35	18.50
B & H	3	0	115	51	38.33

CAREER: BATTING

	I.	N.O.	R.	H.S.	AV.
TEST					
OTHER FIRST CLASS	584	75	16970	248	33.34
INT	10	4	127	52*	21.17
J.P.L.	205	28	4629	166*	26.15
NAT.W.	26	2	744	118	31.00
B & H	54	4	1486	105	29.72

LAST SEASON: BOWLING

	O.	M.	R.	W.	AV.
TEST					
OTHER FIRST CLASS	220.1	50	668	19	35.16
INT					
J.P.L.	54	1	290	5	58.00
NAT.W.					
B & H	19	2	88	1	–

CAREER: BOWLING

	O.	M.	R.	W.	AV.
TEST					
OTHER FIRST CLASS	5824.1	1562	15065	555	27.14
INT	18	0	93	1	–
J.P.L.	1203.1	75	5562	237	23.46
NAT.W.	292	48	967	38	25.45
B & H	432.4	59	1493	59	25.31

Q. 65. Who is the only Englishman to have made over 400 runs in one first-class innings, and how many exactly for which side, where and when?

MALONE, S.J.

Full Name: Steven John Malone.
Role: Right-hand bat, right arm fast
medium bowler, outfielder.
Born: 19 October 1953, Chelmsford.
Height: 6' 1" **Weight:** 12st.
Nickname: Piggy, Beaker.
County debut: 1980 (Hampshire).
County cap: No.
Test debut: —
No. of Tests: 0.
No. of One-Day Internationals: 0.
1000 runs in a season: 0.
50 wickets in a season: 0.
1st-Class 50s scored: 0.
1st-Class 100s scored: 0.
1st-Class 200s scored: 0.
1st-Class 5 w. in innings: 2.
1st-Class 10 w. in match: 1.
One-day 50s: 0.
One-day 100s: 0.

Place in batting averages: — average: —; (1983: — average: —).
Place in bowling averages: — average: —; (1983: 106 average: 37.44).
1st-Class catches 1984: 2 (career: 11).
Parents: John and Norma Malone.
Wife and date of marriage: Elizabeth, 14 March 1981.
Education: King's School, Ely; St Edmund's Preparatory School, Ipswich.
Qualifications: HNC building construction.
Jobs outside cricket: Salesman and interior designer.
Off season 1984–85: Playing cricket in Pinetown, Natal, South Africa.

LAST SEASON: BATTING

	I.	N.O.	R.	H.S.	AV.
TEST					
OTHER FIRST CLASS	2	0	4	4	2.00
INT					
J.P.L.					
NAT.W.					
B & H					

CAREER: BATTING

	I.	N.O.	R.	H.S.	AV.
TEST					
OTHER FIRST CLASS	40	14	178	23	6.85
INT					
J.P.L.	11	5	16	8*	2.67
NAT.W.	3	3	11	7*	–
B & H	8	4	19	16	4.75

LAST SEASON: BOWLING

	O.	M.	R.	W.	AV.
TEST					
OTHER FIRST CLASS	65	17	204	6	34.00
INT					
J.P.L.	16	0	82	4	20.50
NAT.W.					
B & H	9	3	28	2	14.00

CAREER: BOWLING

	O.	M.	R.	W.	AV.
TEST					
OTHER FIRST CLASS	1091.1	236	3582	105	34.11
INT		.			
J.P.L.	312.5	15	1607	64	25.10
NAT.W.	77.4	23	224	12	18.67
B & H	111	20	359	21	17.09

Equipment used: Gunn and Moore.
Overseas teams played for: Collegians in Durban, South Africa 1981–82; and Pinetown, Natal, 1982–83, 1983–84; 1984–85.
Cricketers particularly learnt from: John Lever at Essex and Peter Sainsbury at Hampshire.
Cricketers particularly admired: "John Lever for his non-stop trying."
Other sports: Football, squash, swimming and golf.
Relaxations: Watching television, listening to music, reading.
Extras: Joined Essex staff for 1978 and 1979 seasons after having played a number of 2nd XI games since 1974. Made 1st XI debut for Essex in 1975 v Cambridge University. Played also in 1978, again v Cambridge University. Released end of 1979 season and joined Hampshire for 1980 season. Equalled Derek Shackleton's record for Hants by taking 10 wickets in a day v Oxford Univ. 13 May 1982. Released by Hampshire at end of 1984 season.
Opinions on cricket: "The game should go back to original times instead of 117 overs per day, and also bring back over rate fines, as some matches were going on until 8.00 p.m."
Best batting performance: 23 Hampshire v Kent, Bournemouth 1981.
Best bowling performance: 7-55 Hampshire v Oxford University, Oxford 1982.

MARSHALL, M.D.

Full Name: Malcolm Denzil Marshall.
Role: Right-hand bat, right arm fast bowler.
Born: 18 April 1958, Barbados.
Height: 5′ 11″ **Weight:** 12st.
Nickname: Denz, Maco, Marshie.
County debut: 1979.
County cap: 1981.
Test debut: 1978–79.
No. of Tests: 31.
No. of One-Day Internationals: 44.
1000 runs in a season: 0.
50 wickets ina season: 4.
1st-Class 50s scored: 12.
1st-Class 100s scored: 4.
1st-Class 200s scored: 0.
1st-Class 5 w. in innings: 0.
1st-Class 10 w. in match: 0.
One-day 50s: 1.
One-day 100s: 0.
Place in batting averages: 262 average: 11.44; (1983: 19 average: 46.92).

Place in bowling averages: 3 average: 16.15; (1983: 3 average: 16.59).
1st-Class catches 1984: 3 (career: 62).
Parents: Mrs. Eleanor Inniss.
Marital status: Single.
Education: Parkinson Comprehensive School, Barbados.
Jobs outside cricket: Promoter of banks products.
Family links with cricket: Cousin plays for Texaco as a fast bowler.
Overseas tours: With West Indies to India and Sri Lanka 1978–79; Australia 1979–80; Pakistan 1980–81, India 1983–84.
Overseas teams played for: Barbados debut 1977–78.
Cricketers particularly learnt from: "The West Indies team."
Other sports: Tennis, basketball, darts, softball cricket.
Relaxations: Soul-music, reggae.
Extras: Took nine wickets in debut match v Glamorgan in May 1979. The fact that it snowed "almost sent him home to the West Indies." Scored his first first-class century (109) in Zimbabwe, October 1981, for the West Indies against Zimbabwe. Most wickets in the Shell Shield Competition (25) by a Barbadian. Broke record of number of wickets taken in 22 match season (i.e. since 1969) with 133. Former record of 131 held by Lance Gibbs for Warwickshire in 1971. Top of Hampshire first-class bowling averages in 1982 and 1983.
Opinions on cricket: "All counties should have a qualified physiotherapist at all games and also training like Warwickshire and Sussex, which will be helpful to the recovery of injured players."
Best batting performance: 116* Hampshire v Lancashire, Southampton 1982.
Best bowling performance: 7-53 West Indies v England, Leeds 1984.

LAST SEASON: BATTING

	I.	N.O.	R.	H.S.	AV.
TEST	5	0	47	29	9.40
OTHER FIRST CLASS	4	0	56	34	14.00
INT	2	0	24	20	12.00
J.P.L.					
NAT.W.					
B & H					

CAREER: BATTING

	I.	N.O.	R.	H.S.	AV.
TEST	38	2	536	92	14.89
OTHER FIRST CLASS	169	22	3469	116*	23.60
INT	26	8	281	56*	15.61
J.P.L.	36	11	486	46	19.44
NAT.W.	6	5	64	21*	–
B & H	13	1	135	21	11.25

LAST SEASON: BOWLING

	O.	M.	R.	W.	AV.
TEST	167.4	50	437	24	18.21
OTHER FIRST CLASS	93	25	209	16	13.06
INT	27	2	88	5	17.60
J.P.L.					
NAT.W.					
B & H					

CAREER: BOWLING

	O.	M.	R.	W.	AV.
TEST	1092.4	236	3117	133	23.44
OTHER FIRST CLASS	3863.5	1131	9849	576	17.10
INT	397	42	1259	58	21.71
J.P.L.	416	55	1324	59	22.44
NAT.W.	113.4	23	288	11	26.18
B & H	161	36	436	23	18.96

MARU, R.G.

Full Name: Rajesh Govind Maru.
Role: Right-hand batsman, slow left
arm spinner, close fielder.
Born: 28 October 1962, Nairobi,
Kenya.
Height: 5′ 6″ **Weight:** 10st. 7lbs.
Nickname: Roland or Raj.
County debut: 1980 (Middlesex);
1984 (Hampshire).
County cap: No.
Test debut: —
No. of Tests: 0.
No. of One-Day Internationals: 0.
1000 runs in a season: 0.
50 wickets in a season: 0.
1st-Class 50s scored: 0.
1st-Class 100s scored: 0.
1st-Class 200s scored: 0.
1st-Class 5 w. in innings: 2.
1st-Class 10 w. in match: 0.
One-day 50s: 0.
One-day 100s: 0.
Place in batting averages: 239 average: 15.38; (1983: — average: —).
Place in bowling averages: 100 average: 35.40; (1983: — average: —).
1st-Class catches 1984: 22 (career: 36).
Parents: Jamnadass and Prabhavati Maru.
Family links with cricket: Brother has played for Middlesex 2nd XI.
Qualifications: Cricket coach.
Jobs outside cricket: Cricket coach.

LAST SEASON: BATTING

	I.	N.O.	R.	H.S.	AV.
TEST					
OTHER FIRST CLASS	20	4	246	36	15.38
INT					
J.P.L.	–	–	–	–	–
NAT.W.					
B & H					

CAREER: BATTING

	I.	N.O.	R.	H.S.	AV.
TEST					
OTHER FIRST CLASS	36	7	393	36	13.55
INT					
J.P.L.	1	1	3	3*	–
NAT.W.					
B & H					

LAST SEASON: BOWLING

	O.	M.	R.	W.	AV.
TEST					
OTHER FIRST CLASS	549.4	129	1664	47	35.40
INT					
J.P.L.	–	–	–	–	–
NAT.W.					
B & H					

CAREER: BOWLING

	O.	M.	R.	W.	AV.
TEST					
OTHER FIRST CLASS	744.4	191	2164	66	32.79
INT					
J.P.L.	8	0	41	2	20.25
NAT.W.					
B & H					

Off-season 1984–85: Kenya.
Cricketing superstitions: Nelsons. 111, 222 and 333.
Equipment used: Duncan Fearnley.
Overseas tours: Young England tour of West Indies 1980, N.C.A. tour of Canada, Barbican International XI to Dubai, Middlesex to Zimbabwe 1980–81.
Cricketers particularly learnt from: Jack Robertson, Derek Underwood, David Graveney, Nick Pocock, Fred Titmus.
Cricketers particularly admired: Derek Underwood, Fred Titmus.
Other sports: "Badminton, table tennis, squash, swimming, hockey and anything else."
Significant injuries in 1984: Hit in the mouth.
Relaxations: Music and wine bars.
Extras: Played for Middlesex 1980–83.
Opinions on cricket: "Get rid of 117 overs a day — too many."
Best batting performance: 36 Hampshire v Sussex, Bournemouth 1984.
Best bowling performance: 7-79 Hampshire v Middlesex, Bournemouth 1984.

MIDDLETON, T.C.

Full Name: Tony Charles Middleton.
Role: Right-hand opening bat, slow left arm bowler.
Born: 1 February 1964, Winchester, Hampshire.
Height: 5′ 10½″ **Weight:** 11st.
Nickname: Roo.
County debut: 1984.
County cap: No.
Test debut: —
No. of Tests: 0.
No. of One-Day Internationals: 0.
1000 runs in a season: 0.
50 wickets in a season: 0.
1st-Class 50s scored: 0.
1st-Class 100s scored: 0.
1st-Class 200s scored: 0.
1st-Class 5 w. in innings: 0.
1st-Class 10 w. in match: 0.
One-day 50s: 0.
One-day 100s: 0.

Place in batting averages: — average: —; (1983: — average: —).
Place in bowling averages: — average: —; (1983: — average: —)
Parents: Peter John and Molly Caroline Middleton.

Marital status: Single.
Education: Weeke County Junior School; Montgomery of Alamein School, Winchester; Peter Symonds Sixth Form College, Winchester.
Qualifications: 5 O-levels, 1 A-level (biology).
Jobs outside cricket: Spent a winter as a domestic appliance engineer.
Off-season 1984–85: Playing club cricket in South Africa.
Cricketing superstitions: Always wears 'good luck' chain.
Equipment used: Gunn & Moore.
Cricketers particularly admired: Barry Richards.
Other sports: Played football and squash at college.
Significant injuries in 1984: Out for six weeks with a broken left hand.
Relaxations: Visiting and going out with friends.
Extras: Played for England Schools 1982.
Opinions on cricket: "Too much first class cricket played. Each county should play every other county once in the championship."
Best batting performance: 10 Hampshire v Kent, Bournemouth 1984.

LAST SEASON: BATTING

	I.	N.O.	R.	H.S.	AV.
TEST					
OTHER FIRST CLASS	2	0	15	10	7.50
INT					
J.P.L.					
NAT.W.					
B & H					

CAREER: BATTING

	I.	N.O.	R.	H.S.	AV.
TEST					
OTHER FIRST CLASS	2	0	15	10	7.50
INT					
J.P.L.					
NAT.W.					
B & H					

LAST SEASON: BOWLING

	O.	M.	R.	W.	AV.
TEST					
OTHER FIRST CLASS					
INT					
J.P.L.					
NAT.W.					
B & H					

CAREER: BOWLING

	O.	M.	R.	W.	AV.
TEST					
OTHER FIRST CLASS					
INT					
J.P.L.					
NAT.W.					
B & H					

Q. 66. What is the longest recorded innings by one batsman in first-class cricket? Who made it, when and where?

Q. 67. More than 100 cricketers have scored over 300 runs in one first-class innings. True or false?

NICHOLAS, M.C.J.

Full Name: Mark Charles Jefford
Nicholas.
Role: Right-hand bat, right arm
fast medium bowler.
Born: 29 September 1957, London.
Height: 5' 11½" **Weight:** 12st. 7lbs.
Nickname: Albert, Busby, M.C.J.
County debut: 1978.
County cap: 1982.
Test debut: —
No. of Tests: 0.
No. of One-Day Internationals: 0.
1000 runs in a season: 3.
50 wickets in a season: 0.
1st-Class 50s scored: 25.
1st-Class 100s scored: 12.
1st-Class 200s scored: 1.
1st-Class 5 w. in innings: 1.
1st-Class 10 w. in match: 0.
One-day 50s: 10.
One-day 100s: 1.
Place in batting averages: 87 average: 33.89; (1983: 66 average: 37.32).
Place in bowling averages: — average: —; (1983: 59 average: 28.67).
1st-Class catches 1984: 15 (career: 76).
Parents: Anne Nicholas.
Marital status: Single.
Education: Fernden Prep. School; Bradfield College.
Qualifications: Three A-levels, eight O-levels.
Jobs outside cricket: Worked in Classified Advertising for the *Observer*; sales
for agencies; writing for papers and magazines; P.R.; publishing.
Family links with cricket: Grandfather played for Essex as batsman and
wicket-keeper and toured with the M.C.C.
Overseas tours: Toured South Africa with Dragons (Public Schools team)
1976–77 as Captain. With M.C.C. to Bangladesh, February 1981; with
M.C.C. to East and Central Africa October 1981. Dubai with Cricketer
International XI, November 1981 and Dubai and Bahrain with "England XI",
March 1981.
Overseas teams played for: Captain of Southern Lakes in Australia 1978–79
and Grosvenor/Fynnland Durban 1982–83, 1983–84.
Cricketing superstitions: "Kit and clothing must fit."
Cricketers particularly learnt from: Barry Richards, Mike Brearley, Graham
Gooch.
Off-season 1984–85: Publishing and P.R. with Hampshire.
Equipment used: Duncan Fearnley, and Adidas clothing.

Other sports: Regular football with Old Bradfieldians (Arthurian League).

Relaxations: Theatre, contemporary music, writing, Spurs, golf, Richmond Rugby Club.

Significant injuries in 1984: Missed one game with thigh muscle tear. Constant back problem prevents bowling.

Extras: Scored 155 not out before lunch in 2nd XI match v Hants Cricket League at the start of the 1980 season. Appointed captain 1984.

Opinions on cricket: "Our problems are self-inflicted. Banning of 'rebels', 40 overs cricket ruins technique. We play too much, so too mediocre."

Best batting performance: 206* Hampshire v Oxford University, Oxford 1982.

Best bowling performance: 5-45 Hampshire v Worcestershire, Southampton 1983.

LAST SEASON: BATTING

	I.	N.O.	R.	H.S.	AV.
TEST					
OTHER FIRST CLASS	48	2	1559	158	33.89
INT					
J.P.L.	15	2	558	108	42.92
NAT.W.	2	0	71	63	35.50
B & H	4	1	117	49	39.00

CAREER: BATTING

	I.	N.O.	R.	H.S.	AV.
TEST					
OTHER FIRST CLASS	208	25	6003	206*	32.80
INT					
J.P.L.	61	8	1418	108	26.75
NAT.W.	13	1	280	63	23.33
B & H	19	1	349	49	19.39

LAST SEASON: BOWLING

	O.	M.	R.	W.	AV.
TEST					
OTHER FIRST CLASS	129	23	438	7	62.57
INT					
J.P.L.	69.3	0	368	9	40.89
NAT.W.	19	5	66	1	–
B & H	28	1	140	2	70.00

CAREER: BOWLING

	O.	M.	R.	W.	AV.
TEST					
OTHER FIRST CLASS	427.4	97	1297	36	36.03
INT					
J.P.L.	139.3	1	742	26	28.53
NAT.W.	24.2	5	91	2	45.50
B & H	74	4	310	10	31.00

Q. 68. What is the highest score ever recorded by one batsman in one innings?

Q. 69. What have A.W. Lilley (Essex), D.G. Aslett (Kent) and M.D. Moxon (Yorkshire) in common?

PARKS, R.J.

Full Name: Robert James Parks.
Role: Right-hand bat, wicket-keeper.
Born: 15 June 1959, Cuckfield,
Sussex.
Height: 5' 7¾" **Weight:** 10st.
Nickname: Bobby.
County debut: 1980.
County cap: 1982.
Test debut: —
No. of Tests: 0.
No. of One-Day Internationals: 0.
1000 runs in a season: 0.
50 wickets in a season: 0.
1st-Class 50s scored: 5.
1st-Class 100s scored: 0.
1st-Class 200s scored: 0.
1st-Class 5 w. in innings: 0.
1st-Class 10 w. in match: 0.
One-day 50s: 0.
One-day 100s: 0.
Place in batting averages: 221 average: 17.76; (1983: 220 average: 13.85).
Place in bowling averages: — average: —; (1983: — average: —)
Education: Eastbourne Grammar School; Southampton Institute of Technology.
Qualifications: 9 O-levels, 1 A-level, O.N.D. and H.N.D. in Business Studies.
Family links with cricket: Father, Jim Parks, played for Sussex and England,
as did his grandfather, J.H. Parks. Uncle, H.W. Parks, also played for Sussex.
Jobs outside cricket: Training in accountancy.
Off-season 1984–85: Working for Jardine Air Cargo.

LAST SEASON: BATTING

	I.	N.O.	R.	H.S.	AV.
TEST					
OTHER FIRST CLASS	34	9	444	89	17.76
INT					
J.P.L.	5	4	16	6*	–
NAT.W.	2	1	30	25	–
B & H	3	2	18	11*	–

CAREER: BATTING

	I.	N.O.	R.	H.S.	AV.
TEST					
OTHER FIRST CLASS	121	27	1537	89	16.35
INT					
J.P.L.	27	14	268	36*	20.61
NAT.W.	6	2	55	25	13.75
B & H	13	3	6	11*	6.80

LAST SEASON: WICKET KEEPING

	C.	ST.			
TEST					
OTHER FIRST CLASS	61	10			
INT					
J.P.L.	13	4			
NAT.W.	2	–			
B & H	4	–			

CAREER: WICKET KEEPING

	C.	ST.			
TEST					
OTHER FIRST CLASS	243	33			
INT					
J.P.L.	74	15			
NAT.W.	15	1			
B & H	17	3			

Cricketing superstitions: Left pad on first.
Cricketers particularly learnt from: A. Knott, J. Rice.
Cricketers particularly admired: R. Taylor, N. Pocock.
Other sports: Squash, football.
Relaxations: Backgammon and reading.
Extras: Broke the Hampshire record for the number of dismissals in a match, against Derbyshire in 1982 (10 catches).
Opinions on cricket: "An effort should be made to liaise with the football Association in order to curtail the increased overlapping of their season into ours."
Best batting performance: 89 Hampshire v Cambridge University, Cambridge 1984.

POCOCK, N.E.J.

Full Name: Nicholas Edward Julian Pocock.
Role: Right-hand bat, left arm medium bowler.
Born: 15 December 1951, Maracaibo, Venezuela.
Height: 6′ 1″ **Weight:** 13st 7lbs.
Nickname: Pokers.
County debut: 1976.
County cap: 1980.
Test debut: —
No. of Tests: 0.
No. of One-Day Internationals: 0.
1000 runs in a season: 0.
50 wickets in a season: 0.
1st-Class 50s scored: 18.
1st-Class 100s scored: 2.
1st-Class 200s scored: 0.
1st-Class 5 w. in innings: 0.
1st-Class 10 w. in match: 0.
One-day 50s: 3.
One-day 100s: 0.
Place in batting averages: 203 average: 19.63; (1983: 111 average: 27.96).
Place in bowling averages: — average: —; (1983: — average: —).
1st-Class catches 1984: 13 (career: 124).
Parents: Carmichael Charles Peter Pocock, deceased, and Nina Alice Hilary.
Wife and date of marriage: Gina Mary, 11 September 1976.
Children: Emma Mary, 10 July 1979, Matthew Robert Carmichael 25 November 1981.
Education: Sandroyd School, near Salisbury, Wiltshire; Shrewsbury School.

Qualifications: Insurance A.C.I.I. exams. Three A-levels, seven O-levels.
Jobs outside cricket: Insurance with Holmwoods & Back & Manson (Schools) Ltd., working for Colin Ingleby-Mackenzie.
Family links with cricket: Father and Uncle played for Rossall School 1st XI. Uncle, Duncan Pocock, played for the Army after the war.
Overseas tours: M.C.C. tour to Far East (Hong Kong, Bangkok, Singapore) October–November 1981.
Cricketers particularly learnt from: A.C.D. Ingleby-Mackenzie, R.M.C. Gilliat.
Equipment used: Gray-Nicolls.
Other sports: Squash, tennis, Eton fives, follow National Hunt racing.
Relaxations: Music (Jackson Brown, Springstein, Meat Loaf, Stevie Nicks etc.), family.
Extras: Five years in Shrewsbury School cricket XI. Scored 60 not out in his first match, v Uppingham. Writes weekly cricket article for Evening Echo. Retired during 1984 season.
Best batting performance: 164 Hampshire v Lancashire, Southampton 1982.

LAST SEASON: BATTING

	I.	N.O.	R.	H.S.	AV.
TEST					
OTHER FIRST CLASS	18	2	314	55	19.63
INT					
J.P.L.	5	4	115	48*	–
NAT.W.	2	1	35	33*	–
B & H	3	0	51	25	17.00

CAREER: BATTING

	I.	N.O.	R.	H.S.	AV.
TEST					
OTHER FIRST CLASS	186	22	3790	164	23.11
INT					
J.P.L.	59	20	889	53*	22.79
NAT.W.	14	6	261	73*	32.63
B & H	17	1	196	43*	12.25

LAST SEASON: BOWLING

	O.	M.	R.	W.	AV.
TEST					
OTHER FIRST CLASS	11	1	61	0	–
INT					
J.P.L.					
NAT.W.					
B & H					

CAREER: BOWLING

	O.	M.	R.	W.	AV.
TEST					
OTHER FIRST CLASS	63.2	18	258	3	86.00
INT					
J.P.L.	1	0	1	0	–
NAT.W.					
B & H	2	0	8	0	–

Q. 70. W.G. Grace never scored a century abroad. True or false?

Q. 71. What cricketer has scored two first-class hundreds in the same match the most times?

REIFER, E.L.

Full Name: Elvis Leroy Reifer.
Role: Left-hand bat, left arm fast
medium bowler. Fields gully or any-
where close.
Born: 21 March 1961, St George,
Barbados.
Height: 6′ 2″ **Weight:** 12st. 7lbs.
Nickname: Carew, Fruit, Joe.
County debut: 1984.
County cap: No.
Test debut: —
No. of Tests: 0.
No. of One-Day Internationals: 0.
1000 runs in a season: 0.
50 wickets in a season: 0.
1st-Class 50s scored: 0.
1st-Class 100s scored: 0.
1st-Class 200s scored: 0.
1st-Class 5 w. in innings: 2.
1st-Class 10 w. in match: 0.
One-day 50s: 0.
One-day 100s: 0.

Place in batting averages: 202 average: 19.83; (1983: — average: —).
Place in bowling averages: 101 average: 35.94; (1983: — average: —).
1st-Class catches 1984: 6 (career: 6).
Parents: Mrs. Eulene Reifer.
Marital status: Single.
Children: Dwayne Leroy, 2 October 1980.
Family links with cricket: Brothers Errol and Tony played for Barbados Colts,
Leslie and twin George both played for Barbados and West Indies Youth team,
and three others played club cricket.
Education: St George's Boys' School; St George's Secondary School; S.J.
Prescod Polytechnic; Barbados Community College.
Qualifications: 5 O-levels; 1 A-level; City and Guild O.T.D. in Building and
Civil Engineering and Construction.
Jobs outside cricket: Architectural Draughtsman, Building Technician.
Off-season 1984– 85: Working and playing club cricket in Barbados.
Equipment used: Duncan Fearnley.
Overseas teams played for: Combined Schools, Barbados 1979; Pickwick
1980 until present (Barbados).
Cricketers particularly learnt from: Brothers, Seymore Nurse.
Cricketers particularly admired: Malcolm Marshall, Laurance Rowe.
Other sports: Football, volley ball; watches hockey.

Significant injuries in 1984: Shin soreness and strained muscles in the back and right side.

Relaxations: Listening to music, watching good movies, going to beach and also bird watching.

Opinions on cricket: County cricketers play too much cricket. Also the minimum of 117 overs required to be bowled in one day is too much, soon players will be asking for an overtime clause in their contracts.

Best batting performance: 47 Hampshire v Somerset, Southampton 1984.

Best bowling performance: 4-43 Hampshire v Cambridge University, Cambridge 1984.

LAST SEASON: BATTING

	I.	N.O.	R.	H.S.	AV.
TEST					
OTHER FIRST CLASS	26	8	357	47	19.83
INT					
J.P.L.	8	4	28	10*	7.00
NAT.W.	2	0	7	6	3.50
B & H	3	1	34	14*	17.00

CAREER: BATTING

	I.	N.O.	R.	H.S.	AV.
TEST					
OTHER FIRST CLASS	26	8	357	47	19.83
INT					
J.P.L.	8	4	28	10*	7.00
NAT.W.	2	0	7	6	3.50
B & H	3	1	34	14*	17.00

LAST SEASON: BOWLING

	O.	M.	R.	W.	AV.
TEST					
OTHER FIRST CLASS	524.5	100	1761	49	35.94
INT					
J.P.L.	70.3	2	347	8	43.38
NAT.W.	21	4	77	5	15.40
B & H	36.2	8	122	6	20.33

CAREER: BOWLING

	O.	M.	R.	W.	AV.
TEST					
OTHER FIRST CLASS	524.5	100	1761	49	35.94
INT					
J.P.L.	70.3	2	347	8	43.38
NAT.W.	21	4	77	5	15.40
B & H	36.2	8	122	6	20.33

Q. 72. Who has scored the most first-class hundreds?

Q. 73. Who is the only player to score two first-class double centuries in the same match, where and when?

Q. 74. What is the only occasion on which father and son both hit first-class centuries in the same innings?

Q. 75. What is the longest recorded hit of a cricket ball without bouncing?

SMITH, C.L.

Full Name: Christopher Lyall Smith.
Role: Right-hand bat.
Born: 15 October 1958, Durban, South Africa.
Height: 5' 11" **Weight:** 12st 12lbs.
Nickname: Kippy.
County debut: 1980 (Hampshire).
County cap: 1981.
Test debut: 1983.
No. of Tests: 7.
No. of One-Day Internationals: 4.
1000 runs in a season: 3.
50 wickets in a season: 0.
1st-Class 50s scored: 28.
1st-Class 100s scored: 18.
1st-Class 200s scored: 0.
1st-Class 5 w. in innings: 0.
1st-Class 10 w. in match: 0.
One-day 50s: 18.
One-day 100s: 1.
Place in batting averages: 133 average: 28.21; (1983: 12 average 53.42).
Place in bowling averages: — average: —; (1983: 79 average: 32.18).
1st-Class catches 1984: 13 (career: 69).
Parents: John Arnold and Elaine Jessie Smith.
Marital status: Single.
Education: Northlands High School, Durban, South Africa.
Qualifications: Matriculation (2 A-level equivalents).
Jobs outside cricket: Sales representative for horse-racing company.
Family links with cricket: Grandfather, Vernon Lyall Shearer, played for Natal, brother Robin, also plays for Hampshire.
Overseas tours: Toured U.K. with Kingsmead Mynahs (Natal under-25s under another name) 1976; with England to New Zealand and Pakistan 1983–84.
Overseas teams played for: Kingsmead Mynahs; Natal Schools 1975; South African Schools 1976; Natal B debut 1978.
Off-season 1984–85: Commercial work with Hampshire.
Cricketers particularly admired: Barry Richards, Graeme Pollock.
Equipment used: Gray-Nicolls and Adidas.
Other sports: League squash, golf (handicap 5).
Relaxations: "Bathing on Durban beaches in free time." Soul, jazz, reggae.
Extras: Made debut for Glamorgan in 1979, leaving to join Gorseinon Hampshire at end of season. Made Hampshire debut 1980. Played for Gorseinon in South Wales League in 1979. Became eligible to play for England in 1983. Captained Hampshire 2nd XI in 1981.

Opinions on cricket: "I feel that the counties should play each other once and that the games should be played over 4 days, Monday to Thursday with Friday off– Saturday either a Benson and Hedges game or NatWest fixture, and Sunday should remain John Player. Also feel that the game is not marketed properly. It could probably learn from some of the South African or Australian marketing men who promote games in those countries. I feel that each county should have a highly motivated sales personnel (apart from secretaries) to sell the game. So much money could be made and so many companies exploited to make money for the county game but it is not being done. Players should be able and allowed to sell themselves, i.e. by wearing advertising when playing. I do agree that it should only be allowed to be a certain size. Counties should be allowed to play 2 overseas players. It will raise the general standard of play by having other Test players involved and will therefore raise the standard of the English players. Also there are too many arm-chair critics on the game – particularly in South Africa. I find that sort of person unbearable."

Best batting performance: 193 Hampshire v Derbyshire, Derby 1983.

Best bowling performance: 3-35 Hampshire v Glamorgan, Southampton 1983.

LAST SEASON: BATTING

	I.	N.O.	R.	H.S.	AV.
TEST					
OTHER FIRST CLASS	49	3	1298	125	28.21
INT					
J.P.L.	16	4	720	95	60.00
NAT.W.	2	0	6	4	3.00
B & H	4	1	114	82*	38.00

CAREER: BATTING

	I.	N.O.	R.	H.S.	AV.
TEST	12	1	358	91	32.55
OTHER FIRST CLASS	193	20	6566	193	37.95
INT	4	0	109	70	27.25
J.P.L.	44	4	1592	95	39.80
NAT.W.	8	2	231	101*	38.50
B & H	11	2	295	82*	32.78

LAST SEASON: BOWLING

	O.	M.	R.	W.	AV.
TEST					
OTHER FIRST CLASS	158	19	687	9	76.33
INT					
J.P.L.	3.3	1	10	2	5.00
NAT.W.					
B & H					

CAREER: BOWLING

	O.	M.	R.	W.	AV.
TEST	17	4	39	3	13.00
OTHER FIRST CLASS	438	74	1608	28	57.43
INT	6	0	28	2	14.00
J.P.L.	3.3	1	10	2	5.00
NAT.W.					
B & H					

Q. 76. It is a curious fact that the most number of runs hit off a 6-ball over is greater than the most hit off an 8-ball over. True or false?

SMITH, R.A.

Full Name: Robin Arnold Smith.
Role: Right-hand bat.
Born: 13 September 1963,
Durban, South Africa.
Height: 5′ 11½″ **Weight:** 15st.
Nickname: Judge.
County debut: 1982.
County cap: No.
Test debut: —
No. of Tests: 0.
No. of One-Day Internationals: 0.
1000 runs in a season: 0.
50 wickets in a season: 0.
1st-Class 50s scored: 9.
1st-Class 100s scored: 4.
1st-Class 200s scored: 0.
1st-Class 5 w. in innings: 0.
1st-Class 10 w. in match: 0.
One-day 50s: 1.
One-day 100s: 1.
Place in batting averages: 25 average: 48.30; (1983: 16 average: 48.22).
Place in bowling averages: — average: —; (1983: — average: —).
1st-Class catches 1984: 4 (career: 13).
Parents: John Arnold and Joy Lyall Smith.
Marital status: Single.
Education: Clifton Primary School; Northlands Boys High, Durban.
Qualifications: "Highly qualified with regard to my educational studies."
Jobs outside cricket: Horse-racing company.
Off-season 1984–85: Playing for Natal and coaching in Durban, South Africa.
Family links with cricket: Grandfather played for Natal in Currie Cup.
Brother Chris plays for Hampshire, Natal and England.
Cricket superstitions: "Always have a big night out before a game."
Overseas teams played for: Natal B: 1980–81; Natal A: 1981–82.
Cricketers particularly admired: Barry Richards, Viv Richards, Graeme
Pollock.
Equipment used: Gray-Nicolls.
Other sports: Rugby; athletics (Junior Springbok Athletics).
Significant injuries in 1984: Operation on left hand caused him to miss the
start of the season.
Extras: Played rugby for Natal Schools, 1980. South Africa Schools Cricket,
1979–80. Still holds South African shot-putt and hurdles Under-19 records.
Opinions on cricket: "I would like to see the 4-day game introduced into
English county cricket."
Best batting performance: 132 Hampshire v Sri Lanka, Southampton 1984.

LAST SEASON: BATTING

	I.	N.O.	R.	H.S.	AV.
TEST					
OTHER FIRST CLASS	13	3	483	132	48.30
INT					
J.P.L.	6	0	181	104	30.17
NAT.W.					
B & H					

CAREER: BATTING

	I.	N.O.	R.	H.S.	AV.
TEST					
OTHER FIRST CLASS	62	11	1895	132	37.16
INT					
J.P.L.	8	1	216	104	30.86
NAT.W.					
B & H	1	0	9	9	–

LAST SEASON: BOWLING

	O.	M.	R.	W.	AV.
TEST					
OTHER FIRST CLASS					
INT					
J.P.L.					
NAT.W.					
B & H					

CAREER: BOWLING

	O.	M.	R.	W.	AV.
TEST					
OTHER FIRST CLASS	4	0	30	0	–
INT					
J.P.L.					
NAT.W.					
B & H					

TERRY, V.P.

Full Name: Vivian Paul Terry.
Role: Right-hand bat; right arm medium bowler, slip or cover fielder.
Born: 14 January 1959, Osnabruck, West Germany.
Height: 6' 0" **Weight:** 12st. 6lbs.
County debut: 1978.
County cap: 1983.
Test debut: 1984.
No. of Tests: 2.
No. of One-Day Internationals: 0.
1000 runs in a season: 2.
50 wickets in a season: 0.
1st-Class 50s scored: 11.
1st-Class 100s scored: 8.
1st-Class 200s scored: 0.
1st-Class 5 w. in innings: 0.
1st-Class 10 w. in match: 0.
One-day 50s: 4.

One-day 100s: 2.
Place in batting averages: 24 average: 48.32; (1983: 46 average: 40.59).
Place in bowling averages: — average: —; (1983: — average: —).
1st-Class catches 1984: 17 (career: 41).
Parents: Michael and Patricia Terry.
Marital status: Single.

Education: Durlston Court, Barton-on-Sea, Hampshire; Millfield School, Somerset.
Qualifications: 1 A-level, 8 O-levels.
Off-season 1984–85: Coaching cricket and squash.
Overseas tours: E.S.C.A. tour to India 1977–78, Gordon Greenidge, benefit tour to Paris and Isle of Wight.
Overseas teams played for: "Played in Sydney 1978–79 and in New Zealand 1980–81."
Equipment used: Duncan Fearnley.
Cricketers particularly learnt from: Chris Smith.
Cricketers particularly admired: Robin Smith, Gordon Greenidge.
Other sports: Golf, squash, soccer.
Significant injuries in 1984: Broken arm in Test caused absence from rest of season.
Relaxations: Music, sleeping.
Best batting performance: 175* Hampshire v Gloucestershire, Bristol 1984.

LAST SEASON: BATTING

	I.	N.O.	R.	H.S.	AV.
TEST	3	0	16	8	5.33
OTHER FIRST CLASS	25	3	1192	175*	48.32
INT					
J.P.L.	8	0	335	110	41.88
NAT.W.	2	0	50	50	25.00
B & H	4	0	166	72	41.50

CAREER: BATTING

	I.	N.O.	R.	H.S.	AV.
TEST	3	0	16	8	5.33
OTHER FIRST CLASS	87	13	2657	175*	35.91
INT					
J.P.L.	45	10	964	110	27.54
NAT.W.	7	0	91	50	13.00
B & H	11	0	295	72	26.82

LAST SEASON: BOWLING

	O.	M.	R.	W.	AV.
TEST					
OTHER FIRST CLASS					
INT					
J.P.L.					
NAT.W.					
B & H					

CAREER: BOWLING

	O.	M.	R.	W.	AV.
TEST					
OTHER FIRST CLASS	13.5	4	39	0	–
INT					
J.P.L.					
NAT.W.					
B & H					

Q. 77. Who scored the most first-class runs in one day, where, for whom and when?

Q. 78. Which first-class player has done the most hat-tricks and how many?

Q. 79. Who took the most first-class wickets ever in one season?

TREMLETT, T.M.

Full Name: Timothy Maurice Tremlett.
Role: Right-hand bat; right arm medium bowler.
Born: 26 July 1956, Wellington, Somerset.
Height: 6′ 2″ **Weight:** 13st.7lbs.
Nickname: Hurricane, Trooper, R2.
County debut: 1976.
County cap: 1983.
Test debut: —
No. of Tests: 0.
No. of One-Day Internationals: 0.
1000 runs in a season: 0.
50 wickets in a season: 2.
1st-Class 50s scored: 15.
1st-Class 100s scored: 0.
1st-Class 200s scored: 0.
1st-Class 5 w. in innings: 5.
1st-Class 10 w. in match: 0.
One-day 50s: 0.
One-day 100s: 0.
Place in batting averages: 211 average: 18.25; (1983: 188 average: 18.79).
Place in bowling averages: 7 average: 20.34; (1983: 14 average: 21.37).
1st-Class catches 1984: 4 (career: 51).
Parents: Maurice Fletcher and Melina May Tremlett.
Wife and date of marriage: Carolyn Patricia, 28 September 1979.
Children: Christopher Timothy, 2 September 1981; Alastair Jonathan, 1 February 1983; Benjamin Paul, 2 May 1984.
Education: Shirley Infants' School; Bellemoor Secondary Modern; Richard Taunton Sixth Form College.
Qualifications: 1 A-level, 5 O-levels. Advanced coaching certificate.
Jobs outside cricket: "One winter spent labouring on building site for muscle-building (did not seem to work)." Furrier.
Family links with cricket: Father played for Somerset and England 1947–48 against West Indies in the West Indies. Captained Somerset 1958–60. Younger brother plays in local club cricket for Deanery C.C.
Overseas teams played for: Oudtshoorn Teachers' Training College, Western Cape, South Africa 1978–79.
Cricketers particularly learnt from: "My father, and in general watching and listening to other cricketers, first-class or club players."
Cricketers particularly admired: Vincent Van der Bijl, Mike Hendrick.
Cricket superstitions: "I always like to be the last to leave the dressing room when taking the field. However, due to a run of defeats in 1980, nobody seemed

too keen on taking the field."

Other sports: Golf, (handicap 7), table-tennis, squash, swimming and badminton.

Relaxations: Collecting cricket books, record collecting, gardening, cinema.

Significant injuries in 1984: "Sore feet!! Torn knee ligaments at end of August."

Extras: Member of local cricket club, Deanery. Batted in almost every position for Hants in batting order from 1 to 11 in 1979. Hampshire C.C.C. colleague, John Southern, was best man at his wedding. Captained both his school and sixth-form college at cricket.

Opinions on cricket: I think it would be a good idea to give sides points, if they lose so many hours (through rain), during a county championship match. They might be awarded points:–

There are 19 hours cricket possible each match. For losing the full 3 days,– 4 points.

Example 1.

15 hours – 1 point, 16 hours – 2 points etc.

Example 2.

10 or 11 hours – 1 point, 12 or 13 hours – 2 points, 14 or 15 hours – 3 points etc.

I realise the weather is all part of the game, but some counties, e.g. Gloucestershire 1981, lose a lot more time than others. Perhaps these extra points, just over one fifth of the total in a match, would help to counter any unfavourable geographical position. Futhermore, is it not time for neutral umpires in Test matches?

Best bowling performance: 88 Hampshire v Lancashire, Old Trafford 1981.

Best bowling performance: 6-82 Hampshire v Derbyshire, Portsmouth 1983.

LAST SEASON: BATTING

	I.	N.O.	R.	H.S.	AV.
TEST					
OTHER FIRST CLASS	31	7	438	74	18.25
INT					
J.P.L.	9	5	67	35	16.75
NAT.W.	2	0	20	17	10.00
B & H	1	0	17	17	–

CAREER: BATTING

	I.	N.O.	R.	H.S.	AV.
TEST					
OTHER FIRST CLASS	151	25	2516	88	19.97
INT					
J.P.L.	39	15	245	35	10.21
NAT.W.	10	1	63	17	7.00
B & H	14	3	128	29	11.64

LAST SEASON: BOWLING

	O.	M.	R.	W.	AV.
TEST					
OTHER FIRST CLASS	669.5	210	1444	71	20.34
INT					
J.P.L.	110.5	2	525	17	30.88
NAT.W.	22	4	68	4	17.00
B & H	43	8	138	5	27.60

CAREER: BOWLING

	O.	M.	R.	W.	AV.
TEST					
OTHER FIRST CLASS	2199.2	674	5031	214	23.51
INT					
J.P.L.	542.4	28	2451	86	28.90
NAT.W.	131.2	24	393	15	26.20
B & H	197	34	598	25	23.92

TURNER, D.R.

Full Name: David Roy Turner.
Role: Left-hand bat, right arm
medium bowler, cover fielder.
Born: 5 February 1949, Corsham,
near Chippenham, Wiltshire.
Height: 5' 6" **Weight:** 11st 8lbs.
Nickname: Birdy, Fossil.
County debut: 1966.
County cap: 1970.
Test debut: —
No. of Tests: 0.
No. of One-Day Internationals: 0.
Benefit: £23,011 in 1981.
1000 runs in a season: 7.

50 wickets in a season: 0.
1st-Class 50s scored: 69.
1st-Class 100s scored: 24.
1st-Class 200s scored: 0.
1st-Class 5 w. in innings: 0.
1st-Class 10 w. in match: 0.
One-day 50s: 50.
One-day 100s: 3.
Place in batting averages: 45 average: 41.36; (1983: 37 average: 42.72).
Place in bowling averages: — average: —; (1983: — average: —).
1st-Class catches 1984: 7 (career: 172).
Parents: Robert Edward and Evelyn Peggy Turner.
Wife and date of marriage: Henriette, 18 February 1977.
Children: Nicola Marianna, 15 March 1984.
Education: Chippenham Boys' High School.
Qualifications: O-levels.
Jobs outside cricket: Player-coach for the Paarl C.C., South Africa 1972–80, 1982–85.
Overseas tours: With Derrick Robins XI to South Africa 1972–73.
Overseas teams played for: Played for Western Province in the winning 1977–78 Currie Cup Competition side.
Cricketers particularly learnt from: Roy Marshall.
Cricketers particularly admired: Mike Procter.
Off-season 1984–85: Player-coach Paarl C.C., South Africa.
Cricket records: Shared in an unbeaten partnership of 283 with C.G. Greenidge, a record in any one-day competition. Benson & Hedges Cup, Hampshire v Minor Counties South at Amersham in 1973.
Equipment used: Stuart Surridge.
Other sports: Golf, football.
Relaxations: Chess, gardening, reading, television, watching war films.

Significant injuries in 1984: Pulled leg muscle.

Extras: Played for Wiltshire in 1965. Took a hat-trick in a Lambert & Butler 7-a-side floodlit tournament at Ashton Gate (Bristol) on 17 September 1981 against Glamorgan. "One of the great out-fielders of modern cricket"– Gordon Greenidge. Captained his school at soccer, rugger and cricket.

Opinions on cricket: "I would like the cricket authorities to try for one season, 16 4-day Championship matches, coupled with a Saturday 60-overs limited cricket league, along with the usual Sunday John Player League. The 117 overs a day rule should be scrapped and there should be tighter controls on overseas players."

Best batting performance: 181* Hampshire v Surrey, The Oval 1969.

LAST SEASON: BATTING

	I.	N.O.	R.	H.S.	AV.
TEST					
OTHER FIRST CLASS	37	4	1365	153	41.36
INT					
J.P.L.	14	1	511	114	39.31
NAT.W.	2	0	21	20	10.50
B & H	3	0	130	50	43.33

CAREER: BATTING

	I.	N.O.	R.	H.S.	AV.
TEST					
OTHER FIRST CLASS	581	53	15435	181*	29.23
INT					
J.P.L.	197	18	5254	114	29.35
NAT.W.	28	2	712	86	27.38
B & H	54	8	1602	123*	34.83

LAST SEASON: BOWLING

	O.	M.	R.	W.	AV.
TEST					
OTHER FIRST CLASS	5	1	9	0	–
INT					
J.P.L.	1	0	5	0	–
NAT.W.					
B & H					

CAREER: BOWLING

	O.	M.	R.	W.	AV.
TEST					
OTHER FIRST CLASS	96.4	26	332	9	36.89
INT					
J.P.L.	1.3	0	11	0	–
NAT.W.					
B & H	0.2	0	4	0	–

COUNTY QUIZ

Q. 1. When was the club founded?

Q. 2. Who made the most first-class runs for the county last season, and how many?

Q. 3. What's the highest ever county total, and against whom?

Q. 4. Who took most wickets for the county last season, and how many?

Q. 5. What's the highest individual score for the county, who hit it, and when?

Q. 6. What's the highest scoring partnership for the county for any wicket?

Q. 7. How many times has the club won the County Championship?

Q. 8. What's the lowest ever total made by the county in one innings, when, and against whom?

Q. 9. Which bowler took the most first-class wickets in one season, when, and how many?

Q. 10. Which batsman hit the most runs in one season, when and how many?

Kent

ALDERMAN, T.M.

Full Name: Terence Michael
Alderman.
Role: Right-hand bat, right arm
bowler.
Born: 12 June 1956, Perth, Western
Australia.
Height: 6′ 3″ **Weight:** 13st 7lbs.
Nickname: Clem.
County debut: 1984.
County cap: No.
Test debut: 1981.
No. of Tests: 19.
No. of One-Day Internationals: 18.
1000 runs in a season: 0.
50 wickets in a season: 1.
1st-Class 50s scored: 1.
1st-Class 100s scored: 0.
1st-Class 200s scored: 0.
1st-Class 5 w. in innings: 0.
1st-Class 10 w. in match: 0.
One-day 50s: 0.

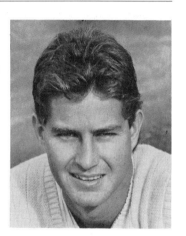

One-day 100s: 0.
Place in batting averages: 234 average: 15.72; (1983: — average: —).
Place in bowling averages: 18 average: 22.69; (1983: — average: —).
1st-Class catches 1984: 29 (career: 100).
Parents: William and Joan Alderman.
Wife and date of marriage: Jane Elizabeth, 1977.
Family links with cricket: Grandfather umpire; father W.A. colts team; sister
Australian ladies.
Education: Aquinas College, Perth; Churchlands College of Advanced
Education.
Qualifications: Teacher's Certificate.
Jobs outside cricket: Corporate officer for Town and Country W.A. Building
Society (Perth).
Off-season 1984-85: Playing for W.A. and Australia.

Equipment used: Symonds.
Equipment endorsed: Adidas.
Overseas teams played for: Watsonians (Scotland) 1980 and Western Australia.
Cricketers particularly learnt from: Dennis Lillee.
Other sports: Golf, Aussie rules football, squash. Watch all sports.
Significant injuries in 1984: Hamstring injury.
Relaxations: Antique hunting, old cars, golf, wine.
Extras: Played one season for Kent while Eldine Baptiste was on West Indies tour of England. Would have played for Worcestershire in 1983 had not been injured.
Best batting performance: 52* Sussex v Kent, Hastings 1984.
Best bowling performance: 7-28 W. Australia v New South Wales, Perth 1981-82.

LAST SEASON: BATTING

	I.	N.O.	R.	H.S.	AV.
TEST					
OTHER FIRST CLASS	27	13	220	52*	15.72
INT					
J.P.L.	5	4	21	11	–
NAT.W.					
B & H	2	1	4	4*	–

CAREER: BATTING

	I.	N.O.	R.	H.S.	AV.
TEST	27	14	79	21*	6.08
OTHER FIRST CLASS	94	47	458	52*	9.74
INT	7	3	19	9*	4.75
J.P.L.	5	4	21	11	–
NAT.W.					
B & H	2	1	4	4*	–

LAST SEASON: BOWLING

	O.	M.	R.	W.	AV.
TEST					
OTHER FIRST CLASS	559.4	149	1725	76	22.69
INT					
J.P.L.	105	9	477	21	22.71
NAT.W.	57	10	222	10	22.20
B & H	40	7	113	7	16.14

CAREER: BOWLING

	O.	M.	R.	W.	AV.
TEST	796.4	171	2258	70	32.26
OTHER FIRST CLASS	952.2 1503.1	176 389	7748	344	22.52
INT	170	27	598	25	23.92
J.P.L.	105	9	477	21	22.71
NAT.W.	57	10	222	10	22.20
B & H	40	7	113	7	16.14

Q. 80. When was the last time a bowler took 200 wickets in a season? Who was it?

Q. 81. Who has taken 100 first-class wickets in a season most times?

Q. 82. Which cricketer scored 111 in the first innings of a first-class county game, 117 n.o. in the second; took six for 70 in the first innings and five for 45 in the second, for whom, against whom, where and when?

ASLETT, D.G.

Full Name: Derek George Aslett.
Role: Right-hand bat, leg-break
bowler.
Born: 12 February, 1958, Dover.
Height: 6' **Weight:** 12st.
Nickname: Spacko and variations.
County debut: 1981.
County cap: 1983.
No. of Tests: 0.
No. of One-Day Internationals: 0.
1000 runs in a season: 2.
50 wickets in a season: 0.
1st-Class 50s scored: 18.
1st-Class 100s scored: 8.
1st-Class 200s scored: 1.
1st-Class 5 w. in innings: 0.
1st-Class 10 w. in match: 0.
One-day 50s: 7.
One-day 100s: 1.
Place in batting averages: 76 average: 35.50; (1983: 31 average: 43.54).
Place in bowling averages: — average: —; (1983: — average: —).
1st-Class catches 1984: 15 (career: 46).
Parents: George and Jean Aslett.
Wife and date of marriage: Bernadine 17 November 1984.
Education: Dover Grammar School, Leicester University.
Qualifications: B.A. (Hons) History.
Family links with cricket: Father played club cricket for Dover.
Jobs outside cricket: Postman, orderly, window cleaner for Jim Day
International.
Off-season 1983–84: Cricket and holiday in Australia.
Equipment endorsed: Slazenger.
Overseas teams played for: West Perth, C.C. 1981 and 1982, Bayswater C.C.
1983–84 on Whitbread Scholarship.
Cricketers particularly learnt from: Father, Nigel Sutton, Andy Froude,
Graham Mart, and senior Kent players.
Cricketers particularly admired: Mark Benson, Bob Woolmer, C.B. Fry.
Other sports: Rugby, hurling, tennis and diving.
Relaxations: Reading, yoga, music.
Extras: Scored 146 in debut v Hampshire, 168 & 119 v Derbyshire, 1983.
Wears spectacles.
Opinions on cricket: "The English cricket season is far too strenuous to enable
players and teams to produce 100% all the way through. It is important to be
able to build oneself up for a game, but when one possibly finishes a game at 8
o'clock, then has to travel 200 miles to the next venue and play the following

morning, that becomes virtually impossible. If the number of games was reduced players could think more about the game, and have a few more days off to recuperate and rebuild enthusiasm."

Best batting performance: 221* Kent v Sri Lanka, Canterbury 1984.
Best bowling performance: 4-119 Kent v Sussex, Hove 1982.

LAST SEASON: BATTING

	I.	N.O.	R.	H.S.	AV.
TEST					
OTHER FIRST CLASS	45	3	1491	221*	35.50
INT					
J.P.L.	14	0	333	72	23.79
NAT.W.	5	0	123	67	24.60
B & H	4	0	146	46	36.50

CAREER: BATTING

	I.	N.O.	R.	H.S.	AV.
TEST					
OTHER FIRST CLASS	113	11	3910	221*	38.33
INT					
J.P.L.	31	1	871	100	29.03
NAT.W.	10	0	225	67	22.50
B & H	6	0	171	46	28.50

LAST SEASON: BOWLING

	O.	M.	R.	W.	AV.
TEST					
OTHER FIRST CLASS	18.4	1	92	0	–
INT					
J.P.L.					
NAT.W.					
B & H					

CAREER: BOWLING

	O.	M.	R.	W.	AV.
TEST					
OTHER FIRST CLASS	139.5	16	653	10	65.30
INT					
J.P.L.					
NAT.W.	0.5	0	0	1	–
B & H					

BAPTISTE, E.A.E.

Full Name: Eldine Ashworth Elderfield Baptiste.
Role: Right-hand bat, right arm fast bowler.
Born: 12 March 1960, Liberta, Antigua.
Height: 6′ 1″ **Weight:** 12st.
Nickname: Big John, Man or Soca.
County debut: 1981.
County cap: 1983.
Test debut: 1983–84.
No. of Tests: 9.
No. of One-Day Internationals: 23.
1000 runs in a season: 0.
50 wickets in a season: 1.
1st-Class 50s scored: 7.
1st-Class 100s scored: 0.
1st-Class 200s scored: 0.
1st-Class 5 w. in innings: 0.

1st-Class 10 w. in match: 0.
One-day 50s: 0.
One-day 100s scored: 0.
Place in batting averages: 163 average: 24.50; (1983: 72 average: 35.95).
Place in bowling averages: 42 average: 27.21; (1983: 31 average: 23.74).
1st-Class catches 1984: 1 (career: 39).
Parents: Gertrude and Samuel Baptiste.
Children: Forbes Liam Baptiste, born 30 December 1981.
Family links with cricket: Father played for Liberta 1940–48. Brother, Rowan, played for Liberta at School level.
Education: Liberta Primary; All Saints Secondary School.
Jobs outside cricket: Sports officer in the Sports Department of The Ministry of Education.
Off-season 1984–85: Touring Australia with West Indies.
Cricketing superstitions: The numbers 49 and 13.
Equipment used and endorsed: Stuart Surridge.
Overseas tours: With Leeward Youths to Barbados 1978; to Australia, St Lucia, St Kitts, St Thomas and Montserat with Antigua National team in 1979; and to England with Antigua Youth in 1979; India 1983 with W.I.
Cricketers particularly learnt from: Guy Yearwood, Viv Richards and Andy Roberts.
Other sports: Playing football, running and exercising, watching netball. Tennis. Volleyball.
Relaxations: Watching movies, music – especially calypso – and meeting people.
Extras: Awarded Viv Richards Schools Cricket Trophy for the Most Outstanding Cricketer 1979, Sportsman of the Year in Antigua 1979. Hat-trick twice for Liberta School v. Cobbs Cross School. Scored 201 for Kent 2nd XI v. Surrey at Oval, 1982.
Best batting performance: 136* Kent v Yorkshire, Sheffield 1983.
Best bowling performance: 5-37 Kent v Lancashire, Maidstone 1981.

LAST SEASON: BATTING

	I.	N.O.	R.	H.S.	AV.
TEST	6	1	174	87*	34.80
OTHER FIRST CLASS	3	0	22	16	7.33
INT	2	0	45	26	22.50
J.P.L.					
NAT.W.					
B & H					

CAREER: BATTING

	I.	N.O.	R.	H.S.	AV.
TEST	10	1	224	87*	24.89
OTHER FIRST CLASS	89	17	2016	136*	28.00
INT	9	2	111	28*	15.86
J.P.L.	19	3	264	47	16.50
NAT.W.	5	0	57	22	11.40
B & H	1	0	1	1	–

LAST SEASON: BOWLING

	O.	M.	R.	W.	AV.
TEST	125	39	265	8	33.13
OTHER FIRST CLASS	96.1	25	252	11	22.91
INT	32	3	109	4	27.25
J.P.L.					
NAT.W.					
B & H					

CAREER: BOWLING

	O.	M.	R.	W.	AV.
TEST	204	55	485	15	32.33
OTHER FIRST CLASS	1353.3	297	4302	159	27.06
INT	203	13	786	23	34.17
J.P.L.	166	8	690	28	24.64
NAT.W.	61	12	209	10	20.90
B & H	11	2	28	0	–

BENSON, M.R.

Full Name: Mark Richard Benson.
Role: Left-hand bat.
Born: 6 July 1958, Shoreham, Sussex.
Height: 5′ 10″ **Weight:** 12st 10lbs.
Nickname: Benny.
County debut: 1980.
County cap: 1981.
Test debut: —
Number of Tests: 0.
No. of One-Day Internationals: 0.
1000 runs in a season: 3.
50 wickets in a season: 0.
1st-Class 50s scored: 29.
1-Class 100s scored: 12.
1st-Class 200s scored: 0.
1st-Class 5 w. in innings: 0.
1st-Class 10 w. in match: 0.
One-day 50s: 12.
One-day 100s: 1.

Place in batting averages: 61 average: 38.08; (1983: 27 average: 44.56).
Place in bowling averages: — average: —; (1983: — average: —).
1st-Class catches 1984: 7 (career: 40).
Parents: Frank and Judy Benson.
Marital status: Single.
Education: Sutton Valence School.
Qualifications: O- and A-levels and 1 S level.
Jobs outside cricket: Marketing assistant with Shell U.K. Oil.
Off-season 1984–85: Johannesburg.

LAST SEASON: BATTING

	I.	N.O.	R.	H.S.	AV.
TEST					
OTHER FIRST CLASS	26	2	914	127	38.08
INT					
J.P.L.	7	0	320	88	45.72
NAT.W.	4	1	281	113*	93.67
B & H					

CAREER: BATTING

	I.	N.O.	R.	H.S.	AV.
TEST					
OTHER FIRST CLASS	142	15	4840	152*	38.11
INT					
J.P.L.	46	0	1421	97	30.89
NAT.W.	12	1	471	113*	42.82
B & H	14	4	275	65	27.50

LAST SEASON: BOWLING

	O.	M.	R.	W.	AV.
TEST					
OTHER FIRST CLASS					
INT					
J.P.L.					
NAT.W.					
B & H					

CAREER: BOWLING

	O.	M.	R.	W.	AV.
TEST					
OTHER FIRST CLASS	13	1	72	0	–
INT					
J.P.L.					
NAT.W.					
B & H					

Family links with cricket: Father played for Ghana.
Equipment used: Duncan Fearnley.
Overseas teams played for: Balfour Guild C.C. 1979–80, Johannesburg Municipals, 1980–81, Port Adelaide C.C. 1981–82.
Cricketers particularly admired: Derek Aslett.
Other sports: Tennis, golf, hockey. Follows horse racing.
Significant injuries in 1984: Cartilage operation restricted appearances to latter half of season.
Extras: Scored 1000 runs in first full season; record for most runs in career and season at Sutton Valence School.
Opinions on cricket: "Believe 4-day County Championship matches should operate. Each county plays each other once during the season."
Best batting performance: 152* Kent v Warwickshire, Edgbaston 1983.

COWDREY, C.S.

Full Name: Christopher Stuart Cowdrey.
Role: Right-hand bat, right arm medium bowler.
Born: 20 October 1957, Farnborough, Kent.
Height: 6' 0" **Weight:** 13st.
Nickname: Cow.
County debut: 1977.
County cap: 1979.
Test debut: —
No. of Tests: 0.
No. of One-Day Internationals: 0.
1000 runs in a season: 2.
50 wickets in a season: 0.
1st-Class 50s scored: 31.
1st-Class 100s scored: 8.
1st-Class 200s scored: 0.
1st-Class 5 w. in innings: 1.
1st-Class 10 w. in match: 0.
One-day 50s: 19.
One-day 100s: 2.

Place in batting averages: 117 average: 30.56; (1983: 7 average: 56.83).
Place in bowling averages: 62 average: 29.71; (1983: 131 average: 61.08).
1st-Class catches 1984: 22 (career: 145).
Parents: Michael Colin and Penelope Susan Cowdrey.
Education: Wellesley House, Broadstairs; Tonbridge School.
Jobs outside cricket: Director, Personality Sports Promotions. Representative for Stuart Canvas Products, Warrington, Cheshire.

Off season 1984–85: Tour to India and Australia with England.

Family links with cricket: Grandfather, Stuart Chiesman, on Kent Committee, twelve years as Chairman. Pavilion on Kent's ground at Canterbury named after him. Father played for Kent and England, brother made Kent debut 1984.

Overseas tours: Captained Young England to West Indies, 1976. Toured with Derrick Robins XI to Far East, South America and Australasia (1979–80).

Cricketers particularly learnt from: Derek Underwood and his "Foxgrove Slog". Frank Woolley, Paul Downton, Nick Kemp.

Equipment used: Duncan Fearnley.

Other sports: Golf, tennis, squash. "Anything!"

Relaxations: Watching Chelsea F.C., horse-racing, playing cards, listening to music—mainly Bob Dylan.

Extras: Played for Kent 2nd XI at age 15. Best man at Kim Barnett's wedding. Fourth wicket partnership record for Kent in Benson & Hedges with Alan Ealham. Vice-captain 1984, Captain 1985.

Best batting performance: 125* Kent v Essex, Colchester 1984.

Best bowling performance: 3-17 Kent v Hampshire, Bournemouth 1980.

LAST SEASON: BATTING

	I.	N.O.	R.	H.S.	AV.
TEST					
OTHER FIRST CLASS	37	3	1039	125*	30.56
INT					
J.P.L.	11	1	420	75	42.00
NAT.W.	5	0	194	71	38.80
B & H	1	0	5	5	–

CAREER: BATTING

	I.	N.O.	R.	H.S.	AV.
TEST					
OTHER FIRST CLASS	234	37	6163	125*	31.28
INT					
J.P.L.	95	13	1976	95	24.09
NAT.W.	18	3	516	122*	34.40
B & H	27	4	600	114	26.09

LAST SEASON: BOWLING

	O.	M.	R.	W.	AV.
TEST					
OTHER FIRST CLASS	271.1	57	832	28	29.71
INT					
J.P.L.	78	0	364	13	28.00
NAT.W.	54	2	162	4	40.50
B & H	7	1	20	1	–

CAREER: BOWLING

	O.	M.	R.	W.	AV.
TEST					
OTHER FIRST CLASS	845.2	163	2775	73	38.01
INT					
J.P.L.	237.3	3	1126	33	34.12
NAT.W.	106	12	337	16	21.06
B & H	71	1	302	6	50.33

Q. 83. Which wicket-keeper made the most first-class dismissals in one season?

Q. 84. Which wicket-keeper has taken the most dismissals in his career?

COWDREY, G.R.

Full Name: Graham Robert
Cowdrey.
Role: Right-hand bat, right arm
medium bowler. Slip or cover
fielder.
Born: 27 June 1964,
Farnborough, Kent.
Height: 5' 11" **Weight:** 13st.
Nickname: Cow, Van.
County debut: 1984.
County cap: No.
Test debut: —
No. of Tests: 0.
No. of One-Day Internationals: 0.
1000 runs in a season: 0.
50 wickets in a season: 0.
1st-Class 50s scored: 0.
1st-Class 100s scored: 0.
1st-Class 200s scored: 0.
1st-Class 5 w. in innings: 0.
1st-Class 10 w. in match: 0.
One-day 50s: 0.
One-day 100s 0.
Place in batting averages: — average: —; (1983: — average: —).
Place in bowling averages: — average: —; (1983: — average —).
1st-Class catches 1984: 1 (career: 1).
Parents: Michael Colin and Penelope Susan Cowdrey.
Marital status: Single.
Family links with cricket: Father played for England, brother Chris on
England tour to India 1984–85.
Education: Wellesley House, Broadstairs; Tonbridge School; Durham
University.
Qualifications: University entrance, 3 A-levels, 8 O-levels.
Off-season 1984–85: Playing for Avendale C.C. Cape Town.
Equipment used: Duncan Fearnley.
Overseas tours: Australia with Tonbridge School in 1980.
Overseas teams played for: Avendale C.C. Cape Town 1983–84.
Cricketers particularly learnt from: Chris Cowdrey, Bob Woolmer, Mark
Benson.
Cricketers particularly admired: Chris Cowdrey, Graham Gooch, Greg
Chappell, Paul Downton.
Other sports: Squash; rackets—most ball sports. Follow racing.
Significant injuries in 1984: Eye problem—have to wear contact lenses.
Relaxations: Reading novels; theatre; music, world authority on Van Morrison

(Irish musician)—seen him 25 times in concert in 3 years. Ambition to see him 100 times in concert.

Extras: Played for Young England and Australia. 1000 runs for Kent II 1st season on staff, captain of Kent II in 1984. Very interested in psychology of cricket.

LAST SEASON: BATTING

	I.	N.O.	R.	H.S.	AV.
TEST					
OTHER FIRST CLASS	1	0	7	7	–
INT					
J.P.L.					
NAT.W.					
B & H					

CAREER: BATTING

	I.	N.O.	R.	H.S.	AV.
TEST					
OTHER FIRST CLASS	1	0	7	7	–
INT					
J.P.L.					
NAT.W.					
B & H					

LAST SEASON: BOWLING

	O.	M.	R.	W.	AV.
TEST					
OTHER FIRST CLASS	7	0	22	1	–
INT					
J.P.L.					
NAT.W.					
B & H					

CAREER: BOWLING

	O.	M.	R.	W.	AV.
TEST					
OTHER FIRST CLASS	7	0	22	1	–
INT					
J.P.L.					
NAT.W.					
B & H					

DILLEY, G.R.

Full Name: Graham Roy Dilley.
Role: Left-hand bat, right arm fast bowler.
Born: 18 May 1959, Dartford.
Height: 6′ 4″ **Weight:** 15st.
Nickname: Picca.
County debut: 1977.
County cap: 1980.
Test debut: 1979–80.
No. of Tests: 18.
No. of One-Day Internationals: 18.
1000 runs in a season: 0.
50 wickets in a season: 1.
1st-Class 50s scored: 4.
1st-Class 100s scored: 0.
1st-Class 200s scored: 0.
1st-Class 5 w. in innings: 9.
1st-Class 10 w. in match: 1.
One-day 50s: 0.
One-day 100s: 0.

Place in batting averages: — average: —; (1983: 217 average: 14.25).
Place in bowling averages: — average: —; (1983: 19 average: 21.97).
1st-Class catches 1984: 0 (career: 53).
Parents: Geoff and Jean Dilley.
Wife and date of marriage: Helen, 6 November 1980.
Education: Dartford West Secondary School.
Qualifications: Three O-levels.
Jobs outside cricket: Diamond setter.
Family links with cricket: Father and grandfather both played local cricket.
His wife is his Kent colleague Graham Johnson's sister.
Equipment used: Gunn & Moore.
Overseas tours: With England to Australia 1979–80, West Indies 1981 and
India 1981–82; New Zealand and Pakistan 1983–84.
Cricketers particularly learnt from: Dennis Lillee, John Snow.
Other sports: Golf, squash, badminton.
Significant injuries in 1984: Returned early from winter tour due to numbness
in side and missed 1984 season.
Relaxations: Music.
Extras: Got sacked from his first job with a Hatton Garden diamond firm after
taking time off to play for Kent 2nd XI. Suffered from glandular fever at end of
1980 season, causing him to miss Centenary Test. Voted Young Cricketer of the
Year, 1980 by Cricket Writers' Club. Lost form and confidence in middle of
1981 season and was dropped from both England and Kent 1st XI but England
selectors kept faith in his ability by choosing him for India in 1981–82.
Best batting performance: 81 Kent v Northamptonshire, Northampton 1979.
Best bowling performance: 6-66 Kent v Middlesex, Lords 1979.

LAST SEASON: BATTING

	I.	N.O.	R.	H.S.	AV.
TEST					
OTHER FIRST CLASS					
INT					
J.P.L.					
NAT.W.					
B & H					

CAREER: BATTING

	I.	N.O.	R.	H.S.	AV.
TEST	28	8	330	56	16.50
OTHER FIRST CLASS	91	34	875	81	15.35
INT	11	3	96	31*	12.50
J.P.L.	19	6	213	33	16.38
NAT.W.	7	1	43	19	7.17
B & H	19	5	111	37*	7.93

LAST SEASON: BOWLING

	O.	M.	R.	W.	AV.
TEST					
OTHER FIRST CLASS					
INT					
J.P.L.					
NAT.W.					
B & H					

CAREER: BOWLING

	O.	M.	R.	W.	AV.
TEST	517.4	103	1564	49	31.92
OTHER FIRST CLASS	1543.4	460	6127	220	27.85
INT	162	14	595	18	33.06
J.P.L.	290.3	27	1140	52	21.92
NAT.W.	93	17	296	15	19.73
B & H	208.5	26	730	35	20.86

ELLISON, R.M.

Full Name: Richard Mark Ellison.
Role: Left-hand bat, right arm
medium bowler, outfielder.
Born: 21 September 1959,
Ashford, Kent.
Height: 6′ 3″ **Weight:** 14st 7lbs.
Nickname: Plank, Snooker,
Bungalow, Elly ("changing all the
time").
County debut: 1981.
County cap: 1983.
Test debut: 1984.
No. of Tests: 2.
No. of One-Day Internationals: 0.
1000 runs in a season: 0.
50 wickets in a season: 2.
1st-Class 50s scored: 5.
1st-Class 100s scored: 1.
1st-Class 200s scored: 0.
1st-Class 5 w. in innings: 2.
1st-Class 10 w. in match: 0.
One-day 50s: 4.
One-day 100s: 0.
Place in batting averages: 159 average: 24.80; (1983: 142 average: 24.50).
Place in bowling averages: 16 average: 22.42; (1983: 61 average: 29.24).
1st-Class catches 1984: 8 (career: 29).
Parents: Peter Ellison (deceased) and Bridget Ellison.
Marital status: Single (engaged).

LAST SEASON: BATTING

	I.	N.O.	R.	H.S.	AV.
TEST	3	1	74	41	37.00
OTHER FIRST CLASS	29	6	546	108	23.74
INT					
J.P.L.	11	1	411	84	41.10
NAT.W.	5	4	138	49*	–
B & H	4	1	144	72	48.00

CAREER: BATTING

	I.	N.O.	R.	H.S.	AV.
TEST	3	1	74	41	37.00
OTHER FIRST CLASS	72	22	1305	108	26.10
INT					
J.P.L.	29	13	526	84	32.87
NAT.W.	10	5	184	49*	36.80
B & H	9	1	190	72	23.75

LAST SEASON: BOWLING

	O.	M.	R.	W.	AV.
TEST	79	16	200	6	33.33
OTHER FIRST CLASS	456.5	126	1123	53	21.19
INT					
J.P.L.	84	2	380	17	22.35
NAT.W.	54	11	171	6	28.50
B & H	37	9	88	8	11.00

CAREER: BOWLING

	O.	M.	R.	W.	AV.
TEST	79	16	200	6	33.33
OTHER FIRST CLASS	1279.4	346	3191	124	25.73
INT					
J.P.L.	233.4	10	1018	43	23.67
NAT.W.	105	21	317	15	21.13
B & H	96	20	256	14	18.29

Family links with cricket: Grandfather played with the Grace brothers. Brother Charles Christopher Ellison played for Cambridge University in 1982.
Education: Friars Prep. School; Tonbridge School; St Luke's College, Exeter University.
Qualifications: Two A-levels, 8 O-levels, various teaching awards. Bachelor of Education (Teacher).
Jobs outside cricket: Coal yard worker, two months in 1978.
Off-season 1984–85: England tour of India and Australia.
Equipment used: Gray-Nicolls.
Cricketers particularly learnt from: Derek Underwood, Bob Woolmer, Ray Dovey.
Cricketers particularly admired: "Too many to mention."
Other sports: "Hockey. Anything apart from horse-racing and show-jumping."
Relaxations: "Any music; taking the mickey out of Graham Johnson."
Extras: Public Schools Cricketer of the Year 1978. U.A.U. Cricket Team 1980–81. Young England and E.S.C.A. 1978. Invited to tour with M.C.C. to Bangladesh (1980) and East and Central Africa (1981) but unable to go due to studies. Scored 55 not out on debut. "Overweight, so Chris Cowdrey and Mark Benson keep telling me – but who are they to know?"
Opinions on cricket: "117 overs a day too many; leads to long days and late finishes. Would like 17 4-day championship matches."
Best batting performance: 108 Kent v Oxford University, Oxford 1984.
Best bowling performance: 5-27 Kent v Essex, Canterbury 1984.

HINKS, S.G.

Full Name: Simon Graham Hinks
Role: Left-hand bat; "right-arm cannon fodder."
Born: 12 October, 1960, Northfleet, Kent.
Height: 6′ 2″ **Weight:** 13st 4lbs.
Nickname: Hinksy.
County debut: 1982.
County cap: No.
Test debut: —
No. of Tests: 0.
No. of One-Day Internationals: 0.
1000 runs in a season: 0.
50 wickets in a season: 0.
1st-Class 50s scored: 1.
1st-Class 100s scored: 0.
1st-Class 200s scored: 0.
1st-Class 5 w. in innings: 0.
1st-Class 10 w. in match: 0.

One-day 50s: 1.
One-day 100s: 0.
Place in batting averages: 261 average: 11.57; (1983: 136 average: 25.30).
Place in bowling averages: — average: —; (1983: — average: —).
1st-Class catches 1984: 3 (career: 6).
Parents: Mary and Graham Hinks.
Marital status: Single.
Education: Dover Road Infant and Junior Schools, Northfleet; St. George's C. of E. School, Gravesend.
Qualifications: 5 0 levels, 1 A level.
Jobs outside cricket: Menswear manager, By One, Gravesend, Sheepskin and Leatherwear sales representative. Gardener.
Off-season 1984–85: Coaching in Tasmania.
Family links with cricket: Father captained Gravesend C.C. and is now chairman. Brother Jonathan plays for Gravesend and Kent Under-19s.
Cricket superstitions: "Put gear on in set order."
Overseas teams played for: Pirates, Johannesburg, 1981–82.
Cricketers particularly learnt from: "Learnt from my father and members of local club, Gravesend. Admire Clive Lloyd's style and power and anyone who has proved themselves over a long period."
Equipment used: Stuart Surridge.
Other sports: Most ball games.
Relaxations: T.V., music, sleep.
Extras: Broke Kent 2nd XI record of total runs scored in championship cricket (2nd XI) previously held by David Laycock, Bernard Julien, and David Constant, with 1159 runs in 26 innings in 1982.
Opinions on cricket: "Deeper look at South African cricket, regarding admission into international cricket. Should be major sponsorships for schoolboy cricket and development of 'grass-root' areas for home-bred players."
Best batting performance: 87 Kent v Glamorgan, Cardiff 1983.

LAST SEASON: BATTING

	I.	N.O.	R.	H.S.	AV.
TEST					
OTHER FIRST CLASS	14	0	162	39	11.57
INT					
J.P.L.	5	2	109	52*	36.33
NAT.W.					
B & H					

CAREER: BATTING

	I.	N.O.	R.	H.S.	AV.
TEST					
OTHER FIRST CLASS	28	1	450	87	16.67
INT					
J.P.L.	7	2	122	52*	24.40
NAT.W.					
B & H					

LAST SEASON: BOWLING

	O.	M.	R.	W.	AV.
TEST					
OTHER FIRST CLASS	16	3	53	2	26.50
INT					
J.P.L.	8	1	36	1	—
NAT.W.					
B & H					

CAREER: BOWLING

	O.	M.	R.	W.	AV.
TEST					
OTHER FIRST CLASS	17.4	4	58	2	29.00
INT					
J.P.L.	8	1	36	1	—
NAT.W.					
B & H					

JARVIS, K.B.S.

Full Name: Kevin Bertram Sidney Jarvis.
Role: Right-hand bat, right arm fast medium bowler.
Born: 23 April 1953, Dartford, Kent.
Height: 6′ 3″ **Weight:** 13st.
Nickname: Jarvo.
County debut: 1975.
County cap: 1977.
Test debut: —
No. of Tests: 0.
No. of One-Day Internationals: 0.
1000 runs in a season: 0.
50 wickets in a season: 6.
1st-Class 50s scored: 0.
1st-Class 100s scored: 0.
1st-Class 200s scored: 0.
1st-Class 5 w. in innings: 16.
1st-Class 10 w. in match: 3.
One-day 50s: 0.
One-day 100s: 0.
Place in batting averages: — average: —; (1983: — average: —).
Place in bowling averages: 27 average: 24.83; (1983: 129 average: 52.63).
1st-Class catches 1984: 6 (career: 50).
Parents: Herbert John and Margaret Elsie Jarvis.
Wife and date of marriage: Margaret Anne, 16 September 1978.
Education: Springhead School, Northfleet, Kent; Thames Polytechnic.

LAST SEASON: BATTING

	I.	N.O.	R.	H.S.	AV.
TEST					
OTHER FIRST CLASS	25	13	41	19	3.42
INT					
J.P.L.	4	1	2	2*	0.67
NAT.W.					
B & H	2	2	2	1*	—

CAREER: BATTING

	I.	N.O.	R.	H.S.	AV.
TEST					
OTHER FIRST CLASS	150	65	275	19	3.24
INT					
J.P.L.	37	21	53	8*	3.31
NAT.W.	10	4	14	5*	2.33
B & H	21	14	14	4	2.00

LAST SEASON: BOWLING

	O.	M.	R.	W.	AV.
TEST					
OTHER FIRST CLASS	570.5	128	1788	72	24.83
INT					
J.P.L.	74.5	6	353	11	32.09
NAT.W.	60	12	151	8	18.88
B & H	38.3	3	139	8	17.38

CAREER: BOWLING

	O.	M.	R.	W.	AV.
TEST					
OTHER FIRST CLASS	4999	1104	15718	543	28.95
INT					
J.P.L.	806.1	74	3318	148	22.41
NAT.W.	197.5	26	696	34	20.47
B & H	461.1	65	1579	73	21.63

Qualifications: Three A-levels, six O-levels. NCA coach. I.S.M.A., M.A.M.S.A.
Jobs outside cricket: Accountancy.
Overseas tours: Derrick Robins XI to Far East 1977. Jamaica 1982.
Overseas teams played for: Played and coached for South Melbourne, Australia.
Off-season 1984–85: Preparing for 1985 season.
Other sports: Squash, golf, badminton, tennis.
Relaxations: Reading, music.
Best batting performance: 19 Kent v Derbyshire, Maidstone 1984.
Best bowling performance: 8-97 Kent v Worcestershire, Worcester 1978.

JOHNSON, G.W.

Full Name: Graham William Johnson.
Role: Right-hand bat, off-break bowler.
Born: 8 November 1946, Beckenham, Kent.
Height: 6′ 1″
Nickname: Johno, Coat-hanger, Prat.
County debut: 1965.
County cap: 1970.
Test debut: —
No. of Tests: 0.
No. of One-Day Internationals: 0.
Benefit: 1983.
1000 runs in a season: 3.
50 wickets in a season: 3.
1st-Class 50s scored: 53.
1st-Class 100s scored: 11.
1st-Class 200s scored: 0.
1st-Class 5 w. in innings: 22.
1st-Class 10 w. in match: 3.
One-day 50s: 25.
One-day 100s 1.

Place in batting averages: 190 average: 21.35; (1983: 144 average: 24.29).
Place in bowling averages: 75 average: 31.28; (1983: 83 average: 32.39).
1st-Class catches 1984: 26 (career: 305).
Parents: Bill and Mamie Johnson.
Education: Malcolm Primary, Penge; Beckenham & Penge Grammar School; Shooter's Hill Grammar School; London School of Economics, London University.

Qualifications: B.Sc. Economics. Eleven O-levels, three A-levels. Qualified coach.

Jobs outside cricket: Investment analyst with Selection Trust Ltd (mining finance company), Bradstock, Blunt and Barney (insurance brokers) and currently with Barclays Bank/Transvaal Cricket Council.

Off-season 1984–85: Working in Johannesburg.

Family links with cricket: "Father played club cricket in Essex and S.E. London and has umpired 2nd XI county cricket. Brother with Brentwood C.C. and Lloyds Insurance, brother-in-law once removed (G. Dilley) has played a bit."

Overseas tours: Derrick Robins XI to South Africa and West Indies; John Player League Champions to West Indies; Kent to West Indies, Canada, Holland and Jersey.

Overseas teams played for: Koh-i-noor Crescents in Premier League in Johannesburg, South Africa for 5 years.

Cricketers particularly learnt from: Coached by Father, Claude Lewis, George Pope, Colin Page and Les Ames—"learnt bits and pieces from most Kent players over last 20 years and by watching other county and test players."

Equipment used: Slazenger.

Other sports: Rugby, football, squash, golf, water-skiing and wind-surfing. Watch most sports except wrestling and horse-racing.

Relaxations: Music, real ale, meeting interesting people, travel, current affairs, ecology.

Significant injuries in 1984: "Minor injuries such as old age and senility for most of the season, and severe shock on September 15th (NatWest final day)."

Extras: "Suffer from hay fever, bad memory for names, tend to get chirpy after taking wickets."

Opinions on cricket: "Let's play 130 overs each day and cut out sleep completely!"

Best batting performance: 168 Kent v Surrey, The Oval 1976.

Best bowling performance: 7-76 Kent v Northamptonshire, Canterbury 1983.

LAST SEASON: BATTING

	I.	N.O.	R.	H.S.	AV.
TEST					
OTHER FIRST CLASS	39	5	726	84	21.35
INT					
J.P.L.	12	5	165	32*	23.57
NAT.W.	4	2	27	21*	13.50
B & H	4	0	107	60	26.75

CAREER: BATTING

	I.	N.O.	R.	H.S.	AV.
TEST					
OTHER FIRST CLASS	582·	73	12549	168	24.65
INT					
J.P.L.	177	25	3606	89	23.72
NAT.W.	31	5	745	120*	28.65
B & H	56	5	1180	85*	23.14

LAST SEASON: BOWLING

	O.	M.	R.	W.	AV.
TEST					
OTHER FIRST CLASS	462.2	117	1220	39	31.28
INT					
J.P.L.	32	1	142	3	47.33
NAT.W.	10	0	32	0	–
B & H					

CAREER: BOWLING

	O.	M.	R.	W.	AV.
TEST					
OTHER FIRST CLASS	6668	1917	17058	555	30.74
INT					
J.P.L.	337.2	20	1511	77	19.62
NAT.W.	71.3	2	277	5	55.40
B & H	115	15	409	16	25.56

KNOTT, A.P.E.

Full Name: Alan Philip Eric Knott.
Role: Right-hand bat, wicket-keeper, can bowl off-breaks.
Born: 9 April 1946, Belvedere, Kent.
Height: 5′ 8″ **Weight:** 10st 10lbs.
Nickname: Knotty, Flea.
County debut: 1964.
County cap: 1965.
Test debut: 1967.
No. of Tests: 95.
No. of One-Day Internationals: 20.
Benefit: £27,037 in 1976.
1000 runs in a season: 2.
50 wickets in a season: 0.
1st-Class 50s scored: 79.
1st-Class 100s scored: 17.
1st-Class 200s scored: 0.
1st-Class 5 w. in innings: 0.
1st-Class 10 w. in match: 0.
One-day 50s: 6.
One-day 100s: 0.

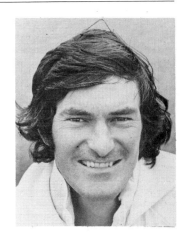

Place in batting averages: 242 average: 14.75; (1983: 50 average: 40.38).
Place in bowling averages: — average: —; (1983: — average: —).
Parents: Eric and Margaret Knott.
Wife and date of marriage: Jan Linda, 21 March 1969.
Education: Northumberland Heath Secondary Modern School, Erith, Kent.
Qualifications: Advanced cricket coach.
Jobs outside cricket: Proprietor of sports shop and gymnasium in Herne Bay.
Family links with cricket: "My father, uncle, brother, cousin and myself have all played for the same club in club cricket, Belvedere C.C. My father was a fine club wicket-keeper who kept me out of the side as keeper. I used to bowl off-spinners while he kept. He taught me cricket from the age of four."
Overseas tours: International Cavaliers 1965; M.C.C. Under-25 tour to Pakistan 1967; West Indies 1967–68 and 1973–74; Ceylon and Pakistan 1968–69; Australia and New Zealand 1970–71, 1974–75; India, Sri Lanka and Pakistan 1972–73; India, Sri Lanka and Australia 1966–67.
Off-season 1984–85: "In my sports shop business."
Equipment used: Slazenger.
Equipment endorsed: Slazenger wicket-keeping gloves and cricket equipment.
Cricketers particularly learnt from: Father, Claude Lewis (Kent coach and ex-player) and Godfrey Evans.
Other sports: Most sports, especially soccer and table-tennis, badminton, squash. Played football for Tooting and Mitcham reserves.
Relaxations: Listening to music, watching movies either on TV or at the

cinema, watching soccer, family.

Extras: Played for World Series cricket and in 6 "Supertests." Set record for more runs in Test cricket than any other wicket-keeper. Dismissed seven batsmen, seven caught, in Test debut v Pakistan (Nottingham 1967).

Best batting performance: 156 M.C.C. v S. Zone, Bangalore 1972–73.

LAST SEASON: BATTING

	I.	N.O.	R.	H.S.	AV.
TEST					
OTHER FIRST CLASS	22	2	295	43	14.75
INT					
J.P.L.	6	1	66	29*	13.20
NAT.W.	2	0	8	7	4.00
B & H	4	1	89	41	29.67

CAREER: BATTING

	I.	N.O.	R.	H.S.	AV.
TEST	149	15	4389	135	32.75
OTHER FIRST CLASS	572	114	13337	156	29.12
INT	14	4	200	50	20.00
J.P.L.	118	26	1567	60	17.03
NAT.W.	34	5	415	46	14.31
B & H	53	6	841	65	17.89

LAST SEASON: WICKET KEEPING

	C.	ST.			
TEST					
OTHER FIRST CLASS	29	1			
INT					
J.P.L.	6	3			
NAT.W.	4	1			
B & H	5	2			

CAREER: WICKET KEEPING

	C.	ST.			
TEST	250	19			
OTHER FIRST CLASS	908	113			
INT	15	1			
J.P.L.	176	34			
NAT.W.	51	6			
B & H	74	9			

MARSH, S.A.

Full Name: Steven Andrew Marsh.
Role: Wicket-keeper, batsman.
Born: 27 January 1961, Westminster.
Height: 5′ 11″ **Weight:** 11st. 9lbs.
Nickname: Marshy, Swampy.
County debut: 1982.
County cap: No.
Test debut: —
No. of Tests: 0.
No. of One-Day Internationals: 0.
1000 runs in a season: 0.
50 wickets in a season: 0.
1st-Class 50s scored: 0.
1st-Class 100s scored: 0.
1st-Class 200s scored: 0.
1st-Class 5 w. in innings: 0.
1st-Class 10 w. in match: 0.
One-day 50s: 0.
One-day 100s 0.

Place in batting averages: — average: —; (1983: — average: —).
Place in bowling averages: — average: —; (1983: — average —).

Parents: Mel Graham and Valerie Ann Marsh.
Marital status: Single.
Education: Walderslade Secondary School for Boys; Mid-Kent College of Higher and Further Education, Maidstone.
Qualificati«ns: 6 O-levels, 2 A-levels. OND in Business Studies.
Cricketing superstitions: "When batting, getting into double figures."
Jobs outside cricket: Office clerk; cricket coach.
Off-season 1984–85: Either coaching in South Africa or any sort of job in England.
Family links with cricket: Father played local cricket for Lordswood.
Overseas tours: Barbados, 1979 with Lordswood C.C. Kent.
Cricketers particularly learnt from: "Alan Knott, and Lindsay Wood for the way he strangles the batsman out!"
Cricketers particularly admired: Gary Sobers.
Equipment used: Reader Sports.
Other sports: Football, golf, snooker, horse-racing.
Relaxations: Watching T.V.
Extras: Won 2nd XI cap 1983.
Opinions on cricket: "Personally I think 117 overs is too many to bowl in one day, because there are too many interruptions not down to the bowling side. The crowd cannot enjoy that either because when I have played till 8 o'clock most of the crowd have gone home anyway."
Best batting performance: 48 Kent v Nottinghamshire, Folkestone 1984.

LAST SEASON: BATTING

	I.	N.O.	R.	H.S.	AV.
TEST					
OTHER FIRST CLASS	7	1	106	48	17.67
INT					
J.P.L.	1	1	1	1*	–
NAT.W.					
B & H					

CAREER: BATTING

	I.	N.O.	R.	H.S.	AV.
TEST					
OTHER FIRST CLASS	10	2	121	48	15.13
INT					
J.P.L.	1	1	1	1*	–
NAT.W.					
B & H					

LAST SEASON: WICKET KEEPING

	C.	ST.			
TEST					
OTHER FIRST CLASS	10	–			
INT					
J.P.L.	1	–			
NAT.W.					
B & H					

CAREER: WICKET KEEPING

	C.	ST.			
TEST					
OTHER FIRST CLASS	16	–			
INT					
J.P.L.	1	–			
NAT.W.					
B & H					

MASTERS, K.D.

Full Name: Kevin David Masters.
Role: Left-hand bat, right arm fast
medium bowler.
Born: 19 May 1961, Chatham, Kent.
Height: 5' 11" **Weight:** 10st. 5lbs.
Nickname: Hod.
County debut: 1983.
County cap: No.
Test debut: —
No. of Tests: 0.
No. of One-Day Internationals: 0.
1000 runs in a season: 0.
50 wickets in a season: 0.
1st-Class 50s scored: 0.
1st-Class 100s scored: 0.
1st-Class 200s scored: 0.
1st-Class 5 w. in innings: 0.
1st-Class 10 w. in match: 0.
One-day 50s: 0.
One-day 100s: 0.
Place in batting averages: — average: —; (1983: — average: —).
Place in bowling averages: — average: —; (1983: — average: —).
1st-Class catches 1984: 0 (career: 2).
Parents: David and Patricia Masters.
Wife: Tracey.
Children: David Daniel, 22 April 1978; Kayley Dawn, 24 February 1983.
Education: Fourt Luton.
Jobs outside cricket: Bricklayer's hod-carrier.

LAST SEASON: BATTING

	I.	N.O.	R.	H.S.	AV.
TEST					
OTHER FIRST CLASS	3	1	0	0*	0.00
INT					
J.P.L.	1	0	0	0	—
NAT.W.					
B & H					

CAREER: BATTING

	I.	N.O.	R.	H.S.	AV.
TEST					
OTHER FIRST CLASS	7	1	1	1	0.17
INT					
J.P.L.	1	0	0	0	—
NAT.W.					
B & H					

LAST SEASON: BOWLING

	O.	M.	R.	W.	AV.
TEST					
OTHER FIRST CLASS	41.5	6	173	4	43.25
INT					
J.P.L.	5.3	0	27	0	—
NAT.W.					
B & H					

CAREER: BOWLING

	O.	M.	R.	W.	AV.
TEST					
OTHER FIRST CLASS	74.5	10	294	6	49.00
INT					
J.P.L.	5.3	0	27	0	—
NAT.W.					
B & H					

Off-season 1984–85: Hodding.
Cricketing superstitions: "Not getting a run."
Equipment used: Duncan Fearnley.
Cricketers particularly learnt from: Colin Page.
Cricketers particularly admired: Derek Underwood.
Other sports: Football, pool, boxing, golf.
Relaxations: Training and T.V.
Extras: "Always keen to find work during the winter, so if you can help please let me know!".
Best bowling performance: 2-85 Kent v Somerset, Taunton 1984.

PENN, C.

Full Name: Christopher Penn.
Role: Left-hand bat, right arm medium fast bowler.
Born: 19 June 1963, Dover.
Height: 6′ 1″ **Weight:** 14st.
Nickname: Penny, Eddy, Cliff.
County debut: 1982.
County cap: No.
Test debut: —
No. of Tests: 0.
No. of One-Day Internationals: 0.
1000 runs in a season: 0.
50 wickets in a season: 0.
1st-Class 50s scored: 1.
1st-Class 100s scored: 1.
1st-Class 200s scored: 0.
1st-Class 5 w. in innings: 0.
1st-Class 10 w. in match: 0.
One-day 50s: 0.
One-day 100s: 0.

Place in batting averages: 167 average: 24.38; (1983: — average: —).
Place in bowling averages: — average: —; (1983: — average: —).
1st-Class catches 1984: 8 (career: 13).
Parents: Reg and Brenda Penn.
Marital status: Single.
Education: River Primary School; Dover Grammar School.
Qualifications: 8 O-levels, 2 A-levels.
Jobs outside cricket: Farm worker, car cleaner for hire company.
Off-season 1984–85: Playing and coaching for Mobil in Johannesburg.
Family links with cricket: Father played club cricket for Dover C.C.
Equipment used: Gunn & Moore.
Overseas tours: N.C.A. tour of Denmark, 1981. Whitbread Scholarship to Australia 1982–83.

Overseas teams played for: Koohinore Crescents, Johannesburg, 1981–82 and 1983–84. West Perth 1982–83, Johannesburg Municipals 1983–84.

Cricketers particularly learnt from: "My father, Colin Page, Brian Luckhurst, Graham Johnson, Barney Lock, the present Kent team."

Other sports: Rugby, football, golf, squash. Follows basketball and tennis.

Relaxations: Music, swimming, art and art history, Indian food.

Extras: Played for Young England v. Young West Indies, August 1982.

Opinions on cricket: "Possibly too much car travel and risk of bad road accident."

Best batting performance: 115 Kent v Lancashire, Old Trafford 1984.

Best bowling performance: 2-11 Kent v Gloucestershire, Canterbury 1984.

LAST SEASON: BATTING

	I.	N.O.	R.	H.S.	AV.
TEST					
OTHER FIRST CLASS	15	2	317	115	24.38
INT					
J.P.L.	8	3	41	13	8.20
NAT.W.					
B & H	3	0	34	17	11.33

CAREER: BATTING

	I.	N.O.	R.	H.S.	AV.
TEST					
OTHER FIRST CLASS	24	6	395	115	21.94
INT					
J.P.L.	14	4	92	40	9.20
NAT.W.	1	0	5	5	–
B & H	5	2	38	17	12.67

LAST SEASON: BOWLING

	O.	M.	R.	W.	AV.
TEST					
OTHER FIRST CLASS	157	25	491	8	61.38
INT					
J.P.L.	63.3	3	344	8	43.00
NAT.W.					
B & H	13	1	42	0	–

CAREER: BOWLING

	O.	M.	R.	W.	AV.
TEST					
OTHER FIRST CLASS	285.4	50	934	17	54.94
INT					
J.P.L.	136	6	698	23	30.34
NAT.W.	12	1	34	1	–
B & H	35	2	124	4	31.00

Q. 85. Has there ever been a case of a wicket-keeper taking a hat-trick behind the stumps?

Q. 86. What is the highest team total in one innings in first-class cricket?

Q. 87. Which non-wicket-keeper took the most first-class catches in his career and how many?

Q. 88. Which non-wicket-keeper took the most first-class catches in one season, and how many?

POTTER, L.

Full Name: Laurie Potter.
Role: Right-hand bat, left hand slow and medium pace bowler, slip fielder.
Born: 7 November 1962, Bexleyheath, Kent.
Height: 6' 1" **Weight:** 14st.
Nickname: Potts and Liz.
County debut: 1981.
County cap: No.
Test debut: —
No. of Tests: 0.
No. of One-Day Internationals: 0.
1000 runs in a season: 0.
50 wickets in a season: 0.
1st-Class 50s scored: 8.
1st-Class 100s scored: 3.
1st-Class 200s scored: 0.
1st-Class 5 w. in innings: 0.
1st-Class 10 w. in match: 0.
One-day 50s: 0.
One-day 100s: 0.
Place in batting averages: 169 average: 23.92; (1983: 149 average: 23.45).
Place in bowling averages: — average: —; (1983: — average: —).
1st-Class catches 1984: 6 (career: 16).
Parents: Ronald Henry Ernest and Audrey Megan Potter.
Marital status: Single.
Education: Kelmscott Senior High School, Perth, Western Australia.

LAST SEASON: BATTING

	I.	N.O.	R.	H.S.	AV.
TEST					
OTHER FIRST CLASS	25	1	574	117	23.92
INT					
J.P.L.	10	1	195	38	21.67
NAT.W.	1	0	41	41	–
B & H					

CAREER: BATTING

	I.	N.O.	R.	H.S.	AV.
TEST					
OTHER FIRST CLASS	63	4	1706	118	28.92
INT					
J.P.L.	25	1	461	45	19.20
NAT.W.	2	0	86	45	43.00
B & H	3	0	84	49	28.00

LAST SEASON: BOWLING

	O.	M.	R.	W.	AV.
TEST					
OTHER FIRST CLASS	63	18	196	5	39.20
INT					
J.P.L.					
NAT.W.					
B & H					

CAREER: BOWLING

	O.	M.	R.	W.	AV.
TEST					
OTHER FIRST CLASS	82	24	243	7	34.72
INT					
J.P.L.	34	2	149	9	16.55
NAT.W.					
B & H					

Qualifications: Australian leaving exams.
Off-season 1984–85: Playing and coaching in South Africa.
Equipment endorsed: Gray-Nicolls.
Overseas tours: With Australian Under-19 team to Pakistan 1981.
Overseas teams played for: Australia Under-19 team West Perth C.C. 1977–82.
Cricketers particularly learnt from: Norm O'Neill, Brian Luckhurst.
Cricketers particularly admired: Derek Underwood.
Other sports: Australian rules football, soccer, squash.
Relaxations: "Music, watching movies (cinema), reading, following sports."
Extras: Captained Australia Under-19 team to Pakistan 1981. Played for Young England v. Young India 1981. Parents emigrated to Australia when he was 4. His mother wrote to Kent in 1978 asking for trial for him. Captained Young Australia as well as Young England.
Best batting performance: 118 Kent v Indians, Canterbury 1982.
Best bowling performance: 2-31 Kent v Oxford University, Oxford 1984.

TAVARÉ, C.J.

Full Name: Christopher James Tavaré.
Role: Right-hand bat, right arm bowler.
Born: 27 October 1954, Orpington, Kent.
Height: 6′ 1½″ **Weight:** 12st.
Nickname: Tav, Rowdy.
County debut: 1974.
County cap: 1978.
Test debut: 1980.
No. of Tests: 30.
No. of One-Day Internationals: 29.
1000 runs in a season: 8.
50 wickets in a season: 0.
1st-Class 50s scored: 81.
1st-Class 100s scored: 25.
1st-Class 200s scored: 0.
1st-Class 5 w. in innings: 0.
1st-Class 10 w. in match: 0.

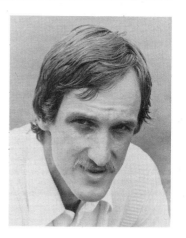

One-day 50s: 28.
One-day 100s: 6.
Place in batting averages: 127 average: 29.21; (1983: 34 average: 42.92).
Place in bowling averages: — average: —; (1983: — average: —).
1st-Class catches 1984: 21 (career: 226).
Parents: Andrew and June Tavaré.

Wife and date of marriage: Vanessa, 22 March 1980.

Education: Riverhead Primary; Sevenoaks School; Oxford University.

Qualifications: Studied zoology.

Family links with cricket: Father, uncle Jack Tavaré, and uncle, Derrick Attwood, all played school and club cricket, father and Uncle Jack at Chatham House, father and Uncle Derrick at Bickley Park C.C. Elder brother, Stephen, and younger brother, Jeremy, both play cricket.

Overseas teams played for: Played for University of Western Australia, Perth, 1977–78. Played for West Perth C.C. for half a season 1978–79.

Equipment used and endorsed: Gray-Nicolls.

Other sports: "Take an interest in most sports."

Relaxations: Music, zoology, playing scrabble, seeing films, gardening, and woodwork.

Extras: Played for England Schools v All-India Schools at Birmingham in 1973, scoring 124 not out. Oxford University cricket blue 1975–76–77. Whitbread Scholarship to Perth, Australia 1978–79. Suffers from asthma and hay-fever. Was top-scorer with 82 not out, and Man of the Match, on debut for England in 55-over match v W. Indies at Headingly, May 1980. "The straightest bat in England"– Sir Len Hutton. According to Peter Roebuck of Somerset, Tavaré, playing for Kent v Somerset, was teased by Botham about his blocking. Botham invited him to hit Marks into the river. Tavaré nodded and smiled and said nothing. Two hours later he hit Marks into the river. Captain 1983–84.

Best batting performance: 168* Kent v Essex, Chelmsford 1982.

LAST SEASON: BATTING

	I.	N.O.	R.	H.S.	AV.
TEST	3	0	79	49	26.33
OTHER FIRST CLASS	38	0	1119	117	29.94
INT					
J.P.L.	14	4	125	34*	12.50
NAT.W.	5	0	185	103	37.00
B & H	4	0	49	31	12.25

CAREER: BATTING

	I.	N.O.	R.	H.S.	AV.
TEST	55	2	1753	149	33.08
OTHER FIRST CLASS	337	38	11711	168*	39.17
INT	28	2	720	83*	27.69
J.P.L.	102	14	2653	136*	30.14
NAT.W.	18	1	700	118*	41.18
B & H	48	2	1228	95	26.69

LAST SEASON: BOWLING

	O.	M.	R.	W.	AV.
TEST	3	3	0	0	–
OTHER FIRST CLASS	2	0	18	0	–
INT					
J.P.L.					
NAT.W.					
B & H					

CAREER: BOWLING

	O.	M.	R.	W.	AV.
TEST	6	3	11	0	–
OTHER FIRST CLASS	51.4	7	282	2	141.0
INT	2	0	3	0	–
J.P.L.					
NAT.W.					
B & H					

TAYLOR, N.R.

Full Name: Neil Royston Taylor.
Role: Right-hand bat, off-break bowler, bat/pad fielder.
Born: 21 July 1959, Farnborough, Kent.
Height: 6' 1" **Weight:** 13st 8lbs.
Nickname: Map.
County debut: 1979.
County cap: 1984.
Test debut: —
No. of Tests: 0.
No. of One-Day Internationals: 0.
1000 runs in a season: 3.
50 wickets in a season: 0.
1st-Class 50s scored: 19.
1st-Class 100s scored: 11.
1st-Class 200s scored: 0.
1st-Class 5 w. in innings: 0.
1st-Class 10 w. in match: 0.
One-day 50s: 5.
One-day 100s: 3.
Place in batting averages: 106 average: 32.29; (1983: 57 average: 38.64).
Place in bowling averages: — average: —; (1983: — average: —).
1st-Class catches 1984: 8 (career: 54).
Parents: Leonard and Audrey Taylor.
Wife: Jane Claire, 25 September, 1982.
Education: Cray Valley Technical High School.
Qualifications: 2 A-levels, 8 O-levels.
Jobs outside cricket: Insurance broker, and clerk with Inland Revenue.
Off-season 1984–85: Playing and coaching in South Africa.
Family links with cricket: Brother Colin played for Kent Under-19s.
Overseas tours: With England Schools Team to India 1977–78, Kent to Vancouver 1979.
Overseas teams played for: Randburg in Johannesburg, South Africa, 1980–83.
Cricketers particularly learnt from: Bob Woolmer, Mark Benson.
Cricketing superstitions: Always puts batting gear on in same order.
Equipment used: Gray-Nicolls.
Other sports: Rugby—played for Kent Under-21 XV—golf, squash.
Relaxations: Listening to records, reading.
Significant injuries in 1984: Injured tendons in left wrist (missed last 2 matches).
Extras: Made 110 on debut match for Kent C.C.C. v Sri Lanka, 1979. Won 4 Man of the Match awards in first 5 matches. Scored highest score by Kent player in Benson and Hedges cricket: 121 v Sussex and Somerset.

Opinions on cricket: "117 overs a day is too high. Why the difference between 18 overs an hour in championship matches and 16 in Tests? Should be cut to 110–108."

Best batting performance: 155* Kent v Glamorgan, Cardiff 1983.

LAST SEASON: BATTING

	I.	N.O.	R.	H.S.	AV.
TEST					
OTHER FIRST CLASS	39	5	1098	139	32.29
INT					
J.P.L.	12	0	309	72	25.75
NAT.W.	5	0	115	49	23.00
B & H	4	0	52	26	13.00

CAREER: BATTING

	I.	N.O.	R.	H.S.	AV.
TEST					
OTHER FIRST CLASS	159	21	4615	155*	33.44
INT					
J.P.L.	34	2	833	74	26.03
NAT.W.	7	0	135	49	19.29
B & H	13	0	563	121	43.31

LAST SEASON: BOWLING

	O.	M.	R.	W.	AV.
TEST					
OTHER FIRST CLASS	15	3	54	0	–
INT					
J.P.L.					
NAT.W.					
B & H					

CAREER: BOWLING

	O.	M.	R.	W.	AV.
TEST					
OTHER FIRST CLASS	80	19	288	5	57.60
INT					
J.P.L.					
NAT.W.					
B & H					

UNDERWOOD, D.L.

Full Name: Derek Leslie Underwood.
Role: Right-hand bat; slow left arm bowler.
Born: 8 June 1945, Bromley, Kent.
Height: 5′ 11″ **Weight:** 12st.
Nickname: Deadly, Unders.
County debut: 1962.
County cap: 1964.
Benefit: 1975: (£24,114).
Test debut: 1966.
No. of Tests: 86.
No. of One-Day Internationals: 26.
1000 runs in a season: 0.
50 wickets in a season: 20.
1st-Class 50s scored: 1.
1st-Class 100s scored: 1.
1st-Class 200s scored: 0.
1st-Class 5 w. in innings: 150.
1st-Class 10 w. in match: 46.
One-day 50s: 0.
One-day 100s: 0.

Place in batting averages: 196 average: 20.75; (1983: 247 average: 10.14).
Place in bowling averages: 6 average: 19.62; (1983: 8 average: 19.28).
1st-Class catches 1984: 11 (career: 249).
Parents: Leslie Underwood, deceased, and Evelyn Underwood.
Wife and date of marriage: Dawn, 6 October 1973.
Children: Heather, 7 February 1976; Fiona, 22 November 1977.
Education: Dulwich College Prep. School; Beckenham & Penge Grammar School.
Jobs outside cricket: Company representative, cricket coach, P.E. schoolmaster. Director of company of Law Stationers.
Family links with cricket: "I played with my father and brother for a local village team, Farnborough. I played for Beckenham with my brother until I played for the Kent 1st XI. My brother now plays for Polok C.C. in Glasgow."
Overseas tours: Pakistan 1966–67; Sri Lanka and Pakistan 1968–69; Australia and New Zealand 1970–71; 1974–75; India, Sri Lanka and Pakistan 1972–73; W. Indies 1973–74; India, Sri Lanka and Australia 1976–77; Australia and India, 1979–80.
Equipment used: Duncan Fearnley.
Other sports: Occasional golf.
Relaxations: Photography, philately, coarse fishing, gardening.
Extras: Second youngest player to receive county cap. Played World Series Cricket 1978–79. Youngest player ever to take 100 wickets in debut season. Banned from Test cricket for 3 years for joining rebel team from England to South Africa. Writes articles for Cricketer International magazine. Top of Kent first-class bowling averages in 1982, 1983 and 1984. Awarded M.B.E. Scored maiden century in 1984 in 618* innings.
Best batting performance: 111 Kent v Sussex, Hastings 1984.
Best bowling performance: 9-28 Kent v Sussex, Hastings 1964.

LAST SEASON: BATTING

	I.	N.O.	R.	H.S.	AV.
TEST					
OTHER FIRST CLASS	33	9	498	111	20.75
INT					
J.P.L.	5	0	8	7	1.60
NAT.W.	2	1	11	11	–
B & H	4	2	17	10	8.50

CAREER: BATTING

	I.	N.O.	R.	H.S.	AV.
TEST	116	35	937	45*	11.57
OTHER FIRST CLASS	523	142	3693	111	9.69
INT	13	4	53	17	5.89
J.P.L.	84	32	353	22	6.78
NAT.W.	31	10	135	28	6.43
B & H	40	18	184	27	8.36

LAST SEASON: BOWLING

	O.	M.	R.	W.	AV.
TEST					
OTHER FIRST CLASS	676.4	250	1511	77	19.62
INT					
J.P.L.	99	11	358	16	22.37
NAT.W.	58	12	159	9	17.67
B & H	41	7	122	6	20.33

CAREER: BOWLING

	O.	M.	R.	W.	AV.
TEST	542.2 2920.4	142 1097	7674	297	25.84
OTHER FIRST CLASS	340.7 17142.1	85 6867	37851	2004	18.89
INT.	6 205	0 26	734	32	22.93
J.P.L.	1382.1	181	5058	315	16.05
NAT.W.	507.3	131	1541	63	24.46
B & H	666.2	141	1820	86	21.16

WATERTON, S.N.V.

Full Name: Stuart Nicholas Varney
Waterton.
Role: Right-hand bat; wicket-keeper.
Born: 6 December 1960, Dartford.
Height: 5' 11½" **Weight:** 11st 7lbs.
Nickname: Buck.
County debut: 1980.
County cap: No.
Test debut: —
No. of Tests: 0.
No. of One-Day Internationals: 0.
1000 runs in a season: 0.
50 wickets in a season: 0.
1st-Class 50s scored: 1.
1st-Class 100s scored: 0.
1st-Class 200s scored: 0.
1st-Class 5 w. in innings: 0.
1st-Class 10 w. in match: 0.
One-day 50s: 0.
One-day 100s: 0.
Place in batting averages: 189 average: 21.44; (1983: — average: —).
Place in bowling averages: — average: —; (1983: — average: —).
Parents: Barry and Olive Waterton.
Marital status: Single.
Family links with cricket: "Father was a magnificent back garden bowler."
Education: St George's Church of England School; Gravesend School for
Boys; London School of Economics, London University.
Qualifications: 3 A-levels, 10 O-levels. N.C.A. Preliminary Coaching Award.
B.Sc. (Economics) Honours.
Off-season 1984–85: Playing and coaching in Johannesburg.
Jobs outside cricket: Civil servant, winter 1979–80.
Cricketers particularly learnt from: "Alan Knott and Bob Taylor, together
with other keepers who have been helpful enough to talk to me about keeping.
Cricketers particularly admired: Taylor, Knott, Glenn Turner.
Cricket superstitions: "I try to do everything the same following a particularly
good day."
Equipment used: John Newbery bat. Readersport soft leather equipment,
Arcass w-k gloves, Brooks footwear.
Other sports: Golf, road-running and cross-country. Follow most sports.
Relaxations: Music, T.V.
Extras: Second wicket-keeper from Gravesend School to play for Kent
C.C.C.—David Nicolls being the other. England Young Wicket Keeper of the
Year 1980. Record individual score for Kent Schools Player, 163 v Sussex
Schools 1979. Record number of runs aggregated in a season for Gravesend

School, 983 runs at average of 75 in 1979. England Young Wicket-keeper of the Year 1980. Played for U.A.U. 1981–83 (captain '83 but did not take the field due to bad weather). Made NatWest debut in 1984 final.

Opinions on cricket: a) Sponsorships are very important for financial stability amongst first class counties—hence it makes sense for the ground facilities to be used twelve months a year. Therefore leisure centres, restaurants etc. should be developed at county headquarters. b) More should be done by county clubs to assist young players in gaining a basis on which they can work in order to develop careers outside of cricket.

Best batting performance: 50 Kent v Lancashire, Old Trafford 1984.

LAST SEASON: BATTING

	I.	N.O.	R.	H.S.	AV.
TEST					
OTHER FIRST CLASS	10	1	193	50	21.44
INT					
J.P.L.	2	1	21	15	–
NAT.W.	1	1	4	4*	–
B & H					

CAREER: BATTING

	I.	N.O.	R.	H.S.	AV.
TEST					
OTHER FIRST CLASS	26	3	364	50	15.83
INT					
J.P.L.	3	1	21	15	10.50
NAT.W.	1	1	4	4*	–
B & H					

LAST SEASON: WICKET KEEPING

	C.	ST.			
TEST					
OTHER FIRST CLASS	11	4			
INT					
J.P.L.	1	2			
NAT.W.	1	–			
B & H					

CAREER: WICKET KEEPING

	C.	ST.			
TEST					
OTHER FIRST CLASS	36	8			
INT					
J.P.L.	2	2			
NAT.W.	1	–			
B & H					

WOOLMER, R.A.

Full Name: Robert Andrew Woolmer.
Role: Right-hand bat; right arm medium bowler.
Born: 14 May 1948, Kanpur, India.
Height: 6′ 0″ **Weight:** 13st 5lbs.
Nickname: Bob, Woolly.
County debut: 1968.
County cap: 1970.
Benefit: 1984.
Test debut: 1975.
No. of Tests: 19.
No. of One-Day Internationals: 6.
1000 runs in a season: 5.
50 wickets in a season: 1.
1st-Class 50s scored: 71.
1st-Class 100s scored: 33.

1st-Class 200s scored: 1.
1st-Class 5 w. in innings: 12.
1st-Class 10 w. in match: 1.
One-day 50s: 15.
One-day 100s: 1.
Place in batting averages: 56 average: 38.82; (1983: 18 average: 47.33).
Place in bowling averages: — average: —; (1983: 5 average: 17.00).
1st-Class catches 1984: 4 (career: 238).
Parents: Clarence (Charles) and Stella Kathleen.
Wife and date of marriage: Gillian Shirley, 9 November 1974.
Children: Dale Robert, 22 March 1979; Russell Christopher, 1 June 1982.
Education: Yardley Court Prep. School; Skinner's School.
Qualifications: 5 O-levels.
Jobs outside cricket: Cricket consultant with Sport and Travel (Twickenham); sports administrator United Hezlia Schools, Cape Town; manager/coach, Avendale C.C. South Africa. Qualified Cricket Coach and Qualified Hockey Coach. Schools Video Coaching Tape.
Family links with cricket: Father played in Ranji Trophy, Uttar Pradesh, against Maharashtra in 1947–48. Also played club cricket for Calcutta, Colombo and Tonbridge C.C.
Overseas tours: India, Sri Lanka, Australia, 1976–77. World Series Cricket 1977–78 and 1978–79. England rebel tour of South Africa 1982. Derick Robbins tour of South Africa 1973–74.
Overseas teams played for: Natal 1973–74 and 1975–76 Currie Cup Competition. Western Province, 1981.
Cricketers particularly learnt from: "Peter Hearn, Colin Page and my father."
Cricketers particularly admired: Colin Cowdrey, Ted Dexter, Fred Trueman, Brian Stratham.
Equipment used: Slazenger.
Equipment endorsed: Reader Sport.
Other sports: Hockey for Tonbridge Hockey Club. Represented Kent A 1969–70. Golf handicap 19. Watching athletics, especially Steve Ovett; Spurs in football.
Relaxations: Photography, theatre. Dining out at the George and Dragon in Speldhurst.
Significant injuries during 1984: Enforced retirement due to severe back injury in 1984.
Extras: When he was a baby his father placed a bat in his hands and said "I hope this will be your life." Played for World Series Cricket in Australia. Hat-trick v. Australia at Lord's for M.C.C. First bowler to take 50 John Player League wickets, in 1970. Only person to bowl more than eight overs in a John Player League match: 8–1 v Hants in 1972. Fractured a cheek-bone after being hit by Malcolm Marshall. Missed several matches. Afterwards, wore a helmet for the first time. Banned from Test cricket for 3 years for joining England rebel tour of South Africa, 1982.
Opinions on cricket: "I am sorry that world cricket will not accept South

LAST SEASON: BATTING

	I.	N.O.	R.	H.S.	AV.
TEST					
OTHER FIRST CLASS	14	3	427	153	38.82
INT					
J.P.L.					
NAT.W.					
B & H	4	0	77	34	19.25

CAREER: BATTING

	I.	N.O.	R.	H.S.	AV.
TEST	34	2	1059	149	33.09
OTHER FIRST CLASS	511	73	14712	203	33.59
INT	4	0	21	9	5.25
J.P.L.	134	23	2054	112*	18.50
NAT.W.	26	6	507	91	25.35
B & H	60	6	1220	79*	22.59

LAST SEASON: BOWLING

	O.	M.	R.	W.	AV.
TEST					
OTHER FIRST CLASS	20	3	51	5	10.20
INT					
J.P.L.					
NAT.W.					
B & H	33	3	102	3	34.00

CAREER: BOWLING

	O.	M.	R.	W.	AV.
TEST	91	16	299	4	74.75
OTHER FIRST CLASS	37 4154.1	4 1112	10569	416	25.66
INT	53.3	3	260	9	28.89
J.P.L.	1162.1	94	4474	220	20.33
NAT.W.	335	58	999	48	20.81
B & H	593.2	92	1654	81	20.42

African cricket back into its fold as I believe that it would be of far more benefit to help South Africa than to isolate it. I also believe that county cricketers play too many games during a season, making a lot of the cricket uninteresting and above all, uneconomical. Over-rate figures are ridiculous considering the financial state of cricket today, and that 18 overs an hour should be the target. I am of the opinion that a large amount of ground work at primary schools level 9-11 age group is necessary. More important that enthusiasm at schoolteacher level has to be increased. The sooner children can learn to love and enjoy cricket the better they will become and the better county and then our Test XI will become. For those who teach at primary schools look out for 'Lets play cricket' a video by Alan Knott, Bob Woolmer and Christopher Martin-Jenkins. It will help!"

Best batting performance: 203 Kent v Sussex, Tunbridge Wells 1982.
Best bowling performance: 7-47 Kent v Sussex, Canterbury 1969.

COUNTY QUIZ

Q. 1. When was the club founded?
Q. 2. Who made the most first-class runs for the county last season, and how many?
Q. 3. What's the highest ever county total, and against whom?
Q. 4. Who took most wickets for the county last season, and how many?
Q. 5. What's the highest individual score for the county, who hit it, and when?
Q. 6. What's the highest scoring partnership for the county for any wicket?
Q. 7. How many times has the club won the County Championship?
Q. 8. What's the lowest ever total made by the county in one innings, when, and against whom?
Q. 9. Which bowler took the most first-class wickets in one season, when, and how many?
Q. 10. Which batsman hit the most runs in one season, when and how many?

Lancashire

ABRAHAMS, J.

Full Name: John Abrahams.
Role: Left-hand bat, off-break bowler. Captain 1984.
Born: 21 July 1952, Capetown, South Africa.
Height: 5′ 7½″ **Weight:** 10st. 4lbs.
Nickname: Abey.
County debut: 1973.
County cap: 1982.
Test debut: —
No. of Tests: 0.
No. of One-Day Internationals: 0.
1000 runs in a season: 3.
50 wickets in a season: 0.
1st-Class 50s scored: 40.
1st-Class 100s scored: 8.
1st-Class 200s scored: 1.
1st-Class 5 w. in innings: 0.
1st-Class 10 w. in match: 0.
One-day 50s: 11.

One-day 100s: 0.
Place in batting averages: 67 average: 36.84; (1983: 55 average: 39.43).
Place in bowling averages: — average: —; (1983: 107 average: 50.62).
1st-Class catches 1984: 19 (career: 127).
Parents: Cecil John and Cynthia Jean Abrahams.
Marital status: "Still single!!"
Education: Moorhouse County Primary School; Heywood Grammar School (later became Heywood Senior High School).
Qualification: A-level biology, nine 0-levels. N.C.A. Preliminary Coaching Certificate.
Jobs outside cricket: Shop manager and representative, Beaverwise Plant Hire, Oldham.
Off-season 1984–85: Coaching and playing in Canberra.
Family links with cricket: Father was professional with Milnrow and Radcliffe in Central Lancashire League. Brother Basil professional at Castleton Moor.

Brother Peter at Milnrow in Central Lancs. League. Basil professional for Heyside in Saddleworth League in 1980.

Overseas teams played for: Player-coach for Mowbray C.C., Tasmania, 1980-81. Western Creek C.C., Canberra 1983-84.

Equipment used: Gunn & Moore.

Cricketers particularly learnt from: Jack Bond and Peter Lever.

Cricketers particularly admired: Clive Lloyd and Mike Brearley.

Other sports: Badminton, golf, watching rugby union on T.V.

Relaxation: "Listening to pop music: Rod Stewart, Fleetwood Mac, for example."

Significant injuries in 1984: Hit in face while fielding at short leg.

Extras: Has lived in UK since 1962. Played as substitute for England in place of Brian Rose in Fifth Test against W. Indies at Headingley in August 1980. "Would very much like to be a physiotherapist when I retire". Gold award winner in 1984 B&H final.

Opinions on cricket: "Cricket managers are necessary in today's game not only to transfer some of the responsibilities from the captain, but also as an extra pair of eyes in a more advantageous position . . . Despite the prolonged discussion on the commercial aspects of the English cricketers' tour to South Africa, on a purely moral basis, there is no way I could tolerate a society which discriminates against some of its people. I do realise that my position is not typical".

Best batting performance: 201* Lancashire v Warwickshire, Nuneaton 1984.

Best bowling performance: 3-27 Lancashire v Worcestershire, Old Trafford 1981.

LAST SEASON: BATTING

	I.	N.O.	R.	H.S.	AV.
TEST					
OTHER FIRST CLASS	39	6	1216	201*	36.84
INT					
J.P.L.	13	0	316	59	24.30
NAT.W.	3	0	64	51	21.33
B & H	7	2	159	66*	31.80

CAREER: BATTING

	I.	N.O.	R.	H.S.	AV.
TEST					
OTHER FIRST CLASS	294	40	7293	201*	28.71
INT					
J.P.L.	93	20	1807	79*	24.75
NAT.W.	17	2	273	51*	18.20
B & H	18	5	353	66*	27.15

LAST SEASON: BOWLING

	O.	M.	R.	W.	AV.
TEST					
OTHER FIRST CLASS	88	19	247	4	61.75
INT					
J.P.L.	6	0	24	0	–
NAT.W.	10	1	45	1	–
B & H	3	0	14	0	–

CAREER: BOWLING

	O.	M.	R.	W.	AV.
TEST					
OTHER FIRST CLASS	849	180	2472	47	52.60
INT					
J.P.L.	57.2	3	317	6	52.83
NAT.W.	14	1	76	1	–
B & H	3	0	14	0	–

ALLOTT, P.J.W.

Full Name: Paul John Walter Allott.
Role: Right-hand bat, right arm fast medium bowler.
Born: 14 September 1956, Altrincham, Cheshire.
Height: 6′ 4″ **Weight:** 14st.
Nickname: Wally.
County debut: 1978.
County cap: 1981.
Test debut: 1981.
No. of Tests: 8.
No. of One-Day Internationals: 10.
1000 runs in a season: 0.
50 wickets in a season: 2.
1st-Class 50s scored: 2.
1st-Class 100s scored: 0.
1st-Class 200s scored: 0.
1st-Class 5 w. in innings: 15.
1st-Class 10 w. in match: 0.
One-day 50s: 0.
One-day 100s: 0.
Place in batting averages: 237 average: 15.52; (1983: 203 average: 16.07).
Place in bowling averages: 5 average: 18.93; (1983: 72 average: 31.00).
1st-Class catches 1984: 8 (career: 34).
Parents: John Norman and Lillian Patricia Allott.
Wife and date of marriage: Helen, 27 October 1979.
Education: Altrincham Grammar School; Bede College, Durham.
Qualifications: Qualified teacher. Cricket coach.
Jobs outside cricket: Teacher. Cricket coach for Manchester Education Committee. Coach in Tasmania for Tasmanian Cricket Association.
Overseas tours: To India with England 1981–82, India and Australia 1984–85; to Jamaica with International XI 1982–83.
Family links with cricket: Father was dedicated club cricketer for 20 years with Ashley C.C. and is now active with Bowdon C.C. (Cheshire County League) as a selector, administrator and junior organiser.
Cricketers particularly learnt from: Dennis Lillee, Steve Murrills.
Equipment used and endorsed: Slazenger.
Other sports: Golf, football, squash, rugby, tennis.
Relaxations: Playing golf, watching all sports, listening to music, eating out, photography.
Extras: Played as goal-keeper for Cheshire schoolboys. Took part in 10th wicket record partnership for England with Bob Willis, 70, v. India, at Lords, June 1982. Wears contact lenses. Forced by injury to return early from Indian tour.

Best batting performance: 52* England v Australia, Old Trafford 1981.
Best bowling performance: 8-48 Lancashire v Northamptonshire, Northampton 1981.

LAST SEASON: BATTING

	I.	N.O.	R.	H.S.	AV.
TEST	7	0	67	26	9.57
OTHER FIRST CLASS	18	4	259	50*	18.50
INT					
J.P.L.	4	2	13	6	6.50
NAT.W.	1	0	7	7	–
B & H	1	1	15	15*	–

CAREER: BATTING

	I.	N.O.	R.	H.S.	AV.
TEST	13	2	186	52*	16.91
OTHER FIRST CLASS	98	27	949	52*	13.37
INT	5	1	13	8	3.25
J.P.L.	29	17	204	32*	17.00
NAT.W.	6	3	36	19*	12.00
B & H	8	3	41	15*	8.20

LAST SEASON: BOWLING

	O.	M.	R.	W.	AV.
TEST	141.5	33	373	15	24.87
OTHER FIRST CLASS	463	138	1123	64	17.55
INT					
J.P.L.	81.4	11	261	14	18.64
NAT.W.	32	4	111	7	15.86
B & H	71.4	10	234	9	26.00

CAREER: BOWLING

	O.	M.	R.	W.	AV.
TEST	257.5	53	787	21	37.48
OTHER FIRST CLASS	2672.3	697	7221	282	25.61
INT	108.3	17	420	13	32.30
J.P.L.	448.5	49	1772	74	23.94
NAT.W.	112.4	21	346	22	15.73
B & H	214.5	36	674	28	24.07

CHADWICK, M.R.

Full Name: Mark Robert Chadwick.
Role: Right-hand bat.
Born: 9 February 1963, Rochdale, Lancs.
Height: 6' 1" **Weight:** 12st 9lbs.
Nickname: Chad.
County debut: 1983.
County cap: No.
Test debut: —
No. of Tests: 0.
No. of One-Day Internationals: 0.
1000 runs in a season: 0.
50 wickets in a season: 0.
1st-Class 50s scored: 2.
1st-Class 100s scored: 0.
1st-Class 200s scored: 0.
1st-Class 5 w. in innings: 0.
1st-Class 10 w. in match: 0.
One-day 50s: 1.
One-day 100s: 0.
Place in batting averages: 193: average: 20.93; (1983: — average: —).
Place in bowling averages: — average: —; (1983: — average: —).

1st-Class catches 1984: 2 (career: 3).
Parents: Robert and Kathleen Chadwick.
Family links with cricket: None.
Education: Moorhouse County Primary School, Milnrow; Rock Valley High School, Milnrow.
Jobs outside cricket: 1979–83 Storeman for diesel engine firm.
Equipment used: Gray Nicolls.
Cricketers particularly learnt from: Geoffrey Boycott – powers of concentration while at the crease.
Other sports: Football, table tennis, badminton, golf.
Relaxations: Listening to music.
Extras: Central Lancs League record run scorer for amateur. 1267 runs for Milnrow C.C. in 1983, beating the previous record of 1205 from 1915. Won gold award in first B&H match (1984 semi-final).
Best batting performance: 61 Lancashire v Nottinghamshire, Blackpool 1984.

LAST SEASON: BATTING

	I.	N.O.	R.	H.S.	AV.
TEST					
OTHER FIRST CLASS	14	0	293	61	20.93
INT					
J.P.L.					
NAT.W.					
B & H	1	0	87	87	–

CAREER: BATTING

	I.	N.O.	R.	H.S.	AV.
TEST					
OTHER FIRST CLASS	16	0	295	61	18.44
INT					
J.P.L.	1	0	10	10	–
NAT.W.					
B & H	1	0	87	87	–

LAST SEASON: BOWLING

	O.	M.	R.	W.	AV.
TEST					
OTHER FIRST CLASS					
INT					
J.P.L.					
NAT.W.					
B & H					

CAREER: BOWLING

	O.	M.	R.	W.	AV.
TEST					
OTHER FIRST CLASS					
INT					
J.P.L.					
NAT.W.					
B & H					

Q. 89. Who has scored the most runs in Tests for England?

Q. 90. Who has scored the most runs in Test matches for Australia?

FAIRBROTHER, N.H.

Full Name: Neil Harvey
Fairbrother.
Role: Left-hand bat, left-hand
medium bowler.
Born: 9 September, 1963,
Warrington, Cheshire.
Height: 5' 9" **Weight:** 11st.
Nickname: Harvey, Farnsbarns
("don't know why!").
County debut: 1982.
County cap: No.
Test debut: —
No. of Tests: 0.
No. of One-Day Internationals: 0.
1000 runs in a season: 1.
50 wickets in a season: 0.
1st-Class 50s scored: 18.
1st-Class 100s scored: 1.
1st-Class 200s scored: 0.
1st-Class 5 w. in innings: 0.
1st-Class 10 w. in match: 0.
One-day 50s: 1.
One-day 100s: 0.
Place in batting averages: 112 average: 31.61; (1983: 69 average: 36.14).
Place in bowling averages: — average: —; (1983: — average: —).
1st-Class catches 1984: 19 (career: 27).
Parents: Leslie Robert and Barbara Fairbrother.
Marital status: Single.

LAST SEASON: BATTING

	I.	N.O.	R.	H.S.	AV.
TEST					
OTHER FIRST CLASS	39	1	1201	102	31.61
INT					
J.P.L.	13	3	229	54*	22.90
NAT.W.	3	0	84	36	28.00
B & H	6	4	141	45*	70.50

CAREER: BATTING

	I.	N.O.	R.	H.S.	AV.
TEST					
OTHER FIRST CLASS	65	6	1960	102	33.22
INT					
J.P.L.	18	3	318	54*	21.20
NAT.W.	3	0	84	36	28.00
B & H	6	4	141	45*	70.50

LAST SEASON: BOWLING

	O.	M.	R.	W.	AV.
TEST					
OTHER FIRST CLASS	4.1	1	20	1	—
INT					
J.P.L.					
NAT.W.					
B & H					

CAREER: BOWLING

	O.	M.	R.	W.	AV.
TEST					
OTHER FIRST CLASS	7.1	3	21	1	—
INT					
J.P.L.					
NAT.W.					
B & H					

Education: St Margaret's Church of England Junior School, Oxford. Lymn Grammar School.
Qualifications: 5 O-levels.
Overseas tours: Denmark 1981 with North of England U-19.
Family links with cricket: Father and two uncles played local league cricket.
Other sports: Rugby, squash. Watch football, rugby union and rugby league.
Equipment used: Gunn and Moore.
Relaxations: Music and reading.
Extras: "I was named after the Australian cricketer Neil Harvey, who was my mum's favourite cricketer." Three Tests and two U-19 One Day Internationals v Young Australians 1983.
Opinions on cricket: "County championships should be 4-day games."
Best batting performance: 102 Lancashire v Derbyshire, Buxton 1984.

FOLLEY, I.

Full Name: Ian Folley.
Role: Right-hand bat, slow left arm bowler.
Born: 9 January, 1963.
Height: 5′ 10″ **Weight:** 12st.
Nickname: Thatch.
County debut: 1982.
County cap: No.
Test debut: —
No. of Tests: 0.
No. of One-Day Internationals: 0.
1000 runs in a season: 0.
50 wickets in a season: 0.
1st-Class 50s scored: 0.
1st-Class 100s scored: 0.
1st-Class 200s scored: 0.
1st-Class 5 w. in innings: 2.
1st-Class 10 w. in match: 0.
One-day 50s: 0.
One-day 100s: 0.

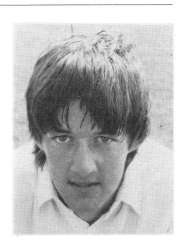

Place in batting averages: 270 average: 10.21; (1983: 193 average: 18.20).
Place in bowling averages: 64 average: 29.85; (1983: — average: —).
1st-Class catches 1984: 6 (career: 12).
Parents: James and Constance Folley.
Marital status: Single.
Education: Mansfield High School, Briersfield, Nelson and Colne College.
Qualifications: Business Studies.
Family links with cricket: None.
Cricketers particularly learnt from: "County team-mates. D. Bloodworth as

coach. Viv Richards, Ian Botham, Alvin Kallicharran and Derek Underwood."

Overseas tours: Barbados 1982 with Lancashire. Denmark 1981 with N.C.A.

Equipment used: Duncan Fearnley.

Other sports: "All, except anything to do with horses. I'm a bad watcher."

Extras: Represented Lancashire Schools U-15s, and U-19s as captain. Represented Lancashire Federation 1979, 1980, 1981. England U-19 v India U-19. 3 "Tests" in 1981. Young England v West Indies (3 "Tests") and 2 1-day "Internationals". Debut for Lancs. v Cambridge University at Fenners. In 1984 changed from left arm medium pace to slow left arm bowler.

Relaxations: Listening to Caribbean music, driving, golf.

Best batting performance: 36 Lancashire v Derbyshire, Old Trafford 1982.

Best bowling performance: 5-65 Lancashire v Glamorgan, Cardiff 1984.

LAST SEASON: BATTING

	I.	N.O.	R.	H.S.	AV.
TEST					
OTHER FIRST CLASS	28	9	194	22*	10.21
INT					
J.P.L.					
NAT.W.					
B & H					

CAREER: BATTING

	I.	N.O.	R.	H.S.	AV.
TEST					
OTHER FIRST CLASS	52	17	450	36	12.86
INT					
J.P.L.	7	5	33	11*	16.50
NAT.W.	1	1	3	3*	–
B & H	5	5	21	11*	–

LAST SEASON: BOWLING

	O.	M.	R.	W.	AV.
TEST					
OTHER FIRST CLASS	374	90	1015	34	29.85
INT					
J.P.L.					
NAT.W.					
B & H					

CAREER: BOWLING

	O.	M.	R.	W.	AV.
TEST					
OTHER FIRST CLASS	874	215	2295	68	33.75
INT					
J.P.L.	106	4	477	8	59.63
NAT.W.	15.3	2	48	4	12.00
B & H	84	17	215	14	15.36

Q. 91. Who has scored the most runs for the West Indies in Test Matches?

Q. 92. Who has scored the most runs for South Africa in Tests?

FOWLER, G.

Full Name: Graeme Fowler.
Role: Left-hand opening bat,
cover fielder, occasional wicket-
keeper.
Born: 20 April 1957, Accrington.
Height: 5′ 9½″ **Weight:** "Near 11st."
Nickname: Fow, Fox, Foxy.
County debut: 1979.
County cap: 1981.
Test debut: 1982.
No. of Tests: 16.
No. of One-Day Internationals: 13.
1000 runs in a season: 4.
50 wickets in a season: 0.
1st-Class 50s scored: 31.
1st-Class 100s scored: 17.
1st-Class 200s scored: 1.
1st-Class 5 w. in innings: 0.
1st-Class 10 w. in match: 0.
One-day 50s: 19.
One-day 100s: 2.
Place in batting averages: 81 average: 34.72; (1983: 13 average: 51.96).
Place in bowling averages: — average: —; (1983: — average: —).
1st-Class catches 1984: 7 (career: 56).
Education: Accrington Grammar School; Bede College, Durham University.
Wife: Stephanie.
Jobs outside cricket: Qualified teacher, swimming teacher. Advanced cricket
coach.

LAST SEASON: BATTING

	I.	N.O.	R.	H.S.	AV.
TEST	11	0	285	106	25.91
OTHER FIRST CLASS	18	0	722	226	40.11
INT	3	0	60	34	20.00
J.P.L.	9	0	389	75	43.22
NAT.W.	3	0	237	122	79.00
B & H	7	0	210	92	30.00

CAREER: BATTING

	I.	N.O.	R.	H.S.	AV.
TEST	29	0	869	106	29.97
OTHER FIRST CLASS	154	9	5675	226	39.14
INT	13	2	488	81*	44.36
J.P.L.	57	4	1312	75	24.75
NAT.W.	10	0	419	122	41.90
B & H	22	1	601	97	28.62

LAST SEASON: BOWLING

	O.	M.	R.	W.	AV.
TEST	1	0	8	0	–
OTHER FIRST CLASS	2.1	0	8	0	
INT					
J.P.L.					
NAT.W.					
B & H					

CAREER: BOWLING

	O.	M.	R.	W.	AV.
TEST	2	0	11	0	–
OTHER FIRST CLASS	17.1	2	71	2	35.50
INT					
J.P.L.	1	0	1	0	–
NAT.W.					
B & H					

Off-season 1984–85: Playing with England in India and Australia.
Overseas tours: Australia and New Zealand 1982–83; New Zealand and Pakistan 1983–84.
Overseas teams played for: Scarborough, Perth, Western Australia, Tasmania, 1981–82.
Equipment used: Duncan Fearnley.
Extras: Has played for 2nd XI since 1973. Played in one John Player League match v Derbyshire at Chesterfield in 1978. At 15 he was the youngest opener in the Lancashire League. Scored two consecutive centuries v Warwickshire in July 1982 with aid of a runner. Never played cricket until he was 12. Played for Accrington and Rawtenstall in Lancashire League. In 1975 and 1976 played for E.S.C.A., N.A.Y.C., and M.C.C. Schools and Young England.
Best batting performance: 226 Lancashire v Kent, Maidstone 1984.

HAYES, F.C.

Full Name: Frank Charles Hayes.
Role: Right-hand bat, right arm medium bowler.
Born: 6 December 1946, Preston, Lancs.
County debut: 1970.
County cap: 1972.
Test debut: 1973.
No. of Tests: 9.
No. of One-Day Internationals: 6.
1000 runs in a season: 6.
50 wickets in a season: 0.
1st-Class 50s scored: 60.
1st-Class 100s scored: 23.
1st-Class 200s scored: 0.
1st-Class 5 w. in innings: 0.
1st-Class 10 w. in match: 0.
One-day 50s: 23.
One-day 100s: 1.
Place in batting averages: — average: —; (1983: 92 average: 32.08).
Place in bowling averages: — average: —; (1983: — average —).
1st-Class catches 1984: 0 (career: 176).
Education: De la Salle College, Salford; Sheffield University.
Overseas tours: West Indies 1973–74. "The Cricketer" Tour of Dubai, 1981–82.
Extras: Hit 34 in one over (six, four, six, six, six, six) off Malcolm Nash v Glamorgan at Swansea in 1977. Scored 94 on Lancs. debut. Scored 106 not out, v W. Indies in Test debut. Broke bone in his left foot in only second

championship match of 1982 season. Lancashire captain 1978–80. Amateur soccer player. Retired from 1st-Class cricket 1984 due to persistent injury.
Best batting performance: 187 Lancashire v Indians, Old Trafford 1974.

LAST SEASON: BATTING

	I.	N.O.	R.	H.S.	AV.
TEST					
OTHER FIRST CLASS	1	0	11	11	–
INT					
J.P.L.					
NAT.W.					
B & H					

CAREER: BATTING

	I.	N.O.	R.	H.S.	AV.
TEST	17	1	244	106*	15.25
OTHER FIRST CLASS	404	57	12774	187	36.81
INT	6	1	128	52	25.60
J.P.L.	127	21	2616	87	24.67
NAT.W.	31	3	711	93	25.39
B & H	47	8	1264	102	32.41

LAST SEASON: BOWLING

	O.	M.	R.	W.	AV.
TEST					
OTHER FIRST CLASS					
INT					
J.P.L.					
NAT.W.					
B & H					

CAREER: BOWLING

	O.	M.	R.	W.	AV.
TEST					
OTHER FIRST CLASS	9.2	3	15	0	–
INT					
J.P.L.					
NAT.W.					
B & H					

HAYES, K.A.

Full Name: Kevin Anthony Hayes.
Role: Right-hand bat; right arm medium bowler.
Born: 26 September 1962, Mexborough, Yorkshire.
Height: 5′ 7″ **Weight:** 11st. 7lbs.
Nickname: Viking, Two-heads, Hazell, Crazy.
County debut: 1980.
County cap: No.
Test debut: —
No. of Tests: 0.
No. of One-Day Internationals: 0.
1000 runs in a season: 0.
50 wickets in a season: 0.
1st-Class 50s scored: 5.
1st-Class 100s scored: 1.
1st-Class 200s scored: 0.
1st-Class 5 w. in innings: 0.
1st-Class 10 w. in match: 0.
One-day 50s: 2.
One-day 100s: 0.

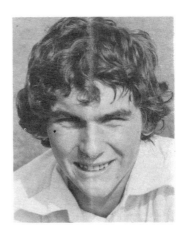

Place in batting averages: 254 average: 13.93; (1983: 221 average: 13.75).
Place in bowling averages: — average: —; (1983: — average: —).
1st-Class catches 1984: 4 (career 12).
Parents: Edward and Pam Hayes.
Marital status: Single.
Education: Queen Elizabeth's School, Blackburn; Merton College, Oxford.
Qualifications: BA(Hons) Chemistry.
Off-season 1984–85: In Australia.
Family links with cricket: Brother, David, played for Lancashire Under-13 and Under-15, and captained Under-15 Schools.
Cricketing superstitions: 111.
Equipment used: Gray-Nicolls.
Other sports: "Any."
Cricketers particularly admired: Richard Hadlee, Viv Richards.
Relaxations: "Listening to most types of music, crosswords."
Extras: Oxford Blue— captain of University in 1984.
Best batting performance: 152 Oxford University v Warwickshire, Oxford 1982.
Best bowling performance: 6-58 Oxford University v Warwickshire, Edgbaston 1983.

LAST SEASON: BATTING

	I.	N.O.	R.	H.S.	AV.
TEST					
OTHER FIRST CLASS	16	1	209	37	13.93
INT					
J.P.L.	2	1	54	53	–
NAT.W.					
B & H	4	0	122	67	30.50

CAREER: BATTING

	I.	N.O.	R.	H.S.	AV.
TEST					
OTHER FIRST CLASS	63	4	1268	152	21.49
INT					
J.P.L.	3	1	59	53	29.50
NAT.W.					
B & H	10	0	164	67	16.40

LAST SEASON: BOWLING

	O.	M.	R.	W.	AV.
TEST					
OTHER FIRST CLASS	99	28	284	9	31.55
INT					
J.P.L.	1	0	5	0	–
NAT.W.					
B & H	39	9	119	4	29.75

CAREER: BOWLING

	O.	M.	R.	W.	AV.
TEST					
OTHER FIRST CLASS	160.1	40	537	17	31.59
INT					
J.P.L.	1	0	5	0	–
NAT.W.					
B & H	39	9	119	4	29.75

Q. 93. Who has scored the most runs for New Zealand in Tests?

HUGHES, D.P.

Full Name: David Paul Hughes.
Role: Right-hand bat, slow left arm orthodox bowler.
Born: 13 May 1947, Newton-le-Willows.
Height: 5′ 11″ **Weight:** 12st.
Nickname: Yozzer.
County debut: 1967.
County cap: 1970.
Test debut: —
No. of Tests: 0.
No. of One-Day Internationals: 0.
Testimonial: 1981.
1000 runs in a season: 2.
50 wickets in a season: 4.
1st-Class 50s scored: 35.
1st-Class 100s scored: 8.
1st-Class 200s scored: 0.
1st-Class 5 w. in innings: 20.
1st-Class 10 w. in match: 2.
One-day 50s: 9.

One-day 100s: 0.
Place in batting averages: 181 average: 22.77; (1983: 177 average: 20.08).
Place in bowling averages: — average: —; (1983: — average: —).
1st-Class catches 1984: 12 (career: 233).
Parents: Both deceased.
Wife and date of marriage: Christine, March 1973.
Children: James, July 1975.
Education: Newton-le-Willows Grammar School.
Qualifications: N.C.A. coaching certificate.
Family links with cricket: Father, Lloyd, a professional with Bolton League Club, Walkden, before and after World War II.
Overseas tours: With Derrick Robins to South Africa 1972–73; England Counties side to West Indies 1974–75.
Overseas teams played for: Played for Tasmania while coaching there in 1975–76 and 1976–77.
Cricketers particularly learnt from: "At the start of my career I spoke to all the leading left arm spin bowlers in the game for help."
Equipment used: Slazenger.
Relaxations: Golf, member of Warrington Golf Club.
Extras: Coached in South Africa 1977–78; coached in Tasmania 1978–79 and 1979–80. Gillette Cup "specialist". Hit 24 runs off John Mortimer v Gloucs in penultimate over in Gillette semi-final in 1972. Hit 26 runs off last over of innings v Northamptonshire in Gillette Final at Lord's 1976. Bowled 13

consecutive maiden overs v Gloucestershire at Bristol, 1980. John Player League 9th wicket partnership of 86 with P. Lever v Essex (Leyton) 1973.
Best batting performance: 153 Lancashire v Glamorgan, Old Trafford 1983.
Best bowling performance: 7-24 Lancashire v Oxford University, Oxford 1970.

LAST SEASON: BATTING

	I.	N.O.	R.	H.S.	AV.
TEST					
OTHER FIRST CLASS	32	1	706	113	22.77
INT					
J.P.L.	14	3	422	91	38.36
NAT.W.	3	0	87	38	29.00
B & H	7	4	206	48*	68.67

CAREER: BATTING

	I.	N.O.	R.	H.S.	AV.
TEST					
OTHER FIRST CLASS	447	82	8201	153	22.47
INT					
J.P.L.	170	41	2385	92	18.48
NAT.W.	33	15	728	71	40.44
B & H	44	13	835	52	26.94

LAST SEASON: BOWLING

	O.	M.	R.	W.	AV.
TEST					
OTHER FIRST CLASS	105	14	261	4	65.25
INT					
J.P.L.					
NAT.W.					
B & H	9	2	40	1	–

CAREER: BOWLING

	O.	M.	R.	W.	AV.
TEST					
OTHER FIRST CLASS	6680.1	23 3 2051	18228	609	29.93
INT.					
J.P.L.	786.1	62	3387	161	21.03
NAT.W.	299.2	29	1161	44	26.39
B & H	218.2	39	702	28	25.07

JEFFERIES, S.T.

Full Name: Steve Jefferies.
Role: Left-hand bat; fast medium left arm bowler.
Born: 8 December 1959, Cape Town, South Africa.
County debut: 1983 (Lancashire).
County cap: No.
Test debut: —
No. of Tests: 0.
No. of One-Day Internationals: 0.
1000 runs in a season: 0.
50 wickets in a season: 0.
1st-Class 50s scored: 6.
1st-Class 100s scored: 0.
1st-Class 200s scored: 0.
1st-Class 5 w. in innings: 10.
1st-Class 10 w. in match: 2.
One-day 50s: 0.
One-day 100s: 0.

Place in batting averages: 156 average: 25.32; (1983: 90 average: 32.50).

Place in bowling averages: 82 average: 32.37; (1983: 35 average: 24.90).
1st-Class catches 1984: 4 (career: 23).
Education: Plumstead High School.
Jobs outside cricket: Physical training instructor with South African Navy.
Off-season 1984–85: In South Africa, in Currie Cup since 1978–79.
Overseas teams played for: Western Province, South Africa.
Extras: Professional with Crompton in Central Lancashire League. Played for South African Schools XI in 1978.
Best batting performance: 75* Lancashire v Essex, Old Trafford 1983.
Best bowling performance: 8-46 Lancashire v Nottinghamshire, Trent Bridge 1983.

LAST SEASON: BATTING

	I.	N.O.	R.	H.S.	AV.
TEST					
OTHER FIRST CLASS	28	3	633	65	25.32
INT					
J.P.L.	10	2	215	35*	26.87
NAT.W.	2	1	23	23*	–
B & H	2	0	41	39	20.50

CAREER: BATTING

	I.	N.O.	R.	H.S.	AV.
TEST					
OTHER FIRST CLASS	97	19	2016	75*	25.85
INT					
J.P.L.	13	3	303	37*	30.30
NAT.W.	2	1	23	23*	–
B & H	2	0	41	39	20.50

LAST SEASON: BOWLING

	O.	M.	R.	W.	AV.
TEST					
OTHER FIRST CLASS	451.2	86	1392	43	32.37
INT					
J.P.L.	93.1	7	394	16	24.62
NAT.W.	21.5	1	88	3	29.33
B & H	75.4	17	220	11	20.00

CAREER: BOWLING

	O.	M.	R.	W.	AV.
TEST					
OTHER FIRST CLASS	2362.1	548	6788	251	27.04
INT					
J.P.L.	117.1	10	497	17	29.23
NAT.W.	21.5	1	88	3	29.33
B & H	75.4	17	220	11	20.00

Q. 94. Who has scored the most runs for India in Tests?
Q. 95. Who scored the most runs in one day in a Test?

LLOYD, C.H.

Full Name: Clive Hubert Lloyd.
Role: Left-hand bat, right arm medium bowler.
Born: 31 August 1944, Georgetown, Guyana.
Height: 6′ 4½″ **Weight:** 14st.
Nickname: Big C, Hubert.
County debut: 1968.
County cap: 1969.
Test debut: 1966–67.
No. of Tests: 105.
No. of One-Day Internationals: 73.
Testimonial: £27,199 in 1977.
1000 runs in a season: 10.
50 wickets in a season: 0.
1st-Class 50s scored: 123.
1st-Class 100s scored: 71.
1st-Class 200s scored: 5.
1st-Class 5 w. in innings: 0.
1st-Class 10 w. in match: 0.
One-day 50s: 53.
One-day 100s: 10.

Place in batting averages: 16 average: 52.00; (1983: 103 average: 29.80).
Place in bowling averages: — average: —; (1983: — average: —).
1st-Class catches 1984: 12 (career: 366).
Parents: Arthur Christopher and Sylvia Thelma Lloyd.
Wife and date of marriage: Waveney, 11 September 1971.
Children: Melissa Monica Simone, 22 February 1974; Samantha Louise, 26 January 1976.
Education: St. Ambrose Primary School, Fountain A.M.E. School and Chatham High School, Georgetown, Guyana.
Qualifications: Cricket coaching certificate. Honorary degrees from Universities of Manchester and Hull.
Jobs outside cricket: Civil servant, Guyana Ministry of Health.
Family links with cricket: Cousin of Lance Gibbs of Warwickshire C.C.C. and West Indies. "My parents had no interest in sport."
Overseas tours: India and Ceylon 1966–67; Australia and New Zealand 1968–69; England 1969, 1973, 1976, 1980 and 1984; Australia 1979–80 and 1984–85; Pakistan 1980–81; India 1983–84.
Equipment endorsed: Gray-Nicolls.
Other sports: Tennis, table tennis, squash, golf, jogging.
Relaxations: Reading, listening to good music. "A bit of soul, a bit of hard rock and a bit of jazz. To say I appreciate Johnny Mathis probably sums it up."
Extras: Played for Haslingden in Lancashire League in 1967. Played for Rest of

the World XI in 1967, 1968, five matches in 1970 and two in 1971 and 1972. Has written articles for Lancashire Evening Post and Bolton Express. Has had knee injury problems since 1976. Was strong supporter of World Series Cricket. Published (by Stanley Paul) "Living for Cricket" in 1980. Eye-sight deteriorated after he tried to separate two boys fighting, at age 12, and received a blow in the eye, and has worn spectacles ever since, including when playing cricket. Has scored 6 centuries v. Yorks.— a Lancs. record. Scored 201 not out in 120 minutes for West Indies v Glamorgan at Swansea, 1976, to equal record for fastest double century in first-class cricket. Captain of Lancashire since 1981. Captain of West Indies since 1974, and announced retirement at end of 1984–85 tour of Australia.

Opinions on cricket: "Cricket has moulded me as a person and, I would like to think, for the better. It has certainly broadened my outlook on life, teaching me self-discipline, and making me appreciate people from all walks of life, of diverse nationalities, races, religions and cultures."

Best batting performance: 242* West Indies v India, Bombay 1974–75.
Best bowling performance: 4-48 Lancashire v Leicestershire, Old Trafford 1970.

LAST SEASON: BATTING

	I.	N.O.	R.	H.S.	AV.
TEST	6	1	255	31	51.00
OTHER FIRST CLASS	3	1	109	72	54.50
INT	2	0	60	52	30.00
J.P.L.	1	0	5	5	–
NAT.W.					
B & H					

CAREER: BATTING

	I.	N.O.	R.	H.S.	AV.
TEST	167	13	7159	242*	46.49
OTHER FIRST CLASS	532	79	22706	217*	50.12
INT	59	14	1609	102	35.76
J.P.L.	145	37	4310	134*	39.90
NAT.W.	34	5	1635	126	56.38
B & H	40	4	1099	124	30.53

LAST SEASON: BOWLING

	O.	M.	R.	W.	AV.
TEST					
OTHER FIRST CLASS					
INT					
J.P.L.					
NAT.W.					
B & H					

CAREER: BOWLING

	O.	M.	R.	W.	AV.
TEST	39 234	6 69	622	10	62.20
OTHER FIRST CLASS	34 1263	7 302	3482	104	33.48
INT	3 55.3	0 7	210	7	30.00
J.P.L.	221	16	935	36	25.97
NAT.W.	92.3	16	320	12	26.67
B & H	83.3	18	302	12	25.17

Q. 96. Who bowled the most balls in Test matches?

Q. 97. How many players have played Test cricket at the age of 50 or over, and who were they?

MAKINSON, D.J.

Full Name: David John Makinson.
Role: Right-hand bat, left arm
medium bowler, outfielder.
Born: 12 January 1961, Eccleston,
Lancs.
Height: 6′ 3″ **Weight:** 12st. 7lbs.
Nickname: "Too many to write here."
County debut: 1984.
County cap: No.
Test debut: —
No. of Tests: 0.
No. of One-Day Internationals: 0.
1000 runs in a season: 0.
50 wickets in a season: 0.
1st-Class 50s scored: 0.
1st-Class 100s scored: 0.
1st-Class 200s scored: 0.
1st-Class 5 w. in innings: 0.
1st-Class 10 w. in match: 0.
One-day 50s: 0.
One-day 100s: 0.
Place in batting averages: — average: —; (1983: — average: —).
Place in bowling averages: — average: —; (1983: — average: —).
Parents: Thomas Andrew and Rhoda.
Wife and date of marriage: Susan, 9 April 1983.
Education: St. Mary's Primary, St. Mary's Junior, St. Mary's High School,
Leyland Mts. Technical College, Bolton Institute of Technology.

LAST SEASON: BATTING

	I.	N.O.	R.	H.S.	AV.
TEST					
OTHER FIRST CLASS	5	2	18	9	6.00
INT					
J.P.L.	4	2	4	2*	2.00
NAT.W.					
B & H					

CAREER: BATTING

	I.	N.O.	R.	H.S.	AV.
TEST					
OTHER FIRST CLASS	5	2	18	9	6.00
INT					
J.P.L.	4	2	4	2*	2.00
NAT.W.					
B & H					

LAST SEASON: BOWLING

	O.	M.	R.	W.	AV.
TEST					
OTHER FIRST CLASS	93	17	313	7	44.72
INT					
J.P.L.	77	1	346	16	21.62
NAT.W.					
B & H					

CAREER: BOWLING

	O.	M.	R.	W.	AV.
TEST					
OTHER FIRST CLASS	93	17	313	7	44.72
INT					
J.P.L.	77	1	346	16	21.62
NAT.W.					
B & H					

Qualifications: 4 O-levels, ONC in Mechanical Engineering; HNC in Automobile Engineering. Qualified Engineering Technician.
Jobs outside cricket: Draughtsman (Leyland Trucks).
Off-season 1984–85: Playing and coaching in Maroochudore, near Brisbane.
Equipment used: "Anything that's handy."
Cricketers particularly learnt from: "Watching most top class players."
Cricketers particularly admired: Ian Botham, Tony Greig, Clive Lloyd.
Other sports: Football, running and exercising, swimming. Watches most sports on television except horse-racing.
Significant injuries in 1984: Shin soreness.
Relaxations: Sunbathing, watching television, listening to records.
Opinions on cricket: "English wickets should be prepared to encourage bowlers to try and bowl quicker (i.e. more pace and bounce). Too much cricket is played; a reduction would mean more time for players to work out problems in nets."
Best batting performance: 9 Lancashire v Gloucestershire, Bristol 1984.
Best bowling performance: 2-49 Lancashire v Essex, Southend 1984.

MAYNARD, C.

Full Name: Christopher Maynard.
Role: Right-hand bat, wicket-keeper, occasional right arm medium bowler.
Born: 8 April 1958, Haslemere, Surrey.
Height: 5' 11½" **Weight:** 11st. 7lbs.
Nickname: Tosh.
County debut: 1982 (Lancashire).
County cap: No.
Test debut: —
No. of Tests: 0.
No. of One-Day Internationals: 0.
1000 runs in a season: 0.
50 wickets in a season: 0.
1st-Class 50s scored: 7.
1st-Class 100s scored: 0.
1st-Class 200s scored: 0.
1st-Class 5 w. in innings: 0.
1st-Class 10 w. in match: 0.
One-day 50s: 1.
One-day 100s: 0.
Place in batting averages: 157 average: 25.13; (1983: 198 average: 17.38).
Place in bowling averages: — average: —; (1983: — average: —).
Parents: John and Joan Maynard.
Marital status: Single.

Family links with cricket: Father and brother, Steve, used to play for Sutton Coldfield C.C. Now in South Africa.
Education: Bishop Vesey's Grammar School, Sutton Coldfield.
Qualifications: Ten O-levels, one A-level.
Jobs outside cricket: Has been salesman and has worked for jewellery firm. "Anything anyone will let me do."
Equipment used: Slazenger.
Overseas tours: Australia with Derrick Robins Under-23 XI in 1979–80.
Overseas teams played for: West Rand (Johannesburg) 1981–82.
Other sports: Anything — mainly hockey in the winter.
Relaxations: Reading, taking it easy.
Significant injuries in 1984: Dislocated and fractured thumb when hit by a ball from Le Roux.
Extras: Was on Warwickshire staff for 6 years. Made debut for Warwicks in 1979, and then having been on Warwicks. staff in 1982, also played for Lancashire in the same season, making debut v. Hants in June 1982 in an unusual but not unique feat. Only played 26 matches in 6 years for Warwicks.
Best batting performance: 85 Warwickshire v Kent, Edgbaston 1979.

LAST SEASON: BATTING

	I.	N.O.	R.	H.S.	AV.
TEST					
OTHER FIRST CLASS	21	5	402	50*	25.13
INT					
J.P.L.	4	1	68	26	22.67
NAT.W.	1	1	5	5*	–
B & H	3	1	35	14	17.50

CAREER: BATTING

	I.	N.O.	R.	H.S.	AV.
TEST					
OTHER FIRST CLASS	97	17	1613	85	20.16
INT					
J.P.L.	45	8	563	46	15.21
NAT.W.	4	1	22	16	7.33
B & H	10	3	152	60	21.72

LAST SEASON: WICKET KEEPING

	C.	ST.			
TEST					
OTHER FIRST CLASS	28	5			
INT					
J.P.L.	13	–			
NAT.W.	–	–			
B & H	11	–			

CAREER: WICKET KEEPING

	C.	ST.			
TEST					
OTHER FIRST CLASS	114	17			
INT					
J.P.L.	51	7			
NAT.W.	25	2			
B & H	52	2			

Q. 98. Who was the first batsman to reach 2000 runs in England in the 1984 season?

McFARLANE, L.L.

Full Name: Leslie Leopold
McFarlane.
Role: Right-hand bat; right
arm fast medium bowler.
Born: 19 August 1952, Jamaica.
Nickname: Les.
County debut: 1982 (Lancs.).
County cap: No.
Test debut: —
No. of Tests: 0.
No. of One-Day Internationals: 0.
1000 runs in a season: 0.
50 wickets in a season: 0.
1st-Class 50s scored: 0.
1st-Class 100s scored: 0.
1st-Class 200s scored: 0.
1st-Class 5 w. in innings: 1.
1st-Class 10 w. in match: 0.
One-day 50s: 0.
One-day 100s: 0.
Place in batting averages: — average: —; (1983: — average: —).
Place in bowling averages: 50 average: 28.22; (1983: 126 average: 49.47).
1st-Class catches 1984: 2 (career: 9).
Equipment used: Gray-Nicolls.
Extras: Played in Northampton Town league. Made debut for Northamptonshire in 1979, but left at end of season. Played for Bedfordshire.
Best batting performance: 15* Lancashire v Northamptonshire, Southport 1984.
Best bowling performance: 6-59 Lancashire v Warwickshire, Southport 1982.

LAST SEASON: BATTING

	I.	N.O.	R.	H.S.	AV.
TEST					
OTHER FIRST CLASS	15	7	41	15*	5.13
INT					
J.P.L.					
NAT.W.	–	–	–	–	–
B & H	–	–	–	–	–

CAREER: BATTING

	I.	N.O.	R.	H.S.	AV.
TEST					
OTHER FIRST CLASS	36	18	115	15*	6.39
INT					
J.P.L.	7	2	16	6	3.20
NAT.W.	–	–	–	–	–
B & H	–	–	–	–	–

LAST SEASON: BOWLING

	O.	M.	R.	W.	AV.
TEST					
OTHER FIRST CLASS	272.5	45	875	31	28.23
INT					
J.P.L.					
NAT.W.					
B & H	11	0	50	0	–

CAREER: BOWLING

	O.	M.	R.	W.	AV.
TEST					
OTHER FIRST CLASS	713.2	126	3132	86	36.42
INT					
J.P.L.	137	6	598	23	26.00
NAT.W.	12	4	18	1	–
B & H	15	0	68	0	–

NASIR ZAIDI

Full Name: Syed Mohammed Nasir
Zaidi.
Role: Right-arm bat, right arm
leg spin and googly.
Born: 25 March 1961, Karachi,
Pakistan.
Height: 5′ 4½″ **Weight:** 8st. 7lbs.
Nickname: Zebedee or Zeb.
County debut: 1983.
County cap: No.
Test debut: —
No. of Tests: 0.
No. of One Day Internationals: 0.
1000 runs in a season: 0.
50 wickets in a season: 0.
1st-Class 50s scored: 1.
1st-Class 100s scored: 0.
1st-Class 200s scored: 0.
1st-Class 5 w. in innings: 0.
1st-Class 10 w. in match: 0.
One-day 50s: 0.
One-day 100s: 0.
Place in batting averages: — average: —; (1983: 168 average: 19.55).
Place in bowling averages: — average: —; (1983: 86 average: 33.13).
1st-Class catches 1984: 6 (career: 15).
Parents: Asim and Akhtar Zaidi.
Family links with cricket: Brother plays League Cricket, father played Club
Cricket.

LAST SEASON: BATTING

	I.	N.O.	R.	H.S.	AV.
TEST					
OTHER FIRST CLASS	6	3	98	36	16.33
INT					
J.P.L.					
NAT.W.					
B & H					

CAREER: BATTING

	I.	N.O.	R.	H.S.	AV.
TEST					
OTHER FIRST CLASS	22	9	313	51	24.08
INT					
J.P.L.					
NAT.W.					
B & H					

LAST SEASON: BOWLING

	O.	M.	R.	W.	AV.
TEST					
OTHER FIRST CLASS	80	12	297	3	99.00
INT					
J.P.L.					
NAT.W.					
B & H					

CAREER: BOWLING

	O.	M.	R.	W.	AV.
TEST					
OTHER FIRST CLASS	271.3	70	827	19	43.53
INT					
J.P.L.					
NAT.W.					
B & H					

Qualifications: Seven O-levels. Did A-level courses in History and Economics.
Jobs outside cricket: In family Import and Export Manufacturing business.
Equipment used: Stuart Surridge.
Overseas teams played for: Played cricket in Malta between 1979–82, and Australia 1983–84.
Cricketers particularly learnt from: "Don Wilson, Chief Coach at Lord's, has helped me all the way."
Other sports: Squash, table tennis, badminton.
Extras: Formerly on Lord's groundstaff. Won M.C.C. Young Cricketers Single Wicket competition in 1979. Won Cross Arrows Cricketer of the Year 1982.
Opinions on cricket: "Like to see more spinners in County Cricket, especially leg spinners."
Best batting performance: 51 Lancashire v Somerset, Old Trafford 1983.
Best bowling performance: 3-27 Lancashire v Sussex, Hove 1983.

ORMROD, J.A.

Full Name: Joseph Alan Ormrod.
Role: Right-hand bat, off-break bowler.
Born: 22 December 1942, Ramsbottom, Làncashire.
County debut: 1962 (Worcestershire). 1984 (Lancashire).
County cap: 1966 (Worcestershire).
Test debut: —
No. of Tests: 0.
No. of One-Day Internationals: 0.
Benefit: £19,000 in 1977.
1000 runs in a season: 13.
50 wickets in a season: 0.
1st-Class 50s scored: 111.
1st-Class 100s scored: 30.
1st-Class 200s scored: 2.
1st-Class 5 w. in innings: 1.
1st-Class 10 w. in match: 0.
One-day 50s: 34.
One-day 100s: 1.

Place in batting averages: 103 average: 32.41; (1983: 133 average: 25.45).
Place in bowling averages: — average: —; (1983: — average: —).
1st-Class catches 1984: 10 (career: 396).
Education: Kirkcaldy High School.
Jobs outside cricket: Runs his own contract flooring business, specialising in gymnasiums.

Off-season 1984–85: Working in his own business.
Equipment used: Duncan Fearnley.
Overseas tours: Pakistan 1966–67.
Extras: Topped Worcestershire batting averages in 1981 but only played five first-class innings. Broke his arm early in 1981 season and did not play again. Reached 20,000 runs in first-class cricket, but "I have never been a man for statistics. The spirit and flavour of the game has always meant much more to me than plain figures." Record J.P.L. partnership for any wicket, with Dipak Patel, of 224 v. Hants at Southampton, August 1982.
Best batting performance: 204* Worcestershire v Kent, Dartford 1973.
Best bowling performance: 5-27 Worcestershire v Gloucestershire, Bristol 1972.

LAST SEASON: BATTING

	I.	N.O.	R.	H.S.	AV.
TEST					
OTHER FIRST CLASS	40	3	1199	139*	32.41
INT					
J.P.L.	8	0	176	57	22.00
NAT.W.	3	0	63	40	21.00
B & H	4	0	38	24	9.50

CAREER: BATTING

	I.	N.O.	R.	H.S.	AV.
TEST					
OTHER FIRST CLASS	839	95	23151	204*	31.12
INT					
J.P.L.	184	17	4074	110*	24.39
NAT.W.	34	2	697	59	21.78
B & H	58	6	1625	124*	31.25

LAST SEASON: BOWLING

	O.	M.	R.	W.	AV.
TEST					
OTHER FIRST CLASS					
INT					
J.P.L.					
NAT.W.					
B & H					

CAREER: BOWLING

	O.	M.	R.	W.	AV.
TEST					
OTHER FIRST CLASS	299	53	1094	25	43.76
INT					
J.P.L.	19	0	105	3	35.00
NAT.W.					
B & H	6.3	0	29	1	–

> **Q. 99.** Who was the first bowler to reach 100 wickets in England in the 1984 season?
>
> **Q. 100.** What was the club cap that D.R. Jardine wore as captain of England during the Bodyline Series in 1932–33, which so infuriated the Australians?

O'SHAUGHNESSY, S.J.

Full Name: Steven Joseph
O'Shaughnessy.
Role: Right-hand bat, right arm
medium bowler.
Born: 9 September 1961, Bury,
Lancashire.
Height: 5′ 10½″.
County debut: 1980.
County cap: No.
Test debut: —
No. of Tests: 0.
No. of One-Day Internationals: 0.
1000 runs in a season: 1.
50 wickets in a season: 0.
1st-Class 50s scored: 12.
1st-Class 100s scored: 5.
1st-Class 200s scored: 0.
1st-Class 5 w. in innings: 0.
1st-Class 10 w. in match: 0.
One-day 50s: 4.
One-day 100s: 1.
Place in batting averages: 83 average: 34.32; (1983: 120 average: 27.40).
Place in bowling averages: 113 average: 39.63; (1983: 87 average: 33.20).
1st-Class catches 1984: 11 (career: 22).
Education: Harper Green Secondary School, Farnworth, Lancashire.
Overseas tours: Canada 1979 with N.C.A. Under-19 XI; West Indies 1980
with England Young Cricketers.
Equipment used: Stuart Surridge.

LAST SEASON: BATTING

	I.	N.O.	R.	H.S.	AV.
TEST					
OTHER FIRST CLASS	38	4	1167	159*	34.32
INT					
J.P.L.	16	4	382	101*	31.83
NAT.W.	3	0	40	21	13.33
B & H	7	0	186	51	26.57

CAREER: BATTING

	I.	N.O.	R.	H.S.	AV.
TEST					
OTHER FIRST CLASS	108	18	2726	159*	30.29
INT					
J.P.L.	41	11	652	101*	21.73
NAT.W.	8	3	108	49*	21.60
B & H	12	0	231	51	19.25

LAST SEASON: BOWLING

	O.	M.	R.	W.	AV.
TEST					
OTHER FIRST CLASS	214.3	39	753	19	39.63
INT					
J.P.L.	81	7	309	14	22.07
NAT.W.	36	5	117	3	39.00
B & H	71	15	213	9	23.67

CAREER: BOWLING

	O.	M.	R.	W.	AV.
TEST					
OTHER FIRST CLASS	791.3	143	2708	83	32.63
INT					
J.P.L.	266	11	1232	35	35.20
NAT.W.	68	7	267	6	44.50
B & H	107	23	318	15	21.20

Relaxations: Snooker.
Extras: Scored 100 in 35 minutes v. Leicestershire, 11 September 1983 to equal the fastest first-class century scored by Percy Fender in 1920 (the bowling to O'Shaughnessy was not of the highest standard).
Best batting performance: 159* Lancashire v Somerset, Bath 1984.
Best bowling performance: 4-66 Lancashire v Nottinghamshire, Trent Bridge 1982.

PATTERSON, B.P.

Full Name: Balfour Patrick Patterson.
Role: Right arm fast bowler.
Born: 15 September 1961, Portland, Jamaica.
Height: 6′ 2½″ **Weight:** 13st. 3lbs.
County debut: 1984.
County cap: No.
Test debut: —
No. of Tests: 0.
No. of One-Day Internationals: 0.
1000 runs in a season: 0.
50 wickets in a season: 0.
1st-Class 50s scored: 0.
1st-Class 100s scored: 0.
1st-Class 200s scored: 0.
1st-Class 5 w. in innings: 0.
1st-Class 10 w. in match: 0.
One-day 50s: 0.
One-day 100s: 0.

Place in batting averages: — average: —; (1983: — average: —)
Place in bowling averages: — average: —; (1983: — average: —).
1st-Class catches 1984: 0 (career: 1).
Parents: Maurice and Emelda Patterson.
Marital status: Single.
Family links with cricket: Father and grandfather played for parish in Jamaica.
Education: Happy Grove High School; Wolmers High School for Boys.
Qualifications: Jamaica School Certificates, O-levels.
Jobs outside cricket: Accounts clerk.
Off-season 1984–85: Playing in Tasmania.
Overseas tours: Leeward Island 1983 with Jamaica Shell Shield team.
Cricketers particularly learnt from: Anderson Roberts.
Cricketers particularly admired: Present West Indian team; Dennis Lillee.
Other sports: Basketball, football, squash, table tennis, for fitness and pleasure. Watches football.
Relaxations: Swimming, listening to music, watching television.

Best batting performance: 10 Lancashire v Northamptonshire, Southport 1984.
Best bowling performance: 2-26 Jamaica v Leewards, Montserrat 1983–84.

LAST SEASON: BATTING

	I.	N.O.	R.	H.S.	AV.
TEST					
OTHER FIRST CLASS	2	0	10	10	5.00
INT					
J.P.L.					
NAT.W.	1	0	4	4	–
B & H					

CAREER: BATTING

	I.	N.O.	R.	H.S.	AV.
TEST					
OTHER FIRST CLASS	5	0	16	10	3.20
INT					
J.P.L.					
NAT.W.	1	0	4	4	–
B & H					

LAST SEASON: BOWLING

	O.	M.	R.	W.	AV.
TEST					
OTHER FIRST CLASS	21	3	51	0	–
INT					
J.P.L.					
NAT.W.	12	0	69	1	–
B & H					

CAREER: BOWLING

	O.	M.	R.	W.	AV.
TEST					
OTHER FIRST CLASS	59	8	179	4	44.75
INT					
J.P.L.					
NAT.W.	12	0	69	1	–
B & H					

SIMMONS, J.

Full Name: Jack Simmons.
Role: Right-hand bat, off-break bowler, slip fielder.
Born: 28 March 1941, Clayton-le-Moors, near Accrington.
Height: 6′ 1″ **Weight:** 14st 7lbs.
Nickname: Simmo, Flat Jack.
County debut: 1968.
County cap: 1971.
Test debut: —
No. of Tests: 0.
No. of One-Day Internationals: 0.
Benefit: 1980. £128,000.
1000 runs in a season: 0.
50 wickets in a season: 7.
1st-Class 50s scored: 31.
1st-Class 100s scored: 5.
1st-Class 200s scored: 0.
1st-Class 5 w. in innings: 33.
1st-Class 10 w. in match: 4.
One-day 50s: 6.
One-day 100s: 0.
Place in batting averages: 152 average: 25.79; (1983: 151 average: 23.41).

Place in bowling averages: 36 average: 26.10; (1983: 47 average: 26.57).
1st-Class catches 1984: 15 (career: 284).
Parents: Ada and Robert Simmons.
Wife and date of marriage: Jacqueline, 23 March 1963.
Children: Kelly Louise, 28 January 1979.
Education: Accrington Technical School, Blackburn Technical College.
Qualifications: 5 O-levels; O.N.C., City & Guilds in Quantities.
Jobs outside cricket: Draughtsman with Accrington Brick & Tile Co. Ltd., and Lancashire County Surveyors' Department. Partnership with Clive Lloyd as Agents for cricketers, also partnership with Pat Pocock in managing cricket matches for club cricketers at La Manga in Spain.
Off-season 1984–85: "First time in 12 winters, apart from benefit year in 1980, that I will not be going to Tasmania. Hoping to open a cricket school early in 1985."
Cricketing superstitions: "I always like to be last on the field. To do the same things again if successful once i.e. clothes or eating habits."
Family links with cricket: Father, Robert, played with Enfield, Lancashire League. Grandfather, Robert, also played for Enfield since 1887, "giving 92 years' association with the same club."
Overseas tours: Rhodesia and South Africa with Whitbread Wanderers 1975. Mike Brearley Invitation XI to Calcutta 1981.
Overseas teams played for: Played for Tasmania from 1972–73 to 1978–79— where he is "a bit of a folk hero". Captained Tasmania to Gillette Cup for first time in 1979, and when they first entered Sheffield Shield (1978).
Cricketers particularly learnt from: "Coached by Clyde Walcott when I was a youngster. Learnt from Clive Lloyd with Lancashire. Jack Bond; Ray Illingworth, plus many more off-spinners."
Cricketers particularly admired: "Clive Lloyd (team man always), Viv Richards, Chappell brothers and great bowlers Dennis Lillee and Michael Holding."
Equipment used: Stuart Surridge.
Relaxations: Soccer, golf, horse-racing, "plus eating, playing cards, watching television and going on holiday."
Extras: "I didn't play for a couple of years because I broke my leg three times in ten months and the previous year broke my arm quite badly, all playing soccer— except one broken leg, which was broken going down to the football ground just after I had it out of plaster for the first time." Made debut for 2nd XI in 1959. Hat-trick v Nottinghamshire (Liverpool) 1977.
Opinions on cricket: "I feel the 3-day and 1-day competitons are fine. Maybe the 3-day should be reduced by a couple of games, taking a little pressure off fast bowlers, and giving a few more rest days to get over injuries or re-charge batteries."
Best batting performance: 112 Lancashire v Sussex, Hove 1970.
Best bowling performance: 7-59 Tasmania v Queensland, Brisbane 1978–79.

LAST SEASON: BATTING

	I.	N.O.	R.	H.S.	AV.
TEST					
OTHER FIRST CLASS	34	5	748	72*	25.79
INT					
J.P.L.	11	4	127	45*	18.14
NAT.W.	3	2	24	13*	–
B & H	3	1	4	3*	2.00

CAREER: BATTING

	I.	N.O.	R.	H.S.	AV.
TEST					
OTHER FIRST CLASS	454	117	7953	112	23.60
INT					
J.P.L.	153	45	1725	65	15.97
NAT.W.	30	13	414	54*	24.35
B & H	39	14	516	64	20.64

LAST SEASON: BOWLING

	O.	M.	R.	W.	AV.
TEST					
OTHER FIRST CLASS	619.4	177	1644	63	26.10
INT					
J.P.L.	104	10	382	16	23.88
NAT.W.	36	6	116	6	19.33
B & H	55	12	158	9	17.56

CAREER: BOWLING

	O.	M.	R.	W.	AV.
TEST					
OTHER FIRST CLASS	466.2 8342.1	94 2482	22482	822	27.35
INT					
J.P.L.	1486.4	122	5951	236	25.21
NAT.W.	447.5	71	1494	67	22.30
B & H	518.2	106	1451	63	23.03

STANWORTH, J.

Full Name: John Stanworth.
Role: Right-hand bat, wicket-keeper.
Born: 30 September 1960, Oldham, Lancs.
Height: 5′ 10″ **Weight:** 10st. 7lbs.
Nickname: Stanny, Stick.
County debut: 1983.
County cap: No.
Test debut: —
No. of Tests: 0.
No. of One-Day Internationals: 0.
1000 runs in a season: 0.
50 wickets in a season: 0.
1st-Class 50s scored: 0.
1st-Class 100s scored: 0.
1st-Class 200s scored: 0.
1st-Class 5 w. in innings: 0.
1st-Class 10 w. in match: 0.
One-day 50s: 0.
One-day 100s: 0.
Place in batting averages: — average: —; (1983: — average: —).
Place in bowling averages: — average: —; (1983: — average: —).
Parents: Robert and Freda Stanworth.
Marital status: Single.
Education: Chadderton Grammar School; North Cheshire College, Warrington.
Qualifications: 8 O-levels, 1 A-level, Bachelor of Education Degree. Physical Education teacher (B.Ed.).

Jobs outside cricket: Health and fitness programmer, P.E. teacher.

Equipment used: Gunn & Moore.

Overseas tours: Australia 1978, playing and coaching in Grade cricket. West Indies 1981, British Colleges Sports Association.

Cricketers particularly learnt from: "Bob Blair (ex New Zealand and Wellington) gave me a kick up the pants in my formative years."

Cricketers particularly admired: Alan Knott, for his dedication. Bob Taylor for his "ease" behind the wicket.

Other sports: Rugby.

Relaxations: Car mechanics, T.V., music and films.

Extras: Instigated pre-season training for the squad.

Opinions on cricket: (1) Not enough time is given in state schools to the game, consequently there are no pitches of any quality nor teachers of any real concern. Result being not the same amount of good young players coming through the schools. (2) Poor pitches in county cricket generally. (3) Tea-interval lengthened to 30 minutes. (4) Gradually replace one of one-day competitions with night cricket.

Best batting performance: 31* Lancashire v Essex, Old Trafford 1983.

LAST SEASON: BATTING

	I.	N.O.	R.	H.S.	AV.
TEST					
OTHER FIRST CLASS	10	3	18	6	2.57
INT					
J.P.L.	1	0	0	0	–
NAT.W.					
B & H					

CAREER: BATTING

	I.	N.O.	R.	H.S.	AV.
TEST					
OTHER FIRST CLASS	16	5	108	31*	9.82
INT					
J.P.L.	1	0	0	0	–
NAT.W.					
B & H					

LAST SEASON: WICKET KEEPING

	C.	ST.			
TEST					
OTHER FIRST CLASS	16	1			
INT					
J.P.L.	7	–			
NAT.W.	2	–			
B & H	1	–			

CAREER: WICKET KEEPING

	C.	ST.			
TEST					
OTHER FIRST CLASS	18	1			
INT					
J.P.L.	8	–			
NAT.W.	2	–			
B & H	1	–			

Q. 101. When were England first defeated five Tests in a row, against whom, and who was the English captain?

VAREY, D.W.

Full Name: David William Varey.
Role: Right-hand bat.
Born: 15 October 1961, Darlington.
County debut: 1984.
County cap: No.
Test debut: —
No. of Tests: 0.
No. of One-Day Internationals: 0.
1000 runs in a season: 0.
50 wickets in a season: 0.
1st-Class 50s scored: 5.
1st-Class 100s scored: 1.
1st-Class 200s scored: 0.
1st-Class 5 w. in innings: 0.
1st-Class 10 w. in match: 0.
One-day 50s: 0.
One-day 100s: 0.

Place in batting averages: 217 average: 18.08; (1983: 193 average: 18.00).
Place in bowling averages: — average: —; (1983: — average: —).
1st-Class catches 1984: 3 (career: 14).
Education: Birkenhead School; Pembroke College, Cambridge.
Family links with cricket: Twin brother, Jonathan, is an Oxford Blue.
Extras: Played for Cheshire 1977, Lancashire 2nd XI debut 1980. Blues in 1982 and 1983. Secretary C.U.C.C. 1983.
Best batting performance: 156* Cambridge University v Northamptonshire, Cambridge 1982.

LAST SEASON: BATTING

	I.	N.O.	R.	H.S.	AV.
TEST					
OTHER FIRST CLASS	14	1	235	61	18.08
INT					
J.P.L.					
NAT.W.					
B & H	2	0	29	27	14.50

CAREER: BATTING

	I.	N.O.	R.	H.S.	AV.
TEST					
OTHER FIRST CLASS	56	6	1206	156*	24.12
INT					
J.P.L.					
NAT.W.					
B & H	2	0	29	27	14.50

LAST SEASON: BOWLING

	O.	M.	R.	W.	AV.
TEST					
OTHER FIRST CLASS					
INT					
J.P.L.					
NAT.W.					
B & H					

CAREER: BOWLING

	O.	M.	R.	W.	AV.
TEST					
OTHER FIRST CLASS	1	0	4	0	–
INT					
J.P.L.					
NAT.W.					
B & H					

WATKINSON, M.

Full Name: Michael Watkinson.
Role: Right-hand bat, right arm
medium bowler.
Born: 1 August 1962, Westhoughton.
Height: 6″ 1½′ **Weight:** 13st.
County debut: 1982.
County cap: No.
Test debut: —
No. of Tests: 0.
No. of One-Day Internationals: 0.
1000 runs in a season: 0.
50 wickets in a season: 0.
1st-Class 50s scored: 4.
1st-Class 100s scored: 0.
1st-Class 200s scored: 0.
1st-Class 5 w. in innings: 3.
1st-Class 10 w. in match: 0.
One-day 50s: 0.
One-day 100s: 0.
Place in batting averages: 128 average: 29.04; (1983: 243 average: 10.50).
Place in bowling averages: 124 average: 42.37; (1983: 46 average: 26.54).
1st-Class catches 1984: 7 (career: 9).
Parents: Albert and Marian Watkinson.
Marital status: Single.
Education: Rivington and Blackrod High School, Horwich.
Qualifications: 8 O-levels; H.T.C. Civil Engineering.
Jobs outside cricket: Draughtsman.
Off-season 1984–85: Playing and coaching in Canberra, Australia.

LAST SEASON: BATTING

	I.	N.O.	R.	H.S.	AV.
TEST					
OTHER FIRST CLASS	29	6	668	77	29.04
INT					
J.P.L.	9	4	98	32*	19.60
NAT.W.	2	1	8	6	–
B & H	1	1	2	2*	–

CAREER: BATTING

	I.	N.O.	R.	H.S.	AV.
TEST					
OTHER FIRST CLASS	49	10	836	77	21.44
INT					
J.P.L.	16	8	156	32*	19.50
NAT.W.	3	1	8	6	4.00
B & H	2	1	5	3	–

LAST SEASON: BOWLING

	O.	M.	R.	W.	AV.
TEST					
OTHER FIRST CLASS	359	73	1229	29	42.37
INT					
J.P.L.	95.1	6	440	15	29.33
NAT.W.	29	3	140	3	46.67
B & H	69	7	257	15	17.13

CAREER: BOWLING

	O.	M.	R.	W.	AV.
TEST					
OTHER FIRST CLASS	691.3	146	2203	65	33.89
INT					
J.P.L.	178	11	810	32	25.31
NAT.W.	49	5	187	4	46.75
B & H	97	11	357	20	17.85

Family links with cricket: "None."
Equipment used: Slazenger.
Other sports: Football.
Extras: Played with Cheshire C.C.C. in Minor Counties, and NatWest Trophy (v. Middlesex) 1982 season.
Best batting performance: 77 Lancashire v Middlesex, Liverpool 1984.
Best bowling performance: 6-39 Lancashire v Leicestershire, Leicester 1984.

COUNTY QUIZ

Q. 1. When was the club founded?
Q. 2. Who made the most first-class runs for the county last season, and how many?
Q. 3. What's the highest ever county total, and against whom?
Q. 4. Who took most wickets for the county last season, and how many?
Q. 5. What's the highest individual score for the county, who hit it, and when?
Q. 6. What's the highest scoring partnership for the county for any wicket?
Q. 7. How many times has the club won the County Championship?
Q. 8. What's the lowest ever total made by the county in one innings, when, and against whom?
Q. 9. Which bowler took the most first-class wickets in one season, when, and how many?
Q. 10. Which batsman hit the most runs in one season, when and how many?

Leicestershire

ADDISON, J.P.

Full Name: Jonathan Paul Addison.
Role: Right-hand bat, slow left-arm spinner.
Born: 14 November 1965, Leek, Staffordshire.
Height: 6′ 0″ **Weight:** 13st.
County debut: 1983.
County cap: No.
Test debut: —
No. of Tests: 0.
No. of One-Day Internationals: 0.
1000 runs in a season: 0.
50 wickets in a season: 0.
1st-Class 50s scored: 1.
1st-Class 100s scored: 0.
1st-Class 200s scored: 0.
1st-Class 5 w in innings: 0.
1st-Class 10 w in match: 0
One-day 50s: 0.
One-day 100s: 0

Place in batting averages: — average: —; (1983: — average: —)
Place in bowling averages: — average: —; (1983: — average: —).
1st-Class catches 1984: — (career: 1).
Parents: Paul Anthony and Beryl Addison.
Marital status: Single.
Family links with cricket: Father still plays in the North Staffordshire and District League.
Education: Beeches Junior School, Blythe Bridge High School.
Qualifications: GCE '0' levels.
Jobs outside cricket: Working in the pottery industry.
Off-season 1984–85: Coaching in S. Africa; Young England tour to W. Indies.
Cricketing superstitions: "Too numerous to mention."
Equipment used: Duncan Fearnley.
Cricketers particularly learnt from: Ken Higgs, Mike Haysman and father.
Cricketers particularly admired: Brian Davison, Garfield Sobers.

Other sports: Football, tennis, squash, golf.

Relaxations: "I find that listening to music is the best way to unwind."

Extras: Made debut in Leicester 2nd XI in 1981. Best bowling 7-24 and 8-80 v Derbyshire 2nd XI 1983. Best batting 68 v Lancashire 2nd XI 1983. 66 not out v Worcestershire 2nd XI. Signed as professional for Caverswall who play in the North Staffordshire and South Cheshire League. They were champions in season 1983. Youngest professional in League.

Opinions on cricket: "Will have more opinions when I have played more first class cricket."

Best batting performance: 51 Leicester v New Zealanders, Leicester 1984.

LAST SEASON: BATTING

	I.	N.O.	R.	H.S.	AV.
TEST					
OTHER FIRST CLASS					
INT					
J.P.L.	–	–	–	–	–
NAT.W.					
B & H					

CAREER: BATTING

	I.	N.O.	R.	H.S.	AV.
TEST					
OTHER FIRST CLASS	2	0	67	51	33.50
INT					
J.P.L.	1	0	10	10	–
NAT.W.					
B & H					

LAST SEASON: BOWLING

	O.	M.	R.	W.	AV.
TEST					
OTHER FIRST CLASS					
INT					
J.P.L.					
NAT.W.					
B & H					

CAREER: BOWLING

	O.	M.	R.	W.	AV.
TEST					
OTHER FIRST CLASS					
INT					
J.P.L.	1	0	16	0	–
NAT.W.					
B & H					

Q. 102. When did an England side win all the matches in a Test series, against whom, and who was the England captain?

Q. 103. Which England Test cricketer, who also played soccer for England, was, on good authority, officially offered a job as King of Albania?

AGNEW, J.P.

Full Name: Jonathan Philip Agnew.
Role: Right-hand bat, right arm fast bowler, outfielder.
Born: 4 April 1960, Macclesfield, Cheshire.
Height: 6' 4½" **Weight:** 12st 7lbs.
Nickname: Spiro (after former US Vice-President Spiro Agnew).
County debut: 1978.
County cap: 1984.
Test debut: 1984.
No. of Tests: 2.
No. of One-Day Internationals: 0.
1000 runs in a season: 0.
50 wickets in a season: 1.
1st-Class 50s scored: 0.
1st-Class 100s scored: 0.
1st-Class 200s scored: 0.
1st-Class 5 w. in innings: 7.
1st-Class 10 w. in match: 1.
One-day 50s: 0.
One-day 100s: 0.
Place in batting averages: — average: —; (1983: — average: —).
Place in bowling averages: 54 average: 28.72; (1983: 117 average: 32.47).
1st class catches 1984: 4 (career: 23).
Parents: Philip and Margaret Agnew.
Wife and date of marriage: Beverley, 8 October 1983.
Education: Uppingham School.
Qualifications: Nine O-levels, two A-levels.
Jobs outside cricket: Cricket Coach. Spent 1981-82 off-season coaching at Sindia High School, Zimbabwe. Production control at T.L. Bennett's Windows Ltd.
Off-season 1984-85: Official reserve for England tour; commercial work with Leicestershire. Then called to India to replace injured Paul Allott.
Cricketing superstitions: "I never use a bowling marker so am never popular with groundsmen!"
Equipment used: Duncan Fearnley.
Cricketers particularly learnt from: Ken Higgs, Andy Roberts, Frank Tyson. "I owe much of last season's success to Peter Willey."
Cricketers particularly admired: Imran Khan.
Family links with cricket: First cousin, Mary Duggan, Captain of England's Women's XI in 1960s.
Overseas Tours: Young England tour of Australia 1978–79. Leicestershire C.C.C. to Zimbabwe, 1981.

Overseas teams played for: Whitbread scholarship, 1978, playing for Essendon C.C., Melbourne, and in 1980. Alexandra C.C., Salisbury, Zimbabwe, 1981-82, Central Cumberland District Cricket Club, Sydney 1982-83.

Other sports: Hockey, badminton, squash, table tennis.

Relaxations: Music (all kinds). Playing piano and tuba. Coaching cricket. "I became very interested in game viewing in Zimbabwe. I spent days driving around to study and photograph— particularly elephants."

Extras: Played for Surrey 2nd XI 1976–77. Back trouble in 1979 season. Esso/Mail on Sunday Bowler of the Month, May 1984.

Opinions on cricket: "Nice to see the change in over-rate structure to a number of overs to be bowled in a day. I think 110 overs per day would be a more realistic figure, but it certainly beats the old system."

Best batting performance: 56 Leicestershire v Worcestershire, Worcester 1982.

Best bowling performance: 8-47 Leicestershire v Cambridge University, Cambridge 1984.

LAST SEASON: BATTING

	I.	N.O.	R.	H.S.	AV.
TEST	3	2	8	5	–
OTHER FIRST CLASS	20	5	148	30	9.87
INT					
J.P.L.	3	1	5	4	2.50
NAT.W.	1	1	4	4*	–
B & H	2	1	26	23*	–

CAREER: BATTING

	I.	N.O.	R.	H.S.	AV.
TEST	3	2	8	5	–
OTHER FIRST CLASS	76	12	592	56	9.25
INT					
J.P.L.	5	2	8	4	2.67
NAT.W.	1	1	4	4*	–
B & H	3	2	26	23*	–

LAST SEASON: BOWLING

	O.	M.	R.	W.	AV.
TEST	69	20	274	4	68.50
OTHER FIRST CLASS	601.1	107	2139	80	26.74
INT					
J.P.L.	78	7	416	11	37.82
NAT.W.	29	3	108	5	21.60
B & H	38	6	120	10	12.00

CAREER: BOWLING

	O.	M.	R.	W.	AV.
TEST	69	20	274	4	68.50
OTHER FIRST CLASS	1744.4	314	6263	207	30.26
INT					
J.P.L.	112.3	7	616	15	41.07
NAT.W.	29	3	108	5	21.60
B & H	50	8	167	12	13.92

Q. 104. Who was the first English Test cricketer to score three centuries in successive Tests against the West Indies?

BALDERSTONE, J.C.

Full Name: John Christopher Balderstone.
Role: Right-hand bat, slow left-arm orthodox bowler, slip fielder.
Born: 16 November 1940 Huddersfield, Yorkshire.
Height: 6′ 2″ **Weight:** 12st. 7lbs.
Nickname: Baldy, Chris, Dad.
County debut: 1971 (Leicestershire).
County cap: 1973.
Testimonial: 1984 (with Ken Higgs).
Test debut: 1976.
No. of Tests: 2.
No. of One-Day Internationals: 0.
1000 runs in a season: 10.
50 wickets in a season: 0.
1st-Class 50s scored: 95.
1st-Class 100s scored: 29.
1st-Class 200s scored: 0.
1st-Class 5 w. in innings: 5.
1st-Class 10 w. in match: 0.
One-day 50s: 27.
One-day 100s 6.
Place in batting averages: 65 average: 37.06; (1983: 53 average: 39.95).
Place in bowling averages: — average: —; (1983: — average: —).
1st-Class catches 1984: 14 (career: 197).
Parents: Frank and Jenny Balderstone.
Wife and date of marriage: Madeline, April 1962.
Children: Sally Victoria, 15 September 1970; Michael James, 3 January 1973.
Education: Paddock County School, Huddersfield.
Qualifications: Advanced cricket coach, soccer coach.
Jobs outside cricket: Professional footballer with Huddersfield Town, Carlisle United, Doncaster Rovers, Queen of the South, Enderby Town. Representative for a sports shop.
Off-season 1984–85: Representative for Suffolk Sovereign Chicken Ltd.
Family links with cricket: None.
Overseas tours: To Zimbabwe March 1981 with Leicester and to Oman 1984.
Cricketers particularly learnt from: "Everyone."
Equipment endorsed: Gunn & Moore.
Other sports: Golf, professional football.
Relaxations: Do-it-yourself, golf, reading and all sports.
Extras: Played for Yorkshire 1961–70. Once played first-class cricket match and a league football match on the same day, 15 September 1975 (Leicestershire v Derbyshire at Chesterfield 11.30 am to 6.30 pm and

Doncaster Rovers v Brentford at Doncaster 7.30 pm to 9.10 pm). Former Chairman of Cricketers' Association.

Best batting performance: 181* Lecicestershire v Gloucestershire, Leicester 1984.

Best bowling performance: 6-25 Leicestershire v Hampshire, Southampton 1978.

LAST SEASON: BATTING

	I.	N.O.	R.	H.S.	AV.
TEST					
OTHER FIRST CLASS	36	2	1260	181*	37.06
INT					
J.P.L.					
NAT.W.	1	0	33	33	–
B & H	2	0	2	2	1.00

CAREER: BATTING

	I.	N.O.	R.	H.S.	AV.
TEST	4	0	39	35	9.75
OTHER FIRST CLASS	552	55	17314	181*	34.84
INT					
J.P.L.	118	23	2556	96	26.90
NAT.W.	28	2	730	119*	28.08
B & H	50	10	1787	113*	44.68

LAST SEASON: BOWLING

	O.	M.	R.	W.	AV.
TEST					
OTHER FIRST CLASS	19	5	69	2	34.50
INT					
J.P.L.					
NAT.W.					
B & H					

CAREER: BOWLING

	O.	M.	R.	W.	AV.
TEST	16	0	80	1	–
OTHER FIRST CLASS	3127	945	7869	306	25.72
INT					
J.P.L.	58.3	2	296	12	24.67
NAT.W.	42.5	9	167	8	20.88
B & H	30	4	103	5	20.60

BOON, T.J.

Full Name: Timothy James Boon.
Role: Right-hand bat.
Born: 1 November 1961, Doncaster, South Yorkshire.
Height: 6′ 0″ **Weight:** 12st.
Nickname: "Ted Moon, Cod, amongst others."
County debut: 1980.
County cap: No.
Test debut: —
No. of Tests: 0.
No. of One-Day Internationals: 0.
1000 runs in a season: 1.
50 wickets in a season: 0.
1st-Class 50s scored: 9.
1st-Class 100s scored: 4.
1st-Class 200s scored: 0.
1st-class 5 w. in innings: 0.
1st-Class 10 w. in match: 0.

One:day 50s: 0.
One-day 100s: 0.
Place in batting averages: 52 average: 39.73; (1983: — average: —).
Place in bowling averages: — average: —; (1983: — average: —).
1st-Class catches 1984: 9 (career: 19).
Parents: Jeffrey and Elizabeth.
Marital status: Single.
Education: Mill Lane Primary; Edlington Comprehensive. Three months at Doncaster Art School.
Qualifications: One A-level, six O-levels. Coaching qualifications.
Family links with cricket: Father played club cricket.
Overseas tours: Toured the Caribbean with England Young Cricketers 1980, as captain. Leicestershire C.C.C. tour of Zimbabwe, March 1981.
Overseas teams played for: Old Hararians, Zimbabwe, 1980–81. Ceylon C.C., Colombo 1981–82; Pirates C.C. Durban 1982–83.
Off-season 1984–85: Playing and coaching in Durban.
Cricketing superstitions: "Constantly changing."
Equipment used: Duncan Fearnley.
Cricketers particularly learnt from: The late Mike Fearnley, Ken Higgs, Chris Balderstone, Peter Willey.
Other sports: "Enjoy playing and watching all sports."
Relaxations: Sleeping.
Extras: Captain England Young Cricketers Tour West Indies 1980; Captain England Young Cricketers v. Indian Young Cricketers 1981. Most Promising Schoolboy Cricketer 1979.
Best batting performance: 144 Leicestershire v Gloucestershire, Leicester 1984.

LAST SEASON: BATTING

	I.	N.O.	R.	H.S.	AV.
TEST					
OTHER FIRST CLASS	37	6	1233	144	39.73
INT					
J.P.L.	9	2	129	48	18.43
NAT.W.	3	2	26	22*	–
B & H	2	2	41	36*	–

CAREER: BATTING

	I.	N.O.	R.	H.S.	AV.
TEST					
OTHER FIRST CLASS	100	12	2383	144	27.08
INT					
J.P.L.	30	7	410	48	17.82
NAT.W.	3	2	26	22*	–
B & H	2	2	41	36*	–

LAST SEASON: BOWLING

	O.	M.	R.	W.	AV.
TEST					
OTHER FIRST CLASS					
INT					
J.P.L.					
NAT.W.					
B & H					

CAREER: BOWLING

	O.	M.	R.	W.	AV.
TEST					
OTHER FIRST CLASS	16	5	57	0	–
INT					
J.P.L.	2	0	14	0	–
NAT.W.					
B & H					

BRIERS, N.E.

Full Name: Nigel Edwin Briers.
Role: Right-hand bat, cover fielder.
Born: 15 January 1955, Leicester.
Height: 6' 0" **Weight:** 12st 5lbs.
Nickname: Kudu.
County debut: 1971 at age of 16 yrs 104 days.
County cap: 1981.
Test debut: —
No. of Tests: 0.
No. of One-Day Internationals: 0.
1000 runs in a season: 3.
50 wickets in a season: 0.
1st-Class 50s scored: 30.
1st-Class 100s scored: 8.
1st-Class 200s scored: 1.
1st-Class 5 w. in innings: 0.
1st-Class 10 w. in match: 0.
One-day 50s: 19.
One-day 100s: 3.

Place in batting averages: 215 average: 18.12; (1983: 51 average: 40.28).
Place in bowling averages: 13 average: 22.00; (1983: — average: —).
1st-Class catches 1984: 9 (career: 68).
Parents: Leonard Arthur Roger and Eveline Briers.
Wife and date of marriage: Suzanne Mary Tudor, 3 September 1977.
Children: Michael Edward Tudor 25 March 1983.
Education: Lutterworth Grammar School; Borough Road College.
Qualifications: Qualified teacher (Certificate of Education). B.Ed. Hons. M.C.C. Advanced Coach.
Jobs outside cricket: Lecturer in Physical Education at Leicester Polytechnic. Taught P.E. at Ludgrove School.
Family links with cricket: Father was captain and wicket-keeper of Narborough and Littlethorpe Cricket Club, first division of Leicestershire League, for 15 years. Mother was scorer for team. Father was Captain of South Leicestershire representative XI and played for the Royal Marines in the same team as Trevor Bailey. Cousin, Norman Briers, played for Leicestershire once in 1967.
Overseas tours: Toured South America with Derrick Robins XI in 1978–79. M.C.C. tour to the Far East 1981. Toured Zimbabwe with Leics. 1981.
Equipment used: Duncan Fearnley.
Cricketers particularly learnt from: Maurice Hallam, Jack Birkenshaw and Ray Illingworth.
Cricketers particularly admired: Barry Richards.
Other sports: Rugby, basketball, squash, hockey.
Relaxations: "Eating good food"; cinema.

Extras: Former Captain of England Young Cricketers, England Schoolboys and British Colleges XI. Record 5th wicket partnership for Leicestershire of 233 with R.W. Tolchard v Somerset at Leicester in 1979. Youngest player to appear for Leicestershire at 16 years, 104 days.

Best batting performance: 201* Leicestershire v Warwickshire, Edgbaston 1983.

Best bowling performance: 3-48 Leicestershire v Lancashire, Leicester 1984.

LAST SEASON: BATTING

	I.	N.O.	R.	H.S.	AV.
TEST					
OTHER FIRST CLASS	37	3	616	73	18.12
INT					
J.P.L.	14	2	428	108	35.67
NAT.W.	3	0	86	59	28.67
B & H	4	0	117	42	29.25

CAREER: BATTING

	I.	N.O.	R.	H.S.	AV.
TEST					
OTHER FIRST CLASS	265	26	6672	201*	27.92
INT					
J.P.L.	93	12	2778	119*	34.29
NAT.W.	15	1	233	59	16.64
B & H	22	2	352	71*	17.60

LAST SEASON: BOWLING

	O.	M.	R.	W.	AV.
TEST					
OTHER FIRST CLASS	109	24	264	12	22.00
INT					
J.P.L.	9	1	68	3	22.67
NAT.W.	7	0	32	1	–
B & H	22	2	93	1	–

CAREER: BOWLING

	O.	M.	R.	W.	AV.
TEST					
OTHER FIRST CLASS	233.1	51	607	22	27.59
INT					
J.P.L.	56.2	5	248	9	27.56
NAT.W.	12	0	67	5	13.40
B & H	38	3	183	2	91.50

BUTCHER, I.P.

Full Name: Ian Paul Butcher.
Role: Right-hand bat.
Born: 1 July 1962, Farnborough, Kent.
Height: 6′ 0″ **Weight:** 12st.
Nickname: Butch, Dog.
County debut: 1980.
County cap: 1984.
Test debut: —
No. of Tests: 0.
No. of One-Day Internationals: 0.
1000 runs in a season: 1.
50 wickets in a season: 0.
1st-Class 50s scored: 7.
1st-Class 100s scored: 8.
1st-Class 200s scored: 0.
1st-Class 5 w. in innings: 0.
1st-Class 10 w. in match: 0.

One-day 50s: 3.
One-day 100s: 0.
Place in batting averages: 97 average: 32.90; (1983: 84 average: 33.55).
Place in bowling averages: — average: —; (1983: — average: —).
1st-Class catches 1984: 19 (career: 41).
Parents: Ray and Jackie Butcher.
Wife and date of marriage: Marie, 12 March 1983.
Education: John Ruskin High School.
Jobs outside cricket: Football coach, Cumnor House School South Croydon. "Government artist (draw the dole!)".
Family links with cricket: Brother, Alan, Surrey C.C.C. and England. Brother, Martin, M.C.C. Young Pros.
Overseas tours: England Young Cricketers tour of West Indies 1980.
Cricket superstitions: " I have many! . . . If I score runs I like to do everything (if possible) the same, the following day. I always wear a sweatband on left wrist while batting."
Off-season 1984–85: Playing football.
Cricketers particularly learnt from: Brian Davison and Graham Gooch.
Equipment endorsed: Slazenger.
Other sports: Football, golf. "Try my hand at anything!"
Relaxations: Sunbathing, a good disco, listening to records. Enjoy a good meal.
Extras: Made his debut for Leicestershire C.C.C. in the John Player League 1979 v. Surrey, the team for which his brother, Alan Butcher, plays. Made his county debut 1980 v. Oxford University. Scored century on championship debut at Grace Road.
Best batting performance: 139 Leicestershire v Nottinghamshire, Leicester 1983.

LAST SEASON: BATTING

	I.	N.O.	R.	H.S.	AV.
TEST					
OTHER FIRST CLASS	42	1	1349	130	32.90
INT					
J.P.L.	13	1	186	35	15.50
NAT.W.	2	0	111	81	55.50
B & H	4	0	119	43	29.75

CAREER: BATTING

	I.	N.O.	R.	H.S.	AV.
TEST					
OTHER FIRST CLASS	83	5	2560	139	32.82
INT					
J.P.L.	31	2	591	71	20.38
NAT.W.	4	0	127	81	31.75
B & H	4	0	119	43	29.75

LAST SEASON: BOWLING

	O.	M.	R.	W.	AV.
TEST					
OTHER FIRST CLASS	2	1	13	0	—
INT					
J.P.L.					
NAT.W.					
B & H					

CAREER: BOWLING

	O.	M.	R.	W.	AV.
TEST					
OTHER FIRST CLASS	4	1	15	1	—
INT					
J.P.L.					
NAT.W.					
B & H					

CARMICHAEL, I.R.

Full Name: Ian Robert Carmichael
Role: Left-hand bat, left arm
fast-medium bowler.
Born: 17 December 1960, Hull.
County debut: 1984.
County cap: No.
Test debut: —
No. of Tests: 0.
No. of One-Day Internationals: 0.
1000 runs in a season: 0.
50 wickets in a season: 0.
1st-Class 50s scored: 0.
1st-Class 100s scored: 0.
1st-Class 200s scored: 0.
1st-Class 5 w. in innings: 4.
1st-Class 10 w. in match: 0.
One-day 50s: 0.
One-day 100s: 0.
Place in batting averages: — average: —; (1983: — average: —).
Place in bowling averages: 110 average: 38.88; (1983: — average: —).
1st-Class catches 1984: 3 (career: 5).
Off-season 1984–85: Playing in Australia.
Overseas teams played for: South Australia.
Extras: Came to England on Esso scholarship to Essex; signed by
Leicestershire when it was realised he held English birth qualifications and
played in 2nd half of season.
Best batting performance: 4* Leicestershire v Lancashire, Leicester 1984.
Best bowling performance: 6-112 S. Australia v Tasmania, Devonport
1983-84.

LAST SEASON: BATTING

	I.	N.O.	R.	H.S.	AV.
TEST					
OTHER FIRST CLASS	6	3	6	4	2.00
INT					
J.P.L.					
NAT.W.					
B & H					

CAREER: BATTING

	I.	N.O.	R.	H.S.	AV.
TEST					
OTHER FIRST CLASS	17	6	17	4	1.55
INT					
J.P.L.					
NAT.W.					
B & H					

LAST SEASON: BOWLING

	O.	M.	R.	W.	AV.
TEST					
OTHER FIRST CLASS	208	40	661	17	38.88
INT					
J.P.L.					
NAT.W.					
B & H					

CAREER: BOWLING

	O.	M.	R.	W.	AV.
TEST					
OTHER FIRST CLASS	716	154	2107	58	36.33
INT					
J.P.L.					
NAT.W.					
B & H					

CLIFT, P.B.

Full Name: Patrick Bernard Clift.
Role: Right-hand bat, right arm medium bowler.
Born: 14 July 1953, Salisbury, Zimbabwe.
Height: 6' 1" **Weight:** 14st.
Nickname: Paddy, Paddles.
County debut: 1975.
County cap: 1976.
Test debut: —
No. of Tests: 0.
No. of One-Day Internationals: 0.
1000 runs in a season: 0.
50 wickets in a season: 6.
1st-Class 50s scored: 26.
1st-Class 100s scored: 1.
1st-Class 200s scored: 0.
1st-Class 5 w. in innings: 22.
1st-Class 10 w. in match: 2.

One-day 50s: 1.
One-day 100s: 0.
Place in batting averages: 179 average: 23.00; (1983: 91 average: 32.42).
Place in bowling averages: 31 average: 25.52; (1983: 7 average: 19.18).
1st-Class catches 1984: 6 (career: 126).
Parents: George Neville and Ivy Susan Clift.
Wife and date of marriage: Penelope Anne, 28 May 1975.
Children: Robert William Patrick, 16 September 1982.
Education: St. Michael's; Hartmann House, St George's College.
Qualifications: O-level.
Jobs outside cricket: Accounting, insurance.
Family links with cricket: None.
Overseas tours: Rhodesia Ridgebacks 1974 U.K. tour.
Overseas teams played for: Rhodesia. Natal.
Cricketers particularly learnt from: Robin Jackman, Mike Procter, Duncan Fletcher, Jack Birkenshaw, Roger Tolchard, Ken Higgs, Jim Cornford, school coach at St. George's College.
Equipment used: Gray-Nicolls.
Other sports: Squash, golf, tennis, jogging.
Relaxations: Stamp collecting, reading, listening to records.
Extras: Debut for Rhodesia 1971–72. Took 8 wickets for 17 in opening match in 1976 season v M.C.C. Performed hat-trick in 1976 at Grace Road v Yorkshire. Suffered from injury in 1981 and 1982 season. Rhodesian 7th wicket partnership record of 174 with Howie Gardiner v Western Province, and Rhodesian 9th wicket partnership of 154 with Robin Jackman v Eastern

Province, both in Currie Cup Competition, South Africa.
Best batting performance: 100 * Leicestershire v Sussex, Hove 1983.
Best bowling performance: 8-17 Leicestershire v MCC, Lords 1976.

LAST SEASON: BATTING

	I.	N.O.	R.	H.S.	AV.
TEST					
OTHER FIRST CLASS	28	7	483	58	23.00
INT					
J.P.L.	8	5	94	30*	31.33
NAT.W.	3	2	32	18*	–
B & H					

CAREER: BATTING

	I.	N.O.	R.	H.S.	AV.
TEST					
OTHER FIRST CLASS	359	80	6651	100*	23.84
INT					
J.P.L.	72	25	1040	51*	22.12
NAT.W.	14	5	234	48*	26.00
B & H	18	2	322	91	20.13

LAST SEASON: BOWLING

	O.	M.	R.	W.	AV.
TEST					
OTHER FIRST CLASS	623.1	165	1608	63	25.54
INT					
J.P.L.	77.3	5	433	14	30.93
NAT.W.	31	4	114	3	38.00
B & H					

CAREER: BOWLING

	O.	M.	R.	W.	AV.
TEST					
OTHER FIRST CLASS	6775.3	1774	17094	698	24.49
INT					
J.P.L.	732.2	51	3011	136	22.13
NAT.W.	138.3	15	523	14	37.36
B & H	256.4	32	876	32	27.38

COBB, R.A.

Full Name: Russell Alan Cobb.
Role: Right-hand bat; slow
left arm bowler.
Born: 18 May 1961, Leicester.
Height: 5' 11" **Weight:** 11st 5lbs.
Nickname: Cobby, Youth.
County debut: 1980.
County cap: No.
Test debut: —
No. of Tests: 0.
No. of One-Day Internationals: 0.
1000 runs in a season: 0.
50 wickets in a season: 0.
1st-Class 50s scored: 1.
1st-Class 100s scored: 0.
1st-Class 200s scored: 0.
1st-Class 5 w. in innings: 0.
1st-Class 10 w. in match: 0.
One-day 50s: 0.
One-day 100s: 0.

Place in batting averages: — average: —; (1983: 238 average: 11.00).
Place in bowling averages: — average: —; (1983: — average: —).

1st-Class catches 1984: 2 (career: 26).
Parents: Alan and Betty Cobb.
Marital status: Single.
Education: Woodbank School, Leicester; Trent College, Nottingham.
Qualifications: Seven O-levels, N.C.A. Advanced coaching certificate.
Family links with cricket: Father a club cricketer. Godfather Maurice Hallam, former Leicestershire captain.
Jobs outside cricket: Clerk for British Shoe Corporation, Leicester. Worked on promotion for Leicestershire.
Off-season 1984-85: Playing and coaching at the Teachers' Training College, Pretoria.
Cricketing superstitions: "Always put my left pad on first. Must wear either helmet or cap when batting."
Equipment used: Gray-Nicolls.
Overseas tours: Australia with Young England in 1979; West Indies with Young England in 1980; Zimbabwe with Leicestershire in 1981.
Overseas teams played for: Glenelg in Adelaide, S. Australia, in 1980-81.
Cricketers particularly learnt from: Jack Birkenshaw and Chris Balderstone.
Cricketers particularly admired: "All who have played top class cricket for a number of years."
Other sports: Squash, badminton, watching rugby.
Relaxations: "A little reading, walking, eating out with friends."
Significant injuries in 1984: Shoulder injury (2 weeks); broken bone in hand (1 month).
Best batting performance: 63 Leicestershire XI v Zimbabwe, Leicester 1982.

LAST SEASON: BATTING

	I.	N.O.	R.	H.S.	AV.
TEST					
OTHER FIRST CLASS	5	0	142	48	28.40
INT					
J.P.L.					
NAT.W.					
B & H					

CAREER: BATTING

	I.	N.O.	R.	H.S.	AV.
TEST					
OTHER FIRST CLASS	68	1	1335	63	19.93
INT					
J.P.L.	3	1	49	24	24.50
NAT.W.					
B & H					

LAST SEASON: BOWLING

	O.	M.	R.	W.	AV.
TEST					
OTHER FIRST CLASS					
INT					
J.P.L.					
NAT.W.					
B & H					

CAREER: BOWLING

	O.	M.	R.	W.	AV.
TEST					
OTHER FIRST CLASS	4	2	5	0	–
INT					
J.P.L.					
NAT.W.					
B & H					

COOK, N.G.B.

Full Name: Nicholas Grant Billson
Cook.
Role: Right-hand bat, slow left arm
orthodox bowler, backward short
leg fielder.
Born: 17 June 1956, Leicester.
Height: 6′ 0″ **Weight:** 12st.
Nickname: Beast.
County debut: 1978.
County cap: 1982.
Test debut: 1983.
No. of Tests: 9.
No. of One-Day Internationals:1.
1000 runs in a season: 0.
50 wickets in a season: 4.
1st-Class 50s scored: 2.
1st-Class 100s scored: 0.
1st-Class 200s scored: 0.
1st-Class 5 w. in innings: 18.
1st-Class 10 w. in match: 2.
One-day 50s: 0.

One-day 100s 0.
Place in batting averages: 257 average: 12.19; (1983: 225 average: 10.58).
Place in bowling averages: 119 average: 41.89; (1983: 73 average: 25.47).
1st-Class catches 1984: 17 (career: 91).
Parents: Peter and Cynthia Cook.
Wife and date of marriage: Janet Elizabeth, 3 November 1979.
Education: Stokes Croft Junior; Lutterworth High; Lutterworth Upper.
Qualifications: One A-level, seven O-levels, advanced cricket coach.
Jobs outside cricket: Has worked for Leicestershire C.C.C. on promotions,
organizing lotteries, sponsored walks, general fund-raising projects. Also
coaching.
Family links with cricket: Father played club cricket.
Overseas tours: Whitbread Scholarship to Perth, Australia, 1980–81; Far
East tour with M.C.C. to Bangkok, Singapore, Hong Kong, 1981. Australia
and New Zealand with Derrick Robins XI, 1980. Zimbabwe with
Leicestershire C.C.C., 1981 and Dubai, 1982 with Barbican XI, America with
M.C.C. 1982–83, Kuwait 1983; New Zealand and Pakistan with England
1983–84.
Overseas teams played for: Claremont-Cottesloe C.C., 1st Grade cricket,
Perth, November 1980-February 1981.
Cricketers particularly learnt from: Jack Birkenshaw and Roger Tolchard.
Other sports followed: Soccer, rugby, horse-riding.
Equipment used: Slazenger.

Relaxations: Crosswords, watching horse-racing and football, especially Leicester City, and most sporting events, reading, especially Wilbur Smith, good comedy programmes and good food.

Extras: Played for E.S.C.A. 1975. Played for Young England v Young West Indies 1975. Played for M.C.C. v. Middlesex at start of 1981 season. Played for England B Team v. Pakistan, August 1982.

Opinions on cricket: "Would like to see 16 4-day county cricket matches ... Basically O.K.!"

Best batting performance: 75 Leicestershire v Somerset, Taunton 1980.

Best bowling performance: 7-63 Leicester v Somerset, Taunton 1982.

LAST SEASON: BATTING

	I.	N.O.	R.	H.S.	AV.
TEST	6	0	25	13	4.17
OTHER FIRST CLASS	24	9	231	44	15.40
INT					
J.P.L.	4	1	23	13	7.67
NAT.W.					
B & H	2	1	26	23	

CAREER: BATTING

	I.	N.O.	R.	H.S.	AV.
TEST	15	1	101	26	7.21
OTHER FIRST CLASS	141	46	1192	75	12.55
INT					
J.P.L.	9	4	52	13*	10.40
NAT.W.					
B & H	3	1	29	23	14.50

LAST SEASON: BOWLING

	O.	M.	R.	W.	AV.
TEST	95	15	297	5	59.40
OTHER FIRST CLASS	674.3	194	1756	44	39.91
INT					
J.P.L.	30	1	165	3	55.00
NAT.W.	12	4	33	2	16.50
B & H	39	6	129	3	43.00

CAREER: BOWLING

	O.	M.	R.	W.	AV.
TEST	498.2	162	1212	40	30.30
OTHER FIRST CLASS	4515.3	1448	10897	387	28.16
INT	8	0	34	1	–
J.P.L.	164.2	17	735	18	40.83
NAT.W.	36	8	131	4	32.75
B & H	67	11	224	4	56.00

Q. 105. Which famous international cricketer was named after an English soccer club?

Q. 106. Which current county cricketer's nick-name is Spiro?

FERRIS, G.J.F.

Full Name: George John Fitzgerald
Ferris.
Role: Right-hand bat, right arm fast
bowler.
Born: 18 October 1964, Urlings
Village, Antigua.
Height: 6′ 3″ **Weight:** 13st. 7lbs.
Nickname: Ferro.
County debut: 1983.
County cap: No.
Test debut: —
No. of Tests: 0.
No. of One-Day Internationals: 0.
1000 runs in a season: 0.
50 wickets in a season: 1.
1st-Class 50s scored: 0.
1st-Class 100s scored: 0.
1st-Class 200s scored: 0.
1st-Class 5 w. in innings: 3.
1st-Class 10 w. in match: 1.
One-day 50s: 0.
One-day 100s: 0.
Place in batting averages: — average: —; (1983: — average: —).
Place in bowling averages: — average: —; (1983: 25 average: 22.74).
1st-Class catches 1984: 0 (career: 3).
Cricketers particularly learnt from: Andy Roberts (neighbour in Antigua).
Overseas tours: With Young West Indies to Zimbabwe 1983.
Overseas teams played for: Leeward Islands.

LAST SEASON: BATTING

	I.	N.O.	R.	H.S.	AV.
TEST					
OTHER FIRST CLASS	1	0	0	0	–
INT					
J.P.L.					
NAT.W.					
B & H					

CAREER: BATTING

	I.	N.O.	R.	H.S.	AV.
TEST					
OTHER FIRST CLASS	22	10	84	26	7.00
INT					
J.P.L.					
NAT.W.					
B & H					

LAST SEASON: BOWLING

	O.	M.	R.	W.	AV.
TEST					
OTHER FIRST CLASS	21	4	83	0	–
INT					
J.P.L.	8	0	46	1	–
NAT.W.					
B & H					

CAREER: BOWLING

	O.	M.	R.	W.	AV.
TEST					
OTHER FIRST CLASS	480.4	94	1650	67	24.63
INT					
J.P.L.	24	0	107	3	35.67
NAT.W.					
B & H					

Significant injuries in 1984: Missed almost entire season because of knee injury.
Relaxations: Listening to music.
Best batting performance: 26 Leewards v Guyana, Nevis 1982–83.
Best bowling performance: 7-42 Leicestershire v Glamorgan, Hinckley 1983.

GARNHAM, M.A.

Full Name: Michael Anthony Garnham.
Role: Right-hand bat, wicket-keeper.
Born: 20 August 1960, Johannesburg, South Africa.
Height: 5' 10½" **Weight:** 11st.
Nickname: Fred.
County debut: 1980 (Leicestershire).
County cap: No.
Test debut: —
No. of Tests: 0.
No. of One-Day Internationals: 0.
1000 runs in a season: 0.
50 wickets in a season: 0.
1st-Class 50s scored: 10.
1st-Class 100s scored: 0.
1st-Class 200s scored: 0.
1st-Class 5 w. in innings: 0.
1st-Class 10 w. in match: 0.
One-day 50s: 2.
One-day 100s: 0.
Place in batting averages: 129 average: 28.96; (1983: — average: —).
Place in bowling averages: — average: —; (1983: — average: —).
Parents: Pauline Anne and Robert Arthur Garnham (divorced).
Wife and date of marriage: Lorraine, 15 September 1984.
Education: Camberwell Grammar, Melbourne, Australia; Scotch College, Perth, Australia; Park School, Barnstaple, North Devon; North Devon College; University of East Anglia (for one year).
Qualifications: Two A-levels, ten O-levels.
Off-season 1984–85: Working in Leicester.
Family links with cricket: Father was a club cricketer in Essex. He lost the sight of an eye keeping wicket.
Overseas tours: England Schools tour of India 1977–78; Young England tour of Australia 1979.
Overseas teams played for: Melbourne University & North Sydney 1979–80 (as prize for Young Keeper of the Year award, 1979). Glenelg, S. Australia, 1980–81.
Equipment used: Duncan Fearnley.

Cricketers particularly learnt from: Brian Roe (ex-Somerset), Alan Knott and Bob Taylor.
Other sports: Squash. Follow athletics.
Relaxations: Carpentry, D.I.Y., music, reading.
Significant injuries in 1984: Damaged finger and thumb.
Extras: Moved to England in 1975 after living in Australia for 10 years and in South Africa for four years. Played for Devon in 1976, 1977 (possibly youngest ever) before joining Gloucs. Summer Staff in 1978. Signed for Leicestershire 1980 season and was banned by the registration committee from competitive first team cricket for a month for breach of registration regulations. Played for Gloucestershire 2nd XI since 1976, making John Player League debut in 1978 v Warwickshire at Birmingham and Championship debut in 1979.
Opinions on cricket: "We should experiment with 4-day cricket."
Best batting performance: 84 Leicestershire v Surrey, The Oval 1984.

LAST SEASON: BATTING

	I.	N.O.	R.	H.S.	AV.
TEST					
OTHER FIRST CLASS	29	6	666	84	28.96
INT					
J.P.L.	10	6	113	26*	28.25
NAT.W.	3	1	29	19	14.50
B & H	2	0	20	14	10.00

CAREER: BATTING

	I.	N.O.	R.	H.S.	AV.
TEST					
OTHER FIRST CLASS	78	14	1541	84	24.08
INT					
J.P.L.	54	11	714	79*	16.60
NAT.W.	7	1	93	25	15.50
B & H	14	4	245	55	24.50

LAST SEASON: WICKET KEEPING

	C.	ST.			
TEST					
OTHER FIRST CLASS	45	3			
INT					
J.P.L.	9	2			
NAT.W.	2	1			
B & H	1	–			

CAREER: WICKET KEEPING

	C.	ST.			
TEST					
OTHER FIRST CLASS	107	16			
INT					
J.P.L.	64	9			
NAT.W.	5	1			
B & H	15	–			

Q. 107. Which current county cricketer's nick-name is Rocky?
Q. 108. Which current county cricketer's nick-name is Animal?

GOWER, D.I.

Full Name: David Ivon Gower.
Role: Left-hand bat, off-break bowler.
Vice-captain of Leics. 1982–83,
captain 1984–.
Born: 1 April 1957, Tunbridge Wells,
Kent.
Height: "5' 11¾" and a bit more."
Weight: 11st 11lbs.
Nickname: Stoat, Lubo, Lu.
County debut: 1975.
County cap: 1977.
Test debut: 1978.
No. of Tests: 65.
No. of One-Day Internationals: 66.

1000 runs in a season: 5.
50 wickets in a season: 0.
1st-Class 50s scored: 76.
1st-Class 100s scored: 27.
1st-Class 200s scored: 1.
1st-Class 5 w. in innings: 0.
1st-Class 10 w. in match: 0.
One-day 50s: 32.
One-day 100s: 13.
Place in batting averages: 73 average: 35.67; (1983: 22 average: 46.41).
Place in bowling averages: — average: —; (1983: — average: —).
1st-Class catches 1984: 17 (career: 149).
Parents: Richard Hallam and Sylvia Mary Gower.
Marital status: Single.
Education: Marlborough House School; King's School, Canterbury; University
College, London (did not complete law course).
Qualifications: Three A-levels, eight O-levels.
Jobs outside cricket: Worked at Bostik Ltd.
Family links with cricket: Father was club cricketer.
Cricketing superstitions: "They change every time they go wrong."
Overseas tours: Toured South Africa with English Schools XI 1974–75 and
West Indies with England Young Cricketers 1976; Derrick Robins to Canada
1976 and to Far East 1977. With England to Australia 1978–79 and 1979–80;
to West Indies 1980–81; India 1981–82, Australia and New Zealand 1982–
83. New Zealand 1983–84.
Overseas teams played for: Claremont-Cottesloe, Perth, Australia 1977–78.
Cricketers particularly learnt from: "Ray Illingworth and Jack Birkenshaw,
amongst many others whose advice has come my way."
Cricketers particularly admired: Graeme Pollock and many others.
Off-season 1984–85: England tour of India and Australia.

Equipment endorsed: Gray-Nicolls, (bats), Bukta (clothing), Sondico (pads and gloves), Patrick (boots), Jockey (leisurewear).

Other sports: Golf, squash, water and snow skiing.

Relaxations: Music, photographs, beaches, vintage port and crosswords.

Extras: Played for King's Canterbury 1st XI for three years. Has written "Anyone for Cricket" jointly with Bob Taylor about the 1978–79 Australian tour. Also "With Time to Spare", an autobiography published in 1980. Published "Heroes and Contemporaries" (Collins) 1983. Writes regular column for Wisden Cricket Monthly. Sir Len Hutton said of him: "He makes batting look as easy as drinking tea". Appointed England captain 1984.

Significant injuries in 1984: Blood poisoning.

Opinions on cricket: "Still very much in favour of 4-day cricket for our main competitions."

Best batting performance: 200* England v India, Edgbaston 1979.

Best bowling performance: 3-47 Leicestershire v Essex, Leicester 1977.

LAST SEASON: BATTING

	I.	N.O.	R.	H.S.	AV.
TEST	11	1	226	57*	22.60
OTHER FIRST CLASS	19	1	773	117*	42.94
INT	3	0	80	36	26.67
J.P.L.	8	1	216	75	30.86
NAT.W.	3	0	257	156	85.67
B & H					

CAREER: BATTING

	I.	N.O.	R.	H.S.	AV.
TEST	113	10	4486	200*	43.55
OTHER FIRST CLASS	265	25	9145	187	38.10
INT	63	7	2172	158	38.79
J.P.L.	93	14	3147	135*	29.83
NAT.W.	20	3	863	156	50.76
B & H	30	3	765	114*	28.33

LAST SEASON: BOWLING

	O.	M.	R.	W.	AV.
TEST					
OTHER FIRST CLASS					
INT					
J.P.L.					
NAT.W.					
B & H					

CAREER: BOWLING

	O.	M.	R.	W.	AV.
TEST	2	1	2	1	–
OTHER FIRST CLASS	34	4	178	3	59.33
INT	0.3	0	5	0	–
J.P.L.					
NAT.W.					
B & H					

Q. 109. Which current county cricketer's nick-name is Picca?

Q. 110. Which current county cricketer's nick-name is Canny or Gadge?

HAYSMAN, M.D.

Full Name: Michael Donald
Haysman.
Role: Right-hand bat, off-spin
bowler, gully fielder.
Born: 22 April 1961, Adelaide,
Australia.
Height: 6′ 2″ **Weight:** "14st. (plus a
bit)".
Nickname: Prince.
County debut: 1984.
County cap: No.
Test debut: —
No. of Tests: 0.
No. of One-Day Internationals: 0.
1000 runs in a season: 0.
50 wickets in a season: 0.
1st-Class 50s scored: 7.
1st-Class 100s scored: 4.
1st-Class 200s scored: 0.
1st-Class 5 w. in innings: 0.
1st-Class 10 w. in match: 0.
One-day 50s: 0.
One-day 100s 0.

Place in batting averages: 58 average: 38.33; (1983: — average: —).
Place in bowling averages: — average: —; (1983: — average: —).
1st-Class catches 1984: 10 (career: 33).
Parents: Margaret and Don.
Marital status: Single.
Education: Brighton High School, Adelaide.
Qualifications: A number of coaching certificates through South Australia
Cricket Association.
Jobs outside cricket: Junior co-ordinator for I.C.A. (indoor cricket arenas) in
Adelaide.
Off-season 1984–85: Playing 1st-Class in Australia.
Cricketing superstitions: "Too many to list."
Equipment used: Duncan Fearnley and Adidas.
Overseas tours: Australian U-25 tour to Zimbabwe.
Overseas teams played for: South Australia 1982–85.
Cricketers particularly learnt from: John Inverarity, Andrew Hilditch, Paddy
Clift.
Cricketers particularly admired: Ian Chappell.
Other sports: Australian Rules football; follow all sport.
Relaxations: Music, golf, sleeping.
Extras: Scored century on 1st-Class debut in both Australia and England.

Opinions on cricket: "Four-day cricket is the only way to play."
Best batting performance: 153 South Australia v Victoria, St. Kilda 1982–83.

LAST SEASON: BATTING

	I.	N.O.	R.	H.S.	AV.
TEST					
OTHER FIRST CLASS	10	4	230	102*	38.33
INT					
J.P.L.	–	–	–	–	–
NAT.W.					
B & H	4	1	68	28*	22.67

CAREER: BATTING

	I.	N.O.	R.	H.S.	AV.
TEST					·
OTHER FIRST CLASS	44	7	1520	153	41.08
INT					
J.P.L.	–	–	–	–	–
NAT.W.					
B & H	4	1	68	28*	22.67

LAST SEASON: BOWLING

	O.	M.	R.	W.	AV.
TEST					
OTHER FIRST CLASS					
INT					
J.P.L.					
NAT.W.					
B & H					

CAREER: BOWLING

	O.	M.	R.	W.	AV.
TEST					
OTHER FIRST CLASS	78	18	219	0	–
INT					
J.P.L.					
NAT.W.					
B & H					

PARSONS, G.J.

Full Name: Gordon James Parsons.
Role: Left-hand bat, right arm
medium bowler.
Born: 17 October 1959, Slough.
Height: 6′ 1″ **Weight:** 13st. 6lbs.
("Give or take a lb. or two").
Nickname: Bullhead, Triangle.
County debut: 1978.
County cap: 1984.
Test debut: —
No. of Tests: 0.
No. of One-Day Internationals: 0.
1000 runs in a season: 0.
50 wickets in a season: 2.
1st-Class 50s scored: 10.
1st-Class 100s scored: 0.
1st-Class 200s scored: 0.
1st-Class 5 w. in innings: 4.
1st-Class 10 w. in match: 0.
One-day 50s: 0.
One-day 100s: 0.

Place in batting averages: 126 average: 29.41; (1983: 199 average: 17.25).
Place in bowling averages: 81 average: 32.30; (1983: 56 average: 28.38).
1st-Class catches 1984: 8 (career: 38).

Parents: Dave and Evelyn Parsons.
Marital status: Single.
Education: Woodside County Secondary School, Slough.
Qualifications: Five O-levels.
Jobs outside cricket: Worked as clerk at J.L. Bennett, Ratby, Leicester.
Family links with cricket: Father played club cricket.
Off-season 1984–85: Coaching in Stellenbosch, S. Africa.
Overseas tours: Australasia with Derrick Robins Under-23 XI in 1979–80.
E.S.C.A. tour to India 1977–78. Zimbabwe with Leicestershire in 1981.
Overseas teams played for: Maharaja's in Sri Lanka, 1979, 1981–82, 1982–83. Boland (S.A.) 1983–84.
Cricketers particularly learnt from: "Alf Gover, Ken Higgs. Roger Tolchard and Andy Roberts have given me plenty of good advice. Plus too many to mention— particularly in the team."
Equipment used: Duncan Fearnley.
Other sports: Golf, squash.
Extras: Played for Leicester 2nd XI since 1976 and also for Buckinghamshire in 1977.
Opinions on cricket: "Like all bowlers who take a long run, I am of the opinion that 19.0 overs per hour is too high. Any successful side who rely on pace bowlers are certainly struggling to reach the number of overs required per hour."
Best batting performance: 63 Leicestershire v Yorkshire, Bradford 1984.
Best bowling performance: 5-25 Leicestershire v Essex, Leicester 1982.

LAST SEASON: BATTING

	I.	N.O.	R.	H.S.	AV.
TEST					
OTHER FIRST CLASS	39	10	853	63	29.41
INT					
J.P.L.	7	0	78	22	11.15
NAT.W.	2	0	24	23	12.00
B & H	2	0	10	7	5.00

CAREER: BATTING

	I.	N.O.	R.	H.S.	AV.
TEST					
OTHER FIRST CLASS	142	33	2077	63	19.06
INT					
J.P.L.	31	9	188	23	8.54
NAT.W.	5	0	54	23	10.80
B & H	8	4	87	29*	21.75

LAST SEASON: BOWLING

	O.	M.	R.	W.	AV.
TEST					
OTHER FIRST CLASS	662.1	140	2164	67	32.30
INT					
J.P.L.	92.5	3	488	10	48.80
NAT.W.	25.4	4	87	4	21.75
B & H	44	4	166	2	83.00

CAREER: BOWLING

	O.	M.	R.	W.	AV.
TEST					
OTHER FIRST CLASS	2390	498	7913	252	31.40
INT					
J.P.L.	425.2	24	1870	62	30.16
NAT.W.	93.4	9	402	9	44.67
B & H	163.5	22	528	22	24.00

ROBERTS, A.M.E.

Full Name: Anderson Montgomery Everton Roberts.
Role: Right-hand bat; right arm fast bowler.
Born: 29 January 1951; Urlings Village, Antigua.
Height: 6′ 1″ **Weight:** 13st. 7lbs.
Nickname: Andy, Fruit.
County debut: 1981 (Leicestershire).
County cap: No.
Test debut: 1973–74.
No. of Tests: 47.
No. of One-Day Internationals: 56.
1000 runs in a season: 0.
50 wickets in a season: 3.
1st-Class 50s scored: 8.
1st-Class 100s scored: 0.
1st-Class 200s scored: 0.
1st-Class 5 w. in innings: 47.
1st-Class 10 w. in match: 7.
One-day 50s: 1.
One-day 100s: 0.
Place in batting averages: 175 average: 23.50; (1983: — average —).
Place in bowling averages: 20 average: 23.30; (1983: — average: —).
1st-Class catches 1984: 2 (career: 52).
Parents: Isabelle and Joseph Roberts.
Wife and date of marriage: Janet, 3 November 1979.
Children: Kareem, 21 May 1981.
Education: Princess Margaret School, Antigua.
Family links with cricket: Cousin of W. Indies Test opener, Gordon Greenidge.
Relaxations: Music: soul, reggae and calypso.
Overseas teams played for: Leeward Islands, Combined Islands, New South Wales, 1976–77.
Overseas tours: With W. Indies to India, Pakistan and Sri Lanka, 1974–75; Australia 1975–76, and 1981–82; England 1976 and 1980; Australia and New Zealand, 1979–80. India 1983–84.
Cricketers particularly learnt from: Learned from them ALL — by WATCHING."
Other sports: Badminton.
Extras: First played for Hants in 1973 and capped in 1974. Attended Alf Gover's cricket school in 1972. Does not smoke or drink. Played Lancashire League cricket for Haslingden in 1981. Joined Leicestershire 1981, after leaving Hants in 1978. Wisden Player of the Year, 1974. Top of Leicestershire

first-class bowling averages in 1982 and 1983. Retired at end of 1983 but came back during 1984.

Best batting performance: 89 Leicestershire v Glamorgan, Swansea 1984.
Best bowling performance: 8-47 Hampshire v Glamorgan, Cardiff 1974.

LAST SEASON: BATTING

	I.	N.O.	R.	H.S.	AV.
TEST					
OTHER FIRST CLASS	12	4	188	89	23.50
INT					
J.P.L.	3	0	34	19	11.33
NAT.W.	3	0	28	19	9.33
B & H					

CAREER: BATTING

	I.	N.O.	R.	H.S.	AV.
TEST	62	11	762	68	14.94
OTHER FIRST CLASS	229	56	2754	89	15.92
INT	32	9	231	37*	10.04
J.P.L.	41	19	427	59*	19.40
NAT.W.	12	2	149	46	14.90
B & H	17	4	166	29	12.78

LAST SEASON: BOWLING

	O.	M.	R.	W.	AV.
TEST					
OTHER FIRST CLASS	265	70	769	33	23.30
INT					
J.P.L.	53.4	1	243	8	30.38
NAT.W.	24.1	2	100	2	50.00
B & H					

CAREER: BOWLING

	O.	M.	R.	W.	AV.
TEST	231.6 1546.5	27 354	5174	202	25.61
OTHER FIRST CLASS	125.4 5570.1	15 1322	13504	687	19.66
INT.	4 515.1	0 75	1771	87	20.36
J.P.L.	492	53	1587	93	17.05
NAT.W.	150	32	1197	56	21.37
B & H	277.5	60	687	46	14.94

TAYLOR, L.B.

Full Name: Leslie Brian Taylor.
Role: Right-hand bat; right arm fast medium bowler.
Born: 25 October 1953, Earl Shilton, Leicestershire.
Height: 6' 3½" **Weight:** 14st 7lbs.
Nickname: Les.
County debut: 1977.
County cap: 1981.
Test debut: —
No. of Tests: 0.
No of One-Day Internationals: 0.
1000 runs in a season: 0.
50 wickets in a season: 3.
1st-Class 50s scored: 0.
1st-Class 100s scored: 0.
1st-Class 200s scored: 0.
1st-Class 5 w. in innings: 12.
1st-Class 10 w. in match: 1.
One-day 50s: 0.
One-day 100s: 0.

Place in batting averages: — average: —; (1983: 171 average: 20.83).
Place in bowling averages: 105 average: 36.90; (1983: 11 average: 20.02).
1st-Class catches 1984: 0 (career: 32)
Parents: Peggy and Cyril Taylor.
Wife and date of marriage: Susan, 12 July 1973.
Children: Jamie, 24 June 1976; Donna, 10 November 1978.
Education: Heathfield High School, Earl Shilton.
Qualifications: Qualified carpenter and joiner.
Family links with cricket: Relation of the late Sam Coe, holder of highest individual score for Leicestershire, 252 not out v Northants. at Leicester in 1914.
Overseas tours: South America with Derrick Robins XI in 1978–79 off-season.
Other sports: Swimming and football.
Relaxations: Game-shooting and fox-hunting with the Atherstone Hunt.
Extras: Was banned from Test cricket for 3 years for joining rebel England tour of South Africa in 1982.
Best batting performance: 47 Leicestershire v Derbyshire, Derby 1983.
Best bowling performance: 7-28 Leicestershire v Derbyshire, Leicester 1981.

LAST SEASON: BATTING

	I.	N.O.	R.	H.S.	AV.
TEST					
OTHER FIRST CLASS	5	1	37	16*	9.25
INT					
J.P.L.	2	1	0	0*	–
NAT.W.					
B & H	2	1	1	1*	–

CAREER: BATTING

	I.	N.O.	R.	H.S.	AV.
TEST					
OTHER FIRST CLASS	117	51	673	47	10.20
INT					
J.P.L.	19	15	68	15*	17.00
NAT.W.	4	3	12	5*	–
B & H	7	3	11	5	2.75

LAST SEASON: BOWLING

	O.	M.	R.	W.	AV.
TEST					
OTHER FIRST CLASS	142	42	369	10	36.90
INT					
J.P.L.	21.2	0	99	3	33.00
NAT.W.					
B & H	37	10	161	3	53.67

CAREER: BOWLING

	O.	M.	R.	W.	AV.
TEST					
OTHER FIRST CLASS	3547.4	869	9787	401	24.41
INT					
J.P.L.	553.4	49	2340	126	18.57
NAT.W.	93.1	15	323	20	16.15
B & H	206.3	45	706	31	22.77

Q. 111. Who scored the first double-century in one-day cricket in England, for whom against whom, when and how much?

WHITAKER, J.J.

Full Name: John James Whitaker.
Role: Right-hand bat, off-break
bowler.
Born: 5 May 1962, Skipton,
Yorkshire.
Height: 6'0" **Weight:** 13st.
County debut: 1983.
County cap: No.
Test debut: —
No. of Tests: 0.
No. of One-Day Internationals: 0.
1000 runs in a season: 1.
50 wickets in a season: 0.
1st-Class 50s scored: 7.
1st-Class 100s scored: 2.
1st-Class 200s scored: 0.
1st-Class 5 w. in innings: 0.
1st-Class 10 w. in match: 0.
One-day 50s: 3.
One-day 100s: 2.
Place in batting averages: 69 average: 36.57; (1983: 134 average: 25.42).
Place in bowling averages: — average: —; (1983: — average: —).
1st-Class catches 1984: 20 (career: 24).
Parents: Rowland and Anne Whitaker.
Education: Uppingham School.
Jobs outside cricket: Employee of Whitakers Chocolates Ltd., groundsman,
Adelaide 1982–83; cricket coach and farmer, Tasmania 1983.
Family links with cricket: Father plays club cricket.

LAST SEASON: BATTING

	I.	N.O.	R.	H.S.	AV.
TEST					
OTHER FIRST CLASS	32	2	1097	160	36.57
INT					
J.P.L.	13	2	503	132	45.72
NAT.W.	2	0	171	155	85.50
B & H	4	0	139	46	34.75

CAREER: BATTING

	I.	N.O.	R.	H.S.	AV.
TEST					
OTHER FIRST CLASS	48	6	1402	160	33.38
INT					
J.P.L.	15	3	595	132	49.58
NAT.W.	2	0	171	155	85.50
B & H	4	0	139	46	34.75

LAST SEASON: BOWLING

	O.	M.	R.	W.	AV.
TEST					
OTHER FIRST CLASS					
INT					
J.P.L.					
NAT.W.	1	0	5	0	—
B & H					

CAREER: BOWLING

	O.	M.	R.	W.	AV.
TEST					
OTHER FIRST CLASS					
INT					
J.P.L.					
NAT.W.	1	0	5	0	—
B & H					

Overseas tours: To Australia 1982–82 with Uppingham School.
Overseas teams played for: Glenelg C.C. Adelaide 1982–83, Old Scotch C.C. Tasmania 1983–84.
Cricketers particularly learnt from: Maurice Hallam (coach at Uppingham) and Brian Davison.
Cricketing superstitions: Pack gear in same way every game, left pad first.
Equipment used: Gunn & Moore.
Other sports: Rugby, hockey, tennis, golf, exercising and keeping fit.
Relaxations: Music, discos, socialising, watching movies.
Extras: "I have learnt a great deal from playing in Australia where cricket is only at weekends and where it is played very hard."
Opinions on cricket: "I do not think 4-day cricket will improve anybody's standard, so we should keep 3-day cricket. People try to complicate cricket too much; it should be kept as simple as possible and played as simply as possible. I think both umpiring and wickets should be more consistent."
Best batting performance: 160 Leicestershire v Northamptonshire, Leicester 1984.

WHITTICASE, P.

Full Name: Philip Whitticase.
Role: Right-hand bat, wicket-keeper.
Born: 15 March 1965, Birmingham.
Height: 5′ 8″ **Weight:** 10st.
Nickname: Jasper, Tracy.
County debut: 1984.
County cap: No.
Test debut: —
No. of Tests: 0.
No. of One-Day Internationals: 0.
1000 runs in a season: 0.
50 wickets in a season: 0.
1st-Class 50s scored: 0.
1st-Class 100s scored: 0.
1st-Class 200s scored: 0.
1st-Class 5 w. in innings: 0.
1st-Class 10 w. in match: 0.
One-day 50s: 0.
One-day 100s: 0.
Place in batting averages: — average: —; (1983: — average: —).
Place in bowling averages: — average: —; (1983: — average: —).
Parents: Larry Gordon and Ann Whitticase.
Marital status: Single.
Family links with cricket: Grandfather and father club cricketers (both wicket-keepers).

Education: Belle Vue Primary; Buckpool Secondary; Crestwood Comprehensive.
Qualifications: 5 O-levels, 4 C.S.E.s
Jobs outside cricket: Worked for Asda Superstores; Inland Revenue.
Off-season 1984–85: Working for Inland Revenue; taking cricket coaching course; playing soccer.
Equipment used: Slazenger.
Overseas teams played for: South Bunbury, W. Australia 1983.
Cricketers particularly learnt from: D. Collins, Stourbridge Cricket Club.
Cricketers particularly admired: Bob Taylor, Alan Knott.
Other sports: Football, table tennis, golf. Follow football (used to be on Schoolboy Forms with Birmingham City F.C.).
Relaxations: "Football, golf, listening to music. I find most sports interesting and relaxing.
Opinions on cricket: "I think that sport in general should not be governed by political matters. Anybody ought to be able to play any sport, wherever they like, without being disciplined for their actions. This not only jeopardises the individual himself but also the spectator.
Best batting performance: 14 Leicestershire v Lancashire, Leicester 1984.

LAST SEASON: BATTING

	I.	N.O.	R.	H.S.	AV.
TEST					
OTHER FIRST CLASS	9	2	35	14	5.00
INT					
J.P.L.	1	1	5	5*	–
NAT.W.					
B & H					

CAREER: BATTING

	I.	N.O.	R.	H.S.	AV.
TEST					
OTHER FIRST CLASS	9	2	35	14	5.00
INT					
J.P.L.	1	1	5	5*	–
NAT.W.					
B & H					

LAST SEASON: WICKET KEEPING

	C.	ST.			
TEST					
OTHER FIRST CLASS	18	–			
INT					
J.P.L.	1	–			
NAT.W.					
B & H					

CAREER: WICKET KEEPING

	C.	ST.			
TEST					
OTHER FIRST CLASS	18	–			
INT					
J.P.L.	1	–			
NAT.W.					
B & H					

Q. 112. Which was the only first-class county to lose to which Minor county in the 1984 NatWest competition; and when, and against whom, was the first time this happened in the equivalent Gillette competition?

WILLEY, P.

Full Name: Peter Willey.
Role: Right-hand bat; off-break
bowler.
Born: 6 December 1949, Sedgefield,
County Durham.
Height: 6' 1" **Weight:** 13st.
Nickname: Chin, Will.
County debut: 1966 (Northants.).
County cap: 1971 (Northants.)
1984 (Leicestershire).
Test debut: 1976.
No. of Tests: 20.

No. of One-Day Internationals: 19.
Benefit: 1981, £31,400.
1000 runs in a season: 5.
50 wickets in a season: 3.
1st-Class 50s scored: 67.
1st-Class 100s scored: 30.
1st-Class 200s scored: 1.
1st-Class 5 w. in innings: 22.
1st-Class 10 w. in match: 3.
One-day 50s: 45.
One-day 100s: 6.
Place in batting averages: 71 average: 35.90; (1983: 14 average: 48.31).
Place in bowling averages: 66 average: 30.02; (1983: 71 average: 30.97).
1st-Class catches 1984: 17 (career: 163).
Parents: Oswald and Maisie Willey.
Wife and date of marriage: Charmaine, 23 September 1971.
Education: Secondary School, Seaham, County Durham.
Jobs outside cricket: Has worked as a groundsman, labourer and in a shoe
factory. Coached in South Africa 1978–79.
Family links with cricket: Father played local club cricket in County Durham.
Overseas tours: Toured Australia with England 1979–80. W. Indies, 1981.
Equipment endorsed: Slazenger.
Other sports: Golf, shooting, follow all sports.
Relaxations: Reading, taking Irish Setter for long walks and shooting.
Extras: With Wayne Larkins, received 2016 pints of beer (7 barrels) from a
brewery in Northampton as a reward for their efforts in Australia with England
in 1978–79. Reputed to be one of the strongest men in county cricket, being able
to defeat Ian Botham at arm-wrestling. Hit a six off his first ball v Middlesex in
J.P.L., 26 July 1981. Shared in fourth wicket partnership record for county, 370
with R.T. Virgin v Somerset at Northampton in 1976. Youngest player ever to
play for Northants. C.C.C. at 16 years 180 days v Cambridge in 1966. Banned
from Test cricket for 3 years for joining England rebel tour of South Africa in

1982. Left Northants. at end of 1983 and moved to Leicestershire as vice-captain.

Best batting performance: 227 Northamptonshire v Somerset, Northampton 1976.

Best bowling performance: 7-37 Northamptonshire v Oxford University, Oxford 1975.

LAST SEASON: BATTING

	I.	N.O.	R.	H.S.	AV.
TEST					
OTHER FIRST CLASS	45	4	1472	167	35.90
INT					
J.P.L.	14	2	592	106	49.33
NAT.W.	3	0	55	26	18.33
B & H	4	1	239	88*	79.67

CAREER: BATTING

	I.	N.O.	R.	H.S.	AV.
TEST	38	5	923	102*	27.97
OTHER FIRST CLASS	618	90	16037	227	30.37
INT	18	1	475	64	27.94
J.P.L.	195	15	5199	107	28.88
NAT.W.	33	4	874	89	30.14
B & H	46	6	1036	88*	25.90

LAST SEASON: BOWLING

	O.	M.	R.	W.	AV.
TEST					
OTHER FIRST CLASS	544.1	163	1291	43	30.02
INT					
J.P.L.	100	8	395	15	26.33
NAT.W.	36	1	112	4	28.00
B & H	35	7	102	0	–

CAREER: BOWLING

	O.	M.	R.	W.	AV.
TEST	177.5	49	441	6	73.50
OTHER FIRST CLASS	7134.4	32.6 1976	17016	585	29.09
INT	126	6	481	9	53.44
J.P.L.	1131.5	103	4547	172	26.43
NAT.W.	310.3	43	962	24	40.08
B & H	414.4	77	1090	29	37.59

COUNTY QUIZ

Q. 1. When was the club founded?

Q. 2. Who made the most first-class runs for the county last season, and how many?

Q. 3. What's the highest ever county total, and against whom?

Q. 4. Who took most wickets for the county last season, and how many?

Q. 5. What's the highest individual score for the county, who hit it, and when?

Q. 6. What's the highest scoring partnership for the county for any wicket?

Q. 7. How many times has the club won the County Championship?

Q. 8. What's the lowest ever total made by the county in one innings, when, and against whom?

Q. 9. Which bowler took the most first-class wickets in one season, when, and how many?

Q. 10. Which batsman hit the most runs in one season, when and how many?

Middlesex

BARLOW, G.D.

Full Name: Graham Derek Barlow.
Role: Left-hand bat, right arm medium bowler.
Born: 26 March 1950, Folkestone, Kent.
Height: 5′ 10½″ **Weight:** 12st 12lbs.
Nickname: "Take your pick! Eddy, Gladys, Duncan."
County debut: 1969.
County cap: 1976.
Benefit: 1984.
Test debut: 1976–77.
Number of Tests: 3.
No. of One-Day Internationals: 6.
1000 runs in a season: 6.
50 wickets in a season: 0.
1st-Class 50s scored: 55.
1st-Class 100s scored: 19.
1st-Class 200s scored: 0.
1st-Class 5 w. in innings: 0.
1st-Class 10 w. in match: 0.
One-day 50s: 29.
One-day 100s: 5.

Place in batting averages: 149 average: 26.56; (1983: 15 average: 48.28).
Place in bowling averages: — average: —; (1983: — average: —).
1st-Class catches 1984: 10 (career: 128).
Parents: Derek Albert and Millicent Louise (Betty) Barlow.
Education: Woolverstone Hall; Ealing Grammar School; Loughborough College of Education.
Qualifications: Certificate of Education for Physical Education and English.
Jobs outside cricket: P.E. teacher, Brentside School, Greenford 1973–74. NCA qualified coach to Wynberg Boys' School, Capetown 1975–76. Printing representative for Hildesley Ltd. 1974–75. Captain and coach, Greenpoint C.C., Melbourne, Australia 1978–79. Abbey Life Assurance Co. Ltd.

Family links with cricket: "Negligible. Distant great uncle played good club cricket, but that's it."
Overseas tours: India, Sri Lanka and Australia 1976–77.
Equipment endorsed: Duncan Fearnley bats and sporting goods.
Other sports: General fitness and particularly squash and running, especially when away in the winter. Played rugby for Loughborough.
Relaxations: "Music—cross-section of taste from Beethoven and particularly Sibelius to 'Yes' on the 'heavier' side. Reading when time permits, likewise cinema and, to a lesser extent, theatre."
Extras: Played rugby union for Loughborough Colleges, Leicestershire, England Under-23 and, briefly, Rosslyn Park. Played in M.C.C. Schools matches in 1968. Spent 1979–80 off-season coaching and playing in Cape Town. Runs pre-season training for Middlesex.
Best batting performance: 177 Middlesex v Lancashire, Southport 1981.

LAST SEASON: BATTING

	I.	N.O.	R.	H.S.	AV.
TEST					
OTHER FIRST CLASS	36	2	903	96	26.56
INT					
J.P.L.	13	0	345	53	26.53
NAT.W.	4	0	218	158	54.50
B & H	3	0	6	5	2.00

CAREER: BATTING

	I.	N.O.	R.	H.S.	AV.
TEST	5	1	17	7*	4.25
OTHER FIRST CLASS	361	53	10833	177	35.17
INT	6	1	149	80*	29.80
J.P.L.	135	13	3459	114	28.35
NAT.W.	27	3	841	158	35.04
B & H	40	4	873	129	24.25

LAST SEASON: BOWLING

	O.	M.	R.	W.	AV.
TEST					
OTHER FIRST CLASS					
INT					
J.P.L.					
NAT.W.					
B & H					

CAREER: BOWLING

	O.	M.	R.	W.	AV.
TEST					
OTHER FIRST CLASS	16.1	2	54	3	18.00
INT					
J.P.L.	15.3	0	91	4	22.75
NAT.W.					
B & H	4	0	18	1	–

Q. 113. Who was the first bowler to take 300 wickets in the John Player Special League?

Q. 114. Who was the longest serving England Test captain of all time?

BROWN, K.R.

Full Name: Keith Robert Brown.
Role: Batsman/wicket-keeper.
Born: 18 March 1963, Edmonton.
Height: 5' 11" **Weight:** 13st.
Nickname: Browny, Gloves.
County debut: 1984.
County cap: No.
Test debut: —
No. of Tests: 0.
No. of One-Day Internationals: 0.
1000 runs in a season: 0.
50 wickets in a season: 0.
1st-Class 50s scored: 0.
1st-Class 100s scored: 0.
1st-Class 200s scored: 0.
1st-Class 5 w. in innings: 0.
1st-Class 10 w. in match: 0.
One-day 50s: 0.
One-day 100s: 0.
Place in batting averages: — average: —; (1983: — average: —).
Place in bowling averages: — average: —; (1983: — average: —).
1st-Class catches 1984: 1 (career: 1).
Parents: Kenneth William and Margaret Sonia.
Wife and date of marriage: Marie, 3 November 1984.
Family links with cricket: Brother Gary is on Middlesex staff as well.
Education: Chace Boys' School.
Jobs outside cricket: Plasterer, light engineering.
Off-season 1984–85: Plastering and playing rugby.

LAST SEASON: BATTING

	I.	N.O.	R.	H.S.	AV.
TEST					
OTHER FIRST CLASS	1	0	6	6	—
INT					
J.P.L.					
NAT.W.					
B & H					

CAREER: BATTING

	I.	N.O.	R.	H.S.	AV.
TEST					
OTHER FIRST CLASS	1	0	6	6	—
INT					
J.P.L.					
NAT.W.					
B & H					

LAST SEASON: BOWLING

	O.	M.	R.	W.	AV.
TEST					
OTHER FIRST CLASS					
INT					
J.P.L.					
NAT.W.					
B & H					

CAREER: BOWLING

	O.	M.	R.	W.	AV.
TEST					
OTHER FIRST CLASS					
INT					
J.P.L.					
NAT.W.					
B & H					

Cricketing superstitions: "None, but it's nice to get off the mark. I bite my gloves when keeping."
Equipment used: Stuart Surridge.
Overseas tours: N.C.A. tour to Denmark in 1981. Played for South of England.
Cricketers particularly learnt from: Father and Don Bennett (county coach).
Cricketers particularly admired: Clive Radley—admire his approach to the game and never say die attitude.
Other sports: Rugby, golf, tennis, snooker, but follow all of them.
Relaxations: Playing snooker and drinking a pint of best bitter.
Extras: Had promising boxing career but gave it up in order to concentrate on cricket.

BUTCHER, R.O.

Full Name: Roland Orlando Butcher.
Role: Right-hand bat, right arm medium bowler.
Born: 14 October 1953, East Point, St Philip, Barbados.
Height: 5′ 7″ **Weight:** 12st.
Nickname: Butch.
County debut: 1974.
County cap: 1979.
Test debut: 1980–81.
No. of Tests: 3.
No. of One-Day Internationals: 3.
1000 runs in a season: 2.
50 wickets in a season: 0.
1st-Class 50s scored: 42.
1st-Class 100s scored: 12.
1st-Class 200s scored: 0.
1st-Class 5 w. in innings: 0.
1st-Class 10 w. in match: 0.
One-day 50s: 18.
One-day 100s: 1.
ace in batting averages: 50 average: 40.18; (1983: 43 average: 41.06).
Place in bowling averages: — average: —; (1983: — average: —).
1st-Class catches 1984: 17 (career: 205).
Parents: Robert and Doreen Butcher.
Wife: Cheryl Denise Butcher.
Children: Paul Nicholas Roland Butcher.
Education: Secondary.
Qualifications: Advanced Cricket Coaching Certificate. Football Association Preliminary Coaching Certificate.

Jobs outside cricket: Coaching. Played semi-professional soccer for Biggleswade and Stevenage. Football coach. Insurance salesman.
Family links with cricket: Cousin is Basil Butcher, of Guyana and West Indies.
Overseas teams played for: Played for Barbados 1974–75 Shell Shield Competition. Spent 1979–80 off season playing cricket in Barbados.
Equipment used: Slazenger.
Other sports: Football.
Relaxations: Television, horse-racing,, cinema.
Extras: Arrived in England aged 13. Does work for Inter-Action Group in deprived areas of London. A devout member of the Anglican church. Regarding his decision to register for England: "There were so many factors to be taken into consideration. I had been settled in England for 13 years, and I had made my home here for my family. There was also a qualification problem if I should ever be picked for the West Indies. That would immediately make me an overseas player again as far as the registration rules are concerned and it could affect my registration with Middlesex. What finally made up my mind was my son whose future is in this country."
Best batting performance: 197 Middlesex v Yorkshire, Lord's 1982.

LAST SEASON: BATTING

	I.	N.O.	R.	H.S.	AV.
TEST					
OTHER FIRST CLASS	40	7	1326	116	40.18
INT		.			
J.P.L.	15	2	319	82	24.53
NAT.W.	4	0	32	15	8.00
B & H	2	0	12	8	6.00

CAREER: BATTING

	I.	N.O.	R.	H.S.	AV.
TEST	5	0	71	32	14.20
OTHER FIRST CLASS	273	25	7746	197	31.23
INT	3	0	58	52	19.33
J.P.L.	102	9	2150	100	23.11
NAT.W.	17	2	222	50*	14.80
B & H	12	2	267	85	26.70

LAST SEASON: BOWLING

	O.	M.	R.	W.	AV.
TEST					
OTHER FIRST CLASS					
INT					
J.P.L.					
NAT.W.					
B & H					

CAREER: BOWLING

	O.	M.	R.	W.	AV.
TEST					
OTHER FIRST CLASS	14	3	76	0	–
INT					
J.P.L.	0.4	0	4	0	–
NAT.W.	2	0	18	1	–
B & H					

Q. 115. How many times did England's longest serving Test captain captain England?

CARR, J.D.

Full Name: John Donald Carr.
Role: Right-hand bat, off-break bowler.
Born: 15 June 1963, St. John's Wood, London N.W.8.
Nickname: Carsi.
County debut: 1983.
County cap: No.
Test debut: —
No. of Tests: 0.
No. of One-Day Internationals: 0.
1000 runs in a season: 0.
50 wickets in a season: 0.
1st-Class 50s scored: 2.
1st-Class 100s scored: 1.
1st-Class 200s scored: 0.
1st-Class 5 w. in innings: 2.
1st-Class 10 w. in match: 0.
One-day 50s: 2.
One-day 100s: 0.
Place in batting averages: 92 average: 33.43; (1983: 237 average: 11.17).
Place in bowling averages: 115 average: 40.23; (1983: — average: —).
1st-Class catches 1984: 9 (career: 14).
Education: Repton School and Oxford University.
Family links with cricket: Father, D.B. Carr, is secretary of T.C.C.B. and played for Oxford University, Derbyshire and England, captaining all three at some stage.
Extras: Played for Oxford in last year's Varsity Match. Secretary of University

LAST SEASON: BATTING

	I.	N.O.	R.	H.S.	AV.
TEST					
OTHER FIRST CLASS	14	0	468	123	33.43
INT					
J.P.L.					
NAT.W.					
B & H	4	0	134	66	33.50

CAREER: BATTING

	I.	N.O.	R.	H.S.	AV.
TEST					
OTHER FIRST CLASS	24	4	535	123	26.75
INT					
J.P.L.	1	1	0	0*	–
NAT.W.					
B & H	5	1	176	66	44.00

LAST SEASON: BOWLING

	O.	M.	R.	W.	AV.
TEST					
OTHER FIRST CLASS	343	94	885	22	40.23
INT					
J.P.L.					
NAT.W.					
B & H	29.2	1	111	5	22.20

CAREER: BOWLING

	O.	M.	R.	W.	AV.
TEST					
OTHER FIRST CLASS	513	143	1361	31	43.90
INT					
J.P.L.					
NAT.W.					
B & H	40.2	5	145	5	29.00

in 1984. Came on as substitute fielder for Middlesex in the 1983 Benson and Hedges Cup Final, holding a vital catch to help his side defeat Essex. Received special clearance to play in the match having previously appeared for Combined Universities in the same competition.
Best batting performance: 123 Oxford University v Lancashire, Oxford 1984.
Best bowling performance: 5-57 Oxford University v Gloucestershire, Oxford 1984.

COOK, C.R.

Full Name: Colin Roy Cook.
Role: Right-hand bat.
Born: 11 January 1960.
Height: 5' 11" **Weight:** 12st. 6lbs.
Nickname: Cooky, Zoot.
County debut: 1981.
County cap: No.
Test debut: —
No. of Tests: 0.
No. of One-Day Internationals: 0.
1000 runs in a season: 0.
50 wickets in a season: 0.
1st-Class 50s scored: 1.
1st-Class 100s scored: 0.
1st-Class 200s scored: 0.
1st-Class 5 w. in innings: 0.
1st-Class 10 w. in match: 0.
One-day 50s: 1.
One-day 100s: 0.
Place in batting averages: — average: —; (1983: — average: —).
Place in bowling averages: — average: —; (1983: — average: —).
1st-Class catches 1984: 1 (career: 8).
Parents: Laurence Alan Charles and Yvonne Marie Cook.
Marital status: Single.
Family links with cricket: Father on organisational side of Middlesex Colts Cricket Association; brother club cricketer. Sister married to Bill Athey of Gloucestershire.
Education: St John's Northwood, Preparatory; Merchant Taylor's, Northwood; Durham University.
Qualifications: University entrance, 3 A-levels, 8 O-levels.
Jobs outside cricket: Advertising assistant, Swan Brewery, Australia (1980–81, 1981–82 off-seasons).
Cricketing superstitions: "The umpire's index finger!"
Equipment used: Slazenger.
Overseas tours: England Young Cricketers tour to Australia 1979.

Overseas teams played for: Claremont-Cottesloe C.C., Perth, Western Australia, 1980–81 and 1981–82.

Cricketers particularly learnt from: Father, and Jack Robertson as coach, and specially admire Michael Holding, and Imran Khan for rhythm and fitness.

Other sports: Rugby Union.

Relaxations: Watching motor racing, visiting country pubs, supporting local rugby club.

Extras: Has played for Pinner C.C. and Southgate C.C. Played rugby for Middlesex Under-19s. Released at end of 1984 season.

Best batting performance: 79 Middlesex v Lancashire, Southport 1981.

LAST SEASON: BATTING

	I.	N.O.	R.	H.S.	AV.
TEST					
OTHER FIRST CLASS	3	0	106	47	35.33
INT					
J.P.L.	2	1	10	9*	–
NAT.W.					
B & H					

CAREER: BATTING

	I.	N.O.	R.	H.S.	AV.
TEST					
OTHER FIRST CLASS	18	2	393	79	24.56
INT					
J.P.L.	9	2	187	73	26.72
NAT.W.					
B & H					

LAST SEASON: BOWLING

	O.	M.	R.	W.	AV.
TEST					
OTHER FIRST CLASS					
INT					
J.P.L.					
NAT.W.					
B & H					

CAREER: BOWLING

	O.	M.	R.	W.	AV.
TEST					
OTHER FIRST CLASS					
INT					
J.P.L.					
NAT.W.					
B & H					

Q. 116. Name the first-class counties for which R.D.V. Knight has played.

Q. 117. Who was the first cricketer to score 1000 runs in the English county season of 1984?

COWANS, N.G.

Full Name: Norman George Cowans.
Role: Right-hand bat, right arm fast medium bowler.
Born: 17 April 1961, Enfield St Mary, Jamaica.
Height: 6′ 3″ **Weight:** 14st.
Nickname: The Flash, Diamond Two, Persil, Cool Breeze.
County debut: 1980.
County cap: 1984.
Test debut: 1982–83.
No. of Tests: 13.
No. of One-Day Internationals: 13.
1000 runs in a season: 0.
50 wickets in a season: 1.
1st-Class 50s scored: 1.
1st-Class 100s scored: 0.
1st-Class 200s scored: 0.
1st-Class 5 w. in innings: 8.
1st-Class 10 w. in match: 0.
One-day 50s: 0.
One-day 100s: 0.

Place in batting averages: 263 average: 11.20; (1983: — average: —).
Place in bowling averages: 11 average: 21.82; (1983: 66 average: 30.40).
1st-Class catches 1984: 9 (career: 31).
Parents: Gloria and Ivan Cowans.
Marital status: Single.
Education: Park High Secondary, Stanmore, Middlesex.
Qualifications: Qualified coach.
Jobs outside cricket: Squash and real tennis professional. Glassblower with Whitefriars hand-made glass.
Overseas tours: Young England tour to Australia 1979; Middlesex tour to Zimbabwe 1980; "Cricketer" tour to Dubai 1981, England to Australia and New Zealand 1982–83 and New Zealand and Pakistan 1983–84. International tour to Jamaica 1983.
Overseas teams played for: Claremont-Cottesloe C.C., Perth, Australia.
Cricketers particularly learnt from: Dennis Lillee, Michael Holding, Wayne Daniel. "The aggression of Lillee, the power of Daniel, and the smoothness of Holding."
Off-season 1984–85: Playing for England in India and Australia.
Equipment used: Slazenger.
Other sports: Basket ball, squash, table tennis, swimming, tennis, real tennis.
Relaxations: Dancing, reading, being with friends, listening to music. Reggae. Arsenal F.C.

Extras: Two Young England Tests, one One-Day Youth International. Has won athletics championship in sprinting and javelin throwing.
Best batting performance: 66 Middlesex v Surrey, Lord's 1984.
Best bowling performance: 6-64 Middlesex v Warwickshire, Lords 1984.

LAST SEASON: BATTING

	I.	N.O.	R.	H.S.	AV.
TEST	2	0	14	14	7.00
OTHER FIRST CLASS	23	1	269	66	12.23
INT					
J.P.L.	3	0	19	10	6.33
NAT.W.	3	1	23	12	11.50
B & H	3	1	16	6	8.00

CAREER: BATTING

	I.	N.O.	R.	H.S.	AV.
TEST	23	5	143	36	7.94
OTHER FIRST CLASS					
INT	5	2	9	4*	3.00
J.P.L.	8	4	41	14*	10.25
NAT.W.	7	2	28	12*	5.60
B & H	3	1	16	6	8.00

LAST SEASON: BOWLING

	O.	M.	R.	W.	AV.
TEST	19	2	76	0	–
OTHER FIRST CLASS	474.1	74	1517	73	20.78
INT					
J.P.L.	56	0	249	7	35.57
NAT.W.	39	7	157	4	39.25
B & H	39.1	5	124	5	24.80

CAREER: BOWLING

	O.	M.	R.	W.	AV.
TEST	360.3	66	1248	35	35.66
OTHER FIRST CLASS	1111.2	254	3467	155	22.37
INT	116.3	11	496	11	45.09
J.P.L.	151.2	5	703	26	27.04
NAT.W.	110	18	386	16	24.13
B & H	72.2	9	250	15	16.67

DANIEL, W.W.

Full Name: Wayne Wendell Daniel.
Role: Right-hand bat, right arm fast bowler.
Born: 16 January 1956, St Philip, Barbados.
Nickname: Diamond.
County debut: 1977.
County cap: 1977.
Benefit: 1985.
Test debut: 1975–76.
No. of Tests: 5.
No. of One-Day Internationals: 10.
1000 runs in a season: 0.
50 wickets in a season: 8.
1st-Class 50s scored: 2.
1st-Class 100s scored: 0.
1st-Class 200s scored: 0.
1st-Class 5 w. in innings: 27.
1st-Class 10 w. in innings: 7.
One-day 50s· 0.
One-day 100s: 0.

Place in batting averages: — average: —; (1983: — average: —).
Place in bowling averages: 41 average: 27.09; (1983: 27 average: 23.00).
1st-Class catches: 4 (career: 47).
Marital status: Single.
Equipment used: Stuart Surridge.
Relaxations: Enjoys listening to soul music.
Extras: Toured England with West Indies Schoolboys team 1974. Played for Middlesex 2nd XI 1975. Debut for Barbados 1975–76. Toured with West Indies to England 1976. Spent 1979–80 off-season in Barbados playing island cricket. Best bowling record for Benson & Hedges Competition 1978 with 7 for 12 v Minor Counties East at Ipswich.
Best batting performance: 53* Barbados v Jamaica, Bridgetown 1979–80; 53* Middlesex v Yorkshire, Lord's 1981.
Best bowling performance: 9-61 Middlesex v Glamorgan, Swansea 1982.

LAST SEASON: BATTING

	I.	N.O.	R.	H.S.	AV.
TEST					
OTHER FIRST CLASS	24	14	87	16*	8.70
INT					
J.P.L.	4	2	5	2*	2.50
NAT.W.	2	1	1	1	–
B & H	3	1	7	5*	3.50

CAREER: BATTING

	I.	N.O.	R.	H.S.	AV.
TEST	11	4	46	11	6.57
OTHER FIRST CLASS	178	81	1260	53*	12.99
INT	5	4	49	16*	–
J.P.L.	34	12	79	14	3.59
NAT.W.	14	7	29	14	4.14
B & H	14	5	46	20*	5.11

LAST SEASON: BOWLING

	O.	M.	R.	W.	AV.
TEST					
OTHER FIRST CLASS	462	86	1463	54	27.09
INT					
J.P.L.	107.1	7	426	29	14.69
NAT.W.	53.4	7	156	11	14.18
B & H	26.5	6	96	8	12.00

CAREER: BOWLING

	O.	M.	R.	W.	AV.
TEST	292	61	910	36	25.28
OTHER FIRST CLASS	4601.5	956	13312	634	21.00
INT	152	17	595	23	25.87
J.P.L.	676	66	2402	136	17.66
NAT.W.	295.3	53	847	56	15.12
B & H	292.4	58	791	62	12.76

Q. 118. Which county won the first county championship and when?

Q. 119. Which county has won the county championship most times and how many?

DOWNTON, P.R.

Full Name: Paul Rupert Downton.
Role: Right-hand bat; wicket-keeper.
Born: 4 April 1957, Farnborough,
Kent.
Height: 5' 10" **Weight:** 11st. 9lbs.
County debut: 1980 (Middlesex)
1977 (Kent).
County cap: 1981.
Test debut: 1980–81.
No. of Tests: 10.
No. of One-Day Internationals: 1.
1000 runs in a season: 0.
50 wickets in a season: 0.
1st-Class 50s scored: 13.
1st-Class 100s scored: 0.
1st-Class 200s scored: 0.
1st-Class 5 w. in innings: 0.
1st-Class 10 w. in match: 0.
One-day 50s: 2.
One-day 100s: 0.
Place in batting averages: 153 average: 25.75; (1983: 162 average: 22.08).
Place in bowling averages: — average: —; (1983: — average: —).
Parents: George Charles and Jill Elizabeth Downton.
Marital status: Single.
Education: Sevenoaks School; Exeter University.
Qualifications: Law degree (LLB); three A-levels, nine O-levels. N.C.A.
coaching course.
Family links with cricket: Father kept wicket for Kent 1948–49.

LAST SEASON: BATTING

	I.	N.O.	R.	H.S.	AV.
TEST	11	1	220	56	22.00
OTHER FIRST CLASS	22	8	398	88	28.43
INT					
J.P.L.	8	2	47	20	7.83
NAT.W.	4	0	115	62	28.75
B & H	4	1	80	28	26.67

CAREER: BATTING

	I.	N.O.	R.	H.S.	AV.
TEST	18	2	279	56	17.44
OTHER FIRST CLASS	175	35	2776	90*	19.83
INT	–	–	–	–	–
J.P.L.	53	20	609	58*	18.45
NAT.W.	15	2	242	62	18.62
B & H	14	6	145	28	18.13

LAST SEASON: WICKET KEEPING

	C.	ST.			
TEST	13	–			
OTHER FIRST CLASS	29	6			
INT					
J.P.L.	4	1			
NAT.W.	6	1			
B & H	3	–			

CAREER: WICKET KEEPING

	C.	ST.			
TEST	21	–			
OTHER FIRST CLASS	326	48			
INT	1	–			
J.P.L.	83	22			
NAT.W.	27	4			
B & H	22	4			

Overseas tours: England tour of Pakistan and New Zealand 1977; West Indies 1980–81. England Young Cricketers tour of West Indies (Vice-Captain) 1976.
Overseas teams played for: Sandgate, Redcliffe 1981–82; Stellenbosch University 1983–4.
Cricketers particularly learnt from: Father, Alan Knott, Bob Taylor.
Equipment used: Slazenger.
Off-season 1984–85: On England tour of India and Australia.
Other sports: Rugby—played in England Under-19 squad 1975, Exeter University 1st XV.
Relaxations: Reading.
Extras: Made debut for Kent C.C.C. in 1977, gaining cap in 1979. Played for Kent 2nd XI at age 16.
Opinions on cricket: "There are things I want to do outside cricket and an eventual business career in the City is something I find appealing. But I am keen to give the game my full attention for a while yet."
Best batting performance: 90* Middlesex v Derbyshire, Uxbridge 1980.

EDMONDS, P.H.

Full Name: Phillippe Henri Edmonds.
Role: Right-hand bat, slow left arm orthodox bowler.
Born: 8 March, 1951, Lusaka, Zambia.
Height: 6' 2".
Nickname: Goat, Henry, Rommel, Duke.
County debut: 1971.
County cap: 1974.
Test debut: 1975.
No. of Tests: 23.
No. of One-Day Internationals: 11.
1000 runs in a season: 0.
50 wickets in a season: 10.
Benefit: 1983 (£80,000).
1st-Class 50s scored: 22.
1st-Class 100s scored: 3.
1st-Class 200s scored: 0.
1st-Class 5 w. in innings: 45.
1st-Class 10 w. in match: 9.
One-day 50s: 2.
One-day 100s: 0.

Place in batting averages: 197 average: 20.69; (1983: 226 average: 13.00).
Place in bowling averages: 43 average: 27.22; (1983: 15 average: 21.46).
1st-Class catches 1984: 20 (career: 286).

Wife: Frances.
Education: Gilbert Rennie High School, Lusaka; Skinner's School, Tunbridge Wells; Cranbrook School; Cambridge University.
Jobs outside cricket: Has worked for sports promotion and finance company.
Overseas tours: Pakistan and New Zealand 1977–78; Australia 1978–79.
Overseas teams played for: Eastern Province in 1975–76 Currie Cup Competition.
Off-season 1984–85: With England in India and Australia.
Other sports: Played rugby for Cambridge but missed blue. Squash.
Relaxations: "Read *Financial Times* avidly at breakfast", crosswords.
Extras: Cambridge cricket blue 1971-72-73, Captain 1973. Constantly listening to News programmes in the dressing-room. Vice-captain of Middlesex, 1980.
Best batting performance: 142 Middlesex v Glamorgan, Swansea 1984.
Best bowling performance: 8-53 Middlesex v Hampshire, Bournemouth 1984.

LAST SEASON: BATTING

	I.	N.O.	R.	H.S.	AV.
TEST					
OTHER FIRST CLASS	33	4	600	142	20.69
INT					
J.P.L.	9	3	71	25*	11.83
NAT.W.	4	1	54	30	18.00
B & H	1	0	11	11	–

CAREER: BATTING

	I.	N.O.	R.	H.S.	AV.
TEST	28	6	430	64	19.55
OTHER FIRST CLASS	373	62	6136	142	19.73
INT	6	2	31	15	7.75
J.P.L.	108	27	1246	52	15.38
NAT.W.	24	8	367	63*	22.94
B & H	34	8	480	44*	18.46

LAST SEASON: BOWLING

	O.	M.	R.	W.	AV.
TEST					
OTHER FIRST CLASS	823.3	233	2096	77	27.22
INT					
J.P.L.	85	7	373	14	26.64
NAT.W.	41	3	138	3	46.00
B & H	4	1	22	0	–

CAREER: BOWLING

	O.	M.	R.	W.	AV.
TEST	199 604.4	48 213	1733	59	29.38
OTHER FIRST CLASS	287 10025.3	72 3046	22815	962	23.71
INT.	28 43.2	1 8	230	11	20.91
J.P.L.	870.4	68	3646	160	22.78
NAT.W.	338.2	60	983	37	26.46
B & H	357.3	74	1010	45	22.44

Q. 120. In what year were the Laws of Cricket first set out for all England?

Q. 121. When was the M.C.C. Code of Laws first adopted?

ELLIS, R.G.P.

Full Name: Richard Gary Peter
Ellis.
Role: Right-hand bat.
Born: 20 December 1960,
Paddington.
Height: 6′ 1″ **Weight:** 12st.
Nickname: Hermie.
County debut: 1982.
County cap: No.
Test debut: —
No. of Tests: 0.
No. of One-Day Internationals: 0.
1000 runs in a season: 0.
50 wickets in a season: 0.
1st-Class 50s scored: 11.
1st-Class 100s scored: 2.
1st-Class 200s scored: 0.
1st-Class 5 w. in innings: 0.
1st-Class 10 w. in match: 0.
One-day 50s: 1.
One-day 100s: 0.
Place in batting averages: — average: —; (1983: 119 average: 27.42).
Place in bowling averages: — average: —; (1983: — average: —).
1st-Class catches 1984: 0 (career: 18).
Parents: Peter and Lilian Ellis.
Family links with cricket: Father on Lord's ground staff; played one first class
game v. Cambridge and was a pro. in Scotland.
Education: Oxford University; Haileybury College.

LAST SEASON: BATTING

	I.	N.O.	R.	H.S.	AV.
TEST					
OTHER FIRST CLASS	3	0	54	33	18.00
INT					
J.P.L.					
NAT.W.					
B & H					

CAREER: BATTING

	I.	N.O.	R.	H.S.	AV.
TEST					
OTHER FIRST CLASS	71	3	1997	105*	29.37
INT					
J.P.L.	11	0	191	52	17.36
NAT.W.	1	1	15	15*	–
B & H	8	0	54	16	6.75

LAST SEASON: BOWLING

	O.	M.	R.	W.	AV.
TEST					
OTHER FIRST CLASS					
INT					
J.P.L.					
NAT.W.					
B & H					

CAREER: BOWLING

	O.	M.	R.	W.	AV.
TEST					
OTHER FIRST CLASS	83	20	264	4	66.00
INT					
J.P.L.					
NAT.W.					
B & H					

Qualifications: Studying for B.A. in History; 4 A-levels; 9 O-levels.
Jobs outside cricket: Squash professional, labourer, teacher.
Cricketing superstitions: The number 111.
Equipment used: Gray-Nicolls.
Cricketers particularly admired: Tony Greig.
Other sports: Squash, rackets, real tennis, golf.
Relaxations: Reading, watching television, music.
Extras: Captain, Oxford University C.C. 1982. Also won blues in squash and rackets. Captain of Middlesex 2nd XI on return from university, 2nd XI cap in 1980. Played for England Under-15 as an off-break bowler but no longer bowls. Released at end of 1984 season.
Best batting performance: 105* Oxford University v Surrey, Oxford 1982.

EMBUREY, J.E.

Full Name: John Ernest Emburey.
Role: Right-hand bat, off-break bowler, slip or gully fielder.
Born: 20 August 1952, Peckham, London.
Height: 6' 2" **Weight:** 13st. 12lbs.
Nickname: Embers, Ernie.
County debut: 1973.
County cap: 1977.
Test debut: 1978.
No of Tests: 22.
No. of One-Day Internationals: 8.
1000 runs in a season: 0.
50 wickets in a season: 8.
1st-Class 50s scored: 15.
1st-Class 100s scored: 2.
1st-Class 200s scored: 0.
1st-Class 5 w. in innings: 43.
1st-Class 10 w. in match: 8.
One-day 50s: 1.
One-day 100s: 0.
Place in batting averages: 223 average: 17.54; (1983: 112 average: 27.93).
Place in bowling averages: 45 average: 27.47; (1983: 6 average: 17.89).
1st-Class catches 1984: 17 (career: 217).
Parents: John and Rose Emburey.
Wife and date of marriage: Susie, 20 September 1980.
Children: Clare, 1 March 1983 (Cape Town).
Education: Peckham Manor Secondary School.
Qualifications: Advanced Cricket Coaching Certificate. O-levels.
Jobs outside cricket: "No other jobs. Have been abroad coaching most years."

Family links with cricket: "An uncle, Charles Roff, was a very good cricketer. His father made him take an apprenticeship which stopped him going any further with cricket." Brother, Stephen, represented London Schools Colts in 1977.

Overseas tours: With England to Australia 1979–80 (following injury to Geoff Miller); with England to West Indies 1981. With England to India 1981–82.

Overseas teams played for: St Kilda C.C., Victoria, Australia, 1979–80.

Off-season 1984–85: St Kilda C.C., Melbourne.

Equipment used: Symonds.

Cricketers particularly learnt from: F.J. Titmus and K. Barrington.

Other sports: Golf. Follows most.

Relaxations: Fishing, reading.

Significant injuries in 1984: Persistent back ailment. Knee. Gallstone operation in April.

Extras: Played for Surrey Young Cricketers 1969–70. Middlesex Vice Captain since 1983. Banned from Test cricket for 3 years after playing for England rebels in South Africa. Hit 6 sixes in 7 balls for Western Province v Eastern Province 1983–84 (52 n.o. in 22 balls).

Best batting performance: 133 Middlesex v Essex, Chelmsford 1983.

Best bowling performance: 7-6 Middlesex v Cambridge University, Cambridge 1977.

LAST SEASON: BATTING

	I.	N.O.	R.	H.S.	AV.
TEST					
OTHER FIRST CLASS	35	2	579	57	17.54
INT					
J.P.L.	10	4	96	23*	16.00
NAT.W.	4	1	68	31	22.67
B & H	4	0	109	50	27.25

CAREER: BATTING

	I.	N.O.	R.	H.S.	AV.
TEST	33	6	326	57	12.07
OTHER FIRST CLASS	261	60	4361	133	21.70
INT	7	1	31	18	5.17
J.P.L.	88	31	905	40*	15.87
NAT.W.	16	6	262	36*	26.20
B & H	22	6	299	50	18.69

LAST SEASON: BOWLING

	O.	M.	R.	W.	AV.
TEST					
OTHER FIRST CLASS	865.3	255	1978	72	27.47
INT					
J.P.L.	95.1	10	381	23	16.56
NAT.W.	48	5	95	5	19.00
B & H	44	11	95	1	–

CAREER: BOWLING

	O.	M.	R.	W.	AV.
TEST	144.4 637.3	49 203	1696	56	30.29
OTHER FIRST CLASS	155.1 7790.4	39 2357	17807	774	23.01
INT.	72.3	9	262	5	52.40
J.P.L.	872.5	79	3617	166	21.78
NAT.W.	290	54	720	23	31.30
B & H	270.5	49	707	20	35.35

FRASER, A.R.C.

Full Name: Angus Robert Charles
Fraser.
Role: Right-hand bat, right arm
medium fast bowler.
Born: 8 August 1965, Billinge,
Lancashire.
County debut: 1984.
County cap: No.
Test debut: —
No. of Tests: 0.
No. of One-Day Internationals: 0.
1000 runs in a season: 0.
50 wickets in a season: 0.
1st-Class 50s scored: 0.
1st-Class 100s scored: 0.
1st-Class 200s scored: 0.
1st-Class 5 w. in innings: 0.
1st-Class 10 w. in match: 0.
One-day 50s: 0.
One-day 100s: 0.
Place in batting averages: — average: —; (1983: — average: —).
Place in bowling averages: — average: —; (1983: — average: —).
Extras: Appeared for Middlesex in final of the Warwick Pool Under-25
competition.

LAST SEASON: BATTING

	I.	N.O.	R.	H.S.	AV.
TEST					
OTHER FIRST CLASS					
INT					
J.P.L.					
NAT.W.					
B & H					

CAREER: BATTING

	I.	N.O.	R.	H.S.	AV.
TEST					
OTHER FIRST CLASS					
INT					
J.P.L.					
NAT.W.					
B & H					

LAST SEASON: BOWLING

	O.	M.	R.	W.	AV.
TEST					
OTHER FIRST CLASS	34	7	124	1	–
INT					
J.P.L.					
NAT.W.					
B & H					

CAREER: BOWLING

	O.	M.	R.	W.	AV.
TEST					
OTHER FIRST CLASS	34	7	124	1	–
INT					
J.P.L.					
NAT.W.					
B & H					

GATTING, M.W.

Full Name: Michael William Gatting.
Role: Right-hand bat, right arm
medium bowler. Captain of
Middlesex 1983–.
Born: 6 June 1957, Kingsbury,
Middlesex.
Height: 5′ 10″ **Weight:** 13st 8lbs.
Nickname: Gatt.
County debut: 1975.
County cap: 1977.
Test debut: 1977–78.
No. of Tests: 30.
No. of One-Day Internationals: 31.
1000 runs in a season: 6.
50 wickets in a season: 0.
1st-Class 50s scored: 66.
1st-Class 100s scored: 29.
1st-Class 200s scored: 2.
1st-Class 5 w. in innings: 2.
1st-Class 10 w. in match: 0.
One-day 50s 30.
One-day 100s 2.

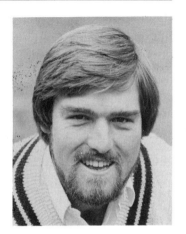

Place in batting averages: 4 average: 68.39; (1983: 3 average: 64.96).
Place in bowling averages: — average: —; (1983: — average: —).
1st-Class catches 1984: 24 (career: 207).
Parents: Bill and Vera Gatting.
Wife and date of marriage: Elaine, September 1980.
Children: One son (Andrew).
Education: Wykeham Primary School; John Kelly Boys' High School.
Jobs outside cricket: "Running my sports shop in Radlett."
Off-season 1984–85: With England in India and Australia.
Family links with cricket: Father used to play club cricket.
Overseas tours: Toured West Indies with England Young Cricketers 1979–80.
With England in W. Indies, 1981; in India 1981–82; New Zealand and
Pakistan 1983–84.
Overseas teams played for: Club cricket in Sydney, Australia, off-season
1979–80.
Equipment used: Newbery bats. Readers soft leather goods.
Other sports: Football, table-tennis, tennis, swimming, golf, offered soccer
trials but turned them down in favour of cricket. Supports Spurs.
Relaxations: Reading—(expert on the books of Tolkien), crosswords, cinema.
Extras: Played for England Young Cricketers 1974. Topped Middlesex first-
class batting averages, 1981, 1982, 1983, and 1984 and bowling averages in
1982. Scored fastest 1st-Class century in 1984—79 minutes v Kent.

Best batting performance: 258 Middlesex v Somerset, Bath 1984.
Best bowling performance: 5-34 Middlesex v Glamorgan, Swansea 1982.

LAST SEASON: BATTING

	I.	N.O.	R.	H.S.	AV.
TEST	2	0	30	29	15.00
OTHER FIRST CLASS	41	10	2227	258	71.84
INT	2	0	6	6	3.00
J.P.L.	13	1	538	103*	44.83
NAT.W.	5	1	215	88*	53.75
B & H	4	0	120	47	30.00

CAREER: BATTING

	I.	N.O.	R.	H.S.	AV.
TEST	52	4	1144	81	23.83
OTHER FIRST CLASS	295	52	11689	258	48.10
INT	29	8	604	96	28.76
J.P.L.	105	10	2676	103*	28.16
NAT.W.	30	7	851	95*	37.00
B & H	35	9	1064	95*	40.92

LAST SEASON: BOWLING

	O.	M.	R.	W.	AV.
TEST					
OTHER FIRST CLASS	87	20	205	8	25.63
INT					
J.P.L.	41.3	0	206	8	25.75
NAT.W.	11	4	22	3	7.33
B & H	21.4	0	94	6	15.67

CAREER: BOWLING

	O.	M.	R.	W.	AV.
TEST	1 36	0 11	115	2	57.50
OTHER FIRST CLASS	19.7 926.3	3 221	2590	103	25.15
INT	21.2	4	95	4	23.75
J.P.L.	361.1	11	1751	66	26.53
NAT.W.	124	17	481	15	32.07
B & H	161.4	12	621	33	18.81

HUGHES, S.P.

Full Name: Simon Peter Hughes.
Role: Right-hand bat; right arm
fast-medium bowler
Born: 20 December 1959, Kingston,
Surrey.
Height: 5' 10" **Weight:** 11st 7lbs.
Nickname: Yozzer, Heinz (57
varieties).
County debut: 1980.
County cap: 1981.
Test debut: —
No. of Tests: 0.
No. of One-Day Internationals: 0.
1000 runs in a season: 0.
50 wickets in a season: 0.
1st-Class 50s scored: 0.
1st-Class 100s scored: 0.
1st-Class 200s scored: 0.
1st-Class 5 w. in innings: 6.
1st-Class 10 w. in match: 0.
One-day 50s: 0.
One-day 100s: 0.

Place in batting averages: 248 average: 14.40; (1983: — average: 3.25).
Place in bowling averages: 67 average: 30.03; (1983: 37 average: 25.28).
1st-Class catches 1984: 5 (career: 16).
Parents: Peter and Erica Hughes.
Marital status: Single.
Education: Latymer Upper School, Hammersmith; Durham University.
Qualifications: Four A-levels, 10 O-levels. Degree in Geography and Anthropology.
Jobs outside cricket: Writes regular sports column in local weekly paper, and monthly for the Cricketer.
Off-season 1984–85: Playing for Auckland University in New Zealand.
Family links with cricket: Father very keen coach and player who owns indoor cricket school in Chiswick and is a qualified coach.
Overseas tours: Personal overseas spell playing in Sri Lanka 1979. Middlesex C.C.C. tour to Zimbabwe winter 1980. With Overseas XI (captained by J.M. Brearley) December 1980– January 1981 to Calcutta (v Indian XI).
Overseas teams played for: Colts C.C., Colombo, Sri Lanka, and Sri Lanka Board President's XI. Northern Transvaal, 1982–83. Grosvenor-Fynaland 1983–84.
Equipment used: Slazenger.
Cricketers particularly learnt from: Father, Jack Robertson, Mike Brearley and Mike Selvey.
Cricketers particularly admired: John Emburey, Clive Radley.
Other sports: Soccer (for university), tennis, golf.
Relaxations: "Travelling, particularly by train; old comedy films (e.g. Laurel and Hardy); music— plays organ and piano; writing; addicted to curry."
Extras: Took 4-82 v Kent on Championship debut, plus played in County Championship and Gillette Cup winning sides (Lord's Final) in 1980 in first season. Selected for England U-25 XI v Sri Lanka (Trent Bridge) July 1981. Awarded cap after only 20 matches. Took 4 for 28 in bowling Somerset out for

LAST SEASON: BATTING

	I.	N.O.	R.	H.S.	AV.
TEST					
OTHER FIRST CLASS	14	4	144	41*	14.40
INT					
J.P.L.					
NAT.W.	1	1	1	1*	—
B & H	3	1	12	8*	6.00

CAREER: BATTING

	I.	N.O.	R.	H.S.	AV.
TEST					
OTHER FIRST CLASS	64	29	274	41*	7.83
INT					
J.P.L.	4	2	11	9	5.50
NAT.W.	1	1	1	1*	—
B & H	3	1	12	8*	6.00

LAST SEASON: BOWLING

	O.	M.	R.	W.	AV.
TEST					
OTHER FIRST CLASS	314.2	53	1051	35	30.03
INT					
J.P.L.	20	0	100	4	25.00
NAT.W.	17	2	78	3	26.00
B & H	31	4	109	2	54.50

CAREER: BOWLING

	O.	M.	R.	W.	AV.
TEST					
OTHER FIRST CLASS	1516.4	286	4989	184	27.11
INT					
J.P.L.	122.1	4	626	19	32.94
NAT.W.	17	2	78	3	26.00
B & H	31	4	109	2	54.50

57 in only 14 overs (all 10 wickets fell in 46 balls) at Weston-Super-Mare, 1982.

Opinions on cricket: "There are so many good players still in county 2nd XIs that there is scope for an 18th county. Everyone plays better when they have a settled place in a side."

Best batting performance: 41* Middlesex v Gloucestershire, Lords 1984.

Best bowling performance: 6-32 Middlesex v Gloucestershire, Bristol 1983.

JAMES, K.D.

Full Name: Kevan David James.
Role: Left-hand bat; left arm fast medium bowler.
Born: 18 March 1961, Lambeth, South London.
Height: 6' 0½" **Weight:** 11st 7lbs.
Nickname: Jambo, Jaimo.
County debut: 1980.
County cap: No.
Test debut: —
No. of Tests: 0.
No. of One-Day Internationals: 0.
1000 runs in a season: 0.
50 wickets in a season: 0.
1st-Class 50s scored: 0.
1st-Class 100s scored: 0.
1st-Class 200s scored: 0.
1st-Class 5 w. in innings: 1.
1st-Class 10 w. in match: 0.
One-day 50s: 0.
One-day 100s: 0.

Place in batting averages: — average: —; (1983: 148 average: 23.50).
Place in bowling averages: — average: —; (1983: — average: —).
1st-Class catches 1984: 0 (career: 3).
Parents: David and Helen James.
Marital status: Single.
Education: Edmonton County High School.
Qualifications: Five O-levels; qualified coach.
Jobs outside cricket: "I write a column in the 'Club Cricketer' magazine."
Off-season 1984–85: Coaching and playing in Wellington, New Zealand.
Family links with cricket: Father and brother play club cricket in North London.
Equipment used: Stuart Surridge.
Overseas tours: Young England tour of Australia, 1978–79; Young England tour of West Indies 1979–80.

Overseas teams played for: Canterbury Province Under-23, New Zealand, 1980; Sydenham C.C., Christchurch, New Zealand 1980–81, Wellington, New Zealand 1983.

Other sports: Soccer. Watch American football.

Cricketers particularly learnt from: Don Bennett, Middlesex coach. All the Middlesex 1st XI.

Relaxations: "Watching Spurs; anything that does not involve cricket."

Extras: Released by Middlesex at end of 1984 season.

Best batting performance: 34 Middlesex v Northamptonshire, Northampton 1983.

Best bowling performance: 5-28 Middlesex v Cambridge University, Cambridge 1983.

LAST SEASON: BATTING

	I.	N.O.	R.	H.S.	AV.
TEST					
OTHER FIRST CLASS	2	1	30	28*	–
INT					
J.P.L.					
NAT.W.					
B & H	1	0	14	14	–

CAREER: BATTING

	I.	N.O.	R.	H.S.	AV.
TEST					
OTHER FIRST CLASS	16	6	220	34	22.00
INT					
J.P.L.	6	3	66	25	22.00
NAT.W.					
B & H	2	0	17	14	8.50

LAST SEASON: BOWLING

	O.	M.	R.	W.	AV.
TEST					
OTHER FIRST CLASS	41	16	106	4	26.50
INT					
J.P.L.	4	1	11	0	–
NAT.W.					
B & H	8	0	28	0	–

CAREER: BOWLING

	O.	M.	R.	W.	AV.
TEST					
OTHER FIRST CLASS	196.5	53	494	25	19.76
INT					
J.P.L.	84.2	4	384	9	42.66
NAT.W.					
B & H	32	3	113	4	28.25

STOP PRESS: K.D. James moved to Hampshire at the end of the 1984 season.

Q. 122. How can a batsman be "timed out"?

Q. 123. How many ways can a batsman officially be given out, and what are they?

METSON, C.P.

Full Name: Colin Peter Metson.
Role: Right-hand bat, wicket-keeper.
Born: 2 July 1963, Cuffley, Hertfordshire.
Height: 5' 7" **Weight:** 10st. 2lbs.
Nickname: Dempster, Meto, Jody.
County debut: 1981.
County cap: No.
Test debut: —
No. of Tests: 0.
No. of One-Day Internationals: 0.
1000 runs in a season: 0.
50 wickets in a season: 0.
1st-Class 50s scored: 2.
1st-Class 100s scored: 0.
1st-Class 200s scored: 0.
1st-Class 5 w. in innings: 0.
1st-Class 10 w. in match: 0.
One-day 50s: 0.
One-day 100s: 0.
Place in batting averages: 158 average: 25.00; (1983: — average: —).
Place in bowling averages: — average: —; (1983 — average: —).
Parents: Denis Alwyn Metson and Jean Mary.
Marital status: Single.
Family links with cricket: Father played good club cricket and for M.C.C.; brother plays club cricket.
Education: Stanborough School, Welwyn Garden City; Enfield Grammar School; in final year at Durham University.
Qualifications: 10 O-levels, 5 A-levels.

LAST SEASON: BATTING

	I.	N.O.	R.	H.S.	AV.
TEST					
OTHER FIRST CLASS	17	5	300	96	25.00
INT					
J.P.L.	3	2	22	15*	–
NAT.W.					
B & H					

CAREER: BATTING

	I.	N.O.	R.	H.S.	AV.
TEST					
OTHER FIRST CLASS	18	6	338	96	28.17
INT					
J.P.L.	3	2	22	15*	–
NAT.W.					
B & H					

LAST SEASON: WICKET KEEPING

	C.	ST.		
TEST				
OTHER FIRST CLASS	28	2		
INT				
J.P.L.	4	2		
NAT.W.				
B & H				

CAREER: WICKET KEEPING

	C.	ST.		
TEST				
OTHER FIRST CLASS	29	2		
INT				
J.P.L.	6	2		
NAT.W.				
B & H				

Jobs outside cricket: Student studying BA Hons Economic History. Trainee accounts clerk.

Off-season 1984–85: Socialising, drinking and relaxing — generally being lazy at Durham.

Cricketing superstitions: Always put right pad on before left; try and use the same equipment right through the season if possible, especially wicketkeeping gloves.

Equipment used: Slazenger.

Cricketers particularly learnt from: "Jack Robertson, Bob Taylor, my father."

Cricketers particularly admired: Bob Taylor, Rod Marsh, Greg Chappell, Mike Brearley.

Other sports: Football for Durham 1st XI, hockey occasionally, tennis, squash, golf. Follows American football, football, golf.

Significant injuries in 1984: Bad knock on finger in June which never really cleared.

Relaxations: Watching films; listening to music; 'The Duncow', Durham; sleeping.

Extras: Young Wicketkeeper of the Year 1981; three Young England Tests v India 1981. Captain Durham University 1984, losing finalists in UAU competition. Beat Cambridge University twice. Had to play for 1st XI during term time at Durham.

Best batting performance: 96 Middlesex v Gloucestershire, Lord's 1984.

MILLER, A.J.T.

Full Name: Andrew John Trevor Miller.

Role: Opening bat, left-hander.

Born: 30 May 1963, Chesham.

Height: 5' 11" **Weight:** 12st.

Nickname: Dusty.

County debut: 1983.

County cap: No.

Test debut: —

No. of Tests: 0.

No. of One-Day Internationals: 0.

1000 runs in a season: 1.

50 wickets in a season: 0.

1st-Class 50s scored: 7.

1st-Class 100s scored: 2.

1st-Class 200s scored: 0.

1st-Class 5 w. in innings: 0.

1st-Class 10 w. in match: 0.

One-day 50s: 0.

One-day 100s: 0.
Place in batting averages: 216 average: 18.07; (1983: 30 average: 43.57).
Place in bowling averages: — average: —; (1983: — average: —)
1st-Class catches 1984: 2 (career: 3).
Parents: John Innes and Sheila Mary Miller.
Marital status: Single.
Education: Belmont School; Haileybury; Oxford University.
Qualifications: 10 O-levels, 3 A-levels and success at Oxbridge exam.
Jobs outside cricket: Clerk for travel agents between school and university.
Off season 1984–85: Studying at Oxford (final year).
Cricketing superstitions: "Always put left pad on first and like to use same kit twice if I've got a few first innings."
Equipment used: Slazenger.
Cricketers particularly learnt from: Opening partners Richard Ellis (Oxford) and Graham Barlow (Middlesex).
Cricketers particularly admired: The majority of international players.
Other sports: Rugby and squash.
Significant injuries in 1984: Badly bruised finger in mid-July — out for a week.
Relaxations: "I love playing and watching rugby, playing squash, music, having a drink with team-mates and friends."
Extras: "First Oxonian since 1975 to score a century in the Varsity Match. First century by Combined Universities batsman in Benson and Hedges competition. Got maiden 1st-Class wicket in maiden over (4th ball) — unlikely to ever bowl again! (I'm that bad)." Captain of Oxford University 1985. Scored 231 v Combined Services 1984.
Opinions on cricket: "1) First team county players are expected to play too much cricket — perhaps 4-day championship matches would be the answer. 2) Surely a fairer championship would ensue if counties played each other once and once only."
Best batting performance: 128* Oxford University v Cambridge University, Lord's 1984.

LAST SEASON: BATTING

	I.	N.O.	R.	H.S.	AV.
TEST					
OTHER FIRST CLASS	15	1	253	128	18.07
INT					
J.P.L.					
NAT.W.	1	0	0	0	–
B & H	4	0	236	101	59.00

CAREER: BATTING

	I.	N.O.	R.	H.S.	AV.
TEST					
OTHER FIRST CLASS	43	4	1275	128*	32.69
INT					
J.P.L.					
NAT.W.	1	0	0	0	–
B & H	4	0	236	101	59.00

LAST SEASON: BOWLING

	O.	M.	R.	W.	AV.
TEST					
OTHER FIRST CLASS	1	0	4	1	–
INT					
J.P.L.					
NAT.W.					
B & H					

CAREER: BOWLING

	O.	M.	R.	W.	AV.
TEST					
OTHER FIRST CLASS	1	0	4	1	–
INT					
J.P.L.					
NAT.W.					
B & H					

RADLEY, C.T.

Full Name: Clive Thornton Radley.
Role: Right-hand bat, leg-break
bowler.
Born: 13 May 1944, Hertford.
Height: 5' 10" **Weight:** 12st.
Nickname: Radders.
County debut: 1964.
County cap: 1967.
Test debut: 1977–78.
No. of Tests: 8.
No. of One-Day Internationals: 4.
Benefit: £26,000 in 1977.
1000 runs in a season: 15.
50 wickets in a season: 0.
1st-Class 50s scored: 121.
1st-Class 100s scored: 41.
1st-Class 200s scored: 0.
1st-Class 5 w. in innings: 0.
1st-Class 10 w. in match: 0.

One-day 50s: 51.
One-day 100s: 7.
Place in batting averages: 82 average: 34.58; (1983: 108 average: 29.47).
Place in bowling averages: — average: —; (1983: — average: —).
1st-Class catches 1984: 21 (career: 485).
Parents: Laura Radley and late Arthur Radley.
Wife and date of marriage: Linda, 22 September 1973.
Children: Louise, 18 September 1978; Paul Craig Thornton, 26 July 1980.
Education: King Edward VI Grammar School, Norwich.
Jobs outside cricket: Has coached in South Africa and Australia.
Family links with cricket: Father played club cricket.
Overseas tours: Pakistan and New Zealand 1977–78; Australia 1978–79.
Equipment used: Stuart Surridge.
Other sports: Squash, golf.
Extras: Played for Norfolk under former Middlesex and England player W.J.
Edrich, who eased his way to Middlesex. Shared in the 6th wicket partnership
record for Middlesex, 227 with F. Titmus v South Africa at Lord's in 1965.
First fielder to hold 50 catches in J.P.L. Gold Award winner in 1983 Benson
and Hedges Final.
Best batting performance: 171 Middlesex v Cambridge University,
Cambridge 1976.

LAST SEASON: BATTING

	I.	N.O.	R.	H.S.	AV.
TEST					
OTHER FIRST CLASS	38	7	1072	128	34.58
INT					
J.P.L.	14	1	417	62	32.07
NAT.W.	5	2	184	67	61.33
B & H	3	1	73	65*	36.50

CAREER: BATTING

	I.	N.O.	R.	H.S.	AV.
TEST	10	0	481	158	48.10
OTHER FIRST CLASS	786	113	23420	171	34.80
INT	4	1	250	117*	83.33
J.P.L.	223	21	6063	133*	30.16
NAT.W.	50	6	1373	105*	31.20
B & H	57	11	1472	121*	32.00

LAST SEASON: BOWLING

	O.	M.	R.	W.	AV.
TEST					
OTHER FIRST CLASS					
INT					
J.P.L.					
NAT.W.					
B & H					

CAREER: BOWLING

	O.	M.	R.	W.	AV.
TEST					
OTHER FIRST CLASS	31	7	122	6	20.33
INT.					
J.P.L.	3.4	1	13	1	–
NAT.W.					
B & H					

ROSE, G.D.

Full Name: Graham David Rose.
Role: Right-hand bat, right arm fast medium bowler.
Born: 12 April 1964, Tottenham.
Height: 6' 3".
County debut: 1983.
County cap: No.
Test debut: —
No. of Tests: 0.
No. of One-Day Internationals: 0.
1000 runs in a season: 0.
50 wickets in a season: 0.
1st-Class 50s scored: 0.
1st-Class 100s scored: 0.
1st-Class 200s scored: 0.
1st-Class 5 w. in innings: 0.
1st-Class 10 w. in match: 0.
One-day 50s: 0.
One-day 100s: 0.

Place in batting averages: — **average:** —; (1983: — average: —).
Place in bowling averages: — average: —; (1983: — average: —).
Extras: Played for Young England v Young Australia 1983.

LAST SEASON: BATTING

	I.	N.O.	R.	H.S.	AV.
TEST					
OTHER FIRST CLASS					
INT					
J.P.L.					
NAT.W.					
B & H	1	0	3	3	3.00

CAREER: BATTING

	I.	N.O.	R.	H.S.	AV.
TEST					
OTHER FIRST CLASS					
INT					
J.P.L.	1	0	33	33	33.00
NAT.W.					
B & H	1	0	3	3	3.00

LAST SEASON: BOWLING

	O.	M.	R.	W.	AV.
TEST					
OTHER FIRST CLASS					
INT					
J.P.L.					
NAT.W.					
B & H	4	0	15	0	–

CAREER: BOWLING

	O.	M.	R.	W.	AV.
TEST					
OTHER FIRST CLASS					
INT					
J.P.L.	16	0	67	1	–
NAT.W.					
B & H	4	0	15	0	–

SLACK, W.N.

Full Name: Wilfred Norris Slack.
Role: Left-hand bat, right arm medium bowler.
Born: 12 December 1954, Troumaca, St. Vincent, West Indies.
Height: 6′ 0″ **Weight:** 13st 2lbs.
Nickname: Wilf, Slacky.
County debut: 1977.
County cap: 1981.
Test debut: —
No. of Tests: 0.
No. of One-Day Internationals: 0.
1000 runs in a season: 4.
50 wickets in a season: 0.
1st-Class 50s scored: 35.
1st-Class 100s scored: 10.
1st-Class 200s scored: 2.
1st-Class 5 w. in innings: 0.
1st-Class 10 w. in match: 0.
One-day 50s: 15.
One-day 100s: 0.

Place in batting averages: 38 average: 42.92; (1983: 33 average: 43.08).
Place in bowling averages: — average: —; (1983: — average: —).
1st-Class catches 1984: 23 (career: 95).
Parents: Grafton and Doreen Slack.
Marital status: Single.
Education: Wellesbourne Secondary, High Wycombe, Bucks.

Qualifications: City & Guilds: Radio and T.V. mechanics. Qualified N.C.A. Advanced Coach.
Jobs outside cricket: Digital electronics test engineer.
Equipment used and endorsed: Gunn & Moore.
Overseas tours: To Pakistan with Rohan Kanhai's World XI in September 1981.
Overseas teams played for: Played in Auckland, New Zealand, in 1979–80, World XI in Pakistan 1981.
Cricketers particularly learnt from: Don Bennett, Clive Radley.
Other sports: Plays basketball for Bucks and Wycombe Pirates; tennis, squash, badminton, football.
Relaxations: Building electronic projects. Relaxing in a sauna and swimming pool. "Lying in bed".
Extras: Played for Buckinghamshire in 1976. At 16 played for Wycombe Colts. Played for Freith in Haig Village Cricket Competition. Then joined High Wycombe; then Buckinghamshire in 1976; then Middlesex in 1977. Qualified to play both for West Indies and England.
Best batting performance: 248* Middlesex v Worcestershire, Lord's 1981.
Best bowling performance: 3-17 Middlesex v Leicestershire, Uxbridge 1982.

LAST SEASON: BATTING

	I.	N.O.	R.	H.S.	AV.
TEST					
OTHER FIRST CLASS	46	8	1631	145	42.92
INT					
J.P.L.	14	3	220	71	20.00
NAT.W.	5	0	196	79	39.20
B & H	4	0	48	14	12.00

CAREER: BATTING

	I.	N.O.	R.	H.S.	AV.
TEST					
OTHER FIRST CLASS	219	23	7213	248*	36.80
INT					
J.P.L.	54	7	1183	77	25.17
NAT.W.	15	1	505	79	36.07
B & H	15	1	288	60*	20.57

LAST SEASON: BOWLING

	O.	M.	R.	W.	AV.
TEST					
OTHER FIRST CLASS	28	3	76	0	–
INT					
J.P.L.	53	1	258	8	32.25
NAT.W.	27	2	90	3	30.00
B & H	5	0	18	0	–

CAREER: BOWLING

	O.	M.	R.	W.	AV.
TEST					
OTHER FIRST CLASS	165.5	29	462	18	25.67
INT					
J.P.L.	136.4	1	664	29	22.89
NAT.W.	79	6	276	8	34.50
B & H	5	0	18	0	–

TOMLINS, K.P.

Full Name: Keith Patrick Tomlins.
Role: Right-hand bat.
Born: 23 October 1957, Kingston-upon-Thames.
Height: 5' 9½" **Weight:** 11st 10lbs.
Nickname: Tommo.
County debut: 1977.
County cap: 1983.
Test debut: —
No. of Tests: 0.
No. of One-Day Internationals: 0.
1000 runs in a season: 0.
50 wickets in a season: 0.
1st-Class 50s scored: 12.
1st-Class 100s scored: 4.
1st-Class 200s scored: 0.
1st-Class 5 w. in innings: 0.
1st-Class 10 w. in match: 0.
One-day 50s: 3.
One-day 100s: 0.
Place in batting averages: 191 average: 21.35; (1983: 96 average: 30.45).
Place in bowling averages: — average: —; (1983: — average: —).
1st-Class catches 1984: 8 (career: 57).
Parents: Royston John and Joan Muriel Tomlins.
Marital status: Single.
Education: St Mary Magdalen's Primary School, Mortlake. St Benedict's School, Ealing; College of St Hilda and St Bede, Durham University.
Qualifications: 3 A-levels, 5 O-levels.
Family links with cricket: Father and eldest brother play for Wycombe House C.C. in Osterley, Middlesex.
Jobs outside cricket: Stage-hand at Richmond Theatre. Sports and music management with Williams Maloney Associates, ship hand with B.P. on survey ship.
Off season 1984-85: Working at Richmond Theatre.
Overseas tours: South America with Derrick Robins XI in 1979. West Indies with British Colleges 1978; Ealing C.C. 1980; Zimbabwe with Middlesex C.C.C. 1980.
Overseas teams played for: Played for Greenpoint C.C., Cape Town, 1979–80. Merewether D.C.C., Newcastle, New South Wales, 1980–81.
Equipment used: Gray-Nicolls.
Other sports: Playing member of Richmond Rugby Club, golf.
Relaxations: Reading, music.
Best batting performance: 146 Middlesex v Oxford University, Oxford 1982.

LAST SEASON: BATTING

	I.	N.O.	R.	H.S.	AV.
TEST					
OTHER FIRST CLASS	18	1	363	103*	21.35
INT					
J.P.L.	12	4	163	59	20.37
NAT.W.					
B & H	4	0	87	40	21.75

CAREER: BATTING

	I.	N.O.	R.	H.S.	AV.
TEST					
OTHER FIRST CLASS	108	13	2529	146	26.62
INT					
J.P.L.	42	8	557	59	16.38
NAT.W.	5	0	193	80	38.60
B & H	6	0	103	40	17.17

LAST SEASON: BOWLING

	O.	M.	R.	W.	AV.
TEST					
OTHER FIRST CLASS	5	1	9	0	–
INT					
J.P.L.	1	0	2	0	–
NAT.W.					
B & H					

CAREER: BOWLING

	O.	M.	R.	W.	AV.
TEST					
OTHER FIRST CLASS	94.3	21	317	4	79.25
INT					
J.P.L.	62	2	307	11	27.91
NAT.W.					
B & H					

WILLIAMS, N.F.

Full Name: Neil Fitzgerald Williams.
Role: Right-hand bat; right arm fast bowler.
Born: 2 July 1962, Hopewell, St. Vincent, West Indies.
Height: 5″ 11′ **Weight:** 11st. 7lbs.
Nickname: Nelly, Joe.
County debut: 1982.
County cap: 1984.
Test debut: —
No. of Tests: 0.
No. of One-Day Internationals: 0.
1000 runs in a season: 0.
50 wickets in a season: 1.
1st-Class 50s scored: 2.
1st-Class 100s scored: 0.
1st-Class 200s scored: 0.
1st-Class 5 w. in innings: 1.
1st-Class 10 w. in match: 0.
One-day 50s: 0.
One-day 100s: 0.
Place in batting averages: 232 average: 15.83; (1983: 160 average: 22.61).
Place in bowling averages: 91 average: 33.74; (1983: 45 average: 26.33).
1st-Class catches 1984: 6 (career: 16).
Parents: Alexander and Aldreta Williams.
Marital status: Single.

Education: Cane End Primary School, St. Vincent. Acland Burghley School.
Qualifications: School Leavers Certificate, 6 O-levels, 1 A-level.
Family links with cricket: "Uncle Joe was 12th man for St. Vincent."
Off-season 1984–85: Playing Shell Shield in West Indies.
Equipment used: Morrant.
Overseas teams played for: Windward Islands 1983; Tasmania 1983–84.
Cricketers particularly admired: Viv Richards, Andy Roberts, Michael Holding, Dennis Lillee.
Other sports: Follow most.
Extras: Was on stand-by for England in New Zealand and Pakistan 1983–84.
Best batting performance: 63 Middlesex v Worcestershire, Worcester 1983.
Best bowling performance: 5-77 Middlesex v Yorkshire, Leeds 1983.

LAST SEASON: BATTING

	I.	N.O.	R.	H.S.	AV.
TEST					
OTHER FIRST CLASS	21	3	285	44	15.83
INT					
J.P.L.	5	2	25	17*	8.33
NAT.W.	2	1	13	10	–
B & H	3	1	43	23	21.50

CAREER: BATTING

	I.	N.O.	R.	H.S.	AV.
TEST					
OTHER FIRST CLASS	64	16	938	63	19.54
INT					
J.P.L.	12	6	99	31*	16.50
NAT.W.	4	1	16	10	5.33
B & H	5	2	68	23	22.67

LAST SEASON: BOWLING

	O.	M.	R.	W.	AV.
TEST					
OTHER FIRST CLASS	474.1	95	1653	49	33.74
INT					
J.P.L.	73	2	303	12	25.25
NAT.W.	27	6	89	2	44.50
B & H	23	1	109	1	–

CAREER: BOWLING

	O.	M.	R.	W.	AV.
TEST					
OTHER FIRST CLASS	1357.2	264	4498	152	29.52
INT					
J.P.L.	162.3	6	710	28	25.35
NAT.W.	59	10	220	10	22.00
B & H	85.3	10	341	13	26.23

COUNTY QUIZ

Q. 1. When was the club founded?
Q. 2. Who made the most first-class runs for the county last season, and how many?
Q. 3. What's the highest ever county total, and against whom?
Q. 4. Who took most wickets for the county last season, and how many?
Q. 5. What's the highest individual score for the county, who hit it, and when?
Q. 6. What's the highest scoring partnership for the county for any wicket?
Q. 7. How many times has the club won the County Championship?
Q. 8. What's the lowest ever total made by the county in one innings, when, and against whom?
Q. 9. Which bowler took the most first-class wickets in one season, when, and how many?
Q. 10. Which batsman hit the most runs in one season, when and how many?

Northamptonshire

BAILEY, R.J.

Full Name: Robert John Bailey.
Role: Right-hand bat; off-spin bowler.
Born: 28 October 1963 Biddulph,
Stoke-on-Trent.
Height: 6′ 3″ **Weight:** 14st.
Nickname: Bailers or Blaster.
County debut: 1982.
County cap: No.
Test debut: —
No. of Tests: 0.
No. of One-Day Internationals: 0.
1000 runs in a season: 1.
50 wickets in a season: 0.
1st-Class 50s scored: 8.
1st-Class 100s scored: 3.
1st-Class 200s scored: 0.
1st-Class 5 w. in innings: 0.
1st-Class 10 w. in match: 0.
One-day 50s: 5.

One-day 100s: 0.
Place in batting averages: 62 average: 37.97; (1983: — average: —).
Place in bowling averages: — average: —; (1983: — average: —).
1st-Class catches 1984: 14 (career: 20).
Parents: John and Marie Bailey.
Marital status: Single.
Education: Biddulph High School.
Qualifications: 6 C.S.E.s; 1 O-level.
Jobs outside cricket: "Worked for 3 winters in electrical trade."
Off-season 1984–85: Coaching in South Africa.
Family links with cricket: Father played in North Staffordshire League for 30 years, for Knypersley and Minor Counties cricket for Staffordshire as wicket-keeper.
Overseas teams played for: Rhodes University (Grahamstown, S.A.) 1982–83. Witenhage C.C. (S.A.) 1983–84.
Cricketers particularly learnt from: My father; Stan Crump.

Equipment used: Slazenger.
Other sports: Badminton, football, golf.
Relaxations: Listening to music.
Extras: Played for Young England v Young Australia, 1983. Scored 2 hundreds in match v Middlesex II 1984.
Best batting performance: 114 Northamptonshire v Somerset, Northampton 1984.

LAST SEASON: BATTING

	I.	N.O.	R.	H.S.	AV.
TEST					
OTHER FIRST CLASS	45	8	1405	114	37.97
INT					
J.P.L.	16	4	375	77*	31.25
NAT.W.	3	2	82	56*	–
B & H	4	0	235	77	58.75

CAREER: BATTING

	I.	N.O.	R.	H.S.	AV.
TEST					
OTHER FIRST CLASS	53	9	1515	114	34.43
INT					
J.P.L.	30	4	471	77*	29.43
NAT.W.	4	2	103	56*	51.50
B & H	4	0	235	77	58.75

LAST SEASON: BOWLING

	O.	M.	R.	W.	AV.
TEST					
OTHER FIRST CLASS	21	6	45	1	
INT					
J.P.L.					
NAT.W.	1	0	14	0	–
B & H					

CAREER: BOWLING

	O.	M.	R.	W.	AV.
TEST					
OTHER FIRST CLASS	36	11	80	4	20.00
INT					
J.P.L.	5	0	49	0	–
NAT.W.	1	0	14	0	–
B & H					

BAMBER, M.J.

Full name: Martin John Bamber.
Role: Opening bat.
Born: 7 January 1961.
Height: 5′ 7″ **Weight:** 12st.
Nickname: Erco.
County debut: 1982.
County cap: No.
Test debut: —
No. of Tests: 0.
No. of One-Day Internationals: 0.
1000 runs in a season: 0.
50 wickets in a season: 0.
1st-Class 50s scored: 3.
1st-Class 100s scored: 0.
1st-Class 200s scored: 0.
1st-Class 5 w. in innings: 0.
1st-Class 10 w. in match: 0.
One-day 50s: 1.

One-day 100s: 0.
Place in batting averages: 165 average: 24.44; (1983: 46 average: 27.69).
Place in bowling averages: — average: —; (1983: — average: —).
1st-Class catches 1984: 1 (career: 6).
Parents: John and Mavis Bamber.
Marital status: Single.
Education: Carshalton High School; Millfield School.
Qualifications: 6 0 levels.
Jobs outside cricket: Salesman; coach.
Family links with cricket: "Father and mother's father both played."
Cricketers particularly learnt from: Geoff Boycott, Dennis Lillee.
Equipment used: Stuart Surridge.
Other sports: Football, golf, squash, tennis.
Relaxations: Tropical fish; gardening; dogs; yoga.
Opinions on cricket: "Better to play 4-day games once a week rather than two 3-day games."
Best batting performance: 77 Northamptonshire v Cambridge University, Cambridge 1983.

LAST SEASON: BATTING

	I.	N.O.	R.	H.S.	AV.
TEST					
OTHER FIRST CLASS	10	1	220	51	24.44
INT					
J.P.L.	2	0	35	26	17.50
NAT.W.					
B & H	3	0	86	40	28.67

CAREER: BATTING

	I.	N.O.	R.	H.S.	AV.
TEST					
OTHER FIRST CLASS	26	2	638	77	26.58
INT					
J.P.L.	4	0	119	71	29.75
NAT.W.					
B & H	3	0	86	40	28.67

LAST SEASON: BOWLING

	O.	M.	R.	W.	AV.
TEST					
OTHER FIRST CLASS	2.3	1	3	0	—
INT					
J.P.L.					
NAT.W.					
B & H					

CAREER: BOWLING

	O.	M.	R.	W.	AV.
TEST					
OTHER FIRST CLASS	2.3	1	3	0	—
INT					
J.P.L.					
NAT.W.					
B & H					

Q. 124. Who has taken the most first-class hat-tricks?

Q. 125. Who was the first player to achieve first-class 1000 runs and 100 wickets in one season, and when?

BOYD-MOSS, R.J.

Full Name: Robin James Boyd-Moss.
Role: Right-hand bat; slow left-arm bowler.
Born: 16 December 1959, Hatton, Sri Lanka.
Height: 5' 10½" **Weight:** 12st 9lbs.
Nickname: Mossy, Mouse.
County debut: 1980.
County cap: No.
Test debut: —
No. of Tests: 0.
No. of One-Day Internationals: 0.
1000 runs in a season: 2.
50 wickets in a season: 0.
1st-Class 50s scored: 30.
1st-Class 100s scored: 9.
1st-Class 200s scored: 0.
1st-Class 5 w. in innings: 1.
1st-Class 10 w. in match: 0.
One-day 50s: 3.
One-day 100s: 0.
Place in batting averages: 121 average: 30.17; (1983: 74 average: 35.05).
Place in bowling averages: — average: —; (1983: — average: —).
1st-Class catches 1984: 11 (career: 45).
Parents: Michael and Shelagh Boyd-Moss.
Marital status: Single.
Education: Bedford School; Cambridge University.
Qualifications: Three A-levels. B.A. in Land Economy.

LAST SEASON: BATTING

	I.	N.O.	R.	H.S.	AV.
TEST					
OTHER FIRST CLASS	32	2	905	105	30.17
INT					
J.P.L.	11	1	383	99	38.30
NAT.W.	2	0	15	15	7.50
B & H	1	0	17	17	–

CAREER: BATTING

	I.	N.O.	R.	H.S.	AV.
TEST					
OTHER FIRST CLASS	171	13	4892	139	30.96
INT					
J.P.L.	32	4	668	99	23.85
NAT.W.	2	0	15	15	7.50
B & H	15	0	215	58	14.33

LAST SEASON: BOWLING

	O.	M.	R.	W.	AV.
TEST					
OTHER FIRST CLASS	55	12	268	1	–
INT					
J.P.L.					
NAT.W.					
B & H					

CAREER: BOWLING

	O.	M.	R.	W.	AV.
TEST					
OTHER FIRST CLASS	412	94	1498	33	45.39
INT					
J.P.L.					
NAT.W.					
B & H	12	1	49	0	–

Equipment used: Slazenger.
Other sports: Rugby football. Played centre for Cambridge v. Oxford in 100th Varsity Match. Double Blue.
Relaxations: Wildlife, photography.
Best batting performance: 139 Cambridge University v Oxford University, Lord's 1983.
Best bowling performance: 5-27 Cambridge University v Oxford University, Lord's 1983.

CAPEL, D.J.

Full Name: David John Capel.
Role: Right-hand bat, right arm medium bowler, gulley fielder.
Born: 6 February 1963, Northampton.
Height: 6′ **Weight:** 12st. 4lbs.
Nickname: Capes.
County debut: 1981.
County cap: No.
Test debut: —
No. of Tests: 0.
No. of One-Day internationals: 0.
1000 runs in a season: 0.
50 wickets in a season: 0.
1st-Class 50s scored: 10.
1st-Class 100s scored: 1.
1st-Class 200s scored: 0.
1st-Class 5 w. in innings: 0.
1st-Class 10 w. in match: 0.
One-day 50s: 2.
One-day 100s: 0.
Place in batting averages: 84 average: 34.30; (1983: 110 average: 28.00).
Place in bowling averages: 125 average: 42.44; (1983: — average: —).
1st-Class catches 1984: 8 (career: 28).
Parents: John and Angela Janet Capel.
Marital status: Single (engaged to Debbie).
Education: Roade Primary and Roade Comprehensive School.
Family links with cricket: Father and brother played in county league.
Qualifications: Three O-levels, five C.S.E.s. Took NCA Coaching Certificate September 1984.
Jobs outside cricket: Surgical shoemaker, including hand-made cricket boots.
Overseas teams played for: Played and coached in South Africa 1981–82. Latrobe, Tasmania, 1982–83, on Whitbread Scholarship. Westview C.C. Port Elizabeth 1983–84.
Overseas tours: Dubai with "The Cricketer", March 1983.
Equipment used: Stuart Surridge.

Cricketers particularly learnt from: Peter Willey, Geoff Cook, Wayne Larkins. "Admire Barry Richards, Imran Khan, Richard Hadlee."

Other sports: "Occasionally golf and enjoy playing crown green bowls when I get the chance. I like watching most sports on TV except horse racing and wrestling."

Significant injuries in 1984: Ligaments and tendons in left ankle hampered bowling for most of season (missed 6 weeks).

Relaxations: Enjoys sea swimming, body surfing, most types of music, loves Indian food and barbecues.

Extras: Played for Young England v. Young West Indies, August 1982, scoring 117 in 2nd "Test".

Opinions on cricket: "I would prefer it if the rules were to be changed so that a maximum of one overseas player only can be played in championship matches, but a county can sign as many overseas players as they wish. I would also like to see S. Africa accepted back into Test cricket; too much politics in sport and everything seems hypocritical. As a cricketing nation we seem to bow down far too easily to other countries' demands."

Best batting performance: 109* Northamptonshire v Somerset, Northampton 1983.

Best bowling performance: 5-28 Northamptonshire v Surrey, The Oval 1984.

LAST SEASON: BATTING

	I.	N.O.	R.	H.S.	AV.
TEST					
OTHER FIRST CLASS	28	5	789	81	34.30
INT					
J.P.L.	10	5	182	53*	36.40
NAT.W.	2	2	32	23*	–
B & H	2	1	22	17*	–

CAREER: BATTING

	I.	N.O.	R.	H.S.	AV.
TEST					
OTHER FIRST CLASS	76	15	1820	109*	29.84
INT					
J.P.L.	31	11	430	79	21.50
NAT.W.	4	2	74	27	37.00
B & H	5	1	81	28	20.25

LAST SEASON: BOWLING

	O.	M.	R.	W.	AV.
TEST					
OTHER FIRST CLASS	155	20	679	16	42.44
INT					
J.P.L.	48	1	301	12	25.08
NAT.W.					
B & H	19	1	89	3	29.67

CAREER: BOWLING

	O.	M.	R.	W.	AV.
TEST					
OTHER FIRST CLASS	322.4	44	1343	25	53.72
INT					
J.P.L.	90	2	547	23	23.78
NAT.W.					
B & H	32	4	119	6	19.83

Q. 126. Who is the youngest player ever to achieve a first-class double of 1000 runs and 100 wickets?

COOK, G.

Full Name: Geoffrey Cook.
Role: Right-hand bat, slow left arm orthodox bowler.
Born: 9 October 1951, Middlesbrough, Yorkshire.
Height: 6' 0" **Weight:** 12st 10lbs.
Nickname: Geoff.
County debut: 1971.
County cap: 1975.
Benefit: 1985.
Test debut: 1981–82.
No. of Tests: 7.
No. of One-Day Internationals: 6.
1000 runs in a season: 9.
50 wickets in a season: 0.
1st-Class 50s scored: 86.
1st-Class 100s scored: 26.
1st-Class 200s scored: 0.
1st-Class 5 w. in innings: 0.
1st-Class 10 w. in match: 0.

One-day 50s: 32.
One-day 100s: 2.
Place in batting averages: 53 average: 39.46; (1983: 54 average: 39.74).
Place in bowling averages: — average: —; (1983: — average: —).
1st-Class catches 1984: 15 (career: 348).
Parents: Harry and Helen Cook.
Wife and date of marriage: Judith, 22 November 1975.
Children: Anna, 21 May 1980.
Education: Middlesbrough High School.
Qualifications: Six O-levels, one A-level.
Jobs outside cricket: Has taught at Spratton Hall Prep School.
Off-season 1984–85: "Playing golf".
Family links with cricket: Father and brother, David, very keen club cricketers. "Father was virtually 'Mr Cricket' in Middlesbrough cricket in the 1960s. (President, Secretary, Chairman, of various leagues)."
Equipment used: Duncan Fearnley.
Overseas teams played for: Eastern Province, 1978–81.
Overseas tours: With England to India 1981–82, Australia 1982–83.
Cricketers particularly learnt from: Wayne Larkins.
Cricketers particularly admired: Clive Rice.
Significant injuries in 1984: Broken right foot (when hit by a drive from partner, Allan Lamb); broken jaw (hit by ball from D.J. Thomas of Surrey).
Other sports: "All sports when given opportunity." Football with Wellingborough in the Southern League.

Relaxations: Walking, reading, crosswords.

Extras: "Great believer in organised recreation for young people. Would enjoy time and scope to carry my beliefs through." Was one of very few opening batsmen not to wear a helmet. Does excellent impersonations of bowlers. Captain since 1981. Chairman of the Cricketers Association.

Best batting performance: 172 E. Province v N. Transvaal, Port Elizabeth 1979–80.

LAST SEASON: BATTING

	I.	N.O.	R.	H.S.	AV.
TEST					
OTHER FIRST CLASS	43	4	1539	102	39.46
INT					
J.P.L.	12	0	253	64	21.08
NAT.W.	3	0	43	23	14.33
B & H					

CAREER: BATTING

	I.	N.O.	R.	H.S.	AV.
TEST	13	0	203	66	15.61
OTHER FIRST CLASS	593	43	17415	172	31.66
INT	6	0	106	32	17.67
J.P.L.	172	13	3802	85	23.91
NAT.W.	29	1	988	114*	35.29
B & H	44	3	1148	96	28.00

LAST SEASON: BOWLING

	O.	M.	R.	W.	AV.
TEST					
OTHER FIRST CLASS	15.1	1	99	0	–
INT					
J.P.L.					
NAT.W.					
B & H					

CAREER: BOWLING

	O.	M.	R.	W.	AV.
TEST	7	3	27	0	–
OTHER FIRST CLASS	75.1	13	642	14	45.86
INT					
J.P.L.	1	0	6	0	–
NAT.W.					
B & H					

GRIFFITHS, B.J.

Full Name: Brian James Griffiths.

Role: Right-hand bat, right arm medium bowler.

Born: 13 June 1949, Wellingborough.

Height: 6' 1" **Weight:** 14st 6lbs.

Nickname: Jim.

County debut: 1974.

County cap: 1978.

Test debut: —

No. of Tests: 0.

No. of One-Day Internationals: 0.

1000 runs in a season: 0.

50 wickets in a season: 5.

1st-Class 50s scored: 0.

1st-Class 100s scored: 0.

1st-Class 200s scored: 0.

1st-Class 5 w. in innings: 12.

1st-Class 10 w. in match: 0.

One-day 50s: 0.
One-day 100s: 0.
Place in batting averages: average: —; (1983: — average: —).
Place in bowling averages: 73 average: 30.98; (1983: 58 average: 28.48).
1st-Class catches 1984: 5 (career: 32).
Parents: James and Muriel Griffiths.
Wife and date of marriage: Paula, 30 September 1972.
Children: Rachel, 26 June 1973, Leighton, 6 November 1975.
Education: Irthlingborough Secondary School.
Jobs outside cricket: Has worked for a haulage firm, and as a bank porter.
Family links with cricket: Uncle played occasionally for Northamptonshire.
Equipment used: Stuart Surridge.
Other sports: Football, darts.
Relaxations: Reading, quizzes and crosswords.
Best batting performance: 16 Northamptonshire v Gloucestershire, Bristol 1982.
Best bowling performance: 8-50 Northamptonshire v Glamorgan, Northampton 1981.

LAST SEASON: BATTING

	I.	N.O.	R.	H.S.	AV.
TEST					
OTHER FIRST CLASS	21	9	48	12	4.00
INT					
J.P.L.	1	0	0	0	–
NAT.W.					
B & H					

CAREER: BATTING

	I.	N.O.	R.	H.S.	AV.
TEST					
OTHER FIRST CLASS	123	44	255	16	3.23
INT					
J.P.L.	26	14	60	11*	5.00
NAT.W.	4	2	2	1*	1.00
B & H	9	3	15	6	2.50

LAST SEASON: BOWLING

	O.	M.	R.	W.	AV.
TEST					
OTHER FIRST CLASS	474	114	1332	43	30.98
INT					
J.P.L.	64.4	3	277	5	55.40
NAT.W.	5	1	19	0	–
B & H	44	2	215	2	107.5

CAREER: BOWLING

	O.	M.	R.	W.	AV.
TEST					
OTHER FIRST CLASS	3970.4	945	11240	391	28.75
INT					
J.P.L.	760.4	61	3089	114	27.09
NAT.W.	162	18	638	22	29.00
B & H	283.2	37	1009	39	25.86

Q. 127. What wicket-keeper made the most dismissals in one innings, when and where?

HANLEY, R.W.

Full Name: Rupert William Hanley.
Role: Right-hand bat, right arm fast
medium bowler.
Born: 29 January 1952, Port
Elizabeth, South Africa.
Nickname: Spook.
County debut: 1984.
County cap: No.
Test debut: —
No. of Tests: 0.
No. of One-Day Internationals: 0.
1000 runs in a season: 0.
50 wickets in a season: 0.
1st-Class 50s scored: 0.
1st-Class 100s scored: 0.
1st-Class 200s scored: 0.
1st-Class 5 w. in innings: 20.
1st-Class 10 w. in match: 3.
One-day 50s: 0.
One-day 100s: 0.
Place in batting averages: — average: —; (1983: — (average: —).
Place in bowling averages: 80 average: 31.95; (1983: — average: —).
1st-Class catches 1984: 3 (career: 39).
Family links with cricket: Father, A.W.D. Hanley, played for Border in South
Africa.
Overseas teams played for: Eastern Province 1970–71; Orange Free State
1975–76; Transvaal 1976–date. D.H. Robins XI v Pakistan 1974.
Significant injuries in 1984: Knee injury.

LAST SEASON: BATTING

	I.	N.O.	R.	H.S.	AV.
TEST					
OTHER FIRST CLASS	21	7	131	33*	9.36
INT					
J.P.L.	2	1	9	6*	—
NAT.W.	1	1	3	3*	—
B & H	1	1	1	1*	—

CAREER: BATTING

	I.	N.O.	R.	H.S.	AV.
TEST					
OTHER FIRST CLASS	96	43	314	33*	5.92
INT					
J.P.L.	2	1	9	6*	—
NAT.W.	1	1	3	3*	—
B & H	1	1	1	1*	—

LAST SEASON: BOWLING

	O.	M.	R.	W.	AV.
TEST					
OTHER FIRST CLASS	401.1	87	1182	37	31.95
INT					
J.P.L.	53.4	3	257	12	21.42
NAT.W.	11	0	46	2	23.00
B & H	42	10	158	6	26.33

CAREER: BOWLING

	O.	M.	R.	W.	AV.
TEST					
OTHER FIRST CLASS	2910.1	682	8326	398	20.92
INT					
J.P.L.	53.4	3	257	12	21.42
NAT.W.	11	0	46	2	23.00
B & H	42	10	158	6	26.33

Extras: Member of the Transvaal side which won SAB Currie Cup 1982–83.
Best batting performance: 33* Northamptonshire v Warwickshire, Northampton 1984.
Best bowling performance: 7-31 Transvaal v E. Province, Johannesburg 1983–84.

LAMB, A.J.

Full Name: Allan Joseph Lamb.
Role: Right-hand bat.
Born: 20 June 1954, Langebaanweg, Cape Province, South Africa.
Height: 5′ 8″ **Weight:** 12st 12lbs.
Nickname: Lambie, Legger.
County debut: 1978.
County cap: 1978.
Test debut: 1982.
No. of Tests: 27.
No. of One-Day Internationals: 32.
1000 runs in a season: 6.
50 wickets in a season: 0.
1st-Class 50s scored: 82.
1st-Class 100s scored: 39.
1st-Class 200s scored: 0.
1st-Class 5 w. in innings: 0.
1st-Class 10 w. in match: 0.
One-day 50s: 33.
One-day 100s: 7.

Place in batting averages: 49 average: 40.30; (1983: 8 average: 56.00).
Place in bowling averages: — average: —; (1983: — average: —).
1st-Class catches 1984: 14 (career: 157).
Parents: Michael and Joan Lamb.
Wife and date of marriage: Lindsay St Leger, 8 December 1979.
Education: Wynberg Boys' High School, Abbotts College.
Qualifications: Matriculation.
Jobs outside cricket: Timber representative. Promotions and selling.
Family links with cricket: Father played in the Boland League; brother played for Western Province 'B'. Brother-in-law, Tony Bucknall, won 10 caps for England at rugger.
Overseas tours: With England to Australia and New Zealand 1982–83; New Zealand and Pakistan 1983–84.
Overseas teams played for: Western Province in Currie Cup Competition, 1972–81.
Off-season 1984–85: Playing for England in India and Australia.

Cricketing superstitions: "I try to use the same batting shirt which I have scored runs in".

Cricketers particularly learnt from: "Everyone."

Equipment used: Slazenger.

Other sports: Squash, golf. Follows most sports.

Relaxations: Shooting, fishing.

Extras: Made first-class debut for Western Province in 1972–73 Currie Cup. Applied to be registered as English in 1980 but application deferred. Was top batting averages 1980. Was primarily a bowler when first played schoolboy cricket in South Africa. Missed two years of first-class cricket because of military training. Qualified to play for England 1982. "My aim is always to score a century." Topped Northamptonshire first-class batting averages, 1981 and 1982.

Opinions on cricket: "County cricket should be played over four days. Then each county would play each other once, a far better reflection on who wins the county championship. By doing this clubs would not have to doctor their pitches in getting results. I am sure this would develop our younger players. 117 overs a day is a joke, and we do not need a captain as the game turns out to be a limited overs match. We should base the county game as the way Test cricket is played. I am definitely in favour of 4-day cricket."

Best batting performance: 178 Northamptonshire v Leicestershire, Leicester 1979.

LAST SEASON: BATTING

	I.	N.O.	R.	H.S.	AV.
TEST	11	1	493	110	49.30
OTHER FIRST CLASS	23	3	716	133*	35.80
INT	3	0	86	75	28.67
J.P.L.	9	2	446	99	63.71
NAT.W.	3	0	117	65	39.00
B & H	4	1	258	92	86.00

CAREER: BATTING

	I.	N.O.	R.	H.S.	AV.
TEST	49	4	1714	137*	38.09
OTHER FIRST CLASS	325	60	13344	178	50.36
INT	31	5	1235	118	47.50
J.P.L.	82	12	2496	127*	35.65
NAT.W.	18	1	601	101	35.35
B & H	27	4	1088	106*	47.30

LAST SEASON: BOWLING

	O.	M.	R.	W.	AV.
TEST	1	0	6	0	–
OTHER FIRST CLASS					
INT					
J.P.L.					
NAT.W.					
B & H					

CAREER: BOWLING

	O.	M.	R.	W.	AV.
TEST	2	1	6	0	–
OTHER FIRST CLASS	25.2	5	92	4	23.00
INT					
J.P.L.					
NAT.W.					
B & H					

LARKINS, W.

Full Name: Wayne Larkins.
Role: Right-hand bat, right arm
medium bowler.
Born: 22 November 1953.
Height: 5′ 11″ **Weight:** 12st.
Nickname: Ned.
County debut: 1972.
County cap: 1976.
Test debut: 1979–80.
No. of Tests: 6.
No. of One-Day Internationals: 6.
1000 runs in a season: 7.
50 wickets in a season: 0.
1st-Class 50s scored: 58.
1st-Class 100s scored: 32.
1st-Class 200s scored: 2.
1st-Class 5 w. in innings: 1.
1st-Class 10 w. in match: 0.
One-day 50s: 32.
One-day 100s: 8.
Place in batting averages: 70 average: 36.00; (1983: 40 average: 42.24).
Place in bowling averages: — average: —; (1983 — average: —)
1st-Class catches 1984: 11 (career: 127).
Parents: Mavis Larkins (father deceased).
Wife and date of marriage: Jane Elaine, 22 March 1975.
Children: Philippa Jane, 30 May 1981.
Education: Bushmead, Eaton Socon, Huntingdon.

LAST SEASON: BATTING

	I.	N.O.	R.	H.S.	AV.
TEST					
OTHER FIRST CLASS	49	3	1656	183*	36.00
INT					
J.P.L.	16	0	475	79	29.69
NAT.W.	3	0	135	77	45.00
B & H	4	0	189	83	47.25

CAREER: BATTING

	I.	N.O.	R.	H.S.	AV.
TEST	11	0	176	34	16.00
OTHER FIRST CLASS	439	27	14478	252	35.14
INT	6	0	84	34	14.00
J.P.L.	153	10	3680	172*	25.73
NAT.W.	24	2	770	92*	35.00
B & H	43	3	1356	132	33.90

LAST SEASON: BOWLING

	O.	M.	R.	W.	AV.
TEST					
OTHER FIRST CLASS	68	19	175	6	29.17
INT					
J.P.L.	17	0	94	2	47.00
NAT.W.	7.5	0	32	0	–
B & H	13	1	71	1	–

CAREER: BOWLING

	O.	M.	R.	W.	AV.
TEST					
OTHER FIRST CLASS	404.5	79	1360	38	35.79
INT	2	0	21	0	–
J.P.L.	245.5	7	1221	47	25.97
NAT.W.	49.5	5	170	1	–
B & H	105.3	14	413	16	25.81

Family links with cricket: Father was umpire. Brother, Melvin, "played for Bedford Town for many years."
Equipment used: Stuart Surridge.
Overseas tours: England tour to Australia and India 1979–80.
Cricketers particularly learnt from: Mushtaq Mohammad.
Other sports: Golf, football (has played semi-pro), squash.
Relaxations: Gardening.
Extras: Northants considered releasing him in 1974. With Peter Willey, received 2016 pints of beer (7 barrels) from a Northampton brewery as a reward for their efforts in Australia in 1979–80. Hat-trick for Northants. v Cambridge and Oxford, Benson & Hedges, 1980. Banned from English Test Cricket for 3 years for joing rebel tour of S. Africa in 1982.
Best batting averages: 252 Northamptonshire v Glamorgan, Cardiff 1983.
Best bowling performance: 5-59 Northamptonshire v Worcestershire, Worcester 1984.

MALLENDER, N.A.

Full Name: Neil Alan Mallender.
Role: Right-hand bat; right arm fast medium bowler.
Born: 13 August 1961, Kirk Sandall, Nr. Doncaster.
Height: 6' 0" **Weight:** 12st. 12lbs.
Nickname: Ghostie.
County debut: 1980.
County cap: 1984.
Test debut: —
No. of Tests: 0.
No. of One-Day Internationals: 0.
1000 runs in a season: 0.
50 wickets in a season: 2.
1st-Class 50s scored: 1.
1st-Class 100s scored: 0.
1st-Class 200s scored: 0.
1st-Class 5 w. in innings: 5.
1st-Class 10 w. in match: 1.
One-day 50s: 0.
One-day 100s: 0.

Place in batting averages: 268 average: 10.44; (1983: 196 average: 17.78).
Place in bowling averages: 83 average: 32.62; (1983: 62 average: 29.32).
1st-Class catches 1984: 7 (career: 37).
Parents: Ron and Jean Mallender.
Wife and date of marriage: Caroline, 1 October 1983.
Education: Beverley Grammar School, East Yorkshire.

Qualifications: Seven O-levels.
Family links with cricket: Brother, Graham, used to play good representative cricket before joining the R.A.F.
Equipment used: Hunts County bats.
Cricket superstitions: Left boot on first.
Overseas tours: Young England tour to West Indies January/February 1980.
Overseas teams played for: Belmont D.C.C., New South Wales, 1980–81. Bathurst, N.S.W., 1982–83. Otago and Kaikorai C.C. 1983–84.
Cricketers particularly learnt from: Peter Willey.
Cricketers particularly admired: Richard Hadlee.
Other sports: Golf. Watching rugby league (especially Hull F.C.).
Significant injuries during 1984: "Exploratory operation on right knee in May kept me out for one month. Nothing serious found."
Relaxations: Playing golf. Modern music.
Opinions on cricket: "I think four-day county cricket should be introduced for one year, letting both players and public decide whether it is or could be a successful venture."
Best batting performance: 71* Northamptonshire v Oxford University, Oxford 1983.
Best bowling performance: 7-41 Northamptonshire v Derbyshire, Northampton 1982.

LAST SEASON: BATTING

	I.	N.O.	R.	H.S.	AV.
TEST					
OTHER FIRST CLASS	30	5	261	33*	10.44
INT					
J.P.L.	4	4	20	8*	–
NAT.W.	1	0	10	10	–
B & H	1	0	7	7	–

CAREER: BATTING

	I.	N.O.	R.	H.S.	AV.
TEST					
OTHER FIRST CLASS	109	34	887	71*	11.83
INT					
J.P.L.	23	10	126	22	9.69
NAT.W.	5	1	25	11*	6.25
B & H	6	2	19	7	4.75

LAST SEASON: BOWLING

	O.	M.	R.	W.	AV.
TEST					
OTHER FIRST CLASS	508	114	1533	47	32.62
INT					
J.P.L.	95.2	8	490	18	27.22
NAT.W.	36	9	89	9	9.89
B & H	42	3	166	4	41.50

CAREER: BOWLING

	O.	M.	R.	W.	AV.
TEST					
OTHER FIRST CLASS	2284.5	546	7115	234	30.41
INT					
J.P.L.	348	22	1721	68	25.30
NAT.W.	129.4	24	371	22	16.86
B & H	118.2	17	376	13	28.92

Q. 128. Who scored the most first-class runs, and how many, in his career?

RIPLEY, D.

Full Name: David Ripley.
Role: Right-hand bat, wicket-keeper.
Born: 13 September 1966, Leeds.
Height: 5' 10" **Weight:** 11st.
Nickname: Rippers, Gripper, Puppy.
County debut: 1984.
County cap: No.
Test debut: —
No. of Tests: 0.
No. of One-Day Internationals: 0.
1000 runs in a season: 0.
50 wickets in a season: 0.
1st-Class 50s scored: 1.
1st-Class 100s scored: 0.
1st-Class 200s scored: 0.
1st-Class 5 w. in innings: 0.
1st-Class 10 w. in match: 0.
One-day 50s: 0.
One-day 100s: 0.
Place in batting averages: 236 average: 15.61; (1983: — average: —).
Place in bowling averages: — average: —; (1983: — average: —).
Parents: Arthur and Brenda Ripley.
Marital status: Single.
Education: Woodlesford Primary and Royds High, both Leeds.
Qualifications: 5 O-levels.
Off-season 1984–85: At home in Leeds and Young England tour of West Indies.

LAST SEASON: BATTING

	I.	N.O.	R.	H.S.	AV.
TEST					
OTHER FIRST CLASS	21	3	281	61	15.61
INT					
J.P.L.	6	3	51	24	17.00
NAT.W.	1	1	27	27*	–
B & H					

CAREER: BATTING

	I.	N.O.	R.	H.S.	AV.
TEST					
OTHER FIRST CLASS	21	3	281	61	15.61
INT					
J.P.L.	6	3	51	24	17.00
NAT.W.	1	1	27	27*	–
B & H					

LAST SEASON: WICKET KEEPING

	C.	ST.			
TEST					
OTHER FIRST CLASS	26	12			
INT					
J.P.L.	6	2			
NAT.W.	3	–			
B & H					

CAREER: WICKET KEEPING

	C.	ST.			
TEST					
OTHER FIRST CLASS	26	12			
INT					
J.P.L.	6	2			
NAT.W.	3	–			
B & H					

Cricketing superstitions: If having a good run will not have my hair cut; left pad first.
Equipment used: Slazenger.
Cricketers particularly learnt from: Brian Reynolds, Jim Yardley, Ian Stein, Billy Rhodes, Roy Wills.
Cricketers particularly admired: Alan Knott, Bob Taylor.
Other sports: Soccer, golf, pool. Follow soccer (Leeds United) and rugby league (Castleford).
Relaxations: Driving, listening to records.
Extras: Youngest wicket-keeper playing 1st-Class cricket 1984 season aged 17.
Opinions on cricket: "I would like to see the county championship split into 2 divisions with 2 counties gaining promotion and 2 being relegated. Also I would like to see the return of uncovered wickets at least for a trial season."
Best batting performance: 61 Northamptonshire v Surrey, Northampton 1984.

SHARP, G.

Full Name: George Sharp.
Role: Right-hand bat, wicket-keeper, can also bowl slow left arm.
Born: 12 March 1950, Hartlepool, County Durham.
Height: 6′ 0″ **Weight:** 14st.
Nickname: Sharpie, Blunt or Chicken George.
County debut: 1968.
County cap: 1973.
Benefit: 1982 (£25,000).
Test debut: —
No. of Tests: 0.
No. of One-Day Internationals: 0.
1000 runs in a season: 0.
50 wickets in a season: 0.
1st-Class 50s scored: 21.
1st-Class 100s scored: 0.
1st-Class 200s scored: 0.
1st-Class 5 w. in innings: 0.
1st-Class 10 w. in match: 0.
One-day 50s: 1.
One-day 100s: 0.

Place in batting averages: 253 average: 14.00; (1983: 85 average: 33.50).
Place in bowling averages: — average: —; (1983: — average: —).
Parents: George and Grace Sharp.
Wife and date of marriage: Audrey, 14 September 1974.

Education: Elwick Road Secondary Modern, Hartlepool.
Qualifications: N.C.A. Coaching Certificate.
Equipment used: Slazenger.
Cricketers particularly learnt from or admired: K.V. Andrew, B. Taylor, A. Knott.
Jobs outside cricket: Peter Bennie Ltd.
Other sports: Football, squash.
Relaxations: Gardening.
Significant injuries in 1984: Damaged thumb minutes after hearing a public address announcement that his wife had given birth to their first child — a son. He then went into the same hospital for treatment!
Extras: Bowled for only the second time in his 12-year career v Yorkshire, 1980 and took Richard Lumb's wicket. Vice-captain of Northants.
Best batting performance: 94 Northamptonshire v Lancashire, Southport 1980.

LAST SEASON: BATTING

	I.	N.O.	R.	H.S.	AV.
TEST					
OTHER FIRST CLASS	12	0	168	28	14.00
INT					
J.P.L.	4	2	21	8*	10.50
NAT.W.					
B & H	3	1	33	22*	16.50

CAREER: BATTING

	I.	N.O.	R.	H.S.	AV.
TEST					
OTHER FIRST CLASS	383	80	6143	98	20.27
INT					
J.P.L.	146	38	1646	51*	15.24
NAT.W.	18	4	280	41*	20.00
B & H	35	8	424	43	15.70

LAST SEASON: WICKET KEEPING

	C.	ST.		
TEST				
OTHER FIRST CLASS	15	2		
INT				
J.P.L.	1	2		
NAT.W.				
B & H	2	–		

CAREER: WICKET KEEPING

	C.	ST.		
TEST				
OTHER FIRST CLASS	548	87		
INT				
J.P.L.	162	37		
NAT.W.	28	5		
B & H	47	7		

Q. 129. Who took most first-class catches in his career?
Q. 130. For how many years did W.G. Grace captain Gloucestershire?

STEELE, D.S.

Full Name: David Stanley Steele.
Role: Right-hand bat, slow left arm orthodox bowler.
Born: 29 September 1941, Stoke-on-Trent.
Nickname: Stainless, Steelo, Stan, Crime.
County debut: 1963.
County cap: 1965.
Test debut: 1975.
No. of Tests: 8.
No. of One-Day Internationals: 1.
Benefit: £25,000 in 1975.
1000 runs in a season: 10.
50 wickets in a season: 4.
1st-Class 50s scored: 117.
1st-Class 100s scored: 30.
1st-Class 200s scored: 0.
1st-Class 5 w. in innings: 26.
1st-Class 10 w. in match: 3.
One-day 50s: 20.
One-day 100s: 1.

Place in batting averages: 161 average: 24.58; (1983: 158 average: 22.76).
Place in bowling averages: 97 average: 34.43; (1983: 16 average: 21.47).
1st-Class catches 1984: 29 (career: 546).
Parents: Alfred and Grace Steele.
Wife: Carol.
Children: Son, Arran.
Education: Enden Secondary Modern, Stoke-on-Trent. Six-year apprenticeship with printers.
Jobs outside cricket: Sales representative for printing company.
Family links with cricket: Younger brother, J.F. Steele, plays for Glamorgan. Cousin, B.S. Crump, played for Northamptonshire C.C.C. Uncle, Stan Crump, played as professional in Lancashire League.
Equipment used and endorsed: Duncan Fearnley, Sondico International.
Cricketers paticularly learnt from or admired: "Admired Tom Graveney and the attitudes of John Edrich."
Other sports: Table-tennis. Played soccer for Northampton Town League at age 35. Follow all sports.
Relaxations: Sleep.
Extras: Played for Staffordshire 1958–62. Debut for Northamptonshire C.C.C. in 1963, captain 1965. Joined Derbyshire as County Captain in 1979, but gave up captaincy to Geoff Miller half-way through the season. Had match double of 100 runs and 10 wickets (130, 6 for 36, 5 for 39) v Derbyshire at

Northampton in 1978. Cricket was not played at his school. Admits to being amongst the worst car drivers in cricket. Got a steak from a local butcher for every run he made for England in 1975. Wears spectacles. Took hat-trick v Glamorgan, 1980. Returned to Northamptonshire at end of 1981 season. Published autobiography "Come In, Number Three" in 1977. Retired at end of 1984.

Opinions on cricket: Good balance at the moment between first class 3-day and the limited over games. Would like to see 4-day first-class championship matches – which would then bring the game very close to Test cricket.

Best batting performance: 140* Northamptonshire v Worcestershire, Worcester 1971.

Best bowling performance: 8-29 Northamptonshire v Lancashire, Northampton 1966.

LAST SEASON: BATTING

	I.	N.O.	R.	H.S.	AV.
TEST					
OTHER FIRST CLASS	39	13	639	78*	24.58
INT					
J.P.L.	2	1	15	14	–
NAT.W.					
B & H	3	2	20	12	–

CAREER: BATTING

	I.	N.O.	R.	H.S.	AV.
TEST	16	0	673	106	42.06
OTHER FIRST CLASS	796	124	21673	140*	32.25
INT	1	0	8	8	–
J.P.L.	144	24	2416	76	20.13
NAT.W.	31	4	916	109	33.92
B & H	46	6	1023	71	25.58

LAST SEASON: BOWLING

	O.	M.	R.	W.	AV.
TEST					
OTHER FIRST CLASS	732	227	2100	61	34.43
INT					
J.P.L.	23	1	134	3	44.67
NAT.W.					
B & H	41	2	171	7	24.43

CAREER: BOWLING

	O.	M.	R.	W.	AV.
TEST	14.4	5	39	2	19.50
OTHER FIRST CLASS	5504	2025	15472	621	24.92
INT	1	0	9	0	–
J.P.L.	239.4	15	1132	43	26.32
NAT.W.	110.3	13	418	12	34.83
B & H	190.4	30	702	26	27.00

Q. 131. Who was the first professional to captain England?

Q. 132. Who and when is the only all-rounder to score 2000 runs and take 200 wickets in the same season?

WALKER, A.

Full Name: Alan Walker.
Role: Left-hand bat, right arm fast medium bowler, outfielder.
Born: 7 July 1962, Emley, Nr. Huddersfield.
Height: 5′ 11″ **Weight:** 12st 7lbs.
Nickname: Arthur Scargill.
County debut: 1983.
County cap: No.
Test debut: —
No. of Tests: 0.
No. of One-Day Internationals: 0.
1000 runs in a season: 0.
50 wickets in a season: 0.
1st-Class 50s scored: 0.
1st-Class 100s scored: 0.
1st-Class 200s scored: 0.
1st-Class 5 w. in innings: 0.
1st-Class 10 w. in match: 0.
One-day 50s: 0.
One-day 100s: 0.

Place in batting averages: — average: —; (1983: — average: —).
Place in bowling averages: 118 average: 41.41; (1983: 44 average: 26.27).
1st-Class catches 1984: 4 (career: 7).
Parents: Malcolm and Enid Walker.
Wife and date of marriage: Janice, 17 September 1983.
Education: Emley Junior School, Kirkburton Middle School, Shelley High (Huddersfield) School.
Qualifications: 2 O-levels, 4 C.S.E.s.
Jobs outside cricket: Miner.
Off-season 1984–85: Coaching in South Africa.
Equipment used: Duncan Fearnley.
Overseas tours: Denmark, with N.C.A. U-19s North of England 1980.
Overseas teams played for: Utinhage (South Africa) 1984.
Cricketers particularly learnt from: David Steele, Rupert Hanley.
Cricketers particularly admired: Dennis Lillee, Richard Hadlee.
Other sports: Football; follow rugby league.
Significant injuries during 1984: Torn muscle in left side.
Relaxations: Watching T.V., listening to music, D.I.Y.
Best batting performance: 19 Northamptonshire v Sussex, Horsham 1984.
Best bowling performance: 4-50 Northamptonshire v Middlesex, Lord's 1984.

LAST SEASON: BATTING

	I.	N.O.	R.	H.S.	AV.
TEST					
OTHER FIRST CLASS	15	4	64	19	5.82
INT					
J.P.L.	1	0	7	7	–
NAT.W.					
B & H					

CAREER: BATTING

	I.	N.O.	R.	H.S.	AV.
TEST					
OTHER FIRST CLASS	19	7	82	19	6.83
INT					
J.P.L.	2	0	20	13	10.00
NAT.W.					
B & H					

LAST SEASON: BOWLING

	O.	M.	R.	W.	AV.
TEST					
OTHER FIRST CLASS	308.5	52	1118	27	41.41
INT					
J.P.L.	87.1	5	371	17	21.82
NAT.W.	28.5	3	112	3	37.33
B & H					

CAREER: BOWLING

	O.	M.	R.	W.	AV.
TEST					
OTHER FIRST CLASS	474.3	82	1696	49	34.61
INT					
J.P.L.	103.4	5	444	18	24.67
NAT.W.	28.5	3	112	3	37.33
B & H					

WILD, D.J.

Full Name: Duncan James Wild.
Role: Left-hand bat; right arm medium bowler.
Born: 28 November 1962, Northampton.
Height: 6' 0" **Weight:** 12st 7lbs.
Nickname: Oscar.
County debut: 1980.
County cap: No.
Test debut: —
No. of Tests: 0.
No. of One-Day Internationals: 0.
1000 runs in a season: 0.
50 wickets in a season: 0.
1st-Class 50s scored: 2.
1st-Class 100s scored: 2.
1st-Class 200s scored: 0.
1st-Class 5 w. in innings: 0.
1st-Class 10 in match: 0.
One-day 50s: 1.
One-day 100s: 0.
Place in batting averages: 86 average: 34.20; (1983: 195 average: 18.00).
Place in bowling averages: 87 average: 32.90; (1983: — average: —).
1st-Class catches 1984: 5 (career: 9).
Parents: John and Glenys Wild.
Marital status: Single.
Education: Cherry Orchard Middle; Northampton School for Boys.

Qualifications: 7 O-levels.
Jobs outside cricket: Law costs draughtsman.
Family links with cricket: Father played for Northants.
Overseas tours: With England Young Cricketers to West Indies 1980.
Off-season 1984–85: Studying and working in law.
Equipment used: Gray-Nicolls.
Extras: Played for England Young Cricketers v Young India in 3-Test series 1981. Also for Young England v. Young West Indies, August 1982.
Best batting performance: 144 Northamptonshire v Lancashire, Southport 1984.
Best bowling performance: 3-15 Northamptonshire v Hampshire, Southampton 1984.

LAST SEASON: BATTING

	I.	N.O.	R.	H.S.	AV.
TEST					
OTHER FIRST CLASS	27	2	855	144	34.20
INT					
J.P.L.	12	3	175	51	19.44
NAT.W.	3	0	17	11	5.67
B & H	3	1	63	48	31.50

CAREER: BATTING

	I.	N.O.	R.	H.S.	AV.
TEST					
OTHER FIRST CLASS	55	7	1258	144	26.21
INT					
J.P.L.	23	8	245	51	16.33
NAT.W.	3	0	17	11	5.67
B & H	4	1	65	48	21.67

LAST SEASON: BOWLING

	O.	M.	R.	W.	AV.
TEST					
OTHER FIRST CLASS	91.4	18	329	10	32.90
INT					
J.P.L.	93	1	420	17	24.70
NAT.W.	35	6	122	4	30.50
B & H					

CAREER: BOWLING

	O.	M.	R.	W.	AV.
TEST					
OTHER FIRST CLASS	260.1	50	945	19	49.74
INT					
J.P.L.	186	4	855	28	30.54
NAT.W.	35	6	122	4	30.50
B & H	8	1	41	0	–

Q. 133. What was the length of Harold's Larwood's run?
Q. 134. Who is the oldest man to play Test cricket, for which country, at what age?

WILLIAMS, R.G.

Full Name: Richard Grenville
Williams.
Role: Right-hand bat; off-break
bowler.
Born: 10 August 1957, Bangor,
Caernarvonshire.
Height: 5' 6"
Nickname: Chippy.
County debut: 1974.
County cap: 1979.
Test debut: —
No. of Tests: 0.
No. of One-Day Internationals: 0.
1000 runs in a season: 6.
50 wickets in a season: 0.
1st-Class 50s scored: 36.
1st-Class 100s scored: 13.
1st-Class 200s scored: 0.
1st-Class 5 w. in innings: 6.
1st-Class 10 w. in match: 0.
One-day 50s: 15.
One-day 100s: 0.
Place in batting averages: 102 average: 32.49; (1983: 32 average: 43.50).
Place in bowling averages: 121 average: 42.13; (1983: 20 average: 22.04).
1st-Class catches 1984: 9 (career: 71).
Education: Ellesmere Port Grammar School.
Overseas tours: Australasia in February and March 1980 with Derrick Robins
Under-23 XI. West Indies with England Young Cricketers 1976.

LAST SEASON: BATTING

	I.	N.O.	R.	H.S.	AV.
TEST					
OTHER FIRST CLASS	37	4	1072	169	32.49
INT					
J.P.L.	12	4	295	81*	36.88
NAT.W.	3	0	130	94	43.33
B & H	2	0	17	12	8.50

CAREER: BATTING

	I.	N.O.	R.	H.S.	AV.
TEST					
OTHER FIRST CLASS	296	36	7990	175*	30.73
INT					
J.P.L.	98	17	1945	82	24.01
NAT.W.	19	4	428	94	28.53
B & H	21	5	462	83	28.88

LAST SEASON: BOWLING

	O.	M.	R.	W.	AV.
TEST					
OTHER FIRST CLASS	442.2	104	1348	32	42.13
INT					
J.P.L.	77	3	393	8	49.13
NAT.W.	25	8	62	1	–
B & H	13	1	68	0	–

CAREER: BOWLING

	O.	M.	R.	W.	AV.
TEST					
OTHER FIRST CLASS	2938.4	764	8225	246	33.44
INT					
J.P.L.	306.5	23	1444	50	28.88
NAT.W.	106	18	281	14	20.07
B & H	101	17	333	10	33.30

Overseas teams played for: Club cricket in Sydney, Australia, on Whitbread Scholarship.

Extras: Debut for 2nd XI in 1972 aged 14yrs 11mths. Made maiden century in 1979 and then scored four centuries in five innings. Hat-trick v Gloucester, at Northants, 1980. Was first player to score a century against the 1980 W. Indies touring team. Was stand-by for England in India, 1981.

Best batting performance: 175* Northamptonshire v Leicestershire, Leicester 1980.

Best bowling performance: 7-73 Northamptonshire v Cambridge University, Cambridge 1980.

COUNTY QUIZ

Q. 1. When was the club founded?

Q. 2. Who made the most first-class runs for the county last season, and how many?

Q. 3. What's the highest ever county total, and against whom?

Q. 4. Who took most wickets for the county last season, and how many?

Q. 5. What's the highest individual score for the county, who hit it, and when?

Q. 6. What's the highest scoring partnership for the county for any wicket?

Q. 7. How many times has the club won the County Championship?

Q. 8. What's the lowest ever total made by the county in one innings, when, and against whom?

Q. 9. Which bowler took the most first-class wickets in one season, when, and how many?

Q. 10. Which batsman hit the most runs in one season, when and how many?

Nottinghamshire

AFFORD, J.A.

Full Name: John Andrew Afford.
Role: Right-hand bat, slow left arm bowler.
Born: 12 May 1964, Crowland, Nr. Peterborough.
Height: 6′ 1½″ **Weight:** 13 st.
Nickname: Aff.
County debut: 1984.
County cap: No.
Test debut: —
No. of Tests: 0.
No. of One-Day International: 0.
1000 runs in season: 0.
50 wickets in a season: 0.
1st-Class 50s scored: 0.
1st-Class 100s scored: 0.
1st-Class 200s scored: 0.
1st-Class 5 w. in innings: 0.
1st-Class 10 w. in match: 0.
One-day 50s: 0.
One-day 100s: 0.
Place in batting averages: — average: —; (1983: — average: —).
Place in bowling averages: — average: —; (1983: — average: —).
1st-Class catches 1984: 1 (career: 1).
Parents: Jill Afford.
Marital Status: Single.
Education: Spalding Grammar School, Stamford College for Further Education.
Qualifications: 5 O-levels.
Off-season 1984-85: "Looking for work".
Cricketing superstitions: Wear the same shirt and trousers getting wickets.
Equipment used: Gunn & Moore.
Cricketers particularly learnt from: Mike Bore and Eddie Hemmings at Notts and David Johnson at Bourne C.C.
Cricketers particularly admired: Richard Hadlee, Bishen Bedi, Derek Underwood.

Other sports: "Play any sport within reason — possibly one of the worst golfers in the world!! Enjoy watching most sports as long as horses aren't involved."
Relaxations: Enjoy listening to music. Play bass guitar.
Opinions on cricket: "I think that the standard of 2nd XI umpiring should be be brought up to a more consistent level — more in line with 1st class."
Best batting performance: —.
Best bowling performance: 2-49 Nottinghamshire v Lancashire, Old Trafford 1984.

LAST SEASON: BATTING

	I.	N.O.	R.	H.S.	AV.
TEST					
OTHER FIRST CLASS					
INT					
J.P.L.					
NAT.W.					
B & H					

CAREER: BATTING

	I.	N.O.	R.	H.S.	AV.
TEST					
OTHER FIRST CLASS					
INT					
J.P.L.					
NAT.W.					
B & H					

LAST SEASON: BOWLING

	O.	M.	R.	W.	AV.
TEST					
OTHER FIRST CLASS	88.3	32	256	7	36.57
INT					
J.P.L.					
NAT.W.					
B & H					

CAREER: BOWLING

	O.	M.	R.	W.	AV.
TEST					
OTHER FIRST CLASS	88.3	32	256	7	36.57
INT					
J.P.L.					
NAT.W.					
B & H					

BIRCH, J.D.

Full Name: John Dennis Birch.
Role: Right-hand bat, slip fielder.
Born: 18 June 1955, Nottingham.
Height: 6' 1" **Weight:** 13st.
Nickname: Bonk.
County debut: 1973.
County cap: 1981.
Test debut: —
No. of Tests: 0.
No. of One-Day Internationals: 0.
1000 runs in a season: 2.
50 wickets in a season: 0.
1st-Class 50s scored: 35.
1st-Class 100s scored: 5.
1st-Class 200s scored: 0.
1st-Class 5 w. in innings: 1.
1st-Class 10 w. in match: 0.
One-day 50s: 12.

One-day 100s: 0.
Place in batting averages: 105 average: 32.32; (1983: 100 average: 30.17).
Place in bowling averages: — average: —; (1983: — average: —).
1st-Class catches 1984: 20 (career: 129).
Parents: Bill and Mavis Birch.
Wife and date of marriage: Linda, 23 May 1980.
Children: Nathalie and Daniel (twins), 21 January 1981.
Education: William Crane Bilateral School.
Qualifications: O-levels.
Family links with cricket: Father was a local cricketer.
Jobs outside cricket: Runs a small building firm with a friend and brothers.
Equipment used: Stuart Surridge, Gunn & Moore.
Cricketers particularly learned from: Clive Rice.
Cricketers particularly admired: Clive Rice, Richard Hadlee, Geoffrey Boycott.
Other sports: Playing soccer (player/manager of local team), golf, snooker, and watching any other sports.
Relaxations: "Gardening and fishing."
Significant injuries in 1984: Missed last month of season with torn hamstring.
Extras: "Would like to thank Frank Woodhead for giving me the chance to play for Notts and all who have helped me at the club."
Opinions on cricket: "I would like to see South Africa return to Test cricket."
Best batting performance: 125 Nottinghamshire v Leicestershire, Trent Bridge 1982.
Best bowling performance: 6-64 Nottinghamshire v Hampshire, Bournemouth 1975.

LAST SEASON: BATTING

	I.	N.O.	R.	H.S.	AV.
TEST					
OTHER FIRST CLASS	33	5	905	110*	32.32
INT					
J.P.L.	10	2	276	72*	34.50
NAT.W.	2	1	3	3	–
B & H	6	2	72	30*	18.00

CAREER: BATTING

	I.	N.O.	R.	H.S.	AV.
TEST					
OTHER FIRST CLASS	252	38	5856	125	27.37
INT					
J.P.L.	106	25	2063	92	25.46
NAT.W.	13	2	133	32	12.09
B & H	27	4	456	85	19.83

LAST SEASON: BOWLING

	O.	M.	R.	W.	AV.
TEST					
OTHER FIRST CLASS	3	0	20	0	–
INT					
J.P.L.					
NAT.W.					
B & H					

CAREER: BOWLING

	O.	M.	R.	W.	AV.
TEST					
OTHER FIRST CLASS	477.5	68	1856	38	48.84
INT					
J.P.L.	152	12	719	20	35.95
NAT.W.	14	1	73	1	–
B & H	54	7	201	8	25.13

BORE, M.K.

Full Name: Michael Kenneth Bore.
Role: Right-hand bat, left arm bowler, spin and seam.
Born: 2 June 1947, Hull.
Height: 5′ 11″ **Weight:** 13st.
Nickname: Noddy.
County debut: 1979(for Notts); 1969 (for Yorkshire).
County cap: 1980.

Test debut: —
Number of Tests: 0.
No. of Tests: 0.
No. of One-Day Internationals: 0.
1000 runs in a season: 0.
50 wickets in a season: 1.
1st-Class 50s scored: 0.
1st-Class 100s scored: 0.
1st-Class 200s scored: 0.
1st-Class 5 w. in innings: 9.
1st-Class 10 w. in match: 0.
One-day 50s: 0.
One-day 100s: 0.
Place in batting averages: — average: —;(1983: 234 average: 12.00).
Place in bowling averages: — average: —; (1983: 112 average: 38.52).
1st-Class catches 1984: 1 (career: 50).
Parents: Kenneth Gordon and Cicely May Bore.
Wife and date of marriage: Ann, 30 September 1972.
Children: Christopher Mark, 17 July 1977; Suzanne, 23 July 1979.
Education: Maybury High School, Hull.
Qualifications: N.C.A. Staff coach. R.S.A./G.C.E. O-level.
Jobs outside cricket: Various clerical jobs, spanning ten years, in off-seasons, five of which were spent in the Civil Service at the Department of Health and Social Security.
Off-season 1984–85: Employed by Nottinghamshire C.C.C. to promote cricket and coaching throughout the area.
Family links with cricket: Father played in local amateur league in Hull as left arm spinner and opening bat.
Cricketing superstitions: "Always prefer to follow the keeper on to the field from the changing room. Put right pad on first when batting."
Equipment used: Gunn and Moore.
Cricketers particularly learnt from: "Most fellow professionals, especially my colleagues at Notts."
Cricketers particularly admired: G. Boycott, C. Rice, R. Hadlee, D. Underwood.

Overseas tours: 1977 to Gibraltar with Yorkshire.

Other sports: Competitive badminton, snooker, table tennis, squash, golf. Follows football and rugby league.

Relaxations: "Spending what spare time I have with my family, and gardening, especially on my allotment."

Extras: Made debut for Yorkshire County Cricket Club in 1969. Started bowling seamers in one-day cricket in 1979. "Now that I've taken over as 2nd XI Captain and the running of a Notts Colts side on Saturday afternoons my role now with Notts is to bring on young talent in the area, and due to my greater involvement with coaching during the winter, both roles now complement each other. Chairman of the Notts Assoc. of Cricket Coaches. I took 5 wickets in 6 balls against Derby's 2nd XI."

Opinions on cricket: "I would like to see some sponsorship for 2nd XI competition, thus enabling the grass roots to survive the present climate of economical cuts that most counties are adopting, especially as the TCCB are trying to reduce the number of overseas players."

Best batting performance: 37* Yorkshire v Nottinghamshire, Bradford 1973.

Best bowling performance: 8-89 Nottinghamshire v Kent, Folkestone 1979.

LAST SEASON: BATTING

	I.	N.O.	R.	H.S.	AV.
TEST					
OTHER FIRST CLASS	2	0	28	27	14.00
INT					
J.P.L.					
NAT.W.					
B & H					

CAREER: BATTING

	I.	N.O.	R.	H.S.	AV.
TEST					
OTHER FIRST CLASS	151	51	856	37*	8.56
INT					
J.P.L.	32	14	129	28*	7.17
NAT.W.	7	4	9	4*	3.00
B & H	10	7	27	7*	9.00

LAST SEASON: BOWLING

	O.	M.	R.	W.	AV.
TEST					
OTHER FIRST CLASS	151.2	40	413	13	31.77
INT					
J.P.L.	2	0	19	0	–
NAT.W.					
B & H					

CAREER: BOWLING

	O.	M.	R.	W.	AV.
TEST					
OTHER FIRST CLASS	4451.5	1501	10858	359	30.25
INT					
J.P.L.	734	81	2932	94	31.19
NAT.W.	109.2	19	327	11	29.73
B & H	259.4	59	736	29	25.83

Q. 135. What was Sobers' full name?

Q. 136. Which player has most often captained which Test team?

BROAD, B.C.

Full Name: Brian Christopher Broad.
Role: Left-hand bat, right arm medium bowler, outfielder.
Born: 29 September 1957, Bristol.
Height: 6' 4" **Weight:** 14st 7lbs.
Nickname: Norfolk, Wally, Beena, Jessie.
County debut: 1979, (Glos.); 1984 (Nottinghamshire).
County cap: 1981, (Glos.); 1984 (Nottinghamshire).

Test debut: 1984.
No. of Tests: 5.
No. of One-Day Internationals: 0.
1000 runs in a season: 4.
50 wickets in a season: 0.
1st-Class 50s scored: 34.
1st-Class 100s scored: 9.
1st-Class 200s scored: 0.
1st-Class 5 w. in innings: 0.
1st-Class 10 w. in match: 0.
One-day 50s: 14.
One-day 100s: 1.
Place in batting averages: 32 average: 44.5 (1983: 28 average: 42.44).
Place in bowling averages: — average: —; (1983: — average: —).
1st-Class catches 1984: 15 (career: 50).
Parents: Nancy and Kenneth Broad.
Wife and date of marriage: Carole Ann, 14 July 1979.
Education: Colston's School, Bristol; St Paul's College, Cheltenham.
Qualifications: Five O-levels. N.C.A. advanced coach.
Jobs outside cricket: Floor laying, lorry loading.
Family links with cricket: Father and grandfather both played local cricket. Father member of Gloucestershire Committee until retired; father on T.C.C.B. development sub-committee.
Overseas tours: Gloucestershire C.C.C. tour of Malawi 1978 and Barbados 1980; British Colleges to Trinidad and Barbados 1979.
Off-season 1984–85: Working for commercial department at Trent Bridge.
Equipment used: Duncan Fearnley, Arcass.
Other sports: Played rugby for English Colleges, Bristol United, St Paul's College, and now plays for Clifton.
Relaxations: Playing any sport, watching TV with my wife. Running a mail order jewellery business.
Extras: Ended 1979 with a century (129) in last match for Gloucs v Northants, and hit a century (120) for Gloucs v Oxford University in first match of 1980.

Moved from Gloucestershire to Nottinghamshire for 1984 season.
Best batting performance: 145 Gloucestershire v Nottinghamshire, Bristol 1983.

LAST SEASON: BATTING

	I.	N.O.	R.	H.S.	AV.
TEST	9	0	281	86	31.22
OTHER FIRST CLASS	31	5	1268	108*	48.77
INT					
J.P.L.	12	0	319	62	26.58
NAT.W.	2	0	73	65	36.50
B & H	6	0	199	122	33.17

CAREER: BATTING

	I.	N.O.	R.	H.S.	AV.
TEST	9	0	281	86	31.22
OTHER FIRST CLASS	190	14	6072	145	34.50
INT					
J.P.L.	62	0	1652	96	26.64
NAT.W.	8	0	274	98	34.25
B & H	21	0	517	122	24.62

LAST SEASON: BOWLING

	O.	M.	R.	W.	AV.
TEST					
OTHER FIRST CLASS					
INT					
J.P.L.	10	0	70	2	35.00
NAT.W.					
B & H	16.4	0	102	3	34.00

CAREER: BOWLING

	O.	M.	R.	W.	AV.
TEST					
OTHER FIRST CLASS	187	47	656	11	59.64
INT					
J.P.L.	111.3	4	602	19	31.68
NAT.W.					
B & H	50.4	2	282	5	56.40

COOPER, K.E.

Full Name: Kevin Edwin Cooper.
Role: Left-hand bat, right arm fast medium bowler.
Born: 27 December 1957, Sutton-in-Ashfield.
Height: 6′ 1″ **Weight:** 12st 4lbs.
Nickname: Henry.
County debut: 1976.
County cap: 1980.
Test debut: —
No. of Tests: 0.
No. of One-Day Internationals: 0.
1000 runs in a season: 0.
50 wickets in a season: 4.
1st-Class 50s scored: 0.
1st-Class 100s scored: 0.
1st-Class 200s scored: 0.
1st-Class 5 w. in innings: 12.
1st-Class 10 w. in match: 0.
One-day 50s: 0.
One-day 100s: 0.
Place in batting averages: — average: —; (1983: 231 average: 12.70).

Place in bowling averages: 39 average: 26.75; (1983: 55 average: 28.25).
1st-Class catches 1984: 10 (career: 54).
Parents: Gerald Edwin and Margaret Cooper.
Wife: Linda Carol, 14 February 1981.
Children: Kelly Louise 8 April 1982.
Education: Secondary modern.
Jobs outside cricket: Has been warehouseman and maintenance man, also P.R. in free trade department of local brewery.
Family links with cricket: None.
Overseas tours: Toured Australasia with Derrick Robins Under 23 XI in 1979–80 off-season.
Equipment used: Gunn & Moore.
Other sports: Football, golf.
Relaxations: Darts, dominoes, snooker, pool.
Extras: On 23 June 1974, playing for Hucknall Ramblers C.C., took 10 wickets for six runs in one innings against Sutton Coll. in the Mansfield and District League.
Best batting performance: 38* Nottinghamshire v Cambridge University, Cambridge 1982.
Best bowling performance: 7-33 Nottinghamshire v Worcestershire, Worcester 1983.

LAST SEASON: BATTING

	I.	N.O.	R.	H.S.	AV.
TEST					
OTHER FIRST CLASS	19	6	117	19	9.00
INT					
J.P.L.	1	0	31	31	–
NAT.W.					
B & H	1	0	0	0	–

CAREER: BATTING

	I.	N.O.	R.	H.S.	AV.
TEST					
OTHER FIRST CLASS	157	36	1113	38*	9.20
INT					
J.P.L.	28	9	98	31	5.16
NAT.W.	4	1	29	11	9.67
B & H	12	7	62	25*	12.40

LAST SEASON: BOWLING

	O.	M.	R.	W.	AV.
TEST					
OTHER FIRST CLASS	623.2	217	1364	51	26.75
INT					
J.P.L.	118	10	515	12	42.92
NAT.W.	24	8	48	2	24.00
B & H	55	10	161	5	32.20

CAREER: BOWLING

	O.	M.	R.	W.	AV.
TEST					
OTHER FIRST CLASS	3808.1	935	10301	371	27.77
INT					
J.P.L.	569.1	36	2634	80	32.93
NAT.W.	116	29	283	15	18.87
B & H	311.4	53	1132	32	35.38

Q. 137. What former England Test player played in League cricket until he was 61, and took 86 wickets in his last season?

EVANS, K.P.

Full Name: Kevin Paul Evans.
Role: Right-hand bat, right arm
medium bowler.
Born: 10 September 1963, Calverton,
Nottingham.
Height: 6′ 2″ **Weight:** 12st. 8lbs.
Nickname: Kevans.
County debut: 1984.
County cap: No.
Test debut: —
No. of Tests: 0.
No. of One-Day Internationals: 0.
1000 runs in a season: 0.
50 wickets in a season: 0.
1st-Class 50s scored: 0.
1st-Class 100s scored: 0.
1st-Class 200s scored: 0.
1st-Class 5 w. in innings: 0.
1st-Class 10 w. in match: 0.
One-day 50s: 0.
One-day 100s: 0.
Place in batting averages: — average: —; (1983: — average: —).
Place in bowling averages: — average: —; (1983: — average: —).
1st-Class catches 1984: 3 (career: 3).
Parents: Eric and Eileen Evans.
Marital status: Single.
Family links with cricket: Brother taken onto Nottinghamshire staff in 1985.

LAST SEASON: BATTING

	I.	N.O.	R.	H.S.	AV.
TEST					
OTHER FIRST CLASS	4	0	48	42	12.00
INT					
J.P.L.	1	1	27	27*	—
NAT.W.					
B & H					

CAREER: BATTING

	I.	N.O.	R.	H.S.	AV.
TEST					
OTHER FIRST CLASS	4	0	48	42	12.00
INT					
J.P.L.	1	1	27	27*	—
NAT.W.					
B & H					

LAST SEASON: BOWLING

	O.	M.	R.	W.	AV.
TEST					
OTHER FIRST CLASS	48	8	173	2	86.50
INT					
J.P.L.	12	0	74	1	—
NAT.W.					
B & H					

CAREER: BOWLING

	O.	M.	R.	W.	AV.
TEST					
OTHER FIRST CLASS	48	8	173	2	86.50
INT					
J.P.L.	12	0	74	1	—
NAT.W.					
B & H					

Education: William Lee Primary; Colonel Frank Seely Comprehensive School, Calverton.
Qualifications: 9 O-levels, 3 A-levels.
Jobs outside cricket: Bank work.
Off-season 1984–85: Working in a shop.
Cricketing superstitions: Putting left pad on first.
Equipment used: Gunn and Moore.
Cricketers particularly learnt from: Mike Hendrick, Mike Bore, Bob White.
Cricketers particularly admired: Richard Hadlee.
Other sports: Football, tennis, badminton, squash.
Significant injuries in 1984: Chipped bone in finger and strained side. Ended the season two weeks early.
Relaxations: Listening to music, reading.
Best batting performance: 42 Nottinghamshire v Cambridge University, Trent Bridge 1984.

FRASER-DARLING, D.

Full Name: David Fraser-Darling.
Role: Right-hand bat, right arm medium fast bowler.
Born: 30 September 1963, Sheffield.
Height: 6′ 5″ **Weight:** 15st.
Nickname: Meat.
County debut: 1984.
County cap: No.
Test debut: —
No. of Tests: 0.
No. of One-Day Internationals: 0.
1000 runs in a season: 0.
50 wickets in a season: 0.
1st-Class 50s scored: 0.
1st-Class 100s scored: 0.
1st-Class 200s scored: 0.
1st-Class 5 w. in innings: 0.
1st-Class 10 w. in innings: 0.
One-day 50s: 0.
One-day 100s: 0.

Place in bowling averages: — average: —; (1983: — average: —).
Place in bowling averages: — average: —; (1983: — average: —).
1st-Class catches 1984: 1 (career: 1). ·
Parents: Alasdair and Mary.
Marital status: Single.
Education: Edinburgh Academy.
Qualifications: 7 O-levels, 2 A-levels.

Off-season 1984–85: Working in London, decorating and work in off-licence.
Cricketing superstitions: Left sock, shoe, pad etc. on first.
Cricketers particularly learnt from: David Standley, Tony Dyer and all at Notts.
Cricketers particularly admired: Mike Hendrick.
Other sports: Football; used to play rugby. Watches any sport.
Significant injuries in 1984: Shin soreness.
Relaxations: Music, films, drinking.
Extras: Played rugby for Scotland U-19 v England, Wales and Ireland 1981.

LAST SEASON: BATTING

	I.	N.O.	R.	H.S.	AV.
TEST					
OTHER FIRST CLASS					
INT					
J.P.L.					
NAT.W.					
B & H					

CAREER: BATTING

	I.	N.O.	R.	H.S.	AV.
TEST					
OTHER FIRST CLASS					
INT					
J.P.L.					
NAT.W.					
B & H					

LAST SEASON: BOWLING

	O.	M.	R.	W.	AV.
TEST					
OTHER FIRST CLASS	29	9	55	3	18.33
INT					
J.P.L.					
NAT.W.					
B & H					

CAREER: BOWLING

	O.	M.	R.	W.	AV.
TEST					
OTHER FIRST CLASS	29	9	55	3	18.33
INT					
J.P.L.					
NAT.W.					
B & H					

FRENCH, B.N.

Full Name: Bruce Nicholas French.
Role: Right-hand bat, wicket-keeper.
Born: 13 August 1959, Warsop, Notts.
Height: 5′ 8″ **Weight:** 10st.
Nickname: Frog.
County debut: 1976, age 16 yrs 10 mths. (Youngest Notts player).
County cap: 1980.
Test debut: —
No. of Tests: 0.
No. of One-Day Internationals: 0.
1000 runs in a season: 0.
50 wickets in a season: 0.
1st-Class 50s scored: 13.
1st-Class 100s scored: 0.

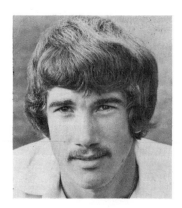

1st-Class 200s scored: 0.
1st-Class 5 w. in innings: 0.
1st-Class 10 w. in match: 0.
One-day 50s: 0.
One-day 100s: 0.
Place in batting averages: 146 average: 26.81; (1983: 190 average: 18.53).
Place in bowling averages: — average: —; (1983: — average: —).
Parents: Maurice and Betty French.
Wife and date of marriage: Ellen Rose, 9 March 1978.
Children: Charles Daniel, 31 August 1978; Catherine Ellen, 28 December 1980.
Education: Meden School, Warsop.
Qualifications: O-level and C.S.E.
Jobs outside cricket: Warehouseman, window cleaner, bricklayer's labourer.
Off-season 1984–85: On tour with England to India and Australia.
Family links with cricket: Brothers, Neil, David, Charlie, Joe, play for Welbeck C.C. Father, Treasurer Welbeck C.C.
Cricketers particularly learnt from: Bob Taylor, Clive Rice.
Cricket superstitions: Right pad on before left when keeping wicket.
Equipment used: Gunn and Moore.
Other sports: Rock climbing, fell walking and all aspects of mountaineering.
Relaxations: Reading, pipe smoking and drinking Theakston's Ale.
Extras: Equalled Notts record for dismissals in match with 10 (7ct. 3 st.), and dismissals in innings with 6 catches. New Notts record for dismissals in a season with 87 (75 ct. 12 st.).
Best batting performance: 98 Nottinghamshire v Lancashire, Trent Bridge 1984.

LAST SEASON: BATTING

	I.	N.O.	R.	H.S.	AV.
TEST					
OTHER FIRST CLASS	32	6	697	98	26.81
INT					
J.P.L.	6	2	43	17*	10.75
NAT.W.	1	0	16	16	–
B & H	4	3	82	48*	–

CAREER: BATTING

	I.	N.O.	R.	H.S.	AV.
TEST					
OTHER FIRST CLASS	221	44	3303	98	18.66
INT					
J.P.L.	42	13	334	25	11.51
NAT.W.	7	2	108	33*	21.60
B & H	18	3	183	48*	12.20

LAST SEASON: WICKET KEEPING

	C.	ST.		
TEST				
OTHER FIRST CLASS	76	11		
INT				
J.P.L.	14	5		
NAT.W.	5	1		
B & H	11	1		

CAREER: WICKET KEEPING

	C.	ST.		
TEST				
OTHER FIRST CLASS	377	41		
INT				
J.P.L.	51	10		
NAT.W.	14	1		
B & H	31	8		

HADLEE, R.J.

Full Name: Richard John Hadlee.
Role: Left-hand bat, right arm fast
bowler.
Born: 3 July 1951, Christchurch,
New Zealand.
Height: 6' 1" **Weight:** 11st 9lbs.
Nickname: Paddles.
County debut: 1978.
County cap: 1978.
Test debut: 1972–73.
No. of Tests: 50.
No. of One-Day Internationals: 63.

1000 runs in a season: 1.
50 wickets in a season: 6 (two 100
wickets in a season).
1st-Class 50s scored: 37.
1st-Class 100s scored: 8.
1st-Class 200s scored: 1.
1st-Class 5 w. in innings: 56.
1st-Class 10 w. in match: 8.
One-day 50s: 8.
One-day 100s: 1.
Place in batting averages: 17 average: 51.26; (1983: 23 average: 45.85).
Place in bowling averages: 1 average: 14.06; (1983: 18 average: 21.74).
1st-Class catches 1984: 23 (career: 136).
Parents: Walter Arnold and Lillius Agnes Hadlee.
Wife and date of marriage: Karen Ann, 24 August 1973.
Children: Nicholas John and Daniel.
Education: Fendalton Primary; Heaton Intermediate; Christchurch Boys'
High School.
Qualifications: School certificate and university entrance.
Jobs outside cricket: Trainee manager, Woolworth's 1970; Dept. trainee
manager, Bing Harris Sargood 1973; Sales manager, Shawn Sports, 1975.
Employed by New Zealand C.C.; managed by International Management
Group, contracted to Leopard Breweries and Armoured Security Services.
Family links with cricket: Father played for New Zealand, 1937–49,
captaining New Zealand on tour of U.K. 1949. Brother, Dayle, played for New
Zealand 1969–78. Brother Barry played for Canterbury. His father, Walter,
has succeeded Gordon Burgess (father of former New Zealand Test captain,
Mark) as president of the New Zealand Cricket council.
Overseas tours: With New Zealand to England 1973, 1978, 1983; Australia
1973–74, 1980–81; India, Pakistan 1976. World Cup in U.K. 1975, 1979,
1983.
Overseas teams played for: Canterbury, New Zealand, 1971–. Tasmania

1979–80. World XI v Australia 1979, World Series Cricket.

Off season 1984–85: Playing in New Zealand.

Cricketers particularly learnt from: "My brother Dayle, Dennis Lillee– Admire his approach to the game– competitive, inspires his team, great bowler."

Cricketers particularly admired: Viv Richards, Sobers, Greg Chappell, Qadir.

Equipment used: Gunn & Moore.

Equipment endorsed: Adidas footwear.

Other sports: Golf. Played goalkeeper for Rangers and for Woolston in New Zealand Southern League, "but I never took it seriously." Follows soccer, rugby, tennis, golf, snooker, etc.

Relaxations: "Watching movies, music, writing weekly newspaper columns."

Extras: Awarded M.B.E. 1980. Hat-trick v Central Districts 1972 at Nelson. Only bowler to take 100 wickets, in 1981 season. Top of English bowling averages 1980, 1981, 1982 and 1984. New Zealand Personality of the Year 1978 and nominated in final 6 on 5 occasions. New Zealand Bowler of the Year 1978–84 inc. Has written autobiography "Hadlee". Author of "Hadlee on Cricket", "Hadlee's Humour" and "Hadlee Hits Out". New Zealand records: (1) Most wickets in Test cricket. (2) Most number of 5 wickets in a Test innings. (3) Most wickets in a Test innings, and in a Test match, 11 for 58. (4) Best bowling in a Test match, 7 for 23 v India 1976. (5) Most number of 10 wickets in a test match, three times. (6) First New Zealand player to take Test double of 100 wickets and 1,000 runs. 1984 did 'double' of 1000 runs and 100 wickets in 1st-Class cricket—first time achieved since F.J. Titmus in 1967.

Opinions on cricket: "Too much cricket played in year—the demand on players physically and mentally is too great and that creates too much mediocrity. Less cricket would create greater desire to play and improve performances because attitudes would change—perhaps 16 3- or 4-day championship games is sufficient along with the Sunday games. For 10 days, in

LAST SEASON: BATTING

	I.	N.O.	R.	H.S.	AV.
TEST					
OTHER FIRST CLASS	31	8	1179	210*	51.26
INT					
J.P.L.	14	5	399	75*	44.33
NAT.W.	1	0	6	6	–
B & H	5	2	120	67*	40.00

CAREER: BATTING

	I.	N.O.	R.	H.S.	AV.
TEST	85	11	1820	103	24.59
OTHER FIRST CLASS	235	43	5967	210*	31.08
INT	52	4	798	79	16.63
J.P.L.	51	14	1040	100*	28.10
NAT.W.	5	2	96	38	32.00
B & H	28	7	694	70	33.00

LAST SEASON: BOWLING

	O.	M.	R.	W.	AV.
TEST					
OTHER FIRST CLASS	772.2	245	1645	117	14.06
INT					
J.P.L.	113	10	426	23	18.52
NAT.W.	24	9	56	4	14.00
B & H	51.2	19	108	8	13.50

CAREER: BOWLING

	O.	M.	R.	W.	AV.
TEST	577.2 1350.3	68 375	5626	235	23.94
OTHER FIRST CLASS	1009 4057.2	163 1209	12715	745	17.07
INT.	277.1 210.4	57 58	1817	86	21.13
J.P.L.	420.2	53	1492	85	17.55
NAT.W.	70.3	19	155	11	14.09
B & H	320.3	69	868	61	14.23

the middle of the season cricket stops and we all have a holiday to freshen up and come back ready to play again—that would help get rid of staleness and players to get over injuries and niggles."

Best batting performance: 210* Nottinghamshire v Middlesex, Lords 1984.
Best bowling performance: 7-23 New Zealand v India, Wellington 1975–76; 7-23 Nottinghamshire v Sussex, Trent Bridge 1979.

HASSAN, S.B.

Full Name: Sheikh Basharat Hassan.
Role: Right-hand bat, right arm medium bowler, occasional wicket-keeper.
Born: 24 March 1944, Nairobi, Kenya.
Height: 5' 11" **Weight:** 10st 10lbs.
Nickname: Basher.
County debut: 1966.
County cap: 1970.
Test debut: —
No. of Tests: 0 (Unofficial Tests: 18 for Kenya and 6 for East Africa.)
No. of One-Day Internationals: 0.
Benefit: £20,000 in 1978.
1000 runs in a season: 5.
50 wickets in a season: 0.
1st-Class 50s scored: 80.
1st-Class 100s scored: 15.
1st-Class 200s scored: 0.
1st-Class 5 w. in innings: 0.
1st-Class 10 w. in match: 0.
One-day 50s: 36.
One-day 100s 3.

Place in batting averages: 187 average: 21.70; (1983: 126 average: 26.97).
Place in bowling averages: — average: —; (1983 — average: —).
1st-Class catches 1984: 23 (career: 304).
Parents: Haji Sarwar Hussain (father) and Sairan Sheikh (mother).
Wife: Dorothy Ann.
Children: Jamil, 22 October 1980, Sarah, 30 June 1982.
Education: City High School, Nairobi.
Qualifications: Advanced coaching certificate.
Jobs outside cricket: Sales representative, printing, cars.
Family links with cricket: Father and brothers all play.
Overseas teams played for: Kenya, 1960–65, East Africa, 1962–65.
Overseas tours: West Indies, Dubai.

Cricket superstitions: "Never take off my 'necklace' which was given to me by my father."

Equipment used: Gunn & Moore.

Cricketers particularly learnt from: M.J.K. Smith, Sir Garfield Sobers, Tom Graveney.

Cricketers particularly admired: Viv Richards, Richard Hadlee.

Other sports: Hockey, football, athletics.

Relaxations: Watching Notts. County and Nottingham Forest football clubs, golf, athletics, gardening.

Extras: Played first Test for Kenya at age of 15½, the youngest in the country. Made debut for East Africa Invitation XI v M.C.C. 1963–64. Played for Kenya against touring sides. Scored a century with the aid of a runner v Kent at Canterbury in 1977. Best sprinter at Notts. Short-listed Kenyan Olympic team in 1960. Wants to be a first-class umpire when retires.

Best batting performance: 182* Nottinghamshire v Gloucestershire, Trent Bridge 1977.

LAST SEASON: BATTING

	I.	N.O.	R.	H.S.	AV.
TEST					
OTHER FIRST CLASS	27	4	499	103*	21.70
INT					
J.P.L.	3	2	37	22	–
NAT.W.					
B & H	3	0	60	25	20.00

CAREER: BATTING

	I.	N.O.	R.	H.S.	AV.
TEST					
OTHER FIRST CLASS	544		53	14285	182*	29.09
INT					
J.P.L.	194	21	5149	120*	29.76
NAT.W.	26	1	551	79	22.04
B & H	48	7	1070	99*	26.10

LAST SEASON: BOWLING

	O.	M.	R.	W.	AV.
TEST					
OTHER FIRST CLASS					
INT					
J.P.L.					
NAT.W.					
B & H					

CAREER: BOWLING

	O.	M.	R.	W.	AV.
TEST					
OTHER FIRST CLASS	141.2	35	407	6	67.83
INT					
J.P.L.	16.3	0	131	2	65.50
NAT.W.	7.1	2	20	3	6.67
B & H					

Q. 138. How old was Ian Botham when he first played for Somerset?

Q. 139. For how many seasons did Geoffrey Boycott captain Yorkshire?

HEMMINGS, E.E.

Full Name: Edward Ernest Hemmings.
Role: Right-hand bat, off-break bowler.
Born: 20 February 1949, Leamington Spa, Warwickshire.
Height: 5' 10" **Weight:** 13st.
Nickname: Eddie.
County debut: 1979 (Notts.).
County cap: 1980 (Notts.).
Test debut: 1982.
No. of Tests: 5.
No. of One-Day Internationals: 5.
1000 runs in a season: 0.
50 wickets in a season: 9.
1st-Class 50s scored: 16.
1st-Class 100s scored: 1.
1st-Class 200s scored: 0.
1st-Class 5 w. in innings: 45.
1st-Class 10 w. in match: 11.
One-day 50s: 1.
One-day 100s: 0.
Place in batting averages: 244 average: 14.59; (1983: 227 average: 13.00).
Place in bowling averages: 22 average: 23.62; (1983: 90 average: 33.89).
1st-Class catches 1984: 7 (career: 150).
Parents: Edward and Dorothy Phyliss·Hemmings.
Wife and date of marriage: Christine Mary, 23 October 1971.
Children: Thomas Edward, 26 July 1977; James Oliver, 9 September 1979.
Education: Campion School, Leamington Spa.
Family links with cricket: Father and father's father played Minor Counties and League cricket.
Overseas tours: Derrick Robins XI tour to South Africa 1975. Tour to Pakistan 1981 with International XI. Australia and New Zealand 1982–83.
Cricketers particularly learnt from: J.A. Jameson.
Off-season 1984–85: Out of work.
Equipment used: Gunn & Moore.
Other sports: Played amateur football, squash.
Relaxations: "Watching football at any level—especially junior. Dining out with my wife."
Extras: Debut for Warwickshire 1966, cap 1974. No longer wears glasses, plays in contact lenses. Started his career as a medium-pacer, and was thought of as a successor to Tom Cartwright. "I was even known as 'Tommy's Ghost' around Edgbaston". Suffers from asthma. Took a hat-trick for Warwickshire in 1977 but had to wait four years to receive the inscribed match ball, when he had

moved to Nottinghamshire. Hit first century— 127 n.o. v. Yorks. at Worksop, July 1982— after 16 years in first-class game.

Best batting performance: 127* Nottinghamshire v Yorkshire, Worksop 1982.

Best bowling performance: 10-175 International XI v West Indies XI, Kingston 1982–83.

LAST SEASON: BATTING

	I.	N.O.	R.	H.S.	AV.
TEST					
OTHER FIRST CLASS	24	7	248	35	14.59
INT					
J.P.L.	5	3	44	17*	22.00
NAT.W.	2	0	29	22	14.50
B & H	2	1	0	0*	–

CAREER: BATTING

	I.	N.O.	R.	H.S.	AV.
TEST	10	1	198	95	22.00
OTHER FIRST CLASS	426	94	6650	127*	20.03
INT	2	0	4	3	2.00
J.P.L.	125	33	1270	44*	13.80
NAT.W.	17	2	168	22	11.20
B & H	32	9	324	61*	14.08

LAST SEASON: BOWLING

	O.	M.	R.	W.	AV.
TEST					
OTHER FIRST CLASS	797.5	234	2220	94	23.62
INT					
J.P.L.	119	4	586	22	26.63
NAT.W.	24	2	87	4	21.75
B & H	58.3	11	163	5	32.60

CAREER: BOWLING

	O.	M.	R.	W.	AV.
TEST	244.4	71	588	12	49.00
OTHER FIRST CLASS	9755.2	2741	26077	920	28.35
INT	41.3	4	175	5	35.00
J.P.L.	1219	84	5601	200	28.01
NAT.W.	241.1	39	794	21	37.81
B & H	529	66	1630	50	32.60

HENDRICK, M.

Full Name: Michael Hendrick.
Role: Right-hand bat, right arm fast medium bowler.
Born: 22 October 1948, Darley Dale, Derbyshire.
Height: 6' 3"
Nickname: Hendo.
County debut: 1969, (for Derbyshire) 1982 (Nottinghamshire).
County cap: 1972.
Test debut: 1974.
No. of Tests: 30.
No. of One-Day Internationals: 22.
Benefit: 1980. £36,060.
1000 runs in a season: 0.
50 wickets in a season: 8.
1st-Class 50s scored: 0.
1st-Class 100s scored: 0.
1st-Class 200s scored: 0.

1st-Class 5 w. in innings: 29.
1st-Class 10 w. in match: 3.
One-day 50s: 0.
One-day 100s: 0.
Place in batting averages: — average: —; (1983: — average: —).
Place in bowling averages: — average: —; (1983: 4 average: 17.00).
1st-Class catches 1984: 2 (career: 176).
Wife: Kathy.
Children: Three.
Jobs outside cricket: Has worked for Electricity Board, Leicester, and as labourer.
Family links with cricket: Father was fast bowler.
Equipment used: Stuart Surridge bat.
Overseas tours: West Indies 1973–74; Australia, New Zealand 1974–75; Pakistan, New Zealand 1977–78; Australia 1978–79 and 1979–80, but returned early through injury. Declined tour of West Indies 1980–81.
Significant injuries in 1984: Knee operation two weeks before start of season.
Other sports: Shooting, fishing, golf.
Extras: Left Derbyshire at his own request at end of 1981 season. Banned from playing for England for joining 'Rebels' in South Africa.
Best batting performance: 46 Derbyshire v Essex, Chelmsford 1973.
Best bowling performance: 8-45 Derbyshire v Warwickshire, Chesterfield 1973.

LAST SEASON: BATTING

	I.	N.O.	R.	H.S.	AV.
TEST					
OTHER FIRST CLASS					
INT					
J.P.L.					
NAT.W.					
B & H					

CAREER: BATTING

	I.	N.O.	R.	H.S.	AV.
TEST	35	15	128	15	6.40
OTHER FIRST CLASS	267	109	1601	46	10.13
INT	10	5	6	2*	1.20
J.P.L.	58	27	299	21	9.65
NAT.W.	10	3	64	18	9.14
B & H	19	9	130	32	13.00

LAST SEASON: BOWLING

	O.	M.	R.	W.	AV.
TEST					
OTHER FIRST CLASS	72.1	33	86	8	10.75
INT					
J.P.L.					
NAT.W.					
B & H	6	0	20	0	—

CAREER: BOWLING

	O.	M.	R.	W.	AV.
TEST	226.6 732.2	42 207	2248	87	25.84
OTHER FIRST CLASS	246.2 5696.5	64 1647	13537	683	19.82
INT.	36 160	2 34	681	35	19.45
J.P.L.	186.1	125	3249	149	21.81
NAT.W.	224.1	51	588	33	17.81
B & H	463.1	108	1125	76	14.81

JOHNSON, P.

Full Name: Paul Johnson.
Role: Right-hand bat, right arm occasional bowler.
Born: 24 April 1965, Newark.
Height: 5' 8" **Weight:** 11st.
Nickname: Johno, Dwarf.
County debut: 1982.
County cap: No.
Test debut: —
No. of Tests: 0.
No. of One-Day Internationals: 0.
1000 runs in a season: 0.
50 wickets in a season: 0.
1st-Class 50s scored: 7.
1st-Class 100s scored: 3.
1st-Class 200s scored: 0.
1st-Class 5 w. in innings: 0.
1st-Class 10 w. in match: 0.
One-day 50s: 0.
One-day 100s: 0.
Place in batting averages: 20 average: 49.78; (1983: 147 average: 23.92).
Place in bowling averages: — average: —; (1983: — average: —).
1st-Class catches 1984: 7 (career: 16).
Parents: Donald and Joyce Johnson.
Marital status: Single.
Family links with cricket: Father played local cricket and is a qualified coach.
Education: Grove Comprehensive School, Newark.
Qualifications: Nine C.S.E.s, senior coaching certificate.

LAST SEASON: BATTING

	I.	N.O.	R.	H.S.	AV.
TEST					
OTHER FIRST CLASS	14	1	647	133	49.78
INT					
J.P.L.	9	2	93	29	13.29
NAT.W.					
B & H	1	0	5	5	–

CAREER: BATTING

	I.	N.O.	R.	H.S.	AV.
TEST					
OTHER FIRST CLASS	49	4	1349	133	29.98
INT					
J.P.L.	18	4	236	44	16.85
NAT.W.					
B & H	2	0	10	5	5.00

LAST SEASON: BOWLING

	O.	M.	R.	W.	AV.
TEST					
OTHER FIRST CLASS	4	0	23	2	11.50
INT					
J.P.L.					
NAT.W.					
B & H					

CAREER: BOWLING

	O.	M.	R.	W.	AV.
TEST					
OTHER FIRST CLASS	4	0	23	2	11.50
INT					
J.P.L.					
NAT.W.					
B & H					

Off-season 1984–85: Coaching, keeping fit, and working for Curtis Tools Ltd.
Cricketing superstitions: Always wear some kind of head wear, left pad on first.
Equipment used and endorsed: Gunn & Moore.
Cricketers particularly learnt from: "Too many to mention."
Other sports: Darts, football, soft tennis, snooker and pool. Follow football and ice-hockey.
Relaxations: Listening to music, watching good comedies and films, watching Forest and County.
Extras: Played for English Schools cricket in 1980–81 season. Youngest member ever to join the Nottinghamshire C.C.C. staff. Hit 16 sixes in School County Cup game v Joseph Whittaker, 195 not out. Played for Young England U-19, 1982 and 1983. Made 235 for Notts. 2nd XI, July 1982, aged 17.
Opinions on cricket: " Play every county once in a 4-day game per season. Counties should make more effort to play 2nd XI games on 1st-Class wickets or of a higher standard."
Best batting performance: 133 Nottinghamshire v Kent, Folkestone 1984.

MEE, S.R.

Full Name: Steven Robert Mee.
Role: Right-hand bat, right arm medium fast bowler.
Born: 6 April 1965, Nottingham.
Height: 6′ 7″ **Weight:** 15st. 9lbs.
Nickname: Pod.
County debut: 1984.
County cap: No.
Test debut: —
No. of Tests: 0.
No. of One-Day Internationals: 0.
1000 runs in a season: 0.
50 wickets in a season: 0.
1st-Class 50s scored: 0.
1st-Class 100s scored: 0.
1st-Class 200s scored: 0.
1st-Class 5 w. in innings: 0.
1st-Class 10 w. in match: 0.
One-day 50s: 0.
One-day 100s: 0.
Place in batting average: — average: —; (1983: — average: —).
Place in bowling averages: — average: —; (1983: — average: —).
Parents: Robert and Bernice Margaret Mee.
Marital status: Single.

Education: Ellis Guildford Comprehensive; High Pavement Sixth Form College.
Qualifications: 6 O-levels.
Jobs outside cricket: Labourer.
Off season 1984–85: Labouring.
Equipment used: Gunn & Moore.
Cricketers particularly learnt from: Mike Bore, Bob Willis ("never gives up").
Cricketers particularly admired: Dennis Lillee, Bob Willis, Derek Randall.
Other sports: Football, basketball, badminton, rugby. Watches American football.
Relaxations: Listening to music; watching good films.
Extras: Shared in record 10th wicket partnership for Notts 2nd XI v Yorkshire 2nd XI, July 1983 (120).
Opinions on cricket: "I don't like to see politics interfering with sport such as the situation with South Africa. This has cost a lot of their players a Test career as well as a number of English 'rebels'."

LAST SEASON: BATTING

	I.	N.O.	R.	H.S.	AV.
TEST					
OTHER FIRST CLASS					
INT					
J.P.L.					
NAT.W.					
B & H					

CAREER: BATTING

	I.	N.O.	R.	H.S.	AV.
TEST					
OTHER FIRST CLASS					
INT					
J.P.L.					
NAT.W.					
B & H					

LAST SEASON: BOWLING

	O.	M.	R.	W.	AV.
TEST					
OTHER FIRST CLASS	23	4	63	2	31.50
INT					
J.P.L.					
NAT.W.					
B & H					

CAREER: BOWLING

	O.	M.	R.	W.	AV.
TEST					
OTHER FIRST CLASS	23	4	63	2	31.50
INT					
J.P.L.					
NAT.W.					
B & H					

Q. 140. What England Test player, when and with what team, won an F.A. Cup-winner's medal?

NEWELL, M.

Full Name: Michael Newell.
Role: Right-hand opening bat, occ.
leg spin bowler or wicket-keeper.
Born: 25 February 1965, Blackburn.
Height: 5' 8" **Weight:** 10st. 7lbs.
Nickname: Sam or Horace.
County debut: 1984.
County cap: No.
Test debut: —
No. of Tests: 0.
No. of One-Day Internationals: 0.
1000 runs in a season: 0.
50 wickets in a season: 0.
1st-Class 50s scored: 1.
1st-Class 100s scored: 0.
1st-Class 200s scored: 0.
1st-Class 5 w. in innings: 0.
1st-Class 10 w. in match: 0.
One-day 50s: 0.
One-day 100s: 0.
Place in batting averages: — average: —; (1983: — average: —).
Place in bowling averages: — average: —; (1983: — average: —).
1st-Class catches 1984: 6 (career: 6).
Parents: Barry and Janet.
Marital status: Single.
Family links with cricket: "Father chairman of local club for which my brother Paul plays."
Education: West Bridgford Comprehensive.
Qualifications: 8 O-levels, 3 A-levels. Qualified coach.

LAST SEASON: BATTING

	I.	N.O.	R.	H.S.	AV.
TEST					
OTHER FIRST CLASS	7	1	109	76	18.17
INT					
J.P.L.					
NAT.W.					
B & H					

CAREER: BATTING

	I.	N.O.	R.	H.S.	AV.
TEST					
OTHER FIRST CLASS	7	1	109	76	18.17
INT					
J.P.L.					
NAT.W.					
B & H					

LAST SEASON: BOWLING

	O.	M.	R.	W.	AV.
TEST					
OTHER FIRST CLASS	4	0	14	0	–
INT					
J.P.L.					
NAT.W.					
B & H					

CAREER: BOWLING

	O.	M.	R.	W.	AV.
TEST					
OTHER FIRST CLASS	4	0	14	0	–
INT					
J.P.L.					
NAT.W.					
B & H					

Jobs outside cricket: Part-time barman; also worked in childrens' home last winter.
Off-season 1984–85: Coaching and working in Nottingham.
Cricketing superstitions: Always puts right pad on first; always bats in short sweater and long-sleeved shirt.
Equipment used: Gunn & Moore.
Overseas tours: N.C.A. U-19 tour to Holland 1983.
Cricketers particularly learnt from: All the batsmen at Notts., Mike Bore and Bob White.
Cricketers particularly admired: Richard Hadlee and Graham Gooch.
Other sports: Football ("of a low standard"); watches rugby union and football.
Relaxations: Good films, music and drinking.
Opinions on cricket: "Championship should keep the 3-day format. Shirt sponsorship should be allowed to be much bigger, like on football shirts."
Best batting performance: 76 Nottinghamshire v Cambridge University, Trent Bridge 1984.

PICK, R.A.

Full name: Robert Andrew Pick.
Role: Left-hand bat, right arm fast medium bowler.
Born: 19 November 1963, Nottingham.
Height: 5′ 10″ **Weight:** 12st. 7lbs.
Nickname: Picky, Toothy, Dad.
County Debut: 1983.
County cap: No.
Test debut: —
No. of Tests: 0.

No. of One-Day Internationals: 0.
1000 runs in a season: 0.
50 wickets in a season: 0.
1st-Class 50s scored: 0.
1st-Class 100s scored: 0.
1st-Class 200s scored: 0.
1st-Class 5 w. in innings: 2.
1st-Class 10 w. in match: 1.
One-day 50s: 0.
One-day 100s: 0.
Place in batting averages: 205 average: 19.20; (1983: — average: —).
Place in bowling averages: 72 average: 30.92; (1983: — average: —)
1st-Class catches 1984: 3 (career: 3).
Parents: Bob and Lillian.

Marital status: Single.
Family links with cricket: Dad, uncles and cousins all play local cricket.
Education: Alderman Derbyshire Comprehensive, High Pavement sixth form.
Qualifications: 6 O-levels, 1 A-level.
Jobs outside cricket: Labourer.
Equipment used: Gunn & Moore.
Cricketers particularly admired: Bob White, Mike Hendrick and Mike Harris.
Other sports: Football, basketball and fishing.
Relaxations: Good food and music.
Extras: Played three tests for Young England against Young Australia 1983.
Opinions on cricket: More freedom for players regarding advertising.
Best batting performance: 27* Nottinghamshire v Oxford University, Oxford 1984.
Best bowling performance: 5-25 Nottinghamshire v Oxford University, Oxford 1984.

LAST SEASON: BATTING

	I.	N.O.	R.	H.S.	AV.
TEST					
OTHER FIRST CLASS	10	5	96	27*	19.20
INT					
J.P.L.	2	1	1	1*	–
NAT.W.	1	1	1	1*	–
B & H					

CAREER: BATTING

	I.	N.O.	R.	H.S.	AV.
TEST					
OTHER FIRST CLASS	18	7	180	27*	16.36
INT					
J.P.L.	3	1	5	4	2.50
NAT.W.	2	2	35	34*	–
B & H					

LAST SEASON: BOWLING

	O.	M.	R.	W.	AV.
TEST					
OTHER FIRST CLASS	243.5	52	773	25	30.92
INT					
J.P.L.	69	1	354	8	44.25
NAT.W.	24	1	103	2	51.50
B & H					

CAREER: BOWLING

	O.	M.	R.	W.	AV.
TEST					
OTHER FIRST CLASS	378.3	68	1273	32	39.78
INT					
J.P.L.	109	1	547	14	39.07
NAT.W.	36	3	163	4	40.75
B & H					

Q. 141. Who had the higher Test batting average, Hobbs or Sutcliffe?

Q. 142. What, when and by whom is the best Test bowling analysis?

RANDALL, D.W.

Full Name: Derek William Randall.
Role: Right-hand bat; specialist fielder.
Born: 24 February 1951, Retford, Nottinghamshire.
Height: 5′ 8½″ **Weight:** 11st.
Nickname: Arkle, Rags.
County debut: 1972.
County cap: 1973.
Benefit: 1983 (£42,000).
Test debut: 1976–77.
No. of Tests: 47.
No. of One-Day Internationals: 48.
1000 runs in a season: 9.
50 wickets in a season: 0.
1st-Class 50s scored: 107.
1st-Class 100s scored: 30.
1st-Class 200s scored: 2.
1st-Class 5 w. in innings: 0.
1st-Class 10 w. in match: 0.
One-day 50s: 36.
One-day 100s: 4.

Place in batting averages: 46 average: 41.29; (1983: 101 average: 29.89).
Place in bowling averages: — average: —; (1983: — average: —).
1st-Class catches 1984: 26 (career: 232).
Parents: Frederick and Mavis Randall.
Wife and date of marriage: Elizabeth, September 1973.
Children: Simon, June 1977.
Education: Sir Frederick Milner Secondary Modern School, Retford.
Qualifications: O.N.C. Mechanical engineering. Mechanical draughtsman.
Jobs outside cricket: Coaching.
Family links with cricket: Father played local cricket, "tried to bowl fast off a long run and off the wrong foot too!"
Overseas tours: India, Sri Lanka and Australia 1976–77, Pakistan and New Zealand 1977–78, Australia 1978–79, Australia and India 79–80. Toured Australia and New Zealand with England 1979–80 and 1982–83. New Zealand and Pakistan 1983–84.
Overseas teams played for: North Perth, Australia.
Cricketers particularly learnt from: Sir Gary Sobers. Tom Graveney was boyhood idol. Reg Simpson.
Equipment used: Gunn & Moore.
Other sports: Football, squash, golf.
Relaxations: Listening to varied selection of tapes. Family man.
Extras: Played in one John Player League match in 1971 for Notts. Before

joining Notts. staff, played for Retford Cricket Club in the Bassetlaw League, and helped in Championship wins of 1968 and 1969. Sings and talks to himself when batting. Earned praise from England tour manager Alec Bedser for walking after an appeal for caught at the wicket v Queensland in December 1979, although appeal turned down by umpire. One of the finest fielders in Test and county cricket. According to his wife Liz: "When we were first married, Derek used to throw the teacups behind his back and catch them. That was one way he got out of doing the dishes!" Scored 174 in Centenary Test v Australia 1977.

Opinions on cricket: Championship needs to return to 100-over first innings.
Best batting performance: 209 Nottinghamshire v Middlesex, Trent Bridge 1979.

LAST SEASON: BATTING

	I.	N.O.	R.	H.S.	AV.
TEST	2	0	1	1	0.50
OTHER FIRST CLASS	38	3	1527	136	43.63
INT	1	0	8	8	–
J.P.L.	12	6	357	66*	59.50
NAT.W.	2	0	75	71	37.50
B & H	6	2	212	103*	53.00

CAREER: BATTING

	I.	N.O.	R.	H.S.	AV.
TEST	79	5	2470	174	33.38
OTHER FIRST CLASS	470	43	15978	209	36.82
INT	44	5	1048	88	26.87
J.P.L.	146	18	3908	107*	30.53
NAT.W.	21	1	484	75	24.20
B & H	56	9	1571	103*	33.21

LAST SEASON: BOWLING

	O.	M.	R.	W.	AV.
TEST					
OTHER FIRST CLASS	9.4	0	43	3	14.33
INT					
J.P.L.					
NAT.W.					
B & H					

CAREER: BOWLING

	O.	M.	R.	W.	AV.
TEST	2	0	3	0	–
OTHER FIRST CLASS	38.1	3	182	6	30.33
INT	0.2	0	2	1	–
J.P.L.	0.3	0	6	0	–
NAT.W.					
B & H	2.5	0	5	0	–

Q. 143. Which wicket-keeper has made most dismissals in Tests?

Q. 144. Who, where and when, bowled most balls in a Test match? And how many?

RICE, C.E.B.

Full Name: Clive Edward Butler Rice.
Role: Right-hand bat, right arm fast medium bowler.
Born: 23 July 1949, Johannesburg, South Africa.
Height: 6' 0" **Weight:** 13st 3lbs.
Nickname: Ricey.
County debut: 1975.
County Cap: 1975.
Benefit: 1982 in South Africa.
Test debut: —
No. of Tests: 0.
No. of One-Day Internationals: 0.
1000 runs in a season: 10.
50 wickets in a season: 4.
1st-Class 50s scored: 97.
1st-Class 100s scored: 30.
1st-Class 200s scored: 3.
1st-Class 5 w. in innings: 20.
1st-Class 10 w. in match: 1.
One-day 50s: 48.
One-day 100s: 7.

Place in batting averages: 22 average: 48.53; (1983: 67 average: 36.64).
Place in bowling averages: 65 average: 29.95; (1983: — average: —).
1st-Class catches 1984: 21 (career: 268).
Parents: Patrick and Angela Rice.
Wife and date of marriage: Susan Elizabeth, 28 February 1975.
Children: Jackie Elizabeth, 27 June 1981, Mark Richard, 11 August 1983.
Education: Sandringham Primary School, St John's College and Damelin College, Johannesburg; Natal University, Pietermaritzburg.
Jobs outside cricket: Director of companies.
Family links with cricket: Grandfather, Phillip Syndercombe Bower, played for Repton and Oxford University. Brother, Richard Patrick Butler Rice, selected for Transvaal B but unavailable because of university exams. Brother, John Cromwell Rice, Captain of school 1st XI.
Overseas tours: World Team in World Series Cricket, Australia 1978–79.
Overseas teams played for: World Series Cricket; Transvaal; Bedfordview C.C., Johannesburg.
Cricketers particularly learnt from: Don Mackay-Coghill and Ali Bacher, Graeme Pollock.
Cricketers particularly admired: Mike Procter, Graeme Pollock, Richard Hadlee, Dennis Lillee.
Cricket superstitions: "111, 222 or 333 on scoreboard."

Off-season 1984–85: Playing in South Africa for Transvaal.
Equipment used: Stuart Surridge.
Other sports: Follow English football, rugby, motor racing.
Relaxations: Reading, listening to music, studying stock markets.
Extras: Writes for local South African newspapers. Captain of Bedfordview C.C., Johannesburg. Made debut for Transvaal in 1969. Professional for Ramsbottom in Lancashire League, 1973. Originally appointed Captain of Nottinghamshire in 1978 but was at first relieved of his appointment after signing for World Series Cricket. Reappointed for 1979. Played 3 "Supertests" for W.S.C. Was sponsored at 5 rands (£2.77) a run, 50 rands (£27) a wicket, and 100 rands (£55) a catch in the 1980–81 Currie Cup competition in S. Africa. Wisden Cricketer of the Year 1981. Most runs in John Player League in a season: 814 in 1977. Highest score for Transvaal in Datsun Shield, 169 v Griqualand West. Highest score for Notts. in John Player League, 120 against Glamorgan. 1984 winner of Silk Cut Challenge all-rounders competition.
Opinions on present state of cricket: "Players need to play a far bigger role in the running of the game, and in its structure in the future. It's about time the banning of players earning a living in South Africa was scrapped and a logical approach was adopted by the authorities and players alike."
Best batting performance: 246 Nottinghamshire v Sussex, Hove 1976.
Best bowling performance: 7-62 Transvaal v W. Province, Johannesburg 1975–76.

LAST SEASON: BATTING

	I.	N.O.	R.	H.S.	AV.
TEST					
OTHER FIRST CLASS	39	7	1553	152*	48.53
INT					
J.P.L.	15	2	504	98*	38.76
NAT.W.	2	1	70	57	–
B & H	6	0	182	94	30.33

CAREER: BATTING

	I.	N.O.	R.	H.S.	AV.
TEST					
OTHER FIRST CLASS	559	85	19099	246	40.29
INT					
J.P.L.	141	25	5069	120*	43.69
NAT.W.	17	1	348	71	21.75
B & H	44	5	1339	130*	34.33

LAST SEASON: BOWLING

	O.	M.	R.	W.	AV.
TEST					
OTHER FIRST CLASS	206	53	569	19	29.95
INT					
J.P.L.	51.4	1	272	9	30.22
NAT.W.					
B & H	43	4	162	14	11.57

CAREER: BOWLING

	O.	M.	R.	W.	AV.
TEST					
OTHER FIRST CLASS	5934	1555	15645	713	21.94
INT					
J.P.L.	674.1	45	2887	129	22.37
NAT.W.	120	19	367	24	15.29
B & H	338	54	1080	62	17.42

Q. 145. What wicket-keeper has got most stumping victims in Test matches?

ROBINSON, R.T.

Full Name: Robert Timothy Robinson.
Role: Right-hand opening bat.
Born: 21 November 1958, Sutton-in-Ashfield, Nottinghamshire.
Height: 5' 11½" **Weight:** 12st 3lbs.
Nickname: Robbo, Chop.
County debut: 1978.
County cap: 1983.
Test debut: —
No. of Tests: 0.
No. of One-Day Internationals: 0.
1000 runs in a season: 2.
50 wickets in a season: 0.
1st-Class 50s scored: 33.
1st-Class 100s scored: 8.
1st-Class 200s scored: 1.
1st-Class 5 w. in innings: 0.
1st-Class 10 w. in match: 0.
One-day 50s: 10.
One-day 100s: 0.
Place in batting averages: 18 average: 50.80; (1983: 44 average: 40.68).
Place in bowling averages: — average: —; (1983: average: —).
1st-Class catches 1984: 16 (career: 55).
Parents: Eddy and Christine Robinson.
Marital status: Single.
Education: Dunstable Grammar School; High Pavement College, Nottingham. Sheffield University.
Qualifications: Honours degree in Accounting and Financial Management.
Family links with cricket: Father, uncle, cousin and brother played local cricket. Brother played for Nottinghamshire Schoolboys.
Jobs outside cricket: Trainee accountant.
Off-season 1984–85: On tour to India and Australia with England.
Cricketing superstitions: Always puts left pad on first.
Equipment used and endorsed: Gunn & Moore.
Overseas tours: N.C.A. Under-19 tour 1976.
Overseas teams played for: Durban Collegians 1980–81 in South Africa.
Cricketers particularly learnt from: Clive Rice, Mike Harris.
Other sports: Soccer, golf, squash, badminton. Follow rugby.
Relaxations: Driving, listening to all music, films, doing nothing.
Extras: Played for Northants 2nd XI in 1974–75 and for Nottinghamshire 2nd XI in 1977. Had soccer trials with Portsmouth, Chelsea and Q.P.R.
Best batting performance: 207 Nottinghamshire v Warwickshire, Trent Bridge 1983.

LAST SEASON: BATTING

	I.	N.O.	R.	H.S.	AV.
TEST					
OTHER FIRST CLASS	47	7	2032	171	50.80
INT					
J.P.L.	14	1	550	97*	42.30
NAT.W.	2	0	67	46	33.50
B & H	6	0	178	71	29.67

CAREER: BATTING

	I.	N.O.	R.	H.S.	AV.
TEST					
OTHER FIRST CLASS	189	24	6117	207	34.95
INT					
J.P.L.	61	7	1585	98*	39.35
NAT.W.	8	1	219	46	31.29
B & H	19	2	379	77*	22.29

LAST SEASON: BOWLING

	O.	M.	R.	W.	AV.
TEST					
OTHER FIRST CLASS					
INT					
J.P.L.					
NAT.W.					
B & H					

CAREER: BOWLING

	O.	M.	R.	W.	AV.
TEST					
OTHER FIRST CLASS	15	0	94	2	47.00
INT					
J.P.L.					
NAT.W.					
B & H					

SAXELBY, K.

Full Name: Kevin Saxelby.
Role: Right-hand bat; right arm medium bowler.
Born: 23 February 1959.
Height: 6′ 2″ **Weight:** 14st.
Nickname: Sax.
County debut: 1978.
County cap: 1984.
Test debut: —
No. of Tests: 0.
No. of One-Day Internationals: 0.
1000 runs in a season: 0.
50 wickets in a season: 1.
1st-Class 50s scored: 1.
1st-Class 100s scored: 0.
1st-Class 200s scored: 0.
1st-Class 5 w. in innings: 3.
1st-Class 10 w. in match: 0.
One-day 50s: 0.
One-day 100s: 0.
Place in batting averages: 220 average: 17.82; (1983: 240 average: 10.96).
Place in bowling averages: 93 average: 33.87; (1983: 49 average: 26.74).
1st-Class catches 1984: 2 (career: 10).
Parents: George Kenneth and Hilda Margaret Saxelby.
Wife: Peta Jean Wendy.
Education: Magnus Grammar School, Newark.

Qualifications: 4 A-levels, 10 O-levels.
Overseas teams played for: North Perth, Australia 1979–80; Durban Collegians, South Africa 1980–81, Alma-Marist (Cape Town) 1982–83.
Off-season 1984–85: Farming.
Significant injuries in 1984: Pelvic strain.
Other sports: Rugby.
Relaxations: "Gardening and drinking Marston's Pedigree at the 'King's Arms', Newark.
Best batting performance: 59* Nottinghamshire v Derbyshire, Chesterfield 1982.
Best bowling performance: 5-43 Nottinghamshire v Middlesex, Lord's 1984.

LAST SEASON: BATTING

	I.	N.O.	R.	H.S.	AV.
TEST					
OTHER FIRST CLASS	19	8	196	27	17.82
INT					
J.P.L.	2	1	6	5*	–
NAT.W.	1	1	1	1*	–
B & H	1	1	3	3*	–

CAREER: BATTING

	I.	N.O.	R.	H.S.	AV.
TEST					
OTHER FIRST CLASS	71	19	671	59*	12.90
INT					
J.P.L.	19	10	90	23*	10.00
NAT.W.	2	1	13	12	–
B & H	8	5	37	13*	12.33

LAST SEASON: BOWLING

	O.	M.	R.	W.	AV.
TEST					
OTHER FIRST CLASS	516.5	140	1592	47	33.87
INT					
J.P.L.	92	4	468	12	39.00
NAT.W.	23.5	9	59	6	9.83
B & H	54.2	9	176	6	29.33

CAREER: BOWLING

	O.	M.	R.	W.	AV.
TEST					
OTHER FIRST CLASS	1341.5	330	4223	148	28.53
INT					
J.P.L.	315	7	1595	54	29.53
NAT.W.	45.5	9	142	9	15.78
B & H	170.2	19	608	24	25.33

Q. 146. Who has made the most catches in Tests? And how many?

Q. 147. When and where was an England Test batsman given out for obstructing the field? And who was he?

SCOTT, C.W.

Full Name: Christopher Wilmot
Scott.
Role: Right-hand bat, wicket-keeper.
Born: 23 January 1964, Lincoln.
Height: 5' 9" **Weight:** 11st.
Nickname: George.
County debut: 1981.
County cap: No.
Test debut: —
No. of Tests: 0.
No. of One-Day Internationals: 0.
1000 runs in a season: 0.
50 wickets in a season: 0.
1st-Class 50s scored: 1.
1st-Class 100s scored: 0.
1st-Class 200s scored: 0.
1st-Class 5 w. in innings: 0.
1st-Class 10 w. in match: 0.
One-day 50s: 0.
One-day 100s: 0.
Place in batting averages: — average: —; (1983: — average: —).
Place in bowling averages: — average: —; (1983: — average: —).
Parents: Kenneth and Kathleen Scott.
Marital status: Single.
Family links with cricket: Father and elder brother play for Collingham C.C.
Younger brother for Lincolnshire Under-19s.
Education: Thorpe-on-the-Hill Primary School; Robert Pattinson Comprehensive School.

LAST SEASON: BATTING

	I.	N.O.	R.	H.S.	AV.
TEST					
OTHER FIRST CLASS	2	1	26	15	—
INT					
J.P.L.	1	0	9	9	—
NAT.W.					
B & H					

CAREER: BATTING

	I.	N.O.	R.	H.S.	AV.
TEST					
OTHER FIRST CLASS	8	2	151	78	25.17
INT					
J.P.L.	1	0	9	9	—
NAT.W.					
B & H					

LAST SEASON: WICKET KEEPING

	C.	ST.		
TEST				
OTHER FIRST CLASS	6	—		
INT				
J.P.L.	2	—		
NAT.W.				
B & H				

CAREER: WICKET KEEPING

	C.	ST.		
TEST				
OTHER FIRST CLASS	13	2		
INT				
J.P.L.	2	—		
NAT.W.				
B & H				

Qualifications: 4 0-levels. 2 C.S.E.s. Cricket coach.
Jobs outside cricket: Farming.
Off-season 1984–85: Looking for any kind of job.
Equipment used: Gunn & Moore.
Overseas teams played for: Poverty Bay C.C. New Zealand 1983–84.
Cricketers particularly learnt from: Everyone at Notts.
Other sports: Rugby Union, soccer.
Relaxations: Watching films, listening to records.
Extras: One of the youngest players to play for Nottinghamshire in County Championship team – made debut at 17 years 157 days.
Best batting performance: 78 Nottinghamshire v Cambridge University, Cambridge 1983.

SUCH, P.M.

Full Name: Peter Mark Such.
Role: Right-hand bat, off-spinner.
Born: 12 June 1964, Helensburgh, Scotland.
Height: 6′ 1″ **Weight:** 11st. 7lbs.
Nickname: Suchy.
County debut: 1982.
County cap: No.
Test debut: —
No. of Tests: 0.
No. of One-Day Internationals: 0.
1000 runs in a season: 0.
50 wickets in a season: 0.
1st-Class 50s scored: 0.
1st-Class 100s scored: 0.
1st-Class 200s scored: 0.
1st-Class 5 w. in innings: 4.
1st-Class 10 w. in match: 0.
One-day 50s: 0.
One-day 100s: 0.
Place in batting averages: — average: —; (1983: — average: —).
Place in bowling averages: 14 average: 22.31; (1983: 110 average: 38.35).
1st-Class catches 1984: 6 (career: 19).
Parents: John and Margaret Such.
Marital status: Single.
Education: Lantern Lane Primary School; Harry Carlton Comprehensive.
Qualifications: 9 0-levels; 3 A-levels. Qualified cricket coach.
Jobs outside cricket: Van driver.

Off-season 1984–85: Van driver.
Family links with cricket: Father and brother village cricketers.
Cricketers particularly admired: Bob White and Eddie Hemmings.
Equipment used: Gunn & Moore.
Overseas teams: Kempton Park C.C. (South Africa) 1982–83.
Other sports: Hockey. Watch most other sports.
Relaxations: Music, T.V., films.
Extras: Played for Young England v Young Australia in 3 'Tests' in 1983.
Best batting performance: 16 Nottinghamshire v Middlesex, Lord's 1984.
Best bowling performance: 6-123 Nottinghamshire v Kent, Trent Bridge 1983.

LAST SEASON: BATTING

	I.	N.O.	R.	H.S.	AV.
TEST					
OTHER FIRST CLASS	10	5	29	16	5.80
INT					
J.P.L.					
NAT.W.					
B & H					

CAREER: BATTING

	I.	N.O.	R.	H.S.	AV.
TEST					
OTHER FIRST CLASS	34	12	45	16	2.05
INT					
J.P.L.	1	1	0	0*	–
NAT.W.					
B & H					

LAST SEASON: BOWLING

	O.	M.	R.	W.	AV.
TEST					
OTHER FIRST CLASS	386.5	122	937	42	22.31
INT					
J.P.L.					
NAT.W.					
B & H					

CAREER: BOWLING

	O.	M.	R.	W.	AV.
TEST					
OTHER FIRST CLASS	833	217	2441	87	28.06
INT					
J.P.L.	7	0	66	0	–
NAT.W.					
B & H					

COUNTY QUIZ

Q. 1. When was the club founded?
Q. 2. Who made the most first-class runs for the county last season, and how many?
Q. 3. What's the highest ever county total, and against whom?
Q. 4. Who took most wickets for the county last season, and how many?
Q. 5. What's the highest individual score for the county, who hit it, and when?
Q. 6. What's the highest scoring partnership for the county for any wicket?
Q. 7. How many times has the club won the County Championship?
Q. 8. What's the lowest ever total made by the county in one innings, when, and against whom?
Q. 9. Which bowler took the most first-class wickets in one season, when, and how many?
Q. 10. Which batsman hit the most runs in one season, when and how many?

Somerset

BOOTH, S.C.

Full Name: Stephen Charles Booth.
Role: Right-hand bat, slow left-arm orthodox bowler.
Born: Leeds, 30 October 1963.
Height: 5′ 9″ **Weight:** 10st 7lbs.
Nicknames: Boothy, Heathcliffe, Eh-up.
County debut: 1983.
County cap: No.
Test debut: —
No. of Tests: 0.
No. of One-Day Internationals: 0.
1000 runs in a season: 0.
50 wickets in a season: 0.
1st-Class 50s scored: 0.
1st-Class 100s scored: 0.
1st-Class 200s scored: 0.
1st-Class 5 w. in innings: 0.
1st-Class 10 w. in match: 0.
One-day 50s: 0.
One-day 100s: 0.

Place in batting averages: 249 average: 14.29; (1983: — average: —).
Place in bowling averages: 69 average: 30.84; (1983: 116 average: 40.43).
1st-Class catches 1984: 13 (career: 20).
Parents: Eric and Kathleen Booth.
Wife and date of marriage: Jane, 20 October 1984.
Family links with cricket: Younger brother, Simon, played Yorkshire Schools U-15.
Education: Boston Spa Comprehensive.
Qualifications: 6 'O' levels.
Off-season 1984–85: Working in Taunton.
Cricketing superstitions: Always puts left pad on first (more through habit).
Equipment used: Gunn & Moore, and Nike.
Cricketers particularly learnt from: Don Wilson, Andy Wagner.
Cricketers particularly admired: "Admire anyone who's played 1st-Class cricket."

Other sports: Football (try any sport).
Extras: Had spleen removed after a football accident in 1982. Released by Yorkshire to take up contract with Somerset.
Opinions on cricket: "Championship should be made into sixteen four-day games."
Best batting performance: 42 Somerset v Derbyshire, Taunton 1984.
Best bowling performance: 4-26 Somerset v Middlesex, Lord's 1983.

LAST SEASON: BATTING

	I.	N.O.	R.	H.S.	AV.
TEST					
OTHER FIRST CLASS	14	7	100	42	14.29
INT					
J.P.L.					
NAT.W.					
B & H					

CAREER: BATTING

	I.	N.O.	R.	H.S.	AV.
TEST					
OTHER FIRST CLASS	26	12	124	42	8.86
INT					
J.P.L.					
NAT.W.					
B & H					

LAST SEASON: BOWLING

	O.	M.	R.	W.	AV.
TEST					
OTHER FIRST CLASS	408.4	117	1172	38	30.84
INT					
J.P.L.					
NAT.W.					
B & H					

CAREER: BOWLING

	O.	M.	R.	W.	AV.
TEST					
OTHER FIRST CLASS	705	202	2021	59	34.25
INT					
J.P.L.					
NAT.W.					
B & H					

BOTHAM, I.T.

Full Name: Ian Terrence Botham.
Role: Right-hand bat, right arm fast medium bowler, slip fielder.
Born: 24 November 1955, Heswall, Cheshire.
Height: 6′ 1″ **Weight:** 14st 7lbs.
Nickname: Guy the Gorilla, Both.
County debut: 1974.
County cap: 1976.
Benefit: 1984.
Test debut: 1977.
No. of Tests: 73.
No. of One-Day Internationals: 72.
1000 runs in a season: 3.
50 wickets in a season: 7.
1st-Class 50s scored: 55.
1st-Class 100s scored: 22.
1st-Class 200s scored: 2.

1st-Class 5 w. in innings: 49.
1st-Class 10 w. in match: 7.
One-day 50s: 20.
One-day 100s: 2.
Place in batting averages: 109 average: 31.88; (1983: 47 average: 40.57).
Place in bowling averages: 38 average: 26.47; (1983: 85 average: 33.09).
1st-Class catches 1984: 7 (career 229).
Parents: Les and Marie Botham.
Wife and date of marriage: Kathryn, 31 January 1976.
Children: Liam James, 26 August 1977; Sarah Lianne, 3 February 1979.
Education: Millford Junior School, Yeovil; Buckler's Mead Secondary School, Yeovil.
Jobs outside cricket: Representative for father-in-law's company, Promuco.
Family links with cricket: Father played for Navy and Fleet Air Arm; mother played for V.A.D. nursing staff.
Overseas tours: Pakistan, New Zealand 1977–78; Australia 1978–79; Australia, India, 1979–80; West Indies 1981, as captain; India 1981–82, Australia and New Zealand, 1982–83.
Cricketers particularly learnt from: "Admired Gary Sobers."
Off-season 1984–85: Playing for Scunthorpe United and resting from cricket.
Cricket records: Holds record for having scored 1,000 runs and taken 100 wickets in fewest Test matches. First player to score a century and take eight wickets in an innings in a Test Match, v Pakistan at Lord's in 1978.
Equipment used: Duncan Fearnley bats; Gola boots; Lyle & Scott shirts.
Equipment endorsed: Duncan Fearnley; Gola; Lyle & Scott; Saab.
Other sports: Captained school soccer team, and has played for Scunthorpe United making debut as striker v Bournemouth in March 1980; Under-16 Somerset champion, badminton doubles. Offered terms by Crystal Palace.
Relaxations: "Time with my family"; golf (handicap 11), shooting, fishing (salmon and trout). First president of Clubworld Angling. Musical taste includes Rolling Stones, and Rod Stewart. Was once beaten by his wife at tennis—according to his wife. Has learned to fly. Racing, owns his own horses.
Significant injuries in 1984: Needed stitches in 3rd finger of left hand after a mishap with a champagne glass.
Extras: Captain of England 1980–81. Took five Australian wickets in his first day of Test Match cricket aged 21. Played for County 2nd XI 1971. On M.C.C. staff 1972–73. Played for county in last two John Player League matches 1973. Honorary townsman of Epworth, South Humberside, where he lives, and Freeman of Yeovil, Somerset. Subject of "This is Your Life" television programme in November 1981. Was Best Man at Viv Richards' wedding in March 1981 in Antigua. Published "The Incredible Tests 1981". Voted BBC TV Sportsview Sporting Personality of 1981. Having a go at baseball in Los Angeles in September 1981 easily exceeded the striking rate of established American baseball stars: he complained that Americans could not pitch the ball fast enough. Scored fastest 100 of 1982 season (131 n.o.) v. Warwickshire in 52 minutes. Scored 200 in 272 minutes for England v. India at Oval, 9 July 1982, third fastest Test century by an Englishman, after Walter Hammond (240 mins.

v. New Zealand in 1932). Denis Compton (245 mins. v. Pakistan in 1954).
Crashed two £12,000 sports cars at 100 m.p.h. in same afternoon in May 1982.
Among the books he chose to take to a desert island was Jack Fingleton's book
on the great Australia cricketer "The Immortal Victor Trumper".
Best batting performance: 228 Somerset v Gloucestershire, Taunton 1980.
Best bowling performance: 8-34 England v Pakistan, Lord's 1978.

LAST SEASON: BATTING

	I.	N.O.	R.	H.S.	AV.
TEST	11	0	353	81	32.09
OTHER FIRST CLASS	15	1	444	90	31.72
INT	3	0	39	22	13.00
J.P.L.	8	0	235	73	29.38
NAT.W.	3	1	45	30*	22.50
B & H	5	1	131	48*	32.75

CAREER: BATTING

	I.	N.O.	R.	H.S.	AV.
TEST	117	3	4159	208	36.48
OTHER FIRST CLASS	270	23	7748	228	31.39
INT	64	8	1147	65	20.48
J.P.L.	109	16	2616	106	28.12
NAT.W.	26	6	724	96*	36.20
B & H	41	6	726	57*	20.74

LAST SEASON: BOWLING

	O.	M.	R.	W.	AV.
TEST	219.2	42	871	26	33.50
OTHER FIRST CLASS	230.2	51	691	33	20.94
INT	28	1	125	3	41.67
J.P.L.	49.3	2	216	9	24.00
NAT.W.	30	6	107	6	17.83
B & H	55	6	212	10	21.20

CAREER: BOWLING

	O.	M.	R.	W.	AV.
TEST	259.4 2466.4	42 595	8191	312	26.25
OTHER FIRST CLASS	190.3 6683	43 1556	13390	540	24.80
INT	38.7 575.1	2 72	2533	96	26.38
J.P.L.	812.2	52	3514	152	23.11
NAT.W.	310.3	54	1042	40	26.05
B & H	484.1	93	1636	76	21.53

BREAKWELL, D.

Full Name: Dennis Breakwell.
Role: Assistant coach, left-hand bat,
slow left-arm bowler.
Born: 2 July 1948, Brierley Hill.
Height: 5' 9" **Weight:** 12st.
Nicknames: Breakley or the Severed
Nerve.
County debut: 1973.
County cap: 1976.
Test debut: —
No. of Tests: 0.
No. of One-Day Internationals: 0.
1000 runs in a season: 0.
50 wickets in a season: 1.
1st-Class 50s scored: 16.
1st-Class 100s scored: 1.
1st-Class 200s scored: 0.
1st-Class 5 w. in innings: 12.

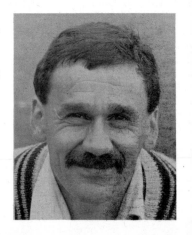

1st-Class 10 w. in match: 1.
One-day 50s: 0.
One-day 100s: 0.
Place in batting averages: — average: —; (1983: — average: —).
Place in bowling averages: — average: —; (1983: — average: —).
1st-Class catches 1984: 0 (career: 81).
Parents: John Morgan and Florence Emily.
Wife and date of marriage: Susan, 11 November 1977.
Children: James Stuart, 12 January 1977; Donna Louise, 8 May 1977.
Family links with cricket: Father and two brothers all good club cricketers.
Education: Ounsdale Comprehensive, Wombourne, Staffs.
Equipment used: Stuart Surridge.
Equipment endorsed: Lyle & Scott.
Cricketers particularly learnt from: My father.
Other sports: Fishing, football, sport in general.
Extras: Debut in 1969 for Northants. Released end of 1981. Assistant coach at Somerset with special responsibilities for schools.
Opinions on cricket: "All groundsmen should have full power and say on pitches and grounds whatever the circumstances."
Best batting performance: 100* Somerset v New Zealanders, Taunton 1978.
Best bowling performance: 8-39 Northamptonshire v Kent, Dover 1970.

LAST SEASON: BATTING

	I.	N.O.	R.	H.S.	AV.
TEST					
OTHER FIRST CLASS					
INT					
J.P.L.					
NAT.W.					
B & H					

CAREER: BATTING

	I.	N.O.	R.	H.S.	AV.
TEST					
OTHER FIRST CLASS	306	64	4792	100*	19.80
INT					
J.P.L.	102	27	1108	44*	14.77
NAT.W.	11	4	88	19*	12.57
B & H	20	4	190	36*	11.88

LAST SEASON: BOWLING

	O.	M.	R.	W.	AV.
TEST					
OTHER FIRST CLASS					
INT					
J.P.L.					
NAT.W.	7	0	45	0	—
B & H					

CAREER: BOWLING

	O.	M.	R.	W.	AV.
TEST					
OTHER FIRST CLASS	5012.4	1518	13008	422	30.83
INT					
J.P.L.	392.1	29	1766	65	27.17
NAT.W.	103	18	352	6	58.67
B & H	150.4	24	477	15	31.80

Q. 148. What was extraordinary about Australia v West Indies at Brisbane, 1960–61?

CROWE, M.D.

Full Name: Martin David Crowe.
Role: Right-hand bat, right arm
medium pace bowler, slip or short leg
fielder.
Born: 22 September 1962,
Auckland, New Zealand.
Height: 6' 1½" **Weight:** 13st. 10lbs.
Nickname: Hogan.
County debut: 1984.
County cap: 1984.
Test debut: 1981–82.
No. of Tests: 13.
No. of One-Day Internationals: 18.
1000 runs in a season: 1.
50 wickets in a season: 0.
1st-Class 50s scored: 25.
1st-Class 100s scored: 17.
1st-Class 200s scored: 0.
1st-Class 5 w. in innings: 2.
1st-Class 10 w. in match: 0.
One-day 50s: 9.

One-day 100s: 2.
Place in batting averages: 13 average: 54.46; (1983: 6 average: 58.50).
Place in bowling averages: 68 average: 30.75; (1983: — average: —).
1st-Class catches 1984: 28 (career: 94).
Parents: David William and Audrey Sybil.
Marital status: Single.
Family links with cricket: Father played for Canterbury and Wellington in
Plunkett Shield; brother Jeff played for South Australia 1977–82, Auckland
and New Zealand 1983–.
Education: Auckland Grammar School.
Qualifications: School Certificate, University entrance, Advanced coach.
Jobs outside cricket: Groundsman for Auckland Grammar and Cornwall
Cricket Club 1980–82. Promotions officer for Hawkes Bay Cricket
Association 1983–84.
Off-season 1984–85: Touring Pakistan, Australia and West Indies with New
Zealand side. Domestic season includes Test series v Pakistan and Central
Districts in Shell Series.
Cricketing superstitions: Left pad on first. When out hit gum away with bat.
Equipment used: Duncan Fearnley.
Equipment endorsed: Mitre footwear.
Overseas tours: New Zealand to England 1983; New Zealand to Sri Lanka
1984; New Zealand to Australia 1982.
Overseas teams played for: Auckland 1979–83 Central Districts 1983–84;

Somerset 1984; D.B. Close's XI 1982, New Zealand.

Cricketers particularly learnt from: Brother Jeff, John Wright, John Wiltshire, Ian Botham.

Cricketers particularly admired: R.J. Hadlee, G.S. Chappell, I.V.A. Richards, I.T. Botham.

Other sports: Squash, tennis, golf, rugby; follow soccer, New Zealand athletics, Aussie rules.

Significant injuries in 1984: Broken left thumb; bruised shin.

Relaxations: "Relaxing in a spa pool; watching videos; music from my Walkman; photography; being around my family."

Extras: New Zealand's 150th Test cricketer and 7th youngest, 3rd youngest to score Test 100. Won scholarship as "New Zealand Young Player of the Year" to Lord's for 1981 season; played for Bradford C.C. in Yorkshire league holding all-time records for batting.

Best batting performance: 190 Somerset v Leicestershire, Taunton 1984.

Best bowling performance: 5-18 Central Districts v Auckland, Auckland 1983–84.

LAST SEASON: BATTING

	I.	N.O.	R.	H.S.	AV.
TEST					
OTHER FIRST CLASS	41	6	1870	190	54.46
INT					
J.P.L.	15	0	457	78	30.46
NAT.W.	3	0	141	114	47.00
B & H	5	1	152	89	38.00

CAREER: BATTING

	I.	N.O.	R.	H.S.	AV.
TEST	21	1	429	100	21.45
OTHER FIRST CLASS	118	20	4930	190	50.31
INT	17	3	547	105*	39.07
J.P.L.	15	0	457	78	30.46
NAT.W.	3	0	141	114	47.00
B & H	5	1	152	89	38.00

LAST SEASON: BOWLING

	O.	M.	R.	W.	AV.
TEST					
OTHER FIRST CLASS	435	101	1353	44	30.75
INT					
J.P.L.	80	3	402	10	40.20
NAT.W.	30	6	75	6	12.50
B & H	49	3	182	10	18.20

CAREER: BOWLING

	O.	M.	R.	W.	AV.
TEST	117	18	225	3	75.00
OTHER FIRST CLASS	711.3	172	2303	78	29.53
INT	52	5	262	9	29.11
J.P.L.	80	3	402	10	40.20
NAT.W.	30	6	75	6	12.50
B & H	49	3	182	10	18.20

Q. 149. What have W.R. Endean of South Africa, A.M.J. Hilditch of Australia, and Mohsin Khan of Pakistan in common?

DAVIS, M.R.

Full name: Mark Richard Davis.
Role: Left-hand bat; left arm
fast medium bowler.
Born: 26 February 1962, Kilve,
Somerset.
Height: 6' ½" **Weight:** 12st. 7lbs.
Nickname: Pooch.
County debut: 1982.
County cap: No.
Test debut: —
No. of Tests: 0.
No. of One-Day Internationals: 0.
1000 runs in a season: 0.
50 wickets in a season: 1.
1st-Class 50s scored: 1.
1st-Class 100s scored: 0.
1st-Class 200s scored: 0.
1st-Class 5 w. in innings: 4.
1st-Class 10 w. in match: 1.
One-day 50s: 0.
One-day 100s: 0.
Place in batting averages: 183 average: 22.25; (1983: 294 average: 10.42).
Place in bowling averages: 24 average: 23.77; (1983: 94 average: 34.92)
1st-Class catches 1984: 6 (career: 15).
Parents: Penelope and Robert Ernest Charles Davis.
Marital status: Single.
Education: Kilve Primary School; Williton First and Middle School; West
Somerset School; Bridgwater College.
Qualifications: 7 O-levels.
Jobs outside cricket: Learning the building trade in my father's firm.
Off-season 1984–85: Building and cricket coaching.
Family links with cricket: "Father and relatives all play for my local club side,
Kilve."
Cricketers particularly learnt from: P.J. Robinson (Somerset coach), M.
Crowe, I. Botham, C. Dredge.
Cricketers particularly admired: I. Botham, M. Crowe.
Equipment used: Stuart Surridge.
Other sports: Squash and follow football.
Significant injuries during 1984: Shoulder injury—missed last month of
season.
Relaxations: "Music, skittles, my local pub."
Opinions on cricket: "County cricket should be on a four-day basis, playing
each county once and allowing players a greater appetite for the game.
Sponsors' names should be allowed on shirts (as in football) to encourage

greater investments from sponsors."

Best batting performance: 60* Somerset v Glamorgan, Taunton 1984.
Best bowling performance: 7-55 Somerset v Northants, Northampton 1984.

LAST SEASON: BATTING

	I.	N.O.	R.	H.S.	AV.
TEST					
OTHER FIRST CLASS	14	6	178	60*	22.25
INT					
J.P.L.	2	2	3	2*	–
NAT.W.	1	1	0	0*	–
B & H	3	0	12	7	4.00

CAREER: BATTING

	I.	N.O.	R.	H.S.	AV.
TEST					
OTHER FIRST CLASS	43	13	368	60*	12.27
INT					
J.P.L.	5	4	15	11	–
NAT.W.	1	1	0	0*	–
B & H	3	0	12	7	4.00

LAST SEASON: BOWLING

	O.	M.	R.	W.	AV.
TEST					
OTHER FIRST CLASS	500.4	108	1569	66	23.77
INT					
J.P.L.	70.5	8	213	9	23.67
NAT.W.	8	3	20	0	–
B & H	53	13	141	3	47.00

CAREER: BOWLING

	O.	M.	R.	W.	AV.
TEST					
OTHER FIRST CLASS	886.1	170	2923	108	28.38
INT					
J.P.L.	119.5	9	464	14	33.14
NAT.W.	8	3	20	0	–
B & H	64	14	166	5	33.20

DENNING, P.W.

Full Name: Peter William Denning.
Role: Left-hand bat, off-break bowler.
Born: 16 December 1949, Wells, Somerset.
Height: 5' 8" **Weight:** 10st 7lbs.
Nickname: Dasher.
County debut: 1969.
County cap: 1973.
Test debut: —
No. of Tests: 0.
No. of One-Day Internationals: 0.
Benefit: 1981.
1000 runs in a season: 6.
50 wickets in a season: 0.
1st-Class 50s scored: 69.
1st-Class 100s scored: 8.
1st-Class 200s scored: 0.
1st-Class 5 w. in innings: 0.
1st-Class 10 w. in match: 0.
One-day 50s: 27.
One-day 100s: 3.
Place in batting averages: 5 average: 67.60; (1983: 155 average: 22.97).

Place in bowling averages: — average: —; (1983: — average: —).
1st-Class catches 1984: 2 (career: 131).
Parents: Thomas Frederick and Maxine Betty Denning.
Wife and date of marriage: Ann, 7 April 1973.
Children: Claire, 28 September 1975; Samantha, 6 July 1978.
Education: Millfield School; St Luke's College, Exeter.
Qualifications: 10 O-levels, 3 A-levels, teacher's certificate.
Jobs outside cricket: Qualified teacher; demolition; civil service.
Other sports: Riding, soccer.
Relaxations: Gardening, decorating, reading.
Extras: Retired at end of 1984.
Best batting performance: 184 Somerset v Nottinghamshire, Trent Bridge 1980.

LAST SEASON: BATTING

	I.	N.O.	R.	H.S.	AV.
TEST					
OTHER FIRST CLASS	8	3	338	90	67.60
INT					
J.P.L.	7	0	109	45	15.57
NAT.W.					
B & H	4	0	120	63	30.00

CAREER: BATTING

	I.	N.O.	R.	H.S.	AV.
TEST					
OTHER FIRST CLASS	447	44	11559	184	28.68
INT					
J.P.L.	184	18	4565	112*	27.50
NAT.W.	28	1	888	145	32.89
B & H	56	7	1339	129	27.33

LAST SEASON: BOWLING

	O.	M.	R.	W.	AV.
TEST					
OTHER FIRST CLASS					
INT					
J.P.L.					
NAT.W.					
B & H					

CAREER: BOWLING

	O.	M.	R.	W.	AV.
TEST					
OTHER FIRST CLASS	24.2	4	96	1	—
INT					
J.P.L.	3	0	31	0	—
NAT.W.	0.1	0	4	0	—
B & H	0.2	0	4	0	—

Q. 150. What player has the highest Test batting average of all time?

Q. 151. How many Tests have Australia played against South Africa?

DREDGE, C.H.

Full Name: Colin Herbert Dredge.
Role: Left-hand bat, right arm medium bowler.
Born: 4 August 1954, Frome, Somerset.
Height: 6' 5" **Weight:** 14st. 7lbs.
Nickname: Herbie.
County debut: 1976.
County cap: 1978.
Test debut: —
No. of Tests: 0.
No. of One-Day Internationals: 0.
1000 runs in a season: 0.
50 wickets in a season: 4.
1st-Class 50s scored: 4.
1st-Class 100s scored: 0.
1st-Class 200s scored: 0.
1st-Class 5 w. in innings: 11.
1st-Class 10 w. in match: 0.
One-day 50s: 0.
One-day 100s: 0.
Place in batting averages: 260 average: 11.89; (1983: 218 average: 14.10).
Place in bowling averages: 55 average: 28.94; (1983: 51 average: 27.56).
1st-Class catches 1984: 12 (career: 70).
Parents: Frederick and Kathleen Dredge.
Wife and date of marriage: Mandy, 9 December 1978.
Children: David, 13 November 1979, Mark, 6 July 1981, Neil, 27 June 1983.
Education: Wesley Methodist School; Milk Street School; Oakfield School.

LAST SEASON: BATTING

	I.	N.O.	R.	H.S.	AV.
TEST					
OTHER FIRST CLASS	26	8	214	25*	11.89
INT					
J.P.L.	6	3	50	16*	16.67
NAT.W.	1	0	9	9	–
B & H	3	2	18	17*	–

CAREER: BATTING

	I.	N.O.	R.	H.S.	AV.
TEST					
OTHER FIRST CLASS	184	58	1749	56*	13.88
INT					
J.P.L.	44	23	233	25*	10.61
NAT.W.	7	3	20	9	5.00
B & H	17	10	65	17*	9.29

LAST SEASON: BOWLING

	O.	M.	R.	W.	AV.
TEST					
OTHER FIRST CLASS	533	125	1534	53	28.94
INT					
J.P.L.	73.3	3	349	10	34.90
NAT.W.	17.2	2	43	3	14.33
B & H	51	2	209	6	34.83

CAREER: BOWLING

	O.	M.	R.	W.	AV.
TEST					
OTHER FIRST CLASS	3960.1	944	11033	380	29.03
INT					
J.P.L.	785.1	39	3476	136	25.55
NAT.W.	208.3	28	704	29	24.28
B & H	355.2	41	1236	52	23.78

Qualifications: Qualified toolmaker. Served apprenticeship Rolls Royce Ltd., Patchway, Bristol.
Jobs outside cricket: Toolmaker.
Family links with cricket: One of ten children, eight boys and two girls; all the brothers have played cricket for Frome C.C.
Cricketers particularly learnt from: Peter White, Peter Robinson.
Off-season 1984–85: Working as a toolmaker. Playing football.
Equipment used: Duncan Fearnley.
Relaxations: "Football, watching TV, playing with my children."
Other sports: Played Western League football for Welton Rovers. Played for Bristol City Reserves 1974–76 and now for Frome Town A.F.C.
Best batting performance: 56* Somerset v Yorkshire, Harrogate 1977.
Best bowling performance: 6-37 Somerset v Gloucestershire, Bristol 1981.

FELTON, N.A.

Full Name: Nigel Alfred Felton.
Role: Left-handed batsman.
Born: 24 October 1960,
Guildford, Surrey.
Height: 5′ 7″ **Weight:** 11st.
Nickname: Will.
County debut: 1982.
County cap: No.
Test debut: —
No. of Tests: 0.
No. of One-Day Internationals: 0.
1000 runs in a season: 0.
50 wickets in a season: 0.
1st-Class 50s scored: 7.
1st-Class 100s scored: 2.
1st-Class 200s scored: 0.
1st-Class 5 w. in innings: 0.
1st-Class 10 w. in match: 0.
One-day 50s: 2.
One-day 100s: 0.

Place in batting averages: 188 average: 21.69; (1983: 80 average: 34.18).
Place in bowling averages: — average: —; (1983: — average: —).
1st-Class catches 1984: 6 (career: 11).
Parents: Ralph and Enid Felton.
Marital status: Single.
Education: Hawes Down Secondary School, West Wickham, Kent; Millfield School, Street, Somerset; Loughborough University.
Qualifications: 6 O-levels, 2 A-levels, B.Sc.(Hons), Cert. of Education P.E./Sports Sciences.

Off-season 1984–85: Grade cricket in Perth, W. Australia.
Overseas teams played for: English Schools Tour of India, 1976–77. Young England in Australia, 1978.
Cricketers particularly learnt from: Peter Denning.
Cricketers particularly admired: Alan Knott, Ian Botham and Viv Richards.
Equipment used: Gray-Nicolls.
Other sports: Football, squash, tennis, most ball games. Watches most sports, excluding show-jumping and racing unless the tipping reliable!
Relaxations: Music, sitting around doing as little as possible, politics and sport.
Extras: Joined Somerset in July 1981. Played a season for Kent in 1980 after leaving Millfield and before going to Loughborough. Left Kent at pre-season training 1981, due to the size of the staff. Joined Somerset at end of first year at Loughborough.
Opinions on cricket: "Despite the financial gains of the one-day game and our dependency on it, the 3-day game must be retained and not undervalued either by the media or the players."
Best batting performance: 173* Somerset v Kent, Taunton 1983.

LAST SEASON: BATTING

	I.	N.O.	R.	H.S.	AV.
TEST					
OTHER FIRST CLASS	24	1	499	101	21.69
INT					
J.P.L.	8	2	176	84*	29.33
NAT.W.	2	0	116	87	58.00
B & H					

CAREER: BATTING

	I.	N.O.	R.	H.S.	AV.
TEST					
OTHER FIRST CLASS	48	2	1221	173*	26.54
INT					
J.P.L.	8	2	176	84*	29.33
NAT.W.	2	0	116	87	58.00
B & H					

LAST SEASON: BOWLING

	O.	M.	R.	W.	AV.
TEST					
OTHER FIRST CLASS	0.1	0	4	0	–
INT					
J.P.L.					
NAT.W.					
B & H					

CAREER: BOWLING

	O.	M.	R.	W.	AV.
TEST					
OTHER FIRST CLASS	0.1	0	4	0	–
INT					
J.P.L.					
NAT.W.					
B & H					

Q. 152. What, where and when was the highest score in a Test, England v Australia?

Q. 153. What, where and when was the highest total of runs ever scored in a Test match?

GARD, T.

Full name: Trevor Gard.
Role: Wicket-keeper, batsman.
Born: 2 June 1957, West Lambrook.
Height: 5" 7' **Weight:** 10st. 7lbs.
Nickname: Gardy.
County debut: 1976.
County cap: 1983.
Test debut: —
No. of Tests: 0.
No. of One-Day Internationals: 0.
1000 runs in a season: 0.
50 wickets in a season: 0.
1st-Class 50s scored: 3.
1st-Class 100s scored: 0.
1st-Class 200s scored: 0.
1st-Class 5 w. in innings: 0.
1st-Class 10 w. in match: 0.
One-day 50s: 0.
One-day 100s: 0.
Place in batting averages: 265 average: 11.00; (1983: 206 average: 15.76).
Place in bowling averages: — average: —; (1983: — average: —).
Parents: David and Brenda Gard.
Wife and date of marriage: Amanda Kay, 29 September, 1979.
Education: Huish Episcopi Comprehensive School.
Qualifications: 0-levels in English and Technical Drawing. Aircraft Engineer Turner.
Jobs outside cricket: Engineering; farm worker.

LAST SEASON: BATTING

	I.	N.O.	R.	H.S.	AV.
TEST					
OTHER FIRST CLASS	24	5	209	26	11.00
INT					
J.P.L.	5	2	21	11	7.00
NAT.W.					
B & H	4	2	28	19	14.00

CAREER: BATTING

	I.	N.O.	R.	H.S.	AV.
TEST					
OTHER FIRST CLASS	73	15	827	51*	14.26
INT					
J.P.L.	8	3	47	14*	9.40
NAT.W.	2	1	17	17	–
B & H	6	2	45	19	11.25

LAST SEASON: WICKET KEEPING

	C.	ST.			
TEST					
OTHER FIRST CLASS	48	10			
INT					
J.P.L.	5	3			
NAT.W.					
B & H	2	–			

CAREER: WICKET KEEPING

	C.	ST.			
TEST					
OTHER FIRST CLASS	115	26			
INT					
J.P.L.	20	4			
NAT.W.	6	3			
B & H	10	2			

Off-season 1984–85: Farming.
Overseas tours: Antigua, 1981 with Somerset.
Cricketers particularly learnt from: Derek Taylor, Bob Taylor.
Cricketing superstitions: "Never keep wicket without wearing county cap".
Equipment used: Hunts County Sports.
Other sports: Field sports, snooker. Watch soccer.
Relaxations: Field sports (hunting, shooting and fishing), rearing pheasants.
Significant injuries in 1984: Broken finger on left hand.
Extras: Made debut for Somerset 2nd XI at 15.
Opinions on cricket: "We play too much".
Best batting performance: 51* Somerset v Indians, Taunton 1979.

GARNER, J.

Full Name: Joel Garner.
Role: Right-hand bat, right arm fast bowler.
Born: 16 December 1952, Barbados.
Height: 6' 8" **Weight:** 17st.
Nickname: Big Bird.
County debut: 1977.
County cap: 1979.
Test debut: 1976–77.
No. of Tests: 42.
No. of One-Day Internationals: 55.
1000 runs in a season: 0.
50 wickets in a season: 2.
1st-Class 50s scored: 4.
1st-Class 100s scored: 1.
1st-Class 200s scored: 0.
1st-Class 5 w. in innings: 41.
1st-Class 10 w. in match: 7.
One-day 50s: 1.
One-day 100s: 0.
Place in batting averages: — average: —; (1983: 129 average: 26.50).
Place in bowling averages: 2 average: 16.00; (1983: 12 average: 20.23).
1st-Class catches 1984: 4 (career: 98).
Marital status: Single.
Education: Boys' Foundation School, Christchurch, Barbados.
Jobs outside cricket: Telegraph operator.
Off-season 1984–85: In Australia with West Indies.
Overseas tours: Toured with West Indies in Australia 1979–80. Pakistan, 1980–81. Australia 1981–82, India 1982–83, England 1980 and 1984.
Overseas teams played for: Made debut for Barbados in Shell Shield Competition in 1975–76.

Equipment used: Duncan Fearnley.
Other sports: Football for Cable & Wireless team in Barbados, as goal-keeper.
Relaxations: Sea-bathing, bird-watching, soul music, jazz. Manchester United.
Extras: Has played as professional for Littleborough in Central Lancashire League. When Garner was bowling at Lords, Mike Brearley reputedly asked if they could heighten the sight-screen at the Nursery End, as the ball was being delivered from such a height, it was being 'lost' in the trees of London Zoo. Topped Somerset first class bowling averages in 1981, 1982 and 1983. Takes size 16 in boots which are custom-built.
Best batting performance: 104 West Indians v Gloucestershire, Bristol 1980.
Best bowling performance: 8-31 Somerset v Glamorgan, Cardiff 1977.

LAST SEASON: BATTING

	I.	N.O.	R.	H.S.	AV.
TEST	6	1	29	10*	5.80
OTHER FIRST CLASS	2	0	32	29	16.00
INT	2	1	9	6*	–
J.P.L.					
NAT.W.					
B & H	.				

CAREER: BATTING

	I.	N.O.	R.	H.S.	AV.
TEST	51	9	519	60	12.36
OTHER FIRST CLASS	113	30	1657	104	19.96
INT	28	12	154	37	9.63
J.P.L.	37	14	326	59*	14.17
NAT.W.	11	4	113	38*	16.14
B & H	7	3	50	17	12.50

LAST SEASON: BOWLING

	O.	M.	R.	W.	AV.
TEST	217.5	60	540	29	18.62
OTHER FIRST CLASS	53	21	84	10	8.40
INT	28	5	57	5	11.40
J.P.L.					
NAT.W.					
B & H					

CAREER: BOWLING

	O.	M.	R.	W.	AV.
TEST	1647.4	458	3924	191	20.59
OTHER FIRST CLASS	3275.4	959	7877	474	16.62
INT	519.2	68	1618	85	19.03
J.P.L.	419.1	61	1327	74	17.93
NAT.W.	224.5	67	522	54	9.67
B & H	167.4	40	405	36	11.25

Q. 154. What, where and when was the lowest total made by an English Test side against Australia?

Q. 155. What, where and when was the lowest score by Australia v England?

MARKS, V.J.

Full Name: Victor James Marks.
Role: Right-hand bat, off-break bowler.
Born: 25 June 1955, Middle Chinnock, Somerset.
Height: 5' 9" **Weight:** 11st. 8lbs.
Nickname: Vic.
County debut: 1975.
County cap: 1979.
Test debut: 1982.
No. of Tests: 6.
No. of One-Day Internationals: 25.
1000 runs in a season: 1.
50 wickets in a season: 4.
1st-Class 50s scored: 47.
1st-Class 100s scored: 4.
1st-Class 200s scored: 0.
1st-Class 5 w. in innings: 24.
1st-Class 10 w. in match: 1.
One-day 50s: 9.
One-day 100s: 0.
Place in batting averages: 14 average: 52.58; (1983: 163 average: 22.08).
Place in bowling averages: 35 average: 25.97; (1983: 78 average: 32.04).
1st-Class catches 1984: 16 (career: 97).
Parents: Harold and Joan Marks.
Wife and date of marriage: Anna, 9 September 1978.
Children: Amy, 27 November 1979.
Education: Blundell's School; Oxford University.
Qualifications: M.A. classics.
Jobs outside cricket: Teaching — but not since March 1981.
Cricketing superstitions: "Always wear a pair of striped underpants."
Family links with cricket: "Father a dangerous village cricketer."
Cricketers particularly learnt from: Tom Cartwright, Arthur Milton, Geoff Boycott, Trevor Gard.
Cricketers particularly admired: Colin Dredge.
Overseas tours: Derrick Robins tour of Canada 1977. England in Australia and New Zealand, 1982–83, and New Zealand and Pakistan 1983–84.
Overseas teams played for: Grade cricket with Bayswater Morley C.C. in Perth, W. Australia 1981–82.
Equipment used: Stuart Surridge.
Other sports: Squash, golf.
Significant injuries in 1984: Bruised hip bone — out for two weeks.
Extras: Half-blue for rugby fives at Oxford University. Debut for Oxford University C.C. 1975, blue 1975–76–77–78, Captain from 1976–77. Somerset vice-captain 1984.

Opinions on cricket: "Starts too early and finishes too late. Hope to keep going until 45."

Best batting performance: 134 Somerset v Worcestershire, Weston 1984.

Best bowling performance: 8-141 Somerset v Kent, Taunton 1984.

LAST SEASON: BATTING

	I.	N.O.	R.	H.S.	AV.
TEST					
OTHER FIRST CLASS	34	10	1262	134	52.58
INT					
J.P.L.	13	3	180	28	18.00
NAT.W.	3	2	34	19*	–
B & H	4	1	122	75*	40.67

CAREER: BATTING

	I.	N.O.	R.	H.S.	AV.
TEST	10	1	249	83	27.67
OTHER FIRST CLASS	308	49	7540	134	29.11
INT	16	3	160	28	12.31
J.P.L.	76	21	1212	72	22.03
NAT.W.	17	6	354	55	32.18
B & H	31	8	653	81*	28.39

LAST SEASON: BOWLING

	O.	M.	R.	W.	AV.
TEST					
OTHER FIRST CLASS	808	226	2233	86	25.97
INT					
J.P.L.	100	11	419	16	26.18
NAT.W.	36	7	81	5	16.20
B & H	48	9	172	1	–

CAREER: BOWLING

	O.	M.	R.	W.	AV.
TEST	180.2	54	484	11	44.00
OTHER FIRST CLASS	4846.5	1606	15668	487	32.17
INT	234	25	796	36	22.11
J.P.L.	502	34	1899	83	22.87
NAT.W.	139.1	18	463	14	33.07
B & H	335.5	63	948	36	26.33

OLLIS, R.L.

Full Name: Richard Leslie Ollis.
Role: Left-hand bat.
Born: 14 January 1961, Bristol.
Height: 6' 1" **Weight:** 13st.
Nickname: 'Aulage.
County debut: 1981.
County cap: No.
Test debut: —
No. of Tests: 0.
No. of One-Day Internationals: 0.
1000 runs in a season: 0.
50 wickets in a season: 0.
1st-Class 50s scored: 3.
1st-Class 100s scored: 0.
1st-Class 200s scored: 0.
1st-Class 5 w. in innings: 0.
1st-Class 10 w. in match: 0.
One-day 50s: 0.
One-day 100s: 0.

Place in batting averages: 271 average: 10.18: (1983: 131 average: 25.85).
Place in bowling averages: — average: —; (1983: — average: —)
1st-Class catches 1984: 8 (career: 13).

Parents: Richard Frederick and Barbara Ann Ollis.
Marital status: Single.
Family links with cricket: Father plays cricket for local club in Keynsham.
Education: Castle County Primary; Wellsway Comprehensive, Keynsham.
Jobs outside cricket: Assistant Distribution Manager in family transport company.
Off season 1984–85: Working for transport company.
Cricketing superstitions: Always put right pad on first.
Equipment used: Duncan Fearnley, Nike Footwear.
Overseas tours: Somerset tour to Antigua, October 1981.
Cricketers particularly learnt from: "My father and Jim King of Keynsham C.C."
Other sports: Football, squash, golf, follows most sports.
Best batting performance: 99* Somerset v Gloucestershire, Bristol 1983.

LAST SEASON: BATTING

	I.	N.O.	R.	H.S.	AV.
TEST					
OTHER FIRST CLASS	12	1	112	20	10.18
INT					
J.P.L.	2	0	8	6	4.00
NAT.W.					
B & H					

CAREER: BATTING

	I.	N.O.	R.	H.S.	AV.
TEST					
OTHER FIRST CLASS	40	3	691	99*	18.68
INT					
J.P.L.	3	0	8	6	2.67
NAT.W.					
B & H					

LAST SEASON: BOWLING

	O.	M.	R.	W.	AV.
TEST					
OTHER FIRST CLASS					
INT					
J.P.L.					
NAT.W.					
B & H					

CAREER: BOWLING

	O.	M.	R.	W.	AV.
TEST					
OTHER FIRST CLASS	1	0	2	0	–
INT					
J.P.L.					
NAT.W.					
B & H					

Q. 156. What is the design of the M.C.C. tie?
Q. 157. What is the design of the I. Zingari tie?

PALMER, G.V.

Full name: Gary Vincent Palmer.
Role: All-rounder.
Born: 1 November, 1965, Taunton, Somerset.
Height: 6' 1' **Weight:** 11st. 7lbs.
Nickname: Pedlar.
County debut: 1982.
County cap: No.
Test debut: —
No. of Tests: 0.
No. of One-Day Internationals: 0.
1000 runs in a season: 0.
50 wickets in a season: 0.
1st-Class 50s scored: 2.
1st-Class 100s scored: 0.
1st-Class 200s scored: 0.
1st-Class 5 w. in innings: 1.
1st-Class 10 w. in match: 0.
One-day 50s: 0.
One-day 100s: 0.
Place in batting averages: 227 average: 16.61; (1983: 241 average: 10.82).
Place in bowling averages: 116 average: 41.03; (1983: 75 average: 31.50).
1st-Class catches 1984: 15 (career: 23).
Parents: Kenneth Ernest and Joy Valerie Palmer.
Marital status: Single.
Education: North Town Junior School; Queen's College, Junior and Senior.
Qualifications: S.R.A. Part 1 Squash Coaching Certificate, N.C.A. Cricket Coaching Award.
Jobs outside cricket: Squash coaching.
Off-season 1984–85: Coaching and playing cricket in South Africa, and West Indies tour with England U-19s.
Family links with cricket: Father, K.E. Palmer played for Somerset and England. Toured Pakistan with Commonwealth team, 1963. Test Umpire. Coach at Somerset C.C.C. in winter. Grandfather did the double for 13 consecutive seasons in club cricket, and scored 25 centuries for Devizes C.C.
Overseas tours: English Schools Under-19, Zimbabwe 1982–83.
Cricketers particularly learnt from: "Learnt from my father from an early age. I admire Viv Richards, Joel Garner, Ian Botham."
Equipment endorsed: Gray-Nicolls.
Other sports: Squash, skiing, tennis.
Relaxations: "Listening to music— the up-to-date variety."
Extras: Somerset Under-19 Squash champion. Youngest professional ever: had summer contract with Somerset at 14. Captain of England Under-15, English Schools Under-16 Cricketer of the Year. Possibly youngest cricketer to play for

England Under-19. Made debut for Somerset 1st XI at 16. Opened his first class career v. Leicestershire by bowling two maidens.
Best batting performance: 78 Somerset v Gloucestershire, Bristol 1983.
Best bowling performance: 5-38 Somerset v Warwickshire, Taunton 1983.

LAST SEASON: BATTING

	I.	N.O.	R.	H.S.	AV.
TEST					
OTHER FIRST CLASS	20	2	299	73*	16.61
INT					
J.P.L.	10	5	92	32*	18.40
NAT.W.	–	–	–	–	–
B & H	1	0	4	4	–

CAREER: BATTING

	I.	N.O.	R.	H.S.	AV.
TEST					
OTHER FIRST CLASS	35	4	451	78	14.55
INT					
J.P.L.	11	6	105	32*	21.00
NAT.W.	–	–	–	–	–
B & H	1	0	4	4	–

LAST SEASON: BOWLING

	O.	M.	R.	W.	AV.
TEST					
OTHER FIRST CLASS	320.3	56	1231	30	41.03
INT					
J.P.L.	69.5	1	369	7	52.72
NAT.W.	20	0	102	1	–
B & H	18	2	79	1	–

CAREER: BOWLING

	O.	M.	R.	W.	AV.
TEST					
OTHER FIRST CLASS	546	98	1918	50	38.36
INT					
J.P.L.	114.5	1	617	12	51.42
NAT.W.	20	0	102	1	–
B & H	18	2	79	1	–

POPPLEWELL, N.F.M.

Full Name: Nigel Francis Mark Popplewell.
Role: Right-hand bat, right arm medium bowler.
Born: 8 August 1957, Farnborough Kent.
Height: 5' 10" **Weight:** 12st. 7lbs.
Nickname: Pops.
County debut: 1979.
County cap: 1983.
Test debut: —
No. of Tests: 0.
No. of One-Day Internationals: 0.
1000 runs in a season: 1.
50 wickets in a season: 0.
1st-Class 50s scored: 15.
1st-Class 100s scored: 3.
1st-Class 200s scored: 0.
1st-Class 5 w. in innings: 1.
1st-Class 10 w. in match: 0.
One-day 50s: 6.
One-day 100s: 0.

Place in batting averages: 99 average: 32.82; (1983: 141 average: 24.61).
Place in bowling average: — average: —; (1983: 91 **average:** 34.17).
1st-Class catches 1984: 27 (career: 100).
Parents: Oliver and Margaret Popplewell.
Wife: Ingrid.
Education: Radley College; Selwyn College, Cambridge University.
Qualifications: B.A. Hons 2:1 in Natural Science. M.A. (Cantab.).
Jobs outside cricket: Teacher.
Off-season 1984-85: Teaching at Taunton School.
Family links with cricket: Father played for Cambridge University for three years, 1949–51. Younger brother has played for Cambridge 2nd XI.
Overseas tours: Australia with Combined Oxford and Cambridge XI.
Equipment used: Gray-Nicolls.
Cricketers particularly learnt from: Peter Roebuck, Trevor Gard.
Other sports: Rugby, squash, boxing, hockey. Played rugby and squash for College. Boxed in a single bout for Cambridge at Middleweight. "Athletics in a very amateur and incompetent manner."
Relaxations: Gardening, brewing.
Extras: Cambridge cricket blue. Played for Hampshire 2nd XI.
Best batting performance: 143 Somerset v Gloucestershire, Bath 1983.
Best bowling performance: 5-33 Somerset v Northamptonshire, Lord's 1983.

LAST SEASON: BATTING

	I.	N.O.	R.	H.S.	AV.
TEST					
OTHER FIRST CLASS	36	2	1116	133	32.82
INT					
J.P.L.	14	3	331	72	30.09
NAT.W.	2	0	25	25	12.50
B & H	5	0	124	67	24.80

CAREER: BATTING

	I.	N.O.	R.	H.S.	AV.
TEST					
OTHER FIRST CLASS	184	25	4006	143	25.20
INT					
J.P.L.	54	9	1073	84	23.84
NAT.W.	10	2	268	68*	33.50
B & H	21	3	317	67	17.61

LAST SEASON: BOWLING

	O.	M.	R.	W.	AV.
TEST					
OTHER FIRST CLASS	125.4	30	370	8	46.25
INT					
J.P.L.	18	0	104	4	26.00
NAT.W.	12	3	49	0	–
B & H					

CAREER: BOWLING

	O.	M.	R.	W.	AV.
TEST					
OTHER FIRST CLASS	1354	304	4284	103	41.59
INT					
J.P.L.	201.1	13	985	34	28.97
NAT.W.	36.2	8	127	4	31.75
B & H	111.1	10	457	10	45.70

Q. 158. How many Test matches have been played between England and Australia, and which country has won how many?

RICHARDS, I.V.A.

Full Name: Isaac Vivian Alexander Richards.
Role: Right-hand bat, off-break bowler.
Born: 7 March 1952, St John's, Antigua.
Height: 5' 11" **Weight:** 13st. 7lbs.
Nickname: Smokey, Viv, Vivvy.
County debut: 1974.
County cap: 1974.
Benefit: 1982 (£56,440).
Test debut: 1974–75.
No. of Tests: 52.
No. of One-Day Internationals: 76.
1000 runs in a season: 10.
50 wickets in a season: 0.
1st-Class 50s scored: 87.
1st-Class 100s scored: 67.
1st-Class 200s scored: 7.
1st-Class 5 w. in innings: 1.
1st-Class 10 w. in match: 0.
One-day 50s: 55.
One-day 100s: 18.

Place in batting averages: 31 average: 44.64; (1983: 1 average: 75.25).
Place in bowling averages: — average: —; (1983: 111 average: 38.50).
1st-Class catches 1984: 12 (career: 309).
Parents: Malcolm and Gratel Richards.
Wife and date of marriage: Miriam, 24 March 1981.
Children: Daughter, Matara and son born on eve of 1983 Nat West final.
Education: St John's Boys School, and Antigua Grammar School.
Jobs outside cricket: Worked as a waiter at D'Arcy's Bar and Restaurant, in St John's, Antigua. Apprentice mechanic. Assistant groundsman.
Family links with cricket: Father played cricket for Antigua as fast-bowler and all-rounder. He also played soccer for Antigua. Half-brother Donald opened bowling for Antigua, and also played for Leeward Islands. Brother Mervyn has played both cricket and soccer for Antigua.
Overseas tours: With West Indies to India, Sri Lanka and Pakistan 1974–75; Australia 1975–76 and 1979–80; England 1976, 1980 and 1984; Pakistan 1980–81. India 1983–84; Australia 1984–85.
Overseas teams played for: Leeward Islands 1971–72; Queensland in 1976–77 Sheffield Shield Competition.
Cricketers particularly learnt from: Father; Pat Evanson; Shandy Perera.
Cricket superstitions: "I'm not a superstitious cricketer".
Equipment used: Duncan Fearnley.

Other Sports: Captained school soccer team as center-half. Invited to go for a trial with Bath City, F.C., the Southern League club, but no offer of terms followed. Played basket-ball for The Knickerbockers in Antigua. Squash.

Relaxations: Music. "I sit for hours listening to my stereo." Has large collection of L.P.s.

Extras: Made debut 1971–72 for Leeward Islands. Has written autobiography with David Foot, entitled "Viv Richards." "I remain a religious person to the delight of my parents. I pray every night before going to sleep; occasionally I pray for success on the field." Helps to sponsor young cricketers, footballers and basketball players in Antigua. "Sounds mad but I'm not a travelling man . . . I hate it in the air. Planes terrify me." Brother Mervyn appointed national soccer coach in Antigua. Attended Alf Gover's cricket school in 1972. Shared in fourth wicket partnership record for Somerset of 251 with P.M. Roebuck v Surrey at Weston-Super-Mare in 1977. Record for most sixes hit in John Player League in one season, 26 in 1977. Took hat-trick v. Essex in J.P.L. at Chelmsford, 1982. Top of Somerset first-class batting averages in 1982 and 1983.

Opinions on cricket: "I have never contemplated wearing a helmet. My personal view is that a helmet with a visor takes a little of the batsman's vision—and just a little of the challenge out of the game."

Best batting performance: 291 West Indies v England, The Oval 1976.

Best bowling performance: 5-88 West Indians v Queensland, Brisbane 1981–82.

LAST SEASON: BATTING

	I.	N.O.	R.	H.S.	AV.
TEST	7	1	250	117	41.67
OTHER FIRST CLASS	8	0	375	170	46.88
INT	3	2	276	189*	–
J.P.L.					
NAT.W.					
B & H					

CAREER: BATTING

	I.	N.O.	R.	H.S.	AV.
TEST	101	5	5237	291	54.55
OTHER FIRST CLASS	424	31	18852	241*	47.97
INT	71	9	3175	189*	51.21
J.P.L.	115	14	3979	126*	39.39
NAT.W.	26	1	1046	139*	41.84
B & H	35	6	1310	132*	45.17

LAST SEASON: BOWLING

	O.	M.	R.	W.	AV.
TEST	1	0	2	0	–
OTHER FIRST CLASS	73	20	181	3	60.33
INT	16	1	68	2	34.00
J.P.L.					
NAT.W.					
B & H					

CAREER: BOWLING

	O.	M.	R.	W.	AV.
TEST	390.5 17.1	2 114	904	17	53.18
OTHER FIRST CLASS	26.3 1728.2	2 442	4824	119	40.54
INT.	2 365	0 8	1690	45	37.56
J.P.L.	270	10	1186	53	22.37
NAT.W.	86.1	12	324	10	32.40
B & H	50.4	10	178	7	25.43

ROEBUCK, P.M.

Full Name: Peter Michael Roebuck.
Role: Right-hand bat, leg-break bowler, outfielder.
Born: 6 March 1956, Oxford, Oxfordshire.
Height: 6′ 0″ **Weight:** 13st 5lbs.
Nickname: Rupert, The Oracle, Robespierre ("called others — I won't mention rude ones").
County debut: 1974.
County cap: 1978.
Test debut: —
No. of Tests: 0.
No. of One-Day Internationals: 0.
1000 runs in a season: 4.
50 wickets in a season: 0.
1st-Class 50s scored: 61.
1st-Class 100s scored: 13.
1st-Class 200s scored: 0.
1st-Class 5 w. in innings: 0.
1st-Class 10 w. in match: 0.
One-day 50s: 17.
One-day 100s: 1.

Place in batting averages: 27 average: 47.28; (1983: 64 average: 37.42).
Place in bowling averages: — average: —; (1983: — average: —).
1st-Class catches 1984: 4 (career: 100).
Parents: James and Elizabeth Roebuck.
Marital status: Single.
Education: Park School, Bath; Millfield School; Emmanuel College, Cambridge University.
Qualifications: 1st Class Hons degree in law.
Jobs outside cricket: Teaching and occasional journalism in Australia.
Family links with cricket: Mother and sister both played for Oxford University Ladies. Young brother, Paul, played for E.S.C.A. Under-15 and now Gloucestershire.
Overseas tours: Toured in Australia with Combined Oxford & Cambridge XI 1979–80.
Overseas teams played for: Played in Perth, Australia, 1979–80. Also in Corfu, Sydney and Fiji.
Cricketers particularly learnt from: Viv Richards, Martin Crowe.
Cricketers particularly admired: Tom Graveney and R.J.O. Meyer.
Off-season 1984–85: Sydney.
Cricket superstitions: "I'm trying to get rid of all these, but I have lots when I'm doing badly."

Equipment used: Duncan Fearnley.
Other sports: "Vague efforts at golf, football, tennis and surfing."
Significant injuries during 1984: "Exhaustion — mental and physical".
Relaxations: "Reading, writing, wining and dining with friends. Also body-surfing."
Extras: Cambridge blue 1975–76–77. Plays in spectacles. Youngest Minor County cricketer, playing for Somerset 2nd XI at age of 13. Shared in fourth wicket partnership record for county of 251 with I.V.A. Richards v Surrey at Weston-Super-Mare in 1977. Books: "Slice of Cricket"; "It Never Rains". Articles in Sunday Independent, Guardian, "and anyone else who asks".
Opinions on cricket: "We play too much, reducing the quality of the cricket. Every game should be a fresh experience, an invigorating challenge, not a routine executed by weary men."
Best batting performance: 159 Somerset v Northamptonshire, Northampton 1984.
Best bowling performance: 6-50 Cambridge University v Kent, Canterbury 1977.

LAST SEASON: BATTING

	I.	N.O.	R.	H.S.	AV.
TEST					
OTHER FIRST CLASS	37	1	1702	159	47.28
INT					
J.P.L.	13	1	454	84	37.83
NAT.W.	3	0	200	98	67.67
B & H	5	0	48	34	9.60

CAREER: BATTING

	I.	N.O.	R.	H.S.	AV.
TEST					
OTHER FIRST CLASS	342	49	9990	159	34.10
INT					
J.P.L.	98	20	2337	105	29.96
NAT.W.	23	2	632	98	30.09
B & H	36	5	783	53*	25.26

LAST SEASON: BOWLING

	O.	M.	R.	W.	AV.
TEST					
OTHER FIRST CLASS	10.2	5	18	0	–
INT					
J.P.L.					
NAT.W.					
B & H					

CAREER: BOWLING

	O.	M.	R.	W.	AV.
TEST					
OTHER FIRST CLASS	732.3	194	2022	42	48.14
INT					
J.P.L.	114.5	1	617	12	51.41
NAT.W.					
B & H	6.2	1	13	2	6.50

Q. 159. What were the full names of the 3 Ws?
Q. 160. When was the first Prudential World Cup? And who won?

ROSE, B.C.

Full Name: Brian Charles Rose.
Role: Left-hand bat, left arm
medium bowler.
Born: 4 June 1950, Dartford, Kent.
Nickname: Rosey or Harry.
County debut: 1969.
County cap: 1975.
Benefit: 1983 (£71,863).
Test debut: 1977–78.
No. of Tests: 9.
No. of One-Day Internationals: 2.
1000 runs in a season: 8.
50 wickets in a season: 0.
1st-Class 50s scored: 49.
1st-Class 100s scored: 21.
1st-Class 200s scored: 2.
1st-Class 5 w. in innings: 0.
1st-Class 10 w. in match: 0.
One-day 50s: 25.
One-day 100s: 3.
Place in batting averages: 124 average: 29.32; (1983: 175 average: 20.44).
Place in bowling averages: — average: —; (1983: — average: —).
1st-Class catches 1984: 5 (career: 118).
Wife and date of marriage: Stephanie, 16 March 1978.
Children: Stuart Charles, 19 March 1979; Jamie Joseph, 14 December 1981.
Education: Weston-Super-Mare Grammar School; Borough Road College,
Isleworth.
Jobs outside cricket: Teacher.

LAST SEASON: BATTING

	I.	N.O.	R.	H.S.	AV.
TEST					
OTHER FIRST CLASS	33	4	856	123	29.52
INT					
J.P.L.	13	0	370	51	28.46
NAT.W.	2	2	90	54*	–
B & H	5	1	116	61	29.00

CAREER: BATTING

	I.	N.O.	R.	H.S.	AV.
TEST	16	2	358	70	25.57
OTHER FIRST CLASS	396	42	11838	205	33.44
INT	2	0	99	54	49.50
J.P.L.	146	20	3274	112*	25.98
NAT.W.	23	4	713	128	37.53
B & H	48	6	1275	137*	30.36

LAST SEASON: BOWLING

	O.	M.	R.	W.	AV.
TEST					
OTHER FIRST CLASS					
INT					
J.P.L.	0.2	0	0	1	–
NAT.W.					
B & H					

CAREER: BOWLING

	O.	M.	R.	W.	AV.
TEST					
OTHER FIRST CLASS	58.1	6	224	6	37.33
INT					
J.P.L.	34	0	152	7	21.72
NAT.W.					
B & H					

Off-season 1984–85: Teaching at Millfield School.
Overseas tours: Pakistan, New Zealand 1977–78. W. Indies 1981.
Overseas teams played for: Claremont-Cottesloe in West Australia in 1979–80.
Relaxations: Gardening.
Extras: Played for English Schools Cricket Association at Lord's in 1968.
Plays in spectacles. Captain 1978–83.
Best batting performance: 205 Somerset v Northamptonshire, Weston 1977.
Best bowling performance: 3-9 Somerset v Gloucestershire, Taunton 1975.

TURNER, M.S.

Full Name: Murray Stewart Turner.
Role: Right-hand batsman, medium
pace seamer, close fielder.
Born: 27 January 1964, Shaftesbury,
Dorset.
Height: 6' 4" **Weight:** 13st. 1lb.
Nickname: Ted.
County debut: 1984.
County cap: No.
Test debut: —
No. of Tests: 0.
No. of One-Day Internationals: 0.
1000 runs in a season: 0.
50 wickets in a season: 0.
1st-Class 50s scored: 0.
1st-Class 100s scored: 0.
1st-Class 200s scored: 0.
1st-Class 5 w. in innings: 0.
1st-Class 10 w. in match: 0.
One-day 50s: 0.
One-day 100s: 0.
Place in batting averages: — average: —; (1983: — average: —).
Place in bowling averages: — average: —; (1983: — average: —).
Parents: John and Kathleen Turner.
Marital status: Single.
Education: Huish Grammar School, Taunton, Somerset.
Qualifications: 3 O-levels.
Jobs outside cricket: Service reception in a main Ford dealer.
Off-season 1984–85: Working/playing local football.
Equipment used: Duncan Fearnley.
Cricketers particularly admired: Dennis Lillee, Michael Holding.
Other sports: Football, darts, snooker, pool, golf. Follows football (Crystal
Palace).
Significant injuries in 1984: Trapped nerve in lower of back.

Relaxations: Rock/pop concerts (especially David Bowie); golf; Steven Spielbergand Dustin Hoffman films.
Extras: "I can bowl right arm seamers and also left arm spin. Scored 101 not out and took 8-35 in same game in 1984 season."
Opinions on cricket: "I hate politics involving itself with sporting matters."

LAST SEASON: BATTING

	I.	N.O.	R.	H.S.	AV.
TEST					
OTHER FIRST CLASS	2	0	1	1	0.50
INT					
J.P.L.					
NAT.W.					
B & H					

CAREER: BATTING

	I.	N.O.	R.	H.S.	AV.
TEST					
OTHER FIRST CLASS	2	0	1	1	0.50
INT					
J.P.L.					
NAT.W.					
B & H					

LAST SEASON: BOWLING

	O.	M.	R.	W.	AV.
TEST					
OTHER FIRST CLASS	29	8	85	0	–
INT					
J.P.L.					
NAT.W.					
B & H					

CAREER: BOWLING

	O.	M.	R.	W.	AV.
TEST					
OTHER FIRST CLASS	29	8	85	0	–
INT					
J.P.L.					
NAT.W.					
B & H					

TURNER, S.J.

Full Name: Simon Jonathan Turner.
Role: Left-hand bat, wicket-keeper.
Born: 28 April 1960, Cuckfield, Sussex.
Height: 6′ 1½″ **Weight:** 12st 10lbs.
County debut: 1984.
County cap: No.
Test debut: —
No. of Tests: 0.
No. of One-Day Internationals: 0.
1000 runs in a season: 0.
50 wickets in a season: 0.
1st-Class 50s scored: 0.
1st-Class 100s scored: 0.
1st-Class 200s scored: 0.
1st-Class 5 w. in innings: 0.
1st-Class 10 w. in match: 0.
One-day 50s: 0.
One-day 100s: 0.

Place in batting averages: — average: —; (1983: — average: —).

Place in bowling averages: — average: —; (1983: — average: —).
Parents: Derek Edward and Doris Lilian Turner.
Marital status: Single.
Family links with cricket: Elder brother Richard captain of Weston-super-Mare; younger brother Robert keeper for Millfield and Somerset Under-19s. Father chairman of Weston-super-Mare C.C.
Education: Uphill Primary; Broadoak Comprehensive; Broadoak Sixth Form; Weston Technical College and Bristol Polytechnic.
Qualifications: 6 O-levels, 6 C.S.E.s. Technical Apprenticeship; City and Guilds Mechanical Engineering Technicians Certificate, B.P.I.C.S. Certificate in Production and Inventory Control.
Jobs outside cricket: 1977 Apprenticeship at Westland Helicopters; 1981 Product Planner at Westlands and 1982 Computer Progammer at Westlands.
Off-season 1984–85: Computer programming at Westland Helicopters.
Equipment used: Gunn & Moore.
Cricketers particularly learnt from: Andy Brassington and Trevor Gard.
Cricketers particularly admired: Alan Knott and Rod Marsh.
Other sports: Squash, football, fitness training.
Relaxations: Woodwork, car maintenance and music playing and listening.
Best batting performance: 27* Somerset v Northamptonshire, Taunton 1984.

LAST SEASON: BATTING

	I.	N.O.	R.	H.S.	AV.
TEST					
OTHER FIRST CLASS	6	3	75	27*	25.00
INT					
J.P.L.	2	1	8	4*	—
NAT.W.	1	0	7	7	—
B & H					

CAREER: BATTING

	I.	N.O.	R.	H.S.	AV.
TEST					
OTHER FIRST CLASS	6	3	75	27*	25.00
INT					
J.P.L.	2	1	8	4*	—
NAT.W.	1	0	7	7	—
B & H					

LAST SEASON: WICKET KEEPING

	C.	ST.		
TEST				
OTHER FIRST CLASS	12	3		
INT				
J.P.L.	—	1		
NAT.W.	1	1		
B & H				

CAREER: WICKET KEEPING

	C.	ST.		
TEST				
OTHER FIRST CLASS	12	3		
INT				
J.P.L.	—	1		
NAT.W.	1	1		
B & H				

Q. 161. What was the middle name of Don Bradman?

Q. 162. What was the middle name of Fred Trueman?

WILSON, P.H.L.

Full Name: Peter Hugh L'Estrange Wilson.
Role: Right-hand bat; right arm fast medium bowler.
Born: 17 August 1958, Guildford, Surrey.
Height: 6′ 5″ **Weight:** 14st 7lbs.
Nickname: Flea.
County debut: 1978 (Surrey), 1983 (Somerset).
County cap: No.
Test debut: —
No. of Tests: 0.
No. of One-Day Internationals: 0.
1000 runs in a season: 0.
50 wickets in a season: 0.
1st-Class 50s scored: 0.
1st-Clas 100s scored: 0.
1st-Class 200s scored: 0.
1st-Class 5 w. in innings: 1.
1st-Class 10 w. in match: 0.
One-day 50s: 0.
One-day 100s: 0.

Place in batting averages: — average: —; (1983: 213 average: 15.00).
Place in bowling averages: — average: —; (1983: 89 average: 33.48).
1st-Class catches 1984: 1 (career: 11).
Parents: Peter Sydney, (Lt-Cdr,R.N.) and Heather Margaret Wilson.
Marital status: Single.
Education: Ludgrove Prep. School, and Wellington College.
Qualifications: O- and A-levels.
Jobs outside cricket: Worked in Estate Agency and as schoolmaster.
Overseas tours: Surrey Tour of Far East, 1979. M.C.C. to Bangladesh, December/January 1981; M.C.C. to Central and East Africa, October 1981.
Overseas teams played for: Northern Transvaal in Currie Cup, 1979–80.
Equipment used: Slazenger.
Other sports: Golf, squash, hockey.
Relaxations: Photography.
Extras: Played for Hampshire 2nd XI 1976–77. Action is often compared with that of Bob Willis and Willis did in fact coach him. Spent 1979–80 off-season in South Africa. First scoring shot in 1st class cricket in England, v Hampshire, and in South Africa, in Currie Cup, v Rhodesia, was a six. Not retained by Surrey at end of 1982 season and released by Somerset at end of 1984. Highest individual score at Wellington of 192 not out, v Haileybury in 1976.
Best batting performance: 29 N Transvaal v Transvaal, Pretoria 1979–80.

Best bowling performance: 5-36 N Transvaal v E Province, Pretoria 1979–80.

LAST SEASON: BATTING

	I.	N.O.	R.	H.S.	AV.
TEST					
OTHER FIRST CLASS	2	0	0	0	0.00
INT					
J.P.L.	1	1	1	1*	–
NAT.W.	–	–	–	–	–
B & H					

CAREER: BATTING

	I.	N.O.	R.	H.S.	AV.
TEST					
OTHER FIRST CLASS	50	25	261	29	10.44
INT					
J.P.L.	12	5	37	18*	5.28
NAT.W.	2	2	17	9*	–
B & H	5	2	0	0*	0.00

LAST SEASON: BOWLING

	O.	M.	R.	W.	AV.
TEST					
OTHER FIRST CLASS	56	14	176	5	35.20
INT					
J.P.L.	29	1	150	6	25.00
NAT.W.	10	1	47	1	–
B & H					

CAREER: BOWLING

	O.	M.	R.	W.	AV.
TEST					
OTHER FIRST CLASS	1138.3	248	3394	110	30.86
INT					
J.P.L.	239.1	11	1159	42	27.59
NAT.W.	34	5	131	5	26.20
B & H	140.2	8	544	25	21.76

WYATT, J.G.

Full Name: Julian George Wyatt.
Role: Right-hand bat, right arm medium bowler.
Born: 19 June 1963, Paulton, Somerset.
Height: 5' 10" **Weight:** 11st. 8lbs.
Nickname: Jules, Earp.
County debut: 1983.
County cap: No.
Test debut: —
No. of Tests: 0.
No. of One-Day Internationals: 0.
1000 runs in a season: 0.
50 wickets in a season: 0.
1st-Class 50s scored: 6.
1st-Class 100s scored: 1.
1st-Class 200s scored: 0.
1st-Class 5 w. in innings: 0.
1st-Class 10 w. in match: 0.
One-day 50s: 0.
One-day 100s: 0.
Place in batting averages: 131 average: 23.79; (1983: 73 average: 35.20).
Place in bowling averages: — average: —; (1983: — average: —).
1st-Class catches 1984: 8 (career: 9).

Parents: Christopher Hedley and Dinah Ruby Wyatt.
Marital status: Single.
Education: Farrington Gurney School (primary) and Wells Cathedral School, Somerset.
Qualifications: 5 O-levels.
Jobs outside cricket: Brandon Tool Hire 1980–83.
Off-season 1984–85: Cricket in Melbourne.
Equipment used: Duncan Fearnley, Nike Footwear.
Cricketer particularly admired: B. Rose, P. Denning, C. Dredge, T. Gard.
Other sports: Squash, football; follow rugby.
Relaxations: "Socialising at the 'Hunter's Rest', Chitton."
Best batting performance: 103 Somerset v Oxford University, Oxford 1984.

LAST SEASON: BATTING

	I.	N.O.	R.	H.S.	AV.
TEST					
OTHER FIRST CLASS	28	0	666	103	23.79
INT					
J.P.L.	3	1	37	21	18.50
NAT.W.	1	0	0	0	–
B & H					

CAREER: BATTING

	I.	N.O.	R.	H.S.	AV.
TEST					
OTHER FIRST CLASS	40	2	1018	103	26.79
INT					
J.P.L.	3	1	37	21	18.50
NAT.W.	1	0	0	0	–
B & H					

LAST SEASON: BOWLING

	O.	M.	R.	W.	AV.
TEST					
OTHER FIRST CLASS	3	1	4	1	–
INT					
J.P.L.					
NAT.W.					
B & H					

CAREER: BOWLING

	O.	M.	R.	W.	AV.
TEST					
OTHER FIRST CLASS	3	1	4	1	–
INT					
J.P.L.					
NAT.W.					
B & H					

COUNTY QUIZ

Q. 1. When was the club founded?
Q. 2. Who made the most first-class runs for the county last season, and how many?
Q. 3. What's the highest ever county total, and against whom?
Q. 4. Who took most wickets for the county last season, and how many?
Q. 5. What's the highest individual score for the county, who hit it, and when?
Q. 6. What's the highest scoring partnership for the county for any wicket?
Q. 7. How many times has the club won the County Championship?
Q. 8. What's the lowest ever total made by the county in one innings, when, and against whom?
Q. 9. Which bowler took the most first-class wickets in one season, when, and how many?
Q. 10. Which batsman hit the most runs in one season, when and how many?

Surrey

BUTCHER, A.R.

Full Name: Alan Raymond Butcher.
Role: Left-hand bat, left arm medium and left arm spin bowler.
Born: 7 January 1954, Croydon, Surrey.
Height: 5' 8" **Weight:** 11st. 7lbs.
Nickname: Butch, Budgie.
County debut: 1972.
County cap: 1975.
Test debut: 1979.
No. of Tests: 1.
No. of One-Day Internationals: 1.
1000 runs in a season: 6.
50 wickets in a season: 0.
1st-Class 50s scored: 61.
1st-Class 100s scored: 25.
1st-Class 200s scored: 1.
1st-Class 5 w. in innings: 1.
1st-Class 10 w. in match: 0.
One-day 50s: 31.
One-day 100s: 4.

Place in batting averages: 59 average: 38.24; (1983: 87 average: 32.90).
Place in bowling averages: — average: —; (1983: — average: —).
1st-Class catches 1984: 11 (career: 114).
Parents: Raymond and Jackie Butcher.
Wife and date of marriage: Elaine, 27 September 1972.
Children: Mark, Gary, Lisa.
Education: Heath Clark Grammar School.
Qualifications: Five O-levels, one A-level.
Jobs outside cricket: Football coach, physical education master, Cumnor House School, South Croydon, Surrey.
Family links with cricket: Brother, Martin, M.C.C. Young Professionals. Brother, Ian, joined Leicestershire, 1979, debut v. Surrey in John Player League.
Other sports: Football.

Relaxations: Most sport, rock music, reading.
Extras: Scored a century before lunch v. Glamorgan at the Oval, 1980.
Best batting performance: 216 Surrey v Cambridge University, Cambridge 1980.
Best bowling performance: 6-48 Surrey v Hampshire, Guildford 1972.

LAST SEASON: BATTING

	I.	N.O.	R.	H.S.	AV.
TEST					
OTHER FIRST CLASS	41	4	1415	135*	38.24
INT					
J.P.L.	14	0	500	73	35.72
NAT.W.	3	1	64	35*	32.00
B & H	4	0	49	17	12.25

CAREER: BATTING

	I.	N.O.	R.	H.S.	AV.
TEST	2	0	71	20	17.00
OTHER FIRST CLASS	414	40	12622	216*	33.75
INT	1	0	14	14	–
J.P.L.	141	15	3567	113*	28.30
NAT.W.	21	3	532	86*	29.56
B & H	43	4	983	80	25.21

LAST SEASON: BOWLING

	O.	M.	R.	W.	AV.
TEST					
OTHER FIRST CLASS	38	9	134	4	33.50
INT					
J.P.L.					
NAT.W.					
B & H	0.3	0	4	0	–

CAREER: BOWLING

	O.	M.	R.	W.	AV.
TEST	2	0	9	0	–
OTHER FIRST CLASS	1249.2	252	4045	103	39.27
INT					
J.P.L.	266	21	1168	25	46.72
NAT.W.	44.2	7	166	3	55.33
B & H	148.3	26	446	18	24.78

CLARKE, S.T.

Full Name: Sylvester Theophilus Clarke.
Role: Right-hand bat, right arm fast bowler, gulley fielder.
Born: 11 December 1955, Lead Vale, Christchurch, Barbados.
Height: 6′ 2″ **Weight:** 15st.
Nickname: Silvers.
County debut: 1979.
County cap: 1980.
Test debut: 1977–78.
No. of Tests: 11.
No. of One-Day Internationals: 10.
1000 runs in a season: 0.
50 wickets in a season: 4.
1st-Class 50s scored: 4.
1st-Class 100s scored: 1.
1st-Class 200s scored: 0.
1st-Class 5 w. in innings: 36.
1st-Class 10 w. in match: 5.
One-day 50s: 0.

One-day 100s: 0.
Place in batting averages: 240 average: 14.95; (1983: 216 average: 14.25).
Place in bowling averages: 10 average: 21.63; (1983: 22 average: 22.44).
1st-Class catches 1984: 22 (career: 45).
Parents: Marjorie and Ashton Smith.
Children: Desiree, 8 December 1974; Dawn, 18 August 1976; Shelly, 2 July 1978.
Education: St Bartholomew Boys' School.
Jobs outside cricket: Carpenter.
Off season 1984–85: Playing in South Africa.
Family links with cricket: Half-brother Damien is professional at Todmorden.
Overseas tours: Toured with West Indies to India and Sri Lanka, 1978–79. Pakistan 1980–81, Australia 1981, and South Africa 1982–83 and 83–84.
Overseas teams played for: Local club in Barbados Cricket League, Transvaal, 'Rebel' West Indians in S. Africa.
Cricketers particularly learnt from: V. Holder.
Equipment used: Slazenger.
Other sports: Football. Watch tennis.
Relaxations: "Music and parties."
Extras: Made fastest century of the 1981 season in 62 mins. v. Glamorgan, 100 n.o. Took first championship hat-trick in 1980 season v. Notts., removing Randall, Rice and Todd. Sponsored at rate of £175 per wicket for Transvaal in Currie Cup.
Best batting performance: 100* Surrey v Glamorgan, Swansea 1981.
Best bowling performance: 7-34 West Indies XI v South Africa, Johannesburg 1983-84.

LAST SEASON: BATTING

	I.	N.O.	R.	H.S.	AV.
TEST					
OTHER FIRST CLASS	25	3	329	35	14.95
INT					
J.P.L.	8	1	77	25*	11.00
NAT.W.	1	0	29	29*	–
B & H	5	1	31	17	7.75

CAREER: BATTING

	I.	N.O.	R.	H.S.	AV.
TEST	16	5	172	35*	15.64
OTHER FIRST CLASS	170	25	2225	100*	15.35
INT	8	2	60	20	10.00
J.P.L.	43	9	405	34*	11.91
NAT.W.	8	3	104	45*	20.80
B & H	21	4	168	39	9.88

LAST SEASON: BOWLING

	O.	M.	R.	W.	AV.
TEST					
OTHER FIRST CLASS	651	165	1687	78	21.63
INT					
J.P.L.	99.4	9	402	16	25.13
NAT.W.	36	9	94	4	23.50
B & H	52	13	147	7	21.00

CAREER: BOWLING

	O.	M.	R.	W.	AV.
TEST	412.5	79	1171	42	27.88
OTHER FIRST CLASS	4658.5	1210	12065	592	20.38
INT	87.2	13	245	13	18.85
J.P.L.	419.2	42	1647	69	23.86
NAT.W.	158.5	37	385	19	20.26
B & H	293.4	70	780	50	15.60

CLINTON, G.S.

Full Name: Graham Selvey Clinton.
Role: Left-hand bat, right arm
medium bowler.
Born: 5 May 1953, Sidcup.
Nickname: Clint.
County debut: 1979 (Surrey).
County cap: 1980 (Surrey).
Test debut: —
No. of Tests: 0.
No. of One-Day Internationals: 0.
1000 runs in a season: 3.
50 wickets in a season: 0.
1st-Class 50s scored: 36.
1st-Class 100s scored: 11.
1st-Class 200s scored: 0.
1st-Class 5 w. in innings: 0.
1st-Class 10 w. in match: 0.
One-day 50s: 8.
One-day 100s: 1.
Place in batting averages: 37 average: 43.09; (1983 154 average: 23.11).
Place in bowling averages: — average: —; (1983: — average: —).
1st-Class catches 1984: 6 (career: 45).
Education: Chislehurst and Sidcup Grammar School.
Family links with cricket: Younger brothers Neil and Tony are regular members of the Blackheath team.
Overseas tours: West Indies with England Young Cricketers 1972.
Extras: Formerly played for Kent, where he made his debut 1974. Left after

LAST SEASON: BATTING

	I.	N.O.	R.	H.S.	AV.
TEST					
OTHER FIRST CLASS	28	6	948	192	43.09
INT					
J.P.L.					
NAT.W.	3	1	107	79*	53.50
B & H	2	0	99	94	49.50

CAREER: BATTING

	I.	N.O.	R.	H.S.	AV.
TEST					
OTHER FIRST CLASS	252	29	6802	192	30.50
INT					
J.P.L.	34	4	761	105*	25.37
NAT.W.	12	1	292	79*	26.55
B & H	26	0	716	94	27.54

LAST SEASON: BOWLING

	O.	M.	R.	W.	AV.
TEST					
OTHER FIRST CLASS	6	1	30	0	–
INT					
J.P.L.					
NAT.W.					
B & H					

CAREER: BOWLING

	O.	M.	R.	W.	AV.
TEST					
OTHER FIRST CLASS	17	1	127	4	31.75
INT					
J.P.L.					
NAT.W.	4	2	2	0	–
B & H	1.2	0	10	0	–

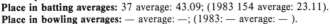

1978 season to join Surrey. Renowned as a dressing-room wit. At age 11, he
played for Kemnal Manor, Kent. Later played club cricket for Sidcup and for
Blackheath.
Best batting performance: 192 Surrey v Yorkshire, The Oval 1984.

CURTIS, I.J.

Full Name: Ian James Curtis.
Role: Slow left-arm bowler "Left-
hand bat, apparently".
Born: 13 May 1959, Purley, Surrey.
Height: 6' 3½" **Weight:** 12st 7lbs.
Nickname: Dot.
County debut: 1983.
County cap: No.
Test debut: —
No. of Tests: 0.
No. of One-Day Internationals: 0.
1000 runs in a season: 0.
50 wickets in a season: 0.
1st-Class 50s scored: 0.
1st-Class 100s scored: 0.
1st-Class 200s scored: 0.
1st-Class 5 w. in innings: 2.
1st-Class 10 w. in match: 0.
One-day 50s: 0.
One-day 100s: 0.
Place in batting averages: — average: —; (1983: — average: —).
Place in bowling averages: — average: —; (1983: 118 average: 40.59).
1st-Class catches 1984: 0 (career: 7).
Parents: Roger James and Patricia Lindsay Curtis.
Marital status: Single.
Family links with cricket: None.
Education: Cumnor House Prep. School, Croydon; Whitgift School, Croydon;
Lincoln College, Oxford.
Qualifications: 4 A-levels, 10 O-Levels. B.A. (Hons) in Agriculture and
Forest Sciences. M.Sc. in Forestry and its Relation to Land Management.
Equipment used: Gunn & Moore.
Overseas teams played for: Papatoetoe C.C. Auckland, New Zealand,
1982–83.
Cricketers particularly admired: "All wrist spinners, and I.V.A. Richards,
who entertains by sheer ability."
Other sports: Rugby fives, squash, rowing.
Relaxations: Photography, drawing, conservation and the environment.
Extras: 1st Class debut for Oxford University, 1980, Blues 1980, 1982.

Combined Universities 1980, 81, 82. Oxford University Rugby Fives Team
1979, 80, 81 (Capt.). Released by Surrey at end of 1984.
Best batting performance: 20* Oxford University v Warwickshire, Oxford
1982.
Best bowling performance: 6-28 Surrey v Oxford University, Oxford 1983.

LAST SEASON: BATTING

	I.	N.O.	R.	H.S.	AV.
TEST					
OTHER FIRST CLASS	1	1	1	1*	—
INT					
J.P.L.					
NAT.W.					
B & H					

CAREER: BATTING

	I.	N.O.	R.	H.S.	AV.
TEST					
OTHER FIRST CLASS	30	14	77	20*	4.81
INT					
J.P.L.	2	2	0	0*	—
NAT.W.					
B & H					

LAST SEASON: BOWLING

	O.	M.	R.	W.	AV.
TEST					
OTHER FIRST CLASS	11.3	3	36	1	—
INT					
J.P.L.					
NAT.W.					
B & H					

CAREER: BOWLING

	O.	M.	R.	W.	AV.
TEST					
OTHER FIRST CLASS	799.1	221	2109	51	41.35
INT					
J.P.L.	16	1	82	1	—
NAT.W.					
B & H					

FALKNER, N.J.

Full Name: Nicholas James Falkner.
Role: Right-hand bat, cover fielder.
Born: 30 September 1962, Redhill.
Height: 5′ 10″**Weight:** 12st. 1lb.
Nickname: Beefy.
County debut: 1984.
County cap: No.
Test debut: —
No. of Tests: 0.
No. of One-Day Internationals: 0.
1000 runs in a season: 0.
50 wickets in a season: 0.
1st-Class 50s scored: 0.
1st-Class 100s scored: 1.
1st-Class 200s scored: 0.
1st-Class 5 w. in innings: 0.
1st-Class 10 w. in match: 0.
One-day 50s: 0.
One-day 100s: 0.

Place in batting averages: — average: —; (1983: — average: —).

Place in bowling averages: — average: —; (1983: — average: —).
Parents: John Holmes Falkner and Barbara May Stocker.
Marital status: Single.
Family links with cricket: Father plays local club cricket.
Education: Yardley Court Prep. School; Reigate Grammar School.
Qualifications: 4 O-levels.
Jobs outside cricket: Assistant in sports shop, 1981; Friends Provident Insurance Co., 1983.
Off-season 1984–85: Either in New Zealand playing club cricket or working in Croydon.
Cricketing superstitions: Always puts pads on before box, thigh pad etc.; always checks stance twice before bowler bowls.
Equipment used: Gunn & Moore.
Overseas tours: Surrey Schools to Australia Christmas 1980–81.
Overseas teams played for: Perth C.C. 1982–83.
Cricketers particularly learnt from: Graham Clinton, Geoff Arnold.
Cricketers particularly admired: Graham Gooch.
Other sports: Squash, fitness and football; watches football, squash and rugby.
Relaxations: Playing chess, reading (books rather than magazines), listening to music.
Extras: Scored 1st-Class 100 on debut v Cambridge University.
Opinions on cricket: "117 overs in a day is too many. 105-110 overs is enough or a 6.30 p.m. finish whichever comes first. One overseas player per county only. Cricketers should be able to travel and play their career anywhere in the world—sport and politics cannot be mixed."
Best batting performance: 101* Surrey v Cambridge University, Banstead 1984.

LAST SEASON: BATTING

	I.	N.O.	R.	H.S.	AV.
TEST					
OTHER FIRST CLASS	1	1	101	101*	–
INT					
J.P.L.	1	0	24	24	–
NAT.W.					
B & H	1	0	2	2	–

CAREER: BATTING

	I.	N.O.	R.	H.S.	AV.
TEST					
OTHER FIRST CLASS	1	1	101	101*	–
INT					
J.P.L.	1	0	24	24	–
NAT.W.					
B & H	1	0	2	2	–

LAST SEASON: BOWLING

	O.	M.	R.	W.	AV.
TEST					
OTHER FIRST CLASS					
INT					
J.P.L.					
NAT.W.					
B & H					

CAREER: BOWLING

	O.	M.	R.	W.	AV.
TEST					
OTHER FIRST CLASS					
INT					
J.P.L.					
NAT.W.					
B & H					

FELTHAM, M.A.

Full Name: Mark Andrew Feltham.
Role: Right-hand bat, right arm fast medium bowler.
Born: 26 June 1963, London.
Height: 6' 2" **Weight:** 13st. 2lbs.
Nickname: Felts, Felpsi or Boff.
County debut: 1983.
County cap: No.
Test debut: —
No. of Tests: 0.
No. of One-Day Internationals: 0.
1000 runs in a season: 0.
50 wickets in a season: 0.
1st-Class 50s scored: 0.
1st-Class 100s scored: 0.
1st-Class 200s scored: 0.
1st-Class 5 w. in innings: 1.
1st-Class 10 w. in match: 0.
One-day 50s: 0.
One-day 100s: 0.

Place in batting averages: 199 average: 20.60; (1983: — average: —).
Place in bowling averages: 77 average: 31.63; (1983: — average: —).
1st-Class catches 1984: 5 (career: 5).
Parents: Leonard William and Patricia Louise Feltham.
Marital status: Single.
Family links with cricket: Mother involved in Ken Barrington Cricket Centre Appeal, brother plays for Surrey Young Cricketers.
Education: Roehampton Church School; Tiffin Boys' School.
Qualifications: 7 O-levels; qualified cricket coach.
Off-season 1984–85: Playing and coaching in Durban with Glenrood Old Boys.
Cricketing superstitions: Left pad on before right.
Equipment used: Slazenger, Gunn & Moore boots.
Overseas tours: Australia, November, December 1980, Surrey Cricket Association U-19s. Barbados, October, November 1981, M.C.C. Young Professionals.
Cricketers particularly learnt from: Sylvester Clarke, Pat Pocock.
Cricketers particularly admired: Ian Botham.
Other sports: Football, darts; watches snooker.
Significant injuries in 1984: Strained back.
Relaxations: Listening to music.
Extras: Played for England Schools at U-15 and U-19 levels. On the M.C.C. Young Professionals Staff 1981–82 seasons.

Opinions on cricket: "4-day county matches; better wickets for 2nd XI matches."
Best batting performance: 44 Surrey v Derbyshire, The Oval 1984.
Best bowling performance: 5-62 Surrey v Warwickshire, Edgbaston 1984.

LAST SEASON: BATTING

	I.	N.O.	R.	H.S.	AV.
TEST					
OTHER FIRST CLASS	15	5	206	44	20.60
INT					
J.P.L.	9	6	23	8*	7.67
NAT.W.	1	0	4	4	–
B & H	4	1	45	22*	15.00

CAREER: BATTING

	I.	N.O.	R.	H.S.	AV.
TEST					
OTHER FIRST CLASS	15	5	206	44	20.60
INT					
J.P.L.	9	6	23	8*	7.67
NAT.W.	1	0	4	4	–
B & H	4	1	45	22*	15.00

LAST SEASON: BOWLING

	O.	M.	R.	W.	AV.
TEST					
OTHER FIRST CLASS	291.2	53	1012	32	31.63
INT					
J.P.L.	56.2	3	302	8	37.75
NAT.W.	13	4	40	1	–
B & H	38.3	6	142	6	23.67

CAREER: BOWLING

	O.	M.	R.	W.	AV.
TEST					
OTHER FIRST CLASS	309.2	58	1056	34	31.06
INT					
J.P.L.	64.2	3	363	8	45.38
NAT.W.	13	4	40	1	–
B & H	38.3	6	142	6	23.67

HOWARTH, G.P.

Full Name: Geoffrey Philip Howarth.
Role: Right-hand bat, off-break bowler, slip fielder.
Born: 29 March 1951, Auckland, New Zealand.
Height: 5' 10½" **Weight:** 12st.
Nickname: Kiwi, Bones.
County debut: 1971.
County cap: 1974.
Test debut: 1974–75.
No. of Tests: 40.
No. of One-Day Internationals: 57.
1000 runs in a season: 4.
50 wickets in a season: 0.
1st-Class 50s scored: 85.
1st-Class 100s scored: 32.
1st-Class 200s scored: 0.
1st-Class 5 w. in innings: 1.
1st-Class 10 w. in match: 0.
One-day 50s: 17.
One-day 100s: 2.

Place in batting averages: 162 average: 24.50; (1983: 56 average: 39.05).
Place in bowling averages: — average: —; (1983: — average: —).

1st-Class catches 1984: 17 (career: 220).
Parents: George and Anne.
Marital status: Separated.
Education: Auckland Grammar School.
Qualifications: New Zealand School Certificate.
Off-season 1984–85: Playing in New Zealand.
Family links with cricket: Younger brother of H.J. Howarth, New Zealand Test cricketer.
Overseas tours: Toured with New Zealand to Pakistan and India, 1976–77; England 1978 and 1983. Australia 1980–81 and 1982–83. Far East, Sri Lanka and South Africa with D.H. Robins XI.
Overseas teams played for: New Zealand Under-23s XI v Auckland at Auckland 1968–69. Auckland.
Equipment used: Slazenger.
Other sports: "Golf, tennis, squash etc. Enjoy watching most sports on T.V."
Relaxations: Music, T.V., reading.
Significant injuries in 1984: Exploratory knee operation in late May.
Extras: Joined Surrey staff 1969. Scored two centuries in a match (122 and 102) for New Zealand v England at Auckland 1977–78. Stayed with Bob Willis's parents during early days with Surrey. Was awarded M.B.E. in 1981. O.B.E. 1984. Captain of New Zealand 1980–. Captain of Surrey 1984–.
Best batting performance: 183 Surrey v Hampshire, The Oval 1979.
Best bowling performance: 5-32 Auckland v Central Districts, Auckland 1973–74.

LAST SEASON: BATTING

	I.	N.O.	R.	H.S.	AV.
TEST					
OTHER FIRST CLASS	37	3	833	113	24.50
INT					
J.P.L.	10	0	160	38	16.00
NAT.W.	3	0	33	18	11.00
B & H	2	0	25	16	12.50

CAREER: BATTING

	I.	N.O.	R.	H.S.	AV.
TEST	71	5	2270	147	34.39
OTHER FIRST CLASS	473	36	14345	183	32.83
INT	54	4	1235	76	24.70
J.P.L.	100	1	2245	122	22.67
NAT.W.	17	0	300	34	17.65
B & H	43	3	1220	80	30.50

LAST SEASON: BOWLING

	O.	M.	R.	W.	AV.
TEST					
OTHER FIRST CLASS	0.4	0	2	0	–
INT					
J.P.L.					
NAT.W.					
B & H					

CAREER: BOWLING

	O.	M.	R.	W.	AV.
TEST	40 40	4 11	254	3	84.67
OTHER FIRST CLASS	565.6 595.1	127 165	3289	109	30.17
INT	14	0	64	2	32.00
J.P.L.	18.2	0	85	5	17.00
NAT.W.	2.1	0	25	2	12.50
B & H					

KNIGHT, R.D.V.

Full Name: Roger David Verdon
Knight.
Role: Left-hand bat, right arm
medium bowler.
Born: 6 September 1946, Streatham.
Height: 6' 3¾" **Weight:** 14st 2lbs.
Nickname: Knighty.
County debut: Originally 1968,
rejoined 1978.
County cap: 1978.
Benefit: 1984.
Test debut: —
No. of Tests: 0.
No. of One-Day Internationals: 0.
1000 runs in a season: 13.
50 wickets in a season: 0.
1st-Class 50s scored: 113.
1st-Class 100s scored: 31.
1st-Class 200s scored: 0.
1st-Class 5 w. in innings: 4.
1st-Class 10 w. in match: 0.
One-day 50s: 39.

One-day 100s: 4.
Place in batting averages: 54 average: 39.19; (1983: 58 average: 38.59).
Place in bowling averages: 95 average: 34.25; 81983: 123 average: 45.13).
1st-Class catches 1984: 19 (career: 294).
Parents: David Verdon and Thelma Patricia Knight.
Wife and date of marriage: Christine Ann McNab, 27 March 1971.
Children: Catherine Elizabeth, 29 November 1972; Graeme Edward Verdon,
16 August 1975.
Education: Dulwich College; Cambridge University.
Qualifications: B.A. Hons (Cantab). MA. Certificate of Education,
Cambridge University. Advanced cricket coach.
Jobs outside cricket: Schoolmaster at Eastbourne College 1970–78.
Schoolmaster at Dulwich College 1978–83. A winter's work at Surrey C.C.C.
dealing with Junior cricket for the county. Housemaster at Cranleigh School,
September 1983— (Master in charge of rugby).
Family links with cricket: Father played for Cambridge University Crusaders.
Overseas tours: Derrick Robins tour of South Africa 1972–73; M.C.C. to East
Africa 1974–75; M.C.C. to West Africa 1975–76; Surrey C.C.C. to
Singapore, Bangkok, Hong Kong 1979; Calcutta, Bengal Golden Jubilee match
December 1980.
Off-season 1984-85: Teaching at Cranleigh.

Cricketers particularly learnt from: Arthur Milton, Tom Cartwright, Colin Cowdrey.

Cricket superstitions: "Not now."

Equipment used: Gray-Nicolls.

Equipment endorsed: Gray-Nicolls bats.

Other sports: Rugby, squash, tennis, swimming, badminton, soccer, volleyball, waterpolo, table-tennis.

Relaxations: Bridge, music (particularly modern jazz), chess, philosophy, French literature, "reading Ogden Nash".

Extras: Played rugby for Cambridge University (no blue), Sussex Rugby XV (Captain 1973). Cambridge cricket blue 1967–70. Following debut for Surrey in 1968 left county after 1970 season and made debut for Gloucestershire 1971, gaining cap in 1971. Left Gloucestershire after 1975 season and made debut for Sussex in 1976, gaining Sussex cap in 1976. Left Sussex after 1977 season and rejoined Surrey in 1978. Most runs in Benson and Hedges competition. Reserve standby for Prudential One-Day International v. India 1982. Captain 1978–83. Not available full-time in 1985, but should be able to play in second half of the season (during school holidays).

Opinions on cricket: "(1) Players representing England should be: (a) British subjects born of British parents; (b) naturalised Britons; (c) *permanent* residents in Britain for at least 12 years. (2) The county programme should be changed. The Championship should be 16 x 4-day games. (3) Under-19 cricket needs to be extended and the various bodies brought together to produce the best youth team. (4) Present county players should be employed to coach in the winter so that young cricketers benefit from their experience."

Best batting performance: 165* Sussex v Middlesex, Hove 1976.

Best bowling performance: 6-44 Gloucestershire v Northamptonshire, Northampton 1974.

LAST SEASON: BATTING

	I.	N.O.	R.	H.S.	AV.
TEST					
OTHER FIRST CLASS	35	3	1254	142	39.19
INT					
J.P.L.	11	2	248	59	27.55
NAT.W.	3	0	54	36	18.00
B & H	5	0	97	37	19.40

CAREER: BATTING

	I.	N.O.	R.	H.S.	AV.
TEST					
OTHER FIRST CLASS	668	59	19518	165*	32.05
INT					
J.P.L.	199	21	4051	127	22.75
NAT.W.	33	1	713	75	22.28
B & H	60	9	2066	117	40.51

LAST SEASON: BOWLING

	O.	M.	R.	W.	AV.
TEST					
OTHER FIRST CLASS	349.4	99	925	27	34.26
INT					
J.P.L.	78	2	401	13	30.84
NAT.W.	33	9	70	5	14.00
B & H	46	7	139	5	27.80

CAREER: BOWLING

	O.	M.	R.	W.	AV.
TEST					
OTHER FIRST CLASS	4601.5	1053	13252	369	35.91
INT					
J.P.L.	1112.4	73	5120	194	26.39
NAT.W.	322	47	1017	46	22.11
B & H	460.4	69	1599	53	30.17

LYNCH, M.A.

Full Name: Monte Allan Lynch.
Role: Right-hand bat, right arm
medium and off-break bowler.
Born: 21 May 1958, Georgetown,
Guyana.
Weight: 12st.
Nickname: Mont.
County debut: 1977.
County cap: 1982.
Test debut: —
No. of Tests: 0.
No. of One-Day Internationals: 0.
1000 runs in a season: 3.
50 wickets in a season: 0.
1st-Class 50s scored: 31.
1st-Class 100s scored: 14.
1st-Class 200s scored: 0.
1st-Class 5 w. in innings: 0.
1st-Class 10 w. in match: 0.
One-day 50s: 13.
One-day 100s: 2.
Place in batting averages: 57 average: 38.65; (1983: 11 average: 53.72).
Place in bowling averages: — average: —; (1983: — average: —).
1st-Class catches 1984: 32 (career: 100).
Parents: Lawrence and Doreen Austin Lynch.
Marital status: Single.
Education: Ryden's School, Walton-on-Thames.

LAST SEASON: BATTING

	I.	N.O.	R.	H.S.	AV.
TEST					
OTHER FIRST CLASS	41	1	1546	144	38.65
INT					
J.P.L.	14	1	495	103	38.07
NAT.W.	3	1	40	19*	20.00
B & H	5	0	100	85	20.00

CAREER: BATTING

	I.	N.O.	R.	H.S.	AV.
TEST					
OTHER FIRST CLASS	239	25	6896	144	32.22
INT					
J.P.L.	85	13	2002	103	27.80
NAT.W.	13	3	281	129	28.10
B & H	21	0	500	85	23.81

LAST SEASON: BOWLING

	O.	M.	R.	W.	AV.
TEST					
OTHER FIRST CLASS	22.3	3	89	4	22.25
INT					
J.P.L.					
NAT.W.					
B & H					

CAREER: BOWLING

	O.	M.	R.	W.	AV.
TEST					
OTHER FIRST CLASS	173.4	30	663	15	44.20
INT					
J.P.L.	4.3	0	41	0	–
NAT.W.	11	5	26	1	–
B & H					

Family links with cricket: "Father and most of family played at some time or another."

Equipment used: Slazenger.

Other sports: Football, table tennis.

Extras: Hitting 141 n.o. for Surrey v. Glamorgan at Guildford in August 1982, off 78 balls in 88 minutes, one six hit his captain's, Roger Knight's, car, denting it. Repeated trick in 1983 v. Worcs. John Player Special League. Joined West Indies "rebels" in South Africa 1983–84.

Best batting performance: 144 Surrey v Leicestershire, The Oval 1984.

Best bowling performance: 3-6 Surrey v Glamorgan, Swansea 1981.

MEDLYCOTT, K.T.

Full Name: Keith Thomas Medlycott.

Role: Right-hand bat, slow left arm bowler.

Born: 12 May 1965, Whitechapel, London.

Height: 5' 10" **Weight:** 12st. 2lbs.

Nickname: Medders.

County debut: 1984.

County cap: No.

Test debut: —

No. of Tests: 0.

No. of One-Day Internationals: 0.

1000 runs in a season: 0.

50 wickets in a season: 0.

1st-Class 50s scored: 0.

1st-Class 100s scored: 1.

1st-Class 200s scored: 0.

1st-Class 5 w. in innings: 0.

1st-Class 10 w. in match: 0.

One-day 50s: 0.

One-day 100s: 0.

Place in batting averages: — average: —; (1983: — average: —).

Place in bowling averages: — average: —; (1983: — average: —).

Parents: Thomas Alfred and June Elizabeth.

Marital status: Single.

Education: Parmiters Grammar School; Wandsworth Comprehensive.

Qualifications: 2 O-levels.

Off-season 1984–85: Coaching abroad.

Equipment used: Newbery.

Cricketers particularly learnt from: G.G. Arnold.

Other sports: Football.

Relaxations: "Sleeping!"

Extras: Scored 100 on debut (117*).
Best batting performance: 117* Surrey v Cambridge University, Banstead 1984.
Best bowling performance: 2-15 Surrey v Kent, The Oval 1984.

LAST SEASON: BATTING

	I.	N.O.	R.	H.S.	AV.
TEST					
OTHER FIRST CLASS	6	5	128	117*	–
INT					
J.P.L.					
NAT.W.					
B & H					

CAREER: BATTING

	I.	N.O.	R.	H.S.	AV.
TEST					
OTHER FIRST CLASS	6	5	128	117*	–
INT					
J.P.L.					
NAT.W.					
B & H					

LAST SEASON: BOWLING

	O.	M.	R.	W.	AV.
TEST					
OTHER FIRST CLASS	98	34	186	7	26.57
INT					
J.P.L.					
NAT.W.					
B & H					

CAREER: BOWLING

	O.	M.	R.	W.	AV.
TEST					
OTHER FIRST CLASS	98	34	186	7	26.57
INT					
J.P.L.					
NAT.W.					
B & H					

MONKHOUSE, G.

Full Name: Graham Monkhouse.
Role: Right-hand bat, right arm medium fast bowler, slip fielder.
Born: 26 April 1955, Carlisle, Cumbria.
Height: 6' 1" **Weight** 13st. 8lbs.
Nickname: Farmer.
County debut: 1981.
County cap: 1984.
Test debut: —
No. of Tests: 0.
No. of One-Day Internationals: 0.
1000 runs in a season: 0.
50 wickets in a season: 1.
1st-Class 50s scored: 2.
1st-Class 100s scored: 1.
1st-Class 200s scored: 0.
1st-Class 5 w. in innings: 1.
1st-Class 10 w. in match: 0.
One-day 50s: 0.
One-day 100s: 0.

Place in batting averages: 213 average: 18.22; (1983: 161 average: 22.38).
Place in bowling averages: 30 average: 25.46; (1983: 21 average: 22.13).
1st-Class catches 1984: 8 (career: 21).
Parents: James Chris and Nancy Monkhouse.
Marital status: Single.
Family links with cricket: Father is chairman and ex-captain of Edenhall C.C., Cumberland Senior League, Division I.
Education: Langwathby C. of E. Primary School; Penrith Queen Elizabeth Grammar School; Nottinghamshire College of Agriculture.
Qualifications: "Various O-levels, O.N.C. Business Studies, H.N.D. Agriculture." N.C.A. Advanced cricket coach.
Jobs outside cricket: Ex-professional footballer. Representative for J. Bibby Agriculture 1976, farm manager 1976–79.
Off-season 1984–85: Building own house in Lake District.
Cricketing habits: "Falling asleep when listening to 'Teddy' Thomas talking cricket."
Equipment used: Slazenger; Nike sports shoes.
Overseas teams played for: Oostelikes C.C., South Africa, 1979–80, 1981–82, Harlequins C.C. 1982–83.
Overseas Tours: McAlpine Tour, South Africa 1984.
Cricketers particularly learnt from: Surrey Cricket Manager, M.J. Stewart, Roy Miles.
Other sports: Played professional football with Workington A.F.C. 4th Division. Other clubs: Carlisle United, Netherfield, Penrith A.F.C. Played county junior tennis, badminton at Under-16 level, and when allowed plays football for Dennis Waterman "Showbiz XI" in charity games in and around London. Plays club cricket for Wimbledon C.C. in the Surrey Championship League when not required by Surrey.
Relaxations: Photography, reading.
Significant injuries in 1984: Virus infection, May.

LAST SEASON: BATTING

	I.	N.O.	R.	H.S.	AV.
TEST					
OTHER FIRST CLASS	25	7	328	100*	18.22
INT					
J.P.L.	4	1	17	16	5.67
NAT.W.	1	0	8	8	–
B & H	3	1	10	4	5.00

CAREER: BATTING

	I.	N.O.	R.	H.S.	AV.
TEST					
OTHER FIRST CLASS	59	21	793	100*	20.87
INT					
J.P.L.	20	11	141	27	15.67
NAT.W.	3	0	15	8	5.00
B & H	6	3	26	12*	8.67

LAST SEASON: BOWLING

	O.	M.	R.	W.	AV.
TEST					
OTHER FIRST CLASS	460.5	120	1273	50	25.46
INT					
J.P.L.	77	1	413	10	41.30
NAT.W.	33.5	4	120	4	30.00
B & H	31	2	145	4	36.25

CAREER: BOWLING

	O.	M.	R.	W.	AV.
TEST					
OTHER FIRST CLASS	1050.5	261	2932	116	25.28
INT					
J.P.L.	279	17	1170	39	30.00
NAT.W.	101.3	9	351	13	27.00
B & H	74	8	285	11	25.91

Extras: Youngest player to be capped by Cumberland in the Minor Counties; Surrey member of Cricketers' Association.
Opinions on cricket: South Africa to be re-instated into Test cricket.
Best batting performance: 63* Surrey v Somerset, The Oval 1982.
Best bowling performance: 7-51 Surrey v Nottinghamshire, The Oval 1983.
Opinions on cricket: "South Africa to be re-instated into Test cricket."
Best batting performance: 100* Surrey v Kent, The Oval, 1984.
Best bowling performance: 7-15 Surrey v Nottinghamshire, The Oval 1983.

NEEDHAM, A.

Full Name: Andrew Needham.
Role: Right-hand bat, off-break bowler.
Born: 23 March 1957, Calow, Derbyshire.
Height: 5' 10" **Weight:** 10st. 8lbs.
Nickname: Needers.
County debut: 1977.
County cap: No.
Test debut: —
No. of Tests: 0.
No. of One-Day Internationals: 0.
1000 runs in a season: 0.
50 wickets in a season: 0.
1st-Class 50s scored: 4.
1st-Class 100s scored: 1.
1st-Class 200s scored: 0.
1st-Class 5 w. in innings: 4.
1st-Class 10 w. in match: 0.
One-day 50s: 1.
One-day 100s: 0.

Place in batting averages: 184 average: 22.21; (1983: — average: —).
Place in bowling averages: 102 average: 36.10; (1983: 34 average: 24.74).
1st-Class catches 1984: 10 (career: 24).
Marital status: Single.
Family links with cricket: Father played in Bassetlaw League.
Education: Ecclesbourne Grammar School, Derbyshire; Paisley Grammar School, Scotland; Watford Grammar School.
Qualifications: Six O-levels.
Cricketing superstitions: Always puts left pad on first.
Equipment used: Stuart Surridge.
Overseas tours: With M.C.C. to Bangladesh 1980–81; with Surrey C.C.C. to Hong Kong, Singapore and Bangkok 1980; with Surrey Y.C. to Antigua.
Cricketers particularly learnt from: Fred Titmus.
Other sports: Watches Chesterfield (football).

Relaxations: "Losing money on horses and cards."
Extras: Made debut for Hampshire in 1977, moving to Surrey for 1981 season. Was dropped in July 1982 for one match by manager Micky Stewart for not being in bed by 10.30 p.m.
Best batting performance: 134* Surrey v Lancashire, Old Trafford 1982.
Best bowling performance: 6-30 Surrey v Oxford University, Oxford 1983.

LAST SEASON: BATTING

	I.	N.O.	R.	H.S.	AV.
TEST					
OTHER FIRST CLASS	30	1	644	70	22.21
INT					
J.P.L.	9	1	78	25*	9.75
NAT.W.					
B & H	4	0	90	30	22.50

CAREER: BATTING

	I.	N.O.	R.	H.S.	AV.
TEST					
OTHER FIRST CLASS	78	10	1141	134*	16.78
INT					
J.P.L.	23	5	267	55	14.83
NAT.W.					
B & H	4	0	90	30	22.50

LAST SEASON: BOWLING

	O.	M.	R.	W.	AV.
TEST					
OTHER FIRST CLASS	328.5	79	1047	29	36.10
INT					
J.P.L.	10	4	31	1	–
NAT.W.					
B & H	8	0	40	0	–

CAREER: BOWLING

	O.	M.	R.	W.	AV.
TEST					
OTHER FIRST CLASS	1036.5	259	3185	80	39.81
INT					
J.P.L.	64.3	4	325	9	36.11
NAT.W.					
B & H	8	0	40	0	–

PAULINE, D.B.

Full Name: Duncan Brian Pauline.
Role: Right-hand opening bat.
Born: 15 December 1960, Aberdeen.
Height: 5′ 11″ **Weight:** 10st. 7lbs.
County debut: 1979.
County cap: No.
Test debut: —
No. of Tests: 0.
No. of One-Day Internationals: 0.
1000 runs in a season: 0.
50 wickets in a season: 0.
1st-Class 50s scored: 10.
1st-Class 100s scored: 1.
1st-Class 200s scored: 0.
1st-Class 5 w. in innings: 0.
1st-Class 10 w. in match: 0.
One-day 50s: 3.
One-day 100s: 0.

Place in batting averages: 164 average: 24.47; (1983: 41 average: 41.90).

Place in bowling averages: — average: —; (1983: — average: —).
1st-Class catches 1984: 9 (career: 14).
Parents: Brian and Vivienne Pauline.
Marital status: Single.
Education: Ashley Road School, Aberdeen; Bishop Fox, East Molesey.
Family links with cricket: Father and uncle both played in Aberdeen.
Overseas tours: Australia with Young England XI in 1978. Surrey C.C.C. Far East Tour, 1979.
Other sports: Football, golf, table-tennis.
Extras: Played for Surrey Schools under-12 and under-15. Played for South-East England under-15. England under-19 v West Indies and v Australia. Opening bat for one of England's oldest clubs, East Molesey, founded 1730. Name is pronounced with the 'ine' to rhyme with 'keen' (Scottish).
Best batting performance: 115 Surrey v Sussex, The Oval 1983.

LAST SEASON: BATTING

	I.	N.O.	R.	H.S.	AV.
TEST					
OTHER FIRST CLASS	16	1	367	88	24.47
INT					
J.P.L.	1	0	9	9	–
NAT.W.					
B & H	4	0	28	19	7.00

CAREER: BATTING

	I.	N.O.	R.	H.S.	AV.
TEST					
OTHER FIRST CLASS	58	4	1411	115	26.13
INT					
J.P.L.	14	1	433	92	33.30
NAT.W.					
B & H	4	0	28	19	7.00

LAST SEASON: BOWLING

	O.	M.	R.	W.	AV.
TEST					
OTHER FIRST CLASS	6	4	6	0	–
INT					
J.P.L.					
NAT.W.					
B & H					

CAREER: BOWLING

	O.	M.	R.	W.	AV.
TEST					
OTHER FIRST CLASS	12	4	28	0	–
INT					
J.P.L.					
NAT.W.					
B & H					

Q. 163. What was the middle name of Victor Trumper?
Q. 164. What was the middle name of Jack Hobbs?

PAYNE, I.R.

Full Name: Ian Roger Payne.
Role: Right-hand bat; right arm medium pace bowler.
Born: 9 May 1958, Kennington.
Height: 5′ 10″ **Weight:** 12st. 7lbs.
Nickname: Clouseau or Freda.
County debut: 1977.
County cap: No.
Test debut: —
No. of Tests: 0.
No. of One-Day Internationals: 0.
1000 runs in a season: 0.
50 wickets in a season: 0.
1st-Class 50s scored: 0.
1st-Class 100s scored: 0.
1st-Class 200s scored: 0.
1st-Class 5 w. in innings: 1.
1st-Class 10 w. in match: 0.
One-day 50s: 0.
One-day 100s: 0.
Place in batting averages: — average: —; (1983: — average: —).
Place in bowling averages: — average: —; (1983: — average: —).
1st-Class catches 1984: 4 (career: 30).
Parents: Richard John and Agnes Ross Payne.
Wife and date of marriage: Julie, 22 September 1979.
Education: Emanuel School, Wandsworth.
Qualifications: Five O-levels. Advanced Cricket Coach.
Jobs outside cricket: Work for travel company.

LAST SEASON: BATTING

	I.	N.O.	R.	H.S.	AV.
TEST					
OTHER FIRST CLASS	3	0	30	17	10.00
INT					
J.P.L.	1	1	9	9*	–
NAT.W.					
B & H	1	0	2	2	–

CAREER: BATTING

	I.	N.O.	R.	H.S.	AV.
TEST					
OTHER FIRST CLASS	37	5	338	43	10.56
INT					
J.P.L.	26	10	239	33*	14.93
NAT.W.	1	0	0	0	–
B & H	2	0	4	2	2.00

LAST SEASON: BOWLING

	O.	M.	R.	W.	AV.
TEST					
OTHER FIRST CLASS	42.5	18	102	3	34.40
INT					
J.P.L.	8	0	55	0	–
NAT.W.					
B & H	11	3	42	2	21.00

CAREER: BOWLING

	O.	M.	R.	W.	AV.
TEST					
OTHER FIRST CLASS	360.4	94	1127	26	43.35
INT					
J.P.L.	198	6	1032	37	27.89
NAT.W.	9	2	34	1	–
B & H	33	6	106	6	17.67

Cricketing superstitions: "Always changing them as they fail, which is very often."
Equipment used: Slazenger.
Overseas teams played for: Nedlands C.C. Perth, 1980–81, 1982–83.
Cricketers particularly learnt from: Craig Sarjeant, D.K. Lillee, B.D. Richards.
Other sports: Soccer.
Relaxations: Reading, music, travelling, T.V. and films.
Extras: Released at end of 1984.
Best batting performance: 43 Surrey v Essex, The Oval 1983.
Best bowling performance: 5-13 Surrey v Gloucestershire, The Oval 1983.

POCOCK, P.I.

Full Name: Patrick Ian Pocock.
Role: Right-hand bat, off-break bowler.
Born: 24 September 1946, Bangor, Caernarvonshire.
Height: 6′ 1½″ **Weight:** 13st.
Nickname: Percy.
County debut: 1964.
County cap: 1967.
Test debut: 1967–68.
No. of Tests: 20.
No. of One-Day Internationals: 0.
Benefit: £18,500 in 1977.
1000 runs in a season: 0.
50 wickets in a season: 16.
1st-Class 50s scored: 1.
1st-Class 100s scored: 0.
1st-Class 200s scored: 0.
1st-Class 5 w. in innings: 59.
1st-Class 10 w. in match: 7.
One-day 50s: 0.
One-day 100s: 0.
Place in batting averages: — average: —; (1983: — average: —).
Place in bowling averages: 33 average: 25.73; (1983: 42 average: 26.07).
1st-Class catches 1984: 8 (career: 175).
Parents: James Reginald and Cecelia Frances Pocock.
Wife and date of marriage: Diane, 8 March 1966.
Children: Samantha, 8 March 1971; Toby 18 May 1973.
Education: Merton C. of E. Secondary Boys' School; Wimbledon Technical School.
Qualifications: M.C.C. Advanced Coach.

Jobs outside cricket: Various posts in sales and marketing. Has own company, Pat Pocock Sports Promotions Ltd.
Family links with cricket: Brothers, Nigel and Tim, are very active members of Merton Cricket Club, London SW20. "W.G. Grace's mother was a Pocock, a relative of mine."
Off-season 1984–85: Touring India with England.
Overseas tours: Toured Pakistan in 1966–67; West Indies 1967–68 and 1973–74; Sri Lanka and Pakistan 1968–69; India, Pakistan and Sri Lanka 1972–73.
Overseas teams played for: Northern Transvaal in 1971–72 Currie Cup Competition.
Other sports: Squash and golf.
Relaxations: "Holidays."
Extras: Organised the Chubb World Double Wicket Championship at Wembley in April 1979, the first time a cricket competition has been televised indoors. Took four wickets in four balls, five in six, six in nine and seven in eleven v Sussex at Eastbourne in 1972. Responsible for the La Manga cricket development in Spain. Recalled to England side during 1984 after 8-year absence.
Best batting performance: 75* Surrey v Nottinghamshire, The Oval 1968.
Best bowling performance: 9-57 Surrey v Glamorgan, Cardiff 1979.

LAST SEASON: BATTING

	I.	N.O.	R.	H.S.	AV.
TEST	5	0	2	2	0.40
OTHER FIRST CLASS	16	6	110	29*	11.00
INT					
J.P.L.	4	2	14	5*	7.00
NAT.W.	1	1	8	8*	–
B & H	5	3	11	8*	5.50

CAREER: BATTING

	I.	N.O.	R.	H.S.	AV.
TEST	32	2	167	33	5.57
OTHER FIRST CLASS	496	136	4376	75*	12.16
INT					
J.P.L.	97	33	476	22	7.43
NAT.W.	17	5	64	14	5.33
B & H	30	16	110	19	7.86

LAST SEASON: BOWLING

	O.	M.	R.	W.	AV.
TEST	123.3	44	298	7	42.57
OTHER FIRST CLASS	515.2	123	1323	56	23.63
INT					
J.P.L.	77.4	10	313	18	17.38
NAT.W.	33	4	117	3	39.00
B & H	48	11	151	3	50.33

CAREER: BOWLING

	O.	M.	R.	W.	AV.
TEST	870.3	228	2321	54	42.98
OTHER FIRST CLASS	14487.4	4295	36670	1452	25.26
INT					
J.P.L.	1289.4	128	5104	194	26.30
NAT.W.	303	66	814	31	26.26
B & H	619.4	113	1943	68	28.86

Q. 165. What was the middle name of Dr. Grace?
Q. 166. What was the middle name of Len Hutton?

RICHARDS, C.J.

Full Name: Clifton James Richards.
Role: Right-hand bat, wicket-keeper.
Born: 10 August 1958, Penzance.
Height: 5' 11" **Weight:** 11st 8lbs.
Nickname: Jack.
County debut: 1976.
County cap: 1978.
Test debut: —
No. of Tests: 0.
No. of One-Day Internationals: 3.
1000 runs in a season: 0.
50 wickets in a season: 0.
1st-Class 50s scored: 17.
1st-Class 100s scored: 3.
1st-Class 200s scored: 0.
1st-Class 5 w. in innings: 0.
1st-Class 10 w. in match: 0.
One-day 50s: 1.
One-day 100s: 1.
Place in batting averages: 120 average: 30.27; (1983: 114 average: 27.81).
Place in bowling averages: — average: —; (1983: — average: —).
Parents: Clifton and Elizabeth June Richards.
Wife: Birgitta, 27 September 1980.
Education: Humphrey Davy Grammar School, Penzance.
Qualifications: 7 O-levels.
Jobs outside cricket: Trainee electrical engineer, apprentice draughtsman.
Family links with cricket: Father a member of Penzance C.C. and Surrey C.C.C.

LAST SEASON: BATTING

	I.	N.O.	R.	H.S.	AV.
TEST					
OTHER FIRST CLASS	38	8	908	109	30.27
INT					
J.P.L.	14	5	166	29	18.44
NAT.W.	2	0	40	38	20.00
B & H	5	0	36	25	7.20

CAREER: BATTING

	I.	N.O.	R.	H.S.	AV.
TEST					
OTHER FIRST CLASS	243	54	4364	117*	23.09
INT	2	0	3	3	1.50
J.P.L.	68	16	627	52	12.05
NAT.W.	9	2	204	105*	29.14
B & H	25	7	214	32	11.89

LAST SEASON: WICKET KEEPING

	C.	ST.			
TEST					
OTHER FIRST CLASS	45	6			
INT					
J.P.L.	12	7			
NAT.W.	3	–			
B & H	5	2			

CAREER: WICKET KEEPING

	C.	ST.			
TEST					
OTHER FIRST CLASS	360	50			
INT	1	–			
J.P.L.	61	25			
NAT.W.	23	4			
B & H	28	5			

Overseas tours: Australia with Derrick Robins Under-23 XI in 1979–80. Far East with Surrey C.C.C. in 1978–79. With England to India 1981–82.
Overseas teams played for: Klaas Vervelde XI 1981.
Equipment used: Slazenger.
Cricketing superstitions: Always last out of the dressing room when fielding.
Other sports: Tennis, golf, rugby, skiing, ice-skating, sailing. Follow most sports, especially American and other foreign sports.
Relaxations: Reading, television, driving.
Opinions on cricket: "Too many matches and too much travelling."
Best batting performance: 117* Surrey v Nottinghamshire, The Oval 1982.

STEWART, A.J.

Full Name: Alec James Stewart.
Role: Right-hand bat, wicket-keeper, short leg fielder.
Born: 8 April 1963, Wimbledon, Surrey.
Height: 5′ 11″ **Weight:** 12st.
County debut: 1981.
County cap: No.
Test debut: —
No. of Tests: 0.
No. of One-Day Internationals: 0.
1000 runs in a season: 0.
50 wickets in a season: 0.
1st-Class 50s scored: 6.
1st-Class 100s scored: 1.
1st-Class 200s scored: 0.
1st-Class 5 w. in innings: 0.
1st-Class 10 w. in match: 0.
One-day 50s: 1.
One-day 100s: 0.
Place in batting averages: 111 average: 31.67; (1983: 49 average: 40.38).
Place in bowling averages: — average: —; (1983: — average: —).
1st-Class catches 1984: 26 (career: 27).
Parents: Michael James and Sheila Marie Macdonald Stewart.
Marital status: Single.
Family links with cricket: Father played for England (1962–64) and Surrey (1954–72). Brother Neil plays club cricket and Surrey 2nd XI.
Education: Coombe Hill Primary School; Tiffin Grammar School.
Qualifications: 4 O-levels.
Overseas tours: 1980–81 tour of Australia with Surrey Under-19.
Off-season 1984–85: Cricket in Perth, Western Australia with Midland-Guildford (1981–85) and work in sports shop.

Equipment endorsed: Slazenger.
Cricketers particularly learnt from: Arthur MacIntyre, Jack Richards, Les Lenham, Kevin Gartrell, Geoff Arnold.
Cricketers particularly admired: Alan Knott, Geoff Boycott.
Other sports: Football. Watch all sports.
Relaxations: "Music, television, Perth beaches, eating out, listening to girl-friend!".
Opinions on cricket: That all, or at least as many 2nd XI games as possible should be played on 1st class grounds rather than club pitches which are a lot lower standard and slower than most county pitches. That all championship matches be played over 4 days, therefore meaning more 'results', and also it would prepare the players better for a 5-day Test Match.
Best batting performance: 118* Surrey v Oxford University, Oxford 1983.

LAST SEASON: BATTING

	I.	N.O.	R.	H.S.	AV.
TEST					
OTHER FIRST CLASS	21	3	570	73	31.67
INT					
J.P.L.	14	1	263	53*	20.23
NAT.W.	–	–	–	–	–
B & H	3	0	22	10	7.33

CAREER: BATTING

	I.	N.O.	R.	H.S.	AV.
TEST					
OTHER FIRST CLASS	42	7	1130	118*	32.29
INT					
J.P.L.	21	4	329	53*	19.35
NAT.W.	–	–	–	–	–
B & H	3	0	22	10	7.33

LAST SEASON: BOWLING

	O.	M.	R.	W.	AV.
TEST					
OTHER FIRST CLASS					
INT					
J.P.L.	0.3	0	4	0	–
NAT.W.					
B & H					

CAREER: BOWLING

	O.	M.	R.	W.	AV.
TEST					
OTHER FIRST CLASS					
INT					
J.P.L.	0.3	0	4	0	–
NAT.W.					
B & H					

Q. 167. Which side won the World Cup in 1983 and who was the captain?

Q. 168. What, where and when is the highest first-class team score in one innings, and who made it?

TAYLOR, N.S.

Full Name: Nicholas Simon Taylor.
Role: Right-hand bat, right arm
fast bowler.
Born: 2 June 1963, Holmfirth,
Yorkshire.
Height: 6′ 4″ **Weight:** 13st. 7lbs.
Nickname: Bond, Harry, Don.
County debut: 1981 (Yorkshire)
1984 (Surrey).
County cap: No.
Test debut: —
No. of Tests: 0.
No. of One-Day Internationals: 0.
1000 runs in a season: 0.
50 wickets in a season: 0.
1st-Class 50s scored: 0.
1st-Class 100s scored: 0.
1st-Class 200s scored: 0.
1st-Class 5 w. in innings: 1.
1st-Class 10 w. in match: 0.
One-day 50s: 0.
One-day 100s: 0.

Place in batting averages: — average: —; (1983: — average: —).
Place in bowling averages: — average: —; (1983: — average: —).
1st-Class catches 1984: 2 (career: 4).
Parents: Kenneth and Avril Taylor.
Marital status: Single.
Education: Gresham's School, Holt, Norfolk.
Qualifications: 3 A-levels, 7 O-levels.
Jobs outside cricket: Squash coach, builder.
Off-season 1984–85: Playing cricket in South Africa.
Family links with cricket: Father, Ken, played for Yorkshire and England.
Cricketers particularly learnt from: Dennis Lillee and Richard Hadlee.
Cricketing superstitions: "Always hold the ball in left hand when starting to
run in to bowl."
Equipment used: Gunn & Moore.
Other sports: Squash (played in British Open Under-19s), swimming, tennis,
running, weight-training. Watch American football.
Relaxations: Fly fishing, shooting, discos, food, reading, parties, T.V., music,
driving fast cars.
Extras: Released by Yorkshire 1983 and joined Surrey for 1984.
Opinions on cricket: "None that could be printed."
Best bowling performance: 5-49 Yorkshire v Sussex, Leeds 1983.

LAST SEASON: BATTING

	I.	N.O.	R.	H.S.	AV.
TEST					
OTHER FIRST CLASS	1	1	6	6*	–
INT					
J.P.L.	1	1	9	9*	–
NAT.W.					
B & H					

CAREER: BATTING

	I.	N.O.	R.	H.S.	AV.
TEST					
OTHER FIRST CLASS	7	2	16	6*	3.20
INT					
J.P.L.	1	1	9	9*	–
NAT.W.					
B & H					

LAST SEASON: BOWLING

	O.	M.	R.	W.	AV.
TEST					
OTHER FIRST CLASS	80	20	254	10	25.40
INT					
J.P.L.	4	0	17	0	–
NAT.W.					
B & H					

CAREER: BOWLING

	O.	M.	R.	W.	AV.
TEST					
OTHER FIRST CLASS	275.2	59	974	32	30.44
INT					
J.P.L.	4	0	17	0	–
NAT.W.					
B & H					

THOMAS, D.J.

Full Name: David James Thomas.
Role: Left-hand bat; left arm medium bowler.
Born: 30 June 1959, Solihull, Warwickshire.
Height: 6′ 0″ **Weight:** 12st. 7lbs.
Nickname: Teddy.
County debut: 1977.
County cap: 1982.
Test debut: —
No. of Tests: 0.
No. of One-Day Internationals: 0.
1000 runs in a season: 0.
50 wickets in a season: 2.
1st-Class 50s scored: 7.
1st-Class 100s scored: 2.
1st-Class 200s scored: 0.
1st-Class 5 w. in innings: 4.
1st-Class 10 w. in match: 1.
One-day 50s: 5.
One-day 100s: 0.
Place in batting averages: 209 average: 18.48; (1983: 70 average: 36.04).
Place in bowling averages: 46 average: 27.57; (1983: 74 average: 31.24).
1st-Class catches 1984: 10 (career: 41).
Parents: Howard James and Heather Thomas.
Wife and date of marriage: Miranda, February 1982.
Education: Eversfield Prep. School, Solihull; Licensed Victuallers' School, Slough.

Jobs outside cricket: Salesman for Securicor Communications.
Off-season 1984–85: Working for Securicor.
Family links with cricket: Father played for R.A.F. Brother, Howard, played for Bucks U-19.
Overseas tours: Surrey C.C.C. tour of the Far East, also Antigua; Cricketer International in Dubai. Whitbread Scholarship in Australia in 1982–83.
Equipment used: Slazenger.
Overseas teams played for: Northern Transvaal 1980–81, Natal 1983–4.
Cricketers particularly learnt from or admired: Mike Procter, Robin Jackman.
Other sports: Golf, squash. Follow: football, rugby, racing.
Significant injuries in 1984: Broken hand and damaged foot.
Extras: Played for England Under-19 v West Indies Under-19, and for Derrick Robins XI v New Zealand Under-25 XI.
Best batting performance: 119 Surrey v Nottinghamshire, The Oval 1983.
Best bowling performance: 6-36 Surrey v Somerset, The Oval 1984.

LAST SEASON: BATTING

	I.	N.O.	R.	H.S.	AV.
TEST					
OTHER FIRST CLASS	28	5	425	48	18.48
INT					
J.P.L.	11	1	230	60	23.00
NAT.W.	2	1	64	53	–
B & H	1	0	19	19	–

CAREER: BATTING

	I.	N.O.	R.	H.S.	AV.
TEST					
OTHER FIRST CLASS	147	29	2385	119	20.21
INT					
J.P.L.	55	12	795	72	18.48
NAT.W.	13	5	197	53	24.63
B & H	8	0	58	19	7.25

LAST SEASON: BOWLING

	O.	M.	R.	W.	AV.
TEST					
OTHER FIRST CLASS	505.4	114	1654	60	27.57
INT					
J.P.L.	85	4	452	11	41.09
NAT.W.	28	5	95	3	31.67
B & H	11	2	67	1	–

CAREER: BOWLING

	O.	M.	R.	W.	AV.
TEST					
OTHER FIRST CLASS	2610.1	589	8132	246	33.06
INT					
J.P.L.	495.5	31	2271	68	33.39
NAT.W.	160.5	20	550	18	30.56
B & H	104.3	16	397	11	36.09

Q. 169. What, where and when is the highest score in one innings by a first-class English county, and who made it?

WARD D.M.

Full Name: David Mark Ward.
Role: Right-hand batsman, short
leg fielder.
Born: 10 February 1961, Croydon.
Height: 6' 1" **Weight:** 12st 7lb.
Nickname: Cocker, Wardy.
County debut: 1984.
County cap: No.
Test debut: —
No. of Tests: 0.
No. of One-Day Internationals: 0.
1000 runs in a season: 0.
50 wickets in a season: 0.
1st-Class 50s scored: 0.
1st-Class 100s scored: 0.
1st-Class 200s scored: 0.
1st-Class 5 w. in innings: 0.
1st-Class 10 w. in match: 0.
One-day 50s: 1.
One-day 100s: 0.
Place in batting averages: — average: —; (1983: — average: —).
Place in bowling averages: — average: —; (1983: — average: —).
Parents: Dora Kathleen and Thomas Ward.
Marital status: Single.
Education: Haling Manor High School; Croydon Technical College.
Qualifications: 2 O-levels. City and Guilds in Carpentry and Joinery.
Jobs outside cricket: Carpenter.
Off-season 1984–85: Playing and coaching abroad.

LAST SEASON: BATTING

	I.	N.O.	R.	H.S.	AV.
TEST					
OTHER FIRST CLASS					
INT					
J.P.L.	2	2	91	59*	—
NAT.W.					
B & H					

CAREER: BATTING

	I.	N.O.	R.	H.S.	AV.
TEST					
OTHER FIRST CLASS					
INT					
J.P.L.	2	2	91	59*	—
NAT.W.					
B & H					

LAST SEASON: BOWLING

	O.	M.	R.	W.	AV.
TEST					
OTHER FIRST CLASS					
INT					
J.P.L.					
NAT.W.					
B & H					

CAREER: BOWLING

	O.	M.	R.	W.	AV.
TEST					
OTHER FIRST CLASS					
INT					
J.P.L.					
NAT.W.					
B & H					

Cricketing superstitions: Dig hole at corner of non striking crease.
Equipment used: Slazenger and Nike boots.
Cricketers particularly learnt from: G.G. Arnold, G. Clinton.
Cricketers particularly admired: G. Gooch and Keith Ebdon.
Other sports: Football and snooker.
Relaxations: Eating out; mellow jazz, any George Benson material; watching T.V.

WATERMAN, P.A.

Full Name: Peter Andrew Waterman.
Role: Right-arm fast bowler.
Born: 26 March 1961, Hendon, London.
Height: 6′ 1½″ **Weight:** 13st. 7lbs.
Nickname: Minder, Dennis, Del Boy.
County debut: 1983.
County cap: No.
Test debut: —
No. of Tests: 0.
No. of One-Day Internationals: 0.
1000 runs in a season: 0.
50 wickets in a season: 0.
1st-Class 50s scored: 0.
1st-Class 100s scored: 0.
1st-Class 200s scored: 0.
1st-Class 5 w. in innings: 0.
1st-Class 10 w. in match: 0.
One-day 50s: 0.
One-day 100s: 0.
Place in batting averages: — average: —; (1983: — average: —).
Place in bowling averages: — average: —; (1983: — average: —).
1st-Class catches 1984: 2 (career: 2).
Parents: Bernard Charles and Bernadette Catherine.
Marital status: Single.
Education: Rooks Heath High School, Pinner Sixth Form College.
Qualifications: 5 O-levels, Higher Technical Education Council Certificate in electronic and electrical engineering.
Jobs outside cricket: Systems analyst since September 1979 with Marconi Space and Defence Systems Ltd.
Off season 1984–85: Playing grade cricket in Sydney.
Overseas tours: Australasia, 1983, Club Cricket conference.
Overseas teams played for: Manly-Warringah 1983–84.
Equipment used: Slazenger.
Cricketers particularly admired: D.K. Lillee, M. Holding.

Other sports: Football, golf, tennis.
Significant injuries during 1984: Strained calf muscle – 10 days.
Relaxations: Live music, reading, travel, videos.
Extras: Hat trick v. Sussex 2nd XI 1983 and sprained ankle in subsequent celebration!
Best bowling performance: 2-16 Surrey v Leicestershire, The Oval 1984.

LAST SEASON: BATTING

	I.	N.O.	R.	H.S.	AV.
TEST					
OTHER FIRST CLASS	2	1	0	0*	–
INT					
J.P.L.					
NAT.W.					
B & H	1	0	2	2	–

CAREER: BATTING

	I.	N.O.	R.	H.S.	AV.
TEST					
OTHER FIRST CLASS	4	2	6	6*	3.00
INT					
J.P.L.	–	–	–	–	–
NAT.W.					
B & H	1	0	2	2	–

LAST SEASON: BOWLING

	O.	M.	R.	W.	AV.
TEST					
OTHER FIRST CLASS	58.2	7	194	5	38.80
INT					
J.P.L.					
NAT.W.					
B & H	10	0	60	0	–

CAREER: BOWLING

	O.	M.	R.	W.	AV.
TEST					
OTHER FIRST CLASS	97.2	14	345	6	57.50
INT					
J.P.L.	13	1	44	1	–
NAT.W.					
B & H	10	0	60	0	–

COUNTY QUIZ

Q. 1. When was the club founded?
Q. 2. Who made the most first-class runs for the county last season, and how many?
Q. 3. What's the highest ever county total, and against whom?
Q. 4. Who took the most wickets for the county last season, and how many?
Q. 5. What's the highest individual score for the county, who hit it, and when?
Q. 6. What's the highest scoring partnership for the county for any wicket?
Q. 7. How many times has the club won the County Championship?
Q. 8. What's the lowest ever total made by the county in one innings, when, and against whom?
Q. 9. Which bowler took the most first-class wickets in one season, when, and how many?
Q. 10. Which batsman hit the most runs in one season, when, and how many?

Sussex

BARCLAY, J.R.T.

Full Name: John Robert Troutbeck Barclay.
Role: Right-hand bat, off-break bowler, slip fielder.
Born: 22 January 1954, Bonn, West Germany.
Height: 5′ 10½″ **Weight:** 11st. 7lbs.
Nickname: Trouters, Trout.
County debut: 1970, aged 16 yrs 6 mths while still at school.
County cap: 1976.
Test debut: —
No. of Tests: 0.
No. of One-Day Internationals: 0.
1000 runs in a season: 4.
50 wickets in a season: 1.
1st-Class 50s scored: 46.
1st-Class 100s scored: 9.
1st-Class 200s scored: 0.
1st-Class 5 w. in innings: 7.
1st-Class 10 w. in match: 1.
One-day 50s: 6.
One-day 100s: 0.
Place in batting averages: 172 average: 23.78; (1983: 166 average: 21.85).
Place in bowling averages: 51 average: 28.42; (1983: 124 average: 45.53).
1st-Class catches 1984: 21 (career: 203).
Parents: C.F.R. Barclay, Mrs J.B. Denman.
Wife and date of marriage: Mary Louise, 16 September 1978.
Children: Georgina Clare, born 9 January 1981.
Education: Summerfields School, Oxford, Eton College.
Jobs outside cricket: Marketing Executive with International Factors Ltd.
Family links with cricket: Great uncle, F.J.J. Ford, played for Middlesex.
Cricketers particularly learnt from: Tony Buss and Stewart Storey.
Overseas tours: India 1970–71 with England Schools Cricket Association (Vice-Captain); England Young Cricketers to West Indies 1972 as Captain.

Overseas teams played for: Orange Free State, 1978–79. Waverley C.C., Sydney, 1981.
Off-season 1984–5: Working for International Factors Ltd.
Equipment used: Gray-Nicolls.
Other sports: Golf, fishing, weightlifting. Watch rugby, golf, racing.
Relaxations: Gardening, music.
Extras: Sussex captain since 1981.
Best batting performance: 119 Sussex v Leicestershire, Hove 1980.
Best bowling performance: 6-61 Sussex v Sri Lankans, Hove 1979.

LAST SEASON: BATTING

	I.	N.O.	R.	H.S.	AV.
TEST					
OTHER FIRST CLASS	35	3	761	82	23.78
INT					
J.P.L.	7	5	51	20*	25.50
NAT.W.	2	2	11	7*	–
B & H	5	0	147	81	29.40

CAREER: BATTING

	I.	N.O.	R.	H.S.	AV.
TEST					
OTHER FIRST CLASS	414	38	9384	119	24.96
INT					
J.P.L.	99	32	1216	48	18.14
NAT.W.	21	2	340	48	17.90
B & H	39	2	1034	93*	27.95

LAST SEASON: BOWLING

	O.	M.	R.	W.	AV.
TEST					
OTHER FIRST CLASS	417	117	1023	36	28.42
INT					
J.P.L.	52	2	243	13	18.69
NAT.W.	20	0	99	7	14.14
B & H	31	2	133	4	33.25

CAREER: BOWLING

	O.	M.	R.	W.	AV.
TEST					
OTHER FIRST CLASS	3183.4	788	8958	293	30.57
INT					
J.P.L.	564	26	2539	99	25.64
NAT.W.	128.3	17	425	23	18.48
B & H	258.5	32	964	35	27.54

Q. 170. What is the highest first-class team score made in the fourth innings to win a match, by whom, where and when?

Q. 171. What is the highest first-class team score in the fourth innings to draw a match, by whom, where and when?

GOULD, I.J.

Full Name: Ian James Gould.
Role: Left-hand bat, wicket-keeper.
Born: 19 August 1957, Taplow, Bucks.
Height: 5′ 7½″ **Weight:** 11st 7lbs.
Nickname: Gouldy, Gunner.
County debut: 1981 (Sussex).
County cap: 1981.
Test debut: —
No. of Tests: 0.
No. of One-Day Internationals: 18.
Benefit: "The year dot!"
1000 runs in a season: 0.
50 wickets in a season: 0.
1st-Class 50s scored: 19.
1st-Class 100s scored: 1.
1st-Class 200s scored: 0.
1st-Class 5 w. in innings: 0.
1st-Class 10 w. in match: 0.
One-day 50s: 8. .
One-day 100s: 0.
Place in batting averages: 178 average: 23.00; (1983: 113 average: 27.88).
Place in bowling averages: — average: —; (1983: — average: —).
Parents: Doreen and George Gould.
Education: Westgate School – "Which some people thought should have been a borstal."
Jobs outside cricket: "Very good dole collector!"

LAST SEASON: BATTING

	I.	N.O.	R.	H.S.	AV.
TEST					
OTHER FIRST CLASS	27	4	529	84	23.00
INT					
J.P.L.	10	1	134	38	14.89
NAT.W.	1	0	31	31	–
B & H	3	0	16	7	5.33

CAREER: BATTING

	I.	N.O.	R.	H.S.	AV.
TEST					
OTHER FIRST CLASS	245	34	4782	128	22.66
INT	14	2	155	42	12.92
J.P.L.	97	13	1376	69*	16.38
NAT.W.	16	0	259	58	16.19
B & H	30	3	451	72	16.70

LAST SEASON: WICKET KEEPING

	C.	ST.			
TEST					
OTHER FIRST CLASS	62	6			
INT					
J.P.L.	8	–			
NAT.W.	–	2			
B & H	6	1			

CAREER: WICKET KEEPING

	C.	ST.			
TEST					
OTHER FIRST CLASS	382	62			
INT	15	3			
J.P.L.	91	20			
NAT.W.	15	6			
B & H	35	2			

Overseas tours: Toured West Indies with England Young Cricketers 1976. With England in Australia and New Zealand, 1982–83.
Overseas teams played for: Auckland, 1980.
Cricketers particularly learnt from: Roger Tolchard: "After seeing him, it makes me feel a lot better because he's such a nice guy!"
Equipment endorsed: Slazenger, Fred Perry.
Other sports: Amateur footballer for Slough Town F.C. at full-back, golf, swimming.
Extras: Was offered contract for 1981 by Middlesex but chose to join Sussex. Made debut for Middlesex in 1975, gaining cap in 1977. "When I had my last medical I found I was as blind as a bat."
Best batting performance: 128 Middlesex v Worcestershire, Worcester 1978.

GREEN, A.M.

Full Name: Allan Michael Green.
Role: Right-hand bat; right arm off-spin.
Born: 28 May 1960, Pulborough, Sussex.
Height: 5′ 11″ **Weight:** 11st.
Nickname: Gilbert.
County debut: 1980.
County cap: No.
Test debut: —
No. of Tests: 0.
No. of One-Day Internationals: 0.
1000 runs in a season: 1.
50 wickets in a season: 0.
1st-Class 50s scored: 11.
1st-Class 100s scored: 0.
1st-Class 200s scored: 0.
1st-Class 5 w. in innings: 0.
1st-Class 10 w. in match: 0.
One-day 50s: 3.

One-day 100s: 0.
Place in batting averages: 150 average: 26.47; (1983: 178 average: 19.72).
Place in bowling averages: — average: —; (1983: — average: —).
1st-Class catches 1984: 12 (career: 30).
Parents: Michael and Sheila Green.
Marital status: Single.
Education: Knoll School, Hove; Brighton Sixth Form College.
Qualifications: Five O-levels.
Jobs outside cricket: Sports shop assistant, labourer.
Family links with cricket: Father played for Findon C.C. "as a fielder."

Cricketers particularly learnt from: Ian Thomson (former Sussex player), Chris Waller, Roger Marshall, Paul Weller.
Equipment used: Duncan Fearnley.
Relaxations: "Sleeping, going to concerts, eating, drinking and listening to records by "The Jam".
Best batting performance: 99 Sussex v Middlesex, Hove 1982.

LAST SEASON: BATTING

	I.	N.O.	R.	H.S.	AV.
TEST					
OTHER FIRST CLASS	40	2	1006	81	26.47
INT					
J.P.L.	8	1	285	83	40.72
NAT.W.					
B & H	2	0	85	74	42.50

CAREER: BATTING

	I.	N.O.	R.	H.S.	AV.
TEST					
OTHER FIRST CLASS	102	5	2441	99	25.12
INT					
J.P.L.	11	3	315	83	39.38
NAT.W.	2	0	85	74	42.50
B & H	4	0	81	30	20.25

LAST SEASON: BOWLING

	O.	M.	R.	W.	AV.
TEST					
OTHER FIRST CLASS	18	2	41	1	–
INT					
J.P.L.					
NAT.W.	1	0	7	0	–
B & H					

CAREER: BOWLING

	O.	M.	R.	W.	AV.
TEST					
OTHER FIRST CLASS	141.4	17	563	13	43.31
INT					
J.P.L.					
NAT.W.	1	0	7	0	–
B & H	3	1	4	1	–

GREIG, I.A.

Full Name: Ian Alexander Greig.
Role: Right-hand bat; right arm medium pace bowler, slip fielder.
Born: 8 December 1955, Queenstown, South Africa.
Height: 5′ 11½″ **Weight:** 12st 7lbs.
Nickname: Washies, Greigy.
County debut: 1980.
County cap: 1981.
Test debut: 1982.
No. of Tests: 2.
No. of One-Day Internationals: 0.
1000 runs in a season: 0.
50 wickets in a season: 3.
1st-Class 50s scored: 17.
1st-Class 100s scored: 4.
1st-Class 200s scored: 0.
1st-Class 5 w. in inngs: 7.
1st-Class 10 w. in match: 2.

One-day 50s: 2.
One-day 100s: 0.
Place in batting averages: 142 average: 27.10; (1983: 71 average: 36.00).
Place in bowling averages: 70 average: 30.85; (1983: 114 average: 40.06).
1st-Class catches 1984: 17 (career: 75).
Parents: Joyce and Sandy Greig.
Wife and date of marriage: Cheryl, 8 January 1982.
Education: Queen's College, Queenstown, South Africa; Downing College, Cambridge.
Qualifications: B.A. (Cantab) in Law.
Family links with cricket: Brother of A.W. Greig, former Captain of Sussex and England. Brother-in-law R.P. Hodson (Cambridge University and Yorkshire).
Overseas tours: Captain of Combined Universities tour to Australia 1979–80.
Overseas teams played for: Debut for Border 1974; also played for Griqualand West while doing national service in South Africa.
Cricketers particularly learnt from: "Coaches at school in South Africa, Colin Milburn, Fred Rumsey, Dennis Amiss, Ian Thompson and Tony Greig. Have learnt a lot from G.G. Arnold."
Jobs outside cricket: Marketing trainee.
Off-season 1984–85: Captain/coach of Waverley C.C., Sydney.
Equipment endorsed: Symonds.
Other sports: Rugby.
Relaxations: "Sleeping—pop music—general outdoor life."
Extras: Three cricket blues at Cambridge University and Captain in 1979; two rugby blues.
Best batting performance: 147* Sussex v Oxford University, Oxford 1983.
Best bowling performance: 7-43 Sussex v Cambridge University, Cambridge 1981.

LAST SEASON: BATTING

	I.	N.O.	R.	H.S.	AV.
TEST					
OTHER FIRST CLASS	35	5	813	106*	27.10
INT					
J.P.L.	13	2	272	48	24.73
NAT.W.	2	0	55	34	27.50
B & H	4	1	69	27	23.00

CAREER: BATTING

	I.	N.O.	R.	H.S.	AV.
TEST	4	0	26	14	6.50
OTHER FIRST CLASS	162	19	3713	147*	25.97
INT					
J.P.L.	50	11	896	48	22.97
NAT.W.	7	0	175	82	25.00
B & H	29	3	450	51	17.31

LAST SEASON: BOWLING

	O.	M.	R.	W.	AV.
TEST					
OTHER FIRST CLASS	648	153	1913	62	30.85
INT					
J.P.L.	83.4	3	461	10	46.10
NAT.W.	23	4	76	2	38.00
B & H	47	2	159	4	39.75

CAREER: BOWLING

	O.	M.	R.	W.	AV.
TEST	31.2	6	114	4	28.50
OTHER FIRST CLASS	2484.2	520	7698	272	28.30
INT					
J.P.L.	352.2	13	1760	55	32.00
NAT.W.	76.5	10	257	12	21.42
B & H	254.2	24	796	26	30.62

IMRAN KHAN

Full Name: Ahmad Khan Niazi Imran.
Role: Right-hand bat, right arm fast bowler.
Born: 25 November 1952, Lahore, Pakistan.
Height: 6′ 0″ **Weight:** 12st 2lbs.
Nickname: Immie.
County debut: 1977 (Sussex).
County cap: 1978.
Test debut: 1971.
No. of Tests: 51.
No. of One-Day Internationals: 48.

1000 runs in a season: 4.
50 wickets in a season: 6.
1st-Class 50s scored: 65.
1st-Class 100s scored: 22.
1st-Class 200s scored: 0.
1st-Class 5 w. in innings: 56.
1st-Class 10 w. in match: 11.
One-day 50s: 31.
One-day 100s: 2.
Place in batting averages: — average: —; (1983: 6 average: 57.57).
Place in bowling averages: — average: —; (1983: 1 average: 7.17).
1st-Class catches 1984: 0 (career: 93).
Marital status: Single.
Education: Aitchison College; Cathedral School, Lahore; Worcester Royal Grammar School; Keble College, Oxford University.
Qualifications: B.A. Hons. in politics and economics.
Jobs outside cricket: "I play cricket all the year round."
Off-season 1984–85: Playing in Australia.
Family links with cricket: Cousin of Pakistan cricketers, Majid Khan and Javed Burki.
Overseas tours: Toured with Pakistan to England in 1971, 1974, 1982 and 1983 World Cup; Australia and West Indies 1976–77; India 1979–80. Australia, 1981–82, 1983–84.
Overseas teams played for: Various Lahore teams.
Cricketers particularly learnt from: John Snow, Basil D'Oliviera, Majid Khan.
Other sports: Squash, swimming, hockey.
Significant injuries in 1984: Stress fracture of shin—long term.
Relaxations: Shooting, listening to music (Western and Eastern).
Extras: Debut for Lahore A 1969–70. Debut for Worcestershire 1971, cap 1976. Left Worcestershire in 1977. Oxford cricket blue 1973–74–75. Captain

in 1974. Scored two centuries in a match, 117 not out and 106, Oxford University v Notts. at Oxford in 1974. Had a match double of 111 not out and 13 for 99 v Lancashire at Worcester in 1976. Played World Series Cricket. Has bad scar on left arm resulting from falling off a slide in Lahore, and cannot fully extend his arm: "It affects my batting a bit. My top hand grip is very strange if I don't bat regularly". Drinks 3½ pints of milk a day. Drinks no alcohol. Does not smoke. "I don't eat pig meat and I wear a verse from the Koran in gold round my neck, which is supposed to protect me. I pray before going to sleep." Top of Sussex first-class batting and bowling averages in 1982 and 1983. Captain of Pakistan 1982–83.

Opinions on cricket: "I've always treated a game of cricket as something to win and if you can't win, you shouldn't be afraid of losing. Most three-day matches are drawn, and I find it dreary playing in games that are heading nowhere. It is unsuitable for the players, and it is unsuitable for spectators. Young people are watching other sports. I see very few young and enthusiastic people watching three-day matches. Who wants to watch draws? Four-day games would be more likely to reach a positive result. It would be necessary to attack. There would be more emphasis on getting batsmen out rather than just containing them. And the crowds would come back."

Best batting performance: 170 Oxford University v Northamptonshire, Oxford 1974.

Best bowling performance: 8-58 Pakistan v Sri Lanka, Faisalabad 1981–82.

LAST SEASON: BATTING

	I.	N.O.	R.	H.S.	AV.
TEST					
OTHER FIRST CLASS					
INT					
J.P.L.					
NAT.W.					
B & H					

CAREER: BATTING

	I.	N.O.	R.	H.S.	AV.
TEST	77	12	2023	123	31.12
OTHER FIRST CLASS	374	58	10110	170	31.99
INT	39	13	907	102*	34.88
J.P.L.	94	14	2258	90	28.23
NAT.W.	22	5	538	114*	31.65
B & H	36	6	1052	72	35.07

LAST SEASON: BOWLING

	O.	M.	R.	W.	AV.
TEST					
OTHER FIRST CLASS					
INT					
J.P.L.					
NAT.W.					
B & H					

CAREER: BOWLING

	O.	M.	R.	W.	AV.
TEST	410 1546.1	68 371	5316	232	22.91
OTHER FIRST CLASS	713.4 5263.5	129 1199	16681	763	21.86
INT.	292.2	42	961	42	22.88
J.P.L.	693.2	56	2573	134	19.20
NAT.W.	209.3	38	662	25	26.48
B & H	354.3	75	994	52	19.11

Q. 172. What is the highest first-class team score in the fourth innings to lose a match, where, when and by whom?

JONES, A.N.

Full Name: Adrian Nicholas Jones.
Role: Left-hand bat, right arm
fast bowler.
Born: 22 July 1961, Woking.
Height: 6′ 2″ **Weight:** 14st.
Nickname: Quincy, Jonah.
County debut: 1981.
County cap: No.
Test debut: —
No. of Tests: 0.
No. of One-Day Internationals: 0.
1000 runs in a season: 0.
50 wickets in a season: 0.
1st-Class 50s scored: 0.
1st-Class 100s scored: 0.
1st-Class 200s scored: 0.
1st-Class 5 w. in innings: 1.
1st-Class 10 w. in match: 0.
One-day 50s: 0.
One-day 100s: 0.

Place in batting averages: — average —; (1983: — average —).
Place in bowling averages: 28 average: 25.44; (1983 — average —).
1st-Class catches 1984: 3 (career: 4).
Parents: William Albert and Emily Doris Jones.
Family links with cricket: Father and brother, Glynne, both fine club cricketers.
Education: Forest Grange Preparatory School; Seaford College.
Qualifications: Two A-levels, 8 O-levels. N.C.A. coaching qualification.
Jobs outside cricket: Working in a warehouse, sales representative.
Off-season 1984–85: Playing for Orange Free State, and coaching Rovers C.C. Welkom, South Africa.
Cricketing superstitions: "Drink lots of tea. Always fold a sweater up before handing to the umpire when bowling."
Equipment used: Duncan Fearnley.
Equipment endorsed: Fred Perry.
Overseas teams played for: Old Selbournians and Bohemians, South Africa, 1981–82, Border 1981–82; Red and White C.C., Haarlem, Holland 1980.
Cricketers particularly learnt from: Geoff Arnold, Imran Khan, Garth Le Roux.
Cricketers particularly admired: John Snow.
Other sports: Rugby, hockey, golf. Watching Indoor Hockey.
Relaxations: "Listening to UB40 all day. Watching Laurel and Hardy films. Driving."
Significant injuries during 1984: Pulled stomach muscle.

Extras: Played for Young England in 1981.
Opinions on cricket: "Groundsmen should pay more attention to bowlers' foot holes during the course of the match."
Best batting performance: 35 Sussex v Middlesex, Hove 1984.
Best bowling performance: 5-29 Sussex v Gloucestershire, Hove 1984.

LAST SEASON: BATTING

	I.	N.O.	R.	H.S.	AV.
TEST					
OTHER FIRST CLASS	7	4	73	35	24.33
INT					
J.P.L.	–	–	–	–	–
NAT.W.	1	1	3	3*	–
B & H					

CAREER: BATTING

	I.	N.O.	R.	H.S.	AV.
TEST					
OTHER FIRST CLASS	27	12	146	35	9.73
INT					
J.P.L.	–	–	–	–	–
NAT.W.	1	1	3	3*	–
B & H	1	0	2	2	–

LAST SEASON: BOWLING

	O.	M.	R.	W.	AV.
TEST					
OTHER FIRST CLASS	208.1	44	636	25	25.44
INT					
J.P.L.	30	2	127	10	12.70
NAT.W.	10	1	49	1	–
B & H					

CAREER: BOWLING

	O.	M.	R.	W.	AV.
TEST					
OTHER FIRST CLASS	423.2	73	1485	54	27.50
INT					
J.P.L.	44	3	218	11	19.82
NAT.W.	10	1	49	1	–
B & H					

LENHAM, N.J.

Full Name: Neil John Lenham.
Role: Right-hand bat, right arm medium bowler.
Born: 17 December 1965, Worthing.
Height: 5' 11" **Weight:** 10st. 12lbs.
Nickname: Spelvin, Nellie.
County debut: 1984.
County cap: No.
Test debut: —
No. of Tests: 0.
No. of One-Day Internationals: 0.
1000 runs in a season: 0.
50 wickets in a season: 0.
1st-Class 50s scored: 0.
1st-Class 100s scored: 0.
1st-Class 200s scored: 0.
1st-Class 5 w. in innings: 0.
1st-Class 10 w. in match: 0.
One-day 50s: 0.
One-day 100s: 0.
Place in batting averages: — average: —; (1983: — average: —).

Place in bowling averages: — average: —; (1983: — average: —).
1st-Class catches 1984: 1 (career 1).
Parents: Leslie John and Valerie Anne Lenham.
Marital status: Single.
Family links with cricket: Father, ex Sussex county cricketer and NCA National Coach.
Education: Broadwater Manor House Prep. School; Brighton College.
Qualifications: 5 O-levels, 2 A-levels.
Off-season 1984–85: Working at Broadwater Manor Prep. School; with Young England team in West Indies, as captain.
Cricketing superstitions: Adjusting all equipment to obtain comfort.
Equipment used: Newbery bats.
Equipment endorsed: Fred Perry.
Overseas tours: 1981 tour to Barbados—Sussex U-16; 1982 tour to Barbados with Sussex Young Cricketers; 1985 England Young Cricketers tour to West Indies.
Cricketers particularly learnt from: Les Lenham, John Spencer.
Cricketers particularly admired: Ken McEwan, Barry Richards.
Other sports: Hockey, squash, golf; follows golf and snooker.
Relaxations: Music, listening to Van Morrison, Neil Diamond and Janis Joplin; reading.
Opinions on cricket: "Too much political interference in sport (especially cricket). All players, touring parties should be left to the county or country's sports governing bodies and no outside influence be allowed."
Extras: Made debut for Young England 1983. Scored double century for Brighton College v Hurstpierpoint 1984. Broke record for number of runs scored in season at a public school in 1984 (1534 Av. 80.74).
Best batting performance: 31 Sussex v Sri Lanka, Hove 1984.

LAST SEASON: BATTING

	I.	N.O.	R.	H.S.	AV.
TEST					
OTHER FIRST CLASS	1	0	31	31	–
INT					
J.P.L.					
NAT.W.					
B & H					

CAREER: BATTING

	I.	N.O.	R.	H.S.	AV.
TEST					
OTHER FIRST CLASS	1	0	31	31	–
INT					
J.P.L.					
NAT.W.					
B & H					

LAST SEASON: BOWLING

	O.	M.	R.	W.	AV.
TEST					
OTHER FIRST CLASS					
INT					
J.P.L.					
NAT.W.					
B & H					

CAREER: BOWLING

	O.	M.	R.	W.	AV.
TEST					
OTHER FIRST CLASS					
INT					
J.P.L.					
NAT.W.					
B & H					

LE ROUX, G.S.

Full Name: Garth Sterling Le Roux.
Role: Right-hand bat, right arm
fast bowler.
Born: 4 September 1955, Capetown,
South Africa.
Height: 6' 3" **Weight:** 15st.
Nickname: Rocky.
County debut: 1978.
County cap: 1981.
Test debut: —
No. of Tests: 0.
No. of One-Day Internationals: 0.
1000 runs in a season: 0.
50 wickets in a season: 3.
1st-Class 50s scored: 16.
1st-Class 100s scored: 0.
1st-Class 200s scored: 0.
1st-Class 5 w. in innings: 29.
1st-Class 10 w. in match: 3.
One-day 50s: 3.
One-day 100s: 0.
Place in batting averages: 219 average: 17.83; (1983: 138 average: 25.06).
Place in bowling averages: 9 average: 21.12; (1983: 39 average: 25.67).
1st-Class catches 1984: 4 (career: 60).
Parents: Pierre and Audrey Le Roux.
Marital status: Single.
Education: Wynberg Boys' High School; Stellenbosch University.

LAST SEASON: BATTING

	I.	N.O.	R.	H.S.	AV.
TEST					
OTHER FIRST CLASS	24	6	321	68*	17.83
INT					
J.P.L.	9	2	158	48	22.57
NAT.W.	1	0	22	22	–
B & H	4	1	63	50	21.00

CAREER: BATTING

	I.	N.O.	R.	H.S.	AV.
TEST					
OTHER FIRST CLASS	191	53	3364	83	24.38
INT					
J.P.L.	43	9	836	88	24.58
NAT.W.	8	1	80	22	11.43
B & H	16	6	334	50	33.40

LAST SEASON: BOWLING

	O.	M.	R.	W.	AV.
TEST					
OTHER FIRST CLASS	604.2	154	1647	78	21.12
INT					
J.P.L.	80.1	7	325	14	23.21
NAT.W.	9	2	13	0	–
B & H	46	6	165	7	23.57

CAREER: BOWLING

	O.	M.	R.	W.	AV.
TEST					
OTHER FIRST CLASS	4628	1062	11892	587	20.26
INT					
J.P.L.	376.2	18	1605	82	19.57
NAT.W.	96.3	18	255	17	15.00
B & H	175.4	19	708	28	25.29

Off-season 1984–85: Playing for Western Province.
Qualifications: B.A. Physical Education.
Overseas tours: World XI in World Series Cricket Tour.
Equipment used: Stuart Surridge.
Other sports: Golf, squash.
Relaxations: Horse-riding, listening to music.
Extras: Played for Packer's World Series cricket.
Best batting performance: 83 Sussex v Surrey, Hove 1982.
Best bowling performance: 8-107 Sussex v Somerset, Taunton 1981.

MENDIS, G.D.

Full Name: Gehan Dixon Mendis.
Role: Right-hand opening bat.
Born: 24 April 1955, Colombo, Sri Lanka.
Height: 5′ 8″ **Weight:** 10st. 4lbs.
Nickname: Mendo, Jack.
County debut: 1974.
County cap: 1980.
Test debut: —
No. of Tests: 0.
No. of One-Day Internationals: 0.
1000 runs in a season: 5.
50 wickets in a season: 0.
1st-Class 50s scored: 48.
1st-Class 100s scored: 15.
1st-Class 200s scored: 2.
1st-Class 5 w. in innings: 0.
1st-Class 10 w. in match: 0.
One-day 50s: 19.
One-day 100s: 6.
Place in batting averages: 90 average: 33.56; (1983: 45 average: 40.60).
Place in bowling averages: — average: —; (1983: — average: —).
1st-Class catches 1984: 9 (career: 83).
Parents: Sam Dixon Charles and Sonia Marcelle Mendis.
Wife and date of marriage: Angela, 12 June 1976.
Education: St Thomas College, Mount Lavinia, Sri Lanka; Brighton, Hove & Sussex Grammar School; Bede College, Durham University.
Qualifications: B.Ed. Mathematics, Durham. N.C.A. coaching certificate.
Jobs outside cricket: Teacher at Rosemead School, Littlehampton, Sussex. Richard Ellis, Perth, W.A.
Overseas teams played for: Maharaja Organisation XI in Sri Lanka 1980–81. Colombo Cricket Club, Sebastianites C.C., and Mount Lawley C.C., W. Australia.

Overseas tours: Maharaja Organisation XI to India 1980. Rohan Kanhai's Invitation XI to Pakistan 1981.

Equipment used: Slazenger.

Cricketers particularly admired: Barry Richards.

Other sports: Played table-tennis for Sussex at junior level, (but "no time for other sports lately.").

Relaxations: Music and getting away from cricket.

Significant injuries in 1984: Torn muscle in right shoulder — out of action for 4 weeks.

Extras: Played for Sussex 2nd XI since 1971. Played Sussex Schools Under 15. Played in one John Player League match 1973. Played for T.C.C.B. XI in 1981. Top of J.P.L. batting averages in 1981 for all counties. Plays in yellow helmet. Has twice turned down invitations to play for Sri Lanka in order to be free to be chosen for England.

Best batting performance: 209* Sussex v Somerset, Hove 1984.

LAST SEASON: BATTING

	I.	N.O.	R.	H.S.	AV.
TEST					
OTHER FIRST CLASS	36	2	1141	209*	33.56
INT					
J.P.L.	11	2	238	58*	26.44
NAT.W.	2	0	81	55	40.50
B & H	5	0	194	56	38.80

CAREER: BATTING

	I.	N.O.	R.	H.S.	AV.
TEST					
OTHER FIRST CLASS	320	27	9865	209*	33.67
INT					
J.P.L.	95	10	2542	125*	29.90
NAT.W.	20	2	724	141*	40.22
B & H	33	1	917	109	28.66

LAST SEASON: BOWLING

	O.	M.	R.	W.	AV.
TEST					
OTHER FIRST CLASS					
INT					
J.P.L.					
NAT.W.					
B & H					

CAREER: BOWLING

	O.	M.	R.	W.	AV.
TEST					
OTHER FIRST CLASS	1.3	0	11	0	–
INT					
J.P.L.					
NAT.W.					
B & H					

Q. 173. What is the lowest score ever made by a first-class team, where, when and by whom?

PARKER, P.W.G.

Full Name: Paul William Giles Parker.
Role: Right-hand bat, leg spin bowler.
Born: 15 January 1956, Bulawayo, Rhodesia.
Height: 5′ 10½″ **Weight:** 12st.
Nickname: Porky, Polly.
County debut: 1976.
County cap: 1979.
Test debut: 1981.
No. of Tests: 1.
No. of One-Day Internationals: 0.
1000 runs in a season: 6.
50 wickets in a season: 0.
1st-Class 50s scored: 49.
1st-Class 100s scored: 23.
1st-Class 200s scored: 1.
1st-Class 5 w. in innings: 0.
1st-Class 10 w. in match: 0.
One-day 50s: 22.
One-day 100s: 3.

Place in batting averages: 28 average: 47.00; (1983: 174 average: 20.48).
Place in bowling averages: — average: —; (1983: — average: —).
1st-Class catches 1984: 23 (career: 132).
Parents: Anthony John and Margaret Edna Parker.
Wife and date of marriage: Teresa, 25 January 1980.
Children: James William Ralph, 6.11.80, Jocelyn Elizabeth, 10.9.84.
Education: Collyer's Grammar School; St Catharine's College, Cambridge.
Qualifications: M.A. (Cantab.).
Family links with cricket: Father played with Essex II. Uncle, David Green, played for Northants. and Worcestershire. Two brothers, Guy and Rupert, "very keen and active cricketers". Father wrote "The Village Cricket Match" and was sports editor of I.T.N.
Overseas tours: Combined Oxford & Cambridge XI tour of Australia 1979–80.
Overseas teams played for: Sturt C.C. in Adelaide, Australia, 1979–80. Natal, South Africa, 1980–81.
Jobs outside cricket: Winter employment with Messrs. Laing & Cruikshank (Stockbrokers) London.
Cricketers particularly learnt from: J. Denman, Sussex C.C.C.
Equipment used: Gray-Nicolls.
Other sports: Most ball games.
Relaxations: Reading, crosswords, bridge, music.
Extras: Was selected for Cambridge against Oxford rugby match in 1977 but

had to withdraw through injury. Tony Greig once said of him, when 17, that he would be "the best cover fielder in the world". Was first reserve for England in Australia tour 1979–80. Vice-captain of Sussex, 1981–83.

Opinions on cricket: Advocates 4-day cricket and the continuance of covered wickets.

Best batting performance: 215 Cambridge University v Essex, Cambridge 1976.

LAST SEASON: BATTING

	I.	N.O.	R.	H.S.	AV.
TEST					
OTHER FIRST CLASS	40	4	1692	181	47.00
INT					
J.P.L.	14	2	387	81*	32.25
NAT.W.	2	0	80	43	40.00
B & H	5	2	210	70	70.00

CAREER: BATTING

	I.	N.O.	R.	H.S.	AV.
TEST	2	0	13	13	6.50
OTHER FIRST CLASS	341	48	10238	215	34.94
INT					
J.P.L.	105	17	2316	121*	26.31
NAT.W.	23	3	633	69	33.32
B & H	36	3	892	77	27.03

LAST SEASON: BOWLING

	O.	M.	R.	W.	AV.
TEST					
OTHER FIRST CLASS	11.1	2	40	2	20.00
INT					
J.P.L.					
NAT.W.	1	0	7	0	–
B & H					

CAREER: BOWLING

	O.	M.	R.	W.	AV.
TEST					
OTHER FIRST CLASS	136.3	23	541	10	54.10
INT					
J.P.L.	5	0	20	2	10.00
NAT.W.	2	0	17	1	–
B & H					

PHILLIPSON, C.P.

Full Name: Christopher Paul Phillipson.

Role: Right-hand bat, right arm medium bowler, slip fielder.

Born: 10 February 1952, Vrindaban, India.

Height: 6'2" **Weight:** 13st 5lbs.

Nickname: Phillipo, Log.

County debut: 1970.

County cap: 1980.

No. of Tests: 0.

No of One-Day Internationals: 0.

1000 runs in a season: 0.

50 wickets in a season: 0.

1st-Class 50s scored: 12.

1st-Class 100s scored: 0.

1st-Class 200s scored: 0.

1st-Class 5 w. in innings: 4.

1st-Class 10 w. in match: 0.
One-day 50s: 6.
One-day 100s: 0.
Place in batting averages: — average: —; (1983: — average: —).
Place in bowling averages: — average: —; (1983: — average: —).
1st-Class catches 1984: 0 (career: 135).
Parents: Rev. Christopher Quentin and Muriel Regina Phillipson.
Wife and date of marriage: Adell, 24 March 1979.
Children: Kirstin Jane, 3 March 1981; Christopher Ross, 14 September 1983.
Education: Prebendal School, Chichester; Ardingly College; Loughborough Colleges.
Qualifications: Teacher's certificate (P.E. and geography), two A-levels. N.C.A. coaching certificate.
Family links with cricket: "My wife's mother's family (Dell) achieved fame in the Eastern Cape in 1908 when they formed a cricket team in Bathurst made up solely of their own family and played as such for several years."
Off-season 1984–85: Promoting Benefit Year.
Equipment used: John Newbery bats, Duncan Fearnley gloves.
Other sports: General fitness training, running, squash and swimming in the off season.
Relaxations: Listening to contemporary music.
Extras: "Acting as 2nd XI captain/coach and while maintaining playing contract and playing a certain amount of limited overs cricket in the county side."
Opinions on cricket: "The current U.K. season is overcrowded to the detriment of playing standards. Players cannot be expected to perform at a consistently high level, and the two extra games last season cannot be beneficial in any way. The only true league system is when each county plays everyone once (like the J.P.L.) over 3 or 4 days."
Best batting performance: 87 Sussex v Hampshire, Hove 1980.
Best bowling performance: 6-56 Sussex v Nottinghamshire, Hove 1972.

LAST SEASON: BATTING

	I.	N.O.	R.	H.S.	AV.
TEST					
OTHER FIRST CLASS					
INT					
J.P.L.	8	1	136	39	19.42
NAT.W.	1	0	2	2	–
B & H	2	0	13	13	6.50

CAREER: BATTING

	I.	N.O.	R.	H.S.	AV.
TEST					
OTHER FIRST CLASS	225	61	3046	87	18.57
INT					
J.P.L.	101	37	1328	71	20.75
NAT.W.	19	7	301	70*	25.08
B & H	29	13	390	66*	24.38

LAST SEASON: BOWLING

	O.	M.	R.	W.	AV.
TEST					
OTHER FIRST CLASS					
INT					
J.P.L.	3	0	21	0	–
NAT.W.					
B & H	0.2	0	0	1	–

CAREER: BOWLING

	O.	M.	R.	W.	AV.
TEST					
OTHER FIRST CLASS	1787	387	5213	153	34.07
INT					
J.P.L.	458.4	29	2141	77	27.80
NAT.W.	64.4	6	261	9	29.00
B & H	122.3	7	532	15	35.47

PIGOTT, A.C.S.

Full Name: Anthony Charles
Shackleton Pigott.
Role: Right-hand bat, right arm fast
bowler.
Born: 4 June 1958, London.
Height: 6' 1" **Weight:** 12st 7lbs.
Nickname: Lester.
County debut: 1978.
County cap: 1982.
Test debut: 1983–84.
No. of Tests: 1.
No. of One-Day Internationals: 0.
1000 runs in a season: 0.
50 wickets in a season: 2.
1st-Class 50s scored: 4.
1st-Class 100s scored: 0.
1st-Class 200s scored: 0.
1st-Class 5 w. in innings: 10.
1st-Class 10 w. in match: 1.
One-day 50s: 0.
One-day 100s: 0.
Place in batting averages: — average: —; (1983: 182 average: 19.43).
Place in bowling averages: — average: —; (1983: 43 average: 26.24).
1st-Class catches 1984: 0 (career: 15).
Parents: Tom and Juliet Pigott.
Wife and date of marriage: Nikki, 26 February 1984.
Children: Elliott, 15 March 1983.
Education: Harrow School.

LAST SEASON: BATTING

	I.	N.O.	R.	H.S.	AV.
TEST					
OTHER FIRST CLASS	–	–	–	–	–
INT					
J.P.L.	–	–	–.	–	–
NAT.W.					
B & H	1	1	3	3*	–

LAST SEASON: BOWLING

	O.	M.	R.	W.	AV.
TEST					
OTHER FIRST CLASS	32	5	96	2	48.00
INT					
J.P.L.	8	1	25	2	12.50
NAT.W.					
B & H	5	2	15	0	–

CAREER: BATTING

	I.	N.O.	R.	H.S.	AV.
TEST	2	1	12	8*	–
OTHER FIRST CLASS	101	20	1216	63	15.01
INT					
J.P.L.	25	9	188	49	11.75
NAT.W.	3	0	70	30	23.33
B & H	10	4	25	6*	4.17

CAREER: BOWLING

	O.	M.	R.	W.	AV.
TEST	17	7	75	2	37.50
OTHER FIRST CLASS	1683.3	290	6288	228	27.58
INT					
J.P.L.	314.5	12	1435	66	21.74
NAT.W.	44	4	157	4	39.25
B & H	129	12	560	19	29.47

Qualifications: Five O-levels. Junior coaching certificate.
Jobs outside cricket: Sportsmaster at Claremont Prep School, Hastings.
Family links with cricket: Father captained club side.
Overseas tours: With Derrick Robins XI to Australasia 1980. Part of England tour to New Zealand 1983–84.
Overseas teams played for: Played for Waverley C.C., Sydney, Australia, for three off-seasons, 1976–77, 1977–78, 1979–80. Went on Whitbread Scholarship 1979–80. Wellington, New Zealand, 1982–83 and 1983–84.
Cricketers particularly admired: G.G. Arnold, J.A. Snow and I.T. Botham.
Equipment used: Duncan Fearnley.
Other sports: Squash, raquets, football, tennis, rugger.
Relaxations: "My son and family and decorating home."
Significant injuries in 1984: Shins injury at beginning of season; back injury ruled out 2nd half of season.
Extras: Public School Raquets Champion 1975. Had operation on back, April 1981, missing most of season, and was told by a specialist he would never play cricket again. First three wickets in first-class cricket were a hat-trick. Postponed wedding to make Test debut when called into England party on tour of New Zealand. Originally going to Somerset for 1984 season, but then remained with Sussex.
Opinions on cricket: "To start playing 4-day county games and only 16 of them. This will make the competition fairer as each side will play each other once."
Best batting performance: 63 Sussex v Hampshire, Eastbourne 1983.
Best bowling performance: 7-74 Sussex v Northamptonshire, Eastbourne 1982.

Q. 174. Who wrote:
"Dr. Grace
Had hair all over his face.
Lord, how the people cheered
When a ball got stuck in his beard!"

REEVE, D.A.

Full Name: Dermot Alexander Reeve.
Role: Right-hand bat, right arm fast
medium bowler.
Born: 2 April 1963, Hong Kong.
Height: 6' 0" **Weight:** 12st.
Nickname: Huck.
County debut: 1983.
County cap: No.
Test debut: —
No. of Tests. 0.
No. of One-Day Internationals: 0.
1000 runs in a season: 0.
50 wickets in a season: 1.
1st-Class 50s scored: 3.
1st-Class 100s scored: 0.
1st-Class 200s scored: 0.
1st-Class 5 w. in innings: 1.
1st-Class 10 w. in match: 0.
One-day 50s: 0.
One-day 100s: 0.
Place in batting averages: 144 average: 27.00; (1983: 230 average: 12.80).
Place in bowling averages: 34 average: 25.82; (1983: 63 average: 29.36).
1st-Class catches 1984: 14 (career: 21).
Parents: Monica and Alexander James Reeve.
Marital status: Single.
Education: King George V. School, Kowloon, Hong Kong.
Qualifications: 7 O-levels.
Off-season 1984–85: Playing cricket for Claremont-Cottesloe C.C. Western
Australia and resting.
Overseas tours: Hong Kong tour to Malaysia and Singapore 1980, Hong Kong
British Forces tour to Malaysia 1982, M.C.C. tour to Holland and Denmark
1983.
Overseas teams played for: Claremont-Cottesloe C.C. Western Australia
1982–83, off season.
Cricketers particularly learnt from: Don Wilson, Andy Wagner and most of
the Sussex senior players.
Cricketers particularly admired: Ian Botham.
Other sports: Soccer, hockey, rugby.
Significant injuries in 1984: "A blow to the head fielding in the gully caused
concussion and 2 weeks off."
Relaxations: "Music, sleeping in".
Extras: Formerly on Lord's groundstaff. Represented Hong Kong in the I.C.C.
Trophy competition June 1982. Hong Kong Cricketer of the Year 1980–81.
Hong Kong's Cricket Sports Personality of the Year 1981.

Opinions on cricket: "117 overs a day is too many, 110 would be more feasible."
Best batting performance: 119 Sussex v Surrey, The Oval 1984.
Best bowling performance: 5-22 Sussex v Cambridge University, Cambridge 1984.

LAST SEASON: BATTING

	I.	N.O.	R.	H.S.	AV.
TEST					
OTHER FIRST CLASS	22	4	486	119	27.00
INT					
J.P.L.	6	4	61	15	30.50
NAT.W.	2	1	13	12	–
B & H	3	0	35	16	11.67

CAREER: BATTING

	I.	N.O.	R.	H.S.	AV.
TEST					
OTHER FIRST CLASS	42	9	678	119	20.55
INT					
J.P.L.	10	6	77	15	19.25
NAT.W.	4	3	35	16*	17.50
B & H	3	0	35	16	11.67

LAST SEASON: BOWLING

	O.	M.	R.	W.	AV.
TEST					
OTHER FIRST CLASS	572.4	175	1420	55	25.82
INT					
J.P.L.	75.1	3	359	20	17.95
NAT.W.	23	3	83	0	–
B & H	47.4	3	213	7	30.43

CAREER: BOWLING

	O.	M.	R.	W.	AV.
TEST					
OTHER FIRST CLASS	1044.5	306	2653	97	27.35
INT					
J.P.L.	160.1	7	723	32	22.59
NAT.W.	55.5	11	154	7	22.00
B & H	47.4	3	213	7	30.43

SMITH, D.J.

Full Name: David James Smith.
Role: Left-hand bat, wicket-keeper.
Born: 28 April 1962, Brighton.
Height: 5' 7½" **Weight:** 10st 2lbs.
Nickname: Smudger, Piglet.
County debut: 1981.
County cap: No.
Test debut: —
No. of Tests: 0.
No. of One-Day Internationals: 0.
1000 runs in a season: 0.
50 wickets in a season: 0.
1st-Class 50s scored: 0.
1st-Class 100s scored: 0.
1st-Class 200s scored: 0.
1st-Class 5 w. in innings: 0.
1st-Class 10 w. in match: 0.
One-day 50s: 0.
One-day 100s: 0.

Place in batting averages: — average: —; (1983: — average: —).
Place in bowling averages: — average: —; (1983: — average: —).

Parents: David Reginald and Isobel Smith.
Marital status: Single.
Education: Hove Grammar School.
Qualifications: 5 0-levels; N.C.A. coaching certificate.
Equipment used: Gunn & Moore.
Overseas tours: With N.C.A. Young Cricketers to Canada 1979.
Cricketers particularly learnt from: Les Lenham, Tony Buss, Chris Waller and "have learnt so much by watching Alan Knott and Bob Taylor."
Other sports: "Most sports, especially squash and football."
Relaxations: Music, eating and sleeping.
Extras: Awarded William Walker Trophy for Best Sussex Under-19 (1980). Made county debut against the touring Australians. Member of the Wicket-keepers Society.
Best batting performance: 13 Sussex v Somerset, Hove 1983.

LAST SEASON: BATTING

	I.	N.O.	R.	H.S.	AV.
TEST					
OTHER FIRST CLASS	2	0	3	2	1.50
INT					
J.P.L.					
NAT.W.					
B & H					

CAREER: BATTING

	I.	N.O.	R.	H.S.	AV.
TEST					
OTHER FIRST CLASS	14	2	29	13	2.42
INT					
J.P.L.	1	1	5	5*	–
NAT.W.					
B & H					

LAST SEASON: WICKET KEEPING

	C.	ST.		
TEST				
OTHER FIRST CLASS	10	–		
INT				
J.P.L.				
NAT.W.				
B & H				

CAREER: WICKET KEEPING

	C.	ST.		
TEST				
OTHER FIRST CLASS	25	–		
INT				
J.P.L.				
NAT.W.				
B & H				

Q. 175. What is the fewest runs scored in a first-class match in a full day's play? Where, when, and by whom?

Q. 176. What, who, where and when was the last occasion in England on which a batsman was dismissed for hitting the ball twice?

STANDING, D.K.

Full Name: David Kevin Standing.
Role: Right-hand bat, right arm
spin bowler.
Born: 21 October, 1963, Brighton,
Sussex.
Height: 5′ 8½″ **Weight:** 10st. 3lbs.
Nickname: Uppers.
County debut: 1983.
County cap: No.
Test debut: —
No. of Tests: 0.
No. of One-Day Internationals: 0.
1000 runs in a season: 0.
50 wickets in a season: 0.
1st-Class 50s scored: 2.
1st-Class 100s scored: 0.
1st-Class 200s scored: 0.
1st-Class 5 w. in innings: 0.
1st-Class 10 w. in match: 0.
One-day 50s: 0.
One-day 100s: 0.
Place in batting averages: — average: —; (1983: 17 average: 48.00).
Place in bowling averages: — average: —; (1983: — average: —).
1st-Class catches 1984: 1 (career: 3).
Parents: David Eric and Valerie Mavis Standing.
Marital status: Single.
Education: Tideway School, Newhaven. Brighton and Hove VIth Form.
Qualifications: 8 O-levels, 1 A-level.

LAST SEASON: BATTING

	I.	N.O.	R.	H.S.	AV.
TEST					
OTHER FIRST CLASS	2	1	12	7	–
INT					
J.P.L.					
NAT.W.					
B & H					

CAREER: BATTING

	I.	N.O.	R.	H.S.	AV.
TEST					
OTHER FIRST CLASS	10	4	252	60	42.00
INT					
J.P.L.					
NAT.W.					
B & H					

LAST SEASON: BOWLING

	O.	M.	R.	W.	AV.
TEST					
OTHER FIRST CLASS					
INT					
J.P.L.					
NAT.W.					
B & H					

CAREER: BOWLING

	O.	M.	R.	W.	AV.
TEST					
OTHER FIRST CLASS	4.3	0	32	0	–
INT					
J.P.L.					
NAT.W.					
B & H					

Equipment used: Gray-Nicolls.
Overseas tours: West Indies with Sussex Young Cricketers.
Cricketers particularly learnt from: Most of Sussex senior players.
Other sports: Football, golf, squash.
Relaxations: Reading, music.
Extras: Captained England Schools Under 15. Played England Schools Under-19.
Opinions on cricket: Review of over-rate — with the possibility of monitoring on a match basis, point/s to be deducted for non-fulfilment of specified requirement.
Best batting performance: 60 Sussex v Worcestershire, Worcester 1983.

WALLER, C.E.

Full Name: Christopher Edward Waller.
Role: Right-hand bat; slow left arm orthodox bowler; gully fielder.
Born: 3 October 1948, Guildford.
Height: 5' 10½" **Weight:** 11st 10lbs.
Nickname: Wal.
County debut: 1974, Sussex.
County cap: 1976.
Benefit: 1984.
Test debut: —
No. of Tests: 0.
No. of One-Day Internationals: 0.
1000 runs in a season: 0.
50 wickets in a season: 4.
1st-Class 50s scored: 2.
1st-Class 100s scored: 0.
1st-Class 200s scored: 0.
1st-Class 5 w. in innings: 21.
1st-Class 10 w. in match: 1.
One-day 50s: 0.
One-day 100s: 0.

Place in batting averages: — average: —; (1983: — average: —).
Place in bowling averages: 29 average: 25.45; (1983: 96 average: 35.34).
1st-Class catches 1984: 13 (career: 131).
Parents: Frederick Edward and Iris Waller.
Wife and date of marriage: Lesley Deborah, 25 March 1972.
Children: Alexandra Lois, 21 August 1975; Stephanie Kate, 16 May 1977; Adrian Paul, 5 August 1979.
Education: St Bede's C. of E. Secondary School, Send, Woking, Surrey.
Qualifications: N.C.A. advanced coach and staff coach.

Jobs outside cricket: Coaching at Alf Gover's Cricket School, Wandsworth; Crystal Palace National Sports Centre; Sussex C.C.C. Indoor School.

Off-season 1984–85: "Coaching at Indoor Cricket School and winding up benefit year."

Family links with cricket: Father played for Horsley C.C. for 47 years as an opening batsman and off-spin bowler. "I first played for Horsley C.C. at the age of 11."

Cricketers particularly learnt from: Norman Gifford and Mickey Stewart.

Cricketers particularly admired: Viv Richards.

Equipment used: Symonds.

Other sports: Squash, football, golf, snooker. Watch all sports.

Relaxations: Listening to records, watching T.V., drinking dark rum and Usher's beer, eating Indian cuisine.

Extras: Debut for Surrey in 1967, cap 1972. Left after 1973 season. Coached 1977–78 in New South Wales, Australia, for World Series Cricket. "I have to navigate as well as drive on our away trips as passenger Colin Wells hasn't a very good sense of direction."

Opinions on cricket: "I feel that the championship should be 16 four-day games as this would be a truer championship playing each other once. Also for the Benson and Hedges to be a league to be played on Saturdays."

Best batting performance: 51* Sussex v Cambridge University, Cambridge 1981.

Best bowling performance: 7-64 Surrey v Sussex, The Oval 1971.

LAST SEASON: BATTING

	I.	N.O.	R.	H.S.	AV.
TEST					
OTHER FIRST CLASS	21	14	56	16*	8.00
INT					
J.P.L.	1	1	3	3*	–
NAT.W.	1	0	1	1	–
B & H	3	2	5	5*	–

CAREER: BATTING

	I.	N.O.	R.	H.S.	AV.
TEST					
OTHER FIRST CLASS	257	108	1444	51*	9.69
INT					
J.P.L.	38	17	169	18*	8.05
NAT.W.	7	2	18	14*	3.60
B & H	13	8	42	11*	8.40

LAST SEASON: BOWLING

	O.	M.	R.	W.	AV.
TEST					
OTHER FIRST CLASS	610.3	221	1349	53	25.45
INT					
J.P.L.	46	0	212	4	53.00
NAT.W.	8	0	40	0	–
B & H	47	6	147	4	36.75

CAREER: BOWLING

	O.	M.	R.	W.	AV.
TEST					
OTHER FIRST CLASS	6798.2	1989	17430	610	28.57
INT					
J.P.L.	566.5	40	2408	83	29.01
NAT.W.	99.2	13	342	9	38.00
B & H	270.3	34	866	28	30.93

WELLS, A.P.

Full Name: Alan Peter Wells.
Role: Right-hand bat,right arm
medium bowler, cover fielder.
Born: 2 October 1961.
Height: 6' 0" **Weight:** 12st. 4lbs.
Nickname: Morph, Bomber.
County debut: 1981.
County cap: No.
Test debut: —
No. of Tests: 0.
No. of One-Day Internationals: 0.
1000 runs in a season: 1.
50 wickets in a season: 0.
1st-Class 50s scored: 14.
1st-Class 100s scored: 2.
1st-Class 200s scored: 0.
1st-Class 5 w. in innings: 0.
1st-Class 10 w. in match: 0.
One-day 50s: 4.
One-day 100s: 0.

Place in batting averages: 101 average: 32.66; (1983: 115 average: 27.71).
Place in bowling averages: — average: —; (1983: — average: —).
1st-Class catches 1984: 10 (career: 24).
Parents: Ernest William Charles and Eunice Mae Wells.
Marital status: Single.
Education: Tideway Comprehensive, Newhaven.
Qualifications: 5 O-levels; N.C.A. Coaching certificate.
Jobs outside cricket: Laboratory assistant. Coached in South Africa.
Off-season 1984–85: Coaching and playing in South Africa.
Family links with cricket: Father played for many years for local club. Eldest
brother, Ray, plays club cricket. Brother of C.M. Wells of Sussex.
Cricketing supersitions: "Have to put bat at junction of return and popping
crease at the end of each over. Never stand inside the return crease when
backing up. When repairing wicket count how many times I tap ground. Double
whirl of arms with bat when going in to bat. Plus many more."
Overseas tours: N.C.A. Under-19 tour of Canada, 1979.
Cricketers particularly learnt from: Father, Chris Waller, Roger Marshall
and Les Lenham.
Equipment used: Slazenger, Fred Perry.
Other sports: Table tennis, squash, darts, snooker, tennis.
Relaxations: Listening to music, eating out, drinking in country pubs.
Extras: Played for England Young Cricketers v. India 1981.
Best batting performance: 127 Sussex v Northamptonshire, Northampton
1984.

LAST SEASON: BATTING

	I.	N.O.	R.	H.S.	AV.
TEST					
OTHER FIRST CLASS	39	7	1045	127	32.66
INT					
J.P.L.	13	1	366	71*	30.50
NAT.W.	2	0	24	24	12.00
B & H	5	1	120	51	30.00

CAREER: BATTING

	I.	N.O.	R.	H.S.	AV.
TEST					
OTHER FIRST CLASS	79	14	2021	127	31.09
INT					
J.P.L.	32	5	640	71*	23.70
NAT.W.	5	1	41	24	10.25
B & H	8	2	164	51	27.33

LAST SEASON: BOWLING

	O.	M.	R.	W.	AV.
TEST					
OTHER FIRST CLASS					
INT					
J.P.L.					
NAT.W.	1	0	1	0	–
B & H					

CAREER: BOWLING

	O.	M.	R.	W.	AV.
TEST					
OTHER FIRST CLASS	12	1	42	0	–
INT					
J.P.L.					
NAT.W.	1	0	1	0	–
B & H	2.1	1	17	1	–

WELLS, C.M.

Full Name: Colin Mark Wells.
Role: Right-hand bat; right arm medium bowler.
Born: 3 March 1960, Newhaven, Sussex.
Height: 6′ 0″ **Weight:** 12st 7lbs.
Nickname: Bomber.
County debut: 1979.
County cap: 1982
Test debut: —
No. of Tests: 0.
No. of One-Day Internationals: 0.
1000 runs in a season: 3.
50 wickets in a season: 1.
1st-Class 50s scored: 22.
1st-Class 100s scored: 9.
1st-Class 200s scored: 1.
1st-Class 5 w. in innings: 2.
1st-Class 10 w. in match: 0.
One-day 50s: 9.
One-day 100s: 1.

Place in batting averages: 36 average: 43.41; (1983: 137 average: 25.21).
Place in bowling averages: 23 average: 23.66; (1983: 97 average: 35.47).
1st-Class catches 1984: 4 (career: 32).
Parents: Ernest William Charles and Eunice Mae Wells.
Marital status: Single.

Education: Tideway Comprehensive School, Newhaven.

Qualifications: 1 A-level, 9 O-levels, two C.S.E.s. M.C.C. Intermediate Coaching Certificate.

Jobs outside cricket: Laboratory assistant.

Family links with cricket: Father, Billy, had trials for Sussex and played for Sussex Cricket Association. Both brothers play cricket and youngest brother, Alan, played for England Schools and toured Canada with N.C.A. 1979, and plays for Sussex.

Cricket superstitions: Left boot and left pad put on first.

Equipment used: Stuart Surridge.

Other sports: Football, rugby, hockey, basketball, tennis, table tennis.

Relaxations: Sea-angling, philately, listening to music.

Extras: Played in three John Player League matches in 1978. Awarded 2nd XI cap in 1980. Was recommended to Sussex by former Sussex player, Ian Thomson.Highest 4th wicket partnership for Sussex v Glamorgan with Imran Khan of 256.

Best batting performance: 203 Sussex v Hampshire, Hove 1984.

Best bowling performance: 5-25 Sussex v Kent, Hastings 1984.

LAST SEASON: BATTING

	I.	N.O.	R.	H.S.	AV.
TEST					
OTHER FIRST CLASS	39	7	1389	203	43.41
INT					
J.P.L.	13	2	216	62	19.63
NAT.W.	2	0	16	14	8.00
B & H	5	0	166	60	33.20

CAREER: BATTING

	I.	N.O.	R.	H.S.	AV.
TEST					
OTHER FIRST CLASS	180	26	5115	203	33.21
INT					
J.P.L.	68	8	1465	104*	24.42
NAT.W.	11	0	141	28	12.82
B & H	21	1	501	80	25.05

LAST SEASON: BOWLING

	O.	M.	R.	W.	AV.
TEST					
OTHER FIRST CLASS	497.2	146	1396	59	23.66
INT					
J.P.L.	98.4	14	307	17	18.05
NAT.W.	24	5	59	1	–
B & H	47	3	169	8	21.12

CAREER: BOWLING

	O.	M.	R.	W.	AV.
TEST					
OTHER FIRST CLASS	1369.4	339	3980	126	31.59
INT					
J.P.L.	316	25	1230	52	23.65
NAT.W.	71.4	12	192	5	38.40
B & H	90	13	319	15	21.27

Q. 177. Who are the only three batsmen ever to have scored 1000 first-class runs *in* May?

WOOD, D.J.

Full Name: David John Wood.
Role: Left-hand bat; slow left arm bowler.
Born: 10 January 1965, Cuckfield.
Height: 5' 7" **Weight:** 9st 7lbs.
Nickname: Pogles, Bod, Woody.
County debut: 1984.
County cap: No.
Test debut: —
No. of Tests: 0.
No. of One-Day Internationals: 0.
1000 runs in a season: 0.
50 wickets in a season: 0.
1st-Class 50s scored: 0.
1st-Class 100s scored: 0.
1st-Class 200s scored: 0.
1st-Class 5 w. in innings: 0.
1st-Class 10 w. in match: 0.
One-day 50s: 0.
One-day 100s: 0.
Place in batting averages: — average: —; (1983: — average: —).
Place in bowling averages: — average: —;(1983: — average: —).
Parents: Frederick George and Jean Wood.
Marital status: Single.
Family links with cricket: Father played club cricket.
Education: Horsted Keynes Primary; Oathall Comprehensive, Haywards Heath.

LAST SEASON: BATTING

	I.	N.O.	R.	H.S.	AV.
TEST					
OTHER FIRST CLASS	3	0	32	15	10.67
INT					
J.P.L.					
NAT.W.					
B & H					

CAREER: BATTING

	I.	N.O.	R.	H.S.	AV.
TEST					
OTHER FIRST CLASS	3	0	32	15	10.67
INT					
J.P.L.					
NAT.W.					
B & H					

LAST SEASON: BOWLING

	O.	M.	R.	W.	AV.
TEST					
OTHER FIRST CLASS					
INT					
J.P.L.					
NAT.W.					
B & H					

CAREER: BOWLING

	O.	M.	R.	W.	AV.
TEST					
OTHER FIRST CLASS					
INT					
J.P.L.					
NAT.W.					
B & H					

Qualification: 3 O-levels.
Jobs outside cricket: Sports shop; mail order firm.
Off-season 1984–85: Fishing and looking for a job.
Equipment used: Gunn & Moore.
Overseas tours: Barbados (2) with Sussex YC's 1982–83 and Australia Sussex
Under-19 1983.
Cricketers particularly learnt from: "My father."
Cricketers particularly admired: Kepler Wessels.
Relaxations: Fishing.
Extras: Compulsive bat feeler; eating Mars bars. Left Sussex staff end of 1984
season.
Best batting performance: 15 Sussex v Surrey, Guildford 1984.

COUNTY QUIZ

Q. 1.   When was the club founded?
Q. 2.   Who made the most first-class runs for the county last season, and how
            many?
Q. 3.   What's the highest ever county total, and against whom?
Q. 4.   Who took most wickets for the county last season, and how many?
Q. 5.   What's the highest individual score for the county, who hit it, and when?
Q. 6.   What's the highest scoring partnership for the county for any wicket?
Q. 7.   How many times has the club won the County Championship?
Q. 8.   What's the lowest ever total made by the county in one innings, when,
            and against whom?
Q. 9.   Which bowler took the most first-class wickets in one season, when, and
            how many?
Q. 10. Which batsman hit the most runs in one season, when and how many?

Warwickshire

AMISS, D.L.

Full Name: Dennis Leslie Amiss.
Role: Right-hand bat, slow left arm chinaman bowler.
Born: 7 April 1943, Harborne, Birmingham.
Height: 5′ 11″ **Weight:** 13st.
Nickname: Sacker.
County debut: 1960.
County cap: 1965.
Test debut: 1966.
No. of Tests: 50.
No. of One-Day Internationals: 18.
1000 runs in a season: 20.
50 wickets in a season: 0.
1st-Class 50s scored: 193.
1st-Class 100s scored: 88.
1st-Class 200s scored: 3.
1st-Class 5 w. in innings: 0.
1st-Class 10 w. in match: 0.
One-day 50s: 62.
One-day 100s: 13.

Place in batting averages: 11 average: 55.97; (1983: 28 average: 44.13).
Place in bowling averages: — average: —; (1983: — average: —).
1st-Class catches 1984: 16 (career: 374).
Benefit: £34,947 in 1975.
Testimonial: 1985 (when part of proceeds will go to schools cricket in Warwickshire).
Wife: Jill.
Children: One son, one daughter.
Family links with cricket: Father, A.F. Amiss, played good club cricket.
Jobs outside cricket: Sales executive for Officescape Ltd. (Interior design and construction group).
Overseas tours: Pakistan 1966–67; India, Pakistan and Sri Lanka 1972–73; West Indies 1973–74; Australia, New Zealand 1974–75; India, Sri Lanka and Australia 1976–77.

Overseas teams played for: World Series Cricket 1978–79.
Equipment used: Fearnley bats. Arcass Sports pads and gloves.
Other sports: Golf, tennis, squash.
Relaxations: Bridge, gardening.
Extras: Scored two centuries in one match, 155 not out and 112 v Worcestershire at Birmingham 1978. Slipped a disc at 17 playing football and the injury means he still has to take precautionary exercise every day. "There is still a stiffness in the back which takes three or four minutes loosening-up work to get rid of." Banned from Test cricket for three years for playing for England rebels in South Africa, 1982.
Opinions on cricket: "For me, nothing beats playing before a full house at Headquarters (Lord's). There is nothing quite like it anywhere in the world."
Best batting performance: 262* England v W. Indies, Kingston 1973–74.
Best bowling performance: 3-21 Warwickshire v Middlesex, Lord's 1970.

LAST SEASON: BATTING

	I.	N.O.	R.	H.S.	AV.
TEST					
OTHER FIRST CLASS	50	10	2239	122	55.97
INT					
J.P.L.	13	1	473	107*	39.41
NAT.W.	4	1	98	73*	32.67
B & H	7	0	366	115	52.29

CAREER: BATTING

	I.	N.O.	R.	H.S.	AV.
TEST	88	10	3612	262*	46.31
OTHER FIRST CLASS	916	102	35506	232*	43.62
INT	18	0	859	137	47.72
J.P.L.	202	17	6098	117*	32.96
NAT.W.	47	5	1705	135	40.59
B & H	56	6	1745	115	34.90

LAST SEASON: BOWLING

	O.	M.	R.	W.	AV.
TEST					
OTHER FIRST CLASS					
INT					
J.P.L.					
NAT.W.					
B & H					

CAREER: BOWLING

	O.	M.	R.	W.	AV.
TEST					
OTHER FIRST CLASS	213.1	32	718	18	39.89
INT					
J.P.L.	3	0	23	1	–
NAT.W.	12.1	0	67	0	–
B & H	0.2	0	4	0	–

Q. 178. Who are the only batsmen, in addition to the three in question above, to have scored 1000 first-class runs *by the end* of May?

ASIF DIN, M.

Full Name: M. Asif Din.
Role: Right-hand bat, leg-break
bowler.
Born: 21 Sept. 1960, Kampala,
Uganda.
Height: 5′ 9″ **Weight:** 9½st.
Nickname: Gunga.
County debut: 1981.
County cap: No.
Test debut: —
No. of Tests: 0.
No. of One-Day Internationals: 0.
1000 runs in a season: 0.
50 wickets in a season: 0.
1st-Class 50s scored: 8.
1st-Class 100s scored: 1.
1st-Class 200s scored: 0.
1st-Class 5 w. in innings: 1.
1st-Class 10 w. in match: 0.
One-day 50s: 6.
One-day 100s: 0.
Place in batting averages: 252 average: 14.14; (1983: 156 average: 22.83).
Place in bowling averages: — average: —; (1983: — average: —).
1st-Class catches 1984: 2 (career: 38).
Marital status: Single.
Family links with cricket: Brother, Abid, plays for Smethwick 1st XI in
Birmingham league.
Education: Ladywood Comprehensive, Birmingham.

LAST SEASON: BATTING

	I.	N.O.	R.	H.S.	AV.
TEST				.	
OTHER FIRST CLASS	9	2	99	35*	14.14
INT					
J.P.L.	4	0	57	22	14.25
NAT.W.					
B & H	3	0	13	9	4.33

CAREER: BATTING

	I.	N.O.	R.	H.S.	AV.
TEST					
OTHER FIRST CLASS	101	11	2243	102	24.92
INT					
J.P.L.	42	7	910	56*	26.00
NAT.W.	6	2	102	45	25.50
B & H	13	2	271	61	24.64

LAST SEASON: BOWLING

	O.	M.	R.	W.	AV.
TEST					
OTHER FIRST CLASS	11.3	1	55	5	11.00
INT					
J.P.L.					
NAT.W.					
B & H					

CAREER: BOWLING

	O.	M.	R.	W.	AV.
TEST					
OTHER FIRST CLASS	449.5	84	1845	33	55.91
INT					
J.P.L.	6	1	37	1	—
NAT.W.					
B & H	2	0	20	0	—

Overseas tours: Bangladesh, 1980–81 with M.C.C. East and Central Africa 1981 with M.C.C.
Other sports: Hockey, squash, badminton.
Extras: Plays in spectacles. Trained on M.C.C. groundstaff at Lords.
Best batting performance: 102 Warwickshire v Middlesex, Coventry 1982.
Best bowling performance: 5-100 Warwickshire v Glamorgan, Edgbaston 1982.

DYER, R.I.H.B.

Full Name: Robin Ian Henry Benbow Dyer.
Role: Right-hand bat.
Born: 22 December 1958, Hertford.
Height: 6′ 4″ **Weight:** 13st.
Nickname: "Dobbin, Donkey, Tuft — generally more nicknames than Christian names!"
County debut: 1981.
County cap: No.
Test debut: —
No. of Tests: 0.
No. of One-Day Internationals: 0.
1000 runs in a season: 1.
50 wickets in a season: 0.
1st-Class 50s scored: 10.
1st-Class 100s scored: 1.
1st-Class 200s scored: 0.
1st-Class 5 w. in innings: 0.
1st-Class 10 w. in match: 0.
One-day 50s: 1.
One-day 100s: 1.
Place in batting averages: 79 average: 34.91; (1983: 176 average: 20.17).
Place in bowling averages: — average: —; (1983: — average: —).
1st-Class catches 1984: 7 (career: 15).
Parents: Ian and Dee Dyer.
Marital status: Single.
Family links with cricket: "Father and mother gave me a lot of encouragement. Also my sister bowls in-swingers although she's not as 'big at the crease' as Sarfraz!"
Education: Wellington College, Berkshire; Durham University.
Qualifications: B.A. Hons in Politics; 3 A-levels.
Jobs outside cricket: Hamper-packer.
Cricketing superstitions: "I don't like changing my kit after scoring runs."
Overseas tours: With English Schools to India 1977–78.

Cricketers particularly learnt from: "Learnt a lot from Fred Berry, the former Surrey player, who was coach at Wellington. Specially admired M.J.K. Smith and Dennis Amiss."

Equipment used: Gray-Nicolls.

Other sports: Golf and squash and watches Rugby Union regularly.

Relaxations: Listening to music (particularly Peter Gabriel), reading good books, watching films, theatre, eating and drinking in sociable situations, travelling.

Extras: Captained Durham University. Wears spectacles.

Opinions on cricket: "I would like to see 4-day championship matches. I believe that County Clubs could and should help more with players' off-season employment. I'm sure that constructive assistance from committees or management would enable more players to spend their winters in worthwhile occupations, in England or abroad."

Best batting performance: 106* Warwickshire v Glamorgan, Cardiff 1984.

LAST SEASON: BATTING

	I.	N.O.	R.	H.S.	AV.
TEST					
OTHER FIRST CLASS	36	2	1187	106*	34.91
INT					
J.P.L.	10	1	160	44	17.78
NAT.W.	4	0	157	119	39.25
B & H	2	0	65	54	32.50

CAREER: BATTING

	I.	N.O.	R.	H.S.	AV.
TEST					
OTHER FIRST CLASS	60	6	1510	106*	27.96
INT					
J.P.L.	15	2	270	44	20.77
NAT.W.	5	0	172	119	34.40
B & H	2	0	65	54	32.50

LAST SEASON: BOWLING

	O.	M.	R.	W.	AV.
TEST					
OTHER FIRST CLASS					
INT					
J.P.L.					
NAT.W.					
B & H					

CAREER: BOWLING

	O.	M.	R.	W.	AV.
TEST					
OTHER FIRST CLASS	1	0	2	0	–
INT					
J.P.L.	2	0	18	0	–
NAT.W.					
B & H					

Q. 179. Which bowler has taken the most first-class wickets in an English season and when?

Q. 180. Which current first-class player has taken the most wickets in a season, and when?

FERREIRA, A.M.

Full Name: Anthonie Michal Ferreira.
Role: Right-hand bat, right arm medium bowler.
Born: 13 April 1955, Pretoria, South Africa.
Height: 6′ 3″ **Weight:** 14st. 10lbs.
Nickname: Yogi—"known as Anton, though."
County debut: 1979.
County cap: 1983.
Test debut: —
No. of Tests: 0.
No. of One-Day Internationals: 0.
1000 runs in a season: 0.
50 wickets in a season: 2.
1st-Class 50s scored: 24.
1st-Class 100s scored: 2.
1st-Class 200s scored: 0.
1st-Class 5 w. in innings: 15.
1st-Class 10 w. in match: 1.
One-day 50s: 2.
One-day 100s: 0.

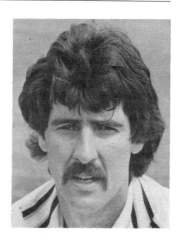

Place in batting averages: 122 average: 29.88; (1983: 132 average: 25.83).
Place in bowling averages: 49 average: 27.94; (1983: 76 average: 31.93).
1st-Class catches 1984: 12 (career: 78).
Parents: Anthonie and Eileen Ferreira.
Wife and date of marriage: Daléne, 28 March, 1981.
Education: Hillview High School, Pretoria; Pretoria University.
Qualifications: B.A.(ed.) Psychology and geography.
Jobs outside cricket: Employed by University of Pretoria as a full time cricket coach and organiser.
Overseas tours: Toured U.K. with Pretoria University in 1975 and in 1978 with a group of young South African players sponsored by Barclays Bank. During tour played twice for Derrick Robins XI.
Cricket superstitions: Joining the rest of the team when the score is on 111, 222 or 333, or hoping either for a wicket when fielding or a run when batting.
Cricketers particularly admired: "Mike Procter more than any other player. I have admired not only his ability but his approach to the game (sportsmanship, conduct, leadership)."
Equipment used: Slazenger, Adidas.
Other sports: "I play golf, squash and tennis—provincial colours in boxing and soccer while still at school. I watch all sports whenever possible (T.V. or live)." Once fought Gerry Coetzee – since professional heavyweight champion.
Relaxations: "Music, movies and a good meal with my wife."

Opinions on cricket: "Obviously as a South African, the issue regarding my country and Test Cricket often crops up. Without using clichés and proverbial statements, may I just say, that I'd like to see the situation resolved one way or another. The really disturbing factor is the ridiculous double standards that exist, and while I hold nothing against the individual/s concerned, I find it amazing that players I've played both with and against in South Africa, are allowed to play Test Cricket for another country other than birthplace, while, e.g., English players are banned because of their involvement. I'm sure my views are shared by many others."

Best batting performance: 112* Warwickshire v Indians, Edgbaston 1982.
Best bowling performance: 8-38 N Transvaal v Transvaal B, Pretoria 1977–78.

LAST SEASON: BATTING

	I.	N.O.	R.	H.S.	AV.
TEST					
OTHER FIRST CLASS	39	13	777	76*	29.88
INT					
J.P.L.	12	5	237	39*	33.85
NAT.W.	4	2	38	21	19.00
B & H	6	1	114	71	22.80

CAREER: BATTING

	I.	N.O.	R.	H.S.	AV.
TEST					
OTHER FIRST CLASS	230	43	5016	112*	26.82
INT					
J.P.L.	53	14	892	52	22.87
NAT.W.	10	4	89	21	14.83
B & H	21	7	319	71	22.79

LAST SEASON: BOWLING

	O.	M.	R.	W.	AV.
TEST					
OTHER FIRST CLASS	772.1	157	2208	79	27.94
INT					
J.P.L.	107	5	516	24	21.50
NAT.W.	35	8	94	5	18.80
B & H	68.5	7	311	8	38.88

CAREER: BOWLING

	O.	M.	R.	W.	AV.
TEST					
OTHER FIRST CLASS	4336.4	1030	12469	414	30.12
INT					
J.P.L.	516.3	24	2553	104	24.54
NAT.W.	137	22	458	24	19.08
B & H	258.5	27	1111	38	29.24

Q. 181. Which bowler has had the most first-class runs hit off him in an innings, and when?

Q. 182. What is the highest first-class score ever made, when, where and by whom?

GIFFORD, N.

Full Name: Norman Gifford.
Role: Left-hand bat, slow left arm orthodox bowler.
Born: 30 March 1940, Ulverston, Cumbria.
Height: 5' 10" **Weight:** 13st 7lbs.
Nickname: Giff.
County debut: 1960 (for Worcs.), 1983 (Warwickshire).
County cap: 1961 (Worcs.), 1983 (Warwickshire).
Test debut: 1964.
No. of Tests: 15.
No. of One-Day Internationals: 0.
Benefit: £11,047, 1974. Testimonial 1981.
1000 runs in a season: 0.
50 wickets in a season: 21.
1st-Class 50s scored: 3.
1st-Class 100s scored: 0.
1st-Class 200s scored: 0.
1st-Class 5 w. in innings: 88.
1st-Class 10 w. in match: 14.
One-day 50s: 0.
One-day 100s: 0.
Place in batting averages: 269 average: 10.43; (1983: 224 average: 13.40).
Place in bowling averages: 60 average: 29.52; (1983: 26 average: 23.01).
1st-Class catches 1984: 10 (career: 302).

LAST SEASON: BATTING

	I.	N.O.	R.	H.S.	AV.
TEST					
OTHER FIRST CLASS	24	10	146	28*	10.43
INT					
J.P.L.	4	2	28	10	14.00
NAT.W.	2	2	8	6*	–
B & H	3	2	13	8	–

CAREER: BATTING

	I.	N.O.	R.	H.S.	AV.
TEST	20	9	179	25*	16.27
OTHER FIRST CLASS	695	217	6470	89	13.54
INT					
J.P.L.	127	55	897	32*	12.45
NAT.W	31	7	219	38	9.12
B & H	38	12	297	33	11.42

LAST SEASON: BOWLING

	O.	M.	R.	W.	AV.
TEST					
OTHER FIRST CLASS	812.4	238	1919	65	29.52
INT					
J.P.L.	95	1	447	15	29.80
NAT.W.	46	9	102	4	25.50
B & H	67.1	7	247	9	27.44

CAREER: BOWLING

	O.	M.	R.	W.	AV.
TEST	514	173	1026	33	31.09
OTHER FIRST CLASS	18581 146.4	6351 14	42530	1856	22.92
INT.					
J.P.L.	1390.1	87	6232	229	27.21
NAT.W.	426	94	1243	50	24.86
B & H	591.3	91	2035	79	25.76

Cricketers particularly learnt from: Charles Hallows (Worcs. coach).
Qualifications: City & Guilds.
Jobs outside cricket: Estimator, industrial decorating.
Family links with cricket: Father played amateur cricket and football, and was also cricket umpire.
Off-season 1984–85: On tour, as assistant manager for England.
Overseas tours: Rest of World to Australia 1971–72; India, Pakistan and Sri Lanka 1972–73.
Other sports: Football, golf.
Relaxations: Horse-racing.
Extras: Was awarded M.B.E. in 1979. Played in one match for Rest of World v Australia 1972. Suffers badly from the sun on overseas tours. Took 100 wickets in a season 4 times. Uncle, Harry Gifford, played rugby union for England. Released by Worcs. at end of 1982 season. England selector, and assistant manager of England side on tour. Appointed Warwickshire Captain 1985.
Best batting performance: 89 Worcestershire v Oxford University, Oxford 1963.
Best bowling performance: 8-28 Worcestershire v Yorkshire, Sheffield 1968.

HUMPAGE, G.W.

Full Name: Geoffrey William Humpage.
Role: Right-hand bat; wicket-keeper; can also bowl right arm medium.
Born: 24 April 1954, Birmingham.
Height: 5′ 9″ **Weight:** 12st 7lbs.
Nickname: Farsley.
County debut: 1974.
County cap: 1976.
Test debut: —
No. of Tests: 0.
No. of One-Day Internationals: 3.
1000 runs in a season: 7.
50 wickets in a season: 0.
1st-Class 50s scored: 59.
1st-Class 100s scored: 21.
1st-Class 200s scored: 2.
1st-Class 5 w. in innings: 0.
1st-Class 10 w. in match: 0.
One-day 50s: 23.
One-day 100s 3.

Place in batting averages: 23 average: 48.49; (1983: 95 average: 31.00).
Place in bowling averages: — average: —; (1983: — average: —).
Parents: Ernest and Mabel Humpage.

Wife and date of marriage: Valerie Anne 14 September 1983 (2nd marriage).
Children: Philip Andrew Guy, 16 November 1977.
Education: Golden Hillock Comprehensive School, Birmingham.
Jobs outside cricket: Former police cadet, then police constable, Birmingham City Police. Coach, Scarborough C.C., Western Australia, 1978–79, sports executive for Pace Insurance Consultants, Birmingham.
Equipment used: Duncan Fearnley and Arcass.
Other sports: Soccer, squash, tennis, swimming, golf, snooker, table-tennis.
Relaxations: Reading, listening to E.L.O.
Extras: Good impressionist, particularly Frankie Howerd. Took part in record Warwickshire, and English first-class fourth wicket partnership of 470 v. Lancs at Southport, July 1982, with Kallicharran making 230 n.o. Humpage made 254 n.o. including 13 sixes. Previous 4th wicket record was 448 for Surrey at Oval v. Yorks. in 1899, by R. Abel and T.W. Hayward. Joined England 'Rebels' in South Africa in 1982.
Opinions on cricket: "Too many players with too short a fuse and taking the game far too seriously instead of enjoying a sport we should all love."
Best batting performance: 254 Warwickshire v Lancashire, Southport 1982.

LAST SEASON: BATTING

	I.	N.O.	R.	H.S.	AV.
TEST					
OTHER FIRST CLASS	47	8	1891	205	48.49
INT					
J.P.L.	13	1	410	109*	34.16
NAT.W.	4	0	101	77	25.25
B & H	7	3	266	100*	66.50

CAREER: BATTING

	I.	N.O.	R.	H.S.	AV.
TEST					
OTHER FIRST CLASS	367	45	11878	254	36.89
INT	2	0	11	6	5.50
J.P.L.	120	18	2531	109*	24.81
NAT.W.	21	4	496	77	29.18
B & H	40	6	1027	100*	30.21

LAST SEASON: BOWLING

	O.	M.	R.	W.	AV.
TEST					
OTHER FIRST CLASS	14	0	57	2	28.50
INT					
J.P.L.					
NAT.W.					
B & H					

CAREER: BOWLING

	O.	M.	R.	W.	AV.
TEST					
OTHER FIRST CLASS	130.1	17	444	10	44.40
INT					
J.P.L.	94.5	2	527	15	35.13
NAT.W.					
B & H	27	2	123	3	41.00

LAST SEASON: WICKET KEEPING

	C.	ST.			
TEST					
OTHER FIRST CLASS	55	11			
INT					
J.P.L.	15	2			
NAT.W.	5	3			
B & H	12	–			

CAREER: WICKET KEEPING

	C.	ST.			
TEST					
OTHER FIRST CLASS	399	49			
INT	2	–			
J.P.L.	77	12			
NAT.W.	21	5			
B & H	48	2			

KALLICHARRAN, A.I.

Full Name: Alvin Isaac Kallicharran.
Role: Left-hand bat, off-cutter.
Born: 21 March 1949, Guyana.
Height: 5′ 4″.
Nickname: Kalli.
County debut: 1971.
County cap: 1972.
Benefit: 1983 (£34,094).
Test debut: 1971–72.
No. of Tests: 66.
No. of One-Day Internationals: 31.
1000 runs in a season: 10.
50 wickets in a season: 0.
1st-Class 50s scored: 111.
1st-Class 100s scored: 69.
1st-Class 200s scored: 6.
1st-Class 5 w. in innings: 1.
1st-Class 10 w. in match: 0.
One-day 50s: 41.
One-day 100s: 9.
Place in batting averages: 15 average: 52.29; (1983: 10 average: 54.57).
Place in bowling averages: — average: —; (1983: — average: —).
1st-Class catches 1984: 17 (career: 276).
Marital status: Married.
Children: One son, Rohan.
Family links with cricket: Brother, Derek Isaac, played for Guyana.
Off-season 1984–85: Playing cricket and coaching in South Africa. Kallicharran has been told he can never again play for the West Indies after two years with Transvaal. Now with Orange Free State.
Overseas tours: With West Indies to New Zealand 1971; England in 1973 and 1976; India, Sri Lanka and Pakistan, 1974–75; Australia 1975–76 and 1979–80; India and Sri Lanka, 1978–79 as Captain. Pakistan, 1980.
Overseas teams played for: Guyana 1966–67 in Shell Shield Competition; Queensland in 1977–78 Sheffield Shield Competition.
Equipment endorsed: Duncan Fearnley.
Extras: Scored 100 not out and 101 in first two innings in Test matches, v New Zealand in 1971. Signed for World Series Cricket but resigned before playing. He made his home in England. With Geoff Humpage took part in record— for Warwickshire and for all English counties — 4th wicket stand of 470 v Lancs at Southport in July 1982. Kallicharran made 230 n.o. Humpage 254 n.o. Previous record was 448 by Abel and Hayward for Surrey v. Yorks at the Oval in 1899. Top of Warwickshire batting averages in 1982 and 1983.
Best batting performance: 235 Warwickshire v Worcestershire, Worcester 1982.
Best bowling performance: 4-48 Warwickshire v Somerset, Edgbaston 1978.

LAST SEASON: BATTING

	I.	N.O.	R.	H.S.	AV.
TEST					
OTHER FIRST CLASS	50	6	2031	200*	52.29
INT					
J.P.L.	13	0	384	73	29.53
NAT.W.	4	0	396	206	99.00
B & H	7	1	351	122*	58.50

CAREER: BATTING

	I.	N.O.	R.	H.S.	AV.
TEST	109	10	4399	187	44.43
OTHER FIRST CLASS	584	63	23657	243*	45.41
INT	28	4	826	78	34.42
J.P.L.	132	16	3380	102*	29.13
NAT.W.	21	2	938	206	49.37
B & H	47	6	1633	122*	39.84

LAST SEASON: BOWLING

	O.	M.	R.	W.	AV.
TEST					
OTHER FIRST CLASS	10	5	12	0	–
INT					
J.P.L.	10	0	76	0	–
NAT.W.	14	4	46	6	7.67
B & H	5	0	11	0	–

CAREER: BOWLING

	O.	M.	R.	W.	AV.
TEST	3.1 63.3	1 13	158	4	39.50
OTHER FIRST CLASS	13.3 856.3	0 123	3280	74	44.32
INT.	17	3	64	3	21.33
J.P.L.	151.5	5	830	11	75.45
NAT.W.	80.5	19	278	11	25.27
B & H	16	0	67	0	–

LETHBRIDGE, C.

Full Name: Christopher Lethbridge.
Role: Right-hand bat, right arm medium bowler.
Born: 23 June 1961, Castleford, Yorkshire.
Height: 5' 10" **Weight:** 13st. 6lbs.
Nickname: Arthur.
County debut: 1981.
County cap: No.
Test debut: —
No. of Tests: 0.
No. of One-Day Internationals: 0.
1000 runs in a season: 0.
50 wickets in a season: 0.
1st-Class 50s scored: 3.
1st-Class 100s scored: 0.
1st-Class 200s scored: 0.
1st-Class 5 w. in innings: 1.
1st-Class 10 w. in match: 0.
One-day 50s: 1.
One-day 100s: 0.
Place in batting averages: 176 average: 23.14; (1983: — average: —).
Place in bowling averages: 86 average: 32.90; (1983: — average: —).
1st-Class catches 1984: 6 (career: 16).
Parents: Chris and Margaret Lethbridge.
Marital status: Single.

Education: Normanton County Secondary School.
Qualifications: Five C.S.E.s. Qualified electrician.
Jobs outside cricket: Mining electrician.
Equipment used: Gunn & Moore.
Cricketers particularly learnt from: David Brown, Don Wilson and Clive Jackson (Junior Coach with Leeds United and Wakefield Trinity).
Cricketers particularly admired: Geoff Boycott.
Other sports: Football.
Relaxations: "Having a drink and a good disco. Watching sport."
Extras: "Dismissed Geoff Boycott with my first ball in first-class cricket and also scored 69."
Opinions on cricket: "First-class counties should only be allowed one overseas player on their staff, because the money they pay the second one could pay for 2 or 3 younger players."
Best batting performance: 87* Warwickshire v Somerset, Taunton 1982.
Best bowling performance: 5-68 Warwickshire v Glamorgan, Cardiff 1982.

LAST SEASON: BATTING

	I.	N.O.	R.	H.S.	AV.
TEST					
OTHER FIRST CLASS	17	3	324	46	23.14
INT					
J.P.L.	4	2	27	17*	13.50
NAT.W.	1	0	19	19	–
B & H	3	0	17	11	5.67

CAREER: BATTING

	I.	N.O.	R.	H.S.	AV.
TEST					
OTHER FIRST CLASS	55	12	949	87*	22.07
INT					
J.P.L.	19	11	208	57*	26.00
NAT.W.	2	0	23	19	11.50
B & H	5	2	34	13*	11.33

LAST SEASON: BOWLING

	O.	M.	R.	W.	AV.
TEST					
OTHER FIRST CLASS	279.5	42	987	30	32.90
INT					
J.P.L.	54	3	305	10	30.50
NAT.W.	24	0	103	1	–
B & H	13	1	50	3	16.67

CAREER: BOWLING

	O.	M.	R.	W.	AV.
TEST					
OTHER FIRST CLASS	767.1	133	2463	72	34.21
INT					
J.P.L.	235.3	8	1207	38	31.76
NAT.W.	76	8	277	7	39.57
B & H	56	5	235	11	21.36

Q. 183. What, where and when is the highest first-class score ever made by an Englishman, and who was he?

LLOYD, T.A.

Full Name: Timothy Andrew Lloyd.
Role: Left-hand bat, right arm
off-spin bowler.
Born: 5 November 1956, Oswestry.
Height: 5′ 10″ **Weight:** 11st. 10lbs.
Nickname: Teflon, Towser.
County debut: 1977.
County cap: 1980.
Test debut: 1984.
No. of Tests: 1.
No. of One-Day Internationals: 3.
1000 runs in a season: 4.
50 wickets in a season: 0.
1st-Class 50s scored: 42.
1st-Class 100s scored: 14.
1st-Class 200s scored: 1.
1st-Class 5 w. in innings: 0.
1st-Class 10 w. in match: 0.
One-day 50s: 30.
One-day 100s: 0.
Place in batting averages: 21 average: 49.16; (1983: 25 average: 45.22).
Place in bowling averages: — average: —; (1983: — average: —).
1st-Class catches 1984: 4 (career: 87).
Marital status: Single.
Education: Oswestry Boys' High School; Dorset College of Higher Education.
Qualifications: H.N.D. Tourism. A-levels and O-levels. N.C.A. Advanced
coach.
Jobs outside cricket: Has played and coached in South Africa; lorry driver.
Overseas tours: Derrick Robins tour to South America 1979; Warwickshire
C.C.C. tour to Zambia 1977; Kingfishers to South Africa 1978; Warwickshire
Wanderers to Barbados 1978.
Overseas teams played for: Orange Free State, Zingari C.C.
Cricketers particularly learnt from: Dennis Amiss. Greatly admired Gary
Sobers.
Equipment used: Duncan Fearnley.
Other sports: Soccer, golf, table-tennis, squash.
Relaxations: "Horse-racing, eating good food, drinking good beer, being on my
own."
Significant injuries in 1984: Hit on head during Test debut and missed rest of
season suffering from blurred vision.
Extras: Scored 202 not out for Shropshire Schools v. Worcs. Played for
Oswestry C.C. at age 17. Played for Shropshire and Warwickshire 2nd XI,
both in 1975. Played in one John Player League match in 1976 v Yorkshire at
Leeds. "Half my first-class wickets are international players."

Best batting performance: 208* Warwickshire v Gloucestershire, Edgbaston 1983.

LAST SEASON: BATTING

	I.	N.O.	R.	H.S.	AV.
TEST	1	1	10	10*	–
OTHER FIRST CLASS	13	1	580	110	48.33
INT	3	0	101	49	33.67
J.P.L.	2	0	14	10	7.00
NAT.W.					
B & H	5	0	195	77	39.00

CAREER: BATTING

	I.	N.O.	R.	H.S.	AV.
TEST	1	1	10	10*	–
OTHER FIRST CLASS	257	29	8355	208*	36.65
INT	3	0	101	49	33.67
J.P.L.	79	11	2207	90	32.45
NAT.W.	14	2	516	81	43.00
B & H	21	2	611	77	32.16

LAST SEASON: BOWLING

	O.	M.	R.	W.	AV.
TEST					
OTHER FIRST CLASS	8	2	41	1	–
INT					
J.P.L.					
NAT.W.					
B & H					

CAREER: BOWLING

	O.	M.	R.	W.	AV.
TEST					
OTHER FIRST CLASS	185	40	740	9	82.22
INT					
J.P.L.	22.1	0	139	1	–
NAT.W.					
B & H	13	1	56	0	–

LORD, G.J.

Full name: Gordon John Lord.
Role: Left-hand bat, slow left arrm bowler.
Born: Birmingham.
Height: 5′ 10″ **Weight:** 11st. 10lbs.
Nickname: Plod.
County debut: 1983.
County cap: No.
Test debut: —
No. of Tests: 0.
No. of One-Day Internationals: 0.
1000 runs in a season: 0.
50 wickets in a season: 0.
1st-Class 50s scored: 2.
1st-Class 100s scored: 0.
1st-Class 200s scored: 0.
1st-Class 5 w. in innings: 0.
1st-Class 10 w. in match: 0.
One-day 50s: 0.
One-day 100s: 0.
Place in batting averages: — average: —; 81983: — average: —).
Place in bowling averages: — average: —; (1983: — average: —).
1st-Class catches 1984: 3 (career: 4).
Parents: Michael David and Christine Frances Lord.
Marital status: Single.

Education: Warwick School, Durham University.
Qualifications: Seven O-Levels, 4 A-Levels and B.A. Gen.
Equipment used: Gray-Nicolls.
Overseas tours: England U-19 tour Australia 1978–79, England U-19 tour West Indies 1979–80.
Cricketers particularly learnt from: Allan Wilkins (school coach), R.N. Abberley (2nd XI coach), Norman Graham (University coach).
Other sports: Squash, tennis, swimming, running. Watches rugby, athletics, boxing.
Relaxations: All forms of music, particularly church organ music. Astronomy, reading, people.
Best batting performance: 61 Warwickshire v Nottinghamshire, Trent Bridge 1983.

LAST SEASON: BATTING

	I.	N.O.	R.	H.S.	AV.
TEST					
OTHER FIRST CLASS	6	0	83	55	13.83
INT					
J.P.L.	2	0	22	21	11.00
NAT.W.					
B & H					

CAREER: BATTING

	I.	N.O.	R.	H.S.	AV.
TEST					
OTHER FIRST CLASS	9	0	174	61	19.33
INT					
J.P.L.	4	0	63	40	15.75
NAT.W.					
B & H					

LAST SEASON: BOWLING

	O.	M.	R.	W.	AV.
TEST					
OTHER FIRST CLASS					
INT					
J.P.L.					
NAT.W.					
B & H					

CAREER: BOWLING

	O.	M.	R.	W.	AV.
TEST					
OTHER FIRST CLASS	8	3	12	0	–
INT					
J.P.L.					
NAT.W.					
B & H					

Q. 184. What, where and when was Don Bradman's highest first-class score?

Q. 185. Who is the only man ever to have scored a double century in each innings of a first-class match, where and when?

MORTON, W.

Full Name: William Morton.
Role: Left-hand bat, slow left arm bowler.
Born: 21 April 1961, Stirling.
County debut: 1984.
County cap: No.
Test debut: —
No. of Tests: 0.
No. of One-Day Internationals: 0.
1000 runs in a season: 0.
50 wickets in a season: 0.
1st-Class 50s scored: 0.
1st-Class 100s scored: 0.
1st-Class 200s scored: 0.
1st-Class 5 w. in innings: 0.
1st-Class 10 w. in match: 0.
One-day 50s: 0.
One-day 100s: 0.
Place in batting averages: — average: —; (1983: — average: —).
Place in bowling averages: 112 average: 39.21; (1983: — average: —)
1st-Class catches 1984: 3 (career: 6).
Jobs outside cricket: Gravedigger.
Extras: Made debut for Scotland in 1982, and played in 1983 Benson & Hedges Cup and NatWest Trophy competitions.
Best batting performance: 13* Warwickshire v Surrey, Edgbaston 1984.
Best bowling performance: 4-85 Warwickshire v Glamorgan, Edgbaston 1984.

LAST SEASON: BATTING

	I.	N.O.	R.	H.S.	AV.
TEST					
OTHER FIRST CLASS	8	2	39	13*	6.50
INT					
J.P.L.	1	0	10	10	—
NAT.W.					
B & H					

CAREER: BATTING

	I.	N.O.	R.	H.S.	AV.
TEST					
OTHER FIRST CLASS	10	2	47	13*	5.88
INT					
J.P.L.	1	0	10	10	—
NAT.W.	1	1	11	11*	—
B & H	3	1	16	11*	8.00

LAST SEASON: BOWLING

	O.	M.	R.	W.	AV.
TEST					
OTHER FIRST CLASS	189.5	46	549	14	39.21
INT					
J.P.L.	4	0	25	0	—
NAT.W.					
B & H					

CAREER: BOWLING

	O.	M.	R.	W.	AV.
TEST					
OTHER FIRST CLASS	256.5	68	765	23	33.26
INT					
J.P.L.	4	0	25	0	—
NAT.W.	12	1	47	4	11.75
B & H	33	10	90	6	15.00

OLD, C.M.

Full Name: Christopher Middleton Old.
Role: Left-hand bat, right arm fast medium bowler.
Born: 22 December 1948, Middlesbrough, Yorkshire.
Height: 6′ 3″ **Weight:** 14st. 7lbs.
Nickname: Chilly, Concorde, Nose.
County debut: 1983 (Warwickshire).
County cap: 1984 (Warwickshire).
Test debut: 1972–73.
No. of Tests: 46.
No. of One-Day Internationals: 32.
Benefit: 1979. £32,916.
1000 runs in a season: 0.
50 wickets in a season: 9.
1st-Class 50s scored: 27.
1st-Class 100s scored: 6.
1st-Class 200s scored: 0.
1st-Class 5 w. in innings: 38.
1st-Class 10 w. in match: 0.
One-day 50s: 13.
One-day 100s: 0.

Place in batting averages: 177 average: 23.12; (1983: 187 average: 18.86).
Place in bowling averages: 56 average: 29.02; (1983: 64 average: 29.42).
1st-Class catches 1984: 8 (career: 213).
Parents: Christopher Middleton Old, deceased, and Phyllis Old.
Wife: Alison.
Children: Juliette Louise, 28 June 1973; Simon Christopher and Paul Edward, 5 November 1975.
Education: Acklam Hall Secondary Grammar School, Middlesbrough.
Jobs outside cricket: Started as a bank clerk.
Family links with cricket: Father played local league cricket in Middlesbrough. Brother, Alan, played cricket for Durham, rugby union for England. On 2 February 1974, Chris played cricket in a Test v West Indies, while Alan played rugger for England v Ireland.
Overseas tours: India, Pakistan, Sri Lanka 1972–73; W. Indies 1973–74; Australia and New Zealand 1974–75; India, Sri Lanka and Australia, 1976–77; Pakistan and New Zealand, 1977–78; Australia 1978–79; W. Indies 1981.
Other sports: Golf, rugby union, squash.
Relaxations: Gardening.
Extras: Joined Yorkshire originally as "a batsman who could bowl". Took four wickets in five balls England v Pakistan, Birmingham in 1978. "Hates the

sunshine." Plagued by injuries: both knees were operated on in 1970 and 1971. Released by Yorkshire at end of 1982 season. Was captain of Yorkshire from 1981–82 having made debut in 1966, and awarded cap in 1969. Banned from Test cricket for 3 years for playing for England rebel team in South Africa in 1982. Declined terms from Glamorgan. Scored century in 37 minutes v Warwickshire at Birmingham in 1977, the second fastest century in first-class cricket at the time.

Best batting performance: 116 Yorkshire v Indians, Bradford 1974.
Best bowling performance: 7-20 Yorkshire v Gloucestershire, Middlesbrough 1969.

LAST SEASON: BATTING

	I.	N.O.	R.	H.S.	AV.
TEST					
OTHER FIRST CLASS	21	4	393	70	23.12
INT					
J.P.L.	8	2	171	58	28.50
NAT.W.	2	0	48	26	24.00
B & H	5	1	109	57	27.25

CAREER: BATTING

	I.	N.O.	R.	H.S.	AV.
TEST	66	9	845	65	14.83
OTHER FIRST CLASS	389	80	6789	116	21.97
INT	25	7	338	51*	18.78
J.P.L.	125	30	1963	82*	20.66
NAT.W.	26	2	348	55*	14.50
B & H	37	8	707	78*	24.38

LAST SEASON: BOWLING

	O.	M.	R.	W.	AV.
TEST					
OTHER FIRST CLASS	496	134	1306	45	29.02
INT					
J.P.L.	94	9	331	8	41.38
NAT.W.	43.1	6	158	6	26.33
B & H	76.4	10	247	10	24.70

CAREER: BOWLING

	O.	M.	R.	W.	AV.
TEST	210.3 1195.5	42 268	4020	143	28.11
OTHER FIRST CLASS	361.5 7516.3	68 1963	20595	915	22.51
INT.	39.2 240.1	2 40	999	45	22.20
J.P.L.	1198.5	125	4563	212	21.52
NAT.W.	353.2	69	1030	49	21.02
B & H	575.5	123	1560	84	18.38

Q. 186. Who scored the most double centuries in what season?
Q. 187. What is the highest first-class innings by a batsman on his debut, where and when?

SMALL, G.C.

Full Name: Gladstone Cleopthas Small.
Role: Right-hand bat, right arm fast medium bowler.
Born: 18 October 1961, St George, Barbados.
Height: 5′ 11″
Nickname: Gladys.
County debut: 1980.
County cap: 1982.
Test debut: —
No. of Tests: 0.
No. of One-Day Internationals: 0.
1000 runs in a season: 0.
50 wickets in a season: 2.
1st-Class 50s scored: 1.
1st-Class 100s scored: 0.
1st-Class 200s scored: 0.
1st-Class 5 w. in innings: 4.
1st-Class 10 w. in match: 0.
One-day 50s: 0.
One-day 100s: 0.

Place in batting averages: 214 average: 18.18; (1983: 233 average: 12.40).
Place in bowling averages: 52 average: 28.55; (1983: 69 average: 34.90).
1st-Class catches 1984: 6 (career: 25).
Parents: Chelston and Gladys Small.
Marital status: Single.
Education: Mosely School and Hall Green Technical College, Birmingham.
Equipment used: Duncan Fearnley, Winit Boots.
Overseas tours: With Young England to New Zealand 1979–80. Derrick Robins XI tour of Australia, Tasmania, New Zealand 1980; Rohan Kanhai International XI tour of Pakistan 1981.
Cricketers particularly learnt from or admired: "I admire Dennis Lillee and have learnt a lot from my manager David Brown."
Extras: In 1980, became youngest bowler to take five J.P.L. wickets in one innings. Was called up for England Test squad v. Pakistan at Edgbaston, July 1982, but did not play. Bowled 18-ball over v. Middlesex in August 1982, with 11 no balls.
Opinions on cricket: "I think it is scandalous that in other sports such as football and tennis, manufacturers' names are visibly displayed whether they are on television or not and we in cricket are not even allowed to advertise individually in a normal championship game. The introduction of managers was a useful step. He can take care of the off-field pressure that the captain and players would otherwise have to look after and therefore they can get on with the actual playing of the game."

Best batting performance: 57* Warwickshire v Oxford University, Oxford 1982.
Best bowling performance: 7-68 Warwickshire v Yorkshire, Edgbaston 1982.

LAST SEASON: BATTING

	I.	N.O.	R.	H.S.	AV.
TEST					
OTHER FIRST CLASS	30	8	400	41*	18.18
INT					
J.P.L.	5	2	68	40*	22.67
NAT.W.	2	1	13	9*	—
B & H	4	1	3	2	1.00

CAREER: BATTING

	I.	N.O.	R.	H.S.	AV.
TEST					
OTHER FIRST CLASS	112	26	1087	57*	12.64
INT					
J.P.L.	26	11	143	40*	9.53
NAT.W.	6	2	72	33	18.00
B & H	12	4	63	19*	7.88

LAST SEASON: BOWLING

	O.	M.	R.	W.	AV.
TEST					
OTHER FIRST CLASS	643.4	127	2027	71	28.55
INT					
J.P.L.	100	2	508	28	18.14
NAT.W.	36	9	99	5	19.80
B & H	61	8	269	10	26.90

CAREER: BOWLING

	O.	M.	R.	W.	AV.
TEST					
OTHER FIRST CLASS	2042.1	370	6966	214	32.55
INT					
J.P.L.	402.2	29	†944	86	22.60
NAT.W.	122.1	25	420	18	23.33
B & H	170.3	31	663	22	30.14

SMITH, K.D.

Full Name: Kenneth David Smith.
Role: Right-hand bat.
Born: 9 July 1956, Newcastle-on-Tyne.
Height: 6′ 2″ **Weight:** 14st.
Nickname: Smithy, K.D.
County debut: 1973.
County cap: 1978.
Test debut: —
No. of Tests: 0.
No. of One-Day Internationals: 0.
1000 runs in a season: 4.
50 wickets in a season: 0.
1st-Class 50s scored: 55.
1st-Class 100s scored: 9.
1st-Class 200s scored: 0.
1st-Class 5 w. in innings: 0.
1st-Class 10 w. in match: 0.
One-day 50s: 20.
One-day 100s: 2.
Place in batting averages: 222 average: 17.74; (1983: 107 average: 29.58).
Place in bowling averages: — average: —; (1983: — average: —).
1st-Class catches 1984: 3 (career: 69).

Parents: Kenneth Desmond and Joy Smith.

Wife and date of marriage: Sally Louise, 9 January 1982.

Education: Heaton Grammar School, Newcastle.

Qualifications: O-levels, N.C.A. cricket coaching award.

Jobs outside cricket: Coaching in Capetown, South Africa and playing in New Zealand.

Family links with cricket: Father played first-class cricket for Leicestershire, 1950–51. Very good minor county cricketer for Northumberland. Brother Paul plays for Warwickshire.

Equipment used: Gray-Nicolls.

Overseas tours: Derrick Robins tour to South America 1979.

Overseas teams played for: Milnerton C.C., Cape Town, 1977–78, 1979–80; Waverley C.C. Melbourne, 1980. Papatoetoe D.C.C. 1982–83.

Cricketers particularly learnt from: "My father and a bit from most people I have played with or against."

Other sports: Squash and watching football (Newcastle United).

Relaxations: "Listening to music, especially Genesis, Phil Collins and Dire Straits; travelling abroad; gardening; listening to Geoff Humpage's sense of humour in the dressing room; watching Willie Hogg bat and then coming into the dressing room and telling us how well he was playing."

Opinions on cricket: "I think we need to play 16 four-day games on covered wickets."

Best batting performance: 140 Warwickshire v Worcestershire, Worcester 1980.

LAST SEASON: BATTING

	I.	N.O.	R.	H.S.	AV.
TEST					
OTHER FIRST CLASS	40	1	692	93	17.74
INT					
J.P.L.	6	0	153	53	25.50
NAT.W.	3	0	180	101	60.00
B & H	3	0	19	11	6.33

CAREER: BATTING

	I.	N.O.	R.	H.S.	AV.
TEST					
OTHER FIRST CLASS	337	28	8614	140	27.88
INT					
J.P.L.	57	3	1136	73	21.03
NAT.W.	16	1	609	113	40.60
B & H	29	2	1020	84	37.78

LAST SEASON: BOWLING

	O.	M.	R.	W.	AV.
TEST					
OTHER FIRST CLASS					
INT					
J.P.L.					
NAT.W.					
B & H					

CAREER: BOWLING

	O.	M.	R.	W.	AV.
TEST					
OTHER FIRST CLASS	2	0	3	0	–
INT					
J.P.L.					
NAT.W.					
B & H					

SMITH, P.A.

Full Name: Paul Andrew Smith.
Role: Right-hand bat; right arm medium bowler.
Born: 15 April 1964.
Height: 6' 2" **Weight:** 11st. 7lbs.
Nickname: Jim, Moonman, Simon, le Bon, Coco.
County debut: 1982.
County cap: No.
Test debut: —
No. of Tests: 0.
No. of One-Day Internationals: 0.
1000 runs in a season: 1.
50 wickets in a season: 0.
1st-Class 50s scored: 13.
1st-Class 100s scored: 1.
1st-Class 200s scored: 0.
1st-Class 5 w. in innings: 0.
1st-Class 10 w. in match: 0.
One-day 50s: 0.
One-day 100s: 0.
Place in batting averages: 134 average: 28.11; (1983: 88 average: 32.72).
Place in bowling averages: 120 average: 41.95; (1983: 115 average: 40.19).
1st-Class catches 1984: 10 (career: 18).
Parents: Kenneth and Joy Smith.
Marital status: Single.
Education: Heaton Grammar School.
Qualifications: 5 O-levels.

LAST SEASON: BATTING

	I.	N.O.	R.	H.S.	AV.
TEST					
OTHER FIRST CLASS	41	4	1040	89	28.11
INT					
J.P.L.	13	5	218	49*	27.25
NAT.W.	4	1	58	41*	19.33
B & H	6	2	64	37	16.00

CAREER: BATTING

	I.	N.O.	R.	H.S.	AV.
TEST					
OTHER FIRST CLASS	74	8	1881	114	28.50
INT					
J.P.L.	27	10	425	49*	25.00
NAT.W.	4	1	58	41*	19.33
B & H	6	2	64	37	16.00

LAST SEASON: BOWLING

	O.	M.	R.	W.	AV.
TEST					
OTHER FIRST CLASS	194.4	23	839	20	41.95
INT					
J.P.L.	18	0	117	1	–
NAT.W.	16.4	0	72	4	18.00
B & H	13.1	0	44	2	22.00

CAREER: BOWLING

	O.	M.	R.	W.	AV.
TEST					
OTHER FIRST CLASS	548.4	73	2219	51	43.51
INT					
J.P.L.	104.4	4	615	18	34.16
NAT.W.	16.4	0	72	4	18.00
B & H	24.1	1	109	3	36.33

Family links with cricket: Father played for Leicestershire and Northumberland. Brother plays for Warwickshire.

Cricket superstitions: "None any more."

Cricketers particularly learnt from: Father, D. Amiss, D.J. Brown, G.W. Humpage; all at Warwickshire.

Equipment used: Gray-Nicolls.

Other sports: "None."

Relaxations: "Listening to music. Talking to Gladstone and Arthur in our flat."

Opinions on cricket: "Don't agree with four-day cricket."

Best batting performance: 114 Warwickshire v Oxford University, Edgbaston 1983.

Best bowling performance: 4-41 Warwickshire v Worcestershire, Edgbaston 1984.

TEDSTONE, G.A.

Full Name: Geoffrey Alan Tedstone.

Role: Right-hand bat; wicket-keeper.

Born: 19 January, 1961, Southport, Lancs.

Height: 5' 7" **Weight:** 10st. 6lbs.

Nickname: Ted.

County debut: 1982.

County cap: No.

Test debut: —

No. of Tests: 0.

No. of One-Day Internationals: 0.

1000 runs in a season: 0.

50 wickets in a season: 0.

1st-Class 50s scored: 1.

1st-Class 100s scored: 0.

1st-Class 200s scored: 0.

1st-Class 5 w. in innings: 0.

1st-Class 10 w. in match: 0.

One-day 50s: 0.

One-day 100s: 0.

Place in batting averages: — average: —; (1983: 189 average: 18.69).

Place in bowling averages: — average: —; (1983: — average: —).

Parents: Ken and Win Tedstone.

Marital status: Single.

Education: Warwick School; St. Paul's College, Cheltenham.

Qualifications: 6 O-levels; 4 A-levels; B.Ed. Degree. Qualified P.E. Teacher.

Jobs outside cricket: Coach, teacher.

Family links with cricket: Father was a keen club cricketer. Sister, Janet plays for England Ladies. Brother, Roger, plays for Leamington C.C.

Overseas tours: 1980, England Young Cricketers to West Indies, 1981; British Colleges, West Indies.
Cricketers particularly admired: Neal Abberley, Geoff Humpage, Bob Taylor.
Equipment endorsed: Gunn & Moore.
Other sports: Hockey for Warwickshire, squash, soccer. Watch Rugby Union and Wolverhampton Wanderers F.C.
Relaxations: Records, films, pubs.
Extras: "Can also bowl vicious in-swingers!"
Best batting performance: 67* Warwickshire v Cambridge University, 1983.

LAST SEASON: BATTING

	I.	N.O.	R.	H.S.	AV.
TEST					
OTHER FIRST CLASS	1	1	0	0*	–
INT					
J.P.L.					
NAT.W.					
B & H					

CAREER: BATTING

	I.	N.O.	R.	H.S.	AV.
TEST					
OTHER FIRST CLASS	22	6	288	67*	18.00
INT					
J.P.L.	2	0	25	13	12.50
NAT.W.					
B & H					

LAST SEASON: WICKET KEEPING

	C.	ST.			
TEST					
OTHER FIRST CLASS	1	1			
INT					
J.P.L.					
NAT.W.					
B & H					

CAREER: WICKET KEEPING

	C.	ST.			
TEST					
OTHER FIRST CLASS	28	6			
INT					
J.P.L.	2	–			
NAT.W.					
B & H					

Q. 188. Which Englishman has scored the most hundreds in consecutive innings, and how many?

Q. 189. What is the fastest double century ever hit by an Englishman in a first-class match, and who was he?

THORNE, D.A.

Full Name: David Anthony Thorne.
Role: Middle order batsman, left arm medium pace bowler.
Born: 12 December, 1964, Coventry.
Height: 6' 0" **Weight:** 11st. 5lbs.
Nickname: Spike, Nat, Napoleon.
County debut: 1983.
County cap: No.
Test debut: —
No. of Tests: 0.
No. of One-Day Internationals: 0.
1000 runs in a season: 0.
50 wickets in a season: 0.
1st-Class 50s scored: 1.
1st-Class 100s scored: 0.
1st-Class 200s scored: 0.
1st-Class 5 w. in innings: 1.
1st-Class 10 w. in match: 0.
One-day 50s: 0.
One-day 100s: 0.
Place in batting averages: 173 average: 23.53; (1983: — average: —).
Place in bowling averages: 108 average: 37.67; (1983: — average: —)
1st-Class catches 1984: 7 (career: 10).
Parents: Dennis and Barbara Thorne.
Marital status: Single.
Family links with cricket: Father is a qualified coach in Warwickshire area. Brothers, Robert and Philip both played for Warwicks. Schools. Mother played for Hinckley Ladies.
Education: Hill Farm Infants School, St. Augustines Primary School, Bablake School Coventry (Grammar School). Keble College, Oxford.
Qualifications: 10 O-levels, 3 A-levels.
Jobs outside cricket: Components packager for Quinton Hazell car components. Worked as a labourer on building site pre-season 1983.
Cricketing superstitions: "Always left pad on first. Hate to have to rush to pad up so usually am ready before I have to be."
Equipment used: Duncan Fearnley.
Cricketers particularly learnt from: "My dad, Neal Abberley and 'the coach' Alan Oakman who taught me to play hard and still enjoy the game as much as before."
Cricketers particularly admired: "Dennis Amiss, Bob Willis and all players I meet who seem unaffected by 'stardom'."
Other sports: Rugby, basketball and pool.
Relaxations: Listening to music, expecially Squeeze. Playing and watching all

other sport, except horse racing. Doing 'boat races' in the Turf Tavern in Oxford.

Extras: "Was hit for 26 in my 3rd over in my first John Player League game by Trevor Jesty. Was out first ball for 0 in my first-class debut v Oxford University. Youngest player to play first class for Warwickshire last season and I believe youngest to make 2nd Team century. Once took 7 for 7 in a school's first XI match including a hat trick and all 7 bowled."

Best batting performance: 69* Oxford University v Kent, Oxford 1984.

Best bowling performance: 5-39 Oxford University v Cambridge University, Lord's 1984.

LAST SEASON: BATTING

	I.	N.O.	R.	H.S.	AV.
TEST					
OTHER FIRST CLASS	16	3	306	69*	23.53
INT					
J.P.L.	3	0	3	2	1.00
NAT.W.	1	0	8	8	–
B & H	4	1	40	28*	13.33

CAREER: BATTING

	I.	N.O.	R.	H.S.	AV.
TEST					
OTHER FIRST CLASS	23	6	368	69*	21.65
INT					
J.P.L.	8	1	112	42	16.00
NAT.W.	1	0	8	8	–
B & H	4	1	40	28*	13.33

LAST SEASON: BOWLING

	O.	M.	R.	W.	AV.
TEST					
OTHER FIRST CLASS	203.1	42	565	15	37.67
INT					
J.P.L.	24	0	139	2	69.50
NAT.W.					
B & H					

CAREER: BOWLING

	O.	M.	R.	W.	AV.
TEST					
OTHER FIRST CLASS	248.1	48	754	17	44.35
INT					
J.P.L.	63.5	1	388	7	55.43
NAT.W.					
B & H					

WALL, S.

Full Name: Stephen Wall.
Role: Right-hand bat, right arm medium-fast bowler.
Born: 10 December 1959, Ulverston, Lancashire.
County debut: 1984.
County cap: No.
Test debut: —
No. of Tests: 0.
No. of One-Day Internationals: 0.
1000 runs in a season: 0.
50 wickets in a season: 0.
1st-Class 50s scored: 0.
1st-Class 100s scored: 0.
1st-Class 200s scored: 0.
1st-Class 5 w. in innings: 0.
1st-Class 10 w. in match: 0.

One-day 50s: 0.
One-day 100s: 0.
Place in batting averages: — average: —; (1983: — average: —).
Place in bowling averages: — average: —; (1983: — average: —).
1st-Class catches 1984: 1 (career: 1).
Extras: Played for Cumberland in 1983 and finished 8th in Minor Counties bowling averages.
Best batting performance: 19 Warwickshire v Hampshire, Edgbaston 1984.
Best bowling performance: 2-65 Warwickshire v Hampshire, Edgbaston 1984.

LAST SEASON: BATTING

	I.	N.O.	R.	H.S.	AV.
TEST					
OTHER FIRST CLASS	9	4	47	19	9.40
INT					
J.P.L.	–	–	–	–	–
NAT.W.					
B & H					

CAREER: BATTING

	I.	N.O.	R.	H.S.	AV.
TEST					
OTHER FIRST CLASS	9	4	47	19	9.40
INT					
J.P.L.	–	–	–	–	–
NAT.W.					
B & H					

LAST SEASON: BOWLING

	O.	M.	R.	W.	AV.
TEST					
OTHER FIRST CLASS	140.4	28	545	9	60.56
INT					
J.P.L.	18	2	98	2	49.00
NAT.W.					
B & H					

CAREER: BOWLING

	O.	M.	R.	W.	AV.
TEST					
OTHER FIRST CLASS	140.4	28	545	9	60.56
INT					
J.P.L.	18	2	98	2	49.00
NAT.W.					
B & H					

Q. 190. What is the fastest first-class triple century ever hit, where, when and by whom?

Q. 191. What is the most runs from one ball, all run, no overthrows and no penalty runs, and who scored them, when?

WILLIS, R.G.D.

Full Name: Robert George Dylan Willis.
Role: Right-hand bat; right arm fast bowler.
Born: 30 May 1949, Sunderland.
Height: 6′ 6″ **Weight:** 14st.
Nickname: Goose, Dylan, Harold, Swordfish.
County debut: 1972 (Warwickshire).
County cap: 1972.
Benefit: £44,951 in 1981.
Test debut: 1970–71.
No. of Tests: 90.
No. of One-Day Internationals: 64.
1000 runs in a season: 0.
50 wickets in a season: 5.
1st-Class 50s scored: 2.
1st-Class 100s scored: 0.
1st-Class 200s scored: 0.
1st-Class 5 w. in innings: 34.
1st-Class 10 w. in match: 2.
One-day 50s: 1.
One-day 100s: 0.
Place in batting averages: 208 average: 18.66; (1983: 201 average: 16.64).
Place in bowling averages: 134 average: 49.80; (1983: 41 average: 25.81).
1st-Class catches 1984: 3 (career: 134).
Education: Royal Grammar School, Guildford.
Family links with cricket: Brother, David, kept wicket for Blackheath C.C.
Overseas tours: Toured Australia, New Zealand 1970–71 and 1974–75; West Indies 1973–74; India, Sri Lanka and Australia 1976–77; Pakistan and New Zealand 1977–78; Australia 1978–79 and 1979–80, as Vice-Captain. West Indies 1981, India 1981–82. Australia and New Zealand as Captain, 1982–83 and New Zealand and Pakistan 1983–84. West Indies 1985 as manager of NCA Young England side.
Other sports: Soccer, tennis, badminton. Played goal-keeper for Guildford City.
Relaxations: Music, classical and popular, especially Bob Dylan.
Equipment endorsed: Winit boots, Duncan Fearnley bat.
Extras: Appointed Captain of Warwickshire 1980. Debut for Surrey 1969. Left staff after 1971 season, to make debut for Warwickshire in 1972. Operations on both knees during 1975 threatened to end his career, but he re-established his England place in 1976. Published "Diary of a Cricket Season" in 1979. Went through hypnotism courses to improve mental attitude. Added third forename, Dylan, by deed poll, because of admiration for songwriter and singer, Bob

Dylan. Writes column for Wisden Cricket Monthly. Published new book "Cricket Revolution" in 1981. Awarded M.B.E., 1981. Shared record 10th wicket partnership for England v. India of 70 with Paul Allott, Lord's, June 1982. Top of Warwickshire 1st class bowling averages in 1982. Captain of England 1982–84. Retired at end of 1984 season.

Opinions on cricket: "I was doubtful about the value of cricket managers when they were first introduced, but having worked with David Brown . . . I have certainly changed my views, and think they are a must for every progressive club."

Best batting performance: 72 Warwickshire v Indians, Edgbaston 1982.

Best bowling performance: 8-32 Warwickshire v Gloucestershire, Bristol 1977.

LAST SEASON: BATTING

	I.	N.O.	R.	H.S.	AV.
TEST	5	3	43	22	21.50
OTHER FIRST CLASS	3	2	13	5	–
INT	2	2	7	6*	–
J.P.L.	2	2	4	3*	–
NAT.W.					
B & H	2	1	2	2	–

CAREER: BATTING

	I.	N.O.	R.	H.S.	AV.
TEST	128	55	840	28*	11.51
OTHER FIRST CLASS	205	90	1794	72	15.60
INT	22	14	83	24	10.38
J.P.L.	56	25	321	52*	10.35
NAT.W.	12	6	46	12*	7.67
B & H	18	2	133	37	8.31

LAST SEASON: BOWLING

	O.	M.	R.	W.	AV.
TEST	85	15	367	6	61.17
OTHER FIRST CLASS	128	27	380	9	42.22
INT	31.2	4	116	3	38.67
J.P.L.	28.4	1	170	4	42.50
NAT.W.	14	5	27	1	–
B & H	57	11	177	6	29.50

CAREER: BOWLING

	O.	M.	R.	W.	AV.
TEST	581.5 2117.4	92 463	8190	325	25.20
OTHER FIRST CLASS	340.6 4641.5	63 1085	14278	574	24.88
INT.	21 571.1	6 91	1968	80	24.60
J.P.L.	957.5	88	3798	176	21.57
NAT.W.	336.2	60	972	57	17.05
B & H	501.2	106	1122	62	18.09

COUNTY QUIZ

Q. 1. When was the club founded?

Q. 2. Who made the most first-class runs for the county last season, and how many?

Q. 3. What's the highest ever county total, and against whom?

Q. 4. Who took most wickets for the county last season, and how many?

Q. 5. What's the highest individual score for the county, who hit it, and when?

Q. 6. What's the highest scoring partnership for the county for any wicket?

Q. 7. How many times has the club won the County Championship?

Q. 8. What's the lowest ever total made by the county in one innings, when, and against whom?

Q. 9. Which bowler took the most first-class wickets in one season, when, and how many?

Q. 10. Which batsman hit the most runs in one season, when and how many?

Worcestershire

BANKS, D.A.

Full name: David Andrew Banks.
Role: Right-hand bat; right arm medium bowler.
Born: 11 January 1961. Pensnett.
Height: 6′3″ **Weight:** 14st.
Nickname: Banksy.
County debut: 1983.
County cap: No.
Test debut: —
No. of Tests: 0.
No. of One-Day Internationals: 0.
1000 runs in a season: 0.
50 wickets in a season: 0.
1st-Class 50s scored: 1.
1st-Class 100s scored: 1.
1st-Class 200s scored: 0.
1st-Class 5 w. in innings: 0.
1st-Class 10 w. in match: 0.
One-day 50s: 0.
One-day 100s: 0.
Place in batting averages: 243 average: 14.67; (1983: 99 average: 30.25).
Place in bowling averages: — average: —; (1983: — average: —).
1st-Class catches 1984: 3 (career: 6).
Parents: William and Betty Banks.
Marital status: Single.
Education: Birds Meadow Infants; St. Mark's Primary School; Pensnett Secondary Modern; Dudley Technical College.
Qualifications: 3 0-levels; 5 C.S.E.s; Certificate of Engineering Craftsmanship City and Guilds; Mechanical and Fabricational Engineering. N.C.A. Coach.
Jobs outside cricket: Craft Apprentice, Gibbons Bros. Ltd., 1977–81, Coached school and club cricket, winter 1981–82.
Off-season 1984–85: Playing in Perth, Western Australia.
Family links with cricket: Father and brother and myself all played club cricket for Brierley Hill Athletic Club; father has retired, but brother still plays.
Cricketing superstitions: Left pad on first.

Overseas tours: Landlsey Green Youth Cricket Club tour to Barbados, October 1981.

Overseas teams played for: Leprechauns Cricket Club (of Dublin) on their annual tour of England, 1982, North Perth C.C. 1983–84.

Cricketers particularly admired: Gordon Greenidge: "Superb technique, tremendous striker of the ball; Richard Hadlee – fine all-rounder, super temperament."

Equipment used: Duncan Fearnley.

Other sports: Football, tennis, table tennis, darts, snooker, "horse racing as the girlfriend's family has race horse."

Relaxations: Reading, movies, listening to music.

Significant injuries in 1984: Groin strain – 3 weeks rest and treatment.

Extras: Century on first-class debut (v. Oxford University) — first Worcester-shire player to do so for 55 years. Also, highest aggregate in a match on Worcestershire debut, with 53 in the 2nd innings.

Opinions on cricket: "(1) Cricketers should have the right to pursue their careers where and whenever possible without the drawbacks of being penalised for doing so. (2) South Africa should be playing Test cricket."

Best batting performance: 100 Worcestershire v Oxford University, Oxford 1983.

LAST SEASON: BATTING

	I.	N.O.	R.	H.S.	AV.
TEST					
OTHER FIRST CLASS	9	0	132	43	14.67
INT					
J.P.L.	3	0	43	23	14.33
NAT.W.					
B & H					

CAREER: BATTING

	I.	N.O.	R.	H.S.	AV.
TEST					
OTHER FIRST CLASS	22	1	495	100	23.57
INT					
J.P.L.	9	1	78	23	9.75
NAT.W.					
B & H					

LAST SEASON: BOWLING

	O.	M.	R.	W.	AV.
TEST					
OTHER FIRST CLASS	4	0	17	0	–
INT					
J.P.L.					
NAT.W.					
B & H					

CAREER: BOWLING

	O.	M.	R.	W.	AV.
TEST					
OTHER FIRST CLASS	4	0	17	0	–
INT					
J.P.L.					
NAT.W.					
B & H					

Q. 192. What is the most number of sixes ever hit in one first-class innings, where, when and by whom?

CURTIS, T.S.

Full Name: Timothy Stephen Curtis.
Role: Right-hand bat. Leg break bowler.
Born: 15 January 1960, Chislehurst Kent.
Height: 5' 11" **Weight:** 12st 5lbs.
Nickname: Tony, T.C.
County debut: 1979.
County cap: 1984.
Test debut: —
No. of Tests: 0.
No. of One-Day Internationals: 0.
1000 runs in a season: 1.
50 wickets in a season: 0.
1st-Class 50s scored: 16.
1st-Class 100s scored: 3.
1st-Class 200s scored: 0.
1st-Class 5 w. in innings: 0.
1st-Class 10 w. in match: 0.
One-day 50s: 3.
One-day 100s: 0.

Place in batting averages: 41 average: 42.57; (1983: 118 average: 24.93).
Place in bowling averages: — average: —; (1983: — average: —).
1st-Class catches 1984: 13 (career: 32).
Parents: Bruce and Betty Curtis.
Marital status: Single.
Education: The Royal Grammar School, Worcester; Durham University. Cambridge University.
Qualifications: Four A-levels, 12 O-levels. Hons. degree in English, and Postgraduate certificate in Education in English and Games.
Family links with cricket: Father played good club cricket in Bristol and Stafford.
Overseas tours: N.C.A. Under-19 tour of Canada 1979.
Equipment used: Duncan Fearnley.
Cricketers particularly learnt from: Glenn Turner.
Other sports: Rugby, tennis, squash, golf.
Significant injuries in 1984: Missed 3 weeks because of torn ankle ligaments.
Extras: Captained Durham University at cricket.
Opinions on cricket: "I am not convinced that 4-day county matches are a good idea because of reduced batting opportunities and the tendency of the increase in time to slow the game down even more. I think the reduction in overseas players was necessary and hope that the consequent reduction in crowd-pulling potential will be made up for by a greater sense of county identity, loyalty and support."

Best batting performance: 129 Worcestershire v Cambridge University, Worcester 1984.

LAST SEASON: BATTING

	I.	N.O.	R.	H.S.	AV.
TEST					
OTHER FIRST CLASS	36	3	1405	129	42.57
INT	10	2	305	75*	38.13
J.P.L.					
NAT.W.	2	1	76	54*	–
B & H	4	0	98	44	24.50

CAREER: BATTING

	I.	N.O.	R.	H.S.	AV.
TEST					
OTHER FIRST CLASS	104	14	2809	129	31.21
INT	20	7	451	75*	34.69
J.P.L.					
NAT.W.	3	1	105	54*	52.50
B & H	7	0	109	44	15.57

LAST SEASON: BOWLING

	O.	M.	R.	W.	AV.
TEST					
OTHER FIRST CLASS	3.3	0	22	0	–
INT					
J.P.L.					
NAT.W.					
B & H					

CAREER: BOWLING

	O.	M.	R.	W.	AV.
TEST					
OTHER FIRST CLASS	13.3	3	50	1	–
INT					
J.P.L.	39	2	232	7	33.14
NAT.W.					
B & H	0.2	0	4	0	–

D'OLIVEIRA, D.B.

Full name: Damian Basil D'Oliveira.
Role: Right-hand bat; slow right arm bowler.
Born: 19 October 1960, Cape Town, South Africa.
Height: 5′ 8″ **Weight:** 11st 8lbs.
Nickname: D.D.
County debut: 1982.
County cap: No.
Test debut: —
No. of Tests: 0.
No. of One-Day Internationals: 0.
1000 runs in a season: 0.
50 wickets in a season: 0.
1st-Class 50s scored: 10.
1st-Class 100s scored: 1.
1st-Class 200s scored: 0.
1st-Class 5 w. in innings: 0.
1st-Class 10 w. in match: 0.
One-day 50s: 2.
One-day 100s: 0.
Place in batting averages: 155 average: 25.67; (1983: 130 average: 26.27).
Place in bowling averages: 94 average: 34.10; (1983: — average: —).
1st-Class catches 1984: 17 (career: 32).

Parents: Basil and Naomi D'Oliveira.
Wife and date of marriage: Tracey, 26 September 1983.
Education: St. George's R.C. Primary School; Blessed Edward Oldcorne Secondary School.
Qualifications: 3 O-levels.
Family links with cricket: Father played for Worcestershire and England.
Overseas teams played for: West Perth C.C. in Western Australia, 1979–80, Christchurch Shirley 1982–83, 1983–84 on a Whitbread scholarship.
Equipment used: Duncan Fearnley.
Cricketers particularly admired: Greg Chappell, Viv Richards, Richard Hadlee.
Other sports: Football and most others.
Relaxations: Watching T.V. and films, and eating out.
Best batting performance: 102 Worcestershire v Middlesex, Worcester 1983.
Best bowling performance: 2-50 Worcestershire v Lancashire, Old Trafford 1984.

LAST SEASON: BATTING

	I.	N.O.	R.	H.S.	AV.
TEST					
OTHER FIRST CLASS	34	3	796	74	25.67
INT					
J.P.L.	11	0	171	36	15.55
NAT.W.	2	1	19	18*	–
B & H	3	0	73	57	24.33

CAREER: BATTING

	I.	N.O.	R.	H.S.	AV.
TEST					
OTHER FIRST CLASS	80	6	1833	102	24.77
INT					
J.P.L.	30	2	463	51*	16.53
NAT.W.	3	1	27	18*	13.50
B & H	6	1	89	57	17.80

LAST SEASON: BOWLING

	O.	M.	R.	W.	AV.
TEST					
OTHER FIRST CLASS	113	24	341	10	34.10
INT					
J.P.L.	17	0	116	3	38.67
NAT.W.					
B & H	21	0	101	0	–

CAREER: BOWLING

	O.	M.	R.	W.	AV.
TEST					
OTHER FIRST CLASS	192	38	603	14	43.07
INT					
J.P.L.	61.2	4	235	13	18.08
NAT.W.	12	4	28	2	14.00
B & H	28	2	114	2	57.00

Q. 193. Who has scored the most first-class runs in an English season, where and how many?

Q. 194. Who last scored 3000 first-class runs in an English season, how many and when?

ELLCOCK, R.M.

Full name: Richard McDonald
Ellcock.
Role: Right-hand bat;
right arm fast bowler.
Born: 17 June 1965, Barbados.
Height: 5' 10" **Weight:** 12st. 7lbs.
Nickname: Ricky.
County debut: 1982.
County cap: No.
Test debut: —
No. of Tests: 0.
No. of One-Day Internationals: 0.
1000 runs in a season: 0.
50 wickets in a season: 0.
1st-Class 50s scored: 0.
1st-Class 100s scored: 0.
1st-Class 200s scored: 0.
1st-Class 5 w. in innings: 0.
1st-Class 10 w. in match: 0.
One-day 50s: 0.
One-day 100s: 0.
Place in batting averages: 147 average: 26.80; (1983: 239 average: 11.00).
Place in bowling averages: 26 average: 24.62; (1983: 105 average: 37.24).
1st-Class catches 1984: 1 (career: 3).
Parents: Everson McDonald (deceased) and Ione Marian Ellcock.
Marital status: Single.
Education: Welches Mixed School, Combermere, Barbados. Malvern College,
England.

LAST SEASON: BATTING

	I.	N.O.	R.	H.S.	AV.
TEST					
OTHER FIRST CLASS	8	3	134	45*	26.80
INT					
J.P.L.	2	0	0	0	0.00
NAT.W.					
B & H	2	1	16	12	–

CAREER: BATTING

	I.	N.O.	R.	H.S.	AV.
TEST					
OTHER FIRST CLASS	33	8	337	45*	13.48
INT					
J.P.L.	5	2	6	5*	2.00
NAT.W.	1	0	6	6	–
B & H	2	1	16	12	–

LAST SEASON: BOWLING

	O.	M.	R.	W.	AV.
TEST					
OTHER FIRST CLASS	221.2	32	714	29	24.62
INT					
J.P.L.	29.1	0	123	7	17.57
NAT.W.					
B & H	18	3	81	2	40.50

CAREER: BOWLING

	O.	M.	R.	W.	AV.
TEST					
OTHER FIRST CLASS	533.4	80	1919	63	30.46
INT					
J.P.L.	61.3	4	235	13	18.08
NAT.W.	10	2	49	3	16.33
B & H	25	4	88	3	29.33

Qualifications: 6 O-levels.
Off-season 1984–85: Playing cricket in Barbados.
Overseas teams played for: Combined Schools, Barbados, 1980, Carlton 1982, 1983, Barbados.
Overseas tours: Jamaica 1983 (Barbados Youth).
Cricketers particularly learnt from: Malcolm Marshall. Admires Alvin Kallicharran.
Equipment used: Duncan Fearnley.
Other sports: Table-tennis and basketball; watches soccer and motor racing.
Relaxations: Movies, music.
Best batting performance: 45* Worcestershire v Essex, Worcester 1984.
Best bowling performance: 4-34 Worcestershire v Glamorgan, Worcester 1984.

HICK, G.A.

Full Name: Graeme Ashley Hick.
Role: Right-hand bat, right arm off spin, slips, gully.
Born: 23 May 1966, Harare, Zimbabwe.
Height: 6′ 3″ **Weight:** 13st. 5lbs.
Nickname: Ash, Thicky.
County debut: 1984.
County cap: No.
Test debut: —
No. of Tests: 0.
No. of One-Day Internationals: 0.
1000 runs in a season: 0.
50 wickets in a season: 0.
1st-Class 50s scored: 1.
1st-Class 100s scored: 0.
1st-Class 200s scored: 0.
1st-Class 5 w. in innings: 0.
1st-Class 10 w. in match: 0.
One-day 50s: 0.
One-day 100s: 0.

Place in batting averages: — average: —; (1983: — average: —).
Place in bowling averages: — average: —; (1983: — average: —).
1st-Class catches 1984: 1 (career: 1).
Parents: John and Eva Hick.
Marital status: Single.
Family links with cricket: Father connected with cricket administration since 1972 and in 1984 elected to Zimbabwe Cricket Union Board of Control.

Education: Banket Primary; Prince Edward Boys' High School, Zimbabwe.
Qualifications: 4 O-levels.
Jobs outside cricket: Zimbabwe Cricket Union coach.
Off-season 1984–85: Coaching in Zimbabwe.
Cricketing superstitions: Left pad always put on first.
Equipment used: Duncan Fearnley.
Overseas tours: Zimbabwe XI 1983 World Cup Zimbabwe v Sri Lanka in Sri Lanka; Zimbabwe U-23 Triangular Tournament, Zambia.
Overseas teams played for: Old Harrarians, Zimbabwe since 1982.
Cricketers particularly learnt from: David Houghton, Basil D'Oliveira, father.
Cricketers particularly admired: Duncan Fletcher (Zimbabwe capt.) for approach and understanding of the game.
Other sports: Golf, hockey, tennis, squash; follows English league football (Liverpool).
Relaxations: Watching movies, television, listening to music.
Extras: Youngest player participating in 1983 Prudential World Cup (17 yrs.); youngest player to represent Zimbabwe. Scored 1234 runs in 1984 Birmingham league season; scored 964 runs in 1984 2nd XI for Worcestershire; scored 185 in Birmingham league highest score since the war; scored 11 centuries (6 in a row) in both above competitions.
Opinions on cricket: "1) Bowling leg side in one-day cricket should be abandoned. 2) Final law on overseas players should be made and stuck to, and not altered every year."
Best batting performance: 82* Worcestershire v Surrey, The Oval 1984.

LAST SEASON: BATTING

	I.	N.O.	R.	H.S.	AV.
TEST					
OTHER FIRST CLASS	1	1	82	82*	–
INT					
J.P.L.					
NAT.W.					
B & H					

CAREER: BATTING

	I.	N.O.	R.	H.S.	AV.
TEST					
OTHER FIRST CLASS	12	3	272	82*	30.22
INT					
J.P.L.					
NAT.W.					
B & H					

LAST SEASON: BOWLING

	O.	M.	R.	W.	AV.
TEST					
OTHER FIRST CLASS	6	0	27	0	–
INT					
J.P.L.					
NAT.W.					
B & H					

CAREER: BOWLING

	O.	M.	R.	W.	AV.
TEST					
OTHER FIRST CLASS	71	18	196	3	65.33
INT					
J.P.L.					
NAT.W.					
B & H					

HUMPHRIES, D.J.

Full Name: David John Humphries.
Role: Left-hand bat, wicket-keeper.
Born: 6 August 1953, Alveley, Shropshire.
Height: 5' 8" **Weight:** 13st.
Nickname: Humpty.
County debut: 1977 (Worcs).
County cap: 1978.
Test debut: —
No. of Tests: 0.
No. of One-Day Internationals: 0.
1000 runs in a season: 0.
50 wickets in a season: 0.
1st-Class 50s scored: 25.
1st-Class 100s scored: 9.
1st-Class 200s scored: 0.
1st-Class 5 w. in innings: 0.
1st-Class 10 w. in match: 0.
One-day 50s: 2.
One-day 100s: 0.
Place in batting averages: 135 average: 28.00; (1983: 167 average: 21.54).
Place in bowling averages: — average: —; (1983: — average —).
Parents: Dennis John and Olive Mary Humphries.
Wife and date of marriage: Lorraine Mary, 7 September 1974.
Children: Rebecca Louise, 10 October 1978.
Education: Bridgnorth Secondary Modern, Wulfrun College, Wolverhampton.
Qualifications: O.N.C. Engineering Part 1, one A-level, six O-levels, eight C.S.E.s.

LAST SEASON: BATTING

	I.	N.O.	R.	H.S.	AV.
TEST					
OTHER FIRST CLASS	32	9	644	133*	28.00
INT					
J.P.L.	8	1	59	17*	8.43
NAT.W.	1	0	0	0	–
B & H	3	0	29	20	9.67

CAREER: BATTING

	I.	N.O.	R.	H.S.	AV.
TEST					
OTHER FIRST CLASS	251	45	5054	133*	24.53
INT					
J.P.L.	94	12	1144	62	13.95
NAT.W.	10	1	178	58	19.78
B & H	28	4	317	41	13.21

LAST SEASON: WICKET KEEPING

	C.	ST.			
TEST					
OTHER FIRST CLASS	36	7			
INT					
J.P.L.	11	6			
NAT.W.	2	–			
B & H	2	–			

CAREER: WICKET KEEPING

	C.	ST.			
TEST					
OTHER FIRST CLASS	291	60			
INT					
J.P.L.	93	23			
NAT.W.	8	3			
B & H	37	8			

Jobs outside cricket: Has been marketing assistant, Kay & Co Ltd., Worcester. Lottery Manager, Worcestershire C.C.C.
Family links with cricket: Father Club Captain of Cannock C.C. and still plays. Brother plays Birmingham League and ex-Staffordshire Schools.
Other sports: Football, golf.
Relaxations: Skittles, darts.
Extras: Played for Shropshire 1971–73, debut for Leicestershire 1974, left county after 1976 season.
Best batting performance: 133* Worcestershire v Derbyshire, Worcester 1984.

ILLINGWORTH, R.K.

Full Name: Richard Keith Illingworth.
Role: Right-hand bat, slow left arm bowler.
Born: 1963, Bradford, Yorkshire.
Height: 5′ 11½″ **Weight:** 11st. 10lbs.
Nickname: Illy, Roo.
County debut: 1982.
County cap: No.
Test debut: —
No. of Tests: 0.
No. of One-Day Internationals: 0.
1000 runs in a season: 0.
50 wickets in a season: 1.
1st-Class 50s scored: 1.
1st-Class 100s scored: 0.
1st-Class 200s scored: 0.
1st-Class 5 w. in innings: 3.
1st-Class 10 w. in match: 0.
One-day 50s: 0.
One-day 100s: 0.
Place in batting averages: 148 average: 26.62; (1983: — average: —).
Place in bowling averages: 85 average: 32.84; (1983: 108 average: 38.12).
1st-Class catches 1984: 9 (career: 21).
Parents: Keith and Margaret Illingworth.
Marital status: Single.
Education: Wrose Brow Middle and Salts Grammar School.
Qualifications: 0-levels in Economics, Geography, Maths, English, Sociology, History. Qualified coach.
Off-season 1984–85: Playing and coaching.
Family links with cricket: Father plays Bradford League cricket. Mother secretary Yorkshire C.A. Centre of Excellence nets.
Overseas tours: Denmark Youth Tournament N.A.Y.C. 1981, Whitbread

scholarship playing for Colts C.C. (Brisbane) 1982–83. Wisden Cricket XI, 1983, Barbados.

Cricketers particularly learnt from: Graham Whyte (Captain of Colts C.C.), father.

Equipment endorsed: Duncan Fearnley.

Other sports: Any ball game.

Relaxations: Listening to music (Dire Straits, various other groups and solo artists). Pint of Tetley's.

Significant injuries in 1984: Split webbing on bowling hand; chipped bone on right hand.

Opinions on cricket: "Closer links between schools and clubs to enhance development of younger players; more professionals to be employed during winter to coach at their own county schools."

Best batting performance: 55 Worcestershire v Leicestershire, Hereford 1983.

Best bowling performance: 5-26 Worcestershire v Gloucestershire, Worcester 1983.

LAST SEASON: BATTING

	I.	N.O.	R.	H.S.	AV.
TEST					
OTHER FIRST CLASS	20	7	346	43*	26.62
INT					
J.P.L.	8	4	28	12*	7.00
NAT.W.	1	0	22	22	–
B & H	2	0	10	10	5.00

CAREER: BATTING

	I.	N.O.	R.	H.S.	AV.
TEST					
OTHER FIRST CLASS	71	17	810	55	15.00
INT					
J.P.L.	17	7	66	21	6.60
NAT.W.	2	0	30	22	15.00
B & H	3	1	21	11*	10.50

LAST SEASON: BOWLING

	O.	M.	R.	W.	AV.
TEST					
OTHER FIRST CLASS	744	220	1872	57	32.84
INT					
J.P.L.	70	3	300	20	15.00
NAT.W.	11.1	2	36	0	–
B & H	21	2	92	2	46.00

CAREER: BOWLING

	O.	M.	R.	W.	AV.
TEST					
OTHER FIRST CLASS	1669.3	451	4513	123	36.69
INT					
J.P.L.	149	7	648	33	19.63
NAT.W.	23.1	6	50	2	25.00
B & H	51	9	168	7	24.00

Q. 195. Who scored most first-class centuries in an English season, and when?

Q. 196. Who has the highest first-class batting average for an English season, what was it, and when?

INCHMORE, J.D.

Full Name: John Darling Inchmore.
Role: Right-hand bat, right arm
fast medium bowler.
Born: 22 February 1949, Ashington,
Northumberland.
Nickname: Inchers.
County debut: 1973.
County cap: 1976.
Benefit: 1985.
Test debut: —
No. of Tests: 0.
No. of One-Day Internationals: 0.
1000 runs in a season: 0.
50 wickets in a season: 2.
1st-Class 50s scored: 7.
1st-Class 100s scored: 1.
1st-Class 200s scored: 0.
1st-Class 5 w. in innings: 18.
1st-Class 10 w. in match: 1.
One-day 50s: 0.
One-day 100s: 0.
Place in batting averages: 210 average: 18.44; (1983: 200 average: 17.41).
Place in bowling averages: 74 average: 31.00; (1983: 60 average: 29.12).
1st-Class catches 1984: 10 (career: 64).
Education: Ashington Grammar School, St. Peter's College, Saltley,
Birmingham.
Qualifications: B.Ed. (physical education).

LAST SEASON: BATTING

	I.	N.O.	R.	H.S.	AV.
TEST					
OTHER FIRST CLASS	24	8	295	34	18.44
INT					
J.P.L.	9	2	101	33*	14.43
NAT.W.	1	0	0	0	–
B & H	3	0	81	29	27.00

CAREER: BATTING

	I.	N.O.	R.	H.S.	AV.
TEST					
OTHER FIRST CLASS	229	49	2982	113	16.57
INT					
J.P.L.	83	22	923	45	15.13
NAT.W.	14	3	118	32*	10.73
B & H	31	8	299	49*	13.00

LAST SEASON: BOWLING

	O.	M.	R.	W.	AV.
TEST					
OTHER FIRST CLASS	497	110	1364	44	31.00
INT					
J.P.L.	90.4	4	349	14	24.93
NAT.W.	24	6	59	3	19.67
B & H	43	4	140	14	10.00

CAREER: BOWLING

	O.	M.	R.	W.	AV.
TEST					
OTHER FIRST CLASS	4471	872	13371	464	28.82
INT					
J.P.L.	837.3	58	3481	145	24.00
NAT.W.	177.3	29	640	26	24.62
B & H	432.4	56	1488	61	24.39

Overseas teams played for: Northern Transvaal in 1976–77 Currie Cup Competition.
Jobs outside cricket: Represents Allied Hambro Financial Management.
Equipment used: Duncan Fearnley.
Cricketers learnt from: Vanburn Holder.
Extras: Played for Northumberland 1970. Played for both Worcestershire and Warwickshire 2nd XIs in 1972 and for Stourbridge in the Birmingham League. Top of Worcestershire first-class bowling averages in 1982. Sponsored by Severn House Publishers Ltd., 4, Brook Street, London W.1. for use of a car.
Best batting performance: 113 Worcestershire v Essex, Worcester 1974.
Best bowling performance: 8-58 Worcetseshire v Yorkshire, Worcester 1977.

KAPIL DEV

Full Name: Kapil Dev.
Role: Right-hand bat, right arm fast bowler.
Born: 6 January 1959, Haryana, India.
Height: 6′ 3″.
Nickname: Haryana Hurricane.
County debut: 1981 (Northants). 1984 (Worcestershire).
County cap: No.
Test debut: 1978–79.
No. of Tests: 62.
No. of One-Day Internationals: 47.
1000 runs in a season: 0.
50 wickets in a season: 0.
1st-Class 50s scored: 27.
1st-Class 100s scored: 8.
1st-Class 200s scored: 0.
1st-Class 5 w. in innings: 29.
1st-Class 10 w. in match: 3.
One-day 50s: 6.
One-day 100s: 1.
Place in batting averages: 40 average: 42.67; (1983: 29 average: 43.63).
Place in bowling averages: 21 average: 23.40; (1983: 32 average: 20.06).
1st-Class catches 1984: 10 (career: 102).
Education: Punjab University.
Marital Status: Married.
Cricketers particularly learnt from: Coach, Desh Prem Azad.
Off-season 1984–85: Playing for India.
Overseas tours: Australia 1980–81, England 1979, World Cup 1983 in England.

Relaxations: Hunting, riding, dancing.

Extras: Played for Nelson in Lancashire League for part of 1981 season. Does not smoke or drink. Started as a spin bowler. Youngest player to take 100 Test wickets at 21 years 25 days, and score 1000 Test runs at 21 years, 27 days. Captain of India, and led them to the 1983 World Cup victory. Played for Northamptonshire 1981–83.

Opinions on cricket: "The first Test Match I ever saw was the first I played in. All I knew was what I had read in books and what my family and friends had told me. I was shattered that opposition players swore and abused me. I have learned to cope now, but I still don't understand it. Test Cricket should be on a plane above all other games– a beautiful sport."

Best batting performance: 193 Haryana v Punjab, Chandigarh 1979–80.
Best bowling performance: 8-38 Haryana v Services Rohtak 1977–78.

LAST SEASON: BATTING

	I.	N.O.	R.	H.S.	AV.
TEST					
OTHER FIRST CLASS	19	4	640	95	42.67
INT					
J.P.L.	8	0	128	40	16.00
NAT.W.	1	0	2	2	–
B & H					

CAREER: BATTING

	I.	N.O.	R.	H.S.	AV.
TEST	92	8	2483	126*	29.55
OTHER FIRST CLASS	126	14	3279	193	29.28
INT	46	6	1048	175*	26.20
J.P.L.	18	0	363	75	20.17
NAT.W.	4	0	22	18	5.50
B & H	2	1	67	49	–

LAST SEASON: BOWLING

	O.	M.	R.	W.	AV.
TEST					
OTHER FIRST CLASS	296.3	75	819	35	23.40
INT					
J.P.L.	59.1	6	229	12	19.08
NAT.W.	22	3	46	1	–
B & H					

CAREER: BOWLING

	O.	M.	R.	W.	AV.
TEST	2225.3	445	6844	247	27.70
OTHER FIRST CLASS	2235.2	505	6478	252	25.71
INT	425.3	67	1536	55	27.91
J.P.L.	126.4	12	484	23	21.04
NAT.W.	62.1	17	138	6	23.00
B & H	34.3	9	94	4	23.50

Q. 197. What Englishman has the highest first-class average for an English season, how much and when?

Q. 198. Who captained Leicestershire at the beginning of the 1984 season in the absence of David Gower through injury?

KING, C.L.

Full Name: Collis Llewellyn King.
Role: Right-hand bat, right arm
medium pace bowler.
Born: 11 June 1951, Barbados.
County debut: 1983 (Worcs.).
County cap: No.
Test debut: 1976.
No. of Tests: 9.
No. of One-Day Internationals: 18.
1000 runs in a season: 0.
50 wickets in a season: 0.
1st-Class 50s scored: 18.
1st-Class 100s scored: 12.
1st-Class 200s scored: 0.
1st-Class 5 w. in innings: 1.
1st-Class 10 w. in match: 0.
One-day 50s: 6.
One-day 100s: 2.
Place in batting averages: —
average: —; (1983: — average: —).
Place in bowling averages: — average: —; (1983: — average: —).
1st-Class catches 1984: 0 (career: 89).
Equipment used: Gray-Nicolls.
Extras: Played for Glamorgan in 1977, and further experience in England in
Lancashire League. Appeared for Worcestershire in 1983 when League
commitment allowed, and registration held for 1984. Played for West Indies in
1979 Prudential World Cup Final, scoring 86. Went to South Africa with West

LAST SEASON: BATTING

	I.	N.O.	R.	H.S.	AV.
TEST					
OTHER FIRST CLASS					
INT					
J.P.L.	1	1	101	101*	–
NAT.W.					
B & H	2	0	83	61	41.50

CAREER: BATTING

	I.	N.O.	R.	H.S.	AV.
TEST	16	3	418	100*	32.15
OTHER FIRST CLASS	156	20	5408	163	39.77
INT	14	2	280	86	23.33
J.P.L.	20	1	586	127	30.84
NAT.W.					
B & H	7	0	167	61	23.86

LAST SEASON: BOWLING

	O.	M.	R.	W.	AV.
TEST					
OTHER FIRST CLASS					
INT					
J.P.L.	3	0	33	0	–
NAT.W.					
B & H	18	5	43	0	–

CAREER: BOWLING

	O.	M.	R.	W.	AV.
TEST	97	24	282	3	94.00
OTHER FIRST CLASS	1259.4	296	3530	126	28.01
INT	124	7	529	11	48.09
J.P.L.	103	5	502	12	41.83
NAT.W.					
B & H	43	9	145	1	–

Indian 'Rebels' and now appears with Natal.

Best batting performance: 163 West Indians v Northamptonshire, Northampton 1976.

Best bowling performance: 5-91 Barbados v Jamaica, Bridgetown 1975–76.

McEVOY, M.S.A.

Full Name: Michael Stephen Anthony McEvoy.

Role: Opening batsman, right arm swing bowler, slip fielder.

Born: 25 January 1956, Jorhat, Assam, India.

Height: 5' 10" **Weight:** 10st. 10lbs.

Nickname: Mac.

County debut: 1976 (Essex),1983 (Worcs.).

County cap: No.

Test debut: —

No. of Tests: 0.

No. of One-Day Internationals: 0.

1000 runs in a season: 0.

50 wickets in a season: 0.

1st-Class 50s scored: 10.

1st-Class 100s scored: 1.

1st-Class 200s scored: 0.

1st-Class 5 w. in innings: 0.

1st-Class 10 w. in match: 0.

One-day 50s: 1.

One-day 100s: 0.

Place in batting averages: 247 average: 14.46; (1983: 157 average: 22.76).

Place in bowling averages: — average: —; (1983: — average: —)

1st-Class catches 1984: 11 (career: 70).

Parents: Anthony Robert and Elizabeth Margaret McEvoy.

Marital status: Single.

Education: Holmwood House, Colchester; Colchester Royal Grammar School; Borough Road College.

Qualifications: Cert. Ed. N.C.A. Advanced coach.

Jobs outside cricket: P.E. teacher.

Equipment used: Duncan Fearnley.

Overseas tours: British Colleges 1978, Barbados, Trinidad and Tobago; Minor Counties 1982, East Africa.

Overseas teams played for: Claremont 1982–83; Northern Goodwood 1983–84 (both Cape Town).

Other sports: "Rugby, hockey, squash, golf, football, etc!"
Relaxations: Eating and drinking.
Extras: Formerly with Essex — released at end of 1981 season and played for Cambridgeshire in 1982, finishing 2nd in Minor Counties averages. Released by Worcestershire at end of 1984.
Best batting performance: 103 Worcestershire v Warwickshire, Edgbaston 1983.
Best bowling performance: 3-20 Essex v Middlesex, Lord's, 1981.

LAST SEASON: BATTING

	I.	N.O.	R.	H.S.	AV.
TEST					
OTHER FIRST CLASS	13	0	188	46	14.46
INT					
J.P.L.	2	1	44	27*	–
NAT.W.					
B & H					

CAREER: BATTING

	I.	N.O.	R.	H.S.	AV.
TEST					
OTHER FIRST CLASS	113	2	2128	103	19.17
INT					
J.P.L.	16	4	169	27*	14.08
NAT.W.	1	0	52	52	–
B & H	4	1	63	24	21.00

LAST SEASON: BOWLING

	O.	M.	R.	W.	AV.
TEST					
OTHER FIRST CLASS					
INT					
J.P.L.					
NAT.W.					
B & H					

CAREER: BOWLING

	O.	M.	R.	W.	AV.
TEST					
OTHER FIRST CLASS	30	8	103	3	34.33
INT					
J.P.L.					
NAT.W.					
B & H					

MOORES, P.

Full Name: Peter Moores.
Role: Wicket-keeper and right-hand bat.
Born: 18 December 1962, Macclesfield, Cheshire.
Height: 6' **Weight:** 12st. 4lbs.
Nickname: Mags.
County debut: 1983.
County cap: No.
Test debut: —
No. of Tests: 0.
No. of One-Day Internationals: 0.
1000 runs in a season: 0.
50 wickets in a season: 0.
1st-Class 50s scored: 0.
1st-Class 100s scored: 0.
1st-Class 200s scored: 0.

1st-Class 5 w. in innings: 0.
1st-Class 10 w. in match: 0.
One-day 50s: 0.
One-day 100s: 0.
Place in batting averages: — average: —; (1983: 209 average: 15.40).
Place in bowling averages: — average: —; (1983: — average: —).
Parents: Bernard and Winifred Moores.
Marital status: Single.
Education: St. Albans Primary; The King Edward VI School, Macclesfield.
Qualifications: 7 O-levels, 3 A-levels.
Jobs outside cricket: Assistant recreational supervisor.
Cricketing superstitions: Always wear same hat when keeping.
Equipment used: Duncan Fearnley.
Cricketers particularly learnt from: Basil D'Oliveira, Don Wilson.
Cricketers particularly admired: Farouk Engineer, Bob Taylor and Clive Lloyd.
Other sports: Football, rugby, squash, badminton, table tennis, general fitness. Watches football, rugby league.
Relaxations: Listening to music, reading sporting autobiographies and watching old movies.
Extras: "Played for H.M.C. Schools, M.C.C. Schools, England Schools and for the National Cricket Association of Young Cricketers. Joined Worcs Staff from the M.C.C. Young Pros staff which I joined at the beginning of the 1982 season." Released at end of 1984.
Best batting performance: 45 Worcestershire v Somerset, Weston 1984.

LAST SEASON: BATTING

	I.	N.O.	R.	H.S.	AV.
TEST					
OTHER FIRST CLASS	4	2	61	45	30.50
INT					
J.P.L.	2	2	14	14*	—
NAT.W.					
B & H					

CAREER: BATTING

	I.	N.O.	R.	H.S.	AV.
TEST					
OTHER FIRST CLASS	15	3	215	45	17.92
INT					
J.P.L.	3	3	24	14*	—
NAT.W.					
B & H					

LAST SEASON: WICKET KEEPING

	C.	ST.
TEST		
OTHER FIRST CLASS	7	4
INT		
J.P.L.	3	1
NAT.W.		
B & H		

CAREER: WICKET KEEPING

	C.	ST.
TEST		
OTHER FIRST CLASS	18	6
INT		
J.P.L.	4	2
NAT.W.		
B & H		

NEALE, P.A.

Full Name: Phillip Anthony Neale.
Role: Right-hand bat, right arm
medium bowler.
Born: 5 June 1954, Scunthorpe.
Height: 5′ 11″ **Weight:** 11st.
Nickname: Phil.
County debut: 1975.
County cap: 1978.
Test debut: —
No. of Tests: 0.
No. of One-Day Internationals: 0.
1000 runs in a season: 6.
50 wickets in a season: 0.
1st-Class 50s scored: 56.
1st-Class 100s scored: 16.
1st-Class 200s scored: 0.
1st-Class 5 w. in innings: 0.
1st-Class 10 w. in match: 0.
One-day 50s: 17.
One-day 100s: 2.

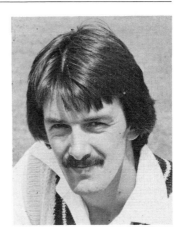

Place in batting averages: 26 average: 47.39; (1983: 42 average: 41.11).
Place in bowling averages: — average: —; (1983: — average: —).
1st-Class catches 1984: 9 (career: 80).
Parents: Geoff and Elsie.
Wife and date of marriage: Christine, 26 September 1976.
Children: Kelly Joanne, 9 November 1979, Craig Andrew, 11 February 1982.
Education: Frederick Gough Grammar School, Scunthorpe; John Leggot
Sixth Form College, Scunthorpe; Leeds University.
Qualifications: B.A. Hons. Russian. Two A-levels, 10 O-levels. Preliminary
football and cricket coaching awards.
Jobs outside cricket: Professional footballer, full-back, with Lincoln City F.C.
Cricketing superstitions: Always puts left pad on first.
Cricketers particularly learnt from: "All the senior players at Worcester."
Equipment endorsed: Duncan Fearnley.
Other sports: Football; enjoys watching all sports and occasionally plays pool,
snooker and squash.
Relaxations: Reading, watching television, "playing with my children".
Extras: Played for Lincolnshire 1973–74. Scored 100 runs before lunch v
Warwickshire at Worcester, 1979. Captain 1983–. Top of Worcs. averages
1983 and 1984. Testimonial season with Lincoln City 1984–85.
Best batting performance: 163* Worcestershire v Nottinghamshire,
Worcester 1979.

LAST SEASON: BATTING

	I.	N.O.	R.	H.S.	AV.
TEST					
OTHER FIRST CLASS	42	6	1706	143	47.39
INT					
J.P.L.	13	5	270	46	33.75
NAT.W.	2	0	20	20	10.00
B & H	3	0	55	23	18.33

CAREER: BATTING

	I.	N.O.	R.	H.S.	AV.
TEST					
OTHER FIRST CLASS	340	40	10514	163*	35.05
INT					
J.P.L.	120	25	2918	102	30.71
NAT.W.	12	0	303	68	25.25
B & H	33	4	797	128	27.48

LAST SEASON: BOWLING

	O.	M.	R.	W.	AV.
TEST					
OTHER FIRST CLASS	1.3	0	11	0	–
INT					
J.P.L.					
NAT.W.					
B & H					

CAREER: BOWLING

	O.	M.	R.	W.	AV.
TEST					
OTHER FIRST CLASS	42.4	3	201	1	–
INT					
J.P.L.	8.2	0	50	2	25.00
NAT.W.					
B & H					

NEWPORT, P.J.

Full name: Philip John Newport.
Role: Right-hand bat; right arm fast medium bowler.
Born: 11 October 1962.
Height: 6' 2" **Weight:** 13st.
Nickname: Newps, Nobbler, Neil Armstrong.
County debut: 1982.
County cap: No.
Test debut: —
No. of Tests: 0.
No. of One-Day Internationals: 0
1000 runs in a season: 0.
50 wickets in a season: 0.
1st-Class 50s scored: 0.
1st-Class 100s scored: 0.
1st-Class 200s scored: 0.
1st-Class 5 w. in innings: 1.
1st-Class 10 w. in match: 0.
One-day 50s: 0.
One-day 100s: 0.
Place in batting averages: 114 average: 31.17; (1983: — average: —).
Place in bowling averages: 84 average: 32.81; (1983: — average: —)
1st-Class catches 1984: 2 (career: 3).
Parents: John and Sheila Diana.
Marital status: Single.
Education: Royal Grammar School, High Wycombe; Portsmouth Polytechnic.

Qualifications: 8 O-levels, 3 A-levels; B.A.(Hons) in geography; basic coaching qualification.

Jobs outside cricket: Schoolmaster.

Off-season 1984–85: Teaching at Worcester R.G.S.

Family links with cricket: "Father is a good club cricketer, my younger brother plays with High Wycombe C.C."

Overseas tours: With N.C.A. to Denmark 1981.

Cricketers particularly learnt from: "I have been helped by numerous people rather than one specific individual."

Equipment endorsed: Duncan Fearnley.

Other sports: Plays soccer, badminton, basketball, volleyball, and fan of American football.

Relaxations: "Listening to music, eating out when possible, and trying to understand the complexities of the Rugby Union laws."

Extras: Had trial as schoolboy for Southampton F.C. Played cricket for N.A.Y.C. England Schoolboys 1981. Also for Bucks. in Minor Counties in 1981, Minor Counties final 1982. Availability for Worcestershire now increased as studies completed. Wears contact lens in left eye only.

Opinions on cricket: "Run-outs should be awarded to fielder involved."

Best batting performance: 41* Worcestershire v Warwickshire, Edgbaston 1983.

Best bowling performance: 5-51 Worcestershire v Warwickshire, Worcester 1984.

LAST SEASON: BATTING

	I.	N.O.	R.	H.S.	AV.
TEST					
OTHER FIRST CLASS	11	5	187	40*	31.17
INT					
J.P.L.	3	1	39	24	19.50
NAT.W.	1	0	25	25	–
B & H					

CAREER: BATTING

	I.	N.O.	R.	H.S.	AV.
TEST					
OTHER FIRST CLASS	20	7	297	41*	22.85
INT					
J.P.L.	5	1	52	34	13.00
NAT.W.	1	0	25	25	–
B & H					

LAST SEASON: BOWLING

	O.	M.	R.	W.	AV.
TEST					
OTHER FIRST CLASS	204.4	36	689	21	32.81
INT					
J.P.L.	32	1	98	6	16.33
NAT.W.	6	0	27	0	–
B & H					

CAREER: BOWLING

	O.	M.	R.	W.	AV.
TEST					
OTHER FIRST CLASS	292.4	40	1045	30	34.83
INT					
J.P.L.	43	1	141	9	15.67
NAT.W.	6	0	27	0	–
B & H					

Q. 199. Which batsman in the 1984 season was run out in both innings of the same match for the same score?

PATEL, D.N.

Full Name: Dipak Narshi Patel.
Role: Right-hand bat, off-break
bowler.
Born: 25 October 1958, Nairobi,
Kenya.
Height: 5' 11½" **Weight:** 10st. 7lbs.
Nickname: Dip or Indian.
County debut: 1976.
County cap: 1979.
Test debut: —
No. of Tests: 0.
No. of One-Day Internationals: 0.
1000 runs in a season: 4.
50 wickets in a season: 2.
1st-Class 50s scored: 34.
1st-Class 100s scored: 14.
1st-Class 200s scored: 0.
1st-Class 5 w. in innings: 12.
1st-Class 10 w. in match: 0.
One-day 50s: 6.
One-day 100s: 1.

Place in batting averages: 89 average: 33.70; (1983: 61 average: 38.45).
Place in bowling averages: 92 average: 33.82; (1983: 104 average: 36.72).
1st-Class catches 1984: 11 (career: 112).
Parents: Narshibhai and Laxmiben Patel.
Wife and date of marriage: Vina, 27 February 1983.
Education: George Salter Comprehensive School, West Bromwich, West
Midlands.
Jobs outside cricket: Sales assistant, Oakfield Tile Co. Ltd., Worcester.
Family links with cricket: Three uncles played for Kenya XI. Cousin,
Harshad, now on Worcester staff.
Overseas tours: Zambia 1977 with Warwickshire, South America 1979 with
Derrick Robins XI and Australia with U-23 XI 1979–80, Trinidad and Tobago
1984 with World Invitation XI.
Overseas teams played for: Played in Australia on Whitbread Scholarship
1979–80 and club cricket in Australia every winter since then.
Equipment used: Duncan Fearnley.
Other sports: Golf, badminton, squash, football. Follows W.B.A.
Cricketers particularly learnt from: Norman Gifford, Glenn Turner, Kapil
Dev.
Significant injuries in 1984: Tore ligaments when twisted both ankles within a
week.
Relaxations: Indian music, D.I.Y. around the house.

Extras: Has lived in UK since 1967. Discovered by Basil D'Oliviera. Shared record J.P.L. partnership of 224 with Alan Ormrod v. Hants. at Southampton, August 1982. Shared in first-class sixth wicket partnership record for county, 227 with E.J.O. Hemsley, v. Oxford University at Oxford, 1976.

Best batting performance: 197 Worcestershire v Cambridge University, Worcester 1984.

Best bowling perforrmance: 7-46 Worcestershire v Lancashire, Worcester 1982.

LAST SEASON: BATTING

	I.	N.O.	R.	H.S.	AV.
TEST					
OTHER FIRST CLASS	41	1	1348	197	33.70
INT					
J.P.L.	15	1	456	98	32.57
NAT.W.	2	0	44	28	22.00
B & H	4	2	195	90*	97.50

CAREER: BATTING

	I.	N.O.	R.	H.S.	AV.
TEST					
OTHER FIRST CLASS	295	19	7863	197	28.49
INT					
J.P.L.	102	9	1818	125	19.54
NAT.W.	9	1	155	42	19.38
B & H	27	4	606	90*	26.35

LAST SEASON: BOWLING

	O.	M.	R.	W.	AV.
TEST					
OTHER FIRST CLASS	770	219	2063	61	33.82
INT					
J.P.L.	106	24	417	19	21.94
NAT.W.	19.2	0	73	5	14.60
B & H	39	4	126	3	42.00

CAREER: BOWLING

	O.	M.	R.	W.	AV.
TEST					
OTHER FIRST CLASS	3813.4	989	10767	300	35.89
INT					
J.P.L.	455.2	14	2134	74	28.83
NAT.W.	55.1	8	196	6	32.67
B & H	178	21	624	20	31.20

PRIDGEON, A.P.

Full Name: Alan Paul Pridgeon.
Role: Right-hand bat, right arm medium bowler.
Born: 22 February, 1954, Wall Heath, Staffordshire.
Height: 6′ 3″ **Weight:** 13st 2lbs.
Nickname: Pridge.
County debut: 1972.
County cap: 1980.
Test debut: —
No. of Tests: 0.
No. of One-Day Internationals: 0.
1000 runs in a season: 0.
50 wickets in a season: 5.
1st-Class 50s scored: 1.
1st-Class 100s scored: 0.
1st-Class 200s scored: 0.
1st-Class 5 w. in innings: 8.

1st-Class 10 w. in match: 1.
One-day 50s: 0.
One-day 100s: 0.
Place in batting averages: 255 average: 13.19; (1983: — average: —).
Place in bowling averages: 61 average: 29.53; (1983: 50 average: 27.47).
1st-Class catches 1984: 14 (career: 62).
Parents: Albert Ernest and Sybil Ruby Pridgeon.
Wife and date of marriage: Jane, 7 October 1978.
Children: Laura, 8 August 1983.
Education: Summerhill Secondary Modern, Kingswinford, West Midlands.
Qualifications: Six C.S.E.s, Qualified F.A. coach and qualified N.C.A. coach.
Jobs outside cricket: Semi-professional footballer, F.A. coach (not full badge), salesman and has worked for Manpower Commission.
Off-season 1984–85: Coach to Howick and Pakuranga C.C. Auckland, New Zealand.
Equipment used: Duncan Fearnley.
Overseas tours: Worcestershire Club tour to Barbados 1980.
Overseas teams played for: Howick and Pakuranga, New Zealand 1983–84.
Cricketers particularly learnt from: I.V.A. Richards, Dennis Lillee, Norman Gifford.
Cricketers particularly admired: Steve Perryman ("fire man").
Other sports: Semi-professional footballer for Dudley Town F.C., West Midlands League, golf, snooker, tennis. Follow horse-racing.
Cricketing superstitions: "Hate batting while Sylvester Clarke is bowling."
Relaxations: Horse-racing, taking dog (Muffin) for walks.
Opinions on cricket: "The 117 over rule should be done away with for 1985, it's ridiculous that pro cricketers should be still out on the park at 8–8.30 on occasions. Also action should be taken about the amount of short-pitched bowling and intimidatory bowling especially against non-recognised batsmen and night-watchmen.
Best batting performance: 67 Worcestershire v Warwickshire, Worcester 1984.

LAST SEASON: BATTING

	I.	N.O.	R.	H.S.	AV.
TEST					
OTHER FIRST CLASS	23	7	211	67	13.19
INT					
J.P.L.	5	4	13	6	–
NAT.W.	1	1	5	5*	–
B & H	2	2	5	3*	–

CAREER: BATTING

	I.	N.O.	R.	H.S.	AV.
TEST					
OTHER FIRST CLASS	185	75	1032	67	9.38
INT					
J.P.L.	48	26	143	17	6.50
NAT.W.	8	5	34	13*	11.33
B & H	16	8	70	13*	8.75

LAST SEASON: BOWLING

	O.	M.	R.	W.	AV.
TEST					
OTHER FIRST CLASS	719.5	168	1949	66	29.53
INT					
J.P.L.	92.5	6	382	9	42.44
NAT.W.	23	3	57	1	–
B & H	36	6	147	4	36.75

CAREER: BOWLING

	O.	M.	R.	W.	AV.
TEST					
OTHER FIRST CLASS	4799	960	14176	417	33.99
INT					
J.P.L.	791.3	40	3642	111	32.81
NAT.W.	105.1	24	347	8	43.38
B & H	305.2	32	1215	23	52.83

Best bowling performance: 7-35 Worcestershire v Oxford University, Oxford 1976.

RADFORD, N.V.

Full Name: Neal Victor Radford.
Role: Right-hand bat, right arm fast medium bowler.
Born: 7 June 1957, Luanshya, Zambia.
Height: 5′ 11″ **Weight:** 12st.
Nickname: Radiz.
County debut: 1980 (Lancashire).
County cap: No.
Test debut: —
No. of Tests: 0.
No. of One-Day Internationals: 0.
1000 runs in a season: 0.
50 wickets in a season: 0.
1st-Class 50s scored: 2.
1st-Class 100s scored: 0.
1st-Class 200s scored: 0.
1st-Class 5 w. in innings: 6.
1st-Class 10 w. in match: 1.
One-day 50s: 0.
One-day 100s: 0.

Place in batting averages: — average: —; (1983: — average: —).
Place in bowling averages: — average: —; (1983: — average: —).
1st-Class catches 1984: 0 (career: 33).
Parents: Edith Joyce and Victor Reginald Radford.
Marital status: Single.
Family links with cricket: Brother Wayne pro for Gowerton (S.W.C.A.) and Glamorgan 2nd XI. Also Orange Free State in Currie Cup.
Education: Rockland Primary School, Blymoor, Athlone Boys High School, Johannesburg.
Qualifications: Matriculation and university entrance. N.C.A. Advanced Coach.
Equipment used: Duncan Fearnley.
Overseas teams played for: Transvaal 1979–83, South African Schools XI, South African Army.
Other sports: Golf, squash (have a bash at most). Follow all sport.
Relaxations: Music, T.V., films.
Best batting performance: 76* Lancashire v Derbyshire, Blackpool 1981.
Best bowling performance: Transvaal B v Griqualand, West Kimberley 1980–81.

LAST SEASON: BATTING

	I.	N.O.	R.	H.S.	AV.
TEST					
OTHER FIRST CLASS	5	1	53	36	13.25
INT					
J.P.L.	3	1	7	4	3.50
NAT.W.					
B & H					

CAREER: BATTING

	I.	N.O.	R.	H.S.	AV.
TEST					
OTHER FIRST CLASS	75	16	1148	76*	19.46
INT					
J.P.L.	16	7	133	48*	14.78
NAT.W.	3	1	29	14	14.50
B & H	2	0	15	14	7.50

LAST SEASON: BOWLING

	O.	M.	R.	W.	AV.
TEST					
OTHER FIRST CLASS	106.4	17	390	10	39.00
INT					
J.P.L.	58.1	4	219	11	19.91
NAT.W.					
B & H					

CAREER: BOWLING

	O.	M.	R.	W.	AV.
TEST					
OTHER FIRST CLASS	1630.5	345	5366	175	30.66
INT					
J.P.L.	169.2	12	686	33	20.78
NAT.W.	34.3	6	105	6	17.50
B & H	25.2	5	83	2	41.50

RHODES, S.J.

Full Name: Steven John Rhodes.
Role: Right-hand,bat, wicket-keeper.
Born: 17 June 1964, Bradford.
Height: 5′ 8″ **Weight:** 11st 9lbs.
Nickname: Wilf.
County debut: 1981 (Yorks.).
County cap: No.
Test debut: —
No. of Tests: 0.
No. of One-Day Internationals: 0.
1000 runs in a season: 0.
50 wickets in a season: 0.
1st-Class 50s scored: 0.
1st-Class 100s scored: 0.
1st-Class 200s scored: 0.
1st-Class 5 w. in innings: 0.
1st-Class 10 w. in match: 0.
One-day 50s: 0.
One-day 100s: 0.
Place in batting averages: — average: —; (1983: — average: —).
Place in bowling averages: — average: —; (1983: — average: —).
Parents: Bill and Norma Rhodes.
Marital status: Single.
Family links with cricket: Father played for Nottinghamshire.
Education: Bradford Moor Junior School; Lapage St Middle; Carlton-Bolling Comprehensive.
Qualifications: 4 O-levels and cricket coaching certificate.

Jobs outside cricket: Trainee manager in sports retailer in winters of 1980–81 and 1981–82.
Off-season 1984–85: "After two seasons abroad I will be staying home and having a rest, possibly coaching."
Equipment used: Slazenger.
Overseas teams played for: Past Brothers Cricket Club, Bundaberg, Queensland, Australia, 1982–83 and 1983–84, and Bundaberg Cricket Association.
Cricketers particularly learnt from: "Phil Carrick, Doug Padgett, Colin Johnson and my father."
Cricketers particularly admired: Bob Taylor.
Other sports: Golf, follows rugby league (Bradford Northern).
Extras: Played for Young England against Young Australia in 1983. Youngest wicket-keeper to play for Yorkshire. Holds record for most victims in an innings for Young England. Played for England Schools U-15s. Released by Yorkshire to join Worcestershire at end of 1984 season.
Best batting performance: 35 Yorkshire v Somerset, Middlesbrough 1984.

LAST SEASON: BATTING

	I.	N.O.	R.	H.S.	AV.
TEST					
OTHER FIRST CLASS	2	1	41	35	–
INT					
J.P.L.	1	0	6	6	–
NAT.W.					
B & H					

CAREER: BATTING

	I.	N.O.	R.	H.S.	AV.
TEST					
OTHER FIRST CLASS	2	1	41	35	–
INT					
J.P.L.	1	0	6	6	–
NAT.W.					
B & H					

LAST SEASON: WICKET KEEPING

	C.	ST.			
TEST					
OTHER FIRST CLASS	3	–			
INT					
J.P.L.	3	–			
NAT.W.					
B & H					

CAREER: WICKET KEEPING

	C.	ST.			
TEST					
OTHER FIRST CLASS	3	–			
INT					
J.P.L.	3	–			
NAT.W.					
B & H					

Q. 200. Which current county and England player had a role in an Oscar-winning film?

Q. 201. What England and Middlesex player said of what other England and Middlesex player that his usual way of calling for a run was "Yes . . . No . . . Wait . . . Sorry . . . Oh, my Gawd!"?

SMITH, D.M.

Full Name: David Mark Smith.
Role: Left-hand bat, right arm fast
medium bowler.
Born: 9 January 1956, Balham.
Height: 6' 4" **Weight:** 14st.
Nickname: Smudger or Smurf.
County debut: 1973 (Surrey),
1984 (Worcestershire).
County cap: 1980 (Surrey), 1984
(Worcestershire).
Test debut: —
No. of Tests: 0.
No. of One-Day Internationals: 0.
1000 runs in a season: 2.
50 wickets in a season: 0.
1st-Class 50s scored: 28.
1st-Class 100s scored: 10.
1st-Class 200s scored: 0.
1st-Class 5 w. in innings: 0.
1st-Class 10 w. in match: 0.
One-day 50s: 10.

One-day 100s: 1.
Place in batting averages: 42 average: 42.04; (1983: 20 average: 46.75).
Place in bowling averages: — average: —; (1983: — average: —).
1st-Class catches 1984: 12 (career: 108).
Parents: Dennis Henry and Tina Smith.
Wife and date of marriage: Jacqui, 7 January 1977, Salisbury, Rhodesia.
Education: Battersea Grammar School.
Qualifications: O-levels in Maths, French and English.
Jobs outside cricket: Two years with insurance company, one year with
Harrods, one year spent in Rhodesia, two years with building firm. Coaching
cricket.
Family links with cricket: Father plays cricket for the B.B.C.
Overseas teams played for: Played in Sydney, Australia, 1980–81.
Equipment endorsed: Gray-Nicolls.
Other sports: Football, kart racing, table tennis.
Relaxations: Reading biographies and historical novels, watching motor racing,
collecting LPs, making video recordings and cine films.
Significant injuries 1984: Groin strain and broken finger.
Extras: Played for Surrey 2nd XI in 1972. Was not retained after 1977 but was
re-instated in 1978. Top of Surrey first-class batting averages in 1982. "Has a
cocker spaniel called Winston." Sacked by Surrey during 1983 season.
Best batting performance: 189* Worcestershire v Kent, Worcester 1984.
Best bowling performance: 3-40 Surrey v Sussex, The Oval 1976.

LAST SEASON: BATTING

	I.	N.O.	R.	H.S.	AV.
TEST					
OTHER FIRST CLASS	31	5	1093	189*	42.04
INT					
J.P.L.	11	3	203	66*	25.38
NAT.W.	1	0	31	31	–
B & H	4	1	39	27	13.00

CAREER: BATTING

	I.	N.O.	R.	H.S.	AV.
TEST					
OTHER FIRST CLASS	246	53	6313	189*	32.71
INT					
J.P.L.	88	20	1660	87*	24.44
NAT.W.	16	5	578	103*	52.55
B & H	30	5	593	45*	23.72

LAST SEASON: BOWLING

	O.	M.	R.	W.	AV.
TEST					
OTHER FIRST CLASS	6	0	22	1	–
INT					
J.P.L.					
NAT.W.					
B & H					

CAREER: BOWLING

	O.	M.	R.	W.	AV.
TEST					
OTHER FIRST CLASS	445	93	1485	28	53.04
INT					
J.P.L.	124.5	6	606	12	50.50
NAT.W.	29	5	113	3	37.67
B & H	56	4	266	8	33.25

WESTON, M.J.

Full Name: Martin John Weston.
Role: Right-hand bat; right arm medium bowler.
Born: 8 April 1959, Worcester.
Height: 6' 1" **Weight:** 14st.
Nickname: Spaghetti, Wesso.
County debut: 1979.
County cap: 1985.
Test debut: —
No. of Tests: 0.
No. of One-Day Internationals: 0.
1000 runs in a season: 1.
50 wickets in a season: 0.
1st-Class 50s scored: 15.
1st-Class 100s scored: 3.
1st-Class 200s scored: 1.
1st-Class 5 w. in innings: 0.
1st-Class 10 w. in match: 0.
One-day 50s: 8.
One-day 100s: 1.
Place in batting averages: 137 average: 27.92; (1983: 152 average: 23.30).
Place in bowling averages: 17 average: 22.50; (1983: — average: —).
1st-Class catches 1984: 15 (career: 33).
Parents: John Franklyn and Sheila Margaret Weston.
Marital status: Single.
Education: St George's C. of E Junior; Samuel Southall Secondary Modern.
Qualifications: City & Guilds and Advance Crafts in Bricklaying.

Overseas tours: 1980 tour to Barbados with Worcestershire C.C.C.
Cricketers particularly learnt from: Dipak Patel.
Equipment used: Duncan Fearnley.
Other sports: Football, darts, dominoes, squash.
Relaxations: Horse-racing.
Extras: Was only Worcester-born cricketer on Worcestershire staff in 1982.
Best batting performance: 145* Worcestershire v Northamptonshire, Worcester 1984.
Best bowling performance: 4-44 Worcestershire v Northamptonshire, Wellingborough 1984.

LAST SEASON: BATTING

	I.	N.O.	R.	H.S.	AV.
TEST					
OTHER FIRST CLASS	41	3	1061	145*	27.92
INT					
J.P.L.	14	0	269	60	19.21
NAT.W.	2	0	11	10	5.50
B & H	4	0	141	53	35.25

CAREER: BATTING

	I.	N.O.	R.	H.S.	AV.
TEST					
OTHER FIRST CLASS	120	6	2764	145*	24.25
INT					
J.P.L.	38	2	788	109	21.89
NAT.W.	4	0	55	23	13.75
B & H	10	0	261	56	26.10

LAST SEASON: BOWLING

	O.	M.	R.	W.	AV.
TEST					
OTHER FIRST CLASS	123.4	29	315	14	22.50
INT					
J.P.L.	18.5	1	69	7	9.86
NAT.W.	12	5	30	4	7.50
B & H					

CAREER: BOWLING

	O.	M.	R.	W.	AV.
TEST					
OTHER FIRST CLASS	250.5	49	760	22	34.55
INT					
J.P.L.	56.1	2	307	10	30.70
NAT.W.	24	6	82	4	20.50
B & H	3	0	15	0	–

COUNTY QUIZ

Q. 1. When was the club founded?
Q. 2. Who made the most first-class runs for the county last season, and how many?
Q. 3. What's the highest ever county total, and against whom?
Q. 4. Who took most wickets for the county last season, and how many?
Q. 5. What's the highest individual score for the county, who hit it, and when?
Q. 6. What's the highest scoring partnership for the county for any wicket?
Q. 7. How many times has the club won the County Championship?
Q. 8. What's the lowest ever total made by the county in one innings, when, and against whom?
Q. 9. Which bowler took the most first-class wickets in one season, when, and how many?
Q. 10. Which batsman hit the most runs in one season, when and how many?

Yorkshire

BAIRSTOW, D.L.

Full Name: David Leslie Bairstow.
Role: Right-hand bat, wicket-keeper, occasional medium pacer. Captain 1984.
Born: 1 September 1951, Bradford.
Height: 5′ 10″ **Weight:** 14st 7lbs.
Nickname: Bluey.
County debut: 1970.
County cap: 1973.
Test debut: 1979.
No. of Tests: 4.
No. of One-Day Internationals: 21.
1000 runs in a season: 2.
50 wickets in a season: 0.
1st-Class 50s scored: 61.
1st-Class 100s scored: 4.
1st-Class 200s scored: 0.
1st-Class 5 w. in innings: 0.
1st-Class 10 w. in match: 0.
One-day 50s: 12.
One-day 100s: 1.

Place in batting averages: 64 average: 37.48; (1983: 62 average: 38.00).
Place in bowling averages: — average: —; (1983: — average: —).
Benefit: 1982.
Wife: Gail Lesley.
Children: Andrew David, Claire Louise.
Education: Hanson Grammar School, Bradford.
Qualifications: 'O' and 'A' levels.
Jobs outside cricket: Sales representative.
Family links with cricket: Father, Lesley, played cricket for Laisterdyke.
Overseas tours: Australia 1978–79. Australia 1979–80. West Indies 1981.
Overseas teams played for: Griqualand West in 1966–67 and 1977–78 as Captain.
Cricketers particularly learnt from: Laurie Bennett, maths and sports master at school. Mike Fearnley.

Equipment used: Morrant Sports.

Cricket superstitions: "I will pat the ground three times or fiddle with my gloves three times. It is ridiculous but I do not want to stop it. I was in a pub a couple of days before the Leeds Test, and a lad I had never seen before gave me a medallion, and told me to keep it in my pocket for luck. Many people would have forgotten completely, but that medallion went into the pocket of my flannels, and stayed there for the whole match."

Relaxations: Gardening.

Other sports: Turned down an offer to play for Bradford City F.C., plays golf.

Significant injuries in 1984: Back strain – affected wicket-keeping.

Extras: Played for M.C.C. Schools at Lord's in 1970. First Yorkshire wicket-keeper to get a 1000 runs in a season (1982) since Arthur Wood in 1935. Set Yorkshire record of seven catches v. Derbyshire at Scarborough, 1982. 133 consecutive John Player League matches. His 145 for Yorkshire v Middlesex is the highest score by a Yorkshire wicket-keeper. Allowed to take an A-level at 6 a.m. at school in order to make Yorkshire debut. Published "A Yorkshire Diary – a year of crisis" 1984.

Best batting performance: 145 Yorkshire v Middlesex, Scarborough 1980.

Best bowling performance: 3-82 Griqualand West v Transvaal B, Johannesburg, 1976–77.

LAST SEASON: BATTING

	I.	N.O.	R.	H.S.	AV.
TEST					
OTHER FIRST CLASS	26	5	787	94	37.48
INT	3	0	30	13	10.00
J.P.L.	13	0	195	42	15.00
NAT.W.	1	0	2	2	–
B & H	4	0	76	39	19.00

CAREER: BATTING

	I.	N.O.	R.	H.S.	AV.
TEST	7	1	125	59	20.83
OTHER FIRST CLASS	501		96	10160	145	25.09
INT	20	6	206	23*	14.72
J.P.L.	167	42	2551	78	20.40
NAT.W.	20	4	348	92	21.75
B & H	41	8	562	103*	17.03

LAST SEASON: BOWLING

	O.	M.	R.	W.	AV.
TEST					
OTHER FIRST CLASS	11	1	39	0	–
INT					
J.P.L.					
NAT.W.					
B & H					

CAREER: BOWLING

	O.	M.	R.	W.	AV.
TEST					
OTHER FIRST CLASS	79	15	247	6	41.17
INT					
J.P.L.					
NAT.W.					
B & H	3	0	17	0	–

LAST SEASON: WICKET KEEPING

	C.	ST.			
TEST					
OTHER FIRST CLASS	39	7			
INT	3	–			
J.P.L.	20	3			
NAT.W.	1	–			
B & H	3	–			

CAREER: WICKET KEEPING

	C.	ST.			
TEST	12	1			
OTHER FIRST CLASS	758	115			
INT	17	4			
J.P.L.	178	17			
NAT.W.	27	2			
B & H	79	3			

BOOTH, P.A.

Full name: Paul Antony Booth.
Role: Left-hand bat; slow
left arm bowler.
Born: 5 September 1965,
Huddersfield.
Height: 6′ **Weight:** 10½st.
Nickname: Boot, Boothy.
County debut: 1982.
County cap: No.
Test debut: —
No. of Tests: 0.
No. of One-Day Internationals: 0.
1000 runs in a season: 0.
50 wickets in a season: 0.
1st-Class 50s scored: 0.
1st-Class 100s scored: 0.
1st-Class 200s scored: 0.
1st-Class 5 w. in innings: 0.
1st-class 10 w. in match: 0.
One-day 50s: 0.
One-day 100s: 0.
Place in batting averages: — average: —; (1983: — average: —).
Place in bowling averages: 126 average: 44.06; (1983: — average: —).
1st-Class catches 1984: 2 (career: 2).
Parents: Colin and Margaret Booth.
Marital status: Single.
Education: Honley High School.

LAST SEASON: BATTING

	I.	N.O.	R.	H.S.	AV.
TEST					
OTHER FIRST CLASS	13	4	78	26	8.67
INT					
J.P.L.					
NAT.W.	1	1	6	6*	—
B & H					

CAREER: BATTING

	I.	N.O.	R.	H.S.	AV.
TEST					
OTHER FIRST CLASS	16	5	78	26	7.09
INT					
J.P.L.					
NAT.W.	1	1	6	6*	—
B & H					

LAST SEASON: BOWLING

	O.	M.	R.	W.	AV.
TEST					
OTHER FIRST CLASS	347	124	749	17	44.06
INT					
J.P.L.					
NAT.W.	11	2	33	2	16.50
B & H					

CAREER: BOWLING

	O.	M.	R.	W.	AV.
TEST					
OTHER FIRST CLASS	374	130	821	17	48.29
INT					
J.P.L.					
NAT.W.	11	2	33	2	16.50
B & H					

Qualifications: School certificate at O-level (maths, woodwork).
Family links with cricket: Father has played local cricket at Meltham for more than 30 years and is still playing.
Jobs outside cricket: Carpenter and joiner.
Off-season 1984–85: Working and Young England tour to West Indies.
Cricketers particularly learnt from: Doug Padgett (county coach).
Equipment used: Stuart Surridge.
Other sports: Football and golf.
Extras: Made county debut at 17 years and 3 days, and first championship wicket was that of Allan Lamb. Played for Yorkshire Schools U. 15's. Represented County U. 19 side which won Oxford and Cambridge Festival 1983.
Opinions on cricket: "(1) Should revert back to uncovered pitches to give more help to the spinners. (2) Would like to see South Africa back in Test cricket and feel that politics should not interfere with cricket and sport."
Best batting performance: 26 Yorkshire v Worcestershire, Scarborough 1984.
Best bowling performance: 3-22 Yorkshire v Northamptonshire, Northampton 1984.

BOYCOTT, G.

Full Name: Geoffrey Boycott.
Role: Right-hand bat, right arm medium bowler.
Born: 21 October 1940, Fitzwilliam Yorkshire.
Height: 5′ 10″ **Weight:** 11st 7lbs.
Nickname: Fiery or Boycs (or Thatch, "but only from Ian Botham").
County debut: 1962.
County cap: 1963.
Test debut: 1964.
No. of Tests: 108. Captain in 4.
No. of One-Day Internationals: 36.
Benefit: £20,639 in 1974.
Testimonial: 1984.
1000 runs in a season: 22.
50 wickets in a season: 0.
1st-Class 50s scored: 221.
1st-Class 100s scored: 133.
1st-Class 200s scored: 10.
1st-Class 5 w. in innings: 0.
1st-Class 10 w. in match: 0.
One-day 50s: 69.
One-day 100s: 7.

Place in batting averages: 8 average: 62.68; (1983: 9 average: 55.46).
Place in bowling averages: — average: —; (1983: — average: —).
1st-Class catches 1984: 13 (career: 250).
Marital status: Single.
Education: Hemsworth Grammar School (7 O-levels).
Jobs outside cricket: Was civil servant, working for Yorkshire Electricity Board.
Family links with cricket: Brothers Peter and Tony both play cricket, but father did not play at all.
Overseas tours: South Africa 1964–65; Australia, New Zealand 1965–66 and 1970–71, returning home early with broken arm; West Indies 1967–68 and 1973–74; Pakistan and New Zealand 1977–78 as Vice-Captain; Australia 1978–79 and 1979–80, West Indies 1981, India 1981–82.
Overseas teams played for: Northern Transvaal 1971–72.
Cricket records: Finished top of the batting averages 1971 with an average of 100.12, the only English batsman ever to have an average of over 100 for a season. Repeated 1979 with average of 102.53. Became highest scoring test batsman of all time when he overtook Sir Gary Sobers' record of 8,032 runs, playing for England v. India in Third Test at Delhi on 23 Dec. 1981. This took him 451 hours 55 minutes in aggregate at the crease. Boycott said of this record: "Records don't mean as much to me as people think. If records were all that concerned me, I would not have spent 3 years and 28 Test Matches out of international cricket."
Players particularly learnt from: "At the start of every season and before I go on tour I visit Johnny Lawrence who has coached me since I was nine years old."
Equipment used: Slazenger, Gola boots.
Other sports: Golf, tennis.
Relaxations: Reading, theatre, cinema. Watching television programmes like the Rockford Files. Enjoys classical ballet "I don't understand modern ballet". Favourite reading includes World Wildlife Fund magazines. "I am a member of the Fund because I believe strongly that we should conserve nature. To me, life, whether human or animal is precious. I've been to most of the major game parks in Africa. They are marvellous places to visit."
Extras: Captained Hemsworth Grammar School and the local Schools XI; at 13, played for Ackworth in Yorkshire Council League; at 15, played for Yorkshire Schoolboys' and Barnsley. Before playing for Yorkshire for first time at age 21, he was top of batting averages for Leeds, Yorkshire Colts and Yorkshire 2nd XI. Plays in contact lenses. Wears cap when bowling. Scored two centuries in a match (103 and 105) v Notts at Sheffield in 1966, and 160 not out and 116 for England v the Rest at Worcester in 1974. On exhibition at Madame Tussaud's. Bowled in the Lord's Test v W. Indies 1980 wearing his cap back to front. Awarded O.B.E. in 1980. Rarely drinks alcohol. Published "Put to the Test", 1979; "Opening Up", 1980; "In the Fast Lane", 1981 and "Master Class", 1982. Also "Geoffrey Boycott's Book for Young Cricketers". Banned from Test cricket for 3 years in 1982 for playing for England rebels in South Africa. Elected to Yorkshire committee in 1984, the 6th man to serve

with the club as player and committee member.
Best batting performance: 261* MCC v Presidents XI, Bridgtown 1973/74.
Best bowling performance: 4-14 Yorkshire v Lancashire, Leeds 1979.

LAST SEASON: BATTING

	I.	N.O.	R.	H.S.	AV.
TEST					
OTHER FIRST CLASS	35	10	1567	153*	62.68
INT					
J.P.L.	13	0	253	67	19.46
NAT.W.	1	0	27	27	–
B & H	6	0	191	106	31.83

CAREER: BATTING

	I.	N.O.	R.	H.S.	AV.
TEST	193	23	8114	246*	47.73
OTHER FIRST CLASS	767	126	37663	261*	58.76
INT	34	4	1082	105	36.07
J.P.L.	155	24	5006	108*	38.21
NAT.W.	36	3	1253	146	37.97
B & H	53	8	1970	142	43.78

LAST SEASON: BOWLING

	O.	M.	R.	W.	AV.
TEST					
OTHER FIRST CLASS	11	0	25	0	–
INT					
J.P.L.	39.2	3	143	0	–
NAT.W.					
B & H					

CAREER: BOWLING

	O.	M.	R.	W.	AV.
TEST	28 120.3	4 41	382	7	54.57
OTHER FIRST CLASS	28.4 424.2	2 132	1038	38	27.32
INT.	28	1	105	5	21.00
J.P.L.	148.5	11	599	14	42.79
NAT.W.	78	15	238	8	29.75
B & H	63	4	227	2	113.50

CARRICK, P.

Full Name: Phillip Carrick.
Role: Right-hand bat, slow left arm
orthodox bowler.
Born: 16 July 1952, Leeds.
Height: 6' 0"**Weight:** 13st 7lbs.
Nickname: Fergie.
County debut: 1970.
County cap: 1976.
Benefit: 1985.
Test debut: —
No. of Tests: 0.
No. of One-day Internationals: 0.
1000 runs in a season: 0.
50 wickets in a season: 6.
1st-Class 50s scored: 22.
1st-Class 100s scored: 3.
1st-Class 200s scored: 0.
1st-Class 5 w. in innings: 33.
1st-Class 10 w. in match: 4.
One-day 50s: 0.
One-day 100s: 0.

Place in batting averages: 224 average: 17.39; (1983: 100 average: 29.04).
Place in bowling averages: 103 average: 36.50; (1983: 54 average: 27.34).
1st-Class catches 1984: 13 (career: 132).
Parents: Arthur and Ivy Carrick.
Wife and date of marriage: Elspeth, 2 April 1977.
Children: Emma Elizabeth, 6 May 1980; Phillipa 11 January 1982.
Education: Bramley C.S.; Intake C.S.; Park Lane College of Physical Education.
Qualifications: Two O-levels, eight C.S.E. N.C.A. coaching certificate.
Jobs outside cricket: Company Director, coach.
Family links with cricket: "Father and brother useful league players."
Overseas tours: Toured with Derrick Robins XI to South Africa 1975–76; Far East 1977.
Overseas teams played for: Eastern Province in 1976–77 Currie Cup Competition, and N. Transvaal 1982–83.
Cricketers particularly learnt from: M.C. Fearnley, Geoff Boycott, Ray Illingworth.
Cricketers particularly admired: D. Underwood, B. Bedi, R. Illingworth.
Cricket superstitions: Left pad on first.
Equipment used: Duncan Fearnley.
Other sports: Golf, follow most.
Opinions on cricket: "Let's go back to uncovered wickets!"
Significant injuries in 1984: Knee—out for 2 weeks.
Best batting performance: 131* Yorkshire v Northamptonshire, Northampton 1980.
Best bowling performance: 8-33 Yorkshire v Cambridge University, Cambridge 1973.

LAST SEASON: BATTING

	I.	N.O.	R.	H.S.	AV.
TEST					
OTHER FIRST CLASS	28	5	400	47*	17.39
INT					
J.P.L.	11	5	181	43*	30.17
NAT.W.	1	0	37	37	–
B & H	3	1	37	24	18.50

CAREER: BATTING

	I.	N.O.	R.	H.S.	AV.
TEST					
OTHER FIRST CLASS	333	64	5826	131*	21.66
INT					
J.P.L.	67	21	658	43*	14.30
NAT.W.	12	2	136	37	13.60
B & H	17	3	132	24	9.43

LAST SEASON: BOWLING

	O.	M.	R.	W.	AV.
TEST					
OTHER FIRST CLASS	665.5	219	1606	44	36.50
INT					
J.P.L.	70	1	326	8	40.75
NAT.W.	12	3	28	1	–
B & H	50	8	175	5	35.00

CAREER: BOWLING

	O.	M.	R.	W.	AV.
TEST					
OTHER FIRST CLASS	7760.6	2545	19307	658	29.34
INT					
J.P.L.	452.5	22	1957	58	33.74
NAT.W.	89	8	284	9	31.55
B & H	196.5	35	663	19	34.89

DENNIS, S.J.

Full Name: Simon John Dennis.
Role: Right-hand bat; fast medium
left arm bowler.
Born: 18 October 1960, Scarborough,
Yorkshire.
Height: 6' 1" **Weight:** 13st.
Nickname: Donkey.
County debut: 1980.
County cap: 1983.
Test debut: —
No. of Tests: 0.
No. of One-Day Internationals: 0.
1000 runs in a season: 0.
50 wickets in a season: 1.
1st-Class 50s scored: 1.
1st-Class 100s scored: 0.
1st-Class 200s scored: 0.
1st-Class 5 w. in innings: 4.
1st-Class 10 w. in match: 0.
One-day 50s: 0.
One-day 100s: 0.
Place in batting averages: 194 average: 20.80; (1983: — average: —).
Place in bowling averages: 109 average: 38.12; (1983: — average: —).
1st-Class catches 1984: 1 (career: 12).
Parents: Margaret and Geoff.
Marital status: Single.
Education: Northstead County Primary School; Scarborough College.
Qualifications: One A-level, seven O-levels.
Jobs outside cricket: Assistant groundsman at Scarborough C.C. Furniture
salesman.
Family links with cricket: Father captained Scarborough for many years.
Uncle, Frank Dennis, played for Yorkshire 1928–33. Uncle, Sir Leonard
Hutton, Yorkshire and England.
Overseas tours: India 1978–79 with E.S.C.A.; Australia 1980 with Young
England. With M.C.C. to East and Central Africa 1981. M.C.C. Tour to
America, 1982. Gibraltar with Sheffield Cricket Lovers 1983.
Overseas teams played for: Orange Free State 1982–83.
Cricketers particularly learnt from: Doug Padgett, Don Wilson, Ray
Illingworth.
Cricketers particularly admired: Dennis Lillee, John Lever.
Cricketing superstitions: "I fasten my pads on the inside instead of outside (not
that it does any good!)".
Equipment used: Slazenger.
Other sports: Rugby, hockey, squash, golf, American football, soccer.

Relaxations: Car maintenance, wine and beer making. Photography and real ale. Home computer, video games. "Also terrible snooker player."
Extras: On debut for Yorkshire v Somerset, at Weston, 1980, got Gavaskar as his first wicket. That was 6 August 1980. Cap awarded 6 August 1983.
Best batting performance: 53* Yorkshire v Nottinghamshire, Trent Bridge 1984.
Best bowling performance: 5-35 Yorkshire v Somerset, Sheffield 1981.

LAST SEASON: BATTING

	I.	N.O.	R.	H.S.	AV.
TEST					
OTHER FIRST CLASS	9	4	104	53*	20.80
INT					
J.P.L.	3	0	13	7	4.33
NAT.W.	1	0	14	14	–
B & H	1	0	10	10	–

CAREER: BATTING

	I.	N.O.	R.	H.S.	AV.
TEST					
OTHER FIRST CLASS	51	20	313	53*	10.10
INT					
J.P.L.	13	6	70	16*	10.00
NAT.W.	2	0	14	14	7.00
B & H	2	0	10	10	5.00

LAST SEASON: BOWLING

	O.	M.	R.	W.	AV.
TEST					
OTHER FIRST CLASS	277.2	48	953	25	38.12
INT					
J.P.L.	29	0	159	1	
NAT.W.	12	1	56	2	28.00
B & H	39	8	129	6	21.50

CAREER: BOWLING

	O.	M.	R.	W.	AV.
TEST					
OTHER FIRST CLASS	1300.1	262	4152	136	30.53
INT					
J.P.L.	198.5	13	916	22	41.63
NAT.W.	40.2	5	163	5	32.60
B & H	76	13	291	7	41.57

FLETCHER, S.D.

Full Name: Stuart David Fletcher.
Role: Right-hand bat, right arm medium bowler.
Born: 8 June 1964, Keighley.
Height: 5' 10" **Weight:** 12st.
Nickname: Fletch, Godber, Norman Stanley.
County debut: 1983.
County cap: No.
Test debut: —
No. of Tests: 0.
No. of One-Day Internationals: 0.
1000 runs in a season: 0.
50 wickets in a season: 0.
1st-Class 50s scored: 0.
1st-Class 100s scored: 0.
1st-Class 200s scored: 0.
1st-Class 5 w. in innings: 0.

1st-Class 10 w. in match: 0.
One-day 50s: 0.
One-day 100s: 0.
Place in batting averages: — average: —; (1983: — average: —).
Place in bowling averages: 90 average: 33.64; (1983: — average: —).
Parents: Brough and Norma Hilda Fletcher.
Marital status: Engaged.
Family links with cricket: Father played in league cricket.
Education: Woodhouse Primary; Reins Wood Secondary.
Qualifications: O-level English and Woodwork. City and Guilds in Coachbuilding.
Jobs outside cricket: Coachbuilder at Reliance Commercial Vehicles Ltd.
Off-season 1984–85: Fitness training after injury.
Equipment used: Gunn & Moore.
Overseas tours: Holland 1983, National Cricket Association U-19s.
Cricketers particularly learnt from: "My father, Phil Carrick, Steve Oldham."
Cricketers particularly admired: Ian Botham, Arnie Sidebottom.
Other sports: Snooker, golf. "I'll try anything." Watches Leeds United.
Relaxations: Watching T.V., music and driving.
Significant injuries in 1984: Dislocated pelvis.
Extras: Played in the Yorkshire U-19s who were the first Yorkshire side to win the Cambridge and Oxford Festival, 1983.
Opinions on cricket: "I think that everybody should leave politics out of the game and let the players get on with playing."
Best batting performance: 28* Yorkshire v Kent, Tunbridge Wells 1984.
Best bowling performance: 4-24 Yorkshire v Somerset, Middlesbrough 1984.

LAST SEASON: BATTING

	I.	N.O.	R.	H.S.	AV.
TEST					
OTHER FIRST CLASS	5	1	35	28*	8.75
INT					
J.P.L.	2	1	13	8	—
NAT.W.					
B & H	—	—	—	—	—

CAREER: BATTING

	I.	N.O.	R.	H.S.	AV.
TEST					
OTHER FIRST CLASS	9	3	49	28*	8.17
INT					
J.P.L.	2	1	13	8	—
NAT.W.					
B & H					

LAST SEASON: BOWLING

	O.	M.	R.	W.	AV.
TEST					
OTHER FIRST CLASS	162	35	471	14	33.64
INT					
J.P.L.	52	0	287	6	47.83
NAT.W.					
B & H	35.3	1	175	3	58.33

CAREER: BOWLING

	O.	M.	R.	W.	AV.
TEST					
OTHER FIRST CLASS	217.4	42	603	22	27.41
INT					
J.P.L.	52	0	287	6	47.83
NAT.W.					
B & H	35.3	1	175	3	58.33

HARTLEY, S.N.

Full Name: Stuart Neil Hartley.
Role: Right-hand bat, right arm
medium bowler, outfielder.
Born: 18 March 1956, Shipley, West
Yorkshire.
Height: 5′ 11½″ **Weight:** 12st 7lbs.
Nickname: Hare, Tommy, Sid.
County debut: 1978.
County cap: 1981.
Test debut: —
No. of Tests: 0.
No. of One-Day Internationals: 0.
1000 runs in a season: 0.
50 wickets in a season: 0.
1st-Class 50s scored: 16.
1st-Class 100s scored: 3.
1st-Class 200s scored: 0.
1st-Class 5 w. in innings: 0.
1st-Class 10 w. in match: 0.
One-day 50s: 8.
One-day 100s: 0.

Place in batting averages: 154 average: 25.70; (1983: 215 average: 14.50).
Place in bowling averages: — average: —; (1983: — average: —).
1st-Class catches 1984: 2 (career: 37).
Parents: Marjorie and Horace Hartley.
Marital status: Divorced.
Education: Beckfoot Grammar School, Bingley; Cannington High, Perth,
West Australia.
Qualifications: Three A-levels, eight O-levels. Exam passes in insurance.
Jobs outside cricket: Trained insurance underwriter.
Family links with cricket: Father played league cricket.
Overseas tours: Captained North of England N.C.A. team in Holland in 1975.
Gibraltar 1981.
Overseas teams played for: Orange Free State, 1981–82.
Cricketers particularly learnt from: Doug Padgett and Mike Fearnley—
Yorkshire County Cricket Club coaching staff.
Off season 1984–85: Playing and coaching in Durban.
Equipment endorsed: Slazenger.
Other sports: Rugby, golf.
Significant injuries in 1984: Broken big toe, damaged back.
Extras: "Started to play cricket in Perth, Western Australia, where I lived for
2½ years, 1967–69. I would like to live in Perth in the future." Amateur football
with Bradford City 1970–75. Rugby Union with Bingley R.U.F.C. Has been
acting captain of Yorkshire.

Best batting performance: 114 Yorkshire v Gloucestershire, Bradford 1982.
Best bowling performance: 3-40 Yorkshire v Glouceestershire, Sheffield 1980.

LAST SEASON: BATTING

	I.	N.O.	R.	H.S.	AV.
TEST					
OTHER FIRST CLASS	21	4	437	104*	25.70
INT					
J.P.L.	12	2	234	73	23.40
NAT.W.	1	0	7	7	–
B & H	4	3	183	65*	–

CAREER: BATTING

	I.	N.O.	R.	H.S.	AV.
TEST					
OTHER FIRST CLASS	144	21	2970	114	24.15
INT					
J.P.L.	63	13	1035	73	20.70
NAT.W.	7	0	146	58	20.86
B & H	14	4	330	65*	33.00

LAST SEASON: BOWLING

	O.	M.	R.	W.	AV.
TEST					
OTHER FIRST CLASS	93	13	359	6	59.83
INT					
J.P.L.	30.3	0	204	6	34.00
NAT.W.	2	0	6	0	–
B & H	27	2	115	4	28.75

CAREER: BOWLING

	O.	M.	R.	W.	AV.
TEST					
OTHER FIRST CLASS	434.5	81	1552	33	47.03
INT					
J.P.L.	171.1	3	992	33	30.06
NAT.W.	48	1	172	7	24.57
B & H	73	3	281	11	25.55

JARVIS, P.W.

Full Name: Paul William Jarvis.
Role: Right-hand bat, right arm fast medium bowler.
Born: 29 June 1965, Redcar, North Yorkshire.
Height: 5' 11½" **Weight:** 12st 4lbs.
Nickname: Gnasher, Jarve, Jarvo, Beaver ("and many more unprintable").
County debut: 1981.
County cap: No.
Test debut: —
No. of Tests: 0.
No. of One-Day Internationals: 0.
1000 runs in a season: 0.
50 wickets in a season: 0.
1st-Class 50s scored: 0.
1st-Class 100s scored: 0.
1st-Class 200s scored: 0.
1st-Class 5 w. in innings: 2.
1st-Class 10 w. in match: 0.
One-day 50s: 0.

One-day 100s: 0.
Place in batting averages: 235 average: 15.70; (1980: — average: —).
Place in bowling averages: 98 average: 34.84; (1983 — average —).
1st-Class catches 1984: 2 (career: 7).
Parents: Malcolm and Marjorie Jarvis.
Marital status: Single.
Family links with cricket: Father has played league cricket for 25 years; brother, Andrew, played for English Schools Under-15s, and also had trials for Northamptonshire and Derbyshire.
Education: Bydales Comprehensive School, Marske.
Qualifications: Four O-levels.
Jobs outside cricket: Trainee groundsman, Marske Cricket Club.
Off-season 1984–85: Playing for Mosman Middle Harbour C.C. in Sydney.
Cricketing superstitions: "The number 111."
Cricketers particularly learnt from: "Learnt a lot from Maurice Hill and Albert Padmore; admire Dennis Lillee."
Equipment used: Gunn & Moore.
Other sports: Football, running and fitness, golf. Follow most sports.
Significant injuries in 1984: Ankle strain in April, followed by shin soreness.
Relaxations: Watching television, films, listening to music.
Extras: Youngest player ever to play for Yorkshire 1st XI in John Player League and County Championships (16 years, 2 months, 1 day in John Player League, 16 years, 2 months, 13 days for County Championship). Hat-trick in JPSL v Deryshire (Derby) 27.6.82. Played for Young England v West Indies 1982 and Australia 1983.
Opinions on cricket: "1. Some sides don't seem to make the effort to bowl the set amount of overs before 6.30 p.m. 2. Non-English born players should not be allowed to qualify or play cricket for England. 3. Sponsorship on shirts etc should be allowed to help revenue to the game."
Best batting performance: 37 Yorkshire v Surrey, The Oval 1984.
Best bowling performance: 6-61 Yorkshire v Lancashire, Old Trafford 1984.

LAST SEASON: BATTING

	I.	N.O.	R.	H.S.	AV.
TEST					
OTHER FIRST CLASS	14	4	157	37	15.70
INT					
J.P.L.	2	1	13	9*	—
NAT.W.					
B & H					

CAREER: BATTING

	I.	N.O.	R.	H.S.	AV.
TEST					
OTHER FIRST CLASS	22	9	186	37	14.31
INT					
J.P.L.	10	6	34	9*	8.50
NAT.W.	—	—	—	—	—
B & H					

LAST SEASON: BOWLING

	O.	M.	R.	W.	AV.
TEST					
OTHER FIRST CLASS	304	53	1115	32	34.84
INT					
J.P.L.	28	1	135	12	11.25
NAT.W.					
B & H					

CAREER: BOWLING

	O.	M.	R.	W.	AV.
TEST					
OTHER FIRST CLASS	498	88	1778	43	41.35
INT					
J.P.L.	139	4	633	37	17.11
NAT.W.	12	0	80	0	—
B & H					

LOVE, J.D.

Full Name: James Derek Love.
Role: Right-hand bat.
Born: 22 April 1955, Leeds.
Height: 6′ 2″ **Weight:** 14st.
Nickname: Jim.
County debut: 1975.
County cap: 1980.
Test debut: —
No. of Tests: 0.
No. of One-Day Internationals: 3.
1000 runs in a season: 2.
50 wickets in a season: 0.
1st-Class 50s scored: 35.
1st-Class 100s scored: 11.
1st-Class 200s scored: 0.
1st-Class 5 w. in innings: 0.
1st-Class 10 w. in match: 0.
One-day 50s: 11.
One-day 100s: 1.
Place in batting averages: 143 average: 27.05; (1983: 86 average: 32.90).
Place in bowling averages: — average: —; (1983: — average: —).
1st-Class catches 1984: 7 (career: 85).
Parents: Derek Oliver and Betty Love.
Marital status: Separated.
Education: Brudenell County Secondary, Leeds.
Jobs outside cricket: Civil servant for three years until left to become professional cricketer.

LAST SEASON: BATTING

	I.	N.O.	R.	H.S.	AV.
TEST					
OTHER FIRST CLASS	23	2	568	112	27.05
INT					
J.P.L.	7	2	183	69*	36.60
NAT.W.					
B & H	6	2	181	88	45.25

CAREER: BATTING

	I.	N.O.	R.	H.S.	AV.
TEST					
OTHER FIRST CLASS	259	38	6869	170*	31.08
INT	3	0	61	43	20.33
J.P.L.	89	11	1682	90	21.56
NAT.W.	11	2	94	61*	10.44
B & H	21	4	616	118*	36.24

LAST SEASON: BOWLING

	O.	M.	R.	W.	AV.
TEST					
OTHER FIRST CLASS					
INT					
J.P.L.					
NAT.W.					
B & H					

CAREER: BOWLING

	O.	M.	R.	W.	AV.
TEST					
OTHER FIRST CLASS	64	15	233	1	—
INT					
J.P.L.	3	0	7	0	—
NAT.W.					
B & H					

Family links with cricket: Father played local cricket; brother Robert plays for Castleford C.C. in Yorkshire League.
Overseas teams played for: Whitbread Scholarship to Mosman Middle Harbour and District C.C. in 1977–78; Scarborough C.C., Perth, Western Australia 1978–79. Mosman Middle Harbour and District C.C. 1982–83.
Off-season 1984–85: Playing for Mosman M.H.C.C. in Sydney.
Cricketers particularly learnt from: Doug Padgett, county coach.
Equipment used: Peter Kippax.
Other sports: Local football, golf.
Relaxations: Shooting.
Significant injuries in 1984: Viral infection and broken finger.
Opinions on cricket: "None—just get on with playing the game!"
Best batting performance: 170* Yorkshire v Worcestershire, Worcester 1979.

LUMB, R.G.

Full Name: Richard Graham Lumb.
Role: Right-hand bat, right arm medium bowler.
Born: 27 February 1950, Doncaster, Yorkshire.
Height: 6′ 3″ **Weight:** 14st.
Nickname: Joe.
County debut: 1970.
County cap: 1974.
Benefit: 1983 (£52,000).
Test debut: —
No. of Tests: 0.
No. of One-Day Internationals: 0.
1000 runs in a season: 4.
50 wickets in a season: 0.
1st-Class 50s scored: 50.
1st-Class 100s scored: 22.
1st-Class 200s scored: 0.
1st-Class 5 w. in innings: 0.
1st-Class 10 w. in match: 0.
One-day 50s: 16.
One-day 100s: 1.

Place in batting averages: 75 average: 35.60; (1983: 150 average: 23.43).
Place in bowling averages: — average: —; (1983: — average: —).
1st-Class catches 1984: 2 (career: 131).
Parents: John Edward Lumb, deceased, and Dorothy Lumb.
Wife and date of marriage: Susan Jane, 4 November 1976, in Johannesburg, South Africa.
Children: Michael John (born Johannesburg 12 February 1980).

Education: Percy Jackson Grammar School; Mexborough Grammar School.
Qualifications: 5 O-levels.
Jobs outside cricket: Assistant hotel manager for three years during off-season. Salesman for engineering company for a year.
Off-season 1984–85: In South Africa, coaching.
Overseas teams played for: Bedfordview 1973–74 and 1979–80. Old Johannians 1980–81 and 1981–82.
Family links with cricket: Grandfather, Joe Thomas Lumb, member of Yorkshire General Committee for 20 years. Joe Lumb Cricket Competition for young cricketers named after him. Brother, John, played for Yorkshire 2nd XI and was with Smethwick in Birmingham League. Brother-in-law, Tony "Titch" Smith, wicket-keeper for Natal in Currie Cup Competition.
Equipment used: Gunn & Moore.
Other sports: Golf, tennis.
Significant injuries during 1984: Arthritis in knees.
Relaxations: Gardening, reading, theatre.
Extras: Played in M.C.C. Schools matches at Lord's in 1968. Missed much of 1981 season through fractured bones in hand. First player to 1000 runs in 1979. Century partnerships for Yorks. with Boycott second only to Holmes and Sutcliffe. The 33rd Yorks. player to reach 10,000 runs for county. Captained Yorks. 3 times. Second only to E. Robinson in taking 5 catches for Yorks. in an innings (Robinson, 6). Played in Test Trial at Bristol in 1976, with top score for The Rest v England in each innings. Retired at end of 1984 season.
Best batting performance: 165* Yorkshire v Gloucestershire, Bradford.

LAST SEASON: BATTING

	I.	N.O.	R.	H.S.	AV.
TEST					
OTHER FIRST CLASS	17	2	534	165*	35.60
INT					
J.P.L.	1	0	39	39	–
NAT.W.					
B & H	1	0	31	31	–

CAREER: BATTING

	I.	N.O.	R.	H.S.	AV.
TEST					
OTHER FIRST CLASS	406	30	11723	165*	31.18
INT					
J.P.L.	75	10	1588	101	24.43
NAT.W.	12	0	222	56	18.50
B & H	34	4	937	90	31.23

LAST SEASON: BOWLING

	O.	M.	R.	W.	AV.
TEST					
OTHER FIRST CLASS	1	0	5	0	–
INT					
J.P.L.					
NAT.W.					
B & H					

CAREER: BOWLING

	O.	M.	R.	W.	AV.
TEST					
OTHER FIRST CLASS	1	0	5	0	–
INT					
J.P.L.					
NAT.W.					
B & H					

METCALFE, A.A.

Full Name: Ashley Anthony Metcalfe.
Role: Right-hand bat, right arm off-spin bowler.
Born: 25 December 1963, Horsforth, Leeds.
Height: 5' 9" **Weight:** 11st. 7lbs.
County debut: 1983.
County cap: No.
Test debut: —
No. of Tests: 0.
No. of One-Day Internationals: 0.
1000 runs in a season: 0.
50 wickets in a season: 0.
1st-Class 50s scored: 2.
1st-Class 100s scored: 1.
1st-Class 200s scored: 0.
1st-Class 5 w. in innings: 0.
1st-Class 10 w. in match: 0.
One-day 50s: 0.
One-day 100s: 0.
Place in batting averages: 228 average: 16.62; (1983: — average: —).
Place in bowling averages: — average: —; (1983: — average: —).
1st-Class catches 1984: 5 (career: 6).
Parents: Tony and Ann.
Wife: Ray Illingworth's daughter, Diane.
Family links with cricket: Father played in local league.
Education: Sandale Primary School; Ladderbanks Middle School; Bradford

LAST SEASON: BATTING

	I.	N.O.	R.	H.S.	AV.
TEST					
OTHER FIRST CLASS	13	0	216	60	16.62
INT					
J.P.L.	11	1	357	115*	35.70
NAT.W.	1	0	0	0	–
B & H					

CAREER: BATTING

	I.	N.O.	R.	H.S.	AV.
TEST					
OTHER FIRST CLASS	15	0	345	122	23.00
INT					
J.P.L.	11	1	357	115*	35.70
NAT.W.	1	0	0	0	–
B & H					

LAST SEASON: BOWLING

	O.	M.	R.	W.	AV.
TEST					
OTHER FIRST CLASS					
INT					
J.P.L.					
NAT.W.					
B & H					

CAREER: BOWLING

	O.	M.	R.	W.	AV.
TEST					
OTHER FIRST CLASS	2	0	6	0	–
INT					
J.P.L.					
NAT.W.					
B & H					

Grammar School; University College, London.
Qualifications: 9 0-levels, 3 A-levels, coaching certificate 1983.
Jobs outside cricket: Worked for Grattan Mail Order Co. during 1983–84 winter.
Off-season 1984–85: Working in England.
Equipment used: Stuart Surridge.
Overseas tours: N.C.A. tour of Denmark 1981.
Cricketers particularly learnt from: Doug Padgett, Ray Illingworth, Don Wilson.
Cricketers particularly admired: Viv Richards, Alan Border, Len Hutton.
Other sports: Squash, rugby, golf. Follows most.
Relaxations: Watching films or T.V., music, holidays.
Extras: "I made 122 on my debut for Yorkshire against Nottinghamshire at Park Avenue in 1983. I was the youngest ever player to do so and it was the highest ever score on a debut."
Opinions on cricket: "Politics should not interfere with sport— South Africa should be eligible for Test Cricket."
Best batting performance: 122 Yorkshire v Nottinghamshire, Scarborough 1983.

MOXON, M.D.

Full Name: Martin Douglas Moxon.
Role: Right-hand bat, right arm medium bowler.
Born: 4 May 1960, Barnsley, Yorkshire.
Height: 6' 0" **Weight:** 13st. 7lbs.
Nickname: Froggy.
County debut: 1980.
County cap: 1984.
Test debut: —
No. of Tests: 0.
No. of One-Day Internationals: 0.
1000 runs in a season: 1.
50 wickets in a season: 0.
1st-Class 50s scored: 16.
1st-Class 100s scored: 6.
1st-Class 200s scored: 0.
1st-Class 5 w. in innings: 0.
1st-Class 10 w. in match: 0.
One-day 50s: 7.
One-day 100s: 0.

Place in batting averages: 74 average: 36.57; (1983: 81 average 33.91).
Place in bowling averages: — average: —; (1983: — average: —)

1st-Class catches 1984: 19 (career: 37).
Parents: Audrey and Derek Moxon.
Marital status: Single.
Education: Holgate Grammar School, Barnsley.
Qualifications: Eight O-levels, 3 A-levels, H.N.C. in Business Studies, N.C.A. Coaching Award.
Family links with cricket: Father and grandfather played local league cricket. Father was coach to Wombwell Cricket Lovers' Society.
Jobs outside cricket: Bank clerk with Barclays Bank for 2 years before turning full-time professional.
Off-season 1984–85: With England touring India and Australia.
Cricketing superstitions: "When getting ready to bat I always follow the same routine."
Equipment used: Gray-Nicolls.
Overseas tours: Captain of North of England Under-19 Tour of Canada, 1979.
Overseas teams played for: Griqualand West in South Africa 1982–83 and 1983–84.
Significant injuries in 1984: Fractured rib in June, so missed making England debut in 2nd Test at Lord's v West Indies.
Cricketers particularly learnt from: Doug Padgett, Ray Illingworth, Phil Carrick.
Cricketers particularly admired: Viv Richards.
Other sports: Plays football in the local league in the winter and "am a keen supporter of Barnsley F.C."
Relaxations: Watching Barnsley F.C., listening to most types of music, having a drink with friends.
Extras: Captained Yorkshire Schools Under-15s and North of England Under-15s. Played for Yorkshire Cricket Federation Under-19s. Captained Yorkshire Senior Schools. Like Yorkshire colleagues, G. Stevenson and A. Sidebottom, he played for Wombwell Cricket Lovers' Society Under-18 side which competes in the Joe Lumb Under-18 Competition. Made Yorks 2nd XI debut in

LAST SEASON: BATTING

	I.	N.O.	R.	H.S.	AV.
TEST					
OTHER FIRST CLASS	32	2	1097	126*	36.57
INT					
J.P.L.	12	0	367	77	30.58
NAT.W.	1	0	16	16	–
B & H	6	0	230	79	38.33

CAREER: BATTING

	I.	N.O.	R.	H.S.	AV.
TEST					
OTHER FIRST CLASS	96	3	3198	153	34.39
INT					
J.P.L.	20	3	445	77	26.12
NAT.W.	4	1	95	78*	31.67
B & H	7	0	252	79	36.00

LAST SEASON: BOWLING

	O.	M.	R.	W.	AV.
TEST					
OTHER FIRST CLASS	98	19	327	4	81.75
INT					
J.P.L.	27	0	180	2	90.00
NAT.W.					
B & H	25	0	111	2	55.50

CAREER: BOWLING

	O.	M.	R.	W.	AV.
TEST					
OTHER FIRST CLASS	183	26	633	7	90.43
INT					
J.P.L.	31	0	197	3	65.67
NAT.W.					
B & H	25	0	111	2	55.50

1978. Made the highest score by a player on his Yorkshire debut– 116 v Essex. First Yorkshire player to make centuries on his first two championship games in Yorkshire: 116 v Essex at Headingly; 111 v Derbyshire at Sheffield. Changed spectacles to contact lenses in 1981. Scored 153 in first 'Roses' innings.
Best batting performance: 153 Yorkshire v Lancashire, Leeds 1983.

OLDHAM, S.

Full Name: Stephen Oldham.
Role: Right-hand bat, right arm fast medium bowler ("up hill").
Born: 26 July 1948, High Green, Sheffield.
Height: 6' 1" **Weight:** 14st. (summer) 15st. (winter).
Nickname: Esso.
County debut: 1980 (Derbyshire), 1974 and 1984 (Yorkshire).
County cap: 1980 (Derbyshire).
Test debut: —
No. of Tests: 0.
No. of One-Day Internationals: 0.
1000 runs in a season: 0.
50 wickets in a season: 1.
1st-Class 50s scored: 1.
1st-Class 100s scored: 0.
1st-Class 200s scored: 0.
1st-Class 5 w. in innings: 4.
1st-Class 10 w. in match: 0.
One-day 50s: 0.
One-day 100s: 0.
Place in batting averages: — average: —; (1983: 222 average: 13.62).
Place in bowling averages: 111 average: 39.06; (1983: 101 average: 36.13).
1st-Class catches 1984: 2 (career: 37).
Parents: Robert and Kathleen.
Wife: Linda.
Children: Sally and Katherine.
Education: Crossfield High Green School.
Qualifications: 6 O-levels, 2 A-levels.
Jobs outside cricket: Qualified engineer. Assistant works manager.
Cricket superstitions: "Always play back to fast bowling."
Equipment used: Slazenger.
Cricketers particularly learnt from: Chris Old, Mike Hendrick.
Cricketers particularly admired: Geoff Boycott.
Other sports: Football, golf.

Relaxations: "Helping to run my local football club. Drinking Tetley's."
Extras: Best man at Graham Stevenson's wedding. Debut for Yorkshire 1974 and left after 1979 season. Returned to Yorkshire 1984.
Opinions on cricket: "Too much one-day cricket, too many poor wickets, too many overseas players."
Best batting performance: 50 Yorkshire v Sussex, Hove 1979.
Best bowling performance: 7-78 Derbyshire v Warwickshire, Edgbaston 1982.

LAST SEASON: BATTING

	I.	N.O.	R.	H.S.	AV.
TEST					
OTHER FIRST CLASS	6	3	85	22	28.33
INT					
J.P.L.	6	5	33	8*	–
NAT.W.	1	0	19	19	–
B & H	2	2	4	3*	–

CAREER: BATTING

	I.	N.O.	R.	H.S.	AV.
TEST					
OTHER FIRST CLASS	96	40	640	50	11.43
INT					
J.P.L.	35	16	165	38*	8.68
NAT.W.	5	2	36	19	12.00
B & H	12	4	18	4*	2.25

LAST SEASON: BOWLING

	O.	M.	R.	W.	AV.
TEST					
OTHER FIRST CLASS	244.5	57	703	18	39.06
INT					
J.P.L.	115.3	6	466	18	25.89
NAT.W.	12	1	44	2	22.00
B & H	62	10	185	13	14.23

CAREER: BOWLING

	O.	M.	R.	W.	AV.
TEST					
OTHER FIRST CLASS	2982	636	8817	269	32.78
INT					
J.P.L.	819	52	3532	142	24.87
NAT.W.	116.5	18	437	20	21.85
B & H	337.4	54	1082	57	18.98

ROBINSON, P.E.

Full Name: Phillip Edward
Robinson.
Role: Right-hand bat, left arm
medium bowler.
Born: 3 August 1963, Keighley.
Height: 5' 10" **Weight:** 13st 7lbs.
Nickname: Red Robbo.
County debut: 1984.
County cap: No.
Test debut: —
No. of Tests: 0.
No. of One-Day Internationals: 0.
1000 runs in a season: 0.
50 wickets in a season: 0.
1st-Class 50s scored: 6.
1st-Class 100s scored: 0.
1st-Class 200s scored: 0.
1st-Class 5 w. in innings: 0.
1st-Class 10 w. in match: 0.
One-day 50s: 0.
One-day 100s: 0.

Place in batting averages: 51 average: 39.79; (1983: — average: —).
Place in bowling averages: — average: —; (1983: — average: —).
1st-Class catches 1984: 7 (career: 7).
Parents: Keith and Margaret Lesley Robinson
Marital status: Single.
Education: Long Lee Primary, Hartington Middle, Greenhead Comprehensive.
Qualifications: O-levels in Maths and English Language.
Jobs outside cricket: Outworker supervisor (Swegmark Nelson Ltd).
Off-season 1984–85: "Hopefully abroad."
Cricketing superstitions: "Always put my left boot on first."
Equipment used: Gunn & Moore.
Cricketers particularly learnt from: "I learn from all cricketers."
Cricketers particularly admired: Gary Sobers ("The best player I've seen.").
Other sports: Football, badminton. "I don't have time to follow any other sports
seriously.".
Relaxations: Watching films; going out with friends.
Extras: Scored the highest score by a Yorkshire 2nd XI player of 233 in 1983 v
Kent at Canterbury.
Opinions on cricket: "I think the 117 overs in a day will never produce home
grown quick bowlers, which is what's missing from English cricket at the
moment."
Best batting performance: 92 Yorkshire v Glamorgan, Bradford 1984.

LAST SEASON: BATTING

	I.	N.O.	R.	H.S.	AV.
TEST					
OTHER FIRST CLASS	24	5	756	92	39.79
INT					
J.P.L.	11	0	191	39	17.36
NAT.W.					
B & H	1	0	4	4	–

CAREER: BATTING

	I.	N.O.	R.	H.S.	AV.
TEST					
OTHER FIRST CLASS	24	5	256	92	39.79
INT					
J.P.L.	11	0	191	39	17.36
NAT.W.					
B & H	1	0	4	4	–

LAST SEASON: BOWLING

	O.	M.	R.	W.	AV.
TEST					
OTHER FIRST CLASS	2	0	12	0	–
INT					
J.P.L.					
NAT.W.					
B & H					

CAREER: BOWLING

	O.	M.	R.	W.	AV.
TEST					
OTHER FIRST CLASS	2	0	12	0	–
INT					
J.P.L.					
NAT.W.					
B & H					

SHARP, K.

Full Name: Kevin Sharp.
Role: Left-hand bat, off-break bowler.
Born: 6 April 1959, Leeds.
Height: 5′ 10″ **Weight:** 12st 9lbs.
Nickname: Lambsy, Poodle.
County debut: 1976.
County cap: 1982.
Test debut: —
No. of Tests: 0.
No. of One-Day Internationals: 0.
1000 runs in a season: 1.
50 wickets in a season: 0.
1st-Class 50s scored: 26.
1st-Class 100s scored: 11.
1st-Class 200s scored: 0.
1st-Class 5 w. in innings: 0.
1st-Class 10 w. in match: 0.
One-day 50s: 10.
One-day 100s: 0.
Place in batting averages: 55 average: 39.05; (1983: 102 average: 29.85).
Place in bowling averages: — average: —; (1983: — average: —).
1st-Class catches 1984: 17 (career: 57).
Parents: Joyce and Gordon Sharp.
Wife and date of marriage: Karen, 1 October 1983.
Education: Green Road Junior School; Abbey Grange C. of E. High School, Leeds.

Qualifications: C.S.E. Grade I Religious Education. Coaching award.

Jobs outside cricket: Plasterer's labourer, warehouseman, driver for film company.

Off-season 1984–85: Decorating, hoping to find winter employment.

Family links with cricket: Father played with Woodhouse in Leeds League for many years. Young brother, David, now playing local cricket.

Overseas tours: Derrick Robins XI to Australasia 1980.

Overseas teams played for: Subiaco Floreat C.C., Perth, Australia. De Beers C.C., Griqualand West, 1981–82.

Cricketers particularly learnt from: Doug Padgett, Yorkshire coach, Mike Fearnley, former assistant Yorkshire coach.

Cricketers particularly admired: Richard Hadlee.

Equipment used: Duncan Fearnley.

Other sports: Golf, soccer, swimming. Watching Leeds United F.C. and athletics.

Relaxations: Crosswords, listening to music, keeping my cricket gear clean.

Extras: 260 not out v Young West Indies 1977. Rested during latter part of 1980 season, on medical advice. Captain of England Under-19 v West Indies Under-19 1978 at Worcester. Winston Churchill Travelling Fellowship to Australia for two months 1978. "I took the first wicket of my career this summer — a feat I never thought possible."

Opinions on cricket: "I have not been too impressed by the new rules introduced i.e. 117 overs in a day. Most think of it as overtime. Some days drag on far too long — 6.30 p.m. is adequate."

Best batting performance: 173 Yorkshire v Derbyshire, Chesterfield 1984.

Best bowling performance: 2-13 Yorkshire v Glamorgan, Bradford 1984.

LAST SEASON: BATTING

	I.	N.O.	R.	H.S.	AV.
TEST					
OTHER FIRST CLASS	39	2	1445	173	39.05
INT					
J.P.L.	15	2	302	74	23.23
NAT.W.	1	0	19	19	–
B & H	6	1	339	87*	67.80

CAREER: BATTING

	I.	N.O.	R.	H.S.	AV.
TEST					
OTHER FIRST CLASS	211	15	6245	173	31.86
INT					
J.P.L.	76	6	1370	74	19.57
NAT.W.	6	1	89	25	17.80
B & H	24	1	650	87*	28.26

LAST SEASON: BOWLING

	O.	M.	R.	W.	AV.
TEST					
OTHER FIRST CLASS	71	18	229	7	32.72
INT					
J.P.L.	0.1	0	1	0	–
NAT.W.					
B & H					

CAREER: BOWLING

	O.	M.	R.	W.	AV.
TEST					
OTHER FIRST CLASS	94.1	22	321	7	45.86
INT					
J.P.L.	0.1	0	1	0	–
NAT.W.	1	0	7	0	–
B & H					

SHAW, C.

Full Name: Christopher Shaw.
Role: Right-hand bat, right arm fast medium bowler.
Born: 17 February 1964, Hemsworth, West Yorkshire.
Height: 6' 0" **Weight:** 12st. 5lbs.
Nickname: Sandy.
County debut: 1984.
County cap: No.
Test debut: —
No. of Tests: 0.
No. of One-Day Internationals: 0.
1000 runs in a season: 0.
50 wickets in a season: 0.
1st-Class 50s scored: 0.
1st-Class 100s scored: 0.
1st-Class 200s scored: 0.
1st-Class 5 w. in innings: 0.
1st-Class 10 w. in match: 0.
One-day 50s: 0.
One-day 100s: 0.
Place in batting averages: — average: —; (1983: — average: —).
Place in bowling averages: — average: —; (1983: — average: —).
Parents: Brian and Betty Shaw.
Marital status: Single.
Family links with cricket: Father good local league cricketer.
Education: Crofton High School.

LAST SEASON: BATTING

	I.	N.O.	R.	H.S.	AV.
TEST					
OTHER FIRST CLASS	5	2	32	17	10.67
INT					
J.P.L.	6	2	58	26	14.50
NAT.W.					
B & H					

CAREER: BATTING

	I.	N.O.	R.	H.S.	AV.
TEST					
OTHER FIRST CLASS	5	2	32	17	10.67
INT					
J.P.L.	6	2	58	26	14.50
NAT.W.					
B & H					

LAST SEASON: BOWLING

	O.	M.	R.	W.	AV.
TEST					
OTHER FIRST CLASS	53.4	5	177	5	35.40
INT					
J.P.L.	33.5	1	178	8	22.25
NAT.W.					
B & H					

CAREER: BOWLING

	O.	M.	R.	W.	AV.
TEST					
OTHER FIRST CLASS	53.4	5	177	5	35.40
INT					
J.P.L.	33.5	1	178	8	22.25
NAT.W.					
B & H					

Qualifications: 5 C.S.E.s; qualified cricket coach.
Jobs outside cricket: Apprentice Electrician (National Coal Board).
Off-season 1984–85: "To complete my apprenticeship."
Equipment used: Slazenger.
Overseas tours: Holland with N.C.A. U-19s North of England 1983; Barbados with Yorkshire Cricket Association April 1984.
Cricketers particularly learnt from: Father, D. Padgett, S. Oldham and J. Lawrence at his cricket school in Rothwell.
Cricketers particularly admired: D. Lillee, M. Holding.
Other sports: Like watching all sports (favourite sport: rugby league); keen supporter of Featherstone Rovers R.L.F.C.
Relaxations: Playing golf, listening to music, driving.
Extras: "On debut at Lords took 4-68 v Middlesex. Took 5-41 in my second JPSL match v Hampshire at Bournemouth.
Best batting performance: 17 Yorkshire v Worcestershire, Scarborough 1984.
Best bowling performance: 4-68 Yorkshire v Middlesex, Lord's 1984.

SIDEBOTTOM, A.

Full Name: Arnold Sidebottom.
Role: Right-hand bat, right arm fast medium bowler, outfielder.
Born: 1 April 1954, Barnsley.
Height: 6′ 2″ **Weight:** 13st 10lbs.
Nickname: Woofer, Red Setter, Arnie.
County debut: 1973.
County cap: 1980.
Test debut: —
No. of Tests: 0.
No. of One-Day Internationals: 0.

1000 runs in a season: 0.
50 wickets in a season: 2.
1st-Class 50s scored: 9.
1st-Class 100s scored: 1.
1st-Class 200s scored: 0.
1st-Class 5 w. in innings: 14.
1st-Class 10 w. in match: 2.
One-day 50s: 1.
One-day 100s: 0.
Place in batting averages: 108 average: 31.94; (1983: 75 average: 35.00).
Place in bowling averages: 8 average: 20.51; (1983: 52 average: 27.69).
1st-Class catches 1984: 1 (career: 39).
Parents: Jack and Florence Sidebottom.
Wife and date of marriage: Gillian, 17 June 1977.

Children: Ryan Jay, 1978; Dale, 1980.
Education: Barnsley Broadway Grammar School.
Jobs outside cricket: Professional footballer Manchester United, five years; Huddersfield Town, two years; Halifax Town.
Family links with cricket: "Father good cricketer."
Equipment used and endorsed: Slazenger.
Cricketers particularly learnt from: Father, Doug Padgett, G. Boycott.
Cricketers particularly admired: S. Oldham, D. Bairstow, G. Stevenson.
Off-season 1984–85: Resting at home.
Overseas tours: Rebel England team in South Africa in 1982.
Other sports: Professional football, tennis, table tennis, badminton. Most sports.
Relaxations: Watching television, horse-racing, playing with sons.
Extras: Played for Yorkshire 2nd XI from 1971. Banned from Test cricket for 3 years for joining rebel team to South Africa in 1982.
Best batting performance: 124 Yorkshire v Glamorgan, Cardiff 1977.
Best bowling performance: 7-18 Yorkshire v Oxford University, Oxford 1980.

LAST SEASON: BATTING

	I.	N.O.	R.	H.S.	AV.
TEST					
OTHER FIRST CLASS	22	6	511	54*	31.94
INT					
J.P.L.	7	2	37	10	7.40
NAT.W.					
B & H	3	2	31	21*	–

CAREER: BATTING

	I.	N.O.	R.	H.S.	AV.
TEST					
OTHER FIRST CLASS	167	40	2987	124	23.52
INT					
J.P.L.	49	17	577	52*	18.03
NAT.W.	10	4	171	45	28.50
B & H	16	6	152	32	15.20

LAST SEASON: BOWLING

	O.	M.	R.	W.	AV.
TEST					
OTHER FIRST CLASS	488.1	105	1292	63	20.51
INT					
J.P.L.	86	4	356	14	25.43
NAT.W.					
B & H	36	6	117	4	29.25

CAREER: BOWLING

	O.	M.	R.	W.	AV.
TEST					
OTHER FIRST CLASS	3002.4	690	8544	364	23.47
INT					
J.P.L.	613.5	25	2655	92	28.85
NAT.W.	137.2	18	404	23	17.57
B & H	265	37	887	35	25.37

Q. 202. What companies sponsored the Test series England v West Indies, the English County Championship and the One-Day Internationals in 1984?

STEVENSON, G.B.

Full Name: Graham Barry Stevenson.
Role: Right-hand bat, right arm fast bowler.
Born: 16 December 1955, Hemsworth, Yorkshire.
Height: 6' 0" **Weight:** 13st.
Nickname: "Several—unprintable!" Moonbeam.
County debut: 1973.
County cap: 1978.
Test debut: 1979–80.
No. of Tests: 2.
No. of One-Day Internationals: 4.
1000 runs in a season: 0.
50 wickets in a season: 5.
1st-Class 50s scored: 15.
1st-Class 100s scored: 2.
1st-Class 200s scored: 0.
1st-Class 5 w. in innings: 18.
1st-Class 10 w. in match: 2.
One-day 50s: 2.
One-day 100s: 0.
Place in batting averages: 259 average: 12.00; (1983: 202 average: 16.50).
Place in bowling averages: 129 average: 46.95; (1983: 36 average: 25.00).
1st-Class catches 1984: 5 (career: 72).
Wife and date of marriage: Angela, 29 October 1977.
Children: Christopher George, 9 January 1982.
Education: Minsthorpe High School, where they did not play cricket.
Jobs outside cricket: Has worked as clerk at Foster Wheeler Power Products Ltd., Snaith, near Goole.
Family links with cricket: Two uncles, Keith and Jack Stevenson, both played local league cricket.
Overseas tours: Australia 1979–80. W. Indies 1981.
Cricketers particularly learnt from: Geoff Boycott: "Boycott has been the biggest help to my career in all ways. He virtually opened my way into county cricket by arranging with Yorkshire for me to attend pre-season nets."
Equipment endorsed: Slazengers.
Other sports: Member of local club snooker team. Golf.
Relaxations: Watching Sheffield Wednesday F.C.
Extras: Toured Australia with England 1979–80, being called in after return to England through injury of Mike Hendrick. Vice-President Townville C.C. Steve Oldham was his best man. Batting No. 11 made 115 n.o. in a record stand of 149 for Yorkshire v Warwickshire, May 1982, with Geoff Boycott, beating

previous Yorkshire record for last wicket by one run, set by Lord Hawke and
David Hunter in 1898.

Best batting performance: 115* Yorkshire v Warwickshire, Edgbaston 1982.

Best bowling performance: 8-57 Yorkshire v Northamptonshire, Leeds 1983.

LAST SEASON: BATTING

	I.	N.O.	R.	H.S.	AV.
TEST					
OTHER FIRST CLASS	16	1	180	27	12.00
INT					
J.P.L.	12	4	229	81*	28.63
NAT.W.	1	0	26	26	–
B & H	1	0	36	36	–

CAREER: BATTING

	I.	N.O.	R.	H.S.	AV.
TEST	2	1	28	27*	–
OTHER FIRST CLASS	220	31	3806	115*	20.14
INT	4	3	43	28*	–
J.P.L.	110	14	1225	81*	12.76
NAT.W.	13	1	190	34	15.83
B & H	23	5	171	36	9.50

LAST SEASON: BOWLING

	O.	M.	R.	W.	AV.
TEST					
OTHER FIRST CLASS	262.3	44	892	19	46.95
INT					
J.P.L.	88.5	5	446	22	20.27
NAT.W.	11	1	46	0	–
B & H	29	0	158	3	52.67

CAREER: BOWLING

	O.	M.	R.	W.	AV.
TEST	52	7	183	5	36.60
OTHER FIRST CLASS	4273.5	960	13498	473	28.54
INT	32	3	125	7	17.86
J.P.L.	983.1	75	4424	180	24.57
NAT.W.	181.3	32	595	28	21.25
B & H	345.3	52	1259	58	21.71

SWALLOW, I.G.

Full Name: Ian Geoffrey Swallow.

Role: Right-hand bat, right arm
off-spin bowler, cover fielder.

Born: 18 December 1962, Barnsley.

Height: 5′ 7″ **Weight:** 9st. 7lbs.

Nickname: Chicken George or Zola.

County debut: 1983.

County cap: No.

Test debut: —

No. of Tests: 0.

No. of One-Day Internationals: 0.

1000 runs in a season: 0.

50 wickets in a season: 0.

1st-Class 50s scored: 0.

1st-Class 100s scored: 0.

1st-Class 200s scored: 0.

1st-Class 5 w. in innings: 0.

1st-Class 10 w. in match: 0.

One-day 50s: 0.

One-day 100s: 0.

Place in batting averages: 182 average: 22.67; (1983: — average: —).

Place in bowling averages: 117 average: 41.33; (1983: — average: —)
1st-Class catches 1984: 8 (career: 9).
Parents: Joyce and Geoffrey Swallow.
Marital status: Single.
Family links with cricket: Father and brother both played for Elsecar village C.C., where I also started my career at the age of 10 years.
Education: Hayland Kirk, Balk, comprehensive school; Barnsley Technical College.
Qualifications: 3 O-levels.
Jobs outside cricket: Stores clerk.
Cricketing superstitions: "Always put left pad on first."
Equipment used: Gray-Nicolls.
Cricketers particularly learnt from: Yorkshire C.C.C. coach (D.E.V. Padgett), P. Carrick, G. Boycott.
Cricketers particularly admired: G. Boycott, I.V.A. Richards, J. Emburey.
Other sports: Football and most sports for fun. Follow Barnsley F.C.
Relaxations: Sports in general, pop music.
Extras: Took hat-trick v Warwickshire 2nd XI 1984. Figures: 4-3-2-4.
Best batting performance: 34* Yorkshire v Somerset, Middlesbrough 1984.
Best bowling performance: 4-52 Yorkshire v Kent, Tunbridge Wells 1984.

LAST SEASON: BATTING

	I.	N.O.	R.	H.S.	AV.
TEST					
OTHER FIRST CLASS	9	3	136	34*	22.67
INT					
J.P.L.	1	0	2	2	–
NAT.W.					
B & H	2	1	8	5	–

CAREER: BATTING

	I.	N.O.	R.	H.S.	AV.
TEST					
OTHER FIRST CLASS	12	5	155	34*	22.14
INT					
J.P.L.	1	0	2	2	–
NAT.W.					
B & H	2	1	8	5	–

LAST SEASON: BOWLING

	O.	M.	R.	W.	AV.
TEST					
OTHER FIRST CLASS	229.1	62	620	15	41.33
INT					
J.P.L.	4	0	31	0	–
NAT.W.					
B & H	25	3	109	2	54.50

CAREER: BOWLING

	O.	M.	R.	W.	AV.
TEST					
OTHER FIRST CLASS	259.5	70	702	17	41.29
INT					
J.P.L.	4	0	31	0	–
NAT.W.					
B & H	25	3	109	2	54.50

COUNTY QUIZ

Q. 1.   When was the club founded?

Q. 2.   Who made the most first-class runs for the county last season, and how many?

Q. 3.   What's the highest ever county total, and against whom?

Q. 4.   Who took most wickets for the county last season, and how many?

Q. 5.   What's the highest individual score for the county, who hit it, and when?

Q. 6.   What's the highest scoring partnership for the county for any wicket?

Q. 7.   How many times has the club won the County Championship?

Q. 8.   What's the lowest ever total made by the county in one innings, when, and against whom?

Q. 9.   Which bowler took the most first-class wickets in one season, when, and how many?

Q. 10. Which batsman hit the most runs in one season, when and how many?

ANSWERS — COUNTY QUIZ

Derbyshire
Q. 1. 1870.
Q. 2. K.J. Barnett; 1703.
Q. 3. 645; 1898; v Hampshire.
Q. 4. G. Miller; 84.
Q. 5. 274; G. Davidson; 1896.
Q. 6. 328; P. Vaulkhard & D. Smith; 1946.
Q. 7. Once.
Q. 8. 16; 1879; v Nottinghamshire.
Q. 9. T.B. Mitchell; 1935; 168.
Q. 10. D.B. Carr; 1959; 2165.

Essex
Q. 1. 1876.
Q. 2. G.A. Gooch; 2281.
Q. 3. 692; 1895; v Somerset.
Q. 4. J.K. Lever; 106.
Q. 5. 343 n.o.; P.A. Perrin; 1904.
Q. 6. 321; G.A. Gooch & K.S. McEwan; 1978.
Q. 7. 3 times.
Q. 8. 30; 1901; v Yorkshire.
Q. 9. T.P.B. Smith; 1947; 172.
Q. 10. J. O'Connor; 1934; 2308.

Glamorgan
Q. 1. 1888.
Q. 2. A.L. Jones; 1550.
Q. 3. 587 for 8 dec.; 1951; v Derbyshire.
Q. 4. J.F. Steele & R.C. Ontong; 65 each.
Q. 5. 287 n.o.; D.E. Davies; 1939.
Q. 6. 330; A. Jones & R.C. Fredericks; 1972.
Q. 7. Twice.
Q. 8. 22; 1922; v Lancashire.
Q. 9. J.C. Clay; 1937; 176.
Q. 10. Javed Miandad; 1981; 2083.

Gloucestershire
Q. 1. 1871,
Q. 2. C.W.J. Athey; 1737.

Q. 3. 653 for 6 dec.; 1928; v Glamorgan.
Q. 4. J.N. Shephard; 72.
Q. 5. 318 n.o.; W.G. Grace; 1876.
Q. 6. 395; D.M. Young & R.B. Nicholls; 1962.
Q. 7. 3 times.
Q. 8. 17; 1896; v Australians.
Q. 9. T.W.J. Goddard; 1937 & 1947; 222.
Q. 10. W.R. Hammond; 1933; 2860.

Hampshire
Q. 1. 1863.
Q. 2. T.E. Jesty; 1329.
Q. 3. 672 for 7 dec.; 1899; v Somerset.
Q. 4. T.M. Tremlett; 67.
Q. 5. 316; R.H. Moore; 1937.
Q. 6. 411; R.M. Poore & E.G. Wynyard; 1899.
Q. 7. Twice.
Q. 8. 15; 1922; v Warwickshire.
Q. 9. A.S. Kennedy; 1922; 190.
Q. 10. C.P. Mead; 1928; 2854.

Kent
Q. 1. 1859.
Q. 2. D.G. Aslett; 1231.
Q. 3. 803 for 4 dec.; 1934; v Essex.
Q. 4. D.L. Underwood; 77.
Q. 5. 332; W.H. Ashdown; 1934.
Q. 6. 352; W.H. Ashdown & F.E. Woolley; 1934.
Q. 7. 6 times.
Q. 8. 18; 1867; v Sussex.
Q. 9. A.P. Freeman; 1933; 262.
Q. 10. F.E. Woolley; 1928; 2894.

Lancashire
Q. 1. 1864.
Q. 2. N.H. Fairbrother; 1163.
Q. 3. 801; 1895; v Somerset.

Q. 4. J. Simmons; 63.
Q. 5. 424; A.C. MacLaren; 1895.
Q. 6. 371; F.B. Watson & G.E. Tyldesley; 1928.
Q. 7. 8 times.
Q. 8. 25; 1871; v Derbyshire.
Q. 9. E.A. McDonald; 1925; 198.
Q. 10. J.T. Tyldesley; 1901; 2633.

Leicestershire
Q. 1. 1879.
Q. 2. P. Willey; 1322.
Q. 3. 701 for 4 dec.; 1906; v Worcestershire.
Q. 4. J.P. Agnew; 72.
Q. 5. 252 n.o.; S. Coe; 1914.
Q. 6. 390; B. Dudleston & J.F. Steele; 1979.
Q. 7. Once.
Q. 8. 25; 1912; v Kent.
Q. 9. J.E. Walsh; 1948; 170.
Q. 10. G.L. Berry; 1937; 2446.

Middlesex
Q. 1. 1863.
Q. 2. M.W. Gatting; 1998.
Q. 3. 642 for 3 dec.; 1923; v Hampshire.
Q. 4. P.H. Edmonds; 77.
Q. 5. 331 n.o.; J.D. Robertson; 1949.
Q. 6. 424 (unbroken); W.J. Edrich & D.C.S.Compton; 1948.
Q. 7. 8 times.
Q. 8. 20; 1864; v M.C.C.
Q. 9. F.J. Titmus; 1955; 158.
Q. 10. W.J. Edrich; 1947; 2650.

Northamptonshire
Q. 1. 1878.
Q. 2. W. Larkins; 1601.
Q. 3. 557 for 6 dec.; 1914; v Sussex.
Q. 4. D.S. Steele; 60.
Q. 5. 300; R. Subba Row; 1958.

Q. 6. 376; R. Subba Row & A. Lightfoot; 1958.
Q. 7. Never.
Q. 8. 12; 1907; v Gloucestershire.
Q. 9. G.E. Tribe; 1955; 175.
Q. 10. D. Brookes; 1952; 2198.

Nottinghamshire
Q. 1. 1841.
Q. 2. R.T. Robinson; 1700.
Q. 3. 739 for 7 dec.; 1903; v. Leicestershire.
Q. 4. R.J. Hadlee; 117.
Q. 5. 312 n.o.; W.W. Keeton; 1939.
Q. 6. 398; W. Gunn & A. Shrewsbury; 1890.
Q. 7. 13 times.
Q. 8. 13; 1901; v Yorkshire.
Q. 9. B. Dooland; 1954; 181.
Q. 10. W.W. Whysall; 1929; 2620.

Somerset
Q. 1. 1875.
Q. 2. M.D. Crewe; 1769.
Q. 3. 675 for 9 dec.; 1924; v Hampshire.
Q. 4. V.J. Marks; 78.
Q. 5. 310; H. Gimblett; 1948.
Q. 6. 346; H.T. Hewitt & L.C.H. Palairet; 1892.
Q. 7. Never.
Q. 8. 25; 1947; v Gloucestershire.
Q. 9. A.W. Wellard; 1938; 169.
Q. 10. W.E. Alley; 1961; 2761.

Surrey
Q. 1. 1845.
Q. 2. M.A. Lynch; 1511.
Q. 3. 811; 1899; v Somerset.
Q. 4. S.T. Clarke; 78.
Q. 5. 357 n.o.; R. Abel; 1899.
Q. 6. 448; R. Abel & T.W. Hayward; 1899.
Q. 7. 18 times.
Q. 8. 14; 1983; v Essex.
Q. 9. T. Richardson; 1895; 252.
Q. 10. T.W. Hayward; 1906; 3246.

Sussex

Q. 1. 1839.
Q. 2. P.W.G. Parker; 1411.
Q. 3. 705 for 8 dec.; 1902; v Surrey.
Q. 4. G.S. le Roux; 76.
Q. 5. 333; K.S. Duleepsinhji; 1930.
Q. 6. 490; E.H. Bewley & John Langridge; 1933.
Q. 7. Never.
Q. 8. 19; 1873; v Nottinghamshire.
Q. 9. M.W. Tate; 1925; 198.
Q. 10. John Langridge; 1949; 2850.

Warwickshire

Q. 1. 1882.
Q. 2. D.L. Amiss; 2137.
Q. 3. 657 for 6 dec.; 1899; v Hampshire.
Q. 4. A.M. Ferreira; 75.
Q. 5. 305 n.o.; F.R. Foster; 1914.
Q. 6. 465 (unbroken); J.A. Jameson & R.B.Kanhai; 1974.
Q. 7. 3 times.
Q. 8. 16; 1913; v Kent.
Q. 9. W.E. Hollies; 1946; 180.
Q. 10. M.J.K. Smith; 1959; 2417.

Worcestershire

Q. 1. 1865.
Q. 2. P.A. Neale; 1692.
Q. 3. 633; 1906; v Warwickshire.
Q. 4. A.P. Pridgeon; 65.
Q. 5. 311 n.o.; G.M. Turner; 1982.
Q. 6. 393; E.G. Arnold & W.B. Burns; 1909.
Q. 7. 3 times.
Q. 8. 24; 1903; v Yorkshire.
Q. 9. C.F. Root; 1925; 207.
Q. 10. H.H.I. Gibbons; 1934; 2654.

Yorkshire

Q. 1. 1863.
Q. 2. G. Boycott; 1567.
Q. 3. 887; 1896; v Warwickshire.
Q. 4. A. Sidebottom; 63.
Q. 5. 341; G.H. Hirst; 1905.
Q. 6. 555; P. Holmes & H. Sutcliffe; 1932.
Q. 7. 31 times.
Q. 8. 23; 1965; v Hampshire.
Q. 9. W. Rhodes; 1900; 240.
Q. 10. H. Sutcliffe; 1932; 2883.

ANSWERS

Q. 1. Warwickshire.

Q. 2. A fox.

Q. 3. Worcestershire. Three pears.

Q. 4. Italy.

Q. 5. Four.

Q. 6. Essex & Gloucestershire.

Q. 7. David Gower of Leics; Laurie Potter of Kent; Bill Athey of Gloucs.

Q. 8. Richard Hadlee of Nottinghamshire; 117 wickets at an average of 14.05.

Q. 9. Mike Gatting of Middlesex; 2257 runs at 68.39 an innings.

Q. 10. Graham Gooch.

Q. 11. Paddy Clift: 8 for 26 for Leics v Warwicks at Edgbaston, on 8 September.

Q. 12. John Steele of Glam: 33.

Q. 13. 306-8. Essex v Herts at Hitchin, 1981.

Q. 14. Sussex v Somerset. Hove, 1983.

Q. 15. 158. Zaheer Abbas. Gloucs v Leics at Leicester, 1983.

Q. 16. 1963.

Q. 17. Sussex.

Q. 18. Middlesex.

Q. 19. 1981.

Q. 20. Derbyshire.

Q. 21. Lancs. 1970, 1971, 1972.

Q. 22. No team.

Q. 23. 350-3. Essex v Comb Univs. Chelmsford, 1979.

Q. 24. 56. Leics v Minor Counties. Wellington, 1982.

Q. 25. 198 not out. G.A. Gooch, Essex v Sussex. Hove, 1982.

Q. 26. 1972.

Q. 27. Leicestershire.

Q. 28. Somerset. 1981, 1982.

Q. 29. 310-5. Essex v Glam. Southend. 1983.

Q. 30. 23. Middx v Yorks. Leeds, 1974.

Q. 31. 176. G.A. Gooch, Essex v Glam. Southend, 1983.

Q. 32. 1969.

Q. 33. Lancashire.

Q. 34. Clive Radley of Middlesex.

Q. 35. 1864.

Q. 36. Surrey.

Q. 37. Surrey. Seven times, 1952–1958.

Q. 38. *Bob Woolmer: Pirate & Rebel?"*

Q. 39. Ray East of Essex.

Q. 40. Peter Roebuck of Somerset.

Q. 41. Derek Randall of Notts & England.

Q. 42. Alan Jones of Glamorgan.

Q. 43. Yorks 1956–59, and Leics 1960–64.

Q. 44. Eleven. D (Derby), C.L. (Hants), D.V. (Sussex), M.J.K. (Oxford, Leics, Warwicks), E.J. 'Tiger" (Warwicks), A. (Warwicks), H. (Gloucs), D.R. (Gloucs), T.P.B. (Essex), C.I.J. (Middx), Sir C.A. (Cambridge & Sussex).

Q. 45. Ranjitsinhji of Sussex & England.

Q. 46. Tim Tremlett.

Q. 47. Mike Gatting. 79 minutes. Middx v Kent, at Lord's, 7 September.

Q. 48. Derbyshire.

Q. 49. 508.

Q. 50. Winston Davis replaced Milton Small.

Q. 51. Ian Botham uses a 3lb bat; Compton & Bradman used bats of only 2lb 2oz.

Q. 52. 91.

Q. 53. True. See Sir Len Hutton's book *Fifty Years in Cricket* p 90–91.

Q. 54. 1954. West Indies.

Q. 55. Mark Nicholas of Hampshire.

Q. 56. Sir Jack Hobbs to the young Alf Gover.

Q. 57. Sir Don Bradman, the Oval, 1948. On his last appearance in a Test Match in England, as Captain of Australia, Bradman was applauded all the way to the wicket by the crowd and the England players. He was much moved. He was then bowled second ball by Eric Hollies.

Q. 58. Six pairs. C.L. & D.C.H. Townsend; Fred & Maurice Tate; Jim Parks, senior & junior; Frank & George Mann; 'Old Joe' & 'Young Joe' Hardstaff; Len & Richard Hutton.

Q. 59. Victor Trumper.

Q. 60. Chris Old. Yorkshire & Warwickshire.

Q. 61. Sir C. Aubrey Smith.

Q. 62. Peter Roebuck of Somerset.

Q. 63. South African cricketer. Played 9 Tests between 1930 and 1938.

Q. 64. 452 not out. D.G. Bradman, 1929–1930. For New South Wales v Queensland at Sydney.

Q. 65. 424. A.C. MacLaren. Lancashire v Somerset, Taunton, 1895.

Q. 66. Hanif Mohammad. 337 runs. Pakistan v West Indies. Bridgetown, 1957–58. 16 hours & 10 mins.

Q. 67. False. Only 93 have.

Q. 68. 628 not out. A.E.J. Collins. A junior house match at Clifton College in 1899.

Q. 69. They all scored a century on their first appearance for their country.

Q. 70. False. He scored one.

Q. 71. Zaheer Abbas. 8 times.

Q. 72. Sir Jack Hobbs. 197.

Q. 73. A.E. Fagg. 244 & 202 n.o. Kent v Essex at Colchester, 1938.

Q. 74. G. Gunn, 183, & G.V. Gunn, 100 n.o. for Notts v Warwicks at Birmingham, 1931.

Q. 75. 175 yards from hit to pitch, by the Rev. W. Fellows at Christ Church, Oxford in 1856.

Q. 76. True. Sir G.S. Sobers (Notts) hit 36 runs in a 6-ball over from M.A. Nash (Glamorgan) in 1968. The most hit off an 8-ball over is 34 by R.M. Edwards (Governor-General's XI) off M.C. Carew (West Indies), Auckland, 1968–69.

Q. 77. C.G. Macartney. 345. Australia v Notts. 1921.

Q. 78. D.V.P. Wright (Kent & England), 7.

Q. 79. A.P. Freeman. 304. 1928.

Q. 80. R. Appleyard. 200. 1951.

Q. 81. W. Rhodes (Yorkshire & England), 23.

Q. 82. G.H. Hirst. Yorks v Somerset, Bath 1906.

Q. 83. L.E.G. Ames (Kent & England), 127 (79 ct, 48 st) in 1929.

Q. 84. Bob Taylor of Derbyshire & England.

Q. 85. Yes, twice. W.H. Brain, 3 stumpings for Gloucs v Somerset, 1893, off C.L.

Townsend; G.O. Dawkes, 3 catches for Derbys v Worcs, 1958, off H.L. Jackson.

Q. 86. 1107. Victoria v New South Wales, 1926–27.

Q. 87. F.E. Woolley, Kent & England. 1018.

Q. 88. W.R. Hammond of Gloucestershire & England, 78.

Q. 89. Geoffrey Boycott of Yorkshire & England. 8114.

Q. 90. Sir Donald Bradman. 6996.

Q. 91. Sir Gary Sobers. 8032.

Q. 92. B. Mitchell. 3471.

Q. 93. B. Congdon. 3448.

Q. 94. Sunil Gavaskar.

Q. 95. Sir Donald Bradman. 309. Australia v England. Leeds, 1930.

Q. 96. Lance Gibbs of West Indies. 27,115.

Q. 97. W. Rhodes, 52 years 165 days, for England, 1929–30.
H. Ironmonger, 50 years 327 days for Australia, 1932–33.
W.G. Grace, 50 years 320 days for England, 1899.
G. Gunn, 50 years 303 days for England, 1929–30.

Q. 98. Graham Gooch of Essex.

Q. 99. John Lever of Essex.

Q. 100. Harlequins.

Q. 101. Australia, 1920–21. J.W.H.T. Douglas.

Q. 102. India, 1959. P.B.H. May.

Q. 103. C.B. Fry, of Sussex, Hampshire & England.

Q. 104. Dennis Amiss – in the West Indies, 1973–74. Allan Lamb was the first to do it in England.

Q. 105. Everton Weekes of West

Indies. On hearing that this was because Weekes' father was a fanatical supporter of Everton F.C. Jim Laker commented "Lucky his father wasn't a supporter of West Bromwich Albion."

Q. 106. J.P. Agnew of Leicestershire.

Q. 107. Garth Le Roux of Sussex.

Q. 108. J.E. Morris of Derbyshire.

Q. 109. Graham Dilley of Kent.

Q. 110. P.W. Romaines of Gloucestershire.

Q. 111. Alvin Kallicharran, 206, for Warwickshire v Oxfordshire, in the NatWest Trophy, 4 July 1984.

Q. 112. Yorkshire lost to Shropshire; in 1973 Yorkshire lost to Durham.

Q. 113. John Lever of Essex & England.

Q. 114. P.B.H. May of Surrey & England.

Q. 115. Forty-one times.

Q. 116. Sussex, Gloucestershire & Surrey.

Q. 157. Equal stripes of black, red and gold.

Q. 158. 251 Test matches, of which England has won 95, and Australia 83.

Q. 159. Clyde Leopold Walcott, Everton De Courcy Weekes, Frank Mortimer Worrell.

Q. 160. 1975. West Indies.

Q. 161. George.

Q. 162. Sewards.

Q. 163. Thomas.

Q. 164. Berry.

Q. 165. Gilbert.

Q. 166. He had no middle name.

Q. 167. India. Kapil Dev.

Q. 168. 1107. Victoria v New South Wales. Melbourne, 1926–27.

Q. 169. 887. Yorkshire v Warwickshire. Birmingham, 1896.

Q. 170. 507 for 7. Cambridge University v M.C.C. Lord's, 1896.

Q. 171. 654 for 5. England v South Africa. Durban, 1938–39.

Q. 172. 604. Maharashtra v Bombay. Poona, 1948–49.

Q. 173. 12. Oxford University v M.C.C. Oxford, 1877.

Q. 174. E.C. Bentley, inventor of the verse form, the clerihew, of which these lines are an example.

Q. 175. 95. Australia, 80 v Pakistan, 15 for 2. Karachi, 1956–57.

Q. 176. J.H. King. Leics v Surrey. Oval, 1906.

Q. 177. W.G. Grace, 1895. W.R. Hammond, 1927. C. Hallows, 1928.

Q. 178. T.W. Hayward, 1900. D.G. Bradman, 1930 & 1928. W.J. Edrich, 1938. G.M. Turner, 1973.

Q. 179. A.P. Freeman. Kent & England. 1928. 304, at av. 18.05.

Q. 180. Derek Underwood. Kent & England. 150. 1966.

Q. 181. A.A. Mailey. New South Wales v Victoria. 1926–27. 362 runs.

Q. 182. Hanif Mohammed. 499. Karachi v Bahawalpur. Karachi, 1958–59.

Q. 183. 424. A.C. MacLaren. Lancs v Somerset. Taunton, 1895.

Q. 184. 452. New South Wales v Queensland. Sydney, 1929–30.

Q. 185. A.E. Fagg. 244 & 202 not out. Kent v Essex. Colchester, 1938.

Q. 186. Don Bradman. Six. 1930.

Q. 187. W.F.E. Marx. 240. Transvaal v Griqualand West. Johannesburg. 1920–21.

Q. 188. C.B. Fry. Sussex & England. Six. 1901. Don Bradman in 1938–39, and Mike Procter, 1970–71, equalled this record.

Q. 189. 120 minutes. G.I. Jessop. Gloucs v Sussex. Hove, 1903. Clive Lloyd exactly equalled this record for West Indies v Glamorgan at Swansea, 1976.

Q. 190. 181 minutes. Denis Compton. M.C.C. v N.E. Transvaal. Benoni, 1948–49.

Q. 191. Nine. Hon. F.G.B. Ponsonby. M.C.C. v Cambridge Univ. Cambridge, 1842.

Q. 192. 15. J.R. Reid. Wellington v Northern Districts. Wellington, 1962–63.

Q. 193. Denis Compton, Middlesex & England. 3816. 1947.

Q. 194. M.J.K. Smith. Warwickshire & England. 1959. 3245.

Q. 195. Denis Compton. Middlesex & England. 18. 1947.

Q. 196. Don Bradman. 115.66. Australian touring team, 1938.

Q. 197. Geoffrey Boycott. Yorkshire & England. 102.53. 1979.

Q. 198. Peter Willey.

Q. 199. John Steele, run out for 33 in both innings, for Glamorgan v Middlesex at Lord's.

Q. 200. Derek Pringle of Essex & England in *Chariots of Fire*.

Q. 201. John Warr about Denis Compton.

Q. 202. Cornhill Insurance, Britannic Assurance & Texaco.